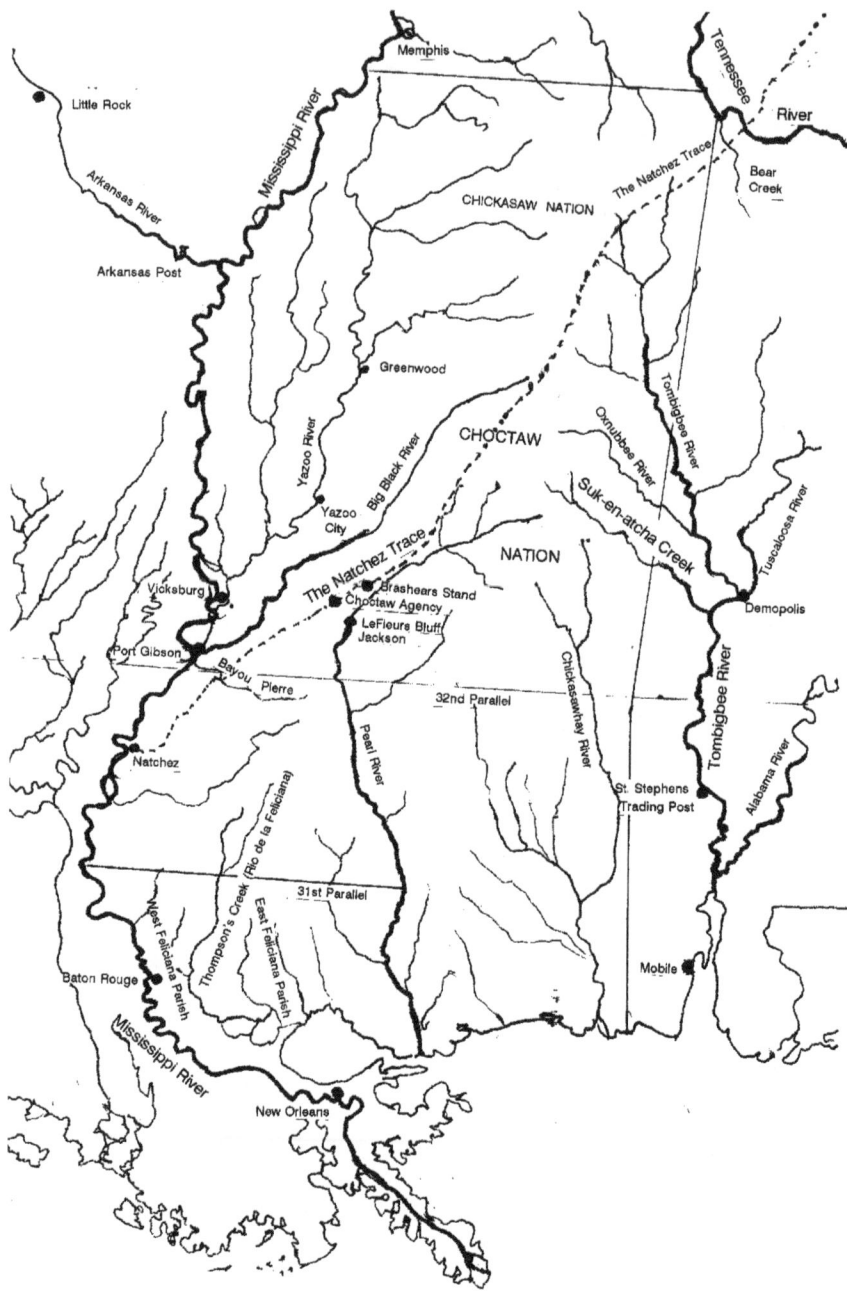

Figure 1: The Lower Mississippi Valley,
showing places where Brashear families lived

A BRASHEAR(S) FAMILY HISTORY,

Descendants of Robert and Benois Brasseur

VOL. 5

Two Brashear(s) Families

of the Lower Mississippi Valley,

Their Choctaw, & Other Descendants

Assembled and published by
Charles Brashear, Books etc
26 Tiffany Place
Santa Rosa, CA 95409

October 31, 2002

ISBN: 0-933362-16-1

A Brashear(s) Family History: Descendants of Robert and Benois Brasseur: Vol. 5: Two Brashear(s) Families of the Lower Mississippi Valley, Their Choctaw and Other Descendants, by Charles Brashear

I am and have been for 30-something years actively engaged in research on the Brashear(s) Family, in all its branches, in all spellings of the surname. Troy Back and Leon Brashear gave me their blessing and permission to "update" their book, THE BRASHEAR STORY, A FAMILY HISTORY, but the more data I collected, the more I realized that this family history will never again fit into one volume, especially if you include the amount and kind of detail that I like to include. I now have working drafts of eight books on the family history; see the end of this book for the plan for and information on these eight volumes, as well as some of my other writing.

CONTENTS

vii

PREFACE

What this book is about:

By the late 1770s, American and European immigrants were already moving into the lower Mississippi Valley in search of new land, even though much of that territory was under Spanish control. Some of them came by ship to Pensacola, Mobile, New Orleans, Baton Rouge, and Natchez, all of which were developed ports under French and Spanish administrations. Others came by flatboat down the Cherokee (Tennessee) River, then proceeded down an ancient, Indian trading path, soon to be known as The Natchez Trace. Still others began floating down the Ohio and Mississippi Rivers to find new land.

Two branches of the Brashear(s) family were among these early immigrants: 1. Benjamin Brashear and all his children except Marsham (who stayed in Louisville, KY) and 2. Jesse Brashears and all of his children. In both cases, one or more members of the family married into the Choctaw tribe and founded large families that are still traceable today. Other of their brothers and cousins founded large, non-Indian families.

In some ways, the period is remarkably well-documented. The French were almost compulsive records-keepers; many of their letters and legal proceedings are extant and translated. The Spanish who followed them were also careful of their records, which have been collected and translated as *The Archives of Spanish West Florida*. During both these administrations, the Catholic church was responsible for recording births, marriages, deaths, estate proceedings, and any other domestic happenings. When the Americans took over, the conflicting interests of previous and new-comer factions made a flood of paper-work necessary, most of which is available in *The American State Papers*.

Treaty negotiations with Indians, especially the Choctaws, generated even more records. The Treaty of Dancing Rabbit

Creek, for instance, required a census of the tribe to determine who was eligible for benefits and who signed up to stay in Mississippi. Land grants to beneficiaries had to be recorded, both in the central government and in the counties where the land actually was. When annuity payments were due, the government again had to take a census. Most of these records are extant and have been micro-filmed as "Choctaw Reserves Records Group 75," literally thousands of rolls of film.

Toward the end of the nineteenth century when the U.S. Government decided to give every Indian an allotment and take away what was left over (for white settlement), a new census was necessary. The records the Dawes Commission generated are staggering. In addition to all the correspondence, the census cards (often abbreviated C.C. in this book) listing and numbering each individual by name are extant and also micro-filmed, as well as the several volumes of the final Dawes Roll. There was considerable litigation about who was to get on the rolls and who wasn't, and these court records have also been preserved.

After Oklahoma statehood, records become conventional: deeds, marriages, births, etc as recorded by the counties in which the events occurred. These have the usual drawbacks of county records everywhere: they leave things out and sometimes get things wrong.

During the Great Depression, the WPA (Works Progress Administration) sponsored writers and journalists to go out into the countryside and interview old-timers, Indians, descendants of slaves, pioneers. These *Oklahoma Indian-Pioneer Interviews* fill over a hundred volumes with life-stories that are frequently very interesting.

I have quoted extensively from many of these records, in an attempt to flesh out the vital statistics and tell the interesting story of *Two Brashear(s) Families of the Lower Mississippi Valley and their Choctaw and Other Descendants.*

A Few Words About My Conventions

Like Troy Back and Leon Brashear, I have marked with an **asterisk** those family lines that are followed up with later, fuller listings or, maybe, a short biographical sketch or some document. Reading genealogies quickly becomes a hopeless, confusing mess; and you just have to flip back and forth between pages, checking birth-dates, wives, etc to trace your line.

Usually, I have put several **generations** in one listing. I've indented and numbered each succeeding generation, thus:

^{1}1. the parents
    ^{2}1. the children
        ^{3}4. the grand-children
            ^{4}1. the great-grandchildren

▸ The **superscripts** in the outlines represent the number of the generation from Robert Brasseur, the Immigrant Huguenot, who arrived in Virginia about 1635. The ordinal numbers indicate the sequence of that person among his/her siblings. Thus ^{2}1 indicates the second generation, first child in a family; ^{3}4 indicates the third generation, fourth child; etc. Sorry if this makes reading difficult. I hope that it's easier than flipping back and forth over dozens of pages.

▸ Also, I have assigned (or rather let my computer assign) a **serial number** to all members of the Brashear(s) family. In most cases, this serial number is at the beginning of a line on which the member appears. The serial number is preceded by some superscripts. Superscript ^{v1} refers to the serial number in vol 1; ^{v2} refers to the serial number in vol 2; etc. Usually, I have also given the serial number assigned by Back and Brashear in parentheses: e.g. Isaac Brashears (Back#168).

▸ I have also tried to **cross-reference** members of the family who married other members of the family, with both their volume serial number and their Back number. It's very hard for me to know when people are cousins, however, and so I apologize in advance for any cross-references I missed.

▸ Maybe the serial numbers will help distinguish several people of exactly the same name. I don't know how many men were named Robert Samuel Brashear(s), but it was a large number. Whenever the family produced a famous person, as for example, Dr. Walter Brashear of Bardstown, KY, who performed the world's first amputation of a leg at the hip joint, or Dr. John Alfred Brashear, who simply made

xiii

the world's finest optics for half a century, there followed a rash of namings for them. There must be a dozen John Alfred Brashears. The only way you can keep them separate is if they happened to have a known nickname, as did Robert Samuel "Old Bob" Brashear," or you nickname them with their serial number. Much the same is true for the many Othos, Basils, Reginalds, not to mention the Johns, Josephs, Jameses, Williams, Roberts, Elizabeths, Marthas, Margarets, Nancys, etc.

▸ I've **boldfaced** only the people whose birth names were some form of the family name: Brashear, Brashears, Brasher, Brashers, Beshears, Boshears, etc. I have tried to give their surnames as they occur in the documents (even when obviously misspelled), sometimes with and sometimes without the "s." So if you see a man's name spelled two ways in the same document, it's likely that's the way it was in the document (I have to confess that I get confused as to who uses the "s" and who doesn't— or when; in many cases a person's name appears in the records both ways).

▸ Spouses are given in bold italics: e.g. **_Phoebe Nicks_**. Often, a wife's maiden name and/or former name is indicated in parentheses; "née" (feminine) or "né" (masculine) (French for "born") indicates the surname at birth; thus Dorothy (née Cager/widow Munroe) Jones.

▸ "Nicknames" are in quotes; e.g. Robert S. "Old Bob" Brashear.

▸ If a person was <u>called by a name</u> other than his/her first, I've underlined that name, e.g. Howard <u>Charles</u> Brashers, who was called "Charles." Underlining is also used occasionally to call the reader's attention to a name or some data.

▸ When all I know are the names of a set of children, I've run them on in a paragraph and separated them by punctuation: e.g. (from a Bell family) Ch: Danny Joe; Karen Lynn; Stanley Farris; and Phillip Drew Bell. The exception (I think) is that all Brashear(s) family members get a bold line of their own.

▸ When I don't know a name, either given or surname, I've offered a **blank**, e.g. Robert Brashier, III, m.1. _____; m.2. c1679, Mrs. Alice Jackson, widow of Thomas Jackson. If you know the name(s) you can fill them in with pen and ink. And, of course, I'd like to receive the data also. These blanks are

NOT indexed.

▸ Information I have reason to believe is accurate, but have **no proof** of, is preceded and/or followed by a question mark; thus "Bill Brashear, b. ?1845" means I'm making an informed guess at his birth date. If you take my information elsewhere, please, please, also take my doubt.

I've used some abbreviations:

HSB = *The Brashear-Brashears Family, 1449-1929*, by Henry Sinclair Brashear (1929), the first book-length history of this family

Back = *The Brashear Story, a Family History, 1637-1963*, by Troy Back and Leon Brashear (1963; 1980), the second book-length history of this family.

BFB = "Br(e)ashe(a)r(s) Family Branches," a newsletter published for more than ten years by Arzella Brashear Spear.

FHL = The Family History Library, Salt Lake City. FHL Arc or ARCfile indicates archive files in that library.

"c" in front of a number means "circa" or about: thus "c1742" should be read "about 1742."

"b." mean "was born on/at," "d." means "died on/at,"

"m." means "married," and sometimes a number is added to indicate which of multiple marriages I'm talking about, as "m.2." indicates a second marriage.

"bur" means "is/was buried at" some cemetery ("cem")

"s/o" "d/o" "gs/o" and the like mean "son of" "daughter of" etc.

I have sometimes abbreviated county names: e.g. PGCo is Prince George's Co, MD; LawrCo is Lawrence Co, TN

SCC (in land records) stands for "Sworn Chain Carrier(s)"

CCC stands for Clerk of the County Court; DC for District Clerk

DS usually mean District Surveyor; sometimes the initials of the county are added, as DSBC might mean "District Surveyor, Bullitt Co."

I.T. and Ind. Terr., or course, stand for Indian Territory.

C.C. stands for Census Card, the records of the Dawes Commission for the five civilized tribes. Sometimes, it is modified with the tribe name: e.g. Choctaw Census Card #____.

Roll #____ stands for the Dawes Rolls, or the Final Rolls of the Commission to the Five Civilized Tribes, usually called simply the Dawes Commission.

CCCC stands for the Choctaw and Chickasaw Citizenship Court, which heard appeals to the Dawes process from 1904 to 1906.

And in places where it struck me as awkward, or lacked clarity, I haven't used these abbreviations.

Thanks to Other Researchers

In many cases, I've followed descending families with other surnames a few generations, especially when someone in that line is an interested and active genealogist, or the lines intermarry later. Many of these people have contributed substantially to what we know about the Brashear(s) Family. As I've said before and will say again, this sort of book cannot be written by one person, because there is simply not enough time in one lifetime to go to all the places, do all the research, and write it up. Any family historian is forced to rely on the research of many a cousin, most of them bearing a different surname. We all owe them heavy thanks for the money and sweat they have expended on our common family history. I'll try to acknowledge each at the spot where they contributed most.

I would also like, especially, to thank:

- The late Dr. Sherburne Anderson, of Baton Rouge, for data on the Brashears of the Natchez and New Orleans areas;
- Judy Berchak, who went to the trouble to Xerox the 1900 and 1910 census Soundex of Louisiana and send the cards to me;
- Joanne Schwilk, for data on Samuel W. Brashears of East Baton Rouge Parish;
- Harley E. Anders, for many documents on Choctaw Affairs, especially concerning Turnbulls, Brashears, and Morans;
- Doug Barkley, for data on Brashears, Daniels, and other families, especially in the Skullyville area;
- Chris Bailey, for invaluable data on Choctaw history and early families;
- Jennifer Mieirs, for data on several families, not least the Traherns;
- Marlene Clark and Sandi Carter, for data on Sampson Moncrief and his descendants;

1. BENJAMIN BRASHEAR
and CATHERINE BELT
Of Maryland and Mississippi

Well before the American Revolution, expanding population and depleted land in the colonies had created a pressure and appetite for new land on the frontiers. In the 1750s, the push had been toward North Carolina and its spill-over into what would one day become Tennessee. In the 1760s and 70s, the thrust was down the Monongahela and Ohio Rivers into the huge watershed of the Ohio River.

In the late 1770s, the rush had already begun on the lower Mississippi Valley, even though much of that territory was under Spanish control. Some of the immigrants to the Mississippi Valley came by ship to Pensacola, Mobile, New Orleans, Baton Rouge, and Natchez, all of which were developed ports under French and Spanish administrations. Others came by flatboat down the Cherokee (Tennessee) River, crossed the slight ridge of land at Bear Creek, then proceeded down the Tombigbee River to Mobile, or traveled the high ground to Natchez on an ancient, Indian trading path, soon to be known as The Natchez Trace. Still others, especially after explorations that were a part of Revolutionary War campaigns in the Ohio and Illinois country— the Old Northwest— began floating down the Ohio and Mississippi Rivers to find new land. One of these early land-grabbers was Benjamin Brashear of Prince George's County, Maryland, and his family.

Benjamin Brashear, VII, (^{v1}536; Back#75), the seventh Brashear named Benjamin and a member of the sixth generation of the family in America, was born 19 Sept 1727, Prince George's Co, MD (PGCo), d. 1809, Russum, Claiborne Co, MS, s/o Samuel Brashear, Jr (^{v1}282; Back#26) and his wife (and double cousin) Elizabeth Brashear (^{v1}258; Back#21).

The line of descent runs as follows:

[#vl]1.   [1]1. **Robert Brasseur**, the Huguenot, b. c1598, France, d. c1667, Nansemond Co, VA (per land records); m. _____? See Vol. 1 for details.

[vl]2.   [2]1. **Benois Brasseur**, (Back#1), also called Bennet, Benoit, Benoist, Benojs, **Benjamin Brashear**, etc. born c1620, France; d. Dec 1662, Calvert Co, MD; m. c1645, *Mary ?Richford*, probably b. England. See Vol. 1 for details.

[vl]81.   [3]1. ***Robert Brasseur/Brashier, III**, (Back#2) b. 1646, Nansemond Co, VA; d. 1712, Prince George's Co, MD; m.1. c1665, _____ (mother of the children); m.2. 1679, *Mrs. Alice Jackson*, wid/o Thomas Jackson. See "Robert, The Improvident," a chapter in Vol. 1.

[vl]231.   [4]1. ***Benjamin Brashear, Sr [III]**, (Back#10) b. 1666, d. 1742 (estate proceedings), m. 1689, *Mary Jones*, d/o William Jones and Dorothy Cager. See separate chapters on him and some of his sons in Vol. 1.

[vl]232.   [4]2. ***Samuel Brashear, Sr**, (Back#11) b. 1673 (51 in 1724), d. Aug 1740, m. c?1694, *Ann Jones*. [Ann and Mary Jones were sisters, just as Benjamin and Samuel Brashear were brothers.] See separate chapters on them and some of their sons in Vol. 1.

[vl]282.   [5]2. ***Samuel Brashear, Jr**, (Back#26) b. 12 Feb 1696/7, d. 1773 Prince George's Co, MD, s/o Samuel Brashear Sr and Ann Jones. He married his "double" cousin, **Elizabeth Brashear** ([vl]258; Back#21), b. 30 March 1701, d. 1775, d/o Benjamin Brashear Sr ([vl]231; Back#10) and Mary Jones.

[vl]536.   [6]6. ***Benjamin Brashear, VII**, (Back#75) b. 19 Sept 1727, Prince George's Co, MD, d. 1809, Russum, Claiborne Co, MS; m. *Catherine Belt*. To Brownsville, PA, c1773; to Bullitt Co, KY, c1778; to Natchez 1780; lived in Spanish territory, now Mississippi. About half of this book is about them and their descendants.

Benjamin and Catherine in Maryland

In 1748, Benjamin Brashear was a member of the "Troop of Horse" in Prince George's County, Maryland; in 1754, Benjamin was a member of Capt. Tobias Belt's Prince George's Co, MD

Militia. (Note that he named a son Tobias.)

About 1750, Benjamin Brashear m. Catherine Belt, b. 18 March 1730, PGCo, d/o John Belt (13 March 1707— 1 Oct 1788) and his wife, Margaret Queen, b. 1709.

Margaret Queen was d/o Samuel Queen (d. 1711) and his wife, Katherine Marsham (1672-1712).

Katherine Marsham was a daughter of Richard Marsham, b. 1638, d. PGCo, 1713 (will) and his wife, Katherine _____, who was "in service" in 1670, i.e. born in England and transported as an indentured servant to Maryland (Patent Bk 12, p.512, Bk 7, p.530, cited in *The Early Settlers of Maryland*, Gust Skordas, Genealogical Publishing Co, Baltimore, 1968).

The story is therefore erroneous that Katherine (Mrs. Richard Marsham) was a Brent, descended from Lt. Gov. Giles Brent and the Piscataway Princess, Mary Kittamaquund, (d/o the Piscataway King, Tayac or Chitomachen). See "Brent-Marsham-Beavan-Blanford: Myth or Mystery," *Md Genealogical Bulletin*, v.36, #1 (Winter 1995) p.81-84, which demonstrates that "The Brent Genealogy" in *Colonial Families of the United States*, v.7, was in error. Katherine (Mrs. Richard Marsham) was NOT a Brent, nor descended from the Piscataway princess, Kittamaquund. She was an indentured servant from England, who married her benefactor.

Catherine Belt came from several prominent and wealthy families of Maryland, including the Marshams, Bealls, and Queens. These family surnames are often used as given names or middle names among their descendants.

Belt Family Connections

Humphrey Belt, b. c1615, the Belt family's progenitor in America, landed in Jamestown, VA, 23 June 1635 on the ship "America," at the age of 20. He lived first in Henrico Co, VA; later in Lower Norfolk Co, VA. He died in Virginia c1698.

a1. John Belt, s/o Humphrey Belt, b. 1654, Norfolk, VA, will dated 13 May 1697, entered probate 17 Nov 1698, Anne Arundel Co, MD (Bk 6, p.175); m. in AACo, Elizabeth Tydings, b. 1672(?), d. 14 Dec 1737, d/o Richard Tydings and Charity Sparrow. The Belt children were thus cousins to Charity and Mary Dowell (daughters of Philip Dowell and Mary Tydings), both of whom married Brashear men. John Belt's will names wife, Elizabeth, and sons, John, Joseph, and Benjamin Belt, daughters Elizabeth, Charity, & Sarah. The widow, Elizabeth (Tydings) Belt, m.2. 25 July 1701, All Hallows Parish, AACo, MD, John Lamb.

Family of John Belt and Elizabeth Tydings:

b1. John Belt, Jr, b. 1678, d. 1761; m. 10 Feb 1700/01, AACo, Lucy Lawrence, (re: West River and Cliff's Meeting, Society of Friends)

b2. *Col. Joseph Belt, b. 1680, d. 26 June 1761, PGCo; m.1. 1706, Esther Beall, m.2. 1727, Margery (Wight) Sprigg, widow of Thomas Sprigg, IV, d. 1725.

b3. *Benjamin Belt, b. 1682, will dated 19 June 1772, prob. 28 May 1773, PGCo; m. Elizabeth Middleton, d/o William and Elizabeth Middleton.

b4. Elizabeth Belt, b. bef 1697, AACo, Christened All Hallows Parish, AACo, 14 Dec 1703

b5. Charity Belt, b. bef 1697, AACo, Christened All Hallows Parish, AACo, 14 Dec 1703

b6. Sarah Belt, b. bef 1697, AACo, Christened All Hallows Parish, AACo, 14 Dec 1703; m. 11 Sept 1718, All Hallows Parish, AACo, Thomas Harwood,

b7. Jeremiah Belt, b. 14 Dec 1698, after father's death, Christened All Hallows Parish, AACo, 14 Dec 1703; m. 21 June 1746, PGCo, Mary Sprigg, b. 15 Dec 1723, d/o Thomas Sprigg, IV and Margery Wight.

b2. Col. Joseph Belt, b. 1680, first owner of the estate "Chevy Chase" in Maryland, d. 26 June 1761; m.1. 1706, Esther Beall, b. 1687, d. 1726, d/o Col. Ninian Beall, who arrived from Scotland in 1650 and amassed a huge estate in Maryland; m.2 Margery Wight, d/o Capt. John Wight, and widow of Thomas Sprigg, IV.

c1. John Belt, b. 13 March 1707; m.1. 4 March 1727/8, Margaret Queen, d/o Samuel Queen, b. ?, d. 1711; m.2. Katherine Marsham, d/o Richard Marsham.

d1. John Belt, Jr, b. 27 April 1729, d. 23 Dec 1814; m. Dinah _____, b. 19 Sept 1739, d. 12 Nov 1799. Moved to Bedford Co, PA.

d2. *Catherine Belt*, b. 18 March 1730, d. 1773; m. c1750, **Benjamin Brashear** ([v1]536), s/o Samuel Brashear, Jr and Elizabeth Brashear

d3. Col. Jeremiah Belt, b. ?, d. bef 1768

d4. Esther Belt, m. c1753, **Jeremiah Brashears, Sr** (ᵛ¹538), s/o Samuel Brashear, Jr and Elizabeth Brashear

d5. Joseph Belt, d. PGCo, 1761; m. Elizabeth _____

d6. Marsham Belt, b. c1735, d. 1801, Fleming Co, KY; m. PGCo c1758, Elizabeth Cross, b. c1740

c2. Mary Belt, m.1. (2nd wife of) Col. Edward Sprigg, m.2. Thomas Spindle,

c3. Joseph Belt, Jr, m. Anne Sprigg, d/o Thomas Sprigg, IV and Margery Wight

c4. Jeremiah Belt, m. 21 June 1746, Mary Sprigg, b. 15 Dec 1723, d/o Thomas Sprigg, IV and Margery Wight.

c5. Rachel Belt, b. 13 Dec 1711 (reg. Queen Anne's Parish), m. 11 July 1727, (2nd wife of) Osborn Sprigg,

b3. Benjamin Belt, b. 1682, will dated 19 June 1772, probate 28 May 1773, PGCo; m. Elizabeth Middleton, d/o William and Elizabeth Middleton.

c1. Middleton Belt. In his will, he named (among others) nephew Middleton Brashears, s/o Basil Brashears.

c2. Anne Belt, m. **Basil Brashears** (ᵛ¹288), b. 1714, s/o Samuel Brashear, Sr and Ann Jones. Volume 6 will be about their descendants.

c3. Elizabeth Belt, m. Basil Waring, III, b. 1717, d. 1776, s/o Col. Basil Waring, II and Martha Greenfield,

c4. Joseph Belt, m. **Rachel Brashears** (ᵛ¹557), d/o Samuel Brashears, III and Rachel Brashears. See Vol 1.

Benjamin Brashear and Catherine Belt lived in Prince George's County, MD, on a plantation called "Pleasant Hill." On 17 Nov 1772, Benjamin sold the plantation, and wife Catherine relinquished dower (Maryland Archives, Land Records, Bk BB3, p.111).

However, when Benjamin released his lease on land called "Land Over" in 1774, preparatory to leaving Prince George's Co, there is no dower release by Catherine, suggesting that she died in 1773, shortly after the birth of Eden Brashear, their last child.

In 1774, just after Catherine probably died, Benjamin and the family were in Brownsville, PA, where several of Benjamin's siblings lived, including Otho Brashear, Ruth (Brashear) Brown,

Elizabeth (Brashear) Brown, and possibly others.

In 1777, in Monongalia Co, VA, now Green Co, PA ("Ten-Mile Creek" area), two of Benjamin's sons, Richard and Tobias, enlisted in Capt. William Harrod's company and were assigned to Gen. [then Col.] George Rogers Clark's command. They spent the winter of 1777 in a fort on "Corn Island" in the Ohio River, just above "the Falls of the Ohio."

The next summer, the civilians who were with Clark, probably including Benjamin and his other sons, built a fort on shore. Benjamin stayed about a year at the "Falls of the Ohio," the site of Louisville in present-day Bullitt Co, KY.

In 1779, Benjamin's son, Marsham Brashear, was a founding commissioner of the town of Louisville and acted as secretary of the commission; he remained in Louisville the rest of his life, while all his siblings and his father moved on. See Vol 4. *Brashear Families of the Ohio Valley* for Marsham's story and family.

Benjamin in Mississippi

In 1780, Benjamin settled in the Natchez area of Spanish West Florida. On 23 May 1780, Benjamin Brashear and others signed a petition, asking that court business be conducted in Natchez for the convenience of its citizens:

Petition to Mr. John Delavillebeuvre (also called Juan de la Villabeuvre), Capt. of Infantry of Louisiana and Commandant of the Fort and District of Natchez:

"We the Subscribing Inhabitants of the above District have the honour to represent to you that agreeable to other British laws established to this country, the --(illegible)- commonly called the Justices of the peace are required to give judgment in any cause that exceeds ten pound sterling, that is forty two dollars, six -- and -- (illegible) the Inhabitants considering the expenses, loss of time, & the difficulty attending those who are obliged to go to the Capital to obtain judgment in all causes which exceeds the above sum, which is of the most pernisious [sic] consequence to their plantations, their families, and those who are obliged to go with them as witnesses. We therefore most earnestly pray that you will be pleased to hear and decide all cases agreeable to the laws of his most Catholic Majesty which shall be brought before you that exceeds the above sum of ten pounds sterling.

"We also most fervently pray that you will be pleased to hear and judge all appeals that may be laid before you from the Court of the Justices of the Peace and freeholders, after Judgment is given by them in order that we may shun the expenses and other inconveniences before-mentioned, being thoroughly convinced not only of your wisdom, integrity, dispatch and of the mildness of the laws of the kingdom of Spain, but at the same time we are confident of the honour, uprightness and purity of conscience with which you will administer them.

"We flatter ourselves that by your meditations Government will grant us these favours and that you will be pleased for the present to act for us in desire."

Signed (among others)

/s/ Benj. Brashear

(*Mississippi Provincial Archives*, Vol. 8)

Benjamin Brashear received a Spanish Land grant near Russum, Mississippi, about five miles south of Port Gibson and close to the boundary of present-day Claiborne and Jefferson

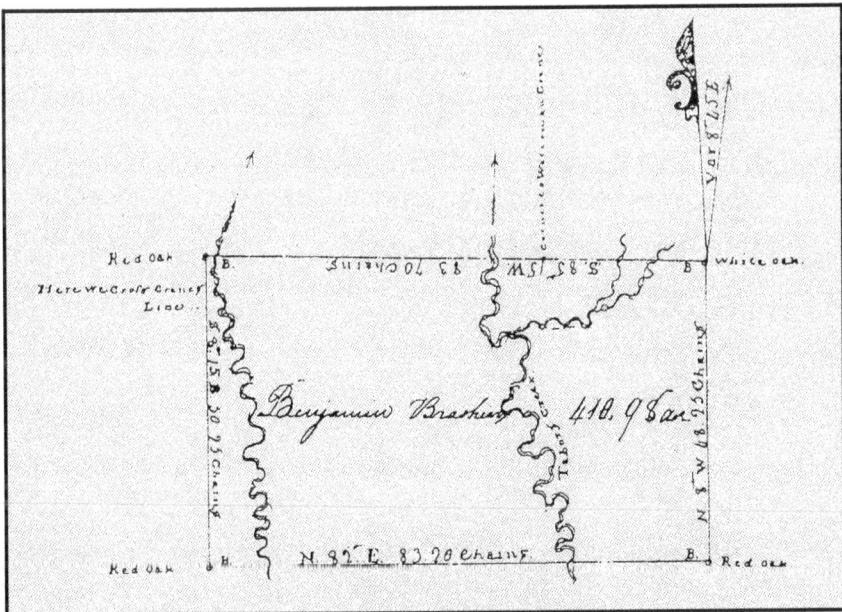

Figure 2: Benjamin Brashears' Spanish Land Grant

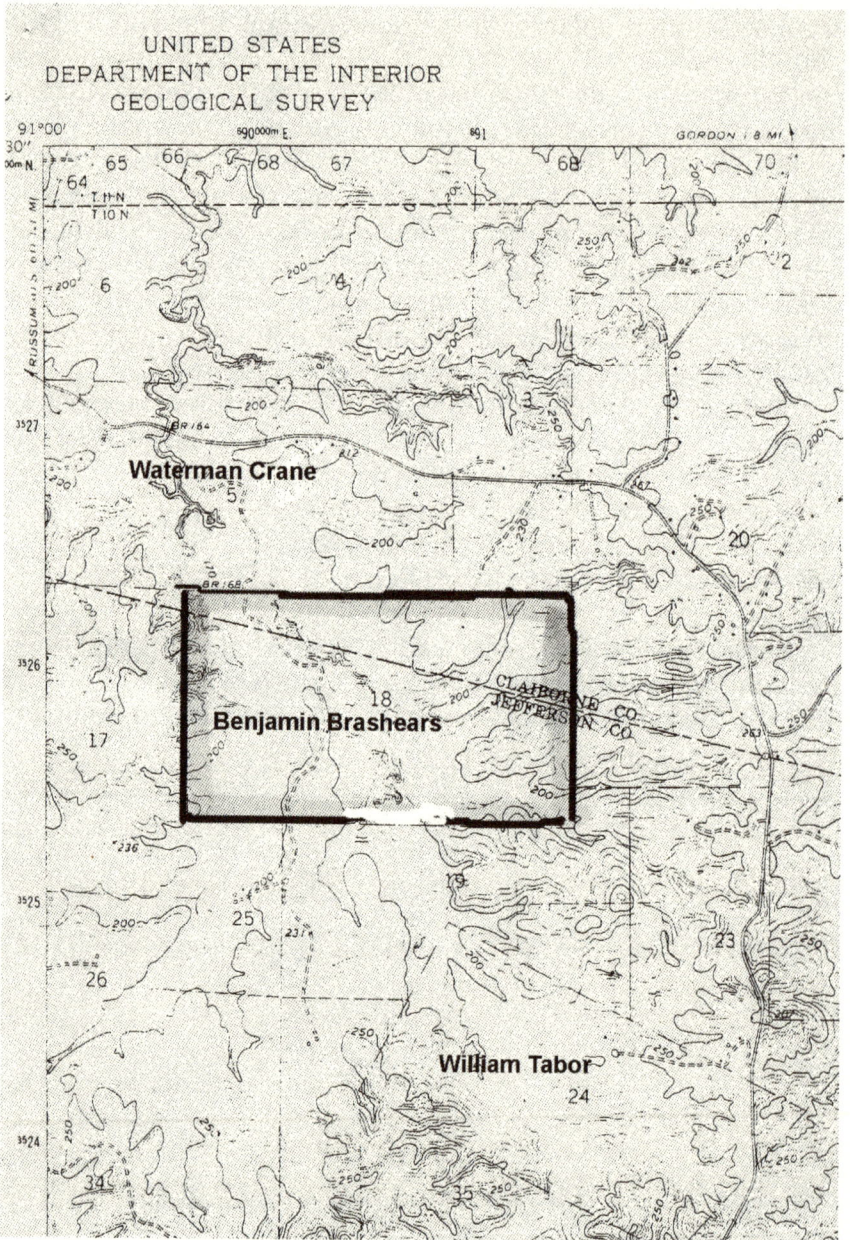

Figure 3: Benjamin Brashears and his neighbors on Bayou Pierre

Counties (once Pickering Co, Mississippi Territory). He received the land grant of 400 arpents on Bayou Pierre, on 20 March 1795. (Thanks to Lanny Headly for the maps.)

After living on his farm under the governments of Spain and the United States, Benjamin died sometime before 3 Oct 1809. (see Back, p.296)

A power of attorney, found in the Smith Coffee Daniell papers, Box 22, Mississippi Archives, lists the children of Benjamin:

Know all men by these presents that Whereas Benjamin Brashear dec'd, late of the State of Mississippi, died leaveing Ten children his legal heirs and representatives and whereas the said Benjamin were he now liveing would have been entitled to [space left blank; some property in Maryland was evidently intended] and whereas also the said ten children of the said Benjamin are named as follows, To wit— Marsham, Richard, Tobias, Turner, Eden, Peggy, Lucy, Sally, Katharine, and Hester, and the said Marsham Brashear having been a Citizen of the County of Bullitt and State of Kentucky and having departed this life leaving his last will and testament and appointing therein the undersigned executors of his said last Will: Now, for and in consideration of the previous and for divers Causes thereunto moveing us, We Anthony Phelps and Lucy [Phelps] Brashear, Executors of the Last Will and Testament of Marsham Brashear, dec'd, do hereby Constitute and appoint Charles A. Wickliffe our true and lawful Attorney for us and in our name to receive and receipt for or sue for and recover any money or property to which the said Marsham would have been entitled in the state of Maryland particulary that portion of the estate of the said [blank] now in the hands of [blank] Duvall of the State of Maryland [something unreadable] ... our said Attorney may lawfully do in the premises. Witness our hands and seals this 17th day of November, 1826

/s/ Anthony Phelps (seal)

/s/ Lucy [X] Brashear (seal)

Filed in Bullitt County Court, Commonwealth of Kentucky, 17 Nov 1826

Charles A. Wycliffe, the attorney, was husband of Margaret Crepps (⁴3022), a granddaughter of Ignatius "Nacy" Brashear (ᵛ¹539; Back#78) of Shepherdsville, KY; Wycliffe was later Governor of Kentucky. The Smith Coffee Daniell papers in the Mississippi Archives also contain a copy of Marsham Brashear's will, dated 28 Feb 1805, and filed in Bullitt Co, KY, 4 Dec 1807.

Figure 4:Windsor Plantation,
from a drawing by a soldier during the Civil War.

Another granddaughter of "Nacy," Nancy (Brashear) Hughes
([v4]3096; Back#217; d/o Ignatius Brashear Jr and Mary Orme),
was great grandmother of Smith Coffee Daniell Jr, of Windsor
Plantation, Claiborne Co, MS.

Benjamin and Catherine's Family

Family of Benjamin Brashear and Catherine Belt all born Prince
George's County, Maryland: (the above document must be the
one sent by Mr. Daniell to Troy Back; "legal documents relating
to the estate of Benjamin Brashear and his son Marsham, filed
in 1826 in Bullitt Co, KY," says Back, p.297): "...and whereas
also the said ten children of the said Benjamin are named as
follows, to wit: Marsham, Richard, Tobias, Turner, Eden, Peggy,
Lucy, Sally, Katherine, and Hester."

[v5]1.   [7]1. ***Marsham Brashear**, (Back#2765) b. c1750-2, MD, d.
1807, Louisville, KY; m. in fall of 1779, at "Bear
Grass," now Louisville, KY, **_Lucy Phelps_**, d/o Thomas
Phelps, Jr. Theirs was the very first marriage in
Louisville, KY. Marsham Brashear, Lucy Phelps, and
their descendants are treated in Vol 4, *Brashear
Families of the Ohio Valley*. See [v4]1300, which is the
same person as this.

[v5]2.   [7]2. ***Richard Brashear**, (Back#2766) b. c1752-4, MD, d.
1822, MS; m. 1782, **_Ann Brocus_**, d/o William Brocus.
Richard was a Capt. in Rev. War; served with Gen.
George Rogers Clark; later in Mississippi.

v53.   73. ***Tobias Brashear**, (Back#2767) b. c1754-6, MD, d. 1807, MS; m. 1780, **Martha Brocus**, d/o John Brocus (she was cousin of Ann Brocus, wife of Capt Richard Brashear, above.) Tobias was a Capt. in Rev. War; served with Gen. George Rogers Clark; later in Mississippi.

v54.   74. **Margaret "Peggy" Brashear**, (Back#2768); m. 1785, Natchez Dist, **?Joseph or Benjamin Newton**,

v55.   75. **Lucy Brashear**, (Back#2769)

v56.   76. ***Sarah "Sally" Brashear**, (Back#2770) b. 1760, m. **Christian Bingaman Jr**,

v57.   77. ***Catherine Brashear**, (Back#2771) b. 1764, Prince George's Co, MD, d. 15 Nov 1833, Claiborne Co, MS; m. 10 Nov 1787, **Waterman Crane**,

v58.   78. ***R.T. "Turner" Brashear**, (Back#2772) b. c1764, Bladenburg, MD, d. 1831, MS; m.1. a full-blood Choctaw Indian, "a daughter of Taboca," (Taboca was the Great Medal Chief of the Oklafalaya, or Western Division, Choctaw Nation), and became an important trader, Indian interpreter, and inn-keeper in Mississippi; m.2. **Oca-ye-mitta**, a full-blood Choctaw.

v59.   79. ***Hester "Esther" Brashear**, (Back#2773) b. 1765, d. 21 Oct 1801, Adams Co, MS; m. 1788, in Adams Co (near Natchez), **Philander Smith**,

v510.   710. ***Eden Brashear**, (Back#2774) b. 1773, PGCo, MD, d. 9 Nov 1839, unmarried; bur Grand Gulf, MS.

SARAH "SALLY" BRASHEAR and CHRISTIAN BINGAMAN Jr

v56. 76. **Sarah "Sally" Brashear**, (Back#2770, d/o Benjamin Brashear and Catherine Belt) b. 1760, d. St Francisville, LA; m. **Christian Bingaman, Jr**, s/o Christian and Charity Bingaman, and grandson of John Bingaman, of German descent, who settled c1755 on the north fork of the Shenandoah River, Augusta Co, VA, where he was killed by Indians. In 1770, the heirs were in Lincoln Co, KY and soon began migrating to Natchez, Mississippi. In 1776, Christian Bingaman, Jr obtained a 600-acre land grant from Spanish authorities, called "Fatherland" in Adams Co, MS. According to descendant Grace Turner Pardue, they lived there a number of years, but saw greater opportunities in old Feliciana Parish, LA. They moved to a plantation near St. Francisville, West Feliciana Parish, and built a home called "Retreat."

Children of Christian Bingaman Sr and Charity ____:
Adam Bingaman, m. Charlotte C. Surget;
Lewis Bingaman;
John Francis Bingaman;
Christian Bingaman Jr, m. **Sarah Brashear**;
Ann Bingaman, m. Benjamin Walker; and
Sarah Bingaman, m. George Banks.

One of Christian Bingaman's sisters was second wife of Col. Stephen Minor, b. 8 Feb 1760, Philadelphia, d. 29 Nov 1815, Mississippi; Col. Minor was confidential aide and companion to Gov. Manuel Gayoso de Lemos, succeeding him as last Spanish governor and known as "Don Estevan Minor." Little wonder that "Don Estevan Minor" was so friendly to the Brashears clan!

In 1819, Christian Bingaman ran for Governor of Louisiana, but was defeated by Gov. Claiborne. He was a Justice of the Peace until his death in 1825.

Family of Christian Bingaman, Jr, and Sarah Brashear:

[v5]11. [8]1. Christian Bingaman, III; m. 1 Oct 1811, Woodville, MS, Martha Bartley. Christian, III, died, leaving no heirs.

[v5]12. [8]2. Adam Bingaman; m. 19 Nov 1806 (Amite Co, MS, Bk A, #147), Louricy Ratliff. Two ch, but only one lived to adulthood.

[v5]13. [9]x. Charlotte Bingaman; m. 27 April 1827, (2nd wife of) Thomas Turner, b. c1800, s/o Mrs. Agatha (Watts) Turner-Brashears, second wife of Levi Brashear ([v1]356) (ancestor of Henry Sinclair Brashear). Thomas Turner m.1. Nettie Brashear, d/o Levi Brashear and his first wife. Nettie's brother, John Brashear m. Sarah Frances Turner, Thomas Turner's sister who d. in Scott Co, KY. After Nettie Brashear's death, Thomas migrated to Louisiana in the early 1820s, worked as an overseer for Adam Bingaman, met and married Charlotte Bingaman in 1827. Seven children, among whom

v5 14.   10x. Dr. Clarence Bingaman Turner; m. 19 July
                1866, Mary Elizabeth Leavens, d/o Thomas
                Leavens and Elizabeth Whately
v5 15.   11x. Richard Leavens Turner; m. Rosalie
                Virginia Ross
v5 16.   12x. Grace Turner; m.1. Walter Brooks;
                   m.2. _____ Pardue. Grace Pardue was
                   a researcher in this line.
v5 17.   83. Lewis Bingaman; m. 29 Nov 1811, Woodville, MS,
         Eliza Cobb,
v5 18.   84. John Bingaman; m. 5 Dec 1818, Mary Cobb,
v5 19.   85. Sarah Bingaman; m.1. 29 April 1807, Stephen Cobb
         (Estevan in Spanish records), d. 1819, s/o Arthur
         Cobb and Susannah _____, of West Feliciana Parish;
         m.2. Capt. Clarence Mulford,
v5 20.   91. Stephen Cobb, Jr,
v5 21.   92. Mary Cobb,
v5 22.   93. Benjamin Cobb,
v5 23.   94. Clarence Cobb,
v5 24.   95. Catherine Mulford,
v5 25.   86. Ann Bingaman; m. John Ratcliff
v5 26.   87. Catherine Bingaman; m.1. 21 Aug 1814, William
         Washington White, s/o William White, a Rev. war
         soldier (Capt Young's 1st Bn, Cumberland, PA), b. 4
         Feb 1743, Lancaster, PA, d. 1813, Knox Co, KY, and
         Ann Mary Lowery. (William White was s/o Moses
         White and Isabell Cochran and grandson of Hugh
         White of Pennsylvania, whose great-grandfather,
         Henry White, was born in London and came to
         Virginia in 1629); m.2. Samuel Wimbush
v5 27.   91. Lilbourne Lowery White, b. 1815; m.1. Eleanor H.
            Davis; m.2. 10 Dec 1849, New Orleans, LA,
            Catherine Alice Purcell, d/o William Purcell (b.
            Ireland, 1787) and Mary Conville, b. New York,
            1784.
v5 28.   92. James White, b. 1816, d. unmarried
v5 29.   93. Sarah Ann White; m. Samuel Doherty
v5 30.   94. Alfred White, b. 1818, d. unmarried
v5 31.   95. Washington Bingaman White, b. 1819; m. Nancy
            Catharine Irwin

CATHERINE BRASHEAR and WATERMAN CRANE

ᵛ⁵7. ⁷7. **Catherine Brashear**, (Back#2771, d/o Benjamin Brashear and Catherine Belt) b. 1764, Prince George's Co, MD, d. 15 Nov 1833, Claiborne Co, MS; m. 10 Nov 1787, in what is now Mississippi, **Waterman Crane**, b. 1768, Hallifax, Nova Scotia, Canada, d. Feb 1826, MS.

Note on the map that Waterman Crane's land adjoined Benjamin's on the north.

Family of Catherine Brashear and Waterman Crane, (Data from *Biography, History, & Memoirs, Mississippi Abstracts*, Goodspeed Publishing Co, 1891; thanks to Mary Snedeker for the data.)

ᵛ⁵32. ⁸1. Elijah Crane, b. 1790, d. 20 March 1810, unm,

ᵛ⁵33. ⁸2. Silas B. Crane, b. 3 June 1792, d. 7 Jan 1820,

ᵛ⁵34. ⁸3. Lucy Crane, b. 1795; m.1. Hector McNeil, m.2. Brooke Hill,

ᵛ⁵35. ⁸4. Clarissa Crane, b. 12 Jan 1798; m.1. William Christie, m.2. Wm. Young,

ᵛ⁵36. ⁸5. Eden Crane, b. 15 Oct 1799, d. 1819, unm,

ᵛ⁵37. ⁸6. James Crane, b. 17 Dec 1800; m. Martha Ragsdale,

ᵛ⁵38. ⁸7. Malinda Crane, b. 21 Feb 1802, d. 1824; m. James Weston,

ᵛ⁵39. ⁸8. Robert Crane, b. 6 Sept 1804, d. 15 Feb 1824.

HESTER BRASHEAR and PHILANDER SMITH

ᵛ⁵9. ⁷9. **Hester "Esther" Brashear**, (Back#2773, d/o Benjamin Brashear and Catherine Belt) b. 1765, Prince George's Co, MD, d. 21 Oct 1801, Adams Co, MS, bur Smith cem, near Natchez, MS; m. 1788, in Adams Co, MS (near Natchez), **Philander Smith**, b. 11 Jan 1765, Granville, MA, d. 29 June 1824, Natchez, Adams Co, MS, s/o Rev. Jedediah Smith and Sara Cook. (NOT the Jedediah Smith who was an early explorer and trapper in the Rocky Mountains and California.)

After Esther Brashear died, Philander m.2. Susanna Miller Scott, widow of John Scott, who had children by her first marriage. Philander Smith's will is found in Book 1, p.330,

Natchez Court House Records; fully quoted in *Carpe Diem*, pp. 75-79.

"Ester was a daughter of Benjamin Brashear & Catherine Belt, pioneers of Claiborne Co, MS, of a French Huguenot family coming to America as early as 1627. The Brashear line has been traced to royalty." (D'Angerville, *Living Descendants of Royal Blood*, Vol IV). "Benjamin and his family came to the Natchez District by way of PA & KY, arriving in 1780. Securing a Spanish land grant, he settled in the area of Russum in So Claiborne Co. In the Spanish Census of 1792, he claims 400 acres." (ref: *The History of the Descendants of the Jersey Settlers of Adams Co, MS*, Vol II, pp.234-5).

This "touch of royalty" depends upon the erroneous link of Katherine, Mrs. Richard Marsham, with Giles Brent and Mary Kittamaquund, which has been disproved.

Philander Smith, b. 11 Jan 1765, Granville, MA, resided in Natchez as early as 1776 (eleven years old); he died in Natchez, 29 June 1824. Philander Smith served as Conservator of the Peace, Justice of the Peace, Captain of Territorial Militia, Member and Speaker of the MS House of Representatives, and was a founding member of the Mississippi Society for the Acquirement and Dissemination of Useful Knowledge. He was foreman of the Grand Jury that indicted Aaron Burr (*The Order of First Families of Mississippi, 1699-1817*, p.71). It is reported his portrait was painted by Gilbert Smith. (Data collected by Ella Mae White, late of Crassett, AR.)

With such accomplishments, who needs a "touch of royalty"?

Family of Hester "Esther" Brashear and Philander Smith:

[v5]40. [8]1. Catherine Smith, b. 1789, d. 17 Jan 1859; m.1. Col. Nathan Swayze; m.2. John H. Van Court,

[v5]41. [8]2. Jedediah Smith, b. 1790, d. 1824; m. 1816, Mary Ann Gray. Jedediah is reported to have been in the War of 1812 and the Battle of New Orleans, Hines Brigade. He is buried at Grace Church cem, St. Francisville, LA

[v5]42. [8]3. Benjamin Smith, b. 12 Jan 1792, d. 1826; m.13 Feb 1816, Anabelle Scott, his step-sister. Benjamin is reported to have been a Sergeant in Hines Battalion in the War of 1812. He was an Elder of Mt. Carmel Church (where?).

[v5]43.   [8]4. Hester Smith, b. 1793, Second Creek, MS, d. there 1825; unm.,
[v5]44.   [8]5. Courtland Smith, b. 1795, Second Creek, MS, d. 13 Feb 1817, Sandy Creek, near Natchez, MS; unm.,
[v5]45.   [8]6. William R. Smith, b. 1797, d. ?; m. 1822, Anna Henderson,
[v5]46.   [8]7. Lewis P. Smith, b. 1801, d. 1821; unm.

EDEN BRASHEAR, Philanthropist

[v5]**10.** [7]10. Eden Brashear, b. 1773, d. 1839, was the last child of Benjamin Brashear and Catherine Belt. He moved to Mississippi with his father and became a businessman.

In 1811, Eden sold his prospective interest in all estates in Kentucky to his nephew, Richard Brashear (s/o Marsham), according to Walter Brashear, Jr (HSB, p.133), and removed to Claiborne Co, MS, where he engaged in mercantile pursuits.

In 1820, he was present at the treaty negotiations between the U.S. Commissioners and the Choctaw Indians. He signed as a witness; his brother, Turner, was one of the official interpreters. In 1834, he was on the tax lists in Claiborne Co, MS. As a merchant, he became quite rich.

Eden died between 15 Oct 1839, when he wrote his will, and 23 Dec 1839, when the will was proved in court and entered probate. In his will, he left a variety of nieces and nephews some 48 slaves and $15,500, collectively. He also left $10,000 to support a Hospital at Grand Gulf, MS, and the residue of his estate to support the Port Gibson Academy. Afterwards, this academy was renamed "The Brashear Female Academy," in recognition of Eden's gift.

The Will of Eden Brashear:
   In the name of God, Amen.
   I, Eden Brashear, being of sound mind but infirm of body, do by this my last Will and Testament dispose of my worldly effects and property in the following manner, to wit:
   First. I do hereby give and bequeath to Catharine and Siloam Crane, the daughters of James Crane, the following Negro slaves, viz: Daniel and his wife Delsey, and Peter, Hester, William, Louisa, Tom, their children, and Tennessee and her children, Grace and an infant child, and do will that if either

Catharine or Siloam die without children, that the above named slaves shall be the property of the survivor, and if both die without children, said slaves to be divided in equal shares among the children of the said James Crane.

Second. I do hereby give and bequeath to Mrs. Margarite Sharbourne (Sherburne), late Margarite Lindsay, and her heirs, the following negroe slaves, viz: Charles, Sally his wife, Millie, Clarissa, Albert, Mary, Stephen, Aaron, Charles, Ann, Brooks, and Warnock, being the children of the aforesaid Charles and Sally.

Third. I do hereby give and bequeath to Mrs. Clarissa Young the following Negro slaves, viz: Barnet and Hannah his wife, Louisa, Jim, and Margaret, their children, Henry, Dinah, Nancy, and Barry.

Fourth. I do hereby give and bequeath to Mrs. Catherine Nelson, late Mrs. Catharine Brashear, the following Negro slaves, viz: Walter and Mariah his wife, Tom and Jerry children, and Paddy, and require that these Negroes be placed in the possession of Mr. Killingsworth, the son-in-law of the said Catharine, in trust for the benefit and use of the said Catharine only, and at the death of said Catharine, said slaves to be the property of Malinda Killingsworth, late Malinda Brashear, and her heirs.

Fifth. I do hereby give and bequeath to Benjamin Lindsey (Lindsay) the following named Negro slaves, viz: Old Peter and his children, viz: Willoughby, John, Amelia and Billy, Judy, Bill's wife Francis and Monday, their children and Dick.

Sixth. I do hereby give and bequeath to William B. Lindsey (Lindsay) the following described Negro slaves, viz: George, Joe, and Sarah, and three thousand Dollars in cash, to be paid out of the first proceeds of my estate and a cancelment of all notes or obligation due me by said William.

Seventh. I Will and bequeath to James B. Lindsey (Lindsay) Six Thousand Dollars, and to his son, Eden Brashear Lindsey (Lindsay), Two thousand Dollars, to be paid out of the first proceeds of my estate.

Eighth. I will and bequeath to Clara and Mary Bertron, the daughters of the late Caroline Bertron, One thousand Dollars each to be held in trust for their use and benefit, by William Young till they or either of them are of legal age or marry.

Ninth. I do hereby give and bequeath to Malinda Brashear,

the daughter of Tobias Eden Brashear, the sum of Five hundred dollars, to be held in trust by William B. Lindsay for her use and benefit till she attains at legal age or marries.

Tenth. I do hereby give and bequeath to William Young and James P. Parker or their heirs, each, One Thousand Dollars.

Eleventh. My executors are hereby authorized to pay over to the Corporation of the Town of Grand Gulf the sum of Ten Thousand Dollars whenever the said Corporation shall have purchased a lot of Ground and have erected thereon a house calculated for a Hospital. I do leave it discretionary with my executors either to pay the above sum in money or to invest it in some safe stock in the name of the trustees of the Grand Gulf Hospital. The dividends of which stock, only shall be applied to defraying the expenses of said Hospital.

Twelvth. It is my will that all my real and personal Estate, excepting what is otherwise hereby disposed of, be sold, leaving the terms of sale subject to the discretion of my executors. And the proceeds of the sale, after defraying the bequests and legacies heretofore made in this instrument, and all debts or liabilities which I may legally owe, be paid over to the trustees of the Academy at Port Gibson, and their successors in office, for the use and benefit of said Academy and to the trustees of any other incorporated literary institution in the town of Port Gibson, in proportion according the discretion of my Executors.

Thirteenth. It is my wish that my place of Burial be substantially enclosed with iron railings and have a plain Tomb, with my name and age only engraved thereon.

Fourteenth. I do hereby constitute and appoint William Young and James P. Parker Executors of this my last will and testament, and having entire confidence in them, it is my wish that they shall not be required to give any security to the Probate Court for the discharge of their duty as Executors.

In witness whereof, I do hereby sign my name and affix my seal to this my last will and testament, revoking all others, this Eighteenth day of October in the year of Our Lord, Eighteen Hundred and thirty nine (1839).

Eden Brashear (seal)

Done in the presence of:
Benj. F. West
Saml R. Bertron
Wm B. Lindsay

Recorded in Will Book B, No. 2, pages 15, 16, 17, 18, this 23rd day of December, A.D., 1839
J. Wetherall, Clk.

The building which housed "Brashear Academy" (a school for girls) still stands at Port Gibson, though it is no longer a school. "Eden is buried at the bluff of Grand Gulf, where a handsome monument was erected to his memory and an iron fence put up, surrounding his square in the quaint old Cemetery. (Letter from A.K. Brashear, s/o Joseph Newton Brashear, to Walter Brashear, 1 Jan 1926; printed in HSB, p.121)

From *The Weekly Southern Reveille*, of 13 June 1857 (see *Claiborne Co, Mississippi—The Promise Land*, by Katy McCaleb Headley, p.166):

Brashear Female Academy—Miss M. Marvin, Principal, Miss S.M. Warner, Assistant Teacher in English, Latin, Drawing, Painting, etc; Miss M. Schalk, Teacher of Music, French, German, and Spanish.

"Miss Marvin takes this method of informing the public that the next session of her school will commence on Wednesday the 1st of October in the above named academy, which is now in the course of erection in the rear of the Presbyterian Church.

"The principal finds it necessary to open a house for the accommodation of herself and teachers, which will enable her to board a limited number of pupils. The scholastic year will be divided into sessions of twenty weeks each. Instruction will be given in English, German, Spanish, and the Latin Languages. Music upon the Piano, Guitar, Organ, also Drawing, Painting, and Needlework taught.

"Port Gibson, Aug 17, 1856"

2. CAPT. RICHARD BRASHEAR, Soldier on the Mississippi

^{v5}**2.** ⁷**2. Richard Brashear(s)**, s/o Benjamin Brashear and Catherine Belt, was born in Prince George's Co, Maryland, about 1754 and died 27 March 1822, in Jackson, Pascagoula Co, MS. As a youth, he gained fame as a Captain in the forces of Gen. George Rogers Clark, but he had an unhappy marriage and a somewhat obscure later life. He was one of those people who, perhaps, ought to have been a professional soldier: everything he did in the army was successful; almost everything he did in civilian life was a failure. In the records, his surname is spelled indiscriminately with and without the final "s."

In 1775, a man named Richard Henderson from North Carolina formed "The Transylvania Company" and tried to buy about 80% of present-day Kentucky from the Cherokee and Shawnee Indians. He offered six wagon-loads of trinkets, blankets, muskets, powder, and lead. This "purchase" was in violation of both Royal law and the will of the budding American states; so his scheme fairly quickly fell through.

However, he did set up a land office late in 1775 and started selling plots of the land. Draper MSS 17CC201 is an account book of the Transylvania Company. It shows that Richard Brashear opened an account in Kentucky on 12 July 1776. This is about the same time as Marsham and Joseph Brashear were prospecting for locations along the Salt River. (The Draper Manuscripts were collected by Dr. Lyman C. Draper, in the 1800's, and are housed at the State Historical Society, Madison, Wisconsin.)

Documents show that Richard Brashears raised a crop of corn on his Transylvania land in 1775, on Fox Run, a branch of Brashears Creek, which was named for him. Brashears Creek branches north off the Salt River at Taylorsville, Kentucky, in present-day Spencer County. Some of its branches headwater north of Shelbyville in Shelby Co.

The Henderson land grants were declared illegal almost at once, but the Virginia authorities (Kentucky was then a part of Virginia) tried to "honor" them with Virginia Land Warrants, if the person had raised a crop on the land or had started or built a cabin.

Virginia Land Grant Surveys, Vol 4, p.391: Surveyed for Richard Brashears 400 acres of land in Jefferson County, By virtue of Certificate of Settlement, on both sides of Fox Run, a branch of Brashears Creek, beginning in Sarah Boone's west line of a 250 acre tract at two sugar trees, thence north 253 poles to black oak & two sugar trees, then west 253 Poles to two sugar trees, thence south 253 poles to two sugar trees, then east 253 poles to the Beginning. Surveyed January 27th 1783. Joseph Helm, Surveyor.

Virginia Land Grant Surveys, Vol.4, pp.396-7: Surveyed for Richard Brashears 500 acres of land in Jefferson by virtue of part of pre-emption warrant Nr. 331, lying on both sides of Fox Run a branch of Brashears Brook, adjoining his settlement on the East, Beginning at Sarah Boone's Northwest corner two sugar trees, thence east 400 poles to two sugar trees on the top of a Ridge, crossing Fox Run at 64 poles, then North 200 poles to a white oak and two sugar trees, then west 400 poles to two sugar trees and an ash, crossing Fox Run at 190 poles, then south 200 poles to the beginning.

Appended to this survey is a certificate of transfer: "For value received I hereby assign the within platt and certificate of survey to Squire Boone, his heirs and assigns and desire patent to be issued accordingly. Witness my hand on this December the 21st 1783," /s/ Richard Brashears. The grant was issued to Boone, 19 Nov 1785.

Squire Boone, brother of Daniel Boone, had land on Gists Creek and Clear Creek "known by the name of the Painted Stone," both branches of Brashears Creek. Squire Boone loved to carve words in rocks, and he was quite skillful. When he staked out his land on Brashears Creek, he carved "Squire Boone" in a rock to mark his corner, then filled in the carved letters with a red paint of his own manufacture. This marker was known as "The Painted Stone" in many land records for more than a generation. What happened to this stone is unknown, but other stones Squire Boone carved are preserved at Bonneville, IL.

Richard Brashears was serving much of this time in the Continental Army, so his brother, Marsham Brashear, took care of his business for him.

On 22 Nov 1779, "Marsham Brasheir for and in behalf of Richd Brashears this day claimed a settlement and preemption to a tract of Land lying on Fox Run a branch of Brashears Creek, a branch of Salt River, about 3 Miles West of the Painted Stone, by the said Brashears raising a crop of Corn in the year 1775 & 1776. Satisfactory proof being made, they are of the opinion that the s'd Breashears has a right to a settlement of 400 acres to include the above location and the preemption of 1000 acres adjoining, and that a Certificate issue accordingly." (*Reg. KY St Hist. Soc*, V.21, p.56)

On 2? Dec 1780, Richard Brashears deeded to Marsham Brashear 400 acres in Jefferson Co, KY, near "the painted stone." (HSB, p.67)

RICHARD'S MILITARY SERVICE

In 1775, Richard Brashear enlisted in a company organized by Col. Michael Cresap of Frederick Co, MD. Cresap had sent one of his lieutenants across the mountains to western Pennsylvania to raise a company of soldiers to march east in support of General George Washington. (*The Tenmile Country and its Pioneers Families*, by Howard L. Leckey, vol. 1, p.14) Cresap's roster, filed with the National Archives, October 7, 1775, lists private Richard Brashear (who was later a Captain with Gen. George Rogers Clark) and private Joseph Brashear (unidentified, but probably the Joseph Brashear, land speculator, who was killed in 1778 at Fort Wheeling) (ibid. p.15).

In 1777, Richard and his brother, Tobias, enlisted in the company of Captain William Harrod, in Monongalia Co, VA, now Green Co, PA; the company was soon assigned to Col. George Rogers Clark.

Annie A. Nunns, Asst Superintendent, State Historical Society, Madison, Wisconsin, responded in a long letter, 23 Feb 1926, to Walter Brashear, of Louisville, KY, and included several details about Richard Brashear: "In the papers of Captain William Harrod of Monongalia County, Virginia, there is an order to Captain William Harrod in January, 1777, to take fifty men and go down the Ohio in search of Captain Linn's Company, bringing powder from New Orleans. This is printed in Twaites and Kellogg's *Revolution on the Upper Ohio* (Madison, 1908, pp. 226-229). But the muster roll is not printed. In the pay roll accompanying this document (Draper MSS 4NN50) appears the name Richard Brashear as sergeant. This would indicate that he lived at this date (1777) near Harrod. Harrod's home was on Ten Mile Creek, tributary of the Monongahela River, now in Green County, Pennsylvania, but then in Monongalia County, Virginia. See map in Thwaites and Kellogg *Frontier and Defense on the Upper Ohio* (Madison, 1912, frontispiece) for the division made October, 1776, of the West Augusta district into three counties of Monongalia, Yohogania, and Ohio. Unfortunately, the records of Monongalia have been burned."

Early in 1778, Richard Brashears was promoted to Lt. in Capt. Harrod's Company in Col. George Rogers Clark's Expedition against Vincennes, a key in the Revolutionary War defenses against the British and Indians in the Old Northwest. On 15 March 1778, Col. Clark wrote a note to Capt. Harrod at Fort Jackson on Ten Mile Creek, calling attention to the fact that the time for starting to Kentucky was drawing near, and that boats should be sent up the river from Wheeling to Monongahela to take in flour; that he had instructed his recruiting officers to send men to Wheeling for that purpose, and that such men should be subjected to no other fatigue duty until their arrival in Kentucky. Lieutenant Richard Brashear was placed in charge of the party, and Captain Harrod was urged to forward men to aid in the work. (William English, *The Conquest of the Country Northwest of the Ohio*; also *George Rogers Clark Papers*, Illinois Historical Association, VIII, 37, 41, 99).

In a letter to Gov. Patrick Henry of Virginia, dated "Kaskaskia, Illinois Country, February 3, 1779," Gen. Clark refers to Lieut. Rich[d] Brashears as one of his trusted officers. When Gen. Clark left to regroup and garner support, he left Lieut. Richard Brashears in command of the stockade at Vincennes.

On 20 March 1779, Capt. Joseph Bowman, who seems to have been Clark's Adjutant, wrote in his journal: "About 4 o'clock the whole embarked, leaving Lieut. Brashier, command[r] of the fort with Lieut. Bayly, Lt. Chaplin, 40 men, serg[t] & Corp includ'd to take care of the Garrison till reliev'd from Kaskaskias."

A short time later, the fort at Vincennes was abandoned and the troops withdrawn. The British immediately took over again. Early the next year, in the midst of winter, Gen. Clark was called upon to capture the fort again. He sent his trusted Lieutenant Richard Brashear with a detachment across country from Kaskaskia, while another detachment was to move up the rivers by boat to the fort.

Lt. Richard Brashear led his men across river after river, often up to their arm-pits in icy waters and amid storms, carrying their powder and lead in bundles on their heads. But his maneuver was immensely successful. He surprised the British completely (they were looking for an attack from downstream), and he captured the entire British garrison.

Richard Brashear was commissioned Captain on 30 May 1780. He served in the army as Captain through 1782.

From *Conquest of the Country Northwest of the Ohio River*, by William English, 1896, reprint: Ann Arbor, 1966: "George Rogers Clark in September, 1779, was at the height of his success in the Illinois country when he wrote Governor Thomas Jefferson his reasons for wanting to locate a fort on the Mississippi near the mouth of the Ohio. Such a post would command navigation and aid communication with the Spanish at New Orleans. One of the chief arguments was that the post would help control the Chickasaws as well as the large number of Tories and deserters constantly heading downstream.

"In January, 1780, Jefferson authorized the new fort and required that compensation be paid the Indians for its site. He seems, however, to have thought of the area as belonging to the Cherokees; for this or some other cause, no negotiations were made with the Chickasaws and no payment was tendered. Clark chose a site at the Iron Bank (now Columbus, Kentucky), five miles south of the Ohio, and set about erecting his stockade in early 1780. Inducements were offered for settlers in the adjacent town, named Clarksville. The stockade was named Fort Jefferson.

"The outraged Chickasaws demanded immediate evacuation of the fort and village. The demand was ignored, but Clark decided belatedly to offer compensation for the land taken. He arranged for a shipment of goods to the Fourth Bluff and sent one of his best captains, Richard Brashear, to take it there. Brashear (whose name appears in a profusion of forms: Brashears, Bashears, Bessiers, and Beshear) was probably a Pennsylvanian [NOTE: They had that wrong; he was born in Maryland, though the family was living in Pennsylvania when he enlisted], and had been made commandant at Vincennes after Clark re-took it from the British.

"When he arrived at the bluff with his goods, he found no Chickasaws on hand to receive it, probably because the warriors were en route to Fort Jefferson to attack it. To shelter the merchandise until it could be called for, and to protect the detachment he had to leave behind as guard, he built a blockhouse "at the upper end" of the bluff. Since the usual landing place was at the mouth of what would later be called Gayoso Bayou, and since the nearest height above flood level was just south of there, Brashear's structure was probably located in what is now the Auction Square vicinity of Memphis. This hasty blockhouse was still standing in 1791. It was the first recorded building within the town limits of early Memphis, and the first anywhere on the bluff since the razing of Fort Assumption, two miles downstream, forty years before." (See also "The Revolutionary War on the Fourth Chickasaw Bluff," *The West Tennessee Historical Society Papers*, vol. V, (Oct 1975), p.10-11, and George Rogers Clark, Clark's Memoirs, reprinted from William Hayden English, *Conquest of the Country Northwest of the Ohio River*, 1896, Ann Arbor, 1966.)

For his Revolutionary War service in the Illinois campaign, Richard Brashears was issued land warrant #2687, for 4000 acres, on 3 March 1784, for having served 3 yrs as a Capt of the Virginia Line (see *Military Warrants, 1782-1793*, Old Kentucky Land Entries and Deeds).

Military Entries, 1784-1797, record that he actually entered the following plots:
1000 acres, 3 Aug 1782, Mouth of Obyan Creek (Book 1, p.12)
1000 acres, 10 Aug 1784, Cumberland River Survey (Book 1, p.79)
1000 acres, 12 Aug 1784, Mayfield Creek (Book 1, p.102)

He also received lots #68, 111, 112, 114, 134, 236, & bu "B" #194 for 234 acres [I think these lots were in Illinois Territory].

(see Wm H. English, *Conquest of the Country Northwest of The River Ohio, 1778-1783*, and *Life of Gen. George Rogers Clark*, 1886, reprint: Heritage Books, Bowie, MD, 1991).

In all, Richard received bounty land grants amounting to 3234 acres. In company with William Pope and Alexander Scott Bullett, Richard bought the bounty claims of Sgt. William Elms (200 acres), Pvt. Stephen Stephenson (100 acres), and Pvt. Daniel Tigard (100 acres). Sgt. William Elms and others founded the town of Hamburg, Illinois, on Tract 108 of the G.R. Clark Grants.

RICHARD IN MISSISSIPPI

On 13 April 1782, Richard Brashear was apparently getting ready to go down the Mississippi again. He gave to Marsham Brashear, his brother, a power of attorney. This was a general power of attorney, and does not state any specific purpose.

POWER OF ATTORNEY
GIVEN BY RICHARD BRASHEAR TO MARSHAM BRASHEAR
Know all men by these present: that I, Richard Brashear, Captain of the Illinois Department, have made, ordained, constituted and appointed, and by these present for me my heirs and assigns do make, ordain, nominate and appoint my friend Marsham Brashear of Louisville in the County of Jefferson and State of Virginia, my true and lawful attorney, to ask, receive, demand of and from all persons or persons, all such sums of money, likewise discharge all debts, dues and demands that shall appear just; and also to act in as full and lawful manner in the premises as if I myself were present; and I do by these presents covenant and grant that I will at all times ratify and confirm all such lawful acts and things as the said Marsham Brashear shall and may do in the premises by virtue thereof. In witness whereof I hereunto set my hand seal this thirteenth day of April, 1782.

/s/ Richard Brashear
Wit: Ben Pope; Jos. Potter; Mark Thomas

In 1782, at Fort Kaskaskia, Illinois Territory, **Richard Brashears** married *Ann (Brocus) Minor*, widow of John Minor and d/o William Brocus, a Virginia Revolutionary soldier and pioneer settler of Claiborne Co, MS. Richard and Ann settled in the Natchez District of Spanish West Florida, and stayed there until 1786, when Richard (having incurred the displeasure of Spanish authorities— see letters below) returned to the United States; he later moved to the Tombigbee River area in the southeast corner of Mississippi. Richard and Ann were divorced 28 Dec 1805, per his pension application.

Richard and Ann's Family

[v5]71. [8]1. **Celeste Ann Brashears**, b. c?1783, d. 1798; m. 1797, *Arthur Carney*, who died young, before Feb 1804, leaving an orphan.

[v5]72. [9]1. Elizabeth Louisiana Carney, b. c1798, m. 1815, Joseph Nicholls and had four children:

[v5]73. [10]1. Joseph Nicholls Jr,

[v5]74. [10]2. William C. Nicholls,

[v5]75. [10]3. Celeste Anne Nicholls, m. _____ Moore,

[v5]76. [10]4. Mary Nicholls, m. Wade Harrison, of Jefferson Co, MS.

In 1785, Richard was in Kentucky; but in 1786 he drifted south—he was at Fort Stephens on the Tombigbee River in present-day Alabama for a time; about Natchez, Adams Co, Mississippi for a time; then settled in Jackson, Pascagoula Co, MS, where he died 27 March 1822. This whole time, Ann was in Claiborne Co, MS, where her father lived. In a court record of 1804, she was referred to as Nannette Harrington; Harrington was the name of her third husband. (See below)

In 1787, Richard was reported to have a Chickasaw trading post of sorts, in company with his brother, Turner Brashears, and about 30 other men; the fort and trading house was on the site where Memphis now stands. They built a block house at the upper end of the bluff, which stood for many years. (*East Tennessee Historical Society Publications*, XXXIV (1962), 32,33.)

Letter, Arturo O'Neill to Senor Don Estevan Miro, Commandant at Pensacola (Confidential) 8 Sept 1787:

By your confidential Letter of the 14th of last month I am informed of the method you prescribed for giving the presents of Munitions to the Indians and at the same time I received your letter of the 12th of the same month in which you mention the passing of the Talapuches, who killed Davenport and the other traders, through the Chickasaw Towns, without having experienced any resentment on the part of the said Towns. I have noted the contents of the letter and I am of the firm belief that, if goods are sold and Peltries are Bought in Mobile at the same prices that prevail here in the Indian trade, we shall assure ourselves forever and exclusively of the friendship of the Chickasaws and Choctaws, but otherwise I foresee that it will be impossible to attract the said Nations later.

At the place on the Mississippi called Chickasaw Bluffs, an American named Buchiers has established himself with some twenty or thirty other Americans. This Town is being increased daily by vagrants from the said Nation, but the only one that trades with the Chickasaws is the aforesaid Buchiers. I report this to you for your consideration.

Antonio Garzon has arrived from the upper Creeks and has sent word to me that Chief Mad Dog of the Town of Tuckabache, who on the 8th of this month, along with several other Towns, decided to support you, has resolved to attack the American Frontiers, and to take vengeance for the injuries done by the Americans to the Indian Nations, particularly the murdering of eleven Indians from the Town of Casista by the Georgians, because up to the present the Indians have waited for a satisfactory reply from the Americans, but not having obtained it have resolved upon what I have stated....

/s/ Arturo O'Neill

to Senior Don Estevan Miro

On 27 Sept 1787, Miro forwarded a portion of this letter to Don Carlos de Grand Pré, Spanish Governor at Baton Rouge. (Reference for these letters: *Archivo General de Indias, Papeles Procedentes de Cuba*, Legajo 86-6-17. Translated and printed in *Papers from the Spanish Archives*, 1783-1800, Corbitt & Corbitt, p.100-101.)

On 26 Oct 1787, Don Carlos de Grand Pré, Governor of Spanish West Florida (i.e. Natchez, Baton Rouge, New Orleans, etc) wrote the following letter to Senor Don Estevan Miro, concerning Richard Brashear's trading house at Chickasaw Bluffs, as well as the unrest among the Indian tribes. (See *Spain in the Mississippi Valley*, by Kinnaird, Vol. III, Part II, p.236)

October 26, 1787

On the 24th of the current month I received Your Lordship's letter of the 25th of last September in which you tell me of the information given to you by the commandant of Pensacola relative to the man named Brashears, who had come down with twenty or thirty Americans by the Mississippi to the place called Chickasaw Bluff, or Barranacas a Margo which is the same. A pirogue with four Americans and one woman arrived [in Mississippi]. They came from Fort Pitt whence they started five weeks ago, and from them I obtained the information which follows.

Richard Brashears is a former inhabitant of this district, where he left his wife, who is the daughter of William Broakas. He went to America on a passport from Lieutenant Colonel Don Francisco Bouligny on the express condition that he should not be permitted to return to this district. This man left the Falls or the Rapids of the Ohio with one of his brothers who was living there and twenty-five or thirty other Americans. They went together down the Mississippi as far as the place called the Chickasaw Bluff in order to establish themselves there and set up trade with the Chickasaw Indians and some of the Choctaws; but the disturbances made by Indians over their territories and the death of Davenport and others who were killed either by the last-named Indians or the Talapoosas, compelled them to abandon this site, and obliged Richard Brashears to retreat to the villages of the Chickasaws, where he is now with seven or eight men. His brother is at the Falls with the rest, where they saw him when they passed by.

The projects of these four Americans for settlement and trade with the Indians have been entirely given up. Their information was confirmed today by two reliable inhabitants who have returned from the Choctaws and Chickasaws where they went with my permission to look for stolen horses. They say that they saw Richard Brashears, but that he had no influence or standing among the Indians.

The four Americans, who are named James Garland, John Wilson, Robert McGuinnes, and David White, also state that the flatboat in which they left Fort Pitt with all their provisions was taken by the Indians twenty-five leagues above the post of Arkansas. At Fort Pitt an officer of the staff of that place ordered them to take with them the two great Chickasaw and Choctaw chiefs who had just arrived there in a coach from Philadelphia at the expense of the General Congress, and to carry them with all the goods and presents which they had to the Barranacas a Margo or Chickasaw Bluff. This they did. They say that these two chiefs were invited by the Congress to go to Philadelphia where a treaty was made with them, forming an alliance against the Talapoosa Indians, and that the two chiefs are to have their people armed immediately so as to join the nine hundred Americans ordered to be raised in the State of Virginia, and are to set out on the march on the second notice that they receive. It has been arranged with the Indians that on the 1st of November this militia should be in the villages of the Chickasaws, where the ceremony is to take place and preparations for the campaign are to be begun.

The two Indian chiefs each received a badge and medal on which their names are stamped. Being asked what their names were, they replied that they could only remember the name of the chief, which is Py Omuttahan [probably Payomataha, also known as Payomingo, Snagbe, and Taboca]. This is all that I could learn on the subject.

In regard to the settlements of the Ohio these same Americans gave the following reports as being also very certain:

The General Congress had sent out without effect repeated orders that all the inhabitants who had established themselves without permission on the right bank of the Ohio would have to leave it immediately. To put the last order into effect, Congress ordered a body of troops to go there. These troops burned all the houses, cut down the corn, and destroyed all the provisions then on hand, so that those families were under the necessity of going to settle on the left bank of the same river, as well as all the inhabitants of Wabash and those of the post of Vincennes. It is the intention and purpose of the Congress, after having reduced or destroyed the Talapoosas, to put on public sale all the lands on the right bank of the Ohio from Fort Pitt to its confluence with the Mississippi. The profit from it is to serve as payment in part for the continental debt.

The aforesaid Americans took here the necessary oath of allegiance until orders are received from Your Lordship whether they are to remain here or not.

God keep Your Lordship many years.

Fort Panmure of Natchez, October 26, 1787

Carlos de Grand-Pré

to Senor Don Estevan Miro

On 12 May 1803, Richard Brashears transferred a power of attorney, in which he acknowledged that his branch of the family knew the other branch of Brashears, who lived among and intermarried with Choctaws:

TRANSFER OF POWER OF ATTORNEY
FROM RICHARD BRASHEARS, AGENT FOR JAMES DANLEY,
TO ZADOC BRASHEARS
(written in Spanish)

Be it known to all who may see this act that I, Richard Brashears, a citizen of the settlement of Washington on the Tombigbee River in the territory of Mississippi, as attorney for James Danley of said settlement and territory, that I depose and give my full power and in particular to my cousin and friend Zadoc Brashears, resident of Thompson's Creek, in the dominions of His Catholic Majesty, in order that in my name and in the name of the said James Danley, have and pass the sale of the following five head of slaves of the property of the said James Danley, named: Rosa, thirty-five years old; Amey, fifteen years old; Milley and Comley eight years of age, and Ana, three years of age, to Christian Bingaman, a resident of New Feliciana in the fourth district, as his property in order that he enjoy them as his slaves and dispose of them as he wishes as his true property, without anyone being able to impede him in any form and in order that this be evident, I sign with the Alcalde John O'Connor and the witnesses of assistance, Solomon Alston, and William Barker, New Feliciana, Fourth District, May 12, 1803.

/s/ Richd Brashers

(*Archives of Spanish West Florida*, v.7, p.356-7)

Christian Bingaman was, of course, Richard's brother-in-law, husband of his sister, Sarah; the Bingamans lived in New Feliciana, Spanish West Florida.

On 1 March 1805, there is a court sale of land near the Court House of Washington Co, AL, on Broad and Main Streets, (probably town of Wakefield, but possibly St. Stephens) "adjacent to the line of Richard Brashears."

On 24 Aug 1805, Richard Brashear received a pre-emption certificate for land on the west side of the Tombigbee River, original Settler: Patrick Brewer. This plot on Sunflower Creek was among the British patents disallowed by U.S. Land Commissioners, 15 March 1804 (American State Papers, Public Lands, v.1, p.?)

On 7 Nov 1805, Richard Brasher endorsed a petition of sundry inhabitants of the County of Washington, in the Mississippi Territory (Alabama Department of Archives & History, Montgomery). The entire Washington Co area, including everything between the Pearl and Chattahoochie Rivers, had only 733 white residents when the county was formed in 1800. All of present-day Alabama was in Mississippi Territory until 1817, when Alabama territory was formed. Alabama became a state in 1819.

31 Dec 1807— Date of entry to land grant East of Pearl River, to Richard Brasher of Washington Co, MS, See p.34, Ledger, Credit System, Huntsville Land Office, 1800-1816. (AL Dept Arc&Hist, Montgomery) See also *Territorial Papers of the United States*, comp & ed by Clarence Edwin Carter, GPO, Wash DC, v.5. See also *Private Land Claims*, on file with the Alabama Secretary of State, v.1, p.21.

ANN (BROCUS) MINOR-BRASHEAR-HARRINGTON-TABOR

Ann Brocus, only child of William Brocus Sr who died 1805, Claiborne Co, MS, was married four times, according to the court records of the settlement of her father's estate and marriage records at Natchez.

Ann m.1. John Minor, who d. prior to 1782; she had two sons by him, Stephen and William Minor (mentioned in her father's will; Stephen d. 1821).

Ann m.2. 1782, at Kaskaskia, IL Terr, **Richard Brashears** (^{v5}2),
by whom she had one child, a daughter; they were divorced
28 Dec 1805, ten years after she married her third husband.
Ann m.3. 1 Jan 1795, at Natchez (wits: George Caughan, Mr.
Ashley), Thomas Harrington, d. bef May 1804, by whom she
had one son, Thomas, and one daughter, Elizabeth, who m.
Thomas B. Mcgruder.
Ann m.4. 21 Feb 1821, in Claiborne Co, MS, William Tabor, but
had no children. This marriage record has her name as Ann
Brashears. Ann d. 1831. Note on the map on page 8 that
William Tabor's land was very near the Spanish Land Grant
to Benjamin Brashear.

Ann Brashears produced a certificate of survey made 11 Nov
1788 by William Thomas and testified that she had a Spanish
warrant for a place called White Ground Lick near Benjamin
Foy's camp on Bayou Pierre. Disallowed by the commissioners
under the act of March 31, 1808, regarding warrants within the
district East of the Pearl River. (*American State Papers, Public
Lands*, v.1, p.?) Bayou Pierre is nowhere near being <u>east</u> of the
Pearl River; it is on the Mississippi, about 10 miles above
Natchez. In 1792, it had 3 houses and about 30 acres in
cultivation. The surrounding area was "pretty thickly inhabited
by settlers from Virginia, the Carolinas, Georgia, and a few
stragglers from the east."

From "Minutes of the Orphans' Court," Claiborne Co, MS,
February Term, 1804 (p.15): Nannette Harrington applies for
letter of Guardianship on Estate and person of Elizabeth
Louisiana Carney, infant daughter of Arthur Carney, dec'd, as
Grandmother of the child. Matilda Carney and Tobias Brashears
make application for the same. William Brocus Sr, the Great-
grandfather of the child makes application also. (p.16):
Guardianship granted to William Brocus Sr. (p.20): Order that
Nannette Brashears & William Brocus Sr be appointed
guardians of Betsy (Elizabeth) and Thomas Cavitt Harrington,
minors, 29 May 1804.

Nannette Harrington is Ann (Brocus-Minor-Brashear)
Harrington, who m. Thomas Harrington after Richard Brashear's
departure. Matilda Carney must be either the dec'd Arthur
Carney's mother or sister. Tobias Brashear, of course, is brother

of Richard Brashear. Harrington must have died early in 1804, leaving the two Harrington children that Ann and her father get custody of in May 1804.

However, Ann continued to use the name Brashear: See Claiborne Co, MS Deeds, Book D, p. 358, 11 July 1814, in which Stephen B. Minor and William B. Minor get the permission of their mother, Ann Brashear, to sell 1000 acres to Samuel Richardson of Adams Co, the land being a tract which William Brocus Sr devised to them in his will, reserving a life interest in the tract to his daughter, Ann Brashear.

Claiborne Deeds, Book D, p.36, 16 Dec 1815, William B. Minor and Elizabeth, his wife, sell 1000 acres on South Fork of Bayou Pierre to William Willis for $3,000, "being the same tract on which William Brocus resided at the time of his death [1805] and gave to Ann Brashears in her lifetime and after her death to her children Stephen B. and William Minor, being a Spanish Grant and recorded in written Evidence, p.135, by John Giroult, Translator & dated 18 June 1792."

Ann [X] Brashears signed to relinquish her rights.

3. CAPT. TOBIAS BRASHEAR and MARTHA BROCUS, of "Pleasant Hill," MS

v53. ⁷3. **Tobias Brashear**, (Back#2767) s/o Benjamin Brashear and his wife, Catherine Belt, was born in Prince George's Co, MD, c1754-56, and died in Dec 1807, at his plantation "Pleasant Hill" on the Big Black River, in Claiborne Co, MS. This plantation was surely named after his father's plantation of the same name in Prince George's Co, MD, where Tobias was born.

Military and Land Records

In 1777, Tobias and his brother, Richard, enlisted as privates in the company of Capt. William Harrod, of Monongalia Co, VA, now Green Co, PA. They served in the Revolution in the forces of Gen. George Rogers Clark, in the Northwest Campaign, 1777-1783.

Apparently, Tobias was a man of considerable talent. His service, as far as we can tell, was all along the Mississippi and at the fort at Kaskaskia, yet he rose to the rank of Captain before the end of the war. His company was charged with the defense of the Mississippi River, but, since no attacks came, he was not involved in a great many battles after the first attack on Vincennes.

From 1786 to 1795, a stockade called "Brashear's Fort" was in use on the banks of the Mississippi River in Monroe Co, IL; it was at the site of present-day Harrisonville, IL, about 25-30 miles downstream from present-day East St. Louis and 40-50 miles upstream from Kaskaskia. The fort was possibly named for Capt. Tobias Brashear, who did duty along the Mississippi near Kaskaskia during the Revolution.

Tobias was discharged shortly before 17 Oct 1780 at Fort

Kaskaskia, with the rank of Captain. He is listed in the DAR Patriot Index, page 81. "Tobias Brashear: b. c1756, d. 12-1807, m. Martha Brookes, Capt. IL". "Brookes" as surname of wife is a mistake; it was Brocus.

In October, 1780, at Fort Kaskaskias, Illinois Territory, he married **Martha Brocus**, b. c1760, VA, d/o John Brocus. (John Brocus was a brother to William Brocus, father of Ann Brocus, Mrs. Richard Brashear; Martha and Ann Brocus were therefore cousins.) Tobias, his wife, and his father-in-law departed for Natchez almost immediately with a Col. Montgomery. (Col. Montgomery was en route to Virginia, via New Orleans, to obtain support, i.e. supplies, for Gen. Clark.)

After about a year in Natchez, Tobias and Martha returned to the Illinois Territory, in 1782, and settled first in the "Village of St. Phillips" and later on a 400-acre farm in present-day St. Clair Co, near Cahokia, IL, (region of East St. Louis) probably his Revolutionary War bounty land. Their first three children were born in Illinois.

Tobias Brashears is listed on a petition (in French) from the Inhabitants of Kaskaskia to the President of the [Continental] Congress, 22 June 1784. (*Index to the Papers of the Continental Congress 1774-1789*, compiled by John P. Butler, v.1, p.566; Nat'l Archives: *M247, r37, i30, p.435*.) He is also on a list of American inhabitants of the Illinois Country, Kaskaskia, in a letter to Barthelemi Tardiveau, 27 Aug 1787 (same ref.; Nat'l Archives: *M247, r62, i48, p.185*.) and on a list of male inhabitants of the Illinois Country, place unspecified, 7 Sept 1787 (same ref.; Nat'l Arc: *M247, r62, i48, p.176*.) [NOTE: Beltashazer Brashears (unidentified) also appears on the last list.]

About 1789, Tobias and his family returned to the Natchez District. "When new settlers wanted land grants, they had to become Spanish subjects. When allegiance was taken to the Spanish King, they most likely had their fingers crossed" (Article in Gen. Helper, Nov/Dec 1983, p.12: Legajo, "Natchez-on-the-Mississippi"). Tobias Brashears appears on a list of "Americans," 3 June–5 July 1789.

The Spanish Census of 1792 shows him living on his plantation, "Pleasant Hill," on Big Black River, Claiborne Co, MS. The Spanish government granted him title to 703 arpents of land on Big Black River, six miles from its mouth, on 29

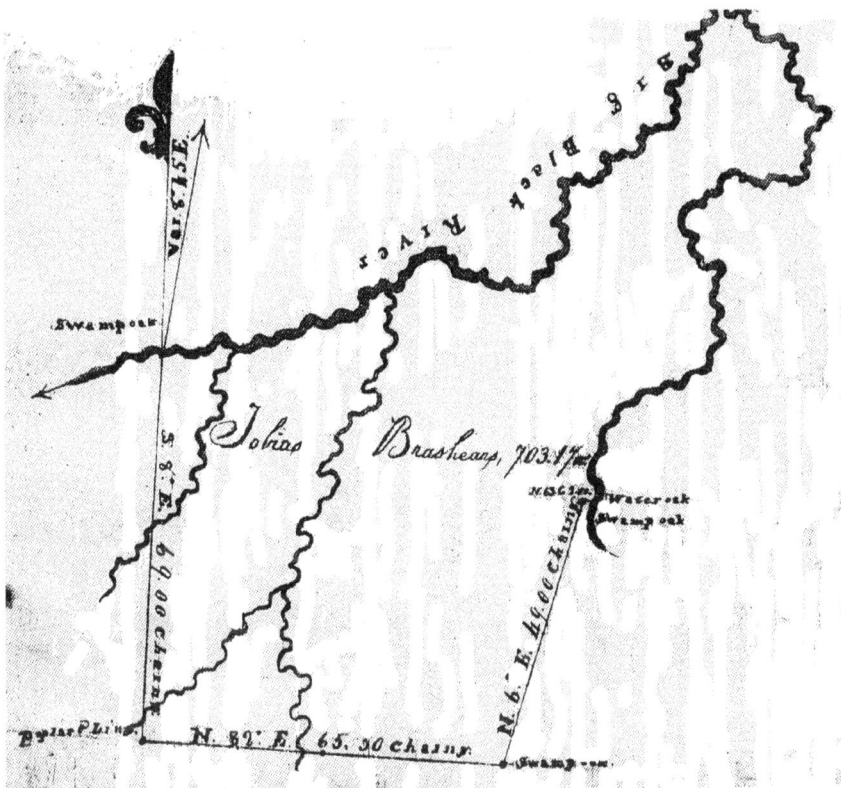

Figure 5: Tobias Brashear's land grant on Big Black River

March 1795. This grant was recognized and certificate of title issued on 20 May 1805 by the United States when it took over (see *American State Papers, Class VIII, Public Lands*, vol.1, 1789-1808, p.52).

Tobias also had two plots of land on Bayou Pierre, where his father's land grant was. On 2 Oct 1805, he was granted certificate of title to 256 (or 220) acres on Bayou Pierre, originally granted to Reuben Proctor by Spanish warrant #308 on 24 Oct 1794 (same ref, p.76). See maps on next pages.

On 3 Sept 1798, Tobias Brashears was listed as Lieutenant of Horse, and Eden Brashears (his brother) as Lieutenant in the Militia (*Territory of United States— Mississippi, 1798-1817*).

On 6 May 1799, Gov. Sargent of the Mississippi Territory appointed Tobias Brashears Judge of the Common Pleas Court of Quarter Sessions and "Conservator of Peace," Pickering Co, MS, 1798-99. He was also Captain of Pickering County Militia;

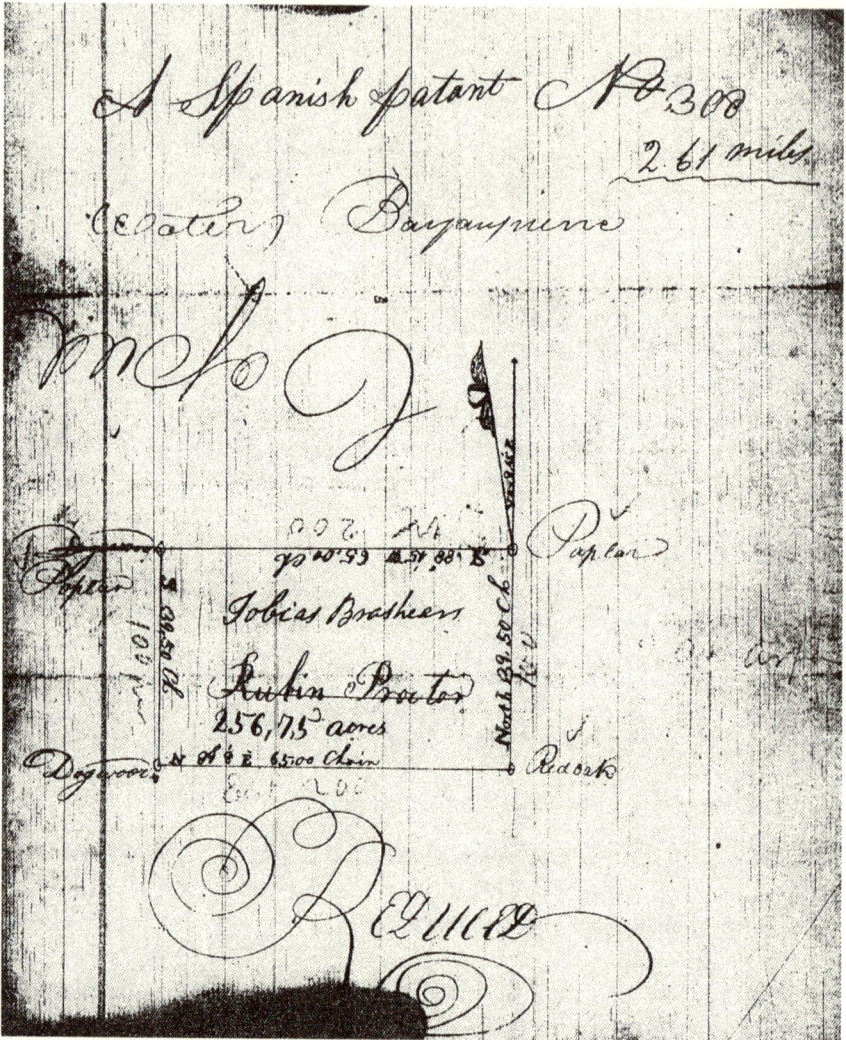

Figure 6: Topbias's Grant from Reuben Proctor

Justice of the Quorum; Judge of Court of General Quarter Sessions and Court of Common Pleas.

Tobias Brashears died at "Pleasant Hill" in Claiborne Co, MS, in 1807, and Martha (Brocus) Brashears died there in Jan 1813.

1820 Census, Claiborne Co, MS:

Ann Brashears	000000-00001-00	ex-wife of Capt. Richard Brashears
Turner B. Brashears	000110-10010-00	Turner Belt Brashears

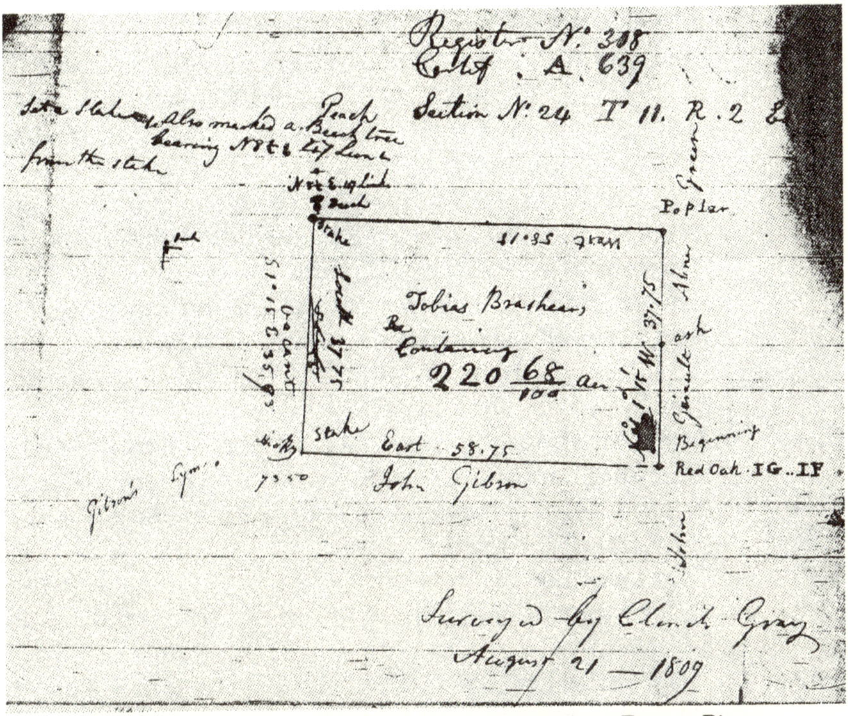

Figure 7: Another version of Tobias's grant on Bayou Pierre

Tobias E. Brashears   000100-00100-00   Tobias Eden Brashears
  1830 Census, Claiborne Co, MS:

Marsham F. Brashears	00100-01000	Marsham Franklin Brashears
Tobias E. Brashears	10100-20100	Tobias Eden Brashears
Turner B. Brashears	11110-01100	Turner Belt Brashears
Eden Brashears	02110-01000	Eden was unmarried, but raised some of Turner Belt Brashear's orphans

Claiborne Co, MS, Tax List, 1834:

Breashears, T. E.	[Tobias Eden Brashears]
Breashears, Eden	[s/o Benjamin Brashear and Catherine Belt]
Breashear, F. B. (estate	[copyist mis-read F. for T.; this is Turner Belt Brashears]
Breshears, M. F. (estate)	[Marsham Franklin Brashears]

Tobias and Martha's Family

[v5]91.   [8]1. ***Turner Belt Brashear**, (Back#2882) b. c1783-5, IL Terr, d. Claiborne Co, MS, 1831-34; m. c1815 in Claiborne Co, MS, **Catherine Newton**, d/o Benjamin Newton. After Turner died, Catherine m.2. 1834,

William Nelson.

^{v5}92.   ⁸2. ***Martha Brashear**, (Back#2883) b. c1788, St. Clair Co, IL Terr., d. 17 July 1821, at Port Gibson, MS; m.1. 1805, at Port Gibson, Claiborne Co, MS, *Judge William Lindsay*, b. Pittsylvania Co, VA, 1769, d. Dec 1817, on the Natchez Trace in the Old Choctaw Nation; m.2. 26 March 1820, at Port Gibson, *John Gibson*, s/o Samuel Gibson, the founder of Port Gibson, MS. No children by the second marriage.

^{v5}93.   ⁸3. **Benjamin Woodward Brashear**, (Back#2884) b. c1789, IL Terr; d. 1813, Claiborne Co, MS (not in his mother's will, written 1813)

^{v5}94.   ⁸4. **Lucy Brashear**, (Back#2886) b. c1791-5, Natchez Dist, MS; d. Claiborne Co, MS; m. bond 18 Oct 1810 in Claiborne Co, *David Lee* (bondsman: James Lee). David Lee d. c1825.

^{v5}95.   ⁹1. David Lee Jr,

^{v5}96.   ⁹2. Catherine Lee, m. William T. Irish, moved to Madison Co, MS

^{v5}97.   ⁹3. Martha Lee, m. John S. Gooch, Claiborne Co, MS

^{v5}98.   ⁹4. Elizabeth Lee, m. John Briscoe, and left MS

^{v5}99.   ⁸5. **Priscilla Brashear**, (Back#2885) b. c1793, Natchez Dist. MS, d. 1814, Claiborne Co, MS

^{v5}100. ⁸6. ***Tobias Eden Brashear**, (Back#2887) b. c1795-7, Natchez Dist. MS; m.1. 29 July (or 3 Aug) 1820 in Claiborne Co, MS, *Matilda Duncan*, who may have died in childbirth with her second child; m.2. 17 Aug 1824, Warren Co, MS, *Martha Ann Sharp*, b. c1809, who was mother of the other child. Gainesville Advocate: 17 July 1837: "died in this place, on Sabbath night last, Martha Ann, wife of Tobias E. Brashears in the 29th year of her age. The deceased was a native of this county."

^{v5}101. ⁸7. **Marsham Franklin Brashear**, (Back#2888) b. c1797, Natchez Dist. MS, d. 1832, Claiborne Co, MS; m. 17 Aug 1824, Warren Co, MS (Book C, p.188), *Lucinda Bullock*, d/o Jonathan Bullock. After Marsham F. Brashear's death, Lucinda (alias Elizabeth) Brashear, m.2. 14 March 1832, Warren Co, MS (Bk D, p.274), William D. Bush, with Jonathan Bullock as surety. That's the same date and place as the marriage of

Tobias E. Brashears m. Martha Ann Sharp.

v5102.   9 1. **William F. Brashear**, b. 1832, after the death of his father, d. 1833, Claiborne Co, MS.

The Will of Martha Brashears, made 15 Nov 1813, recorded 15 Nov 1814, Claiborne Co, MS: names sons: Turner Belt, Tobias Edon, Mersham Franklin, all to have slaves; daughters: Priscilla Brashears and Lucy Lee, to have slaves. Faithful old servant, Peter, to have his freedom. Executors: David Lee, Isaac Repalje, Teisilla Brashear (Priscilla). Witnesses: Thomas Fortner, William E. Campbell, and Lain Cloyd.

Thomas Fortner was French and a relative. David Lee was a son-in-law. Isaac Rapalje was from Holland; he married Elizabeth Ross, the sister of John Ross who died in Claiborne Co, in 1803. He was apparently only a good friend.

Turner Belt Brashears and Catherine Newton

v5**91**. 8 1. **Turner Belt Brashear**, (Back#2882; s/o Tobias Brashear and Martha Brocus), b. c1783-5, IL Terr, d. Claiborne Co, MS, 1831-34; m. c1815 in Claiborne Co, MS, **Catherine Newton**, d/o Benjamin Newton. After Turner died, Catherine m.2. 1834, William Nelson. Turner's great-uncle Eden Brashear took the children, Amelia and Joseph, "to raise," but Amelia was married in her mother's home.

v5103.   9 1. **Amelia Malinda Brashear**, (Back#2991), b. 24 Oct 1819, d. 7 March 1845, age 25 yrs 4 mo 11 days (Killingsworth Cem, Jefferson Co, MS); m. 18 May 1837 (reported in *Port Gibson Correspondent*), **Anon Washington Killingsworth**, b. 18 Feb 1814, d. 12 May 1882, s/o Noel Killingsworth (1778-1831) and his wife, Jane Scott, of Richland Co, SC.

Anon and Amelia's marriage was reported in the *Port Gibson Correspondent*, see *Marr. & Deaths from MS Newspapers*, v.2, p.212: "married on Thursday evening, the 18th, at the residence of Mrs. William Nelson, by N. McDougal, Esq, Mr. Anon W. Killingsworth of Jefferson Co to Miss Amelia M. Brashears of this Co."

Her death was reported in *Port Gibson Herald*, 13

March 1845. see *Marr. & Deaths from MS Newspapers*, v.2, p.243: "died at Red Lick, Jefferson Co, MS, Mrs. Malinda Amelia Killingsworth [sic], only daughter of late E.B. Brashers, age 33." Her tombstone, however, says she was 25 yrs, 4 mo, and 11 days old.

A.W. apparently married again, for there is a child buried in Killingsworth Cem, b. 1861, d. 1865.

^{v5}104. ^{10}1. Uncas Brashears Killingsworth, d. 24 Sept 1840, 2 yrs, 3 mo, 26 days.

^{v5}105. ^{10}2. Katherine N. Killingsworth, m. Benizah Ellis Killingsworth

^{v5}106. ^{10}3. Noel Scott Killingsworth, b. 5 Aug 1843, d. 27 Jan 1862; who served in CSA. His memorial in Killingsworth Cem says "Jefferson Artillery, d. at Bowling Green."

^{v5}107. ^{10}4. William Woods Killingsworth, b. 21 Aug 1861, d. 24 Oct 1865, "s/o A.W. and M. Killingsworth" in Killingsworth Cem.

^{v5}108. ^{9}2. **Margaret Newton Brashear**, (Back#2990) b. 1817, d. 16 March 1819, "age 19 months, 10 days," bur Brashears Cem, south of Port Gibson.

^{v5}109. ^{9}3. **Benjamin Albert Woodward Brashear**, (Back# 2992), b. 1822, d. 23 Aug 1823, "age 1 yr 5 mos", bur Brashears Cem, south of Port Gibson.

^{v5}110. ^{9}4. ***Joseph Newton Brashears**, (Back#2993) b. 27 Nov 1823; m. **Martha Elizabeth Garrett**.

The Will of Turner Belt Brashears

The last will and testament of Turner Belt Brashears, Planter of the County of Claiborne and State of Mississippi -- I Turner Belt Brashears considering the uncertainty of life and being now of sound and disposing mind and memory, do make and publish and declare this my last will and testament in manner and form following. That is to say, after all my just debts are paid, I give and bequeath all my property both real and personal as follows--

First. I give unto my beloved wife Catharine Brashears during natural life the use of the dwelling house and necessary out houses where we now reside, and one hundred acres of lands adjoining the same as she may select together with the five following negroe Slaves for life, named Ellen, Sylva,

Edmond, Bill, and Leonard, and their increase. Also the whole of my household and kitchen furniture together with all my farming utensils and my whole stock of horses, hogs, cattle, and sheep--

Secondly. At the death of my said wife, I give and bequeath the property aforesaid as herein after mentioned subject to the life estate and reservation in favour of my wife aforesaid--

Thirdly, I give and bequeath unto our dearly beloved daughter, Amelia Malinda, the tract of land and plantation which I have recently purchased and obtained from my kind and respected uncle, Eden Brashears, adjoining my home residence, together with the following negroes, Slaves for life and their increase namely, Betty and Corsa, Eliza and Jim, Manson and Emily, Clarisa, Julia, Susan, Ann, Sabra, Harriet, Martha, and Allan and the three following subject to the life estate of my beloved wife as aforesaid and their increase, namely Ellen, Edmond, and Leonard.

Fourthly, I give and bequeath unto our dearly beloved son, Joseph Newton, the plantation on which I now reside being the home place and a tract of land near the same containing one hundred acres more or less, bought by me from Josiah Rundell, and also, the following negro slaves for live, namely, Dick, Orvil, Sillah, James, Nelson, Abram, Peggy, Levi, Phebe, Creacy, Right, Caleb, Caroline, Alphea, Harrison, and Arab, and the two following, Bill and Silva, subject to the life estate of my beloved wife as aforesaid in the said two negroes last named, and in the dwelling house the one hundred acres of land and the convenient houses as aforesaid--I also give and bequeath to my wife during her natural life, one negro girl named Mary not before disposed of, and at the death of my said wife, I give the last named negro girl Mary to my son Joseph Newton to be a slave for life--

Fifthly, I do hereby declare it as my will that the property herein given to our beloved son Joseph Newton, and all that he may in any manner inherit from me shall not vest absolutely in him in fee simple, until he arrives at the age of thirty years, so that he shall not sell or convey the same in full right until he arrives at such age -- though my will is that he shall have and possess the use and advantages of the same at all times through my Executors, or his guardians until his arrival at the age of twenty one years, and then he shall be entitled to take possession of said property-

Sixthly, should I die without other heirs than those herein provided for and they should both die before arriving at the period and legal possession of the property herein specified and bequeathed, they both dying without legal heirs, children of their own bodies, then in such case it is my will that the whole of said property should return to my beloved wife, Catharine Brashears, should she survive them and be enjoyed by her during her life.

Seventhly, in case of the death of one or the other of my two children, it is my will that the other surviving one should inherit the property of the deceased, he or she dying without legal heirs of his or her body, lawfully begotten--

Eighthly, And it is my will that should both of my said children die without heirs that after the provisions made for my wife in the Article, that all the personal property willed to Amelia Malinda should go and I hereby bequeath the same to James Brashears Lindsey (Lindsay), my nephew, and also will and bequeath to him all the real estate left to my son Joseph Newton, subject to the various provisions already made--

Ninthly, I also give and bequeath to my brother Tobias Eden Brashears' daughter, Malinda, the two following named negroes, to wit Mary and Manson, and to my nephew, Benjamin Lindsay, I give and bequeath one half the plantation formerly owned by Eden Brashears, together with the following named negroes, that is, Creaca, Right, Caleb, Caroline, Alpha, Levi, and Phebe, and to my niece Miss Margaret Sherburn, I give and bequeath one half the plantation formerly owned by Eden Brashears, also the following named negroes, that is, Orrit, (Orvil) Sillah, James, Nelson, Abram, Arab, Harrison, Bill, and Sylva, and their descendants, all the above legacies subject to the various provisions made in the above will--

Tenth, And it is my will that the whole of the personal property given by me to my daughter, Amelia Malinda, shall descend and be vested in her and her heirs lawfully begotten of her, my will and object being to secure and entail the said personal property during her natural life and to her children--

And finally, I do hereby constitute and appoint my beloved wife, Catharine, my Executrix, and my friends James P. Parker, and Benjamin Hughes of Port Gibson, and my nephew, James B. Lindsay Executors of this my last will and testament hereby revoking and annulling all former wills and testaments by me at any time made.

In testimony whereof I have hereunto set my hand and seal this Thirtieth day of May in the year of our Lord one thousand eight hundred and thirty three.

Signed, sealed published by the Testator
as his Last Will in our presence who signed
the same as witnesses in his presence
and in the presence of each other.
Witnesses
Francis Murdock
Ial (?) Alison   Truly Recorded; Fees $2.29
W. McDonald   _____ Lucas (?) Clk

Joseph Newton Brashear and Martha Garrett

[v5]**110.** [9]**4. Joseph Newton Brashear**, (Back#2993; s/o Turner Belt Brashear and Catherine Newton), b. 27 Nov 1823, Claiborne Co, MS, d. there 26 Dec 1899, on plantation "Belton," which he had inherited from his father, Turner Belt Brashear (Back#2882). He married **Martha Elizabeth Garrett**, b. 5 May 1836, d. 29 Oct 1904. They had twelve children (Notes by the late Dr. Sherburne Anderson, Baton Rouge, LA):

[v5]111. [10]1. **Turner Belt Brashear, II**, (Back#3088), b. 26 Dec 1853, d. 21 June 1894, age 38

[v5]112. [10]2. **James Garrett Brashear**, (Back#3089), b. 18 Jan 1855, d. 31 Jan 1905, age 49

[v5]113. [10]3. **Cidic Newton Brashear**, (Back#3090), b. 7 Sept 1857, d. 7 April 1878, age 20

[v5]114. [10]4. **Mary Catherine Brashear**, (Back#3091), b. 31 March 1859, d. 11 April 1875, age 16

[v5]115. [10]5. **Benjamin Newton Brashear**, (Back#3092), b. 10 May 1861, d. 11 May 1861, age one day

[v5]116. [10]6. **Joseph Newton Brashear Jr**, (Back#3093), b. 1 Aug 1863, d. 2 Nov 1922, age 60; m. 25 Nov 1897, Claiborne Co, MS, **S. Cornelia Taylor**, b. 6 Feb 1875, d. 14 March 1948, both bur Wintergreen Cem.

[v5]117. [10]7. **Louis Garrett Brashear**, (Back#3094), b. 26 Nov 1864, d. 27 Nov 1864, age one day

[v5]118. [10]8. **Amelia Malinda Brashear**, (Back#3095), b. 28 Oct 1865

[v5]119. [10]9. **Mordecai Pryor Brashear**, (Back#3096), b. 1 Oct

1867, d. 7 Oct 1867, age 6 days

^{v5}120.   ¹⁰10. **Anon Killingsworth Brashear**, (Back#3097), b. 26 Feb 1869, d. 18 May 1932, age 63; m. 15 April 1896, Claiborne Co, MS, **Nora Cole Foote**, b. 29 July 1873, d. 20 Sept 1950. He is the A. K. Brashear who wrote a letter to Walter Brashear, 1 June 1926, which is included in HSB, p.121.

^{v5}121.   ¹¹1. **Mildred Elizabeth Brashear**, b. 21 March 1901, Jackson, MS

^{v5}122.   ¹¹2. **Anona Vaughn Brashear**, b. 1 Feb 1904, Jackson MS, d. 18 May 1932, age 28

^{v5}123.   ¹¹3. **Elinor Wood Brashear**, b. 7 Feb 1906, Jackson, MS, d. 7 Feb 1909, age 3

^{v5}124.   ¹⁰11. **Phineus Magruder "Daddy Doc" Brashear**, (Back#3098), b. 5 May 1871; **Florence Jane Rumaggi**, b. 1880, ?Salerno, Italy. Data from grandson, "Dr. Bob" Brashear, who writes: "She had been adopted by the Kersey family from St. Peter's Orphanage in Memphis, where she and her siblings were placed after the death of their parents. Her Certificate of Death shows she was born in 1880; Father: John Rumaggi, b. in Italy; Mother: _____ Carmentieri; (Dad said at one time she was born in Salerno, Italy. One of her brothers, Robert J., remained at "St. Pete's" and became a Dominican Priest, who served for many years in campus ministries at Yale University. Another brother, whom my Dad called "Cousin Jake," retired from the US Air Force as a Lieutenant General. (I was never completely sure whose cousin he was.)"

^{v5}125.   ¹¹1. **Pascal Merlin "Mr. Jack" Brashear**, b. Port Gibson, MS, 1901, d. 1968 of complications from Parkinson's disease; m. **Mary Lucille "Mrs. Jack" Lewis**, b. 2 June 1905, Hazlehurst, MS, d. 29 March 1998, age 93. Notes by son, Dr. Bob Brashear: 'Jack' is a monicker. His given name is Pascal Merlin Brashear. He was an auto mechanic. While working on a fellow's car, the customer asked, "What in hell do they call you for supper?" He thought for a minute and said, "Jack," and so it was. Mom was known as "Mrs.

Jack" through all these years. She died March 29, 1998 at 93. For the record, she was born in Hazlehurst, MS, June 2, 1905.

v5126. [12]1. **Paul Merlin Brashear**, b. Memphis, TN, 1927, d. 1998 of cancer; m. 1950, *Betty Lewis*, four children.

v5127. [13]1. **Paul Merlin Brashear, Jr**, two children,

v5128. [14]1. **Michael Brashear**,

v5129. [14]2. **Alicia Brashear**,

v5130. [13]2. **Timothy Brashear**, children unknown to "Dr. Bob"

v5131. [13]3. **Martha Carol Brashear**; m. *"Timmy" Pitman*, one son

v5132. [13]4. **Debra Sue Brashear**, one son.

v5133. [12]2. **Robert Marion "Dr. Bob" Brashear**, b. 10 Jan 1929, Memphis, TN. No ch. 76 Alta Vista Drive, Jackson, TN 38305; 731-424-1385; <bobrash@aeneas.net>

v5134. [12]3. **Carolyn Jane Brashear**, b. Memphis, TN, 23 Jan 1932; m. *Glen E. Jones*, 2805 Westwood, Arlington, TX 76012; two children, Jeffrey and Jana Carolyn Jones.

v5135. [11]2. **Dr. Robert Garland Brashear,** orthopedist and long-time team physician for the U. of Tennessee, Knoxville, TN, and Sports Medicine Hall of Fame inductee in Knoxville; m.1. *Marian McGlothlin* (?) of Memphis, who died of tuberculosis; m.2. *Blanche* _____. No children.

v5136. [11]3. **Linnie Carol Brashear**, m. *Macon Turner*. She was a long-time nurse in the Panama Canal Zone. "Uncle Macon" was an engineer in the Canal Zone. They adopted one son, Johnny.

v5137. [11]4. **Kenneth Brashear**, died at age seventeen from influenza.

Martha Brashears and William Lindsay/ John Gibson

v592. [8]2. **Martha Brashear**, (Back#2883; d/o Tobias Brashear and Martha Brocus) b. c1788, St. Clair Co, IL Terr., d. 17 July 1821, at Port Gibson, MS; m.1. 1805, at Port Gibson, Claiborne

Co, MS, Judge **William Lindsay**, b. Pittsylvania Co, VA, 1769, d. Dec 1817, on the Natchez Trace in the Old Choctaw Nation; m.2. 26 March 1820, at Port Gibson, **John Gibson**, s/o Samuel Gibson, the founder of Port Gibson, MS. No children by the second marriage.

v5138.   91. Dr. William <u>Brashear</u> Lindsay, (Back#2994) b. 13 May 1806, d. 7 Aug 1866, New Orleans; m. 6 Nov 1829, **Ruth Caroline Brashear**, (v43099; Back#218) b. 22 Jan 1807, d. 22 Oct 1866, New Orleans, d/o Ignatius Brashear, Jr, and Mary Orme.

v5139.   101. William Brashear Lindsay, Jr; m. Marie Martha Mouton, b. March 1, 1852, Lafayette, LA, d. May 13, 1930, Lafayette, LA (Thanks for data from Rhonda (Wilson) Whitfield.)

v5140.   111. William Brashear Lindsay, III, b. September 27, 1876, Lafayette, LA, d. March 4, 1943, Lafayette, LA; m. Lena Clotile Toups b. July 2, 1893, Thibodeaux, LA, d. December 18, 1980, Lafayette, LA

v5141.   121. William Brashear Lindsay, IV, b. March 2, 1912, Lafayette, LA, d. August 13, 1996, Philadelphia, PA

v5142.   122. Bonita Lindsay b. November 3, 1913, Lafayette, LA

v5143.   123. Felix Hubert Lindsay b. February 23, 1915, Lafayette, LA, d. 1997, Virginia

v5144.   124. Peggy Irene Lindsay b. October 14, 1927, Lafayette, LA; m. Frank Emmett Wilson, Jr. b. January 31, 1922, Church Point, LA, d. March 29, 1986, Lafayette, LA

v5145.   131. Rhonda Anita Wilson, b. October 17, 1950, born Church Point, LA; m. Ross Elliot Whitfield, b. June 22, 1948, Cincinnati, Ohio

v5146.   141. Ross Stuart Whitfield, b. June 15, 1980, Baton Rouge, LA

v5147.   142. Lindsay Elizabeth Whitfield, b. November 10, 1982, Baton Rouge, LA

v5148.   132. Frank Emmett Wilson, III, b. May 7, 1952, Church Point, LA; m. Janet

Faulk, b. March 18, 1953, Rayne, LA

^{v5}149. ^{14}1. Ashley Rae Wilson, b. December 25, 1979, Crowley, LA

^{v5}150. ^{14}2. Mark Joseph Wilson, b. September 15, 1983, Lafayette, LA

^{v5}151. ^{13}3. William Brian Wilson, b. December 14, 1960, Crowley, LA; m. Elizabeth Leicher, b. September 13, 1962, Folsom, LA

^{v5}152. ^{14}1. Samuel William Wilson, b. September 10, 1991, Slidell, LA

^{v5}153. ^{14}2. John Emmett Wilson, b. May 31, 1994, Slidell, LA

^{v5}154. ^{14}3. Maxwell Brian Wilson, b. October 16, 1998, Rockledge, Florida

^{v5}155. ^{9}2. Benjamin Newton Lindsay, d. Dec 1839, Rosedale, LA; m. Ann Wright,

^{v5}156. ^{9}3. James Brashear Lindsay, living in KY in 1840, had a son, Eden Lindsay

^{v5}157. ^{9}4. Margaret Newton Lindsay, b. 1816 on the Natchez Trace, Claiborne Co, MS, d. 25 July 1850 at "Fontana" Plantation, East Baton Rouge Parish, LA; m. 1832, East Baton Rouge Parish, Eugene Amedee Sherburne, b. 1802, near St. Malo, France, d. 2 Nov 1860 at "Fontana" Plantation.

^{v5}158. ^{10}1. William Lindsay Sherburne, b. 21 May 1835, at Plaquemines Parish, LA, d. 12 Feb 1872, at Zachary, LA; m. 3 May 1861, at Baton Rouge, LA, Sarah Eliza Caston, b. 24 July 1844, Amite Co, MS, d. 8 Sept 1898, Amite Co, MA.

^{v5}159. ^{11}x. Martha Newton Sherburne, b. 23 July 1864, Amite Co, MS, d. 13 Dec 1955, Mangham, LA; m. 1 March 1882, Wilkinson Co, MS, Thomas Calvin Gaulden, b. 21 July 1853, Wilkinson Co, MS, d. 27 Sept 1895.

^{v5}160. ^{12}x. Ethel Eugenia Gaulden, b. 30 June 1883, Wilkinson Co, MS, d. 29 March 1957, Baton Rouge, LA; m. 30 Aug 1905, at Gloster, MS, John Albert Anderson, b. 12 May 1875, Independence, KS, d. 17 May 1941, Baton Rouge, LA.

v5161.   131. Dr. John Sherburne Anderson, b. 19
          May 1905, at Elgin, IL; m. 15 Sept
          1928, at New Orleans, LA, Mary
          Mildred Stone Ware, b. 24 Dec 1904,
          Whitecastle, LA (no ch). The late Dr.
          Sherburne Anderson of Baton Rouge
          did a great deal to collect the
          information we now have on this
          branch of the family.

Tobias Eden Brashear and Matilda Duncan/ Martha Sharp

v5**100.** 86. **Tobias Eden Brashear**, (Back#2887; s/o Tobias
Brashear and Martha Brocus), b. c1795-7, Natchez Dist. MS;
m.1. 29 July (or 3 Aug) 1820 in Claiborne Co, MS, **Matilda
Duncan**, who may have died in childbirth with her second child;
m.2. 17 Aug 1824, Warren Co, MS, **Martha Ann Sharp**, who
was mother of the other child. *Gainesville Advocate*: 17 July
1837: "died in this place, on Sabbath night last, Martha Ann,
wife of Tobias E. Brashears in the 29th year of her age. The
deceased was a native of this county." (Thanks to Michael P.
Cahill, a Cannon descendant, for much of the following
information.)

v5162.   91. **Malinda Woodward Brashear**, b. c1822, d. 16 Sept
          1859, bur Emmanuel Protestant Episcopal Church of
          Plaquemines Parish, LA, d/o Tobias & Matilda; m.
          c1840-42, **Charles James Cannon**, b. c1819, AL, d.
          1889, s/o Nathaniel Cannon of South Carolina. They
          had one child in Mississippi, then Charles & Malinda
          moved to Plaquemines Parish, LA, where the rest of
          the children were born.

v5163.   101. Mary Elizabeth Cannon, b. c1842, MS (17 in
          1860), d. 9 Sept 1896, Grand Prairie, Plaquemines
          Parish, LA; m. c1868, in Plaquemines Parish,
          William Hippolyte Williams Jr, b. c1841, d. 8 Oct
          1888, Plaquemines Parish, LA.

v5164.   102. Alice F. Cannon, b. c1846, LA (13 in 1860); m.
          Felix A. Williams, b. March 1845, d. 3 May 1895,
          Plaquemines Parish, LA

v5165.   103. Clara Gardner Cannon, b. 22 June 1848, LA (12

in 1860), d. 26 Dec 1897, Plaquemines Parish, LA; m. 14 Dec 1871, in New Orleans, LA, David Gould Wire, b. Aug 1844, New Orleans, d. 1 March 1906, Plaquemines Parish. LA

v5166.   [10]4. William Lindsay Cannon, b. 1850, LA (10 in 1860), d. 1892, Williamson Co, TX; m.1. (?) Emma C. Mumson; m.2. c1877 Courtney A. _____, b. Aug 1855, TX, d. after 1919

v5167.   [10]5. Newton Brashear Cannon Sr, b. April 1852 (8 in 1860), Plaquemines Parish, LA; d. 5 Sept 1927, LA; m.1. LA, Sarah Elizabeth Holly, b. c1852, LA, d. bef 1879; m.2. 12 March 1878, in Plaquemines Parish, LA, Charlotte Frederica Conrad, b. 23 Dec 1857, LA, d. 16 Aug 1909, Happy Jack, Plaquemines Parish, LA

v5168.   [10]6. Charles M.(?) Cannon, b. c1854 (6 in 1860), Plaquemines Parish, LA

v5169.   [10]7. Malinda "Linda" Cannon, b. c1856, Plaquemines Parish, LA (4 in 1860), d. bef 1871, LA

v5170.   [9]2? ?son of Tobias and Matilda, no further information.

v5171.   [9]3. **Elizabeth Martha Brashear**, b. 17 Sept 1828, d. 9 Aug 1903, d/o Tobias Brashears & Martha Sharp; m.1. 1846, *Matthew Bryant Gardner*, of Vermont; m.2. 1861, *Charles James Cannon*, widower of her half-sister, Malinda. Charles J. Cannon was b. 15 July 1819, AL, d. 26 Feb 1889, bur Emmanuel Protestant Episcopal Church of Plaquemines Parish, LA, 69y, 7m, 11d.

v5172.   [10]1. John Gardner, b. c1848 (12 in 1860)

v5173.   [10]2. Elizabeth Malinda Gardner, bapt 30 Jan 1852, Emmanuel Protestant Episcopal Church of Plaquemines Parish, LA, d.young

v5174.   [10]3. Julia Cannon, b. July 1863, Plaquemines Parish, LA, d. 1941; m. 18 Jan 1886, Grand Prairie, Plaquemines Parish, LA, Theodore Augustus Brown, b. Feb 1863, Plaquemines Parish, LA, d. after 1919

v5175.   [10]4. Edward Joseph "Eddie" Cannon, b. Jan 1865, Plaquemines Parish, LA, d. 27 Oct 1947, New Orleans, LA; m. 1 Jan 1889, in New Orleans, Elizabeth "Lissie" Kness, b. Feb 1865,

Plaquemines Parish, LA, d. 30 Dec 1925, New Orleans

v5176.   [10]5. Mattie Millard Cannon, b. 3 Jan 1867, Plaquemines Parish, LA, d. 10 Sept 1929, New Orleans; m. 31 Oct 1888, Grand Prairie, Plaquemines Parish, LA, Charles Guillotte Louderbough, b. 24 Aug 1863, Plaquemines Parish, LA, d. 17 Aug 1913, New Orleans

1860 Census, Grand Prairie, Plaquemines Parish, LA, p. 678:

#102/152	Cannon, Charles J.	40, b. AL, planter, 15,000/12,000
	Mary	17, b. LA
	Alice	13, b. LA
	Clara	12, b. LA
	Lindsey	10, b. LA
	Newton	8, b. LA
	Charley	6, b. LA
	Linda	4, b. LA
102/153	Gardner, Mary B.	30, b. MS, 800/5,000
	John	12, b. LA

Obit: Charles J. Cannon (from *Plaquemines Protector*, 9 March 1889; thanks to Michael P. Cahill for this and other copies): In Memoriam: On Tuesday, February 26, 1889, at 1 o'clock at Elmwood, Parish of Plaquemines, C. J. Cannon, aged 69 years 7 months and 11 days. A native of Alabama and a resident of this parish for the past forty-four years. He departed this life at his residence, after an illness of two years, ten months. Mr. Cannon possessed a clear head, a strong will and a sincere heart, which ever beat in simpathy for the well being of others. His real worth was best known and appreciated by those most intimately acquainted with him. Mr. Cannon was twice married, he leaves a widow and nine children (all of whom are married) to mourn his death. He was buried at "The Oaks" by the side of his first wife.

Died (New Orleans Daily Picayune, Sunday 16 Aug 1903) At Elmwood, Plaquemines Parish, LA, on Sunday, Aug. 9, 1903, at 5 o'clock p.m., Elizabeth M. Brashear, wife of the late C.J. Cannon, aged 74 years and 10 months, a native of Grand Gulf, Miss.

Obit: Elizabeth M. Brashear (*Plaquemines Protector*, 15 Aug

1903). Died at her residence in Elmwood, LA, at 5 o'clock Sunday evening, August 9, 1903, Elizabeth M. Brashear, widow of Chas. J. Cannon, aged 74 years, 10 months, and 22 days. Mrs. Cannon was a native of Claiborne Co, Miss, and the daughter of Tobias Eden Brashear and Martha Sharp. Left an orphan at an early age, she became the ward of her then brother-in-law, Chas J. Cannon.

In 1844, Mr. Cannon, accompanied by his family, came to Louisiana and opened up Elmwood. Here, two years later, Miss Brashear became the wife of Matthew Gardner. Losing her husband and children in a few years, she found herself a childless widow.

In 1861, Mrs. Gardner married her brother-in-law, Mr. Cannon, who had himself suffered the loss of his life partner. This union lasted for twenty-eight years, being dissolved by the death of Mr. Cannon in 1889. To this marriage were born two daughters and a son, who survive their mother. Monday evening her mortal remains, accompanied by relatives, were consigned to their last resting place in Union Settlement.

4. R.T. "TURNER" BRASHEAR, The Choctaw Trader

^{v5}8. ^{7}8. **R.T. "Turner" Brashear**, b. c1764, near Bladenburg, Prince George's Co, MD, d. 1831, near Rankin, MS, s/o Benjamin Brashear and Catherine Belt; m.1. "a daughter of Taboca," called "Jane Apuckshunnubbee," a full-blood Choctaw; m.2. **Oca-ye-mitta**, a full-blood Choctaw. I have never seen his first name on a genuine document, though it appears as "Robert" on some spurious documents, and he had several descendants whose given names were "Robert Turner."

SOME CAUTIONS: 1. Turner Brashear (^{v5}8; Back#2772) and Robert Turner Brashear (Back#2904) are the same person. The Robert Turner Brashear and his wife Nancy Vaughn, referred to in "J.W. Hyden v. Choctaw Nation" simply never existed; they were Hyden inventions, part of the fraudulent Hyden hoax to get Choctaw land and annuity payments (see Chapter 16, "The Dawes Disaster and American Chicanery").

There just isn't time in there for another generation:

—>Turner's daughter, Eva (Brashear) Everidge, died in 1879 "about 90 years old," i.e. b. c1789.

—>Turner's daughter, Lucy (Brashear) Patton-Standley, m.2. 1816, Capt. James S. Standley. She had three children by her first marriage to William? Patton. Giving her two years for each child and one between her first marriage and the birth of the first child means her first marriage had to be c1809. Let's say she was 16 or 17 when she married; that would mean she was born 1792-93, when Turner, s/o Benjamin and Catherine, was c28 years old and known to be married to "a daughter of Taboca."

—>Also Turner's granddaughter, Harriet (Everidge) Oakes, d/o Eva Brashear and Thomas Everidge, testified in "J.W. Hyden vs. Choctaw Nation" (see below) that her grandfather, Turner

Brashear, whom she knew and remembered, was a white man, who had brothers named Tobias and Eden.

Caution #2. There are two Turner Brashears in early Mississippi (not to mention later generations); they are fourth cousins and both are involved with the Choctaws. [v5]8. R.T. "Turner" Brashear, s/o Benjamin, lived on the west side of the state, at Natchez, in Yazoo County, and near Jackson; the other Turner Brashears, (I'm going to call him Turner Brashear, II; [v5]841) s/o Zadock Brashear and Susannah Vaughn, lived at "Brashear Bluffs" on the Tombigbee River, in present-day Sumter Co, Alabama. The two groups knew each other and recognized each other as kinsmen. The Tombigbee Turner was probably named for his noted kinsman, the Natchez Turner. R.T. Turner's brother, Richard, had land near St. Stephens Trading Post and once gave his power of attorney to a cousin in the Tombigbee group.

TIME-LINE OF TURNER BRASHEAR

About 1772, Turner Brashear, age 8, s/o Benjamin Brashear and Catherine Belt, moved with his father to Brownsville, PA, and with him to Bullitt Co, KY, and to the Natchez District by 1780. Turner became a favorite of and an advisor to Chief Franchismastabbe (in Choctaw, "Franchismastaba" means "he killed a Frenchman," or— in the idiom of the 1780s frontier: "he took a Frenchman and killed him.") Turner eventually became a noted Choctaw trader, an interpreter, a slaveholder, an innkeeper on the old Natchez Trace (the ancient trading path and road from Nashville to Natchez), and owner and operator of a plantation known as "Brashears Field." He was somewhat famous in his own time; his name appears fairly often in the American State Papers and the Archives of Spanish West Florida.

12 Nov 1786, Turner Brashears vs. James Stoddard. "Turner Brashear, lately of the Choctaw Nation, represents that near three years since, a gray horse was stolen from him, now about six years old in the Choctaw Nation where your petitioner then lived, and having found, two days ago, the said horse near the plantation of a certain James Stoddard, he caught said horse

and led him to the house of said Stoddard who told the petitioner that said horse belonged to him and that he bought him from a certain Griffing who he believed had him from Benjamin Rogers, who had him from St. Germain. Your petitioner can readily prove by Joseph Duncan and his father that said horse belongs to him; he prays that James Stoddard be ordered to restore to your petitioner his said horse." Endorsed: Petitioner will produce sufficient proof that the horse which he claims belongs to him, /s/ [Carlos de] Grand Pré, [Civil and Military Governor of Natchez].

Also on 12 Nov 1786: The annexed certificate being sufficient proof of property, the horse will be restored to claimant, the present possessor having recourse against the seller, and so on. /s/ Grand Pré (*The Natchez Court Records, 1767-1805*, Genealogical Publ Co, 1979, p.245).

According to correspondence in old Spanish records, "Capt. Turner Brashear" was operating a Chickasaw Trading post at Chickasaw Bluffs (now Memphis) in 1787. He was apparently single and "with a colony of 30 to 40 men," which seems to have included his older brother, Capt. Richard Brashear. In fact, there is some confusion as to whether Richard or Turner was in charge. In 1780, near the end of the Revolution, Gen. George Rogers Clark had sent Capt. Richard Brashears to the Chickasaw Bluffs to trade for supplies, which he did successfully; there is evidence that Richard returned after the war, in 1787, built the block (log) house at The Bluffs, and opened a trading post. "By 1792, he [Turner] became a Choctaw trader, attached to the Spanish interests." (*East Tenn Hist Soc Publs.* 12 (1940), 101-102, 115.)

Also in 1787, Juan de la Villabeuvre listed "Tonel Busshiers" (a Spanish rendering of Turner's name) as operating a trading house in Chenoukau (properly "Shenuk Kama," located on Owl Creek, a tributary of Bok Chito), a village in the Grand Party (also Big Party, also known as the Western Division, or Oklafalaya), Choctaw Nation, with one unidentified employee. Oklafalaya District was on the headwaters of the Pearl and Chickasawhay Rivers. The other two main divisions of the Choctaw Nation were the Southern District, or Six Villages, Okla Hunnalli, on the Chickasawhay River, rather downstream from the Oklafalaya, and the Small Part, or Small Party, or Ahepat Okla (which John H. Peterson, author of *A Choctaw Source Book,* says means "potato eating people") which was located on the upper reaches of Suk-en-atcha Creek and the Oxnubbee River.

Also in 1787, Natchez Governor Gayoso de Lemos mentioned Turner Brashear as living in Yazoo, the village of Franchismastabbe, in the Big Party, or Oklafalaya. Yazoo is also listed in 1787 as Yazouz and in 1794 as Yazaux; it was in present-day Holmes Co, MS, considerably west of the main body of the Oklafalaya, but still well within their established hunting grounds. It may have been founded by enterprising Choctaws to facilitate trade with the whites at Natchez. Modern Yazoo on the Big Black River may or may not be the same village. The trader there in 1787, according to Juan de la Villabeuvre's record, was Alexander Frazier, almost certainly the father of the Choctaw Frazier family, who intermarried with the Coles. Testimony of Robert Cole in the 1830s strongly suggests that Alexander Fazier's wife was a sister to Apuckshunnubbee and Shumaka, who married a Cole. Shumaka's son, Robert Cole, was successor to Apuckshunnubbee, in 1824.

In another reference, it is clear that Turner had established a Choctaw trading post near Natchez, about 1792, which roused considerable displeasure among the Spanish authorities, who were debating whether or not to drive him off by force. For example, on 21 July 1792, Manuel Gayoso de Lemos, Governor at Natchez, wrote the Señor Baron de Carondelet, Governor General of Spanish West Florida: "In spite of the fact that Don Juan de la Villabeuvre is going to reside in the Choctaw and Chickasaw Nations as Commissary, I think that now is no time to undervalue the services of Turner Brashears; he has just given proof of his good intentions, and I am of the opinion that it would be best not to displease him; he is an intimate friend of Franchismastabbe, and is married to a daughter of Taboca; and furthermore, as a Trader he has many Indians at his beck and call. A modest pension of thirty pesos per month will make him exceedingly useful to the Commissary who goes there; or want to do to promote the things I must in Fulfillment of my obligations to you. This and other expenses are unavoidable under the present circumstances, for if the necessary steps are not taken at the proper time any others will be useless to counteract the measures used by the Americans." (Letter of 21 July 1792. Text reprinted in *East Tenn Hist Soc Publs*, #27, p.89-90.)

Gayoso added, in the same letter: "On taking leave, Taboca told me that different Nations called him by different names; that some gave him the name he had already, others Snagbe, and others Payo mingo; but that his real name was Payo Mataha."

In the Treaty at Hopewell, SC, 3 Jan 1786, between the United States and the Choctaw, the primary negotiators for the Choctaw are listed as Yokonahoma, great Medal Chief of Soonacoha; Yockehoopoie, leading Chief of Bugtoogoloo; Mingohoopoie, leading Chief of Hashooqua; and Tobocoh (Taboca), great Medal Chief of Congetoo (probably the same village as the Conchito, listed by Juan de la Villabeuvre as a village in the Large Party, or Western District (Oklafalaya) in 1787).

Eva Brashear, Turner's daughter, was born c1789; so Turner probably married "a daughter of Taboca" about 1788, when he was about 24 years old. In the Choctaw clan system, a "daughter of Taboca" would in fact be Taboca's sister's child; the sister could have been married to Apuckshunnubbee, as some of the descendants claim. Apuckshunnubbee, b. 1739, is the right age to have such a wife and daughter.

In 1792, Spanish Governor Manuel Gayoso de Lemos commissioned Lieut. don Esteban Minor (Stephen Minor), Adjutant of the post of Natchez, to visit Chief Franchismastabbe of the Choctaw Nation, with the aim of treating with him on the territory of Nogales. Lieut. Minor elected to have Turner Brashear accompany him on the trip as an interpreter and aide. Franchismastabbe's town was called Yason, or Yazoo. Turner Brashear and John Turnbull both had trading houses in the town, though perhaps not at the same time. George Turnbull and William Turnbull, half-Chickasaw sons of John Turnbull, both married to Choctaw women, later operated the Turnbull warehouse at Yazoo, in competition with Turner Brashear.

However, Turner Brashear and George Turnbull were very close and *may* (no documents) have married sisters. George Turnbull named his first son Turner Brashear Turnbull.

In Baron de Carondelet's diary of 1792, he referred to Turner as "a young man ... moderate, prudent, and favorable to us [the Spanish Government]..." On 3 April 1792, the Baron wrote: "Of all the white traders in this [Choctaw] Nation, the one I met most ardent to our interests is Mr. Turner Brashears with whom I have consulted from time to time on matters relative to my mission, and I have always found him a man of truth and influence in this Nation; he is also an intimate friend of Franchismastabbe and [the one] in whom he [Franchismastabbe] places his greatest confidence, the reason why he sent him [Turner] to Natchez to confer with the [Spanish] Governor." On 21 May 1792, Turner played an important part in the negotiations between the Spanish and the Choctaws at Walnut Hills (now Vicksburg, Mississippi) in confirming the western boundaries of the Choctaw Nation, as they had been fixed by the Treaty of Pensacola in 1765.

On 5 Sept 1792, Juan de la Villabeuvre, the Spanish Commissary to the Choctaw, wrote to Baron de Carondelet that he had "finally arrived at the Choctaw nation after travelling for six days out from Bayou Pierre.... calling an assembly at the Large Part in which I spoke to them on your behalf.... Franchismastabbe spoke after me ... Taboka (Taboca) spoke also and said many fine things. Then the gathering dispersed. When I arrived at the nation, Franchismastabbe had already given the two American medals to Toorner Bichairs (Turner Brashears) for him to send them to the governor at Natchez, who in turn was to send them to you. However, the other large one, which had been given to one of our medal-chiefs named Tloupone Nantla of the village of Canlabatia in the Small Part, is still in his possession. He left immediately for Cumberland upon receiving it and has not returned ...."

De la Villabeuvre is referring to medals the Americans had given the Choctaw chiefs, hoping to secure their allegiance, and to the meeting which William Blount, Governor of the Territory South of the Ohio, had called at Nashville.

"Taskactoca, king of the Chickasaws, had gone to the Talapoosas," de la Villabeuvre went on. "He came back several days ago and sent word to Franchismastabbe that he would come to the Choctaws here one of these days, and that he was to wait for him. The latter was getting ready to leave for Mobile with Tornair Bishairs. He says the commandant is expecting him there. He is being spoilt by being asked everywhere; he will think he is more important than he is and will become more and more troublesome. I made him postpone his trip four or five days, because I believe that the king of the Chickasaws is to come here with Tourneboul (John Turnbull) who went to that nation with a passport from the commandant of Mobile ...."

"Upon arriving at the nation, I went to Yason, Franchismastabbe's village, where Tornair Bichairs was staying. ... In Franchismastabbe's village there are nothing but drunkards who expose one all the time to the risk of being insulted and molested. I believe that it makes no difference in which part I live, since the good of the service does not suffer; besides, Tornair Bichairs, who is trustworthy, will inform me of what is going on in his village, which I can easily get to in two hours...."

"If you could possibly forbid the introduction of liquor into this nation, you would be doing a great good, because it is coming from everywhere and is making the Indians nasty and insolent...." (*Spain in the Mississippi Valley*, v.4, part 3, p.74)

Early in the autumn of 1792, William Blount, Governor of the Territory of the United States South of the River Ohio, sent a military mission to invite the Choctaw and Chickasaw Nations to send delegates to Nashville to negotiate a treaty. Only a few of the Choctaws honored the invitation, and, in a letter to Secretary of War, General Knox, dated 20 Sept 1792, Blount blamed Turner Brashears for the failure.

"I do not know how to explain to you the cause of their being only so few Choctaws, than by enclosing to you the report of Mr. Forster, one of the gentlemen who carried my letter of invitation to them [the Choctaws] to attend. You will observe that he supposed one cause to have been the conduct of one of his colleagues, meaning Captain David Smith, who I engaged to accompany him, and Mr. James Randolph, from a belief that he, David Smith, as he has frequently been in the nation and spoke the tongue, was the most proper man in the territory in all respects to be engaged in such business; in fact, I added him to those who I first employed, fearing if I did not, and any failure should take place, that it may be imputable to me for not having sent him.

"It seems, on the arrival of Mr. Forster and Captain Smith, they found this Mr. Brassheart, who Mr. Forster mentions in his report, there residing, a trader much attached to the Spanish interest; and that Captain Smith and he had been old acquaintances, and not friends; that on meeting, they presently fell into warm dispute concerning the American and Spanish Governments, and their respective consequence and influence in the Choctaw nation: at length each agreed that he would be determined by the number that would accompany Smith to the conference, or that Brassheart should prevent.

"This Brassheart was the only one who possessed any Taffier in the town where the council assembled, and it was no doubt he who made the party drunk, and induced them to break up the council and tear the belts, so that the insult which appeared to be offered to the United States, is justly to be attributed to him and his taffia, and not to the nation....

"Another artifice made use of by Mr. Brassheart was to inform the chiefs that there was something in the letters which had not been explained in council, written in red ink, by which he foresaw the Choctaws, if they went, would be put to death, and as the letters were in his care, it is highly probable he might have inserted some words with red ink. Many are the artifices of this kind made use of by the white people living among the Indians, to the unjury of the best concerted measures of Government, and cannot be counteracted until they have had the pernicious effects intended by their authors. The Spanish interest must unquestionably have had its weight, and in that may justly be included the conduct of Mr. Brassheart. (Blount to Knox, *Documents Legislative and Executive of the Congress of the United States*, v.4, Washington, DC, published by Gales and Seaton, 1832; thanks to Harley D. Anders for a copy).

[Taffia is the Creole name of a West Indies rum, distilled from sugar cane. Blount seems to have been deliberately lying, which he was known to do on several occasions where Cherokees, Chickasaws, and Choctaws were concerned. Another reference has Turner present at Gov. Blount's speech at the "Conference Ground, near Nashville, where Brashears was assuring the Chickasaw and Choctaw of good intentions." (See *American State Papers, Indian Affairs*, I, 284-288, for details.)] Turner most definitely was present, for he wrote a summary of Blount's speech and sent it to Gov. Gayoso (see below).

On 8 Nov 1792, Gov. Blount again wrote to Gen. Knox: "... am told that the Choctaws, on their return home, drove Boshears [sic], the Spanish Agent, from the Choctaw Nation, because he had misrepresented the intentions of the U.S. to them ..."

Blount is either lying again to make himself look good or wishfully thinking, for there is plenty of evidence that Turner remained in the Choctaw Nation for many years and was active in its affairs.

On 25 Nov 1792, Turner faithfully reported the Blount conference to Manuel Gayoso de Lemos, the Spanish Governor at Natchez. Some scholars have called him "nearly illiterate" for his spelling and grammar (*East Tenn. Hist. Soc. Pub.* 28 (1956), 138; see also the original in English in *Papeles Procedentes de Cuba*, Legajo 41:928-9.):

"Dear Sir, I sit heir to Right to You the Perticlar Vews of the Treaty of Comberland Betwen Govner Blunt and the Chactaws and Chicasaws

"I sent for you [here Turner is trying to give Blount's message in Blount's own voice] Out of no Ill desire But to give you Some Smal Preasents to Fullfile Our Promas at the Treaty of Hopewell I sent for you to let you Know that we are not Lyars wee Only want to Convince you of Our Trew Frendship you and the Chicasaws we Don't want to tell Any thing but the Truth as you may go home Satisfied with ous and all your Neighbours and to Love your White-People and to Hold them fast by Hand thare ar the People that find you in Goods and Aminion [Ammunition] Evy thing that you stand in need of tha [they] ar Our Find [?friend] as well as yourn and Go and See them as you shal as befour Genera Washington is Desirous to See Some of Your Head Chief of your Land to Convince you of his Trew Friendship We have Sum Very bad Indians to Deel with heare   tha are People that wishes to be at Peace with nobody I Wish that you will not Beleave Any thing thies Bad Indians Shall Tell you We are desiruous to be at Peace With Evry Bodey We Give you Anvitacion to Come and See Ous in Spring at Nash Vile on Cumberland, it oute of no ill desire it is to Shoo you that we ar your frind and to Convince you that we Don't want to Decev you   The Spanards is Your Friends and Hold them by the Hand and Lisin to What tha Say to you and go and Se them you shal we are Convened [?convinced] that tha ar your friends We have Eat Drunk and Smoked togather Like Brothers and I Hope we will Still Remain Frind and Neighbours to

Geather
 "So no more but still remain
   Your Esteame Frind
   and Umble Servant
   Turn. Brashears"

On 26 Nov 1792, Gayoso (in Natchez) wrote to Baron de Carondelet: "There has just arrived here Turner Brashears with two Indians accompanying a woman and small child whom they rescued in the Choctaw Nation, from the hands of the Talapuches who were on the Big Black. I had talked to the woman and child for two days in my home and they told that the night of the 26th October last found her and all of her family sleeping, when six Talapuches Indians entered her cabin; that one delivered a machete blow to her husband and another fired a shot at his chest, of which results he died; that another killed one of her children ... [continues with a description of the tragedy] and was rescued by Turner Brashears, Jamie Davenport, Henrique Snelgrove and Jaime McAlfee with seven Choctaw Indians. ... This woman has gone to live at Bayou Pierre at the house of the father of Brashears .... to the Indians that arrived with her and to Turner Brashears, he was ordered to give a reward of 50 pesos." (*Papeles Procedentes de Cuba*, Legajo 41:926-6, in Spanish.)

On 10 June 1793, Turner wrote to Gayoso: "Friend, I recived your letter which gave me a grate deel of sattisfaction to heare from you According to your Request I have don and your Friends is mutch Pleased at your talk and the Chicasaws Likewise and Says that tha [they] take you More to be thare Friends now then Ever for tha See you wish them well I Expect you will have a Grate number of this Nation to See you — Inglesh Will [a Choctaw Chief] says you told him to bring all his People with him young And Old and all the Indians of the uper towns talks of Going old Snagle is Expected from the Creeks in Eight Days from now I hope to have the pleasure of Seeing you at the Ball Ground I have no furin nuse [?further news] to tell you of Onley Cornel Robertson Sun has bin in the Chickasaws but his talks I have not heard yet — I Expect PoyaMingo [Piomingo, Chickasaw Chief] will be to See you in afew Days he is on his Jorney to Natchez and Oliyouokubbia [Ogoulayacabe, rival Chickasaw chief] Is to be heare to Meate old Snagle from the Creeks tha ar all willing for peace Sir if you will Oblige me mutch for Proisions is very cearse [scarce] heare we are all on the Point of Deth for the want of Provisions I Beleave that I cant full fill My Promis I have Sarch and inquire but I Cant fiend it Old Snagle had it Last I suppose has mislaid it it is not out of Neglect that you hant got it is not in my Power to find it so no more but Still

Remain with Esteame
your Efectinet friend
/s/ Turner Brashears

(*Papers from the Spanish Archives*, East Tennessee Historical Society Publication No. 33, p.71).

12 April 1794, Manuel Gayoso de Lemos to Baron de Carondelet: "Yesterday Turner Brashears, confidant of Franchsimastabbe, arrived at this place [Natchez], accompanied by two Choctaw Indians on their way to that capital. He brought me a letter from the chief referred to, which I enclose under No. 1 for Your Lordship's information. Its content is confined to expression of friendship and to requests for some small present. For the present, I am giving to the said Brashears a piece of Limbourg [cloth] which has been here for some time, destined for Franchismastabbe. If you find it convenient to give him a little salt, coffee, and sugar for the above-mentioned chief he will take charge of it. — Brashears delivered to me a copy of the message which the Creek Indians, White Lieutenant of Oakfuskees and Mad Dog, sent to the Choctaw nation directed to Toscapotapo, principal chief of the Small Part, and Abecochee, which is the same as Franchismastabbe as he is so called by some of the Creeks. It contains nothing more than what Your Lordship already knows, so you may tell Brashears, the bearer of this letter, whatever pleases you. — I do not doubt that this commission proceeds from the intrigues of Seagrove, as Your Lordship has already been pleased to hint to me. [Note: Seagrove was U.S. Commissioner to the Creek Nation, working against the Spanish interests.] — Brashears had a petition on the part of Franchismastabbe begging Your Lordship to be pleased to transfer the enclosed commission of Payehuma, chief of the small medal, to Paquechenabe (Apuckshunnubbee), his son, of the same village, Octafalaya, as the father is very old and

desires that his son shall occupy his place, since he is the confidential warrior of Franchismastabbe, I believe there is no objection to granting this favor, and it would be very agreeable to the one who solicits it." (*Spain in the Mississippi Valley*, by Kinnaird, v.4, part 3, p.266; thanks again to Harley D. Anders for the text.)

On 23 April 1794, Baron de Carondelet wrote to Juan de la Villabeuvre, in part: "I have seen here Turner Brashears, Franchismastabbe's confidant, and I gave him a present of 150 piastres. I also gave him a barrel of salt, one arroba of sugar, and a half arroba of coffee for the great chief. He seems to me to be quite in favor of the new fort at Confederation and promised to do his best to prevent the Choctaws and the Chickasaws from going to greet Seagrove." (*Spain in the Mississippi Valley*, by Kinniard, b.4, part 3, p.271.)

8 June 1794, Turner Brashears, in the Choctaw Nation, to Gayoso de Lemos, at Natchez: "My dier Friend. This is to inform you of my safe arrival in good health Hoping this may Find you in the Same I have nothing strainge to Inform you of only that Yallow Wood is ded and Old Friday News is very Still Jest now the Lower Towns is gon to Mobile but the uppers has not John Pitchlynn and George James and Several others has gon to Cumberland with Sum heade Men I Stoped the Indians from going to the Creeks Acording to the Govno. General orders to me and I Believe it has Bin on our favor The Creeks thretens the Chicksasw and Says that beteen now and fall tha will kill them I umbly Beg Liefe of his Excelency to Relate the Down fall of the Trade Owing to the Commandant of the Hills According to your word and Orders to me I thaught that the trade of that Plase was Stoped and for that Reason I Baught the Dets he had in the hands of the Indians So that he Should Lose nothing by the stopeage of the Trade But he trades more now than he did befour and has Dammage me mor then one thousend Dollars So I think it is very hard for me to Pay him money for nothing Call the Indians thare and give them trust and in Corrages them to kill Bayr for him instade of Killing Deour for me I beg Leave of His Excellency to Put a Stop to the trade in that Destrict for the Good of the Pour Hunters and the Por Trader of this Land So no more at presant, But I Ever Remain with Esteam Yaw

most Obedient

Friend and umble Servent
Turner Brashears

Also in June, 1794, Turner Brashears and a number of traders in the Choctaw Nation petitioned Manuel Gayoso de Lemos to "ritefy" abuses in the Indian Trade, alluded to in the last letter.

"Firstly, our Indians hunters who are obliged to go to the other Side of the Missispea to kill dier and are fitted out for that purpose by your petitiour are often intersepted on thare return by people who Contrive to get a quntity of Taffee at that particulor Season and by thase means purches the Skins with which the Hunters would pay thar Depts to us ... a grate namber of petty Stors astablesed in the Settlement on the Hunting path on the Same and thareby encorreges a growing vice amongst the Red pople which aught to be put a Stopt to that Supplyes under the managements of Man Schouly we might orselves do better and bring the Indians in time to be mour usefull to Government Another measure destructive to us & of no use to Goverment is the Store of Turnbull at Yassaw which is equally bad in intercepting our Piltry and encouraging the Indians to deceve ous...." Those signing this petition were Janbatis, Turner Brashears, William Stanley, Philip Hay, David Chota, Lewis Ward, Enok Nelson, Mastang the younger, Loui Flos, Michelle, Loui Catens, Edward Rogers, and John Hencock (*Spain in the Mississippi Valley*, Kinniard, v.4, part 3, p.310).

22 July 1794, Juan de la Villabeuvre, in Boukfouka (a village in the Small Part), to Monsieur the Baron de Carondelet, Governor General, in part: "I can do no less than to point out to you once again how much inconvenience there is in giving commissions at Mobile to the traders of the Choctaw nation to trade in various villages. They have discussion every day amongst themselves because the commandant of Mobile cannot possibly know whether the village for which the commission is asked is free or not. He gives it to anyone who asks him for it without knowing whether he is entitled to it, so that dishonest traders often try to displace those more honest than themselves to whom the Indians often owe four or five hundred skins. The result is that once the permission is granted, these poor fellows

must lose everything ... I have asked whether Bishers had given to Franchesmastabe on your behalf the quart of salt, the two pounds of sugar, and the twelve and a half pounds of coffee, as you informed me. He has received none of these things and Bichers tells me that they only wanted to give him six pounds of salt and only a little sugar and coffee. Therefore he refused to take anything, even food supplies." (*Spain in the Mississippi Valley*, Kinniard, v.4, part 3, p.327).

Such abuses had apparently "ruined" the Indian Trade for Turner Brashears. On 2 Sept 1794, he registered his cattle brand "TB" with the Spanish authorities. (*Papeles de Procedentes*, Legajo 41:1225). He may well have been preparing to move to his plantation on the Natchez Trace, where he later opened a "stand," an inn for travelers.

At any rate, the shift-over from Spanish rule to American rule in that portion of the Choctaw Nation where Turner's sympathies resided was already under way, and his loyalties shifted with them. On 3 Jan 1799, Governor Winthrop Sargent wrote to Peter Bryan Bruin: "The Governor has received the note which Judge Bruin has been good enough to send him, enclosing the letter from Mr. Brashears. Will Judge Bruin be so obliging as to signify to Mr. Brashears the Governor's full approbation of his zeal in the service of his country. The sound Judgment of a few such well disposed men as Mr. Brashears will be sufficient to counteract the Machination of more cunning, and more mischievous characters than the Burnet he has mentioned...." (*Mississippi Territorial Archives, 1798-1803*, by Dunbar Rowland, Brandon Publishing Co, Nashville, 1905, v.1, p.95-6; thanks again to Harley D. Anders for the text.)

On 24 Sept 1797, U.S. Commissioner Andrew Ellicott informed Secretary of State Timothy Pickering that he had heard of Choctaw discontent with the United States and had written to Turner Brashear to inquire about it. In 1798, Turner was mentioned in another letter from Ellicott to Pickering.

In 1801, while recommending Turner as U.S. Indian Agent among the Choctaws, Benjamin Hawkins, U.S. Indian Agent for the Southern District, wrote: "Turner Brashear resides among them; he is a native of Maryland, of good character, and understands the Indian language and appears to me to be fit for the appointment." (Hawkins to Dearborn, December 21, 1801.) Turner was "a man whom officials wanted on their side because of the influence he could wield." (*East Tenn. Hist. Soc. Pub.* No. 27 (1955), pp. 87, 87n. 90.)

On 17 Oct 1802, Turner was an interpreter and witness to a treaty with the Choctaws, negotiated by James Wilkinson at Fort Confederation on the Tombigbee River. The Choctaws quit claimed to the United States the area between the Chickasawhay River and the Tombigbee River, as well as agreed to adjust the boundaries near the mouth of the Yazoo River to accommodate encroachers.

On 16 June 1813, Turner was in council with Chief Pushmataha, Chief Musholatubbe, and General Humming Bird of the Choctaw Nation. At that time, Turner was being paid $400 per year as an official Indian interpreter for the United States Government.

In Sept 1816, he was one of the interpreters in treaty negotiations with the Choctaws. (*East Tenn. Hist. Soc. Pub.* 10 (1938), 22.)

The Apuckshunnubbee Connection

For several years, we have believed that Turner's first wife was "Ho-ti-o-ka," a daughter of Apuckshunnubbee, but that conclusion was based on a faulty interpretation of a document. There were two men named Apuckshunnubbee, or one named Apuckshunnubbee and one named Puckshenubbee.

The first Apuckshunnubbee died in Maysville, KY at the age of 85 on 15 Nov 1824 (b. c1739) after he accidentally stepped off a retaining wall near the river and fell 15 to 20 feet to the stone pavement below. He was on his way to Washington, DC, on a diplomatic mission with Pushmataha and Musholatubbe. This event was well-documented, since this Apuckshunnubbee was one of the three "Great Medal" Chiefs of the Choctaws. (See accounts in the Maysville *Eagle*, Weds, 20 Oct 1824, and the Maysville *Republican*, Sat, 9 Oct 1875.)

On 10 April 1831-2 (?? hard to read, but it was after the Treaty at Dancing Rabbit Creek of 1830) several years after the death of the first Apuckshunnubbee, the second Puckshenubbee gave testimony before a U.S. government commission (see *Territorial Papers of the U.S.; Alabama*, 3:78): he swore that he "is a full blood Choctaw, aged 55 years [b. c1777], and that his name is Puck:she:nubbee. He lived at the time of the Treaty [of Dancing Rabbit Creek] at Tala:homa Creek three miles from Che:nock:a:bee town, now Garlandsville. He had then a wife and four children living with him. His wife is still living and is named A:bu:to:na. The names of his children are:

1. E:to:na, female, at home, near 28 years old. Has never been married. [I'll bet "28" is a copyist's error for 18.]
2. Ho:ti:o:ka, female, not here [i.e. not present at the conference], she is 13 years old. Has never been married.
3. Kow:on:ta:chubbee, male, at home, he is 11 years old.
4. Ab:et:is:tu:a, male, at home, he was unable to come here, could not walk on account of _____[a wound] in his thigh. He is 10 years old."

Some family researcher apparently jumped to the conclusion that this second Puckshenubbee's daughter, Ho:ti:o:ka, was the first wife of Turner Brashear, but it would be impossible for a girl born c1818-20 to have been Turner's first wife, who had at least five children in the 1788-1800 period. This second Puckshenubbee is almost certainly the Puckshenubbee who removed to Indian Territory and was shot in the streets of Van Buren, AR, in 1832.

The first Apuckshunnubbee first appears in the records in 1794. In a letter which Turner Brashear wrote on behalf of Choctaw Chief Franchismastabbe, which is quoted in a letter from Gayoso to Carondelet, 12 April 1794, (see *Spain in the Mississippi Valley*, by Kinnaird, v.4, pt.3, p.266), Franchismastabbe requested that the official commission of his "confidential warrior," Payehuma, chief of the small medal "of Octafalaya," be transferred to his son, Paquechenabe.

"Paque:che:nabe" [French orthography] is apparently Apuckshunnubbee, who became one of the three great medal chiefs at about this time. "Octafalaya" refers to Oklafalaya, the general name for all the villages of the Western Division, where Apuckshunnubbee was chief. "His son" almost certainly refers to his sister's son, what we could call Payehuma's nephew, as would be dictated by Choctaw traditions. (Is Payehuma still another name for Taboca-Snagbe-Payomingo-Payomataha?)

A man was not even related to his own blood children, for they were not in his clan; but all his sister's children were in his clan and he was responsible for their education and upbringing. The succession of power also passed to these clan-sons, whom we would call nephews (as for example, in the succession of power from Apuckshunnubbee to his sister Shumaka's son, Robert Cole, in 1824, and from Cole to his sister Nahotima's grandson, Greenwood LeFlore, in 1826; see also Chap 10).

Apuckshunnubbee was famous as a warrior and orator and had considerable influence even outside his district. He is described as a large man, tall and bony, with a "down" look and "was of a religious or superstitious cast of mind." He was considered a good man, given to deep thought, and quite intellectual. He was taciturn and stubborn in negotiations with the whites, even moreso than Pushmataha (See Dr. Gideon Lincecum's descriptions in his *Autobiography* (*Chronicles of Oklahoma*, and his *Life of Apushimataha* (Mississippi Historical Society).

Apuckshunnubbee, Shumaka, and their siblings were born Chakchiumas (or Chocchuma) Indians. This small tribe was massacred by the Chickasaws in the 1840s; the remnants were absorbed into the Choctaw tribe and became the Chakchiumas *iksa*, or clan. Most of this clan seems to have settled along the Yalobusha River valley.

Shumaka (or maybe her name was really Shun Ah Ka, as it is entered in land claims Case 148, p.844, by Joshua T. Brown, her attorney), she was still living in 1838 and was reputed to be 120 years old (b. c1718), "the last of the Chocchuma race." In 1831, she lived in Sec 22, T21N, R7E, where she had improvements. Her grandson, Coleman Cole, gave testimony in her behalf to land commissioners: "Coleman Cole, a 3/4 blood Choctaw, a witness for Claimant, being sworn, deposes as follows: That he is acquainted with Shumaka; she is his grandmother; has known her as long as he can recollect; saw her about 20 days since; she was then at Puttacacowa Creek, where she lived on (witness's land); she is very old; she is represented to be 120 years old; she is unable to travel any distance. And the time of the treaty she lived on Bittupinbogue, about 18 or 19 miles from its mouth. She had then no child living with her; she was visited by her grand-children at that time, but no person lived there. She lived there at and before the treaty, and remained there until the land she lived on was sold by the government at the first land sales at Chocchuma [about

1834], after which a white man required her to move. Before this, she had a house and field, in which she lived. He (witness) assisted her in making a crop. He has no recollection of her husband, his grand-father. He has heard her say she belonged to the Chocchuma tribe; that she was very young at the massacre of her tribe by the Chickasaws and others; she made her husband escape, and got among the Choctaws, who adopted her as a Choctaw. She is the mother of Robert Cole, witness's father. The Chocchumas lived in a village, and were surprised by the Chickasaws at break of day, and were all murdered with few exceptions; they were killing them all day. About 200 escaped among the Choctaws. These were merged in the Choctaw tribe, and the Chocchuma name abandoned. Her faculties are in a great degree unimpaired; she can see to work with her naked eyes, hears well, &c. She belonged to Lewis Perry's company at the date of the treaty. The witness has no interest in her claim. Her name was put on Nelson's list, at the council at Nelson's, by her request, as he heard Nelson say at the time he was taking other names. Nelson told him he was going to put her name down, and he saw him immediately write."

Shumaka is the matriarch of several Choctaw families, among them, the Coles, LeFlores, Belvins, Nelsons, and McCurtains, says Jennifer Mieirs.

The genealogy of *Captain J.S. Standley, Ancestors and Descendants*, claims that Turner's [first] wife was a daughter of Apuckshunnubbee: "James S. Standley, I, was born June 22, 1792, moved from Tennessee, 1814, to the Choctaw Nation in Territory of Mississippi. In 1816, he married the widow, Lucy Patton, née Lucy Breashears, daughter of Turner Breashears, granddaughter of Apuckshunnubbee" (p.1). Since this book was written rather early, before it was fashionable to have Indian ancestors, I tend to lend credence to its assertions. It would be possible for her to be the clan-daughter of Taboca, but the blood-daughter of Taboca's sister and Apuckshunnubbee, but documentation is lacking. Apuckshunnubbee, b. c1739 (age 85 in 1824), would be the right age to have a blood daughter eligible to marry Turner Brashear. The Standley's referred to Turner's first wife as Jane Apuckshunnubbee.

In 1933, Judge R.L. Williams gave a photostatic copy of a Bible to the Oklahoma Historical Society belonging to Captain

James S. Stanley, at that time in possession of his daughter, Mrs. B.S. Smiser. This Bible says that the Stanley family, along with the Everidges and Oakes from near Hugo, OK, are descendants of Chief Apuckshunnubbee. (ref: *Chronicles of Oklahoma*, Vol XI, 1933, p.?)

Turner's Families

Family of R.T. "Turner" Brashear and "a daughter of Taboca," a full-blood Choctaw: (ref: Testimony in "J.W. Hyden vs. Choctaw Nation"; Records of Carlos Patton; 1831 Special Census of the Choctaw Nation; *Register of Choctaw Indians* who were moved to Ft. Towson, from Mississippi, 11 Feb 1832, v.2)

v5201. 81. ***Illiapotubbe, or Eva Brashear**, b. c1789, d. 1879 "about 90 years old" per testimony of her daughter; m. *Thomas Willie Everidge*, of VA.

v5202. 82. ***Lucy Brashear**, b. c1792-3, d. 1829; m.1. c1809, *?William Patton*, and had three children; m.2. 1816, *Capt. James S. Standley*, and had another family.

v5203. 83. ***Elizabeth Brashear**, b. ?c1795, d. young in MS before 1832; m. *Joseph Fisher*, (a white man) in MS, and left two small children.

v5204. 84. ***Lewis Brashear**, b. c1797 (age 34 in Feb 1832); m. twice, full-blood Indians both times (see below).

v5205. 85. ***Benjamin Brashear,** b. c1800 (age 31 in Feb 1832); m. *Illichihana*, b. c1806 (25 in 1832).

Family of R.T. "Turner" Brashear and Oca-ye-mitta, a full-blood Choctaw: (re: testimony of Harriet Oakes in "J.W. Hyden vs. Choctaw Nation")

v5206. 86. **Jefferson Brashear**, b. after 1824; m. _____ *Turnbull*

v5207. 87. **William Brashear**, b. c?1826; m. _____ *Allen*. According to testimony of Harriet Oakes in 1904, _____ Allen, m.1. _____ *Turnbull*, m.2. _____ *Johnson*, m.3. _____, m.4. William "Bill" Brashear. He *may* be the William Brashares, Senior, who is on the 1855 Choctaw Census, with wife, Visa, and children, Ionis, Mary, and Davis.

v5208. 88. ***Tobias Brashear**, b. c1830, "still nursing when his father died", d. early 1880s; m. *Susan* _____, a Chickasaw. Their descendants are on the Chickasaw

Rolls, not the Choctaw. Tobias Brashear, apparently unmarried, is on the 1855 Choctaw Census.

A special 1831 Census of the Choctaw Indian Tribe lists Turner and his two sons by his first marriage in Greenwood LeFlore's District, i.e. Apuckshunnubbee's old District, the Oklafalaya, or Western Division, of the Choctaw Nation; Greenwood LeFlore had succeeded to the chieftainship in 1826, following Robert Cole, 1824-26, who had succeeded Apuckshunnubbee.

In 1831, Ne-Ta-Cha-Chii, ["Son" of Pushmataha (= nephew to us); he was a son of Nahomtima, Pushmataha's sister], was Chief of the Southern District, or Okla Hunnalli, also called Six Villages.

name	# acre	#in fam.	m.16+	m&f>10	# slaves	place
Greenwood LeFlore's Company, Miss.--Yazoo City:						
Benjamin Brashears	14	8	3	4	-	Yazoo valley
Lewis Brashears	12	7	1	3	-	Yazoo valley
Turner Brashears	50	7	1	-	-	Yazoo valley

R.T. "Turner" Brashears died shortly after this census was taken.

BRASHEAR STAND

In 1804, Turner Brashear opened "Brashears Stand," an inn for travelers on the newly-cleared Natchez Trace. (Such inns were generally called "stands.") He advertized in the Natchez *Gazette* of 2 Dec 1806 that he had established "a House of Entertainment on the road leading from Natchez to Nashville" and assured travelers that they could be furnished with "provender and Provisions."

Those travelers who left a record seem to have been more or less pleased with Turner's "Brashears Stand." Rev. Jacob Young, an itinerant Methodist preacher who stopped there in 1807, reported, "Near the line that divided the Choctaw Nation from Mississippi Territory stood a fine public house kept by a man by the name of Bishiers. Although he had an Indian wife, he himself was a gentleman. He had a good many colored people, and appeared to be a man of considerable wealth. He treated us well, but knew how to make a high bill."

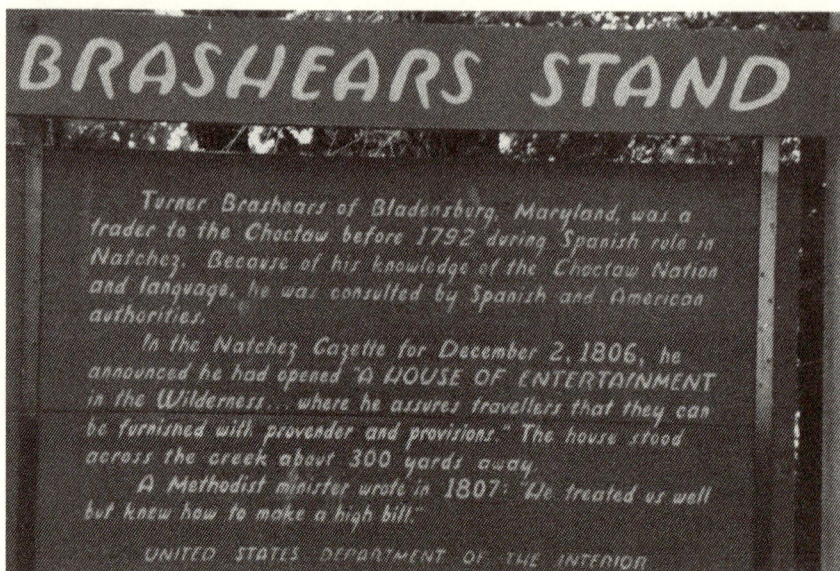

Figure 8: Sign formerly on the Natchez Trace (it has since been removed)

In 1815, another Methodist wrote: "We rode to Brashears. We were well provided for here. Brashears is a white man."

A traveler who seems not to have been favorably impressed with Turner's accommodations was William Richardson, who stayed at the inn on April 3, 1815, while en route from Boston to New Orleans. He reported that he arrived at Beshurs at ten o'clock, where he got "a little venison and some coffee." Perhaps he arrived after the cooks had retired for the night.

Turner's stand on the old Natchez Trace appears as a station with the place-name "Brashears" in gazetteers for all the years from 1812 to 1822. It was located a few miles east of what is now Ridgeland, Mississippi. In later years, Turner's stand became known as "King's Tavern" and still later as "Hawthorne Vale." The large house, built of hand-hewn cypress logs, burned in 1896.

On 24 Nov 1821, the Natchez *Gazette* referred to Turner's place as "the stand of the Late Turner Brashears." Previously, we have assumed he was dead by that time, but apparently only his first wife died at that time and Turner sold out. According to Testimony in "J.W. Hyden vs. Choctaw Nation," he moved to Rankin, about 12 miles from the Pearl River. He married a second time, to Oca-ye-mitta, a full-blood Choctaw, and had three more children. Estate papers (see below) indicate he died in 1831. He received a reservation of land under the Treaty of Dancing Rabbit Creek, 1830, but died soon afterwards. He and his sons by his first marriage were included in a special 1831 Choctaw Census as heads of Choctaw families.

(References: *American State Papers, Indian Affairs*, I; *McBee's Collection* (Abstracts of Natchez Court Records); *Correspondence of the Spanish Governors of LA*, MSS section, La. State Museum; Court records, Madison Co, MS; Carter's *Territorial Papers of the United States*; The *Mississippi Herald* and the Natchez *Gazette*; *Publications of the East Tennessee Historical Society*; Jacob Young's *Autobiography of a Pioneer*, (1859); *Boston to New Orleans by Land, 1815*, publ 1938 by Wm. Bell Wait; *History of Methodism*, (1887) Vol 1; Alsworth's *King's Inn*, MSS, Natchez Trace files; Testimony of ex-slaves Richard Brashear and Elizabeth Nunnelly (1904); Notes by Dr. Sherburne Anderson, Baton Rouge, LA.)

EXHIBIT 'D' of "J.W. HYDEN vs. CHOCTAW NATION"

TO ALL to whom these presents shall come, Oca-ye-mitta of the Choctaw Country, County of Yazoo and State of Mississippi, relict of R. Turner Brashears, late of said Choctaw Country and said County, sends greetings:

Know ye that whereas the said Brashears died intestate leaving three small children and whereas Thomas Everidge, son-in-law of said Brashears, will become chargeable with the sustenance of said children;

Now, this witnesseth that in consideration of the premises and the further consideration of one dollar to me in hand paid, the receipt thereof is duly acknowledged, I, the said Oca-ye-mitta, have granted, remitted, released, and forever quit-claimed, and with these presents do grant, remit, release and forever quit-claim unto the said Thomas Everidge, his heirs and assigns forever, all the dower of thirds and all title of dower of thirds and all other right, title, intent, property claim and demand whatsoever in law and equity of her, the said Oca-ye-mitta, of and to a reservation of land granted to said Brashears by the Supplement to the late Treaty between the Choctaw People and the United States Government, and also all and every the missuages, lands, tenements, and real estate whereof the said R. Turner Brashears died seized and possessed, or to which he was entitled at the time of his death, in law or equity, in possession or expecting, wherever the same may be, so that the said Oca-ye-mitta her heirs, Executors, and Administrators, and assigns, nor any other person or persons for her, them, or any of them, have claim, challenge, or demand, or pretend to have claim, challenge, or demand my dower of thirds, or any other right, title, claim, or demand of mine to the farm or any part thereof, but thereof and therefrom shall be utterly bound and excluded from with these presents—

In Witness whereof, the said Oca-ye-mitta, having had the foregoing release fully explained, read, and interpreted to her by Edmund McKinney, a sworn interpreter, hath hereunto set her hand and seal in the presence of said interpreter and the undersigned witness, the 22nd day of October, 1831,

/s/ Oca-ye-mitta [X] her mark

in presence of
Edmund McKinney, interpreter
A.A. Halsey

State of Mississippi
Yazoo County, C.N. (Choctaw Nation)

This day, personally appeared before me, Thomas Deloach, one of the justices of the peace in and for the said county of Yazoo, Oca-ye-mitta, the person who executed for foregoing release, and through Edmund McKinney, a sworn interpreter, acknowledged the same as her voluntary act and deed for the purposes therein mentioned. Given under my hand and seal, the 22nd day of October, 1831,

/s/ Thos Deloach, JP (Seal)

and at the same time and place, came Edmund McKinney, who, being sworn, deposes and says that he well and truly interpreted and explained in the Choctaw Language the foregoing release of dower executed by the said Oca-ye-mitta and that she fully understands the purport and object thereof and fully agreed thereto and executed the same in her person, and also that he well and truly interpreted the acknowledgment above written, with the Choctaw Language,

Sworn the 22nd day of October,

/s/ Edmund McKinney

before me: Thos Deloach, JP

Turner Brashears applied for a land allotment under Article 19 of the Treaty of Dancing Rabbit Creek, 1830, and was certified as being entitled to 1½ sections. On 11 Nov 1833, he [i.e. his estate] entered 1035.16 acres, being the whole of Sec 13, T16, R1E, and the north half of Sec 24, T16, R1E, Northeastern land district, LeFlore's District, Mississippi. His son, Lewis Brashears, received lot No. 34 under the provision of Article 19, Treaty of Dancing Rabbit Creek: the W ½ of SE ¼ of Sec 12, T16, R12E, and E ½ of SW ¼ of Sec 12, T16, R12E. (Federal Records Center, Microfilm 7RA-116, roll 1).

On 20 Nov 1837, Abraham A. Holsey made deposition that Turner Brashear had sold his land to Thos. Everidge, for money he owed Everidge, plus $2000 to be paid... Everidge became Turner's administrator, paid several claims against the estate, and sold the land to Willie Davis, now (1837) dec'd, for $4000 in three payments, 1st two payments were made in Negroes and perhaps some money. A Note for the last payment of $1300 was in Holsey's hands for collection, about $800 paid and balance secured by deed of trust on 2 or 3 negroes. Wm. M. Givin claims purchase from W. Davis and a transfer from Thos. Everidge, admr of reservee, who acknowledged payment on back of transfer, dated 20 Nov 1837, witnessed by Jno. F. Price and Basil L. LeFlore.

On 25 July 1840, the Office of Indian Affairs, Washington, DC, verified these plots as the right of R.T. Brashears, otherwise known as Turner Brashears.

On 7 Oct 1843, the Office of Indian Affairs, Washington, DC, transmitted with approval of the President of the United States ... two deeds for reservations under the Treaty of 1830, one for "R.T. Brashears, otherwise called Turner Brashears" and one for Richard Holderfield, "patents for which to be issued for the use of Alexander M. Givin, assignee of Wm. M. Givin."

5. JESSE BRASHEARS
and ELIZABETH PRATHER,
of NC, GA, and Pensacola

[6]4. **Jesse Brashears**, son of Robert C. Brashears and Charity Dowell of Prince George's Co, MD, and Guilford Co, NC, was born probably at Brashears Meadows in Prince George's Co, Maryland, about 1733-34, in the sixth generation of Brashears in America. Jesse's Brashear ancestors:

[v1]**1.**   [1]1. **Robert Brasseur/Brashear,** *the Huguenot*, b. France, bef. 1600; to Isle of Thanet, Kent Co, England, c1620-30; to Virginia, bef. 1635; d. 1666-7; m. _____.

[v1]**2**   [2]1. **Benjamin Brassieur,** *the American* (Back#1), also called Benois/ Benoit/ Bennet Brasseur/ Brashear, b. France, c1620; to Virginia with father, c1635; to Maryland, 1658; m. *Mary ?Richford*. Benjamin was naturalized as a citizen of Maryland by Cecil Calvert, 4 Dec 1662; d. c1662.

[v1]**81.**   [3]1. **Robert Brashier, III,** *the Improvident* (Back#2), b. 1646 in Virginia; d. 1712 in Maryland; m.1. _____ (mother of the children); m.2. c1679, *Alice ____,* widow of Thomas Jackson.

[v1]**232.** [4]2. **Samuel Brashear Sr,** *the Maryland Carpenter* (Back#11), b. 1673 in Maryland; d. 1740 in Maryland; m. *Ann Jones*, d/o William Jones and Dorothy (née Cager/ widow Munroe)

[v1]**285.** [5]6. **Robert C. (Cager?) Brashear** (Back#29), b. 1704 in Maryland; to Fairfax Co, Va, c1742; to Orange/Guilford Co, NC, c1750; d. NC, July 1786; m. *Charity Dowell*, d/o Philip Dowell and Mary Tydings.

[v1]**694.** [6]4. **Jesse Brashears,** b. c1734, MD, d. 1788, Pensacola; m. *Elizabeth Prather*, d/o Philip Prather and Margery Hunt,

---

JESSE IN NORTH CAROLINA

On 9 Nov 1754, Jesse Brashears, along with Otho Brashears [a younger brother of Robert C. Brashear], was a sworn chain carrier in the survey of 483 acres for Basil Brashear [another brother of Robert C. Brashear], on the north side of Reedy Fork of Haw River, and on both sides of Brashear's Creek, in Orange (now Guilford) Co, NC (*Orange Co Records*, Granville Proprietary Land Office, Abstracts of Loose Papers, ed by William D. Bennett, publ. Raleigh, NC, 1987, v.1, p.8). If he had to be 21 to take that oath, he was born some time before Nov 1733. On 11 Nov 1754, he was sworn chain carrier in a 640 acre survey for William Blackwood, and on 12 Nov 1754, he was sworn chain carrier in a 256 acre survey for his cousin, Middleton Brashear, s/o Basil Brashear. (same ref.)

On 26 Feb 1755, a Granville warrant was issued to Robert Brashear for 640 acres to be located between Brazil Brashear and Blackwood, and Robert "entered" the land, 30 Dec 1754. On 5 Sept 1755, this plot was surveyed for Jesse Brashear. Robert Brashear and Robert Brashear Jr (Jesse's father and brother) were sworn chain carriers. A deed for 637 acres was made 20 Feb 1756 to Jesse Brashear. (*Orange Co Records*, v.1, p.10). From this, we might conclude that Jesse was under age in Feb 1755, but had reached his majority by Sept 1755, i.e. he was born between Feb and Sept 1734.

The metes and bound of Jesse's Granville Grant #80: "Six hundred and thirty seven acres of land in Orange county, lying on Buffello Creek, Beginning at a white oak, then running South 75 chains to a BlackJack, then West 85 chains to a Beech by Buffelo Creek, then No 75 chains to a white oak Saplin, then East 85 chains to the first station, dated 17th day of July 1760." (Grant Book 14, p.351; NC archives file #402). The plot is quite regular, almost a square.

In 1755, Jesse Brashears is on the tax list of Orange Co, NC (p.108); since he had to be 21 at the time, he was b. 1734 or before. Some time in 1755, his first child, Zadock Brashears, was born. (On 13 Jan 1810, in Baton Rouge, Zadock testified in the estate proceedings of David White that he was 54 years old. See *Archives of Spanish West Florida*, v.17, p.16; also called "The Spanish West Florida Papers.")

(NOTE: The "Spanish West Florida Papers" are the *Archives*

of Spanish West Florida, 1782-1810. The originals are in the Record Room of the 19th Judicial Court, Baton Rouge, and copies are in various places, including the Louisiana State Museum, New Orleans. The records were also published as a W.P.A. Project in the 1930s (Baton Rouge: W.P.A., 1937). They are the official records of the territory south of the 32nd parallel, east of the Mississippi, and west of the Apalachiola River. This area was not included in the Louisiana Purchase and continued to be governed by the Spanish until the "Rebellion of 1810," when the Americans staged a small revolution and took over for about six months, before the area was annexed to the United States. Spanish East Florida, from the Apalachiola River to St. Augustine, continued under Spanish control until 1819.)

Though no records has been found, **Jesse Brashears** married about 1755, *Elizabeth Prather*, surely at Buffalo Presbyterian Church in Orange (now Guilford) Co, NC, where his father was a member. Elizabeth was born 6 May 1739, Anne Arundel Co, Maryland, daughter of Philip Gittings Prather and Margery Hunt (Chancery Paper #2617, Land Office, Annapolis, MD). There is, however, a curious, second marriage record. Elizabeth Prather, m. Jesse Brashear, 8 Dec 1760, in Escambia Co, Florida (Book 1, p.104), according to *Marriage Records of People Named Prather, Prater, Prator, Praytor*, comp. by Anna M. Cartlidge, Baltimore, MD, 1976, p.16. This abstract of the record identifies her as the daughter of Philip Gittings Prather. Why would they be marrying five years after their first child was born? To re-affirm their vows? To make their Protestant marriage legal in a Catholic province? (which did not come into British possession until 1763). Present-day Escambia County, Florida, is the westernmost tip of the Florida panhandle, from Pensacola west; Jesse and Elizabeth later, c1773, moved to a land grant on the Escambia River, which empties into Pensacola Bay. Jesse was later an inn-keeper in Pensacola.

Prather Family

The Prather progenitor of the family in America came from Wiltshire, England, in 1622. I looked in three or four Prather genealogies and found that Philip Gittings (or Philemon) Prather (he's referred to both ways) was the s/o **Thomas Prather**, b. 1671, Calvert Co, MD, d. 1712, PGCo, m. 1698, *Martha Sprigg*,

b. 1677 Calvert Co, d. 13 Nov 1742, Charles Co, MD, d/o Thomas Sprigg, Sheriff of Calvert Co, MD. Martha (Sprigg) Prather's sister, Anne Sprigg, m. Philip Gittings.

Family of Thomas Prather and Martha Sprigg:
1. Elinore Prather, b. 1700, PGCo, d. ?, MD
2. Rachel Prather, b. 1702, PGCo, d. Charles Co, MD
3. Thomas Sprigg Prather, b. 1704, PGCo, d. 1785, Washington Co, MD, named for his maternal grandfather.
4. John Smith Prather, b. 1706, PGCo, d. 3 Sept 1763, Bladenburg, PGCo, MD, named for his grandmother's second husband, who was a loving and supportive step-father to the children.
5. Philip Gittings Prather, b. 1708, PGCo, obviously named for his uncle Philip Gittings; d. 1767, Upper Enoree, SC
6. Aaron Prather, b. 10 Oct 1710, PGCo, d. 1777, Montgomery Co, MD

Philip Gittings Prather was apparently married four times:
m.1. 12 Feb 1725, Catherine Hunt (PGCo Marr. Book 1, p.107), d/o John Hunt. They had three children:
1. Margaret Prather, b. 1730, Queen Anne's Parish, PGCo, MD; m.1. a cousin, Lt Thomas Clagett Prather, b. 1726, killed at battle of Loyahenna, PA, 1758; m.2. Thomas Freeman, Esq, and removed to Fort Harrod, VA
2. Martha Prather, b. 1733
3. John Hunt Prather, b. c1735
m.2. 3 Dec 1737, Margery Hunt, d/o John Hunt. They apparently had only one child:
1. Elizabeth Prather, b. 6 May 1739, Anne Arundel Co, Maryland; m.1. *Jesse Brashear* (^{v1}694); m.2. George Freeland Sr
m.3. Margery Mayfield, by whom he had several children, names unknown to me.
m.4. **Henrietta Brashear** (^{v1}702), d/o Basil Brashear (^{v1}288) and sister of Middleton Brashear (^{v1}701), an extremely close, life-long associate of Jesse and Elizabeth (Prather) Brashears. (Cousins Jesse and Middleton were almost the same age, grew up on adjoining farms, and act almost like twins.) Henrietta Prather, widow of Philip Prather, and Middleton Brashear, brother-in-law of Philip, administered his estate

in 1767 in Laurens Co, SC. No sister of Philip is eligible to be Middleton's wife— they're all 35 years older than he; so I conclude that old man Philip married a much younger Henrietta Brashear, probably in the 1760s in Orange Co, NC. Maryland Chancery Paper #2617, Land Office, Annapolis, MD, establishes that Philip sold land in Augusta Co, VA, in Sept 1756; he was then living in Orange Co, North Carolina.

Through the 1750's, Jesse Brashear was with the Brashear colony in Orange Co, North Carolina, on land that bordered Philip Prather's land and his cousin Middleton Brashear's land (Middleton may also have married a Prather— no documents).

At the May 1761 session of the Orange Co Court of Pleas and Quarter sessions, Jesse Brashear was appointed constable [construction and maintenance foreman] on the head of Haw River. At the same session, "Jesse Brashear and Middleton Brashear, securities for John Pearsons in the suit brought by John Powell against him, came into court and surrendered the principal, whereupon Peter Noey and Benjamin Phillips enters [sic] themselves special bail for the said John Pearson." (*Abstracts of the Minutes of the Court of Pleas and Quarter Sessions of Orange County in the County and Province of North Carolina*, abstracted by Ruth Herndon Shields, p.6).

On 15 May 1764, Jesse sold (or mortgaged?) his 637 acres to Edward Gilbert, a land speculator in Orange Co, NC, with William Anderson as witness.

In 1765, Jesse served on the Orange Co Grand Jury, alongside his father-in-law, Philip Prather. Perhaps he got fed up with the petty squabbles in the courts (he was involved in several small law suits; for details, see *Robert C. Brashear and the North Carolina Interlude*, v.2 of A BRASHEAR FAMILY HISTORY), for he left the area, moving first to Virginia, then to Georgia about January 1767; on 9 Sept 1767, he wrote in a petition in Georgia that he was "eight months out of the province of Virginia," ... and had a wife and five children. (Georgia State Archives, Drawer 40, Microfilm box 55; Volume IX, p.415-416.)

JESSE IN GEORGIA RECORDS

Jesse and Elizabeth were in Georgia, from Jan 1767 to March 1773. Jesse received a 250 acre grant of land in St. Matthews Parish, GA, on 3 March 1767 (Grant Book F, p.95); another grant of 100 ac. in St. Matthews Parish, on 7 June 1768 (Grant Book G, p. 118); and a third grant for 100 ac. on 5 June 1770 (Grant Book I, p.41). There was also a 100 ac. grant on Horse Creek in St. George Parish, Georgia, 2 May 1768 (Grant Book G, p.311).

Sep 1767: "Read a Petition of Jesse Brashear setting forth that he had been about Eight Months in the Province from Virginia had had no Land granted him and was desirous to obtain Land for Cultivation having <u>a Wife, five Children, and a Negroe</u>; Therefore praying for two hundred and fifty acres upon the south side of Horse Creek, about a mile and half above Land surveyed for William Coulsin - -

"RESOLVED That on Condition only that the Petitioner doth take out a Grant for the said Land within seven Months from this Date and that he doth also register the said Grant in the Register's Office of the said Province within six Months from the Date thereof that his Majesty may not be defrauded of his Quit Rents the prayer of the said Petition is granted but no Grant to pass until the Petitioner produces a Certificate of his Character.

ORDERED That the further Consideration of the said Petition be postponed.

GOVERNOR AND COUNCIL

His Excellency the Governor signed the following Grants viz;

Jesse Brashears 150 Acres -- St. Matthew's Parish.

(Georgia State Archive, Drawer 40, Microfilm box 55; Volume IX, p.415-416.)

November 1767, Read a Petition of Jesse Brashear setting forth that he was settled in the Province had had three hundred and fifty Acres of Land granted him and was desirous to Obtain an Additional Tract having <u>a Wife, six Children, and a Negro</u>; Therefore praying for One hundred Acres in St. Mathew's Parish to adjoin Land there already granted him at a Place called Horse Creek.

RESOLVED That on Condition only that the Petitioner doth

take out a Grant for the said Land within Seven Months from this date and that he doth also register the said Grant in the register's Office of the said Province within six Months from the date thereof that his Majesty may not be defrauded of his Quit Rents the prayer of the said Petition is granted.
(Georgia State Archives, Drawer 40, Box 51-39; Volume X, p.446.)

December 1768, GOVERNOR AND COUNCIL

Read a Petition of Jesse Brashears setting forth that he had heretofore had ordered him One hundred Acres of land in St. George's Parish which had been Surveyed and a Plan thereof returned into the Surveyor General's Office but the time was elapsed in which a Grant for the same ought to have passed. Therefore praying that notwithstanding the lapse of time he might be permitted to take out his Majesty's Grant for the said Land and that the Surveyor General might be ordered to prepare and Certify a plan thereof for that purpose.

RESOLVED That on Condition & the prayer of the said Petition is granted
(Georgia State Archive, Drawer 40, Box 51-59, Volume X, p.683-684.)

7 June 1768; Royal Land Grant to Jesse Brashear

George the Third, by the Grace of God, of Great-Britain, France and Ireland, KING, Defender of the Faith, and so forth, To all to whom these presents come, GREETING.

KNOW YE, That WE, of Our special Grace, certain Knowledge, and meer Motion, hereby Given and Granted, and by these presents, for Us, Our Heirs and Successors, do Give and Grant unto Jesse Brasher his Heirs and Assigns all that Tract of Land Containing One hundred acres - situate and being in the Parish of Saint Matthew in Our Province of Georgia bounded on every side by Land vacant. Having such Shape, Form and Marks, as appears by a Plot thereof hereunto annexed, together with all Woods, Underwoods, Timber and Timber-Trees, Lakes, Ponds, (Fishings?), Waters, Water-Courses, Profits, Commodities, Hereditaments, and Appurtenances whatsoever thereunto belonging or is anywise appertaining, together also with Privilege of Hunting, Hawking and Fowling, in and upon the same, and all Mines and Minerals whatsoever; Saving Reserving, nevertheless, to Us, Our Heirs and Successors, all White Pine Trees, if any should be found growing thereon: and also Saving and Reserving, to Us, our Heirs and Successors, One Tenth Part of Mines of Silver and Gold only.

TO HAVE AND TO HOLD the said Tract of One hundred Acres of land and all and singular other the Premises hereby granted, with the Appurtenances, unto the said Jesse Brashear his heirs and Assigns forever in the free and common Soccage, he the said Jesse Brasher his Heirs or Assigns, Yielding and Paying therefor, unto Us, our Heirs and Successors, or to our Receiver-General for the time being, or to his Deputy of Deputies for the Time being, yearly and every Year, on the twenty-fifth day of March at the rate of Two Shillings Sterling for every Hundred Acres, and so in Proportion, according to the Quantity of Acres contained herein, the same to commence at the End and Expiration of two Years from the Date hereof.

PROVIDED ALWAYS, and this present Grant is upon Condition nevertheless, That he the said Jesse Brashear, his Heirs and Assigns, shall and do within three Years after the Date hereof, for every fifty Acres of plantable Land hereby granted, clear and work Three acres at least in that Part thereof as he or they shall judge most convenient and advantageous, or else do clear and drain three Acres of Swamp or sunken Grounds, or drain Three of Marsh, if any such contained herein; and shall and do, within the Time aforesaid, put and keep, upon every fifty Acres thereof accounted (barren?); Three neat Cattle or Six Sheep or Goats, and continue the same thereon until Three Acres for every Fifty Acres be fully cleared and improved, or otherwise, if any Part of the said Tract shall be stony or rocky Ground, and not fit for Planting or Pasture, shall and do, within Three Years as aforesaid, begin to employ thereon, and so continue to work for Three Years then next ensuing, in digging any Stone Quarry, or Coal, or other Mine, One good and able Hand for every Hundred Acres, it shall be accounted sufficient Cultivation and Improvement.

PROVIDED ALSO, That every three Acres which shall be cleared and worked, or cleared and drained as aforesaid, shall be accounted a sufficient Seeding. Planting, Cultivation and Improvement, to save for ever from Forfeiture, Fifty Acres of Land in any Part of the Tract hereby granted. And the Said

Jesse Brasher, his Heirs and Assigns, shall be at Liberty to withdraw his or their Stock, or to forbear working in any Quarry or Mine, in Proportion to such Cultivation and Improvements as shall be made upon the Plantable Lands Swamps, sunken Grounds, or Marshes, herein contained. AND, if the said Rent hereby reserved shall happen to be in Arrear and unpaid, for the Space one Year from the Time it shall become due, and no Distress can be found on the said Lands, Tenements and Hereditaments, hereby granted, that then and in such case, the said Lands, Tenements and Hereditaments, hereby granted, and every Par and Parcel thereof, shall revert to Us, Our Heirs and Successors, as fully and absolutely as if the same had never been granted,

PROVIDED ALSO, if this Grant shall not be duly registered in the Register-Office of our said Province, within Six months from the Date hereof, and a Docquet hereof also entered in the Auditor's Office of the same. That then this Grant shall be void, any Thing herein contained to the contrary notwithstanding. Given, under the Great Seal of the Province of GEORGIA.

Witness Our Truly and Well beloved James Wright, (Cz?) our Captain General & governor in Chief of (-?-)(-?-) Province, the Seventh Day of June in the Year of Our Lord 1768 and in the Eighth Year of Our Reign.

(L. S.) Js. Wright

Signed by his Excellency the Governor in Council.

Cha. Watson, C. C.

Marginal notes appear as follows:
 Jesse Brasher, 100 acres, St. Matthews
 Dated 7 June 1768 Regsd. 16 June 1768

December 1769, - Read a Petition of Jesse Brashear setting forth that he had been long settled in the Province had had four hundred and fifty Acres of Land Granted him and was desirous to obtain an additional Tract having a Wife, seven Children, and two Negroes; Therefore praying for one hundred Acres in St. Matthew's Parish at a Place called Horse Creek to adjoin Land there ordered him --

RESOLVED That on Condition only that the Petitioner doth take out a Grant for the said Land within seven Months from

this date and that he doth also register the said Grant in the Register's Office of this Province within six Months from the date thereof that his Majesty may not be defrauded of his Quit Rent the Prayer of the said Petition is granted--
(Georgia State Archives, Drawer 40, Box 51-59; Volume X, p.963.)

GOVERNOR AND COUNCIL
His Excellency the Governour Signed the following Grants viz;--
Jesse Brashear. . .100 Acres. . .St. Mathew's Parish.
(Georgia State Archives, Drawer 40, Box 51-59, Volume XI, p.84.)

January 1772, "Read a Petition of Jesse Brashear setting forth that he had heretofore five hundred and fifty Acres of Land granted him and no more, that he had a Wife, Ten Children, and three Negroes and was desirous of Obtaining an additional Quantity of Land for Cultivation; Therefore praying for Two hundred and fifty Acres of Land on the north side of great Ogechee a Mile above Horse Creek - -

RESOLVED That on Condition & c the prayer of the said Petition is granted - -
(Georgia State Archives, Microfilm Drawer 40, Box 56, Vol. XI, p.173.)

If Jesse and Elizabeth had ten children by 1772, some of them must have died young; there are only six adults in the estate proceedings in 1804.

31 March 1773 - Jesse Brashears and Elizabeth Brashears sold 250 acres of their land in Georgia:
This indenture made the thirty first day of March in the year of our lord one thousand seven hundred and seventy three and in the thirteenth year of the reign of our sovereign Lord George the Third by the Grace of God of Great Britain, France and Ireland King, defender of the faith and so forth between Jesse Brashear and Elizabeth of St. Matthews parish and province of Georgia of the one part and Robert Hankinson of the parish and province aforesaid of the other part witnesseth that for and in consideration of the sum of one hundred and fifty current money of the province aforesaid to him the said Jesse Brashear in hand at and before the Sealing & delivery of these presents

by the said Robert Hankinson well & truly paid the receipt whereof the said Jesse Brashear doth hereby acknowledge and thereof and of every part and parcel thereof doth acquit release exonerate and discharge the said Robert Hankinson his heirs Executors & Administrators and every of them forever by these presents he the said Jesse Brashear hath granted bargained sold aliened released and confirmed & by these presents doth fully freely clearly and absolutely grant bargain sell alien release and confirm unto the said Robert Hankinson in his actual possession now being by virtue of a bargain and sale to him thereof made by the said Jesse Brashear for one whole year for the consideration of five shillings by an indenture of lease bearing date the day next before the day of the date of these presents to commence from the day next before the day of the date hereof and sealed and delivered before the executing of these presents and also by force of the statute for transferring of (uses?) into possession in that case made and provided and unto his heirs and assigns forever all that said plantation parcel or tract of land containing <u>two hundred & fifty</u> acres situate lying and being in the parish of St. Matthews in the province of Georgia bounded west by (horse) Creek and on all other sides by land vacant having such shape form and marked (Treas?) as are delineated and expressed in a plot (/) the same to the original grant annexed bearing date the third day of March in the year of our Lord one thousand seven hundred and sixty seven which said grant was to the said Jesse Brashear party to these presents and tested by his Excellency James Wright, Esqr Captain (--?--) and Governor in Chief in and over (--?--) said province of Georgia together with all and singular the gardens orchards fences ways wells water, water courses easements profits commodities advantages emoluments hereditaments and appurtenances whatsoever to the said plantation or tract of land containing two hundred and fifty acres belonging or in any way appertaining and the Reversion and reversions remainder and remainders rents (--?--) and profits thereof and of every part and parcel thereof and also all the estate right title interest possession property profit claim and demand whatsoever either in law or equity which they the said Jesse Brashear and his wife Elizabeth now have or ever had or which they or their heirs hereafter shall may can or ought to have of into or out of the said plantation or tract of land containing two hundred acres and other premises with their and every of their appurtenances together with all deeds plats grants charters writings and (muniments?) whatsoever which they said Jesse Brashear and his wife Elizabeth now hath in their custody or possession or can come by without suit in law or equity that do only concern the premises to have and to hold the said plantation of two hundred and fifty acres of land and all and singular other the premises hereby granted and released unto the said Robert Hankinson his heirs and assigns to the only proper use and behoof of the said Robert Hankinson his heirs and assigns forever and the said Jesse Brashear and his wife for themselves and their heirs the said premises hereby bargained sold granted released or meant and intended to be bargained sold granted and released with their and every of their appurtenances unto him the said Robert Hankinson his heirs and assigns against all and all manner of person and persons whatsoever shall and will warrant and forever defend by these presents and the said Jesse Brashear and Elizabeth his wife for themselves and their heirs executors & administrators do covenant promise grant and agree to and with the said Robert Hankinson his heirs and assigns by these presents in manner and form following that is to say that they the said Jesse Brashear and Elizabeth his wife now at the time of the sealing and delivery of these presents is and standeth lawfully and absolutely seized of and in the said plantation or tract of land containing two hundred and fifty acres as aforesaid and all & singular other the premises herein before mentioned and intended to be hereby granted and released and every part and parcel thereof with their and every of their appurtenances of a good sure perfect and absolute estate of inheritance in fee simple without any manner of condition trust proviso power of revocation or limitation of any use or uses or other restraint matter or thing whatsoever to alter change charge defeat or evict the same and also that the said Jesse Brashear and his wife Elizabeth now have in themselves good rightful power and lawful and absolute authority to grand release and confirm the said plantation or tract of land containing two hundred acres aforesaid and all & singular other the premises herein before mentioned and intended to be hereby granted and released and every part & parcel thereof with their and every of their appurtenances unto the said Robert Hankinson his heirs and assigns forever as aforesaid and also that it shall and may be lawful to and for the said Robert Hankinson his heirs and assigns from time to time and at all times forever hereafter peaceably and quietly to enter into have hold occupy possess and enjoy the said plantation or tract of land as aforesaid and all and singular other the premises herein before mentioned & intended to be hereby granted and released and every part & parcel thereof with their and every of their appurtenances without any (the)? lawful (let?) suit trouble molestation eviction or interruption of the said Jesse Brashear and his wife Elizabeth executors or administrators or any other person or persons whatsoever claiming or to claim by from or him her or they under and that free and clear and freely and clearly and absolutely acquitted exonerate & discharged of and from all and all manner of former and other gifts grants bargains sales uses wills entails (jointers?) dowers judgments executions charges and encumbrances whatsoever had made done committed or suffered by the said Jesse Brashear and his wife Elizabeth or any other person or persons whatsoever lawfully claiming or to claim by from or under him or their and lastly that the said Jesse Brashear and Elizabeth his wife their heirs & all & every other person & persons lawfully claiming or to claim any estate right title trust or interest of in or to the said plantation or tract of land aforesaid and all & singular other the premises herein before mentioned and intended to be hereby granted & released or any part or parcel thereof shall and & from and at all times hereafter at the reasonable request and proper costs and charges in the law of the said Robert Hankinson his heirs & assigns make do acknowledge & execute or cause & procure to be made done acknowledged and executed all and every such further & other lawful & reasonable act and acts thing & things conveyances and assurances in the law whatsoever for the further better & more perfect & absolute granting conveying & assuring the said plantation or tract of land containing two hundred & fifty acres & all and singular other the premises herein before mentioned & intended to be hereby granted & released & every part & parcel thereof with their and every of their appurtenances to & for the use and behoof of the said Robert Hankinson his heirs & assigns forever as by him or them or by his or their counsel learned in the law shall be reasonably devised or advised and required in witness whereof the said parties to these presents have hereunto interchangeably set their hands and seals the day and year first above written----

Jesse Brashear (ls)
Elizabeth Brashear (ls)

Signed sealed and delivered
in the presence of
    John Ford   Alexander Newman
Received the day and year first written of the within named Robert Hankinson the sum of Sixty pounds sterling current money of Georgia it being the full consideration money within mentioned (-?-) received by

John Ford   Jesse Brashear (ls)
Alexander Newman   Elizabeth Brashear (ls)

Memorandum that on the fifth day of August in the year of our Lord one thousand seven hundred and seventy three before me Isaac Ford, Esqr. one of his majesty's Justices assigned to keep the peace in the parish of Saint Matthews personally came and appeared John Ford and made oath on the holy Evangelists that he did see the within named Jesse Brashear & Elizabeth Brashear sign seal and as their act and deed deliver the within deed to & for the uses within mentioned & did also see the said Jesse Brashear & Elizabeth Brashear sign the receipt hereon endorsed & did likewise see Alexander Newman subscribe his name as a witness thereunto - ----
    John Ford
Sworn the day and year above mentioned before me
    (?) Isaac Ford
Recorded 19th April 1775 (Conveyances, Book DD 1775-1795, pp.37-46, March 31, 1773.)

1773, March 31 - The same day, Jesse and Elizabeth made a deed for an additional 100 acres for 50 pounds Sterling, also to Robert Hankinson, before the same witnesses. These deeds differ only in specifying the amount of money and the acreage. Recorded 19th April 1775. (Conveyances, Book DD, 1775-1798, pp.37-46, March 31, 1773)

Robert Hankinson had trouble holding onto the land and apparently lost it to taxes or debt:
10 Aug 1774: Whereas the Provost Marshall of this province, by

virtue of a writ of attachment to him directed, did attach the lands, tenements, goods, chattels, monies, debts, and books of account, of Robert Hankinson, have at the parish of Saint George, in the province aforesaid, planter, who is absent from and without the limits of the said province, at the suit of John Ford, in the hands and possession of William Blackman, and particularly one tract of two hundred and fifty acres of land, in the parish of Saint Matthew; one other tract of land, containing one hundred acres in the parish aforesaid; also one other tract containing 100 acres of land in the parish of Saint George (aforesaid?); the whole having been originally granted one Jesse Brashear, his heirs and assigns, and by him sold and conveyed to the said Robert Hankinson; AND WHEREAS the said John Ford HATH, agreeable to the directions of the attachment (Act?), filed his declaration in his Majesty's General Court against the said Robert Hankinson, and HATH obtained the following, viz.

John Ford)

  versus)

Robert Hankinson)

ORDERED. That the defendant do appear and plead within a year and a day, otherwise judgement by default.

(By?) the Court
PRESTON AND PRYCE, C.G.C.

NOTICE therefore is hereby given, That, unless the said Robert Hankinson appear and plead agreeable to the aforesaid rule or order, judgment will be entered against him accordingly.

  (ROBERSON?), Plaintiff's Attorney

To be sold, at the Exchange in Savannah, on Thursday the 16th November next at the usual hour, for (cash?)

[Several tracts, not copied]

Also a Tract of Land, situated in said parish, but by the original grant failed to be in the parish of St. George, bounded, south by land of Jesse Brashears, and on all other sides by land vacant.

The <u>four land tracts originally granted Jesse Brashears</u>, and levied on as the property of the said Brashears and Robert Hankinson.

[Other tracts, not copied. A lot of families seem to have moved on west.]

The whole seized on execution by

LEWIS JOHNSTON, P. M.

(*The Georgia Gazette*, No 566, Wednesday, August 10, 1774.)

JESSE IN SPANISH WEST FLORIDA RECORDS

About March 1773, Jesse and Elizabeth moved to Pensacola. Their son, Philip, had moved to Feliciana Parish, Spanish West Florida, east of the Mississippi River, now in Louisiana.

On 13 March 1776, Jesse Brashear received a Land grant, situated northeasterly about eighteen miles from Pensacola on the Southwest side of the River Escambia, and on the other side by vacant land. Signed Peter Chester, Capt. General Governor of West Florida. Survey by Elias Dumford dated 6 March 1776. (Great Britain Public Records Office, University of Florida, P.K. Yonge Library, Microfilm 5/608:143)

On 23 or 24 Nov 1778, Jesse received a land grant of Lot #36 in Pensacola; Elizabeth also received a grant of lot #35. A Pensacola deed dated 24 Nov 1778, from John Hicktail (Hightail, in other records) to Jessie Brashears, transfers "one part of a town lot of ground, and the whole of garden lot #26." Jesse and Elizabeth kept an inn in Pensacola. (*West Florida Records*, Vol. 8, p.211-219) [See entry under date of March 1, 1805, below.]

In Feb 1780, Jesse Brashear was listed as an inhabitant of the Town of Pensacola (No data given.) (Public Records Office, Great Britain, P.K. Yonge Library, University of Florida, Lockey Collection #5/635:8.) He was later referred to as an Inn-keeper.

On 28 Sept 1781, Jesse Brashier bought lots 172, 173, and 200 in the city of Pensacola, from William Marshall and Henry Beaumont. "Isabelle" Brashier, widow of Jesse, sold these lots to Martin de Madrid on 12 Oct 1788. (See Record Book A, Vol I, pp.209-212, 324-325.)

In 1783, Florida was once again transferred to Spanish control, and the Spanish authorities took a census to determine the extent and make-up of their population.

BUCIERS (BRASHEARS?) Miuel, English	42	Jesse Brashears
PRETA (PRATHER?), Ysabel, his wife	37	Elizabeth Prather
Ysabel, daughter	12	Elizabeth, m. William Taylor
Ysaiar, son	13	Asa Brashears
Juan, son	1 yrs. 6 mos.	John Brashears, d. young?
Lucia, daughter	2 yrs. 8 mos.	Lucy Brashears, d. young?
Lucia, Negro slave	17	"Lucy" in Elizabeth's will
Bob, Negro slave	20	mentioned in Elizabeth's will
Sisa, same	19	"Nell" in Elizabeth's will
Jorge, same	25	"George" in Elizabeth's will

(NOTE: In spite of the variant spellings (Spanish phonetics), the statistics and names, including the names of the slaves, identify this as a census enumeration of Jesse and Elizabeth Prather-Brashears. In the Spanish phonetic rendering of English names, mistakes were probably made. But this also identifies some of the missing children who died young.)

There were 393 free persons and 17 servants, for a total of 410 persons, living in 46 occupied houses in Pensacola that year. The Rural population was 187 and there were 37 convicts, making a total population of 630.

Jesse died in Pensacola in 1788, according to Richard Brashears ([v]5 2), a kinsman who lived at St. Stephens Trading Post in Alabama (Capt. Richard Brashears was s/o Benjamin and Catherine (Belt) Brashears.)

2 Aug 1790

To Messrs Gipson & Brevade of Hagerstown, Md, Merchants:

I am living on Tombigby about 50 miles above Mobile. A Mr. Hoape has come into this country in search of a woman whose maiden name was Elizith Prather and some years past was married to Jesse Brashear, who lived in Pensacola when you was in this country and kept a public house. About 2 years past Jesse died in Pensacola. Elizabeth moved to this river and has lately married a second time and is well and hearty and likely to marry a third time. This, gentlemen, I assure you to be the truth as her first husband was a relation of mine, and this I write in behalf of Mr. Hope, who said that if he could prove that the said woman was alive and the daughter of Philip Prather it would render him a great service, which he can do if writings will be sufficient.

Your humble servant,

/s/ Richard Brashear"

(Chancery Paper #2617, Washington Co, Maryland, 1792.)

1 Sept 1792, - Complaint of Rudolph Hawpe of Augusta County, Virginia.

On 9 Oct 1737, a Van Swearingin of Prince George's County, Maryland, leased 99 acres of Conseocheague (?) Manor (later in Washington County) for his life and the lives of his wife, Elizabeth, and his daughter, Priscilla. On 8 Dec. 1739, he assigned the lease to Philip Prather, who had the names originally on the lease replaced by his and those of his wife, Margery [Hunt] Prather, and his daughter, Elizabeth Prather. In September 1756, Philip Prather assigned the lease to Joseph Rench and moved to North Carolina with his family. In 1778 Hawpe was in possession of the lease and Elizabeth Prather, who was an infant (a minor) when the lease was assigned to her father, was living, Hawpe had recently been informed, in West Florida, but because the intermediate country was partly possessed by the Enemies of America (Britain), he could not safely attempt to find her. Hawpe had discovered that Elizabeth was living on Tombeckbe (Tombigby) River in the Spanish Settlements in Florida. She was then Elizabeth Freeland. Hawpe asks that all the money John Galloway and Samuel Ringgold have received for the use of the land since 1784 be paid to him.

Filed 1 Sept. 1792

[Agreement 1 May 1778, concerning Swearingen Upper Place, 101 acres, as all the lives of the lease are certainly dec'd. except Elizth. Prather's and there is some reason to believe she is also dead, between Rudolphe Haupe and Adam Grave, farmers, of the one part and John Galloway as extc. of Thomas Ringgold, Esq., dec'd. of the other part that Haupe and Grave shall pay 47 pounds per year rent for said land.])

(Chancery Paper #2617, Washington Co, Maryland, 1792.)

Elizabeth (Prather) Brashears m.2. c1800, on the Tombigbee River, George Freeland Sr, and they soon moved to Feliciana Parish, now Louisiana. She and her children owned several parcels of land in present-day Louisiana, just south of Natchez in the vicinity of Sara "Sally" (Brashears) Bingaman, d/o Benjamin Brashears and Catherine Belt. Elizabeth and George Freeland Sr must have separated soon after, however, for Elizabeth returned to the Tombigbee River and lived the rest of her life with her son, Zadock. In her estate papers, she is referred to as "formerly wife of George Freeland Sr" and "a spinster." George Freeland Sr was still living; part of the estate proceedings took place at his house.

In the *Archives of Spanish West Florida*, the will of Elizabeth (née Prather), "relict of Jesse Brashear, now married to George Freeland, Sr," named her and Jesse's children (that is, the ones who lived to adulthood): Zadock, Samuel, Philip, Asa, Elizabeth, and Routh. The will was signed 16 July 1804 and probated 22 Oct 1804 in East Feliciana Parish, now Louisiana. At the time of her death, Elizabeth was living on the Tombigbee River, near her son, Zadock, who operated a trading post and ferry at "Brashear Bluffs." (See *Archives of Spanish West Florida*, v.8, p.211-22.

The <u>Will of Elizabeth Prater</u> appears in the *Archives of Spanish West Florida* in both English and Spanish versions. The English version p.571-573 [or v.8, p.211. The text I have has two sets of numbers]: In the name of God, Amen. I, Elizabeth formerly [p.572] wife of George Freeland of New Feliciana in West Florida, considering the uncertainty of this mortal life and being of perfect sound and disposing mind and memory do make and ordain this my last Will and Testament in manner and form, to wit: I give and Bequeath to my daughter Elizabeth Brashears, wife of William Taylor, a negro girl named Sukey, about fourteen years old, in consideration of her care and attention to me during former and present illnesses. I give and Bequeath to my daughters Elizabeth and Routh Brashears all my wearing apparel, to be equally divided between them. The remainder of my Estate both Real and Personal consisting of Lands, Lots in Pensacola, negroes viz. Lucy, Bob, Nell, George, Jenny, and March, and horned cattle the number not ascertained. I give and Bequeath to my children named Zadock, Philip, Elizabeth, Samuel, Asa, and Routh Brashear to be equally divided amongst them after my decease. And it is my will, that whatever I have formerly given amongst my said children, since the decease of my first husband Jesse Brashears, shall remain as it now is, without any alteration or Second Division. And I do hereby Constitute and Appoint my son Zadock Brashears, Doctor Jacques Raoul, and John Murdoch Executors of this my last Will and Testament, hereby revoking all former wills, ratifying and [p.573] confirming this and no other to be my last Will and Testament. In Testimony whereof I, the said Elizabeth Prater, have hereto made my accustomed Mark, not knowing how to write, in Feliciana aforesaid, the sixteenth day of July, one thousand eight hundred and four in the presence of John Rhea, Champness Terry, Thomas Carney, Marin Bourg, Adwell Atkins, Zachariah Richardson and Americus Brizina, witnesses, inhabitants and residents in the District, for the want of a notary.

JOHN RHEA   MARIN BOURG

C. TERRY   ADWELL ATKINS   ELIZABETH [X] PRATER

THOMAS CARNEY   AMERICUS BRISINA

In Spanish in the Margin: "Will of Elizabeth Prater, wife of George Freeland, 19 of July of 1804." The Spanish version of the will immediately follows.

On 22 Oct 1804, Zadock Brashears petitioned Governor Grand-Pré to open the last will of his mother, "who has been dead about three months" (p.575-6). That is, she died about mid-July.

On 27 Oct 1804, Governor Grand Pré ordered Alcalde Isaac Johnson to proceed with the opening of the will. John Mears, Alcalde, acting in the place of Isaac Johnson, proceeded with the opening of the will of "Mrs. Elizabeth Freeland, formerly Mrs. Elizabeth Prater, Spinster" in the presence of John Rhea, Champness Terry, Zachariah Richardson, Thomas Carney, Adwell Atkins, Americus Briznoe, and Marin Bourg. "The seal being broken and the will read in the presence of the attending witnesses," they all affirmed the will to be Elizabeth's and that she seemed to them in command of her mental faculties. Zadok [B] Brashiers, J. Raoul, and John Murdoch were then confirmed as administrators, and the children petitioned (Written in Spanish): "We supplicate Your Excellency to please order that the executors deliver to us the property due us, because we have all attained the age of majority, are established and married ..." (Baton Rouge, 22 Jan 1805, p.588-89; v.8, p.215)

"His Excellency, Governor Carlos de Grand Pré attended on the first day of March 1805 at the house of Mr. George Freeland Senior to make with the Executors appointed by the last will and testament of Mrs. Elizabeth Freeland (heretofore Brashears and heretofore Prater, late the wife of Mr. George Freeland aforesaid, but now deceased) the dispositions necessary for delivering the legacies to their respective legatees named in the said will; The Executors John Murdoch Esquire, Zadoch Brashears, and Dr. James Raoul having already accepted the appointment; and to proceed according to law do appoint Mr. John Mears and Mr. Marin Bourg my witnesses of assistance to attend on this business till it shall be concluded" (i.e. to conduct an inventory).

The inventory (written in English, p.592-95, v.8, p.218) included:

1. A Negro woman Lucy, aged about forty years, $ 350
2. A negro boy named Bob, aged about twelve years   300
3. A negro girl name Nel, aged about ten years   250
4. A negro boy named George, aged about seven years   230
5. A negro girl named Jenny, aged about four years   120
6. A negro boy named March, aged about fifteen months   80
7. A feather bed and bed clothes, Household goods   20
   Horned Cattle:
8. One cow, one two years old heifer, one bull a year old, one old worn ox, at six dollars each, making together twenty-four dollars   24
9. An old cow, one three year old cow, one two year old heifer, one heifer of one year old, at five dollars each, making twenty   20
10. One part of the town lot of ground, the whole of the garden lot Number 36 in the town of Pensacola, granted to Jesse Brashears by John Hicktail, as appears by the deeds duly executed and under date of 23rd and 24th November 1778. But as it appears that the said lot has been granted away by the Spanish Government of West Florida it appears to us doubtful whether any valuation can be affixed thereon, and do therefore decline valuing the same.

On 2 March 1805, the six children signed an agreement about the disposal of Elizabeth's estate. "Executors shall pay the amount of a note of our late father Jesse Brashear to William Radliffe for the sum of twenty dollars." The slaves were distributed: Philip got Lucy, Samuel got Nel, Asa got George, Zadock got Jenny and March and the feather bed and "bed cloaths," Routh got Bob and four head of horned cattle, Samuel got four more head of cattle. [mistake? Elizabeth wasn't in the division, yet she signed.] The legatees agreed, "for the reason expressed, the Appraisers have judged that no value can be fixt on the lots number 36 in the town of Pensacola, we do mutually and severally agree that the two other Executors shall give full power to the Executor Zadok Brashears to dispose thereof at his discretion, and if any pecuniary consideration shall at any time be obtained for the said town lots, the same may be divided among the said residuary legatees..."[p.600]

On 2 March 1805, the five youngest children executed identical receipts, acknowledging they had received their share. The receipts are written in Spanish, (pp.601-607):

Received New Feliciana, 2d March 1805 of Zadok Brashears, Doctor Raoull and John Murdoch Esquire, Executors of the last will of the late Elizabeth Prater, otherwise Brashears, otherwise Freeland, deceased, my full share as legatee of the residue of the estate; it being the sum of two hundred and thirty two dollars and one third part of a dollar; and in full of all claim and demands of and out of the said estate and do hereby promise to pay one sixth part of the charges agreed by the legatees to be paid by the Executors of the said will.

Wit: Isaac Johnson   his customary
     John Mears   Zadok [B] Brashears
     Marin Bourg   mark

                            his customary
                            Philip [X] Brashears
                            mark

       her customary   his customary
Elizabeth [X] Brashears   Samuel   Brashears
        mark   mark

       her customary   his customary
Routh [X] Brashears   Asa [A] Brashears
        mark   mark

Jesse and Elizabeth's Family

Family of Jesse Brashears and Elizabeth Prather: In Dec 1769, Jesse wrote in a petition that he had a wife and seven children; in Jan 1772, he said he had a wife and ten children. Either he was lying or a good many of his children died young; only six of his and Elizabeth's children reached maturity. (Ref: Elizabeth's

Will, *Archives of Spanish West Florida*, v.8, pp.211-222; data collected by Dr. Sherburne Anderson, Baton Rouge, LA, and Dorothy Elliott, Commerce City, CO, both deceased, supplemented with data from the Spanish census of Pensacola, 20 June 1784, and the *Archives of Spanish West Florida*.)

v5231. 71. ***Zadock Brashears Sr**, b. c1755, North Carolina (on 13 Jan 1810, in court testimony, Zadock stated that he was 54 years old and "of Maryland," which probably reflects the Spanish sense of family origins), d. c1734, Sumter Co, AL. Some reports say he died 18 Dec 1816 in New Feliciana Parish, Louisiana, but that was probably a confusion with a cousin or nephew also named Zadock. Zadock Sr was still alive and on the Census of Choctaw Indians in 1831 and died in Sumter Co, AL, about 1834.

Zadock m.1. **Susannah Vaughn**, a half-blood Choctaw, whose parentage is in controversy: family tradition claims she was a daughter of John Turnbull, but court records say she was d/o Thomas Vaughn and Winifred _____, a Choctaw woman from "Standing Hickory," probably Oksuk Talaya (which Chris Morgan says means literally "Hickory, Standing in"), in the Oklafalaya District; quite possibly she was d/o John Turnbull and Winifred, and her half-siblings and Catherine Rucker Turnbull engaged in some creative lying in the court records, claiming she was d/o Thomas Vaughn. Zadock and Susannah lived on the Tombigbee River, Alabama, where Susannah died before 1824.

Zadock m.2. in 1824, **Rachel Durant**, ex-wife of his brother Samuel and widow of David Walker. The story is erroneous that Zadock got to Anne Arundel County, Maryland, where in July 1776, he was enrolled in the Revolutionary Army as a private, by 2nd Lt. John Sprigg Belt. That Zadock was s/o John and Mary (Dowell) Brashear (*Archives of Maryland*, XVIII:40). Zadock and Susannah had ten children.

v5232. 72. ***Philip Brashears**, b. c175?, d. c1825, moved to New Feliciana, Spanish West Florida, now Louisiana, by 1774. Philip apparently married twice: m.1. _____ and had children Zadock, Samuel, etc. according to

Dorothy Elliott; m.2. **Mary "Polly" White**, and had eight more children. See below. In the 1820 Census, Feliciana Parish, Philip registered 3 males, 7 females, and 5 slaves. He resided between Zadock's daughter, Susanna Stuart/Stewart (3m, 4f, 23s), and George Freeland Jr (4m, 1f, 11s); two doors away: John Brashier (5m, 1f, 1s), Philip's son.

v5233. 73. unknown, b. bef 1767

v5234. 74. ***Samuel Brashears Sr**, b. c?1760-3 (if in mid-20s when marrying), appears in records to about 1810; m. c1788, **Rachel Durant**, d/o Benjamin Durant and Sophia McGillivray, a Creek Indian. Sophia was a sister of Alexander McGillivray; their parents were Sehoy, princess of the Wind Clan, Creek Nation, and Lachlan McGillivray, a Scot. However, Rachel is on the 1831 special census of Choctaws. Samuel and Rachel apparently separated, for Rachel m.2. c?1795, David "Davy" Walker, who d. c1821-24. Rachel m.3. 1824, Zadock Brashears Sr, brother of her first husband.

v5235. 75. unknown, b. bef Sept 1767. In petition of Sept 1767, Jesse had 5 ch

v5236. 76. unknown, b. Sep-Nov 1767, GA; in petition of Nov 1767, he had 6 ch.

v5237. 77. unknown, b. bef Dec 1769, GA. In petition of Dec 1769, Jesse had 7 ch.

v5238. 78. ***Asa Brashears**, b. c1770-1, surely in GA ("Ysaiar"; 13 in June 1784 Spanish census) ?of MD; m. 20 Oct 1806, Baton Rouge, **Cynthia Coulton**, d/o Joseph Coulton and Mary Stevenson.

v5239. 79. **Elizabeth Brashears**, b. c1771-2, ?GA, (12 in June, 1784 Spanish Census); m. **William Taylor**,

v5240. 710. **John Brashears**, b. Dec 1772 ("Juan"; 11 yrs, 6 mos, in 20 June 1784 Spanish Census), d. young? Not in any further records.

v5241. 711. **Lucy Brashears**, b. Oct 1781 ("Lucia"; 2 yrs, 8 mos, in 20 June 1784 Spanish Census), d. young? No further record.

v5242. 712. **Ruth Brashears**, also "Routh," b. c1785 (if about 20 when marrying); m. before 1805, **George Freeland Jr**, her step-brother. In the 1820 Census of Feliciana

Parish, George Freeland Jr registered 4 males, 1 female and 11 slaves. He was next door to Phillip Brashier.

A stray marriage:
Eliza Brashears, m. 16 May 1818, *Thomas Benson*, (Mobile Marriages). Eliza is about the right age to be of this generation; a bit too old to be from the next, e.g. too old to be d/o Alexander Brashears.

References to Jesse and Elizabeth's children appear numerous times in the *Index to the Archives of Spanish West Florida, 1782-1810*:
(All of the citations in Vol. IV involve the estate proceedings of Thomas Vaughn, father of Susannah (Vaughn) Brashears, wife of Zadock Brashears.)

Vol IV:365		Zadock Brashears, deposition of
	370	Vaughn & Brashears, minors, executor Edward Hawes
	403	Thomas Vaughn & Brashears, succession of
	371	Inventory
	165	Citation from Caty Turnbull
V:	210	Theodore Brashears [This one baffles; we don't have a Theodore!]
VI:	147,231	Philip Brashears
	248	Asa Brashears
	231	Samuel, sale of land to James McElroy
VII:	345	Richard Brashears, [a fourth cousin, s/o Benjamin Brashears & Catherine Belt]
	356	" , power of atty from James Denley
	357	" , transfer of power to Zedoc Brashears
	36, 133, 345a	Zedoc Brashears

(The following several entries are the probate of Elizabeth (Prather) Brashears/Freeland's will)

VIII:	211	Asa Brashears
	211	Elizabeth Brashears
	211	Ruth (Routh) Brashears
	211	Samuel Brashears
	211	Zadoc Brashears
	211	Jesse Brashears
	211	Elizabeth Prater Brashears, succession of

ASA BRASHEARS and CYNTHIA COULTON

[v5]**238.** [7]8. **Asa Brashears**, (s/o Jesse Brashear and Elizabeth Prather), b. c1771, surely in Georgia, where his parents were living at the time, ("Ysaiar"; 13 in 1784 Spanish census). In the Spanish West Florida Papers, his name is spelled variously as Asa, Essie, and Jessie. "Essie Bashires" m. 20 Oct 1806, in St. Joseph's Catholic Church in Baton Rouge, **Cynthia Coulton**, d/o Joseph Coulton and Mary Stevenson (*Diocese of Baton Rouge Records*, v.3, 1804-1819, ledger 88, entry 18; witnesses: Henry Collins of NC, age 50 yrs; Pedro (Peter) Sydes of NC, age 53 yrs; & V.T. Dalton). The marriage records state that he was "of Maryland," which may indicate that Jesse and Elizabeth were in Maryland at the time of his birth, or (more probably) it may only indicate a Spanish sense of family origins: both Jesse's and Elizabeth's families were "of Maryland." Asa died before 26 March 1823 in St. Helena Parish, LA, and Cynthia died there 20 April 1825.

Archives of Spanish West Florida, Vol VI, p.248: Cash sale of land (written in Spanish) Robert McFarland to Rhea and Cochran, land located in settlement of Feliciana, being bounded by Feliciana River and the land belonging to Asa Brashear and that belonging to James Foster, which land I have had in my possession since the 10th Oct 1799

3 Jan 1807: *Archives of Spanish West Florida*, Vol XII, p.3: Power of Attorney given by Asa Brashears to Llewellyn Griffith to sell land in Feliciana to John Cason (Written in English):

Know all men by these presents, that I Asa Brashears of the District of Baton Rouge have this day nominated and appointed my trusty friend Llewellyn C. Griffith of the district of New Feliciana my true and lawful attorney for me and in my name to transfer in the office of Baton Rouge to John Cason all my rights and title to a certain parcell of land lying on Thompsons Creek containing four hundred acres the surveys of Robert McFarland and Celey, which tract of land aforesaid I have sold unto the said John Cason for the sum of nine hundred dollars, the payment whereof I do hereby acknowledge to have received and I do hereby ratify and confirm whatsoever my said attorney may lawfully do or cause to be done in the promises in as full a manner as if I were personally present and transacted the same. In testimony whereof I have hereunto set my hand at Feliciana this third day of January in the year One thousand eight hundred and seven.

Asa [A] Brashears, LS

The fifth day of January one thousand eight hundred and seven, personally appeared before me, John Rhea, Alcalde of the first Division of the District of New Feliciana, <u>Asa Brashears</u> and, in the presence of my two assistant witnesses Richard Croshier and Robert Moore, acknowledged the above instrument of writing empowering Llewellyn C. Griffith to act as his true and lawful attorney for the purpose mentioned to be his act and deed—

John Rhea

30 Jan 1807: *Archives of Spanish West Florida*, Vol XII, p.3-7: (Written in Spanish) Jan 30, 1807: Land Sale, Llewellyn C. Griffith to John Cason: Be it known to all who may see this [p.3] act, that I, Llewellyn C. Griffith, acting as attorney for <u>Asa Brashears</u>, as is evident from the power which accompanies this, depose that I sell, really and with effect, in the name of said constituent, to John Cason, a tract of land consisting of four hundred arpents in area, located in the settlement of Feliciana, District of Baton Rouge, bounded by land belonging to Robert McFarland, by others which are vacant, and by the River Feliciana, as is shown by the plat of it made by the surveyor-general in the year of one thousand seven hundred and ninety-nine. ... [Usual disclaimers, warranties, etc. and signatures:]

Carlos de Grand Pré
Thomas Estevan   Llewellyn C. Griffith
Antonio Cruzat   John Cason

12 Aug 1802: *Archives of Spanish West Florida*, Vol VI, p.147: Promise of sale by William and Elizabeth [Brashears] Taylor to Champness Terry, payment to be made when the titles are verified. Parcel bounded on one side by Doctor James Raoul and on the opposite side by Phillip Brashears, 12 Aug 1802.

v5243. [8]1. **Jesse Brashear**, b. c1816, d. c1888, Dunham Springs, LA; m. ***Mary Bandeley***, b. c1827, d. c1895, Dunham Springs, Livingston Parish, LA, d/o Jacob Bendly, of Germany or Holland, and Anna Childs. Jesse and Mary are Fam #166 in 1850 census, Livingston Parish, LA. Three children born to Jessy Brashears and Mary Bandeley are registered in St. Joseph's Church Records, Book 18, p.11; *Diocese of Baton Rouge Records*, v.8, p.104, 1853-1857. Additional data from Jeanell G. Hannula <jhan168532@aol.com>

v5244. [9]1. **Senty (Cynthia) Ann Brashears**, b. 4 May 1846, (bap. 2 April 1853; sponsors: Valery Weaver and Mary Gallegher), d. 3 April 1917; m. ***Howells H. Chambers***, b. 28 July 1844, d. 24 Aug 1881, both bur Chambers cem, Livingston Parish, LA

v5245. [9]2. ***James Henry Brashears**, b. 18 Sept 1847, d. 14 March 1908; m. c1867, ***Phoebe "Phiby" (Dillon) Dykes***, b. 9 July 1851,

v5246. [9]3. **Marguerite Eloisa "Dudie" Brashears**, b. 17 Dec 1849, (bap. 2 April 1853; sponsors: Joseph Cannon and Mary Weaver); d. 4 Nov 1933, Dunham Springs, LA; m. ***John Charles Comeaux***, (or Charles J. Comeaux, per tombstone) b. 29 August 1842, d. 6 Sept 1905, both bur First Baptist ch, Denham Springs, Livingston Parish, LA.

v5247. [8]2. Another son of Asa Brashears and Cynthia Coulton (possibly named **George Brashears**) was lost in the forest; nothing found but his cap.

James Henry Brashears and Phoebe Dillon

v5245. [9]2. **James Henry Brashears**, (s/o Asa Brashear and Cynthia Coulton), b. 18 Sept 1847, (bap. 2 April 1853; sponsors: George Bandeley and Marie Madeleine Robin), d. 14 March 1908; m. c1867, ***Phoebe "Phiby" (Dillon) Dykes***, b. 9 July 1851, Pike Co, MS, d. 6 March 1925, both bur First Baptist ch cem, Denham Springs, Livingston Parish, LA. Phoebe Dillon came to Livingston Parish about 1855 (when she was 4 years old) with Samuel James Hughes; the Dykes family raised her (may have adopted her). (Data from Jeanell Hannula <Jhan168532@aol.com>). Phoebe M. Brashears, 68, is a widow, fam #16/16, in 1920, Livingston Parish, LA.

v5248. 101. **Nancy Elizabeth "Aunt Lizzie" Brashears**, b. 5 Oct 1867, d. 22 Feb 1948; m. 11 Feb 1892, Livingston Parish, LA, **Willie D. Boyer** (pron: Boo-yer), b. 2 Aug 1866, d. 2 March 1952, both bur Denham Springs Memorial, Livingston Parish, LA. Listed in 1910, Livingston Parish, LA, as Willie M. Boyd, 43, fam #199/200, with two ch. Also in the hh: James E. Brashears, 40, brother-in-law.

v5249. 111. Clara Boyer, b. c1893, LA (17 in 1910)

v5250. 112. James Boyer, b. c1896, LA (14 in 1910)

v5251. 102. **James Edward "Eddie" Brashears**, b. 27 Oct 1869, d. 30 March 1950; m. **Ruby** _____, b. 20 Sept 1899, d. 28 Jan 1921, both bur First Baptist Ch cem, Denham Springs, Livingston Parish, LA.

v5252. 111. **James "Jim" Brashears** , b. 1921, d. _____, (s/o James Edward Brashears and Ruby _____. Ruby died in childbirth and Jim was raised in the family of Mary Margaret Brashears and Sylvester Brown); m. **Catherine** _____

v5253. 103. **Leila Brashears**, m. _____ **Miller**

v5254. 104. **Mary Margaret Brashears**, b. 1873, d. 11 March 1954; m. **Daniel Sylvester "Vest" Brown**, b. 14 April 1863, d. 19 April 1935, both bur First Bapt Ch cem, Denham Springs, Livingston Parish, LA.

v5255. 111. Temmie M. Brown, b. 20 November 1888, bur Old Hebron Church Cemetery, Denham Springs, Livingston Parish, LA; m. 20 June 1908, (LA Marr CD - Livingston Parish), Robert P. "R.P." Cooper, b. 14 April 1881, d. 27 June 1968, bur Old Hebron Church Cemetery, Denham Springs, Livingston Parish, LA,

v5256. 112. Sadie Idelle Brown (tombstone of one child called her "I.S." all our records so far indicate "S.I."), b. 27 January 1893, d. 13 March 1970, bur Denham Springs Memorial, Denham Springs, LA, m. Dallas Monroe Tate, b. 13 July 1889, bur Denham Springs Memorial, Denham Springs, LA, son of Wm. M. Tate and W. Josephine Taylor v5257.   11 3. Stella B. Brown, b. 1895, d. 1900, bur First Baptist Church, Denham Springs, Livingston Parish, LA,

v5258.   11 4. Freddie Lorena Brown, b. 18 Feb 1897, probably Liv. Parish, LA, d. 28 March 1993, Baton Rouge, LA, bur Roselawn Memorial Gardens, Baton Rouge, East Baton Rouge Parish, LA; m.1. Charles James Tate (Jeanell Hannula's grandfather, s/o William M. Tate and Wilhelmina Josephine Taylor), b. 21 Sept. 1893, Colyell, Liv. Parish, LA, d. 27 January 1926, Denham Springs, Liv. Parish, LA, bur First Baptist Church, D. S., Liv. Parish, LA; m.2. Eugene J. O'Regan, b. 18 November 1903, d. July 1981, bur Roselawn Memorial Gardens, Baton Rouge, East Baton Rouge Parish, LA,

v5259.   11 5. Eddie Brown, b. 28 Jan 1901, d. 23 Feb 1939, bur Hebron Cemetery, Denham Springs, Livingston Parish, LA; m. 15 Aug 1920, (Livingston Parish, LA, Louisiana Marriages CD - Livingston Parish) Ruth Tyler, b. 23 March 1903, Denham Springs, Livingston Parish, LA. She m.2. _____ Katzes.

v5260.   11 6. Ivy Conley Brown (Uncle Conley), b. 20 Sept 1906, Liv. Parish, La., d. 13 January 1998, D.S., Liv. parish, LA, bur Denham Springs Memorial, D.S., LA; m. Daisy Bourgeois

v5261.   11 7. Daniel Sylvester "D.S." Brown, Jr, b. 1911, bur Hebron Cemetery, Denham Springs, Livingston Parish, LA; m.1. Cora S. ____ (mother of their children), b. 30 July 1917, d. 10 May 1968, bur Hebron Cemetery, Denham Springs, Livingston Parish, LA; m.2. Bessie ____

v5262. 10 5. **Jesse L. Brashears Sr**, b. 31 July 1875, d. 12 Feb 1960; m. **Maude B.** _____, b. 2 July 1896, d. 16 Dec 1968, both bur Denham Springs Memorial, Livingston Parish, LA.

v5263.   11 x. **Jesse L. Brashears Jr**, b. 5 March 1921, d. 24 Jan 1941, bur Denham Springs Memorial

v5264. 10 6. **John P. "J.P." Brashears**, b. 16 Feb 1878, d. 25 May 1968; m. 1 May 1901, Denham Springs,

Livingston Parish, LA, **Sarah Elizabeth "Aunt Lizzie" Watts**, b. 1 May 1883, d. 17 May 1964, both bur Denham Springs Memorial, Livingston Parish, LA. They are fam #475/477 in 1910 census, Livingston Parish, LA; they had been married 9 yrs, had borne 5 ch, 3 of them living. They are fam #71/71 in 1920, Livingston Parish. J.P. was a timber buyer.

[v5]265.   [11]1. _____ (? d. before 1910)

[v5]266.   [11]2. **Muriel A. Brashears**, b. 11 Dec 1903, d. 16 Sept 1905, "daughter of J.P. and S.E. Brashears," bur Denham Springs Memorial

[v5]267.   [11]3. **Murry E. Brashears**, b. c1906, (4 in 1910; 14 in 1920)

[v5]268.   [11]4. **Georgia A. Brashears**, b. c1908, (2 in 1910; 12 in 1920)

[v5]269.   [11]5. **John P. Brashears Jr**, b. c1910 (3/12 in 1910; 9 in 1920)

[v5]270.   [11]6. **Samuel D. Brashears**, b. c1914 (6 in 1920)

[v5]271. [10]7. **Frederica "Aunt Freddie" Brashears**, b. 8 Jan 1886, d. 14 Sept 1974, bur Denham Springs Memorial, Livingston Parish, LA; m. **D.D. Samford**, a merchant marine who disappeared; believed to be lost at sea.

[v5]272.   [11]x. Dudly D. Samford, b. 6 Nov 1913, d. 13 Nov 1913, "son of Mr. and Mrs. D.D. Samford," Denham Springs Memorial cem.

[v5]273. [10]8. **George H. Brashears**, b. 15 Jan 1887, d. 10 Dec 1907, bur First Baptist Cem, Denham Springs, Livingston Parish, LA; m. 11 March 1906, Livingston Parish, LA, **Ida R. Brown**,

[v5]274.   [11]1. **Murphy G. Brashears**, b. 8 May 1907, d. 8 Aug 1907, "son of G.H. and I.R. Brashears,"

[v5]275. [10]9. **Sophie Brashears**, b. c1887; m.1. 29 Feb 1908, Livingston Parish, LA, **Henry M. Haacks**; m.2. _____ **Jones**; m.3. _____ **Wheat**

[v5]276. [10]10. **Sessions Brashears**, b. c1891. In 1910, Livingston Parish, LA, Sassione Brashears, 19, employed in logging, scaling, is a boarder in boarding house of Clara Bourgeois, hh #86/87.

6. PHILIP BRASHEAR
of East Baton Rouge Parish, LA

^{v5}**232.** ⁷2. **Philip Brashear**, b. c175?, d. c1825, s/o Jesse Brashear and Elizabeth Prather, moved to New Feliciana, Spanish West Florida, now Louisiana, by 1774. He and most of his children seem to have lived their whole lives in East Baton Rouge Parish. Philip apparently married twice: m.1. _____ and had children Zadock and Samuel; m.2. **Mary "Polly" White**, niece of David White, and had ten more children.

In August 1803, Philip made 58 claims for land, according to the *American State Papers*. He occupied 255 acres from 1774 to 1814. On 3 May 1801, he sold 490 acres to the heirs of H. Richardson.

Archives of Spanish West Florida, Vol IX, p.840, sale of tract of land to Champness Terry, by Philip Brashears. The wording has been destroyed, except for the signatures: signed by Carlos de Grand Pré,

> signed for Felipe Brashears, by Juan Murdoch
> signed C. Terry

Witnesses: Thomas Estevan, Antonio Cruzat

10 Sept 1804: *Archives of Spanish West Florida*, Vol VII, p.247: Manuel, or Henry William, a mulatto incarcerated in the fort of Baton Rouge, was conditionally handed over to Philip Brashears by Governor de Grand Pré, since he [Manuel] could not prove that he was a free mulatto. (Written in Spanish) No 942: Baton Rouge, September tenth, 1804. Considering the great losses caused by [to?] Philip Brashears [p.668] on account of the prolonged imprisonment of the mulatto Manuel, or Henry Williams, who claims to be free, and that on the other hand he is supposed to belong to a resident of Kentucky named Spolling, that having advised all the American traders who have been seen around this post about said mulatto, and up to the

present, no one claiming him, nor having received the least news from the said Spolling, nor proofs from the said mulatto of his being free, therefore, it being over a year that this affair has [been] pending without the aforesaid Brashears having any legitimate recourse against whoever sold the said mulatto to him, due to the absence of any of the aforementioned proofs, we have determined to deliver unto him the said mulatto, on condition that if he, the said mulatto should present any documents proving the fact that he is free, he will be decreed to be free without any objection being made to it, as well as if the said proofs should show that the said mulatto belongs to the above referred Spolling, the mulatto should be delivered to him, the said Brashears to have his recourse only against his vendor; and so that the delivery of the said mulatto to the above referred Philip Brashears on these conditions be recorded, he made his mark, with the witnesses, the lieutenant of the regiment of Louisiana, Thomas Estavan, and Juan Lut, who signs with me, the civil and military governor of this post and district.

Carlos de Grand Pré   Mark [X] of Philip Brashears
Thomas Estevan
Juan Lut

(Written in Spanish, p.670) With regard to the negro mentioned, and in the prison of this fort, he is not free, but a run-away, and belongs to John Spolling, a resident of Nelson County, Kentucky. Gov. de Grand Pré decrees that the mulatto Manuel is not free and he orders Champness Terry not to pay to anyone who solicits it, the five hundred piastras in his keeping.

A court record dated 27 July 1809, concerning the estate of David White, shows that Philip Brashear's wife, Mary "Polly", was a niece to David White (*Archives of Spanish West Florida*, v.XV, p.313). Polly Brashears and her sister, Nancy Stuart, wife of William Stuart, sued to break the will of David White, "uncle of petitioners," because he left his entire estate to Sylvia Turnbull, a half-Indian girl, wife of David Holsten and daughter of John Turnbull and "an unknown Chickasaw woman."

Nancy and Polly White were ignorant of their Indian relatives. There's plenty of documentation that the "unknown Chickasaw woman" was a Choctaw, Isabel "Belcie" Perry, d/o

Hardy Perry and Anolah, a Choctaw woman. Isabel "Belcie" Perry m.1. John Turnbull; m.2. David White; Sylvia Turnbull was therefore David White's step-daughter.

(written in Spanish)
To His Excellency the Governor,

I, William Stuart, acting for Nancy, my wife, and for Polly [p.866] Brashears, wife of Philip Brashears, heirs of David White, their uncle, present myself before Your Excellency and say that the deceased David White made a will twenty years ago, which is in the archives of this post, in virtue of which the said David White infringed the laws of this government, to the detriment of the said heirs, Nancy and Polly, leaving all his property to a certain Sylvia Turnbull, since that time married to David Holsten, in whose hands the property is, the funds being misapplied; Your Excellency will observe that these being the legitimate heirs, they have all reason to believe that the said will ought to be null, especially when Your Excellency will realize that the said Sylvia is of mixed blood (of Indian), and that the two executors of the said succession are both dead, and have not been replaced since their deaths; I supplicate Your Excellency to observe that the said Holsten has the said property in his possession in trust until others, who may have more right, can prove their claim; also Your Excellency will observe that the surety of the said Holsten owes more to the property of [p.867] the succession than he can pay with his property.

Therefore,

I supplicate Your Excellency, after having deliberated on this affair, to be pleased to give Justice with your Excellency's accustomed equity,

Baton Route, July 27, 1809

> William Stuart
> Mary Brashears
> (and for her husband) Phillip Brashears
> Inhabitants of New Feliciana
> her
> Nancy (X) Stuart
> mark

They were apparently not the only persons trying to break the will of David White:

14 April 1810, New Feliciana - Deposition of Susannah Hawkins who said she had been a neighbor of David White for a good while and that he used to visit deponent and her husband, and that while talking with White he told deponent that Joseph White was not his son and not even a relative, and he was afraid Joseph White would take away some of his property, and leave with it. That he had made his testament and had left everything to Susan (should be Sylvia) Turnbull, now the wife of David Holsten, who he said had more rights to it than any other person. She said she was 38 years old. (*Spanish West Florida Records*, Vol. XI, p.8-12, and 37, as cited in *Women in the Florida Parishes of Louisiana*, by Donna Burge Adams, Shreve Memorial Library, Shreveport, La. p.54.)

13 Jan 1810, - Zadock Brashears gave his deposition in the matter of the legitimate children of David White. In it he stated he was 54 years of age, thus establishing his year of birth as c1755. He stated he was "of" Maryland. (*Spanish Records Translations*, Vol. 17)

18 June 1810, Gov. Delassus decreed that Sylvia Turnbull was the legal heir, since Joseph White had failed to show proper and sufficient evidence to overthrow the testament of David White. (*Spanish West Florida Records*, Vol. XI, p.8-12, and 37, as cited in *Women in the Florida Parishes of Louisiana*, by Donna Burge Adams, Shreve Memorial Library, Shreveport, La. p.54.)

Families of Philip Brashears

In the 1820 Census, Philip Brashears and his wife were listed as over 45 years of age. By the 1830 Census, both Philip and his wife are missing, and a probate shows that he died in 1825 (Feliciana Probate Records, Book A, p.113).

Family of Philip Brashear and 1st wife:

[v5]301. [8]1. **Zedock Brashear**, b. 1790s (40-50 in 1840 Census, East Baton Rouge Parish, Ward #9: (0000001-211101) ?s/o Philip and 1st wife? On 3 May 1811, Zadock Brashears, a resident of East Baton Rouge Parish, sold land in West Feliciana Parish (West

Feliciana Parish Deeds, v.? p.?). On 21 April 1827, Zadock sold 80 acres of land 18 miles north of the city of Baton Rouge, bounded by lands of Mrs. Turnbull (East Baton Rouge Deeds, Bk ?). On 18 June 1828, he bought two tracts of land in East Baton Rouge Parish from Ann Rush of Baton Rouge (same ref). On 18 Dec 1828, he sold these two tracts to O.C. Van Landingham (same). Zadock Brashears was present in East Baton Rouge Parish in 1835 for a family meeting to discuss the disposition of the estate of Samuel Brashears, deceased, father of William Brashears (Probate Records, East Baton Rouge Parish). His family in 1840:

v5302.   wife,   30-40, b. 1800-1810
v5303.   fem.   15-20, b. 1820-25
v5304.   fem.   10-15, b. 1825-30
v5305.   fem.   5-10, b. 1830-35
v5306.   fem.   0-5, b. 1835-40
v5307.   fem.   0-5, b. 1835-40

v5308. [8]2. **Samuel Brashear**, ?Died young? May be the Samuel who d. c1816: probate #151, East Baton Rouge Parish, 7 Nov 1816, Samuel Brashears, ill and not capable of handling property, asks that eldest son, William, be appointed curator; six children, most very young; wife, **Cassandra**, sons **William** and **Laraney**. William Winfree, Esq, named Curator.

Family of Philip Brashear and Mary White: named in probate records in East Feliciana, 12 Feb 1827 (Book A, p.113), according to Loretta Coppick and descendant Gary Robertson, 11519 Lazy Lake Drive, Baton Rouge, LA 70818.

v5309. [8]3. ***John R. Brashear**, b. 1795, New Feliciana, m.1. 1820, West Feliciana Parish, LA, **Sarah Martha Jane McCants**, d/o Samuel McCants; m.2. Nov 1838, **Catherine Shaffett**, d/o John Shaffett. Baton Rouge Diocese Catholic Church Records show that "Jean" Breashers (son of Philippe Breashers and Mary White) was married to Catherine Shaffet in November of 1838 (vol. 5, p.120). Birth record of his daughter, "Suzan," (vol. 5, p.110), gives us John's middle initial.

v5310. [8]4. **Sarah Brashear**, m. _____ **Foster**,
v5311. [8]5. **Ann (Nancy) Brashear**, m. **Francis Millican**,

^{v5}312. ⁸6. **Elizabeth Brashear**, m. _____ *Marbury*,

^{v5}313. ⁸7. **Lavinia Brashear**, m. *Epheus Gibson*,

^{v5}314. ⁸8. ***Robert Lafayette Brashear***, a minor in 1827; married five times; see Bible records below

^{v5}315. ⁸9. **Mary Brashear**, under age in 1827; m. *Isaac Peairs*,

^{v5}316. ⁸10. **Rebecca Brashear**, under age in 1827; m.1. 1827, *Wiley Ingram*, m.2. *Jacob Zug*,

Feliciana Probate Records, Book A, p.113, names the children from John on; no Zadock, no Samuel, though they were in the area at the time, says Loretta Coppick. Some records also give Philip a son, William. No further info. In the 1820 Census of Feliciana Parish, Philip Brashier registered 3 males, 7 females, and 5 slaves. If Samuel and William died or married early, that listing would come close to matching Philip's family.

JOHN R. BRASHEAR and SARAH McCANTS/ CATHERINE SHAFFETT

^{v5}309. ⁸3. **John R. Brashear**, b. 1795, s/o Philip Brashear and Mary White, d. after 1850 Census and before 1860, East Baton Rouge Parish; m.1. 1820, West Feliciana Parish, LA, *Sarah Martha Jane McCants*, b. c1800 ("Mary" in 1830 census), d. after 1830, d/o Samuel McCants (s/o Thomas McCants) and Margaret Packer, d/o John Packer. In 1830, John and Jane sold land which she had inherited through her deceased father's share of the estate of James McCants); m.2. Nov 1838, *Catherine Shaffett*, b. 1816-18, d. after 1880 census, d/o John Shaffett and Mary Shaw. Mary Shaw was d/o William and Mary Ann (Weakley) Shaw. John was at least 20 years older than his second wife; the 1830 and 1840 census indicate children by first wife; the 1850 Census of East Baton Rouge Parish, LA, named the children of John and Catherine. (ref: *The Genealogy of Several Related Families*, by Charles Owen Johnson, Pelican Publishing. For more on McCants, contact Josephine Lindsay Bass, 216 Beach Park Lane, Cape Canaveral, FL 32920 <jbass@digital.net> 407/868-1771, or Becky Bass Bonner, 8209 Canna Lane, Oklahoma City, OK 73132 <rbonner@ imail.ouhsc.edu> 405/728-2050.)

In 1820, John [R.] Brashiers acted as curator for the children of Samuel McCants, who were heirs of their father's share in the estate of James McCants.

State of Louisiana

Parish of Feliciana

I acknowledge to have received of David McCants, curator of the estate of James McCants, decd, the sum of thirty three dollars and nine cents, being the full portion of said Estate accrueing and Heired by Jane <u>Brashiers</u>, Alexander [McCants] and Thomas McCants, children of said McCants decd, in witness whereof I have hereunto set my hand this seventh day of August, 1820.

John Brasher for Jane McCants

and as curator for James and Alexander McCants

Witnesses: E. Eddards, Beverly Down

Wm C. Wade, Parish Judge of Feliciana

Truly Recorded 7 August 1820 (Book B, p.255; thanks to Joanne Schwilk for the Xerox copy.)

Some of the family of John Brashiers and Martha Jane McCants is established by a deed from Mary Jane (Rourk) Hatcher to Louisa Williams, widow of Samuel W. Brashiers:

The State of Louisiana,

Parish of East Feliciana

Know all men by these present that I, Mary Jane Rourk and wife of Hiram M. Hatcher of said parish of the first part, apointed herein by my said husband here present at the signing this act, do here by these presents, grant, bargain, sell, transfer, and let over unto Ms Louisa Williams, surviving widow of Samuel W. Brashiers of the Parish of East Baton Rouge, of the second part, all my right, title, interest and claim in and to the Negro man Oliver since in the possession of Ms Catherine Brashiers, widow of John Brashiers decd, in parish of East Baton Rouge. This being the same slave sold by Philip Brashiers to John Brashiers for the use and benefit of his minor children, Samuel, Ann and John Brashiers, said sale made on the 11th day of April 1825 before John C. White, then a notary public. I this vendor being a daughter of said Ann Brashier, the issue of the marriage with Westley Rourk, decd. This sale is made for and in consideration of the price and sum of three hundred dollars, each paid to us by the purchaser at or before the signing this act, the receipt of which I hearby acknowledge, to have and hold unto the said Ms Louisa Brashiers the said interest all of which I have in and to said slave Oliver from us and my heirs and assigns to her own benefit forever. In testimony of all which I sign my name hereto authorized by my husband and in the presence of C. E. Rogillio and John F. Worsham, subscribing witnesses, on the twenty seventh day of December eighteen hundred and fifty nine (1859).

/s/ M. J. Hatcher.

I authorize my wife to sign the above.. /s/ H. M. Hatcher.

L.T. Brashiers

Witness: C.E. Rogellio... John F. Worsham

Registered the 28th and Recorded on the 31st December 1859 (Book R, p. 45-6; thanks to Joanne Schwilk for the copy.)

John Brashiers died between 1850 and 1860. The 1860 Census listing for his survivors is confusing: Why is Susan Norwood listed in her mother's household? And Philip's wife in Thomas Norwood's?

1860 Census, East Baton Rouge Parish:

#800	Catharine Brashears,	43, b. c1817, LA; widow of John R. Brashears
	Phillip Brashears,	25, b. c1835, LA; son
	Susan Norwood,	17, b. c1843; dau, wife of Thomas L. Norwood,
	Robert Brashears,	15, b. c1845, LA, son
#801	Thomas Norwood,	31, b. c1829, AL; husband of Susan (Brashears) Norwood
	Chapel C. Norwood,	1, b. c1859, LA; s/o Thomas and Susan Norwood
	Joana Brashears,	18, b. c1842, LA; ?wife of Philip Brashears?

Family of John R. Brashear and Sarah Martha Jane McCants: (a deed made by Mary Jane Hatcher, d/o Ann Brashiers, establishes some of these family relationships)

v5317. 9 1. ***Samuel W. Brashiers**, b. 1819, d. 1859; m.1. 18 Aug 1841, **Ezilda R. Foster**, b. 1825, d. 1846; m.2. 28 May 1850, **Louisa T. Williams**, b. 1835; ancestors of Joanne Schwilk <Jovintage@aol. com>

v5318. 9 2. **Ann Brashiers**, b. 1820-25, d. before 1859; m. **Westley Rourk**

v5319. 10 x. Mary Jane Rourk, m. Hiram M. Hatcher.

v5320. 9 3. **John Brashiers**, b. 1820-25, in 1830 census, but not in 1840 census; d. young? (name was re-used in second marriage) v[5]321.   [9]4. female, b. 1820-25, in 1830 census

v[5]322.   [9]5. male, b. 1825-30.

v[5]323.   [9]7. female, b. 1825-30, in 1830 census, but not 1840; d. young?

v[5]324.   [9]8. **Philip Brashears**, b. c1833-35, LA; m. *Joanna Corbel*, b. 1842-45

v[5]325.   [10]1. **Sam Brashear**, b. 1864

v[5]326.   [10]2. **Edward Brashear**, b. 1868

v[5]327.   [10]3. **Elizabeth Brashear**, b. 1870

v[5]328.   [10]4. **Annie Brashear**, b. 1872

v[5]329.   [10]5. **Catherine Brashear**, b. 1877

v[5]330.   [9]9. female, b. 1830-35, in 1840 census, not in 1850; d. young?

Family of John R. Brashear and Catherine Shaffett:

v[5]331.   [9]10. **John Brashear Jr**, b. c1839-40, baptized 20 Sept 1840 (Baton Rouge Diocese Records, vol.5, p.110), in 1840 census, not in 1850; d. young?

v[5]332.   [9]11. **Susan Brashears**, b. Oct 1841, LA (Baton Rouge Diocese Records, vol.5, p.110); m. 1858, *Thomas L. Norwood*, b. 1825, (East Baton Rouge Par. Marriages, Book 5, p.174). In 1880, the four youngest children were in the household of their grandmother, Catherine Brashear, b. c1817.

v[5]333.   [10]1. Chapel C. Norwood, b. 1859

v[5]334.   [10]2. William Norwood, b. 1864, m. 9 April 1888, Mary Frances Devall,

v[5]335.   [10]3. Catherine Norwood, b. 1868, m. 1890, J.E. Carpenter,

v[5]336.   [10]4. Milton Norwood, b. 1870

v[5]337.   [10]5. Robert Norwood, b. 1873

v[5]338.   [10]6. John Norwood, b. 1878 (twin); m. 1891, Mary Selser,

v[5]339.   [10]7. Susan Norwood, b. 1878 (twin)

v[5]340.   [9]12. **Robert Brashears**, b. Dec 1843, LA (Baton Rouge Diocese Records, vol.7, p.90-91), (1841, per 1900, East Baton Rouge Par, sht 5, line 96); m. 1867, (East Baton Rouge Par, Marriages, Book 8, p.18), *Estelle Babin*, b. Dec 1853 (per 1900). In their household in 1870: Mary A. Babbin, b. 1832; she's 74 in 1910 and 90 in 1920, sister-in-law.

v[5]341.   [10]1. **Mary C. Brashears**, b. July 1869 (per 1900) v5342.   [10]2. **Mattie Brashears**, b. 1873

v5343.   [10]3. **Joseph Robert Brashears**, b. Oct 1879 ("Joseph R." 20 in 1900), or b. Jan 1880

v5344.   [10]4. **Susie I. Brashears**, b. March 1886 (per 1900)

v5345. [9]13. **Joseph Greenberry "Green" White Brashear**, b. Jan 1847, LA (Baton Rouge Diocese Records, vol.7, p.90-91), (12 in 1860 Census), (23 in 1870 census), b. 1827 (per 1880 Census, which must be a mistake), d. 5 Sept 1923 (age 78, per death certificate), bur St. Isadore Cem; m. 1873, *Victoria Babin*, (Marr. Rec, East Baton Rouge Par. LA, Book 13, p.497), b. c1848 (In 1910, she's 62 in HH of son, Gilbert, East Baton Rouge Parish), but b. 1837 (acc. 1880 Census, which is surely a mistake. The 1827 reading of Green's birth in the 1880 census is a mistake for 1847, so the 1837 reading for Victoria's is probably a mistake for 1847. The 1847 dates would mean they were about 26 when they married in 1873). They had five children who lived to be over 18 years:

v5346.   [10]1. **Mary Ella Brashear**, b. 1 Sept 1874, d. 12 May 1905; m. *William Daniel Shaw*, (her 1st cousin) s/o William and Ellen (Neville) Shaw, gs/o William and Mary Ann (Weakley) Shaw

v5347.   [10]2. **Olivia Elvena Brashear**, b. 1879, d. 27 Feb 1946; m. *James T. Laney*,

v5348.   [11]1. Mary Lillian Laney, d. 10 Sept 1956; m. _____ *Phillips*, no ch.

v5349.   [10]3. **Buffington Brashear**,

v5350.   [10]4. **Walter Andrew Brashear**, b. 1885 (24 in 1910, East Baton Rouge Parish); m. 1907, *Sarah Amidee Devall*, b. c1888 (22 in 1910)

v5351.   [11]1. **Alice Wilma Brashear**, b. 1908 (2 in 1910); m. *Louis Ourso*,

v5352.   [12]1. Louis Ourso Jr, b. 1931; m. Theresa Gonzales

v5353.   [13]1. Joseph Lynn Ourso, b. 1956

v5354.   [13]2. Louis J. Ourso III, b. 1959

v5355.   [12]2. Carolyn Ourso, b. 1937; m. Harry Lee Daigle, Sr

v5356.   [13]1. Harry Lee Daigle Jr, b. 1956

v5357.   [13]2. Arena Mae Daigle, b. 1959

v5358.   [11]2. **Annie Lucille Brashear**, b. 1910; m. *Elisha Stiles*,
v5359.   [12]1. Betty Stiles, b. 1937; m. Sidney H. Womack
v5360.   [13]1. Terri Lynn Womack, b. 1956
v5361.   [13]2. Debra Ann Womack, b. 1957
v5362.   [13]3. Sidney H. Womack Jr, b. 1959
v5363.   [11]3. **Alma Elvina Brashear**, b. 1914; m. *William Joseph Stiles*,
v5364.   [12]1. Shirley Ann Stiles, b. 1936; m. Billy Joe Haynes
v5365.   [13]1. Vickie Lynn Haynes, b. 1957
v5366.   [12]2. William Joseph Stiles Jr, b. 1939
v5367.   [12]3. Gary Glynn Stiles, b. 1942
v5368.   [12]4. Bradley Dale Stiles, b. 1943
v5369.   [11]4. **Mary Annabelle Brashear**, b. 1915; m. *George Seguin*,
v5370.   [12]1. George Lee Seguin
v5371.   [12]2. Janice Gail Seguin, b. 1944
v5372.   [12]3. Judy Kay Seguin, b. 1948
v5373.   [12]4. Linda Darnell Seguin, b. 1954
v5374.   [12]5. Cyntha Ann Seguin, b. 1956
v5375.   [11]5. **Joseph Andrew Brashear**, b. 1922, m. 12 Sept 1947, **Betty Jane Wicker**, b. 2 Jan 1927. Bonnie McIntyre, 219 E. San Emidio, Taft CA 93268, reported in BFB 31:7 that this data came from *Our Dawson Kin*, p.86, which "was submitted by Ben Wicker of Baton Rouge, LA."
v5376.   [12]1. **Pamela Sue Brashear**, b. 25 Sept 1948
v5377.   [12]2. **Gwendolyn Sherry Brashear**, b. 30 June 1951
v5378.   [12]3. **Patsy Lou Brashear**, b. 22 Jan 1953
v5379.   [12]4. **Walter Andrew Brashear**, b. 3 Sept 1956
v5380. [10]5. **Gilbert I. Brashear**, b. 1 Jan 1891, d. 30 May 1956; m. 30 March 1910, *Luby L. Crumholdt*. Victoria Brashear, 62, his mother, is in their HH in 1910, East Baton Rouge Parish. They had four children:
v5381.   [11]1. **Ollie Brashear**,
v5382.   [11]2. **Joseph Leon Brashear**, b. 21 Jan 1914; m.

	Nellie Lee Taylor, three ch:
v⁵383.	¹²1. **Louise Marie Brashear**, b. 17 Oct 1935; m. *Joseph Raymond Boudreaux*,
v⁵384.	¹³1. Karen Rae Boudreaux, b. 1953
v⁵385.	¹³2. Joseph Leon Boudreaux, b. 10 Jan 1960
v⁵386.	¹²2. **Jean Ann Brashear**, b. 17 Dec 1937; m. 21 Jan 1957, *Ronnie O. Riley*,
v⁵387.	¹³1. Rhonda Ann Riley, b. 18 Sept 1958
v⁵388.	¹²3. **Bobbie Fay Brashear**, b. 29 Aug 1946
v⁵389.	¹¹3. **Charles W. Brashear**, b. 2 March 1918; m. *Loretta M. Perault*,
v⁵390.	¹²1. **Ronald Wayne Brashear**, b. 18 Nov 1947
v⁵391.	¹¹4. **Mary Elma Brashear**, b. 23 Oct 1920; m. *Alder L. Chaney*,
v⁵392.	¹²1. Donald Ray Chaney, b. 3 Feb 1944
v⁵393.	¹²2. Randy Leo Chaney, b. 13 April 1956

SAMUEL W. BRASHIERS and EZILDA R. FOSTER/ LOUISA T. WILLIAMS

v⁵317. ⁹1. **Samuel W. Brashiers**, (surname spelled both Brashears and Brashiers; s/o John R. Brashears and Martha Jane McCants), b. 1819, d. 1859; m.1. 18 Aug 1841, Adams Co, MS, *Ezilda R. Foster*, b. c1825. *Mississippi Free Trader*, 2 Sept 1846: "died in Adams Co, MS, July 31, 1846, Mrs. Ezilda Brashears, consort of Samuel Brashears, and daughter of William J. and Mary Foster, age 21 years."

Samuel m.2. 28 May 1850, *Louisa T. Williams*, b. c1835, d/o Benjamin Williams (3 Nov 1797— 8 April 1858) and his wife, Nancy <u>Ann</u> Rice Christmas (28 March 1807— 19 March 1872). Benjamin Williams was s/o William Williams Sr and Esther McDonald Kimball; Ann Christmas was d/o Thomas Christmas. (data from Joanne Schwilk, 4101 Kenneth Ave, Fair Oaks, CA 95628; 916/967-6157; <jovintage@aol.com>)

Samuel had eight children by his two wives.

Family of Samuel W. Brashier and Ezilda R. Foster:

v⁵394. ¹⁰1. **Mary Jane Brashears**, b. c1842, LA (18 in 1860)

v⁵395. ¹⁰2. **Samuel Foster Brashears**, b. c1844, LA (16 in 1860),

d. c1866

v5396. [10]3. **Ezilda Elizabeth Brashears**, b. c1846, LA (14 in 1860); m. *Benjamin F. McClelland*

Family of Samuel W. Brashier and Louisa T. Williams: (data from Joanne Schwilk <jovintage@aol.com>)

v5397. [10]4. ***Joseph H. Brashears**, b. May 1854; m. *Edith Devall*, b. March 1855.

v5398. [10]5. **Sarah White Brashears**, b. c1854 (6 in 1860), d. unmarried in 1894, leaving an estate valued at $567. (see below)

v5399. [10]6. **Ann W. (or M.) Brashears**, b. c1856 (4 in 1860); apparently died before 1894. no further information.

v5400. [10]7. **John V. (or T.) Brashears**, b. c1857 (3 in 1860); apparently died before 1894. no further information.

v5401. [10]8. **Elizabeth Brashears**, b. c1859 (1 in 1860); apparently died before 1894. no further information.

Ezilda R. Foster was just 16 years old when she married Samuel. A handwritten note attached to the marriage license and certificate reads: "To the Clerk that issues licenses for Marriage, Dear Sir. Mr. Samuel W. Brashiers will apply for license to marry my daughter Ezilda R. Foster. She has my consent. Yours respectfully, Wm. J. Foster."

When Ezilda died, just five years later, the three children of Samuel W. Brashear and Ezilda R. Foster were sent back to her parents, William J. and Mary Foster, in Natchez, Adams Co, Mississippi, where they are in the Foster household in the 1860 Census. These grandparents were very generous to these grandchildren:

This indenture made this Thirteenth day of January in the year of our Lord, One Thousand eight hundred and fifty Six between William J. Foster of the County of Adams and State of Mississippi of the one part and Mary Jane Brashiers, Samuel Foster Brashiers, and Ezilda Elizabeth Brashiers, children under age of Samuel W. Brashier of the Parish of East Baton Rouge and State of Louisiana and grand children of the said William J. Foster, witnesseth:

that the said William J. Foster, for and in consideration of the natural love and affection which he hath ____ts the said grandchildren, hath given, granted, aliened, released and confirmed and by these presents doth give, grant, alien, release and confirm unto the said Mary Jane Brashier, Samuel Foster Brashier, and Ezilda Elizabeth Brashier, to each the one third part as hereinafter designated of all that certain tract or parcel of land situated lying and being in the Parish of East Baton Rouge and State of Louisiana, lying between Cypress and White's Bayou about six miles north northeast of the Fort at Baton Rouge, containing one thousand arpents, bounded on the East by land of Philip Hicky, West by land of Bartel and Kleinpeter, South by Bartel and north by Cavalier and Grand Pré, being the same land conveyed to the said Wm J. Foster by Mrs. Helene Grand Pré Fulton by deed before John Reid, Notary Public, at Baton Rouge, State of Louisiana, on the 18th day of January in the year A.D. 1843, together with all appurtenances....

And the said William J. Foster ... further gives, grants, (etc) to his grandchildren ... for the consideration aforesaid, the following named Negroes, slaves for life, ... on the 7th December 1841 and the 16th September 1843, given by the said Wm J. Foster to his late daughter, Mrs. Ezilda R. Brashier and late wife of the said Samuel W. Brashier ... said slaves being severally named as follows, to wit: Jacob, Ben, Grayson, Elleck, Dick, Irene, Harriet, Louisa, Lucinda & Ginny, and their natural increase since then, to wit: Ellen, Clara, Mary Ann, Emily, Polly, Alice, Scott, Cinthy, Celia, and Minerva. Also the productive increase of said slaves since their delivery, as aforesaid, to the said Ezilda R. Brashier, deceased.

In witness whereof, the said William J. Foster has set his hand and seal the day and year first above written (13 Jan 1856).

/s/ Wm J. Foster

Recorded 26 July 1856
(Thanks to Joanne Schwilk for a Xerox copy)

Know all men by these presents that I, Mary Jane Brashears, of the County of Adams and State of Mississippi, have made constituted and appointed, and by these presents do make constitute and appoint my grandfather, William J. Foster, of said County and State, my sufficient and lawful attorney for me and in my name to enter into and take possession of my third part, being the North end of the tract of land purchased by the said

William J. Foster from Helene de Grand Pré Fulton of the Parish of East Baton Rouge and State of Louisiana, by deed before John Reid, a Notary Public in and for said Parish, dated Baton Rouge January ___, A.D. 1843 and described therein as follows:

A tract of land in this Parish lying between Cypress and White's Bayous about six miles north northeast of the Fort at Baton Rouge, containing one thousand arpents, bounded on the East by land of Philip Hicky, West by land of Bartel and Kleinputer, South by Bartel and north by Cavalier and Grand Pré, being the same granted by the Spanish Government to the vendor and her sister Celeste de Grand Pré and confirmed by an Act of Congress dated 3rd March 1817, and subsequently by an act before Charles W. Crawford this appearing became the sole owner of said land.

And being the same tract conveyed by the said Wm J. Foster as follows: one third thereof at the North end of said tract to me, the South end to my sister, Ezilda E. Brashears, now Mrs. McClelland, and the other third part lying in the middle of said tract to my deceased brother, Samuel Foster Brashears.

And I hereby authorize my said attorney for me and in my name to have my portion as heir at law of my deceased brother, S. Foster Brashear, in and to the middle portion of said tract, partitioned and set off to me; and then to enter upon and take possession thereof in my name, and for me and in my name and stead to lease (demise and to form let) all on my portion of my said land, to such person or persons, for such terms of years, and with a reservation of such rent or rents on for said sums and sums of money annually to be paid as to my said Attorney shall deem expedient for me, and in my name to make, seal and execute ....

this seventeenth day of November, A.D. 1866
Recorded February 2nd, 1867, John McGrath, Recorder
(Thanks to Joanne Schwilk for a Xerox copy)

For and in consideration of the sum of Eight Hundred dollars to me in hand paid by Mary Jane Brashiers, I have sold and delivered to the said Mary J. Brashiers, the following personal property, to wit:

One bay horse mule, branded US and about ten years old;

One light bay mare mule branded 3F and about ten years old;

One bay mare mule branded 3F and about eight years old;

One gray horse colt 3 years old next spring;

One bay mare about 15 years old;

One old buggy;

One shot gun (double barrel); and

One Bed stead and bedding for same.

In witness whereof, I have hereunto set my hand and seal this 19th day of December, A.D. 1866,

/s/Wm J. Foster

in presence of us as witnesses

/s/E.R. Foster

/s/Ravness Conner

Recorded February 2nd 1867, John McGrath, Recorder

(Thanks to Joanne Schwilk for a Xerox copy)

In 1844, Samuel bought land in East Feliciana Parish from his brother-in-law, his sister, Ann's husband, Westley Rourk: Be it remembered that on the day of the date hereof before me, John C. White, notary public in and for the Parish of East Feliciana, State of Louisiana, duly commissioned and sworn, came and appeared Westley Rourk, residing in the State of Mississippi, Adams County, of the one part and Samuel W. Brashiers of the Parish of East Baton Rouge in the State of Louisiana, of the second part. And the said Westly Rourk declared and acknowledged that for and in consideration of the sum of Thirteen hundred and Seventy seven dollars to him in hand paid by the said Samuel W. Brashiers before the sealing and delivery hereof, the receipt whereof is hereby acknowledged ..... Westley Rourk hath granted... [etc]... to Samuel W. Brashiers, all his right, title, [etc] to a certain tract of land situate lying and being in the Parish of East Feliciana, containing about Three hundred and fifty acres, bounded on the East by Hi Comile and John Waddell, on the north and west by Thomas Chapman, and north by Bass, his portion in and to the said tract, being the one half, the one fourth of the other half, and the one fourth of the fourth of the said half, it being the whole amount of the land that has this day been transferred to said Westley by his mother [not named] by an Act of Donation ... <snip>

Done and signed the third day of July, Eighteen hundred and forty four.

Westley Rourk

S.W. Brashier

Witnesses:

Llewellyn T. White

William B. Rourk,

J.C. White, Notary Public

Recorded 17th July 1844 (Book J, p.184-5;
thanks to Joanne Schwilk for the Xerox copy.)

Samuel apparently died young about 1859, for Louisa and their children are in the household of her mother in the 1860 Census, East Baton Rouge Parish, LA, along with Louisa's younger siblings.

<u>1860 Census, East Baton Rouge Parish:</u>

#1007	Ann C. Williams,	52, b. c1808, LA
	Louisa Brashears,	25, b. c1835, [wid/o Samuel W. Brashears]
	Joseph H. Brashears,	7, b. c1853,
	Sarah W. Brashears,	6, b. c1854,
	Ann W. Brashears,	4, b. c1856,
	John T.(?) Brashears,	3, b. c1857,
	Elizabeth Brashears,	1, b. c1859,
	J.D. Williams,	20, b. c1840, [John Dawson Williams]
	Benja. A. Williams,	17, b. c1843, [Benjamin Henderson Williams]
	Josephine Williams,	10, b. c1850, (Josephine Eloise Williams]

Louisa (Williams) Brashier m.2. 24 July 1863, James A. Sullivan, and had several children, including Mary "Mollie", b. c1865 (m. W.T. Law); Keziah, b. c1867 (m. J.H. Lezenby); Josephine (called "Phoenie") Sullivan, b. c1867; and James Sullivan, Jr, b. c1869 (birth years calculated from 1870 census).

State of Louisiana

Parish of East Baton Rouge

Before me, James M. Loudon, a Notary Public in and for the said parish and state, duly commissioned and qualified, on the date hereof (31 Aug 1894), personally came and appeared Mrs. Louisa T. Sullivan, Joseph H. Brashear, Mollie Sullivan, wife of W.T. Law, Keziah Sullivan, wife of John Lezenby, Phoenie Sullivan, and James Sullivan, all residents of the Parish of East Baton Rouge, except Mrs. Mollie Sullivan and Keziah Sullivan, who reside in East Feliciana, who declared that whereas Miss Sarah White Brashears lately died in this Parish, leaving an estate therein, consisting of real and personal property, she being the daughter of Mrs. L.T. Sullivan by a first marriage and sister of the whole blood to Joseph H. Brashear, and sister of the half blood to Mrs. Mollie Law, Mrs. Keziah Lezenby, Miss Phoenie Sullivan, and James Sullivan, and that in order to accept the succession of their deceased relative and to effect a final partition of the same, they have agreed to the following valuation and apportionment of the same, to wit:

1. One quarter of an acre of land in the town of Zachary, with all the buildings and improvements thereon, bounded North by C. R. Ratcliff, East by Robert Flanders, south by Mrs. Chapman, and West by (then 1892) the L.N.O.& T. R.R. Co. right of way, ¼ acre front on said railroad by a depth of one acre, valued at One Hundred and fifty Dollars . . . . $ 150.00
2. Two (2) horses valued at 80.00
3. One buggy 30.00
4. Cash in Bank of Baton Rouge 113.00
5. Fourteen head of cattle (J.H.Brashear) 112.00
Five Hundred and Sixty seven Dollars . . . . $ 567.00
to be divided as follows, to wit:
1. Mrs. Louisa T. Sullivan, the mother, takes ten head of cattle, more or less . . . . $ 80.00
2. Jos H. Brashear, brother of the whole blood of deceased, takes cash in Baton Rouge Bank, one hundred and ninety five dollars 195.00
    one horse, forty dollars 40.00
    one (1) buggy, thirty dollars 30.00
    Four (4) head of cattle @ $8.00 . . . . 32.00
    Total to J.H. Brashear . . . . $ 297.00
3. Mrs. Mollie Law, Mrs. K. Lezenby, Miss Phoenie Sullivan, and Mr. Jas Sullivan take as their part of said property, as joint owners and as sisters and brother of the half blood, to wit:
    the house and land in Zachary as above described, valued at . . . . $ 150.00
    one (1) horse 40.00
    making one hundred and ninety dollars . . . . . . $ 190.00
being five hundred and sixty seven dollars so divided.

And that Mrs. L.T. Sullivan and J.H. Brashear remit in favor of Mrs. Law, Mrs. Lezenby, Phoenie Sullivan and James Sullivan all their right title and interest in and to the quarter acre of land and improvements in Zachary, also to the horse allotted to them; and Mrs. Law, Mrs. Lezenby, Phoenie Sullivan and Jas Sullivan relinquish all their right, title and interest in and to the property allotted to Mrs. Sullivan and J.H. Brashear, each guaranteeing to each other the allotment as made and agreed to herein. The said husbands authorizing their wives.

And it is further agreed and understood and Jos H. Brashear binds and obligates himself to pay all the expenses of last sickness of deceased, and the funeral expenses, and the charges for this petition.

This act was then read to the parties and signed by them and me, notary, in presence of W. W. Douglass and R. J. Douglass, competent witness, who sign as such this 31st day of August, A.D. 1894.

Witnesses:

/s/ W.W. Douglass
/s/ R.J. Douglass

/s/ Louisa T. Sullivan
/s/ J.H. Brashear
/s/ Mollie H. Law
/s/ W.T. Law, to authorize
/s/ Kizzie Lisenbie
/s/ J.H. Lisenbie, to authorize
/s/ Phoenie E. Sullivan
/s/ J.T. Sullivan
/s/ J.M. Loudon, Notary Public

The above and foregoing is the Original, a true copy of which is recorded in my Book of Notorial Acts, pages 16, 17 & 18,

given under my hand and seal of office, at my office, in and for the Parish of East Baton Rouge on this 3d day of Sept 1894,

/s/ J.M. Loudon, Notary Public

Recorded September 4th, 1894, F.A. Woods, by Clerk Recorder
(Thanks to Joanne Schwilk for a Xerox copy)

Joseph H. Brashears and Edith Devall

v^{5}397. ^{10}4. **Joseph H. Brashears**, (s/o Samuel W. Brashiers and Louisa T. Williams), b. May 1854, East Baton Rouge Parish, LA (7 in 1860), d. and bur Quincy, CA; m. **Edith Devall**, b. March 1855 (or Nov 1859, per 1900 census), d/o Richard Devall and Sarah Ann Allen. In 1900 Census, Point Coupe Parish, LA, Joseph and Edith have five children (two others were un-named; the family reports there was a sister named Anna, but we haven't found her yet): Joseph and Edith were in the 1910 census of El Paso, TX.

v5402.   11 1. **Steven F. Brashear**, b. May 1884, LA (16 in 1900);
            m. _____
v5403.   11 2. **Zelda Brashear**, b. July 1885, LA (14 in 1900)
v5404.   11 3. **Louisa Brashear**, b. Jan 1887, LA (13 in 1900)
v5405.   11 4. **Josephine Brashears**, b. Nov 1889, LA (11 in 1900),
            lived and died in Los Angeles, CA; m. *Joseph Mobley*.
            (no ch)
v5406.   11 5. **John Walker Brashear**, b. 24 Sept 1891, Baton
            Rouge, LA (Aug 1892, per 1900), d. 2 June 1969, San
            Jose, CA; m. 10 June 1916, *Laura Florence Keven*,
            b. 11 Sept 1898, Hawaii, d. 12 Feb 1985, San Jose,
            CA, d/o Terrence Robert Keven Sr and Marie
            Encarancao Martins.
v5407.   12 1. **John Brashear**, b. 3 April 1917, d. 1986; m.2. 10
            June 1916, *Rene Brown*, (2 ch); m.2. *Cary
            Cipolla*.
v5408.   13 1. **John David Brashear**, b. 18 July 1945, d. 29
            June 1998; no ch
v5409.   13 2. **Donna Brashear**, has two boys and one girl
v5410.   13 3. **Steven Brashear**, b. 27 Aug 1953, San Jose,
            CA; 3 boys
v5411.   13 4. **Timothy Patrick Brashear**, b. 6 Sept 1956,
            San Jose, CA; no ch
v5412.   13 5. **Jeff Brashear**, b. 12 July 1953, San Jose, CA;
            one girl, one boy
v5413.   13 6. **Kenneth Brashear**, b. 29 Oct 1959, San Jose,
            CA; no ch
v5414.   13 7. **Jeannie Marie Brashear**, b. 9 Oct 1962; San
            Jose, CA; Jeannie had a girl named Gretchen
            and a boy.
v5415.   12 2. **Mercedes Zelma Joan Brashear**, b. 9 Oct 1919,
            Seattle, WA; m. 7 March 1942, *Victor Ross
            Gorin*, b. 14 Sept 1916, Arden, Clark Co, NV, s/o
            James Clay Gorin and Martha Emma Hamann.
v5416.   13 1. Joanne Carole Gorin, b. 18 Feb 1943,
            Klamath Falls, OR; m. Douglas Frederick
            Schwilk, b. 17 June 1942, Hollywood, CA, s/o
            Frederick Henry Schwilk and Sophia Ellen
            "Sandra" Larson.
v5417.   14 1. Dylan Walker Schwilk, b. 10 Dec 1973,
            Hanover, NH

v5418.   142. Erika Larson Schwilk, b. 7 Jan 1977, Sacramento, CA
v5419.   132. Kathleen Sue Gorin, b. 22 Sept 1947, San Jose, CA; m. ____ ; 2 boys: Roshan and Christopher.
v5420.   133. Patricia Jean Gorin, b. 14 Jan 1952, San Jose, CA; m. ___; 2 girls: Lauren and Whitney.

ROBERT LAFAYETTE BRASHIER

v5314. 88. **Robert LaFayette Brashier**, b. c1815 (35 in 1850, East Feliciana Parish, LA), s/o Philip Brashear and Mary White; married five times. About 1875, he bought a Bible and entered his family and the families of several of his children and grandchildren. The family record pages came to be in the possession of a granddaughter, Mrs. Kizzie Brashear Epperson. Copies (as near true as the torn and worn paper would allow) were made in 1961 by Anny Harvey Daniel and published in *Louisiana Bible Records*, "Be It Known and Remembered," Louisiana Genealogical and Historical Association. Additional data from Michele Savage <msava22@aol.com>.

Robert L. Brashier, m.1. 22 March 1836, **Susan Ann Chapman**, b. 14 Feb 1819, d. 29 Aug 1837 (1 Sept 1837, says her stone in Chapman Cem, East Feliciana Parish, a month after son, T.J., was born); m.2. 1 June 1839, **Harriet Barfield**, b. c1816 (34 in 1850, East Feliciana), d. 3 March 1852, after birth of David Barfield Brashier, their sixth child; m.3. 18 Jan 1853, **Louisa Austen**, d. 14 March 1854; m.4. 13 Jan 1857, **Jane E. Bell**, d. ? June 1860?; m.5. ?7 July 1884, **Ann McLee**,.

Child of Robert LaFayette Brashier and Susan Ann Chapman:
v5421.   91. *****Thomas James Brashier**, b. 25 July 1837 (13 in 1850, East Feliciana); m.1. 3 Nov 1859, **Margaret Norwood**, d. 12 May 1862 (they had 2 children); m.2. 19 March 1863, **Sarah A. Witherington**.
Family of Robert LaFayette Brashier and Harriet Barfield: (Fam #187, in 1850, East Feliciana Parish, LA)
v5422.   92. **Hugh Phillip Brashier**, b. 12 March 1840, (10 in 1850, East Feliciana), killed in C.S.A. near Atlanta, GA, 28 July 1864

v5423. [9]3. **Pauline Brashier**, b. 30 March 1842 (8 in 1850, East Feliciana), d. 11 Dec 1876; m. 12 July 1864, *William Wallace*, d. 16 (or 10) March 1882

v5424. [10]1. Robert B. Wallace, b. 10 Oct 186?; d. 13 Nov 1870, at 5:45 p.m., aged 5 yrs, 1 mo, 3 days

v5425. [10]2. Julia E. Wallace, b. 18 Nov 1868; "Julliette Wallace m. _____" ? (too faded to read)

v5426. [10]3. Emmette B. Wallace, b. 5 Feb 1871

v5427. [10]4. Francis "Frank" R. (or B.) Wallace, b. 10 March 1876

v5428. [10]5. Jesse E. Wallace, b. 25 Aug 1879; d. 28 July 1879, aged 5 yrs

v5429. [9]4. **Susan Ann Brashier**, b. 31 July 1843 (7 in 1850, East Feliciana); m. 14 Sept 186?, *Mr. S. Lambert*,

v5430. [9]5. **Emily Jane Brashier**, b. 7 Sept 184?5 (torn) (4 in 1850, East Feliciana)

v5431. [9]6. **Robert LaFayette Brashier Jr**, b. 23 June 1849 (1 in 1850, East Feliciana). Probably father of:

v5432. [10]x. **R.L. Brashier**, b. 14 Sept 1874, listed in Bible, but unidentified. There are no other eligible parents in the right generation.

v5433. [9]7. **David Barfield Brashier**, b. Jan 1852, d. 13 June 1853

Family of Robert LaFayette Brashier and Jane E. Bell:

v5434. [9]8. ***Wiley Dunn Brashier**, b. 9 Nov 1857 (39 in 1910, East Feliciana Parish); m. 30 March 1881, *Emily Lambert*, b. Sept 1861, TX, (per 1900 Census, sht 14, line 26; they lived in 2nd Ward, East Feliciana with their first six children). Wiley Brashear, 63, and Emma, 50, are in 1920 Census, East Feliciana Parish, with son James, and granddaughters, Thelma Dixon, 5, and Mabel Kennedy, b. c1918 (1 2/12)

v5435. [9]10. **Joseph Brashier**, b. 6 Feb 1860, d. near Olive Branch, LA, 5 Oct 1866, at 5:30 p.m.

Family of Wiley Dunn Brashier ([V5]434) and Emily Lambert:

v5436. [10]1. **Robert Beverly Brashier**, B. 17 Aug 1883; m. 31 Dec 1905, *Berta Lisenbee*,

v5437. [10]2. **Kizzie Ella Brashier**, b. 6 Jan 1887; m. ? Dec 1904, *Glen Epperson*. Kizzie Epperson owned the pages from her grandfather's Bible.

v⁵438. ¹⁰3. **Vida May Brashier**, b. 14 April 1889; m. 1 Sept 1910, *Charlie Phares*,

v⁵439. ¹⁰4. **Jane Beatrice Brashier**, b. ?8 Sept 1891; m. 25 July 1912, *Raymond Dixon*,

v⁵440.   ¹¹x. Thelma Dixon, b. c1915 (5 in Wiley's HH in 1920, East Feliciana, and identified as granddaughter)

v⁵441. ¹⁰5. **Lawrance Bell Brashier**, b. 7 Nov 1894 (15 in 1910 Census, East Feliciana Parish. LA)

v⁵442. ¹⁰6. **Emma Dunn Brashier**, b. 2 April 1897; m. 6 Jan 1918, *T.W. Kennedy*,

v⁵443.   ¹¹x. Mabel Kennedy, b. c1918 (1 2/12 in Wiley's HH in 1920, East Feliciana, and identified as granddaughter)

v⁵444. ¹⁰7. **Wiley James Brashier**, b. 6 June 1901

Emily (Lambert) Brashier's parents and siblings:

David Lambert, b. 28 March 1830, d. 1 Nov 1901, (s/o Benjamin Lambert and Christian Gottliegy); m. 22 Dec 1853, in Orange, Texas, Emily Lyons, b. 1 Nov 1837, d. 12 Jan 1884, (d/o John Lyons and Amanda Stanton); their ch:

1. Adela Lambert, b. 3 April 1855, d. 4 Oct 1920; m. _____ Golding,
2. Charles Wesley Lambert, b. 17 April 1857
3. John Lawrence Lambert, b. 30 March 1859, d. 25 Feb (no year shown)
4. Emily Lambert, b. 9 Sept 1861; m. **Wiley Dun Brashier**,
5. Ernistine Amelia Lambert, b. 22 June 1864; m. _____ Tucker,
6. James Montford Lambert, b. 9 Feb 1867, d. 12 June 1883
7. Benjamin Artiss Lambert, b. 9 Jan 1870, d. 25 Aug 1872
8. Vida Lue Lambert, b. 25 Feb 1872, d. 7 July 1942; m. _____ Wallace,
9. Lilly Amanda Lambert, b. 9 Aug 1874
10. Festus Stanton Lambert, b. 5 May 1877

Thomas James Brashier and Margaret Norwood/ Sarah Witherington

v⁵421. ⁹1. **Thomas James Brashier**, (s/o Robert LaFayette Brashier and Susan Ann Chapman), b. 25 July 1837 (13 in 1850, East Feliciana); m.1. 3 Nov 1859, *Margaret Norwood*, d.

---

12 May 1862 (they had 2 children); m.2. 19 March 1863, **Sarah A. Witherington**. Thomas J. Brashear, 62, in 1900 Census, East Feliciana Parish (sht 5, line 65) with three of his grown sons at home. Thomas J. Brashear is 70 in HH of son, Eslet, in 1910, East Feliciana Parish; next door are Hugh T. 46, and Thomas, 27.

Some of the descendants of Thomas Wallace Brashier have it that Thomas James Brashier m.1. Albina Wellington, who d. shortly after birth of their only child; m.2. _____ Ellis, a first cousin of Albina, who had come to Louisiana from Evergreen, AL, during the Civil War to visit, and couldn't get back home; her father was George Ellis. But this story does not agree with the Bible data.

v5445.   10 1. **Hardy Brashier**, b. 25 Nov 1860, d. 29 Nov 1860, age 4 days.

v5446.   10 2. **Maggie L.A. Brashier**, b. 27 Feb 1862, d. 7 June 1862, age 3½ months

v5447.   10 3. **Hugh T. Brashear**, b. 20 Feb 1863, (Feb 1864 per 1900 census; 46 in 1910 Census, East Feliciana); m. **Emma E.** _____, b. March 1870 (per 1900; 36 in 1910). In Patterson Cem, East Feliciana Parish: Hugh S. Brashier, 20 Feb 1863— 4 Jan 1931.

v5448.   11 1. **Jessie R. Brashear** (son), b. June 1894 (per 1900; 15 in 1910)

v5449.   11 2. **Mattie A. Brashear** (dau), b. Jan 1898 (Mattie, age 2 in 1900; Lou A., 12 in 1910)

v5450.   10 4. **Robert Estes Brashear**, (Eslet Brashier in some records), b. c1867 (33 in 1900, son in hh of Thomas J. Brashear; 42 in 1910, East Feliciana; Robert E. Brashear, 52 in 1920); m. 8 Sept 1905, **Clara Lou Barr**, b. c1882, LA (28 in 1910; 36 in 1920). In Robert's HH in 1910: Thomas J. Brashear, 70, father. Additional data from Michele Savage <msava22@aol.com>.

Clara Lou Barr m.1. 27 Aug 190_, Taylor Brashier, brother to Robert Estes Brashier; Taylor and Clara Lou had no children. Taylor died after 8 months, and Clara Lou stayed with another brother and his wife, Thomas and Mattie Brashier, until she m. Robert Estes Brashier.

v5451.   11 1. **Taylor Wiley Brashear**, b. 2 Sept 1906 (3 in

1910; 13 in 1920)

v⁵452.   ¹¹2. **Robert James Brashear**, b. 17 Sept 1908 (1 7/12 in 1910; Robert E. Jr, 12 in 1920)

v⁵453.   ¹¹3. **Clara Ola Brashier**, b. 8 Oct 1910, (9 in 1920)

v⁵454.   ¹¹4. **Lanier Brashier**, b. 5 March 1912, (7 in 1920)

v⁵455.   ¹¹5. **Maggie Gertrude Brashier**, b. 2 July 1914, (5 in 1920)

v⁵456.   ¹¹6. **Pershing Brashier**, b. 13 Sept 1916, (2 6/12 in 1920

v⁵457.   ¹¹7. **Katie Ethel Brashier**, b. 5 Jan 1918, (6/12 in 1920)

v⁵458. ¹⁰5. **Thomas Wallace Brashear**, b. 17 Oct 1871 (or Oct 1872 per 1900, East Feliciana Par, sheet 6, line 86; error: 27 in 1910, East Feliciana), d. 31 Jan 1948; m. *Martha I. "Mattie" Pennington*, b. 28 April 1880, LA (1881 per 1900; 23 in 1910), d. 7 Aug 1961

v⁵459.   ¹¹1. **William Hugh "Willie" Brashear**, b. 17 June 1902 (8 in 1910; 17 in 1920); m. *Addie Mae Hall*, b. 23 Nov 1912, d. 7 Aug 1967

v⁵460.   ¹²1. **William Glenn Brashier**, b. 28 June 1935; m. 23 Dec 1955, *Truly Elane Serbert*,

v⁵461.   ¹¹2. **Edna Brashear**, b. c1911 (11 in 1920)

v⁵462. ¹⁰6. **Wiley Taylor Brashear**, b. Nov 1876 (23 in 1900; son in hh of Thomas J. Brashear); m. *Clara Lou Barr*. Taylor died soon after the marriage, with no children; and Clara later married Taylor's brother, Robert Estes Brashear.

v⁵463. ¹⁰7. **Samuel L. Brashear**, b. April 1879 (21 in 1900; son in hh of Thomas J. Brashear)

LOUISIANA STRAYS

The Register of Patents on Military Bounty Warrants, 1855-1861, in American State Papers, Public Lands, v.1, p.?, lists a warrant for Samuel E. Brasher, 11 Sept 1851, in T6S, R2W, located 8 June 1853; a warrant for William Brasher, 27 July 1848, in T1S, R3, located 27 Sept 1848; and a warrant for Marie Brasseur, 5 April 1852, T6, R1, located 24 May 1853.)

East Feliciana

v5464. **Anna Brashier**, b. Nov 1856, LA (43; 1900 Census, Louisiana, East Feliciana Parish, Ward 2, sht 19, line 49)

v5465.   1. **John L. Brashier**, b. July 1883, LA (16)

v5466.   2. **Emma Brashier**, b. July 1888, LA (12)

v5467.   3. **Katie Brashier**, b. April 1893, LA (7)

This same Anna Brashier is in the 1910 census:

    Anna Brashier, b. c1857 (52 in 1910), w/ children:

        1. **John L. Brashier**, b. c1886 (23 in 1910)

        2. **Emma Brashier**, b. c1888 (21 in 1910)

East Baton Rouge

1860 Census, East Baton Rouge Parish: #906?

v5468. **Charlotte Brashears**,	31, b. c1829, LA; apparently a widow	
v5469. **Thomas Brashears**,	18, b. c1842, LA; ?poss. m. Lucinda Patton,	
v5470. **Eliza A. Brashears**,	16, b. c1844, LA	
v5471. **Charlotte Brashears**,	10, b. c1850, LA	
v5472. Lorenzo Roberson,	21, b. c1849,	
v5473. Archibald Roberson,	25, b. c1845,	
v5474. Eliza A. Roberson,	10/12, b. c1959	
v5475. Mary Ruhelio,	23, b. c1847,	
v5476. Thomas Ruhelio,	5, b. c1855,	
v5477. Andrew J. Ruhelio,	3, b. c1858,	

v5478. #953   Joseph Denhman and family;

v5479. in HH: **Sophia Brashears**,   30, b. c1830

There are a number of Brashear families in the 1900, 1910, and 1920 Censuses of East Baton Rouge Parish, LA, that I can't account for. Help, anyone?

1900 Census, Louisiana, East Baton Rouge Parish, Ward 2, sht 18, line 18

v5480. **Bessie Brashear**, b. Feb 1890, (10 in1900, in Protestant Female Orphan Home)

v5481. **Ruby Brashear**, b. Nov 1892, LA (7 in 1900, in Protestant Female Orphan Home; 17 in 1910, East Feliciana Parish, granddaughter in HH of Wiley Atkinson)

1900 Census, Louisiana, East Baton Rouge Par, Ward 4, sht 23, line 69

v5482. **Leah Brashear**, b. Oct 1878, LA (21); boarder in hh of James E. Foney (or Toney)

v5483. **Joseph Brashear**, b. LA, c1846 (64 in 1910 & 73 in 1920), father-in-law in HH of Leroy James (1910) or James T. Lavey (1920).

v5484. **J.T. Brashear**, b. LA, c1875 (44 in 1920); lived at 1112 Convention, Baton Rouge, with wife, *Maud* _____, b. c1895 (24 in 1920), and dau
v5485. x. **Hilda Brashear**, b. c1917 (2 8/12 in 1920)

v5486. **Joseph B. Brashear**, b. c1881 (29 in 1910, East Baton Rouge Parish); m. *Bessie* _____, b. c1887 (23 in 1910)
　　1. **Lee Ray Brashear**, b. c1907 (3 in 1910)
　　2. **Leo Brashear**, b. c1908 (1 6/12 in 1910)
same family, new name: **Robert Brashear**, 40, and wife "Bess," 33, are in the 1920 Census of East Baton Rouge Parish, with 7 children.
v5487. 1. **Ray Brashear**, b. c1907 (3 in 1910; 13 in 1920)
v5488. 2. **Leo Brashear**, b. c1908 (1 6/12 in 1900; 11 in 1920)
v5489. 3. **Mary Brashear**, b. c1911 (9 in 1920)
v5490. 4. **Elma Brashear**, b. c1913 (7 in 1920)
v5491. 5. **Jessie Brashear**, (son & twin), b. c1915 (5 in 1920)
v5492. 6. **Bessie Brashear**, (dau & twin), b. c1915 (5 in 1920)
v5493. 7. **Maud Brashear**, b. c1917 (3 in 1920)

v5494. **Anna Brashear**, b. c1893 (27 in 1920); sister-in-law to Edgar A. Sanchez, 729 St. Maximillian, Baton Rouge.

7. SAMUEL BRASHEARS, SR and RACHEL DURANT

Samuel Brashears, Sr, was actually the third mature son of Jesse Brashears and Elizabeth Prather, but I'm going to put him here, because his sons made early history that helps to explain (or at least put in context) some of the later family ties.

v5**234. Samuel Brashears Sr**, (s/o Jesse Brashear and Elizabeth Prather), b. ?c1760, m. c1788, **Rachel Durant**, b. c1770, a mixed-blood Creek Indian, d/o Benjamin Durant and Sophia McGillivray (Rachel was, therefore, a niece of Principal Chief Alexander McGillivray of the Creeks).

Samuel and Rachel must have separated; she married, second, Billy McGirth; married third, David Walker; m.4. Zadock Brashears, Sr, Samuel's oldest brother. Her Walker children married in the early 1820's, which would put their births c1795-1805. Samuel and his distinctive signature mark, a heart with a tail curled to the right, continue to appear in the land records to 1806 at least.

20 Jan 1804: *Archives of Spanish West Florida*, Vol VIII, p.6: (Written in Spanish) Be it known to all who see this act that I, Samuel [p.15] Brashear, resident of New Feliciana, execute, really and with effect, a final receipt in favor of James McElroy for the total amount of one thousand one hundred pesos, the purchase price of three hundred arpents of land, which I sold him in the said settlement, which act was passed on the sixth of July of the year one thousand eight hundred and three, discharging him for this said sum which has been delivered to me in due form as he promised, etc. In testimony of which, I receive this final payment in Baton Rouge on the twentieth day of the month of [p.16] January of the year one thousand eight hundred and four.

I, Carlos de Grand Pré, Colonel of the Royal Armies, Political and Military Governor of the Post and Settlement of Baton Rouge, certify that I know the grantor, who does not know how to sign but makes his customary mark, signing with the present witnesses, Francisco Miranda and Juan Perez.

Carlos de Grand Pré   M a r k 💟 of Samuel Brashear
Fran^{co} Miranda
Juan Perez

26 Aug 1806: *Archives of Spanish West Florida*, Vol XI, p.120. (Written in Spanish) Be it known to all who may see this act, that I, Samuel [p.337] Brashears, depose that I sell, really and with effect, to Philip Alston Gray, a negro named John, native of this province, about twenty-eight years old, this being the same one which I acquired from Mr. Vaughn. The said negro is thus being sold free of encumbrance and mortgage for the price and amount of six hundred pesos in cash, which I acknowledge to have received from the purchaser, and for which I hereby give him a formal receipt, through which I relinquish the right of property, possession and dominion which I had on the said negro, all of which I cede and transfer in favor of the purchaser and/or his assigns, to have and to hold, to exchange, sell or encumber at his will as his own, and through this act it shall be seen that he has acquired its possession with- [p.338] out the necessity of any further proofs of which I relieve him, obligating myself in case of eviction and for the security and legality of this sale in due form of law. The payment not being in hand I renounce the laws of the thing not seen nor received, fraud and all others to the same effect. I empower the courts of His Majesty to compel me to its performance with the force of confession of judgment and passed upon the authority of a decided case upon which I renounce the jurisdiction and all rights, privileges and laws in my favor, together with the general one that prohibits it.

And I, Phillip Gray, being present at the execution of this act, accept it in my favor, of my own free will acknowledging that the said land has been delivered to me after having paid in cash to the vendor the amount of six hundred pesos for which it has [p.339] been sold to me. In testimony of which, this act was executed in Baton Rouge on the twenty-sixth day of August, 1806.

I, Don Carlos de Grand Pré, Colonel of the Royal Armies, Civil and Military Governor of the Post and District of Baton Rouge, certify that I know the grantors, the vendor made his mark not knowing how to write, the purchaser signing with Thomas Estevan and Celestin de St. Maxent, as witnesses,

Carlos de Grand Pré   Mark ♡ of the vendor

Celestion de S^n Masent

Thomas Estevan   Phil. A. Gray

The McGillivray Connection

A Frenchman named Marchand came into the Creek nation to live and married Sehoy, beautiful princess of the Wind Clan. Their daughter, Sehoy Marchand, m. Lachlan McGillivray, who came to America from Scotland, 1736, on the ship, *The Prince of Wales*. (Information sent to me by Patty Gambill from "Alabama Records at Texas State Library and from the Secretary of the Choctaw Nation Election Board")

Lachlan McGillivray and Sehoy Marchand had at least 4 children:

a1. Alexander McGillivray, Chief of the Creeks, b. 1740, d. 17 Feb 1793, bur in garden of his good friend and partner, William Panton, in Pensacola; m. Elizabeth Cornell, d/o Joseph Cornell and had six children.

b1. Sarah Ann McGillivray,

b2. Sophia McGillivray,

b3. Rachel McGillivray,

b4. William McGillivray,

b5. Robert McGillivray,

b6. Alexander McGillivray Jr, unborn child mentioned in Will. "The boy, Aleck, is old enough to be sent to Scotland, to School, which I intend to do next year," wrote Panton, several years later. The letter was found in the District Court at New Orleans (see also "Alexander McGillivray, Emperor of the Creeks" *Chronicles of Oklahoma*, v.7 (1929), p.118).

a2. Sophia McGillivray, b. ?c1742 "oldest sister" of Alexander McGillivray; m. Benjamin Durant and had eight children. *Early History of the Creek Indians and Their Neighbors*, by John R. Swanton, p. 242, quoting Benjamin Hawkins's "A

Sketch of the Creek Country," 1799 (thanks to Josephine Bryant <Josephine_Bryant@myfamily.com> for a copy): "Mrs. Durant, the oldest sister, has eight children. She is industrious, but has no economy or management. In possession of fourteen working negroes, she seldom makes bread enough, and they live poorly. She can spin and weave, and is making some feeble efforts to obtain clothing for her family." According to a deposition 9 Aug 1816 by son, Lachlan, Benjamin Durant was killed 30 Aug 1813 in the Massacre at Ft. Mims, when "Red Sticks," traditional Indians from up-river, attacked the fort and killed most of the white and half-breed inhabitants. (See Thomas Woodward [a mixed-blood who knew many of these families], *Woodward's Reminiscences*, 1850s, available in many Alabama libraries; see also Albert Pickett, *History of Alabama*, 1852; additional data from Woodie Wallace, Josephine Bryant <Josephine_ Bryant@myfamily.com>, and Mary Lou Jones <mljones@ WHC.NET>)

b1. Rachel Durant, b. 1770-73 (if she was 16-19 when her first child, Alexander, was born in 1789); m.1. **Samuel Brashears Sr** (^{v5}234); m.2. Billy McGirth; m.3. David Walker; m.4 **Zadock Brashears Sr** (^{v5}231).

b2. Lachlan Durant, b. 1774/75 (Census, Baldwin Co, AL, 1850); m. Mary Hall,

    c1. Sarah Ann Durant, b. 1809-10 (according to FL Census); m. Samuel Adams;

    c2. Martin Madison Durant, b. 1810, lived Baldwin Co, AL (headstone shows birth date); m. Hannah Betty Pollard

    c3. Andrew Jackson "Jack" Durant, b. 14 March 1811, went to Williamson Co, TX (Mary Lou Jones's gggrandfather); m. Sarah Jane McNeil

    c4. Aurelia Durant, b. c1814; m. J. Knox;

    c5. Constantine P. "Bud" Durant, had land in Baldwin Co, AL; never married;

    c6. William H. Durant, b. 1825 (1850 Baldwin Co, AL Census)

    c7. Charles Lachlan Durant, b. 1828 (1850 Baldwin Co, AL Census);

b3. John Durant - in their books, Woodward and Pickett say he died in FL b4. Alexander "Sandy" Durant, (may be the A. Isham Durant, who lived in Texas, says one report; went with Peter McQueen and died in Florida, says another. McQueen was the Red Stick who led the attack and massacre at Fort Mims).

b5. Mary "Polly" Durant, may have drowned with her husband and four of her children when a steamboat sank in 1836 on the way to Indian Territory from Pass Christian on the Mississippi Coast, where the last of the Creeks were assembled in the Removal; m. Tustennuggee Emarthla, (a Creek title of honor) or Cochamay; he was called "Coachman," or "Jim Boy," and was one of the Red Stick leaders who led the Creek contingent in the Seminole War of 1836, later removed to Indian Territory (mentioned in Angie Debo's book, *The Road to Disappearance*). Ch: Ward Coachman, (Creek Roll #5109), b. 1827, Wetumka, AL; m.1. Lizzie Carr; m.2. Lizzie Yaholar, full-blood Creek (Roll #5111); Children included Peter (Roll #3351), Visey, Charles (Roll #5365), and George Coachman (Roll #5110).

b6. Sophia Durant, b. 1787 (per Census); m.1. before 1801, _____ Linder (On 20 Feb 1801, Benjamin and Sophia Durant, of the Creek Nation, State of Georgia, gave their daughter, Sophia Linder, some negro slaves. (Washington Co, AL, Deeds, Book 1, p.23); m.2. before 1815, _____ McComb. (Signed letter in 1815 as Sophia McComb)

b7. Elizabeth "Betsy" Durant, (twin), b. 1790; m.1. Peter McQueen, who led the Red Sticks in the attack on Fort Mims; he and Betsy removed to Seminole territory and he died there, according to Woodward; Betsy then returned and m.2. Willie McQueen, a nephew of her first husband. Pickett says she lived to be an old woman.

b8. Nancy Durant, (twin), b. 1790, killed at Ft. Mims, 30 August 1813, at the same time as her father, Ben. Probates say that she was a sister of Rachel, Sophia, and Lachlan. (Probates available from Mary Lou Jones.) Nancy *MAY* have m.1. _____ Pounds; m.2. James Bailey. Peggy Bailey, James's sister, said that James was inside the Fort with Nancy Pounds with two children by her and one by another woman; and they were all killed. Peggy was claiming James's land on Choctaw Bluff on the west side of the Alabama River, which he had bought from a man named Linder. Lachlan Durant corroborated most of this in a deposition, except he never said Nancy Pounds was the same as his sister, Nancy Durant.

a3. Jeanette McGillivray, b. ?c1744; m. c1784, Leclerc (or Louis) Milfort. Milfort, a young Frenchman, came to the U.S. in 1776, was charmed by Jeannette McGillivray (she is described as a pretty maiden, dressed in silk and linen, wearing earrings, bracelets, and clasps of silver), and married her. Milfort wrote *Sejour dans La Nation Creck*, in which he described his life among the Creeks with great exaggeration and tried to claim Alexander McGillivray's accomplishments as his own.

a4. Sehoy McGillivray, m.1. David Tate; m.2. William Charles Weatherford, a half-breed, who was a Principal Chief among the Upper Creeks after McGillivray's death. *Early History of the Creek Indians and Their Neighbors*, by John R. Swanton, p. 242, quoting Benjamin Hawkins's "A Sketch of the Creek Country," 1799: "The other sister, Sehoi, has about thirty negroes, is extravagant and heedless, neither spins nor weaves, and has no government of her family."

    b1. David Tate, who "has been educated in Philadelphia and Scotland. He promises to be better." (Hawkins, op.cit.); m.1. _____; m.2. Margaret Dyer Powell. Daughter Louisa Tate, m. _____ Tunstall, and had a son, David Tate Tunstall.

    b2. William Weatherford, "Red Eagle," "Lumbo Chat," a chief of the Red Sticks; m. _____ Stiggins, s/o of George Stiggins.

In December 1796, some 2 years after the death of Alexander McGillivray, Benjamin Hawkins, the Indian Agent for the Territory South of the Ohio, was on a tour through the area.

Alexander McGillivray's plantation was at Little Tulsa, three miles above the "falls" of the Coosa River. After his death, the family moved to "Hickory Ground" (Otciapofu or O-che-au-po-fau, from oche-ub 'hickory tree' and po-fau 'in or among'), which was located below the "falls" and near the confluence of the Coosa and Tallapoosa Rivers. In "A Sketch of the Creek Country," 1799, Benjamin Hawkins described it as "two miles above the fork of the river, and one mile below the falls, on a flat of poor land, just below a small stream; the fields are on the right side of the river, on rich flat land; and this flat extends back for two miles, with oak and hickory, then pine forest; the range out in this forest is fine for cattle; reed is abundant in all the branches.... At the termination of the falls there is a fine little stream, large enough for a small mill, called, from the clearness of the water, We-hemt-le, 'good water.' Three and a half miles above the town are ten apple trees, planted by the late General McGillivray; half a mile further up are the remains of Old Tal-e-see (Little Tulsa), formerly the residence of Mr. Lachlan McGillivray. Here are ten apple trees, planted by the father, and a stone chimney, the remains of a house built by the son, and these are all the improvements left by the father and son." (thanks to Josephine_Bryant@myfamily.com for a copy of *Early History of the Creek Indians and Their Neighbors*, by John R. Swanton, p. 242.)

"In 1797, the traders here were James McQueen, the oldest white man in the Creek nation, who had come to Georgia as a soldier under Oglethorpe in 1733, and William Powell.... The Indians who have settled out on the margins and branches of the creek have, several of them, cattle, hogs, and horses, and begin to be attentive to them. The head warrior of the town, Peter McQueen, a half-breed, is a snug trader, has a valuable property in negroes and stock, and begins to know their value." (Swanton, p.244.) "They have forty gunmen." (p.242.)

(From *Benjamin Hawkins, Indian Agent*, by Merritt B. Pound, Athens, GA: University of Georgia Press, 1951, p.110-111). "As he penetrated farther into the country of the Upper Creeks, Hawkins noticed decided improvement. More land was cultivated, stock was better and more numerous, houses cleaner and more comfortable, and the Indians seemed willing, even anxious, to cooperate with the government in a program of farming and handicrafts. The presence of many half-breeds, some of whom held high tribal positions, and white men with Indian families had some influence on the change of tribal customs.

"On December 18, Hawkins and Alexander Cornells [his half-breed assistant] visited Richard Bailey, a white man living five miles down the river. Bailey had an Indian family and was a man of much influence in the nation. On his excellent farm, he gathered honey from twenty beehives and planted cotton which his wife and daughters spun and made into clothes. He possessed seven Negroes, two hundred cattle, one hundred fifty hogs, and one hundred twenty horses. An Englishman, he had formerly worked in Savannah, but had spent forty years pleasantly and profitably among the Creeks.

"The next day on the way to the house of Charles Weatherford, half-breed brother-in-law of McGillivray, Hawkins passed a Uchee village and a half mile farther a Shawnee town. These Indians were living peacefully with the Creeks, though the Shawnees retained the language and customs of their tribesmen of the Northwest. [The Old Northwest was west of the Allegheny Mountains and north of the River Ohio.]

"A day later, Hawkins was at Weatherford's residence on a high bluff on the left bank of the Alabama River below the confluence of the Coosa and Tallapoosa. Weatherford, one of the principal chiefs of the Upper Creeks, was a man of some wealth with a particular interest in breeding fine horses. He maintained a race track near his home. Hawkins thought him a most undesirable character and doubted his legal ownership of some of the horses he raced.

"Near Weatherford lived Mrs. [Sophia] Durant, the oldest sister of Alexander McGillivray, whose husband was a dull man with some Negro blood. With their eight children they were housed in dirty and uncomfortable quarters. They possessed eighty slaves but the Negroes were burdensome because of poor management. Panton, Leslie & Company had refused to supply Mrs. Durant further with goods and this emphasized her poverty."

"The spirit of Christmas had entered the Indian country. It was customary for all the neighboring slaves to gather at the home of Mrs. [Sophia McGillivray] Durant or Mrs. [Sehoy McGillivray] Weatherford on Christmas Day. This year the gathering was at the Durants'. 'And there they had a proper frolic of rum drinking and dancing ... the white people and the Indians met generally at the same place with them and had the same amusements'" (ibid p.112).

Notwithstanding her poverty after the Creek civil war and incursions of the whites, Sophia (McGillivray) Durant had been a wealthy and influential woman. She was in the cattle business and sold beef to the increasing populations of places like

Pensacola, Mobile, and New Orleans. As sister to Alexander McGillivray, she was often his agent and interpreter on business, for example with Panton & Leslie Trading Company in Pensacola, who financed some of her operations. In this capacity she was welcomed by the Spanish governor after Spain occupied Pensacola in 1783. She was often a guest of Spanish Governor O'Neil during the 1780s. While on business in Pensacola, it is said she stayed at Jesse and Elizabeth (Prather) Brashear's Inn, where her daughter, Rachel, met her husband-to-be, Samuel Brashears Sr, son of Jesse and Elizabeth.

The so-called Upper Creeks had settled along the Coosa and Talapoosa Rivers, near their confluence with the Alabama River, around present day Wetumka, and down on the Tensaw and Little Rivers. There was a high percentage of mixed bloods among them, and, as Hawkins discovered, some of wealth and influence. These families were attacked by traditional Creeks from higher up the Coosa and Talapoosa Rivers and by invading whites from down the river.

Benjamin Hawkins wrote: "The situation of the half breeds has been particularly embarrassing. They embraced the plan of civilization first and by their conduct merited the attention of the Agent for Indian Affairs. They would not agree in their mode of living or pursuits with their Indian relatives or the Chiefs generally, which produced continual broils between them. This determined the half breeds to apply for, and after several years, to obtain from the Convention of the nation leave to settle down on the Alabama near the white settlements on the Indian lands. Here they were when the civil war among the Indians commenced." (Grant, ed. 1980, p.768)

The most infamous event of this war was the Massacre at Fort Mims. Traditional "Red Sticks" from up the river attacked the (largely) half-breed "Upper Creeks" and ruthlessly murdered a good many of them. Several of the McGillivray connection were among the victims. After the Creek War, 1813-14, many of the Creeks left this area, sometimes whole towns, and moved down into the Florida panhandle, where many of their descendants still live.

There were no clear boundaries between the Upper Creeks and their attackers, and some families were split between the two sides. Sophia (McGillivray) Durant's daughter, Betsy Durant, had married Peter McQueen, a leader of the attack. Her daughter, Sophia Durant Jr, was married to a prominent white man (McComb) and kept away from the fray. Her daughter, Rachel Durant, and her Brashear, McGirth, and Walker children, were identified with the half-breed Creek Indians along the lower rivers. Rachel lived in the vicinity of Little River, the border between Monroe and Baldwin Counties in Alabama. Fisher's Post Office was located nearby.

On 29 May 1815, eleven of Rachel's family and friends wrote a two and one half page letter to President James Madison and mailed it at Fisher's Post Office. This letter was eventually passed on to the Indian Agent, Benjamin Hawkins, who investigated the matter. The eleven signers were: Rachel (Durant) Walker, Lachlan Durant (Rachel's brother), Samuel Brashiere (Rachel's son), William McGirt (Rachel's son), Sophia (Durant) McComb (Rachel's sister), Peggy Summerlin, Nancy Summerlin (d/o Josiah Fisher and Le-mah-wey), Leonard McGhee, Lemi (or Semi) McGhee, Alex Brashiers (Rachel's son), and Harriet Linder (probably Sophia (Durant) McComb's daughter by her first marriage).

The letter reads, in part: "We the Natives of the Creek Nation, Relations of Alexander McGillivray, most respectfully beg leave to present this our humble petition to the President of the United States for a redress of grievances of the most serious nature that can happen to us.

"After having shown an inviolate atachment [sic] for the Government of the United States through the whole of the last war (The Creek War) in which our property has been destroyed, our lives threatened with indiscriminate carnage, not one of us but who lost Relatives both near and dear to us on the memorable day that Fort Mimms was taken by dreadful massacre that the Hostile Indians made there; we have at all times evinced a willingness and readiness (as many of the Officers of the Army can testify) to cooperate and contribute to every measure that was calculated to prosecute the war with success on behalf of the United States -- and we in common with every good citizen of the Government rejoiced at the fair prospects of peace but our prospects are darkened and we are placed in a most critical situation. Many citizens of the Mississippi Territory have moved over the boundary line betwixt the United States and the Creek Indians on the Alabama River as high up as Fort Claiborne in which distance the greatest number of us who are called Half-breeds were born and raised. They have taken forcible possession of our fields and houses and ordered us off at the risk of our lives. They have reproached us with our origins, insulted us with the most abusive language, and not content with that, they have even proceeded to blows and committed private injury in our stocks and property."

The letter continues that they had sought for redress from local authorities, but that no one yet had jurisdiction. They said further that General Jackson had given them to understand that all actual settlers "...who were natives and descendants of the Indians would be entitled to a lease of six hundred and forty acres of land— some think differently on this subject now, that females with families will not be entitled to any." They petitioned "to remain on our farms which we had occupied for years before the war," and they ended the letter with the usual perfunctory protocol which correspondence demanded at that time.

We believe that Rachel or Alexander Brashears actually wrote this letter. Alexander and Rachel were about the only ones in the settlement with education enough to do it. It is reported that Alexander Brashears identified himself to Col. Ward, the Indian Agent as a warrior of the Creek nation, as did his brother, Samuel Brashears Jr. Note later that Samuel Brashears, Creek Warrior, got the 640 acres that General Jackson had "promised" Creeks for their participation in the Creek War. Rachel and Alexander, at least, soon gave up their land on the Alabama River and joined their Brashears cousins in the Suk-en-Atcha settlement in Sumter Co, AL.

Family of Samuel Brashears, Sr and Rachel Durant

v5521. 81. ***Alexander M. (?McGillivray) Brashears**, b. c1789 (61 in 1850, Mobile Co, AL, #491-491; almost certainly named for Alexander McGillivray, Principal Chief of the Creek Indians, his great uncle); m.1. _____ (probably an Indian woman who was probably killed at Fort Mims—no documents); m.2. **Anne (Brashears) Lyles** (v5834), his cousin, d/o Zadock Brashears Sr and Susannah Vaughn; m.3. 15 July 1826, Marengo Co, AL, **Emiline Jane Winn**, m.4. **Bromly Cravey**, b. c1810-19 (31 in 1850), d/o Hugh Cravey and Kessy Norsworthy. Alexander was a beneficiary under Clause 14 of the Treaty of Dancing Rabbit Creek. See below.

[v5]522. [8]2. **Rachel Brashears**, (There is scant evidence of her existence. In the deed where Rachel, Alexander, and Samuel Brashear deed slaves to their mother, Rachel Brashears, Rachel Brashears signed with a mark (Marengo Co, AL, Deeds, Book A, p.3098). Since her mother, Rachel, was quite literate, I think the one who signed the deed must be a daughter. See the deed below.) Rachel Brashears was head of a household in 1820, Marengo Co, AL, as was a George H. Chrisman. Rachel Brashears m. 12 March 1822, in Marengo Co, AL, **George H. Chrisman**. Josephine Turner Bryant says a George H. Chrisman bought a lot of public property in Illinois.

[v5]523. [8]3. ***Samuel Brashears Jr**, b. c1792; may have married three times, and may have died after 1846. Samuel Jr was recognized by the U.S. Government as a "warrior of the Creek Nation" and was a beneficiary of the treaty of 1814, which ended the Creek War. See below.

Family of Billy McGirth and Rachel Durant:

[v5]524. [8]4. William "Billy" McGirth Jr

Family of David Walker and Rachel Durant: Rachel m.3. 1803, David "Davy" Walker Sr (ref: *The First American Frontier*, by Albert Pickens James, v.2, p.8-11). David "Davy" Walker, died between 1821 (birth of son, David) and 1824 (Rachel's marriage to Zadock Brashears Sr).

[v5]525. [8]5. George W. Walker, m. 19 Jan 1832, (Sumter Co, AL "by Cainon Pistole, JP"), Mrs. Rebecca (Juzan) Bond, d/o Charles Juzan and widow of John Bond; (Rebecca D. Juzan m.1. John Bond, 25 Feb 1825, Marengo Co, AL, Marr. Book A, p.83; Alexander Brashears was security. On 14 Oct 1833, George W. Walker was appointed guardian of Thomas, James L., and Louisa Bond.)

[v5]526. [9]1. Thomas J. Bond, step-son to George Walker

[v5]527. [9]2. James L. Bond, step-son of George Walker

[v5]528. [9]3. Louisa Bond, step-dau of George Walker

v5529.   94. William Walker,

v5530.   86. Benjamin Walker, m. Sybel Juzan, d/o Charles Juzan

v5531.   87. Martha Walker, m. 1. 20 March 1824, William LeFlore, s/o Louis LeFlore and Rebecca Cravatt, grand-niece of Apuckshunnubbee (Marengo Co, AL Marr; Cornelius H. Vawter, Security)

v5532.   88. Sarah Walker, m. 19 Sept 1820, J.H. Miller (Marengo Co, AL; Alex McGrew, bondsman)

v5533.   91. Robert Miller,

v5534.   92. Martha Miller, m. 17 Dec 1838, **Alexander M. Brashears Jr** (v5538), s/o Alexander M. Brashears Sr, s/o Samuel Brashears Sr and Rachel Durant.

v5535.   89. Henrietta Walker,

v5536.   810. Sophia Walker, m. c1830, Dennis Payne, s/o William and Sara Payne, who settled near Demopolis about 1819. Dennis's sister, Sarah Jane Payne, m. William Winn, and was mother of Emiline Jane Winn, third wife of Alexander Brashears Sr.

v5537.   811. David Walker Jr, b. c1821

(Marengo Co, AL, Deeds, Book A, p.3098).

Know all men by these presents that we, Rachel Brasheers, Alexander Brashears, and Samuel Brashears Junior, all of Marengo Co, except Samuel Brashears Jr, who resides in Monroe Co of said state.

We are each of us held and firmly bound to each other for the just and full sum of fifteen hundred dollars each, good and lawful money of said state for the payment of which sum we jointly and firmly bind ourselves, each of our heirs, executors, administrators, and assigns unto each of the above mentioned Rachel Brasheirs, Alexander Brashiers, and Samuel Brasheirs, junior, their heirs, executors, administrators and assigns.

In witness whereof we have set our hands and offered our seals this eleventh day of December, A.D. 1826.

Conditions of the above obligation are that we, the above mentioned Rachel, Alexander, and Samuel Brasheirs are in possession of nine negroes, slaves for life, (viz) Dick, aged about seventy five years, Becky, his wife, aged about fifty five years, Henry, aged about thirty eight years, Ned aged about thirty four years, Will, aged about thirty, Moses, aged about thirteen years,

Dinah, aged about thirteen years, and Anthony, aged about nine years. The above named slaves are the children of the two first named, Dick and Beck, except the ones last named Moses, Dinah, and Anthony, which are the grandchildren of Dick and Beck, which negroes above named were deeded to above Alexander Brashears and Samuel Brashears by our father Samuel Brashears, senior, and we, Alexander and Samuel admit our mother, Racheal Brasheirs to enjoy and possess one third of said negroes, (viz) Beck, Mary, Dinah and Anthony ___xx___ our mother's for her natural life, after which ___xx___ they are to descend to her younger children and the heirs of their body, (viz): the heirs of Sarah [Walker] Miller, deceased, viz, Robert and Martha Miller; Martha [Walker] LeFlore; George Walker; David Walker; Benjamin Walker, Sophia Walker; Henrietta Walker— except the old woman, Beck. At the death of our mother, she is to be free.

The last four slaves, Rachael Brasheirs has at this time in her possession, and Alexander Brasheirs has three of the above named slaves, viz, Dick, Henry, and Moses, and Samuel Brasheirs, Junior, has two of the above named slaves, viz, Ned and Will.

Now, be it well understood that each person, vzt, Rachael, Alexander and Samuel are peaceably to hold, enjoy and inherit the above named slaves respectively as they are named in the possession of each person forever and their heirs and assigns. Now, I Rachel Brasheirs do warrant and defend unto Alexander and Samuel Brasheirs the five negroes they have in possession as they are named in possession of each of them, all my right, title, interest, and claim unto them and their heirs and assigns for ever from me or my heirs, and I, Alexander do warrant and defend the right, title, and interest that I or my heirs could have to Ned and Will, unto Samuel Brasheirs and his heirs forever, and I, Samuel Brasheirs junior, do forever warrant and defend unto Alexander Brasheirs and his heirs and assigns, the above named Dick, Henry and Moses of the above named.

Rachael, Alexander, and Samuel shall respectively hold and peaceably enjoy the above named slaves from each other and the heirs and assigns of each other, forever, then the above obligation to be void. Otherwise to remain in full force and effect. In testimony whereof, we and each of us have set our hands and affixed our seal on the date and day above written.

/Signed 11 December 1826, by/
                Rachel [her mark] Brashears (seal)
                Alexander Brashears (seal)
                Samuel Brashears (seal)
Attest: /s/ C___xx___ W. Vautor; Wm. McGrew

This day came before me, John Gilmore, one of the Justices of the Peace for said County, C_____ W. Vauter and William McGrew and made oath that Rachel Brasheirs, Alexander Brasheirs and Samuel Brasheirs assigned the above instrument of writing. Sworn to this twelfth day of December, 1826,
    /s/ John Gilmore, J.P.
Recorded 12 Dec 1826,
(Marengo Co, AL, Deeds, Book A, p.3098).
Thanks to Dorothy Sims of Mesquite, TX, for the copy.

Mrs. Pauline Gandrud's typed work: "Records of Marengo Co, AL" contains a summarized and defective copy of this deed, which would lead one to believe that Alexander and Samuel Brashears are relinquishing the slaves to their mother and her younger children. But the way I read the deed, the three siblings, Rachel, Alexander, and Samuel Brashears are only allowing their mother (and her younger children) to have the slaves during their mother's life. And since the Rachel of the deed gave the others warranties, took four of the slaves in the long run, and signed the deed (Rachel, the mother, as recipient of property, would NOT have signed), I am concluding that Rachel of the deed was, in fact, a sister to Alexander and Samuel Brashears.

In 1831, Sophia and David Walker are listed as step-children in the household of Rachel's fourth husband, Zadock Brashears Sr, in Sumter Co, AL, with Alexander Brashears and Allen Stanton as witnesses (American State Papers, Indian Affairs).

Rachel (Durant) Brashear received land in Sec. 3, T16 R1W, Sumter Co, AL, under the terms of the Treaty of Dancing Rabbit Creek, 1830. This is two miles south and one mile west of Jesse and Delilah (Juzan) Brashears' farm, and five miles south and one mile east of her son, Alexander Brashears. (See map of "The Brashear Settlement on Suk-En-Atcha Creek."

On 24 Jan 1837, Rachel [Durant] Brashears advertised in *The Voice of Sumter* that she was offering for sale the remainder of her Reserve, adjoining Black Bluff. (*Marriage, Death and Legal Notices from Early Alabama Newspapers, 1819-1893*, compiled by Pauline Jones Gandrud, p.25). This is the land in Sec 3, T16N, R1W, which was her allotment under Article 14 of the Treaty of Dancing Rabbit Creek, 27 Sept 1830.

ALEXANDER BRASHEARS' Families by His Four Wives

[v5]**521.** [8]1. *****Alexander M. (?McGillivray) Brashears**, b. c1789 (61 in 1850 Census, Mobile Co, AL, #491-491, b. "Florida" i.e. Spanish West Florida, possibly Pensacola), d. 6 April 1868, in Mobile Co, AL, probably the first child of Samuel Brashear Sr and Rachel Durant, and surely named for Rachel's illustrious uncle, Alexander McGillivray, Principal Chief of the Creeks. Alexander Brashears' middle name may have been McGillivray.

As a youth, Alexander is said to have received some education at the school established in 1799 by John Pierce at the Boat Yard, ?Pensacola. Loretta Coppick says he took an active part in Creek affairs as a young man, and was called "El Cat" by the Spanish authorities.

On 29 May 1815, following the Creek War, Alexander Brashears (and/or his mother, Rachel) wrote a letter to President James Madison, describing the plight of the Upper Creek people and asking for redress. The letter was mailed from Fisher's Post Office, Mississippi Territory, and several of Alexander's relatives co-signed the letter with their mark. (See text above.)

Some time after the writing of this letter in 1815 and before 1818, Alexander moved to the Choctaw Brashears settlement on Suk-en-Atcha Creek, in Sumter Co, AL, where he rapidly became the care-giver and "leader," probably because he could read and write and was fluent in English, Creek, and Choctaw.

Alexander Brashears married four times:

m.1. _____, possibly an Indian woman, possibly killed at Fort Mims in Aug 1813; and had at least two children;

m.2. ?c1815-18, **Anne (Brashears) Lyles** ([v5]834), his cousin, d/o Zadock Brashears Sr and Susannah Vaughn. In 1818,

Alexander Brashears and Anne Brashears, his wife, both of Pearl River in the Choctaw Nation, sold 400 a. of land on Redwood Creek to Thomas Carney of Feliciana Parish, land that had been given to Anne Lyles by her father, Zadock Brashears, on 7 June 1812, as her dotal portion (Notorial Records, Feliciana Parish, Book A, p.208). Anne apparently d. c1825, because Alexander Brashears,

m.3. 15 July 1826 **Emiline Jane Winn**, (Marengo Co, AL, "by John Gilmore, JP", Marengo Co, AL, Bk A, p.118; also in Sumter Marriage Book 2, p.36), d/o William Winn and Sarah Jane Payne. Emiline b. c1806-11, Kershaw Dist, SC, d. 10 Jan 1841 in Alabama; they had five children;

m.4. 24 Sept 1843 **Bromley Cravey**, (Sumter Co, AL Marr Book 1, p.148, "by Joseph Arrington; Augustus Buckholtz, bondsman"). Bromley, b. c1819, (31 in 1850 Census of Mobile Co, AL), d/o Hugh Cravey and Kessey Norsworthy.

Alexander and his family were beneficiaries under Clause 14 of the Treaty of Dancing Rabbit Creek, 1830; he received 640 acres in T17N, R1W, as a resident who intended to remain more than five years and become a U.S. citizen. He also received nine quarter sections for his Indian children. (He had nine children, three of them over ten in 1830. Children over 10 were to receive a half-section; children under 10, a quarter section.) The land is ½ of section 3, all of section 4, ¾ of section 5, two odd-shaped portions of sec 8, all of Sec 9, ¼ of sec 10, and ½ of Sec 16—see Map No. 1.

Loretta Coppick, late descendant of Jesse Brashears, s/o Zadock Brashears and Susannah Vaughn, reported that, in 1848, Sarah Ann (Brashears) Jones, Sophia (Brashears) Jones, and Rachel (Brashears) Daniels sold land in Sections 4, 9 and 10, T17N, R1W, Sumter Co, AL, for $1200 to James H. Bowman of Hinds Co, Mississippi. (Sumter Co, AL, Deeds, Bk K, p.445.) These plots were some of Alexander's land received for himself and his children under terms of the Treaty of Dancing Rabbit Creek.

In a special Choctaw Census of 1831 (to determine beneficiaries of Articles 14 and 19, Treaty of Dancing Rabbit Creek), Alexander Brashears was farming 30 acres on Suk-en-Atcha Creek, had ten in his family, including 2 males over 16 and 5 children of both sexes under 10.

In another 1831 list of Choctaws who wished to remain in Alabama and become citizens, taken at St. Stephens Trading Post, Alexander Brashears has 3 children under 10 and 2 children over 10 (this was later proven to be an error by the incompetent agent, Col. William Ward, who messed up quite a few Choctaws). Alexander is listed as "Indian half breed." In another place, he is listed as "Half-breed Creek and Half-breed Choctaw."

In the 1840, Sumter Co, AL, census, Alexander Brashers is 40-50 yrs old, wife 20-30 (b. 1810-20), and he has five sons and four daughters (2111001-11201). Application for Enrollment, Choctaw Nation, Case 5187, says he was father of Rachel, Alexander, Harriet, Letta, and Sophia Brashears, according to *Who Was Who Among the Southern Indians*, by Don Martini, p.58.

Probable children of Alexander Brashears and his 1st wife:

[v5]538. [9]1. **Alexander M. Brashears Jr**, b. bef 1815 (over 16 in 1831 Choctaw Census; 20-30 in 1840 and next door to Alexander in Sumter Co, AL) with wife and one daughter (00001-10001). Alexander M. Brashears m.1. 17 Dec 1838, *Martha Miller* ([v5]534), (Marengo Co, AL, Marr. Book 2, p.36; James Lear, bondsman). Martha was a granddaughter of Rachel (Durant) Brashears/ Walker/ Brashears; m.2. 14 Jan 1846, *Rachel W. Harmon*, (Mobile Marr, Book 7, p.736b); m.3. *Elizabeth Rice*, per Loretta Coppick.

Alexander M. Brashears one man, one woman, and one child are on the Roll of Choctaw emigrants of Itoonla's party of 6, landed at Fort Coffee, Indian Territory, on the 12th of Feb. 1847. (ref: *Choctaw Emigration Records*, Vol. 1 & 2 1831-1856, by Olsen; thanks to Pat "Albert Brigance" <brigancepublishing @msn.com> for the data.)

In 1855, Alexander was living in Skullyville Co, I.T., with wife, Rachel, and daughters Almira, Allis, Marian, and Jennett.

Family of Alexander M. Brashears Jr and Martha Miller:

[v5]539. [10]1. **Almira Brashears**, b. c1835-40, indicated by 1840 census

Family of Alexander M Brashears Jr and Rachel W. Harmon:

[v5]540. [10]2. **Allis (?Alice) Brashears**,

^{v5}541.   ¹⁰3. **Marian Brashears**,

^{v5}542.   ¹⁰4. **Jennett Brashears**,

^{v5}543. ⁹2. **William Brazier**, b. bef 1815 (over 16 in 1831 Choctaw Census; 20-30 in 1840 Sumter Co, AL (00001-0001), or Samuel E. Brasher, according to Dr. Larkin E. Wilson, El Dorado, AR; m. *Laura Ann* _____, b. c1820-25 (15-20 in 1840).

Children of Alexander Brashears Sr and Anne Brashears:

^{v5}544. ⁹3. **Harriet Brashears**, b. 1820 or before (over ten on 27 Sept 1830), indicated by census and Choctaw Citizenship case #5187; m.1. 12 Sept 1832, *William Juzan*, "by Canan Pistole, JP, Bond: Canan Pistole (Sumter Co, AL, Marriages, Bk 1, p.265); m.?2. *Joseph Sileskie*, (per Dr. Larkin Wilson, of El Dorado, AR).

^{v5}545. ⁹4. **Letty A.J. Brashears**, b. 1821 (under 10 in 1830; 18+ in 1839; 10-20 in 1840, Sumter Co, AL); m. 11 Sept 1839, *Augustus Buckholtz* (^{v5}961), (Sumter Marriage Book 1, p.112; "by Robt. Goodwyn, JP"). Augustus Buckholtz certified that Alexander Brashears Sr's daughter, Letty A.J., was over 18. Augustus Buckholtz, s/o Elizabeth "Betsy" (Brashears) Buckholtz, was b. c1814, d. c1840-45. There were three girls in their household in 1840: 1 under 5; 1 5-10; and 1 10-15; all of them cannot be Letty's children... nor Augustus's. (Letty m.2. *Ansley Gibbon*, says Dr. Larkin Wilson.)

^{v5}546. ⁹5. ***Sophia Brashears, II**, b. c1820-25; m.1. 7 June 1841, in Marengo Co, AL, *John L. Jones*. Sophia and John Jones moved to Indian Territory, where John died and Sophia married three more times: m.2. *Amos Goins*; m.3. *Sampson Moncrief*, (widower of her aunt, Sophia (Brashears) Moncrief); m.4. _____ *Baker*. Sophia sold her allotment on Suk-en-Atcha Creek in 1848. We call her Sophia, II, to distinguish her from her aunt of exactly the same name.

^{v5}547. ⁹6. **Rachel Brashears**, b. c1820-25; m. 12 Jan 1846, in Mobile Co, AL, *Asa M. Daniels*, (Rachel sold her allotment on Suk-en-Atcha Creek in 1848, and reportedly moved to Indian Territory.)

^{v5}548. ^{9}7. ***Sarah Ann Brashears**, b. 21 Jan 1825 (per descendants; under 10 on 27 Sept 1830), d. 8 June 1890, Baxter Springs, KS; m. 7 Feb 1843, in Marengo Co, AL (p.142), *James F. Jones*, b. c1817, Virginia, d. c1865, Marengo, AL, s/o John Jones and Laura Adams. Sarah Ann and James Jones moved to AR; she sold her allotment on Suk-en-Atcha Creek in 1848.

Family of Alexander Brashears Sr and Emily Jane Winn: (see IGI extracted record F507346/0038 and #1760721; also FHL film 5003708/4)

^{v5}549. ^{9}8. ***Henrietta Jane "Hennie" Brashears**, b. 12 May 1827, Sumter Co, AL, d. 24 Dec 1890, Mobile Co, AL; m. 21 Oct 1844, *John Joseph Jeremiah Boykin*, b. c1817-18, AL

^{v5}550. ^{9}9. ***Dennis Payne Brashears**, b. 18 Oct 1829, Sumter Co, AL, d. 5 March 1863, Factory Bottom Hospital No. 2, Albermarle Co, VA. See his will below; he mentions his brother, William Payne Brashears, his sister, Emaline Jane Smith, his father, Alexander, and stepmother, "Brambly."

^{v5}551. ^{9}10. **William Payne Brashears**, b. 11 Feb 1831, Sumter Co, AL ("Clerk," 28 and living alone, #397, in 1860 Census of Mobile City, AL); was prominent in Mobile in politics and business; never married.

^{v5}552. ^{9}11. ***Emiline Jane Brashears**, b. 1 June 1833, Sumter Co, AL, d. 1 June 1915; m. 24 Dec 1850, at Mobile, AL, *Ira Byrd Smith*, b. 16 Dec 1827, Greene Co, MS, d. 22 Feb 1884, Mobile Co, AL. He was a brother of Nathaniel John Smith, who married Louisa Jane Brashears.

^{v5}553. ^{9}12. ***Louisa Jane Brashears**, b. 26 Dec 1835, Sumter Co, AL, d. 26 Jan 1899, Washington Co, AL; m. 24 Jan 1850, Mobile Co, AL, *Nathaniel John Smith*, b. 13 Jan 1822, Mt Vernon, Mobile Co, AL, d. 8 Aug 1914, Baxterville, Lamar Co, TX. He was a brother of Ira Byrd Smith, who married Emiline Jane Brashears.

^{v5}554. ^{9}13. son, b. 1835-40, per 1840 census [d. young? not in 1850 census]

^{v5}555. ^{9}14. son, b. 1835-40, per 1840 census [d. young? not in 1850 census]

Child of Alexander Brashears Sr and Bromly Cravey:

[v]5556. [9]15. **Retuim C. Brashears**, (male; name in 1850 census looks like "Retares"; middle initial may stand for "Cravey") b. c1845 (5 in 1850, Northern Dist, Mobile Co, AL, fam #491; listed as "C.C. Brashears," 14, in 1860 census, Northern Dist, Mobile Co, AL, fam #95; he signed his marriage license as R.C. Brashears); m. 28 Nov 1866 in Mobile Co, AL, *Mary E. Buford*, b. c1848 (age 18 at marriage; "by P. Imsand, S.J., Catholic Priest"; thanks to Josephine Turner Bryant for a Xerox copy and other information). Simeon E. Buford, probably Mary's father, also signed the marriage bond.

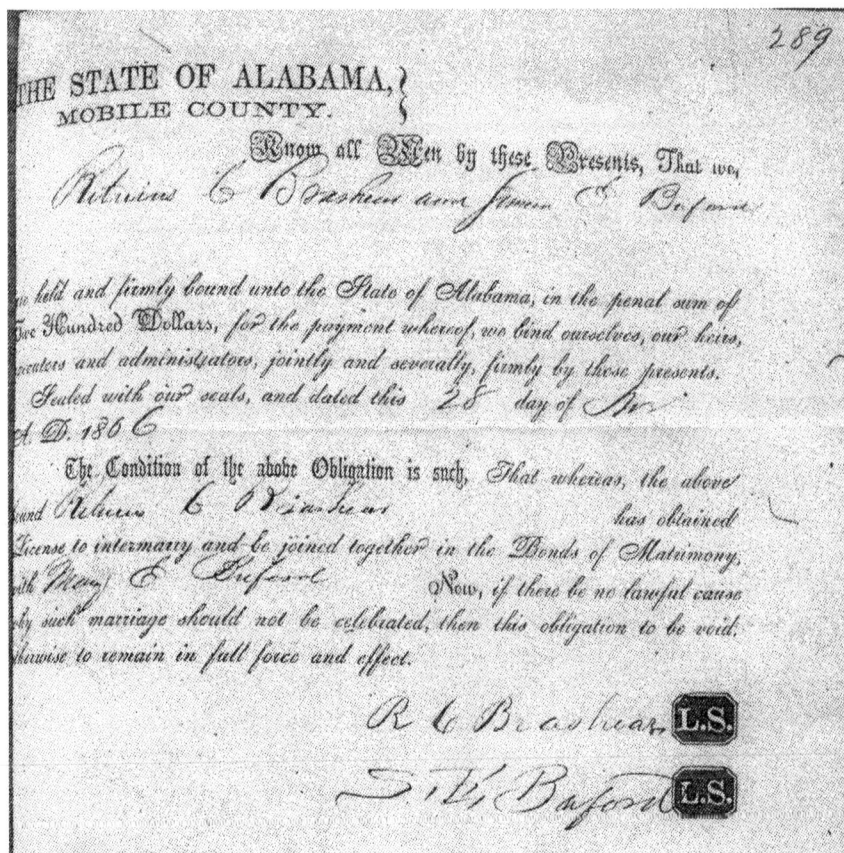

Another name supplied by Dr. Larkin E. Wilson, of El Dorado, AR, but I don't know where to put him:

v5557. x. **Derrill Brashears**, (per Dr. Larkin E. Wilson) b. 1820-25, indicated by census;

I suspect Dr. Wilson is confusing families, and mistaking Derrell Payne for Derrill Brashears:

William Payne and wife Sara moved to Marengo County near Demopolis in 1819. Their children were:

* Derrell Payne, who never married
* Dennis Payne, who married Sophia Walker (v5536), d/o David Walker and Rachel Durant
* Sara Jane Payne, who m. William Winn and was mother of
* Emiline Jane Winn,(who married Alexander Brashears (v5521), and
* Sara Winn

In 1850 Census, Mobile Co, AL, #491-491, p.475:

Alexander Brashears,	61, b. 1789, "Florida" (i.e. "Spanish West Florida")	
Bramby	31, b. AL, c1819	
Dennis	17, b. AL (should be 21, b. 1829)	
Emeline	17, b. AL	
Retares (m)	5, b. AL	
Howard Hale	35, b. AL, Teacher	

Sophia Brashears, II, and John L. Jones

v5546. 95. **Sophia Brashears, II**, (d/o Alexander Brashears and Anne Brashears), b. ?1820-25; m.1. 7 June 1841, in Marengo Co, AL, *John L. Jones*, Bond: Thomas McCormick (Alabama Records, Marriage Records of Marengo Co, AL, by Pauline Jones Gandrud. (Sophia sold her allotment on Suk-en-Atcha Creek in 1848; she had moved earlier to Indian Territory.) Sophia died at age 69 [c1890-95], according to her youngest son, Joseph Moncrief, who was interviewed on August 20, 1937, by Jasper N. Mead for the *Indian-Pioneer History Project of Oklahoma*. Joseph identified his father as Sampson Moncrief and his mother as Sophia Breshears.

Do not confuse this Sophia Brashears with the first Sophia Brashears (v5839), b. c1802, (d/o Zadock Brashears and Susannah Vaughn), who was the first wife of Sampson Moncrief and aunt of this second Sophia Brashears; the first Sophia Brashears was about 25 years older than the second one.

Sophia m.2. **Amos Goins**. In the application of Joseph Moncrief for enrollment as a Choctaw, Nancy A. Hill, d/o Mary Ann (Moncrief) McCarty, testified that Sophia "was a widow by the name of Goins when she married Sampson Moncrief." Annie (Goins) Davis testified that Joseph Moncrief was her half brother and that her father was Amos Goins and her mother was Sophia Goins.

Sophia m.3. c1854-55, at the home of Mary Ann (Moncrief) McCarty, near Skullyville, I.T., **Sampson Moncrief**, b. 1793, d. 1856-7, widower of the first Sophia Brashears and father of Mary Ann (Moncrief) McCarty. This second Sophia (Brashears) Moncrief is #296 on the 1855 census of Choctaws with seven children: Charles Jones, Benjamin Jones, Alexander Jones, Frances Jones, Anne Goins, Mary Goins, and Joseph Moncrief.

Sophia m.4. probably c1857, _____ **Baker**, non-citizen, deceased before 1896 (data from Ann Gray Victery, Ninnekah, Oklahoma <redknight05@hotmail.com>). Their daughter, Ellen Baker, ¼ blood, Choctaw Roll #159, b. c1858 (44 in 1902); m.1. _____ Wilkens; m.2. John Calvin Gray, non-citizen. Sarah Ann (Moncrief) Harlan (v51394) testified that Sophia Brashears had married a Baker, though she probably had the order of Sophia's four marriages wrong.

Family of Sophia Brashears, II, and John L. Jones:
v5558. 101. Charles Jones, b. c?1842 (oldest of seven children on 1855 Choctaw Census)
v5559. 102. Benjamin Franklin Jones, b. c?1843-44, d. 13 Sept 1876, McAlester, I.T.; m. _____. Benjamin Jones was a lighthorseman (Law Officer) for the Choctaw Tribe. He was shot and killed in North McAlester, 13 Sept 1876, bur North McAlester Cem.
v5560. 103. *Alexander Jones, b. 1845, Skullyville, I.T., d. c1875; m. Paralee (Gardenhire) Guy, b. c1847, Crawford Co, AR, d. before 1902, d/o William H. Gardenhire, of TN, and Elizabeth Mary O'Neal.
v5561. 104. *Frances Jones, b. 4 May 1848, Skullyville, I.T., (Choctaw Roll #432), d. 27 May 1932; m.1. William J. Leslie; m.2. Wyley Johnson,
Family of Sophia Brashears, II, and Amos Goins:
v5562. 105. Anne Goins, m. _____ Davis. Annie Davis gave testimony in the application for enrollment as a

Choctaw of her half-brother, Joseph Moncrief.

[v5]563. [10]6. Mary Goins, n.f.i.

Family of Sophia Brashears, II, and Sampson Moncrief:

[v5]564. [10]7. Joseph Moncrief, b. 22 Aug 1854, at Oak Lodge near Skullyville, I.T. (NOTE: *he* thought he was born 1857, but that is probably an erroneous reading of 1854—he was on the 1855 census of Choctaws); m. 12 Aug 1888, Lulu Self, b. 1878 (?1858), d/o Pleasant and Arta Self. Joseph was interviewed 20 Aug 1937 by Jasper N. Mead for the *Indian-Pioneer History Project of Oklahoma*. He was in Sophia's household on the 1855 Census of Choctaws, taken Nov/Dec 1856. Note that all of the children of Sampson Moncrief and the first Sophia Brashears are also Joseph's half-siblings.

Family of Sophia Brashears, II, and _____ Baker:

[v5]565. [10]9. Ellen Toyl (or Toyle/Toil) Baker, ¼ blood, Choctaw Census Card #159, b. c1858 (age 44 as of 25 Sep 1902) or b. June 1861 (per 1900 Census, Grady Co, OK), d. 1922, bur Ninnekah, Grady Co, OK; m.1. _____ Wilkens (no known ch; widowed by 1883); m.2. 18 April 1883, according the J.C. Gray's testimony in citizenship hearing;

Figure 13: John Calvin Gray and Ellen T. Baker

m. 28 Dec 1885, Pickens Co, Chickasaw Nation, I.T., John Calvin Gray, non-citizen (Marr Book, p.87, "by Willis Dickinson, County Judge"; had been married 17 years in 1900 census). John Calvin Gray was b. 18 Oct 1851, Madison Co, AR, d. 15 May 1905, Grady Co, OK, bur Rush Spring Cem, s/o Henry C. Gray of TN and Mary Ann Fritts of AR. (data from Ann Gray Victery, Ninnekah, Oklahoma <redknight05@ hotmail.com>. 1900 Census says Ellen had 9 children, 6 living; only 8 are accounted for. Choctaw

Census Card #159 gives 6 children, all children of John C. Gray. John C. Gray was admitted as an intermarried citizen, then stricken from the rolls, then re-admitted in 1905, after his death.

v⁵566.   ¹¹1. Ella T. Gray, Choctaw Roll #15346, b. 24 Jan 1884, Grady Co, I.T. (19 as of 25 Sep 1902), d. 29 April 1907, Grady Co, OK; m. 17 Aug 1904, Richard Joseph Gray (no relation, though the families knew each other), b. 12 Jan 1882, Dallas Co, TX, d. 19 June 1921, Grady Co, OK.

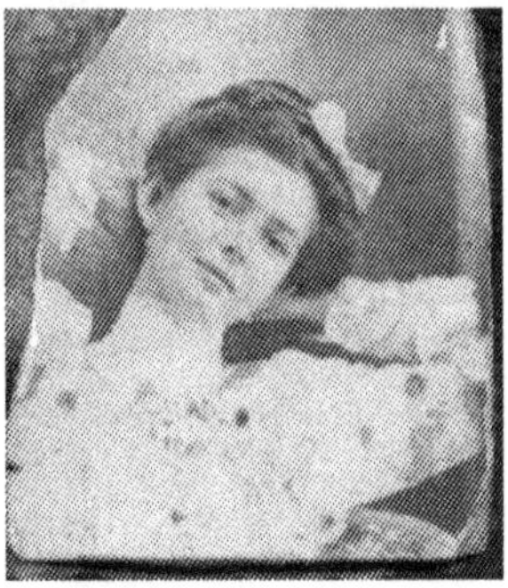

Figure 14: Ella T. Gray

v⁵567.   ¹²1. Luther Emery Gray, b. 20 July1905, Grady Co, I.T., d. 28 Jan1994, Chickasha, OK, bur Rose Hill Cemetery, Chickasha.

v⁵568.   ¹²2. Leonard Joseph Gray , b. 14 April 1907, Grady County, OK, d. 14 Nov 1990, Grady Co, OK, bur Rose Hill Cemetery, Chickasha, OK

v⁵569.   ¹¹2. Laura B. Gray, Choctaw Roll #15347, b. 16 June 1885, I.T. (17 as of 25 Sep 1902), d. 24 Oct 1969, Los Angeles, CA; m.1. 30 Nov 1902, Rufus L. Allen; m.2. 23 May 1906, Clabe Weaver; m.3. Virgil Baccus "Jack" Young, b. 11 Sep 1902, AR, d. 27 Aug 1984, Los Angeles, CA

v⁵570.   ¹¹3. Pearl Gray, Choctaw Roll #15348, b. c1886 (13 as of 25 Sep 1902); m. 8 June 1905, Richard A. Thomas

v⁵571.   ¹¹4. James Gray, b. 7 July 1887, d. 25 June 1893, bur Rush Springs Cem (dates from tombstone)

v⁵572.   ¹¹5. John Gray, b. 25 Sep 1892, d. 29 Aug 1895, bur Rush Springs Cem (dates from tombstone)

v⁵573.   ¹¹6. Elmer Gray, Choctaw Roll #15349, b. 19 Aug 1895 (8 as of 25 Sep 1902), d. mid-1960s, CA

v⁵574.   ¹¹7. Clifford Gray, Choctaw Roll #15350, b. 1 Feb 1897, Rush Springs, I.T. (6 as of 25 Sep 1902), d. 22 Aug 1973, Bakersfield, CA; m. Hattie Emeline Johnson Ireton, Roll #831, b. 26 Sep 1901, I.T., d.

[v5]575.   [11]8. Charles Edward Gray, Choctaw Roll #15351, b. 3
May 1899 (3 as of 25 Sep 1902), d. 24 April 1962,
Kings Co, CA.

In his application for enrollment as a Choctaw, Joseph
Moncrief testified that he was forty-nine, born in 1857 and his
post office address was Savanna, I.T. He was so young when his
father died that he did not remember him. He knew nothing of
his ancestors. He was born near Skullyville at Oak Lodge. He
was about twelve when his half brother, Charles Jones, took
him to GA. He lived in GA, TN, and AL and returned to the
Choctaw Nation in 1896 or 98. He was married 12 Aug 1888.

Sarah Ann (Moncrief) Harlan ([v5]1394) testified that the family
was from the old Choctaw Nation in MS and AL. They were from
Sumter County, AL— Belmont and Demopolis. She, Sarah Ann,
was born in Sumter Co, AL. Her mother was Sampson's first
wife, Sophia Brashears. Joseph's mother was the niece of
Sarah's mother. The grandmother of Joseph was Annie
Brashears and his grandfather, maternal grandfather, was Alex
Brashears, and he possessed Choctaw and Creek blood.

Joe Gardner testified that he knew Joseph for the past 10
years and that he also knew his half brothers, Charles Jones
and Ben Jones. He had often heard them say that Charles
Jones, shortly after the civil war, had taken Joseph to the State
of Georgia and had left him there. He stated he also knew
Joseph's brother, George Moncrief, who lived and died near
Canadian in the Choctaw Nation.

Nancy A. Hill testified that she was sixty years of age and her
post office address was Savanna, I.T. She stated Joseph was her
uncle, her mother's half brother. Her mother was Mary Ann
Moncrief McCarty. She stated Sophia Brashears Moncrief was
the mother of Joseph and that she was a widow by the name of
Goins when she married Sampson. Nancy was born 1846 in
Sumter Co, AL— post office, Demopolis. They moved to
Skullyville Co. on the Arkansas line when she was three. Her
father was Robert McCarty. She remembered her grandfather,
Sampson Moncrief, and he had lived with them when he first
arrived in Skullyville. Sophia, II, lived three or four miles from
their house. Sophia and Sampson were married in the home of
the McCarty's. She believes it was by an Indian preacher by the

name of Folsom. Nancy's mother was still alive at the time of this testimony by Nancy, but was unable to attend.

Family of Alexander Jones (v5560) and Paralee Gardenhire, (Alexander Jones, s/o Sophia Brashears, II and John L. Jones):

v5576. [11]1. Charles Jefferson Jones, b. 1867 (Choctaw Roll #449), d. 1912, bur Lindsey, OK; m.1. Lizzy Young (no ch); m.2. Ellie Reeves (2 daus); m.3. Jo Ella Lawson

v5577. [12]1. Veda Jones (Choctaw Roll #450)

v5578. [12]2. Velda May Jones (Choctaw Roll #451)

v5579. [12]3. Charles Alexander Jones, b. 24 Jan 1905 (Choctaw Roll #509), d. 25 May 1957, Mercy Hosp, San Diego, CA; m. 23 Aug 1930, at Sayre, OK, Linnie Marie Fry, b. 8 Oct 1914, Gowen, OK, d. 4 April 2000. (Data from James A. Jones, P.O.Box 48, Union City, OK 73090-0048)

v5580. [13]1. John Paul Jones, b. 29 May 1931, Carter, OK

v5581. [13]2. James Arthur Jones, b. 3 March 1933, Sayre, OK; m. 1 Aug 1952, at Van Buren, AR, Helen Virginia Green, b. 1 Aug 1934, Wister, OK

v5582. [14]1. Gail Yvonne Jones, b. 13 Sept 1954, Poteau, OK; m.1. Barry Shroeder, s/o Norman and Alma Schroder; m.2. Steve Peacher, s/o Dr. K.L. and Joann Peacher. Ch: Amanda Gail Shroeder (m. Brad Mason; ch: Austin and Dalton Mason); and Brandon Barry Shroeder (m. Christy Meyer; ch: Zak Campbell and Alexander Jones)

v5583. [14]2. Belinda Louellen Jones, b. 23 Dec 1957, Indio, CA; m.1. Billy Hughey, s/o Harold and Bonnie Hughey; m.2. Curt Stanley, s/o LeRoy and Jean Stanley. Ch: Jordan (m. Jayme Merritt; ch: Cale Hughey) and Brooklyn Hughey (m. Gorton).

v5584. [14]3. James Shippey Jones, b. 2 July 1964, El Reno, OK; m. Tonja Jones, d/o Allen and Doris Jones. Ch: Chelsea; Jameson Levi; Joshua Seth; and Sierra Noel Jones

v5585. [13]3. Allie Lee Jones, b. 28 April 1935, Carter, OK

v5586. [13]4. Tom Frank Jones, b. 16 Oct 1936, Sayre, OK

v5587.   135. Robert Bruce Jones, b. 28 March 1939, Carter, OK

v5588.   136. Deanna Carroll Jones, b. 25 March 1941, Sayre, OK

v5589.   112. Alexander Jones Jr, b. Sept 1869 (Choctaw Roll #14983), d. 1918, per stone in Blue Ridge Cem, near Calvin, Hughes Co, OK; m. Mattie L. Smith, (Intermarried Citizen #535), b. 15 March 1871, d. 10 Nov 1941, d/o Jim Smith, of AL, and his wife, Lou Smith, of IN. Mattie had been married previously to white men named _____ White and _____ Waters. Information from posting on www.choctawnation.com by g.g.grandson, Robert R. "Bob" Curlee.

v5590.   111. Vergia "Virgie" Ellen Jones, Choctaw Roll #14984, b. 11 Feb 1902, Celestine, Choctaw Nation, I.T.; m. c1914, Bert Curlee, b. 22 May 1895, Kiowa, Choctaw Nation, I.T., s/o Willis Curlee and Matilda Catherine Cook. (In July 1942, Virgie moved with her son Herschel's family to California; she is buried in Valhalla Cem, Burbank, CA)

v5591.   121. Herschel Walton Curlee, b. 9 Feb 1915 (two days before Virgie's 13th birthday!), Calvin, Hughes Co, OK, d. 13 Aug 1990, bur Greenlawn Cem, Bakersfield, CA; m.1. 1937, in Ada, OK, Nancy Orlena Walker, b. 5 Sept 1918, Lawrence, Pontotoc Co, OK, d. Aug 1972, d/o Robert Roy Walker and Martha "Maddie" Jane Davis; m.2. Violet Meeks Hedge. Herschel was an ordained minister of Pentecostal Holiness Church and pastored a number or churches in OK and CA. He and Orlena had three ch:

v5592.   131. Donald Floyd Curlee, b. 26 Oct 1938, OK

v5593.   132. Barbara Helen Curlee, b. 26 March 1940, OK

v5594.   133. Robert Roy Curlee, b. 13 Oct 1942, San Francisco, CA, who has been accepted as a member of the Choctaw Nation in OK.

v5595.   122. Geneva Curlee,

v5596.   123. Wilma Curlee, died in infancy

v5597.   124. Floyd Curlee, died by drowning at age six
v5598.   125. Virginia Curlee,
v5599.   122. Fred Jones, b. 1911

Figure 15: Frances Jones

v5561. 104. Frances Jones, (d/o Sophia Brashear, II, and John L. Jones), b. 4 May 1848, Skullyville, I.T., (Choctaw Roll #432), d. 27 May 1932, Lebanon, Marshall Co, OK, at the home of her daughter, Laura Lynn, bur Oakland Cem, Madill, OK; m.1. William J. Leslie; m.2. Wyley Johnson, b. 30 June 1820, in MS, d. 16 Feb 1890, Lone Grove, Carter Co, OK (Ind. Terr.) (g-grandfather of Olive Alexander, 638 Newberry Dr, Richardson, TX. 75080, who sent data). Frances, her children and grandchildren were on the final Choctaw Rolls. In 1868, while Frances was pregnant with her first child, William J. Leslie went on a cattle drive to Kansas. She received a letter from him just after the drive had crossed the Canadian River. After that, she never heard from him again. She never knew what happened to him.

Family of Frances Jones and William J. Leslie/ Wyley Johnson:
v5600. 111. William Joseph Leslie Jr, (Choctaw Roll #436), b. Aug 1868, I.T.; m. Mary Florence Smith, d/o C. Smith and Martha J. _____. In W.J. Leslie's household in 1900 in Ardmore, OK, are Frances Johnson, 52, mother, and M.J. Smith, mother-in-law, 64.

Figure 16: Wyley Johnson

v5601.   121. Clifford Lushie Leslie, (fem; Choctaw Roll #437), b. May 1889
v5602.   122. Robert E. Leslie, (Choctaw Roll #438), b. May 1893
v5603.   123. Dewey Leslie, (Choctaw Roll #439), b. 1898, d. 17 June 1899
v5604.   124. Beatrice Leslie, (Choctaw Roll #440), b. 1898

^{v5}605. ^{11}2. Ida Belle Johnson, (Choctaw Roll #396; Olive's grandmother), b. 19 Aug 1870, Whitebead, Garvin Co, I.T., d. 23 Nov 1944, Madill, Marshall Co, OK; m. 16 Oct 1884, in Gainesville, Cooke Co, TX, Elsey Berry Lynn, s/o Jackson Lynn and Lucinda ____

^{v5}606. ^{12}1. Lucinda Frances Lynn, b. 27 April 1887, Fox, Carter Co, I.T., d. there, 5 May 1887.

^{v5}607. ^{12}2. Wiley Ulysses Lynn, (Choctaw Roll #397), b. 28 May 1888, Fox, Carter Co, I.T., d. 19 July 1932, Ardmore, Carter Co, OK

^{v5}608. ^{13}1. Justice Banks Lynn, b. 2 Aug 1906, d. 26 Dec 1975, Ada, Pontotoc Co, OK; m.1. in Ardmore, Carter Co, OK, Ruth Hooks (1ch); m.2. Sylvia Lois Hord (1 ch)

^{v5}609. ^{14}1. Donald Berry Lynn, b. 15 Aug 1933

^{v5}610. ^{15}2. Ronald B. Lynn, b. 11 July 1952; m. Carol Ann McCracken

^{v5}611. ^{13}2. Elzie B. Lynn, b. 22 April 1914, Madill, OK, d. CA

^{v5}612. ^{12}3. William Andrew Lynn, (Choctaw Roll #398), b. 4 Sept 1890, Fox, Carter Co, I.T., d. 29 March 1966, Odessa, Ector Co, TX; m. 13 Sept 1911, in Madill, Marshall Co, OK, Agnes Holford, d/o George Holford and Annie Crenshaw

^{v5}613. ^{13}1. William Alley Lynn, b. 21 July 1914, Madill, OK, d. 2 April 1970, Garland, Dallas Co, TX; m. Edna Lucille Hutchins

^{v5}614. ^{14}1. Linda Joy Lynn, b. 5 Jan 1941, Dallas, TX; m. 17 Oct 1964, in Garland, Dallas Co, TX, Alvin Bernard Albers. Ch: Angela Lynn (m. Richard Keith Tevebauth, Ch: Ryan Keith and Ashley Marie Tevebaugh); Amy Michelle (m. William Randall Tarbett. Ch: Stephanie Rochelle, Kelly Lynn, and Brook Tarbett); and Ann Marie Albers.

^{v5}615. ^{14}2. Juanita Ann Lynn, b. 4 Aug 1951, Garland, Dallas Co, TX; m. 29 June 1974, in Garland, Dallas Co, TX, James Alva Ellis. Ch: Laura Marie; Paul James; and Stephen James Ellis.

^{v5}616. ^{13}2. Olive Ruth Lynn, b. 16 June 1919, Madill,

OK; m. 30 Dec 1939, in El Reno, Canadian Co, OK, William Leslie Alexander, s/o William Alexander and Mabel Wood

v5617.   [14]1. Wayne Leslie Alexander, b. 7 Jan 1948, Dallas, TX; m. 8 June 1968, in Waco, McClelland Co, TX, Carolyn Sue Childs. Ch: Brian Michael (m. Stephanie Nicole Stamper, Ch: Ian Patrick Alexander); and Jason Stephens Alexander.

v5618.   [14]2. Rodney Lynn Alexander, b. 30 Sept 1950, Dallas, TX, d. there, 7 Dec 1997

v5619.   [14]3. Karen Kay Alexander, b. 18 Aug 1956, Dallas, TX

v5620.   [13]3. Ralph David Lynn, b. 28 June 1928, Ardmore, Carter Co, OK; m. 4 June 1945, in Dallas, TX, Betty Jean Dodd,

v5621.   [14]1. Sherry Annette Lynn, b. 7 Jan 1947, Dallas, TX; m.1. 17 March 1969, Houston, TX, Charles Heslep; m.2. 4 May 1985, Conroe, TX, George Melvin Krauskopf. Ch: Stephanie Dawn Heslep (m. David Neal Taylor, Ch: Billy Lynn; Courtney Nicole; and Brittany Dawn Taylor).

v5622.   [14]2. Ralph David Lynn Jr, b. 22 Sept 1949, Denver, CO, d. 22 Feb 2001, Houston, Harris Co, TX; m. in Houston, TX, Terry _____. Ch: Melanie Lynn (Terry's dau by previous marr; adopted by Ralph), and Christofer Lynn.

v5623.   [12]4. Worley Berry Lynn, (Choctaw Roll #399), b. 10 March 1892, Fox, Carter Co, I.T., d. 22 March 1940, Mayo Clinic, Olmsted Co, MN; m. 8 Sept 1912, Madill, Marshall Co, OK, Ella Mabel Jones

v5624.   [13]1. Dorothy Lynn, b. 3 Aug 1913, Madill, OK, d. 1 Sept 1982, Hobart, Kiowa Co, OK; m. in Hobart, OK, Merle Watkins. Ch: David Merle; Gordon Elliot; and Janice Louise (adopted) Watkins.

v5625.   [13]2. Gordon Lynn, b. 30 June 1915, Madill, OK, d. FL; m.1. Marie Conwell; m.2. Evelyn _____

v5626.   [13]3. Worley Berry Lynn Jr, b. 25 June 1922,

Madill, OK, d. 2 Oct 1984, Vian, Sequoyah Co, OK; m. Margaret Kortendick.

$^v5$627. ^{14}1. Laura Lynn, m. David Blackorby. Ch: Page Lynn; and Barton Lynn Blackorby.

$^v5$628. ^{14}2. Steven Craig Lynn, m. Pam Sims. Ch: Lisa Meredith Lynn.

$^v5$629. ^{13}4. Carol Jean Lynn, b. 30 Aug 1927, Enid, Garfield Co, OK, d. 15 Oct 1985, Stuart, St Lucie Co, FL; m.1. in Madill, Marshall Co, OK, Don Welch Jr; m.2. Gardner Pate; m.3. Bill Jack Evans. Ch: Donovan; Tim; and Gaylynn Welch

$^v5$630. ^{12}5. Laura Bell Lynn, (Choctaw Roll #400), b. 24 Sept 1894, Fox, Carter Co, I.T., d. 2 Feb 1922; n.m.

$^v5$631. ^{12}6. Durley Elvie Lynn (Choctaw Roll #14499), b. 17 March 1896, Madill, Marshall Co, I.T., d. 29 May 1991, Dallas, TX; m. Michael Twomey. (No ch).

$^v5$632. ^{12}7. Pearlie Houston Lynn (Choctaw Roll #401), b. 11 Aug 1898, Madill, Marshall Co, I.T. Pearlie never married; he was in WW I in France with the 57th Co, Artillery.

$^v5$633. ^{12}8. Earlie Elzey Lynn, (Choctaw Roll #402), b. 25 Dec 1899; never married.

$^v5$634. ^{12}9. Ada Winnifred Lynn, (Choctaw Roll #403), b. 15 Nov 1901, Madill, Marshall Co, I.T., d. 14 July 1991, Dallas, TX; m.1. in OK city, Paul McCarthy; m.2. Clifton W. Cassidy.

$^v5$635. ^{13}1. Clifton W. Cassidy Jr, b. 1927, Dallas, TX; m. Sally Otis, Ch: Clifton W. III; Elynn; Kelly; and Michael Cassidy.

$^v5$636. ^{12}10. Cecil Maxwell Rudolph "Buster" Lynn, b. 16 Jan 1909, Madill, Marshall Co, OK, d. 23 March 1962, Oklahoma City; m. Ruby Jones. Ch: Michael Berry; Maxwell E.; Dwight; and Patricia Bell Lynn.

$^v5$637. ^{12}11. Marjorie Lynn, b. 30 Dec 1910, Madill, Marshall Co, OK, d. 16 Nov 1998, Dallas, TX; m. Welch Edward Henderson.

$^v5$638. ^{13}1. Welch Edward Henderson Jr, b. 16 Oct 1926, Madill, Marshall Co, OK; m. Karen ___. Ch: Mat David; Lisa Lynn; and Michelle Leigh Henderson v5639. [11]3. Minnie Lee Johnson, b. 12 Dec 1875, d. 26 Dec 1959, Oklahoma City, OK; m. Henry Lee Lynn

v5640. [12]1. Adley Vi Lynn, b. 19 June 1904

v5641. [12]2. Henry Hazel Lynn, b. 30 July 1907

v5642. [12]3. Margaret Lynn, b. 2 Feb 1909

v5643. [12]4. Jack Bill Lynn, b. 10 Jan 1910

v5644. [12]5. John Henry Lynn, b. 10 Sept 1912

v5645. [12]6. Mildred M. Lynn, b. 4 Nov 1914

v5646. [12]7. Lois Dixie Lynn, b. 7 Dec 1915

v5647. [11]4. Laura Lee Johnson, (Choctaw Roll #433), b. 24 Dec 1879, Fox, Carter Co, I.T., d. 8 Jan 1933, Lebanon, Marshall Co, OK; m. George Ernest Lynn (Choctaw Roll #436–intermarried citizen),

v5648. [12]1. Tams Berry Lynn, (Choctaw Roll #434), b. 1 Jan 1901

v5649. [12]2. Maggie Tammy Lynn, (Choctaw Roll #435), b. 11 Jan 1903

v5650. [12]3. Bevie Lynn, b. 3 Dec 1903

v5651. [12]4. Ernest Houston Lynn, b. 23 Nov 1907

v5652. [12]5. Edith Marie Lynn, b. 13 Jan 1912

v5653. [12]6. Mabelle Lynn, b. 26 Feb 1915

Sarah Ann Brashears and Dr. James F. Jones

v5**548**. [9]7. **Sarah Ann Brashears**, (d/o Alexander Brashears and Anne Brashears), b. 21 Jan 1825 (under 10 on 27 Sept 1830), d. 8 June 1890, Baxter Springs, KS; m. 7 Feb 1843, Marengo Co, AL, "by Thomas A. Sharpe, J.P., Bond: Thomas McCormick (Marengo Co, AL, Marriages), **James F. Jones**, b. c1817, Virginia, d. c1865, Marengo, AL. (Sarah sold her allotment on Suk-en-Atcha Creek in 1848; she had moved earlier to Arkansas.) Sarah Ann (Brashears) Jones is recorded as a sister of Emiline Jane (Brashears) Smith in the Guion Miller Rolls. (additional data from Lottie <punkin1@etex.net> and Nora and Frank Martin <lfm8967@centuryinter.net>

Says Nora Martin: We were told by descendants of Lucy Ann (Jones) Smithee that all Sarah's daughter's middle names were Ann; however, this did not seem to be the case when we found the marriage records.

Children of Sarah Ann Brashears and James F. Jones:

[v5]654. [10]1. George Jones, b. 1843, AL

[v5]655. [10]2. *Laura Ann Jones, b. 22 Sept 1844, AR, d. 3 Jan 1927, North McAlester, Pittsburg Co, OK; m. 7 Feb 1843, in Marengo Co, AL, Samuel Stewart

[v5]656. [10]3. Emaline Ann Jones, b. 1850, AR (ancestor of Dr. Larkin E. Wilson, of El Dorado, AR)

[v5]657. [10]4. *Lucy Ann Jones, b. 2 Jan 1852, Indian Territory, d. 12 July 1925, Gandy, Bossier Parish, LA, bur Cottage Grove Cem, Alden Bridge, Bossier, LA (all her husband's were buried in AR); m.1. 2 Jan 1873, Jefferson Co, AR, Warren F. Smithee (ancestors of Frank Martin); m.2. 11 Nov 1885, Pine Bluff, Jefferson Co, AR (Bk E, p.41), John C. Head (no ch); m.3. 5 Oct 1889, Pine Bluff, Jefferson Co, AR (Bk G, p.85), William Patrick Yandell (no ch)

[v5]658. [10]5. Walter Jones, b. c1853, AR

[v5]659. [10]6. *Lugelia Ann "Geet" Jones, b. 1856, AR; m.1 _____ Mitchell; m.2. 2 March 1883, Pine Bluff, Jefferson Co, AR (Bk D, p.21), Charles Cleveland Monk

[v5]660. [10]7. James Samuel "Jim" Jones, b. 1859, AR; m. 8 Nov 1881, Pine Bluff, Jefferson Co, AR (Bk C, p.227), Missouri Belle Monk, d/o Franklin Green Monk, a brother to Charles Cleveland Monk, who m. Lugelia Ann "Geet" Jones, Jim's sister.

[v5]661. [10]8. Clara Ann Jones, b. 1862, AR; m. 23 March 1884, Jefferson Co, AR (Bk D, p.243), R.J. Phillips

[v5]662. [10]9. Sarah "Sallie" Ann Jones, b. 1867, AR

Figure 17: Belle Monk and Jim Jones

[v5]663. [10]10. John William "Willie" Jones, b. c1870, AR

[v5]664. [10]11. Katherine "Kate D." Jones, b. c1872, AR

Family of Laura Ann Jones ([v5]655) and Samuel Stewart, Sr:

[10]2. Laura Ann Jones, (d/o James F. Jones and Sarah Ann Brashears), b. 22 Sept 1844, AR, d. 3 Jan 1927, North

McAlester, Pittsburg Co, OK; m. 7 Feb 1843, in Marengo Co, AL, Samuel Stewart, b. AL. (Data from descendant, Mike Vance <pccowboy@swbell.net>

v5665.   [11]1. James Stewart, b. c1868, AR

v5666.   [11]2. Sarah Stewart, b. c1870, AR

v5667.   [11]3. Samuel Stewart, Jr, b. 11 Jan 1873, AR, d. 15 Nov 1967, Pittsburg Co, OK; m. c1881, in MO, Daisy _____.

v5668.   [12]1. Hattie Stewart, b. c1898, OK

v5669.   [12]2. James Sam Stewart, b. 26 June 1899, AR, d. 40 March 1969; m. Della E. _____, b. 14 Oct 1902

v5670.   [12]3. George Stewart, b. c1901, OK

v5671.   [12]4. Prather Stewart, b. c1906, OK

v5672.   [12]5. Eunice A. Stewart, b. 1908-1909, OK

v5673.   [11]4. Gealy Stewart, b. c1877, AR

v5674.   [11]5. Hattie Stewart, b. 14 Nov 1878, AR, d. 24 April 1957, Bolivar, Polk Co, MO, bur Greenwood Cem in Bolivar, MO; m.1. 15 Aug 1895, in Choctaw Nation, I.T., Walter Scott Mathews, b. 22 Jan 1875, Wingo Station, Graves Co, KY, d. 27 Feb 1963, Corpus Christi, TX; m.2. 15 Aug 1905, in Choctaw Nation, Indian Territory, John F. Smith, b. c1882, I.T., d. before 1957

v5675.   [12]1. Gertrude Mae Mathews, b. 17 Sept 1896, Hartshorne, I.T., d. Jan 1972, Santa Rosa, TX; m.1. 26 Nov 1913, in Wilburton, OK, Tobe Davidson, b. c1894, OK; m.2. 3 May 1915, in Ft Smith, Sebastian Co, AR, Anthony Bernard Magdalena, b. 9 May 1890, Youngstown, OH, d. 12 April 1977, Harlingen, TX

v5676.   [13]1. Walter Anthony "Buddy" Magdalena, b. 16 Feb 1918 in Krebs, Pittsburg Co, OK, d. 9 May 2002 in Harlingen, Cameron Co, TX; m.1. Margaret Lovern, b. 8 Nov ___; m.2. Flora Swabel

v5677.   [13]2. Theodora Lucille Magdalena, b. 17 Aug 1922 in Santa Rosa, Cameron Co, TX, d. 18 June 1991 in Birmingham, AL; m. 20 Feb 1943 in Santa Rosa, TX, Dawson M. Vance, b. 2 March 1917 in Green Co, KY, d. 21 Feb 1999, Houston, TX.

v5678.   133. Mary Jane Magdalena, b. 28 Dec 1924 in Santa Rosa, Cameron Co, TX, d. 27 Feb 1990 in Houston, Harris, TX; m. 20 Feb 1943, in Santa Rosa, Cameron Co, TX, Shelby Arnold Callaway,

v5679.   134. Joe Mike Magdalena; m. 20 May 1952 in Santa Rosa, Cameron Co, TX, Julianne Grace Schmeltekopf,

v5680.   122. Ruby Mathews, b. 3 Dec 1898, Hartshorne, Pittsburg Co, OK, d. 8 Sept 1900, Hartshorne, OK.

v5681.   123. Alfred W. Mathews, b. 1899-1902, d. 1 Jan 1961; m. Ruth _____.

v5682.   124. Laura E. Smith, b. c1907

v5683.   125. Richard S. Smith, b. c1916

v5684.   126. Waurika Smith, b. c1918

Notes on Laura Ann (Jones) Stewart (by Mike Vance):

In the 1880 census, Spring twp, ?Pittsburg Co, I.T., (ED 142, p.11, taken June 18, 1880), she is listed as born in Alabama.

In 1910, Laura's son, Samuel Stewart, Jr, lists his parents as born in AL and OK.

But in 1920, Dow twp, Laura was living with her daughter, Hattie, and her husband, John F. Smith. She is said to be born in Oklahoma, with her parents born in Virginia and Mississippi respectively.

Her death certificate says that she was born in Oklahoma. Dr. Robert L. Browning or Broussard, of Hartshorne, attributed the cause of death. Harry Chaney, apparently the funeral home owner, is listed as the informant. Both the death certificate and funeral home record, which could conceivably be considered the same source in this case, show that she was buried at Red Oak Cemetery. That is located just north of Canadian in the northeast part of Pittsburg County. The cemetery books for there do not list Laura or any other Stewarts, however. Her grave may have been unmarked.

Notes on Gertrude (Mathews) Magdalena (by Mike Vance):

Gertie was raised mostly by her paternal grand-parents. She is enumerated with them in 1910, even though both her parents live in the same county. In the divorce action against her first husband, she said that she had moved back in with her grandparents in 1914, after she was turned out of her home in Craig, OK. That divorce was granted on 24 April 1915. The order forbade either party from marrying for a term of six months, but she was married to Tony Magdalena in Ft. Smith, AR only nine days later.

All family stories indicate that Gertie was very feisty in her younger days. She was sometimes displeased with her sisters-in-law and once picked one of them up and put her in a washtub full of water. She was much larger than the tiny little sisters of her husband, Tony.

Her son, Joe, tells of her estimating a year's cotton crop as being worth more than Tony thought it would be, one time in the late 1940s. He promised to give her the total above his own estimate. When the crop was sold at the gin, Gertie made enough money to buy herself a new silver service and a new crystal service.

Probably starting around 1950, she became a very accomplished china painter. She left a full hand-painted china service for twelve to each of her five grandchildren along with numerous other serving pieces. Her youngest grandson, Mike, has a full nativity scene hand-painted by her, with a creche made by Tony.

Notes on Alfred Mathews (by Mike Vance):

Alfred lived with his grandparents in 1910, even though both parents were still living in the same county. The birthdate from his obituary shows November 24, 1899, but he is not listed with Walter in the 1900 census and his age in 1910 is shown as 8. No SSDI record was found for Alfred Mathews or Frank Murphy. The obituary has other incorrect material, as well.

He entered the service to avoid some as-of-yet-unknown trouble he had gotten into and changed his name to Frank Murphy. Uncle Shelby says that it may have been a car theft. He doesn't know if Alfred was convicted, or if it was before trial, but Alfred took off and began using his new name. I don't know if the name was ever changed legally.

He and his wife, Ruth, owned a restaurant in Anderson, Indiana, named Pine Manor. It was located on Mounds Road, which is described by a librarian there as being on the edge of town, even in 2001. The first appearance of Pine Manor in the city directory was in 1957. The librarian was unsure if that was because it was new then, or because it was in an area not previously considered part of the city of Anderson.

Alfred, by then called Frank Murphy, appears in the Anderson city directories in 1945 and 1947. In 1945, he is listed as an inspector for Delco-Remy, a General Motors company. In 1947, he is listed as a chef, but no restaurant is given. They then disappear from the directories until 1957, when they return, along with the listing for Pine Manor.

Alfred was killed in a car accident, according to my dad, but Uncle Shelby recalls the accident involving their son. The obituary seems to support Uncle Shelby's recollection. An obituary for Frank Murphy ran in the Anderson (IN) Daily Bulletin on January 2, 1961. It perpetuates the idea that his original name was Frank Murphy. The first few lines are missing, but the remainder reads: "of the Pine Manor Restaurant on Ind 32, east of Anderson, died while enroute to St. John's Hospital in the city ambulance after being stricken ill about 7pm Saturday at the restaurant. Mr. Murphy was born Nov 24, 1899 at Haleyville, Okla. He came to Anderson from Indianapolis in 1927. He served in the Marine Corps during World War II. Surviving are: the widow, Ruth E. Murphy; a son, Walter G. Murphy, at home; his father, Walter G. Murphy, Corpus Christi, Texas; three sisters, Mrs. Antonia Magdalena, Santa Rosa, Texas; Mrs. Ray Mathis, Henrietta, Okla; and Mrs. Ray Crawford, Shulter, Okla; and a brother, Richard Smith, Bolivar, Mo. Friends are being received at the Baker Bros Funeral Home. Services will be conducted at 10am Tuesday at the funeral home, with Rev. Monroe G. Schuster, pastor at Central Christian Church, officiating. Burial will be in Anderson Memorial Park Cemetery."

Family of Lucy Ann Jones (^{v5}657) and Warren F. Smithee:

^{v5}685. ^{11}1. Alice L. Smithee, b. 19 Dec 1873, Pine Bluff, Jefferson Co, AR, d. 14 March 1965, Jena, LaSalle, LA, bur Cypress Creek Cemetery, Winn Parish, LA; m.1. 3 Jan 1890, Pine Bluff, Jefferson Co, AR (Bk G, p.150), Charles Samuel Kitchingham (d. 1912); m.2. 10 June 1915, Winn Parish, LA (ML Bk F, p.521), W.W. Barnett; m.3. 3 Oct 1929, Acadia Parish, LA (ML Bk 8, p.423), Allen Thomas Adams. (Nora Martin: Alice and Charles Samuel Kitchingham were my husband's grandparents.)

^{v5}686. ^{12}x. Lillie Ann Kitchingham, m. David D. Arnaud. son: Richard Arnaud

^{v5}687. ^{11}2. Lillie Smithee, b. 22 Dec 1875, Pine Bluff, Jefferson Co, AR, d. TX (lived in Orange, TX); m. 12 Feb 1891, Chicago, IL (not proved), Frank J. Johnson

^{v5}688. ^{11}3. Nancy Ann Smithee, b. 8 Jan 1878, Pine Bluff, Jefferson Co, AR, d. 31 July 1963, Houston, Harris Co, TX, bur Forest Park Cemetery, Shreveport, Caddo Par, LA; m. 12 Jan 1892, LaFayette Co, AR (not proved), John Foley

^{v5}689. ^{11}4. Leon Leroy Smithee, (fem; pronounced lee-own, called "Oney" — Aunt Oney said she must have been the boy!) b. 29 July 1879, Pine Bluff, Jefferson Co, AR, d. 1979, LA (probably Monroe, Ouachita Par, LA as that is where she lived); m. Albirtus "Bert" L. DeLoach

^{v5}690. ^{11}5. Ruth Smithee, b. 6 Oct 1882, Pine Bluff, Jefferson Co, AR, d. 4 July 1983 Columbia, Caldwell Par, LA (she was 100 yrs old); m.1. J.W. Trailer (they lived in AR); m.2. 1912 in Blocker, TX, T.E. Hudgens

Lugelia Ann "Geet" Jones (^{v5}659) and ____ Mitchell; C.C. Monk:
    ^{10}6. Lugelia Ann "Geet" Jones, (d/o James F. Jones and Sarah Ann Brashears), b. 1855/56, AR. d. 1926, Woodson, AR (at home of her dau, Dawnie Monk Bridges), bur Whitehall Cemetery, Jefferson Co, AR; m.1 ____ Mitchell; m.2. 2 March 1883, Pine Bluff, Jefferson Co, AR, Charles Cleveland Monk, b. 25 Sept 1854, Pine Bluff, Jefferson Co, AR, d. there, May 1920, bur Whitehall Cem, s/o Wiley Buck Monk and Mary Louise S. Cherry. C.C. had been married previously to Anna S. Chandler and had one child, Lolly Monk. Two of C.C. and Lugelia's children married Bridges siblings in a double wedding ceremony. (Data and pictures from Lottie <punkin1@etex.net>)

Figure 18: Charles Cleveland Monk and Lugelia "Geet" Jones

Family of Lugelia Ann Jones and _____ Mitchell:
v5691. 111. Lena Mitchell, b. bef 1883, AR
Family of Charles Cleveland Monk & Lugelia Jones:
v5692. 112. Carroll Cleveland Monk (twin), b. 11 Dec 1885, Pine
Bluff, Jefferson Co, AR, d. there, 1 Oct 1966, bur
Whitehall Cem, Jefferson Co, AR; m. 25 Dec 1905,
Jefferson Co, AR, Josie Bridges, b. 9 May 1888,
Jefferson Co, AR, d. there 27 July 1955, bur
Whitehall Cem, Jefferson Co, AR, d/o Joseph Green
Bridges and Laura Anderson.
v5693. 121. stillborn female
v5694. 122. stillborn male
v5695. 123. stillborn female
v5696. 124. Lottie Monk, b. 11 Aug 1912, Pine Bluff, Jefferson
Co, AR, d. 30 Nov 1960, Longview, Gregg Co, TX;
m. 23 Dec 1926, Pine Bluff, Jefferson Co, AR, Guy
Johnson Wickersham (Lottie's grandparents)
v5697. 125. male Stillborn
v5698. 126. Carroll Clarence Monk, b. 20 Jan 1917, Jefferson
Co, AR, d. there, 20 Jan 1986, bur Whitehall
Cem, Jefferson Co, AR; m. 9 May 1944, Jefferson
Co, AR, Helena Dallia Massanelli
v5699. 127. Alma Monk, b. 24 Sept 1916, Jefferson Co, AR,
living in 2001 in Florida; m. 11 Nov 1935, in
Gregg Co, TX, Frank Edgin.
v5700. 128. Laura Lugelia Monk, b. 31 May 1921, Jefferson
Co, AR, living in 2001 in Whitehall, Jefferson Co,
AR; m. 23 April 1941, in Jefferson Co, AR, Ralph
Givens.
v5701. 129. Josie Monk, b. 4 Oct 1928, Jefferson Co, AR, d.
11 Feb 1999, Pine Bluff, Jefferson Co, AR; m.
1944, in Jefferson Co, AR, Leroy Holden
v5702. 113. _____ Monk, (twin) b. & d. 11 Dec 1885
v5703. 114. Victor Monk, b. March 1889, Jefferson Co, AR; m.
Lucille Herring. After Lucille died, Victor went to
California, leaving his children with a lady who
adopted children out. He told her he would return,
but he never did. The boy was adopted out.
v5704. 121. Lugelia Monk, b. Jefferson Co, AR; m. in LA
v5705. 122. Cricket Monk (female; known only by nickname),
b. Jefferson Co, AR; m. in LA

v5706.   [12]3. male Monk, b. Jefferson Co, AR, adopted in Pine Bluff, AR.

v5707. [11]5. Dawnie May Monk, b. 24 May 1891, Whitehall twp, Jefferson Co, AR, d. 15 Feb 1947, Pacific Grove, CA, body returned by train and buried in Whitehall Cem, Jefferson Co, AR; m. 24 Dec 1905, in Jefferson Co, AR, Columbus Marion Bridges, s/o Joseph Green Bridges and Laura Anderson.

v5708.   [12]1. Laura Bridges

Henrietta Jane Brashears and John J.J. Boykin

v5**549.** [9]8. **Henrietta Jane "Hennie" Brashears**, (d/o Alexander Brashears and Emiline Jane Winn), b. 12 May 1827, Sumter Co, AL (22 in 1850, 32 in 1860, Mobile Co, AL), d. 24 Dec 1890, Mobile Co, AL; m. 21 Oct 1844 (Mobile Marr, Book 8, p.44b), *John Joseph Jeremiah Boykin*, b. c1817-18, AL (32 in 1850, 42 in 1860, Mobile Co, AL), d. 8 Sept 1900, Montgomery Co, TX. Ch, per Loretta Coppick:

v5709. [10]1. Mason Boykin, 1845;

v5710. [10]2. Mary Ann Boykin, 1846;

v5711. [10]3. Sarah Jane Boykin, 1847;

v5712. [10]4. Alexander Boykin, 1848;

v5713. [10]5. John Boykin, 1849;

v5714. [10]6. Angelina Boykin, 1850;

v5715. [10]7. Celia Boykin,

v5716. [10]8. Easton Boykin, 1855;

v5717. [10]9. Rowell Boykin, 1859;

v5718. [10]10. Dennis B. Boykin, 1860.

Will of Dennis Payne Brashear

(v5550)[of] Mobile Co, AL.

To brother William Payne Brashear, interest in following slaves: Maria, Hester, Jack, Elias, Anthoney, Henry, Louisa, Clara, Eastra, Pieree, and Pauline, all being children and grandchildren of aforementioned Maria.

To brother, William Payne Brashear, 5000 acres of land situated on Big Lizzard and Little Lizzard Creeks, about 20 Miles from City of Mobile. Also 80 acres on Cedar Creek.

To step-mother, "Brambly" Brashear, after death of my father, Alexander Brashear, land in Section 28, Township 1

North, Range 1 East, in Mobile Co, about 40 acres.

To Emaline Jane [Brashear] Smith, ½ of stock cattle.

Executors: William Payne Brashear and Ira B. Smith.

Witnesses: J.M. Jeffries, P.J. White, N.W. Tatty.

Dated 4 March 1863

Recorded 20 March 1863, Mobile Co, AL, Book ?, pp. 321-25.

Deposition of J.M. Jeffries: Will written in Hospital No. 2, Scottswell, Albemarle Co, Virginia by Peter White. The said Dennis P. Brashear too weak to write, just made his mark. Said Dennis P. Brashear was about 35 years of age.

Deposition of N.W. Tatty: Signing of will took place at the Factory Bottom Hospital No. 2. Mr. Peter White wrote and read will to said Mr. Brashear, and Dr. Jeffries helped him make his mark. Mr. Brashear died the next day.

Emiline Jane Brashears and Ira Byrd Smith

v5**552.** 9**11. Emiline Jane Brashears**, (d/o Alexander Brashears and Emiline Jane Winn), b. 1 June 1833, Sumter Co, AL (17 in 1850; 27 in 1860; 47 in 1880, Mobile Co, AL), d. 1 June 1915, East Brewton, AL, at home of her dau, Margaret Caroline Raley; m. 24 Dec 1850, at Mobile, AL, (Mobile Marr, Book 11, p.106' William Malone, J.P.), **Ira Byrd Smith**, b. 16 Dec 1827, Greene Co, MS, d. 22 Feb 1884, Mobile Co, AL. He was a brother of Nathaniel John Smith, who married Louisa Jane Brashears. The Smith boys were sons of Oliver Merida Smith and Barbara Ellen Byrd. (ref: *They Say the Wind Is Red -- the Alabama Choctaws; Lost in Their Own Land* [book].)

Ira Byrd Smith Sr was a farmer. He and his father-in-law, Alexander M. Brashears Sr were trustees of the 31–Mile Bluff School District in northern Mobile Co, AL.

Of Alexander's first (and second) families, the only one remembered by Emiline Jane was Sara Ann whose birthday she remembered. It is possible that Sara Ann visited or even lived part time with Alexander Brashears in Mobile County. (The two girls were only 8 years apart in age). This would explain Emiline Jane's recording Sarah Ann as her sister in the Guion Miller Rolls. (Research earlier in 1900s by Frank and Tina Wolcott.)

Great-great-granddaughter Josephine Turner Bryant <jtbryant@bellsouth.net> says there were 17 children and that Emiline made application for recognition as a Choctaw in 1906, stating that her grandmother was Rachel (Durant) Brashears/McGirth/Walker.

[v5]719. [10]1. William Franklin Smith, b. 24 Sept 1851, Mount Vernon, AL; m.1. 12 March 1874, Mobile Co, AL (Book 26, p.191, L.H. Norton, J.P.; Edward T. Broadway, Bondsman), Sarah S. Dillard, b. 14 Jan 1857, AL, d. 25 April 1888, AL; m.2. 11 Feb 1891, Chastang, Mobile Co, AL (Book 32, p.468, Walter Vigor, J.P.) Missouri Taylor, b. July 1875, AL.

[v5]720. [10]2. Virginia Missouri Smith, b. 12 Dec 1852, AL; d. June 1938; m. 29 Dec 1880, Mobile Co, AL (Book 28, p.564, Minister: C.H. Kellam; at the bride's parents' home; bondsman: John R. Williams) William Rufus Dillard, b. c1850-51, AL.

[v5]721. [10]3. Rosalie Adelle Smith, b. 25 Aug 1854, Mobile Co, AL; d. 18 Aug 1912, Mobile Co, AL; m. 6 April 1873, Mobile Co, AL (Book 26, p.100 (Minister: J.E. Forest?; at the residence of Jasper J. Botter; bondsman: Jasper J. Botter) Jacob Levi "Jake" Crist

[v5]722. [10]4. Ira Byrd Smith, Jr, b. c1855-56, Mobile Co, AL; d. single.

[v5]723. [10]5. Dennis Payne Smith, b. c1856-57, AL; d. young, after 1870

[v5]724. [10]6. Louisa Jane "Lula" or "Chick" Smith, b. 11 May 1859, AL; m. 3 Sept 1886, Mobile Co, AL (Book 30, p.700 (by A.J. Coleiuaie?; at the bride's mother's home; bondsman: D. Davis) Hamilton Hill Ramey, b. 21 March 1858, d. April 1909, (murdered).

[v5]725. [10]7. Oliver Cromwell Smith, b. 1860; d. Biloxi, Harrison Co, Mississippi (single).

[v5]726. [10]8. Joseph James Smith, b. June 1862, AL; d. (single, as far as Josephine knows).

[v5]727. [10]9. Robert Walker Smith, b. 28 Dec 1863, Mobile Co, AL; d. 1912, Mobile Co, AL; m. 21 June 1886, Mobile Co, AL (Book 30, p.645) Emily Caroline "Emma" Allen, b. c1866-67, AL.

[v5]728. [10]10. Margaret Caroline "Maggie" Smith, b. 15 Oct 1865, Mobile Co, AL; m. 16 Aug 1882, Mobile Co, AL (Book 29, p.275) James Wilson Raley

[v5]729. [10]11. Fannie B. Smith, b. 28 Nov 1868, Mobile Co, AL; d. 6 Jan 1957, Biloxi, Harrison Co, Mississippi; m. 13

October 1886, Mobile Co, AL (Book 30, p.679, Minister: M.S. Anderson; bondsman: Joseph Smith) Henry Boozer Wolcott.

[v5]730.   [11]x. Frank H. Wolcott; m. Jewell Christine "Tina" Lee (Frank and Tina Wolcott were early researchers in this line of the family.)

[v5]731.   [10]12. George Glenn Smith, b. c1868-69; d. New Mexico.

[v5]732.   [10]13. Ebeneezer Hern Smith, b. 18 Aug 1870, Mobile Co, AL; m. 31 Jan 1893, Mobile Co, AL (Book 33, p.218) Emma L. Winters

[v5]733.   [10]14. Martha Smith, stillborn after 1870; (her name was given to Josephine, but has not been verified.)

[v5]734.   [10]15. Emma Nina Smith, b. c1873-74, Mobile Co, AL; d. 1926; m. 23 April 1906, Mobile Co, AL (Book 39, p.559) John Cornstock Bradford.

[v5]735.   [10]16. Alice G. "Jewel" Smith, b. 26 Dec 1875, Mobile Co, AL; d. 9 Dec 1929, Calvert, AL; m. 29 Nov 1892, Mobile, Mobile Co, AL (Book 33, p.165; Pastor of St. Francis St. Methodist Church: W.P. Dickinson; bondsman: G.G. Smith; 17 years of age w/consent of mother; listed as Alice G. Smith on Marr Lic) Daniel Newton Baker

[v5]736.   [10]17. Price Williams "P.W." Smith, b. 17 July 1877, Mobile Co, AL; d. 14 Sept 1956, Mount Vernon, AL; m. c1906-07, Melinda McCloud b. c1888-89, Mississippi.

And two more names, which were given to Josephine, but she has been unable to verify:

[v5]737.   [10]18. Chris Smith,

[v5]738.   [10]19. Baker Smith,

Louisa Jane Brashears and Nathaniel John Smith

[v5]**553.**   [9]12. **Louisa Jane Brashears**, (d/o Alexander Brashears and Emiline Jane Winn), b. 26 Dec 1835, Sumter Co, AL, d. 26 Jan 1899, Washington Co, AL, bur Charity Chapel Cem, Washington Co, AL; m. 24 Jan 1850, at Mount Vernon, Mobile Co, AL, (Mobile Marr, Book 11, p.31), **Nathaniel John Smith**, b. 13 Jan 1822, Mt Vernon, Mobile Co, AL, d. 8 Aug 1914, Baxterville, Lamar Co, TX. He was a brother of Ira Byrd Smith, who married Emiline Jane Brashears. The Smith boys

were sons of Oliver Merida Smith and Barbara Ellen Byrd. (ref: *They Say the Wind Is Red -- the Alabama Choctaws; Lost in Their Own Land* [book].)

Louisa was under age at the time of the marriage; so Alexander sent a note of permission, which is filed with the marriage license: to "Mr. E. Rush, Clerk of Co Court at Mobile: Sir, You may grant license to Nathaniel Smith to marry Louisa Z. Brashears, /signed/ A Brashears." (Thanks to Josephine Turner Bryant for the info. The "z" may be a misreading of a cursive "j".)

According to descendant, Woodie Wallace, they moved out on Bates Creek in the "Big Timber" where they lived among the Cajuns, now known as the MOWA (Mobile, Washington County).

<u>Family of Louisa Jane Brashears and Nathaniel John Smith</u>: (per FHL, Salt Lake City and a family group sheet by Woodie Wallace)

v5739. [10]1. Manson Marion Smith, b. 3 Nov 1852, Citronelle, Washington Co, AL; m. Eliza Ann Reed,

v5740. [11]x. Saphronia Smith, b. 22 Oct. 1881; m.1. Jim Knight who was killed in the cyclone that hit Purvis, Miss, in 1908; m.2. Jefferson Davis Wallace, in 1911.

v5741. [12]x. Woodie Wallace writes: I was born to this marriage on Oct 4, 1913.

v5742. [10]2. Adelia Smith, b. 1858 (in FHL list, but not in Woodie's)

v5743. [10]3. Catherine "Cate" (or Keet) Smith, b. 7 March 1859; m. Joseph King, an Army sergeant at nearby Mt. Vernon Barracks.

v5744. [10]4. Lillian Bromly Smith, b. 1860; m. Henry Rifflet, a soldier from Mt. Vernon Barracks.

v5745. [10]5. John Nathaniel Smith, b. 10 March 1862; m. Barbara Reed, sister to Eliza Ann Reed, Mrs. Manson Smith.

v5746. [10]6. *Benjamin Pearce Smith, b. 12 May 1863, Washington Co, AL; m. Harriette Elizabeth Weaver, b. 21 May 1861, Washington Co, AL

v5747. [10]7. Oliver Emory Smith, b. Dec 1864; m. Mary Parker, a full blood Choctaw, according to their son, a prominent minister of the Gospel in Saraland, Alabama.

^{v5}748. ^{10}8. Barbara Ellen Smith, b. 9 June 1866; m. Frank Cole,

^{v5}749. ^{10}9. George William "Buddy" Smith, b. 9 March 1868 or 1869; m. Francis Weaver,

^{v5}750. ^{10}10. Elizabeth Smith, b. 1870 (in FHL list, but not Woodie's list)

^{v5}751. ^{10}11. Emiline "Pitts" Smith, b. 1870; m.1. John Cole; m.2. Robert "Bob" Lewis

Woodie adds two others, whose birthdates are so late that they must be grandchildren:

^{v5}752. x. Ira Smith, b. Sept 1893; m. Louisa Chastang

^{v5}753. x. Ludlow "Luddy" Smith, d. at age 14.

Family of Benjamin Pearce Smith (^{v5}746) and Harriette Elizabeth Weaver

^{v5}754. ^{11}1. Catherine Smith, b. 22 Nov 1879, Citronelle, Wash Co, AL; m.1. Bobby Nelton, m.2. Rodney Queen,

^{v5}755. ^{11}2. Percy Veil Smith, b. 30 April 1881, Citronelle, Washington, AL; m. Rose Emmer Holder, b. 31 May 1885, Brooklyn, Forrest Co, MS

^{v5}756. ^{12}1. Oscar Ray Smith, b. 14 March 1908, Brooklyn, Forrest Co, MS

^{v5}757. ^{12}2. Richard Howard McCloud Smith, b. 16 Dec 1913, Brooklyn, Forrest Co, MS

^{v5}758. ^{11}3. Kelly Aaron Smith, b. 4 Aug 1883; m. Clara Alice Morris, b. July 1885, Washington Co, AL

^{v5}759. ^{11}4. John Pilgrim Smith, b. 27 April 1885; m. Mamie Emma James,

^{v5}760. ^{11}5. Stella Smith, b. 11 April 1887; m. Dave Merratt,

^{v5}761. ^{11}6. Benjamin Franklin Smith, b. 10 April 1889, St. Stevens, AL; m.1. Isabelle Woodard, b. 23 Jan 1894; m. _____ Mead,

^{v5}762. ^{11}7. Fletcher L. Smith, b. 16 July 1891, Baldwin Co, AL; m. Maggie James McDonald,

^{v5}763. ^{11}8. Lovid Busby Smith, b. 17 Feb 1894, Hurricane Branch, Wash Co, AL; m. Ruthie May,

^{v5}764. ^{11}9. George Herbert Smith, b. 8 March 1896, Citronelle, Wash Co, AL

^{v5}765. ^{11}10. _____

^{v5}766. ^{11}11. Lillie Alfa Smith, b. 16 Aug 1902, Brooklyn, Forrest

Co, MS; m. Joseph John Vojkufka, b. 12 Aug 1887 Lyons, TX

v5767. [12]1. Robert Eugene Vojkufka; m. Viola Louise Henderson,

v5768. [11]12. Mack Smith, b. 13 May 1904

v5769. [11]13. James Matthew Smith, b. 12 Jan 1907

Alexandre Brashear and Cecile Turner

This was probably (no proof) a grandson of Alexander Brashears, possibly through his son, William.

v5770. [10]x. **Alexandre Brashear**, b. Dec 1849, LA, d. Ponchatoula, LA; m. *Cecile Turner*, b. Jan 1855 or 1858, d. 1945, Milton, LaFayette Parish, LA, d/o Alexis Turner Sr and Anastasie Trahan. (data from John Hebert, 221½ Stone Ave, LaFayette, LA 70507-6315.)

1900 Census, [Ponchatoula] Louisiana, Tangipahoa Parish, Ward 7, ed 94, sht 6, line 90:

Alex Brashear,   b. Dec 1849, LA
    Cecilia   (wife), b. Jan 1855, LA
    Ava (or Ana) (dau), b. Feb 1892, LA
    Augustus   (son), b. April 1896, LA (Augustine)
    Amiline   (dau), b. Feb 1897, LA
    Antonio   (son), b. Feb 1899, LA   (Antoine)

Family of Alexandre Brashear and Cecile Turner:

v5771. [11]1. **Ava (or Ana) Brashear**, b. Feb 1892, LA

v5772. [11]2. **Augustine Brashear Sr**, b. 15 April 1896, Ponchatoula, LA, , d. 6 Nov 1977, Milton, LA; m. *Elodia Stephen*, b. 15 Nov 1907, Kaplan, LA, d. 5 Sept 1981, Milton, LA, both bur Milton Catholic Cem.

v5773. [12]1. **Augustine Brashear Jr**

v5774. [12]2. **Francis Brashear**

v5775. [11]3. **Ameline Brashear**, b. Feb 1897, Ponchatoula, LA, d. Abbeville, LA; m. *John Turner Sr*, b. LaFayette Parish, LA, d. 22 Feb 1961, Abbeville, LA, both bur Abbeville, LA.

v5776. [12]1. Clarence Turner

v5777. [12]2. Ida Turner

v5778. [12]3. Margie Turner

v5779. [12]4. Anise Turner

v5780. [12]5. Anna Turner

v5781.	[12]6. Clavelle Turner
v5782.	[12]7. Ana Turner
v5783.	[12]8. John Turner Jr
v5784.	[11]4. **Antoine Brashear**, b. 28 Feb 1899, Ponchatoula, LA, d. 25 July 1982, bur LaFayette, LA; m. ***Odeide Diane Trahan***, b. Milton, LaFayette Parish, LA.
v5785.	[12]1. **Archie Brashear**
v5786.	[12]2. **Gilbert Brashear**
v5787.	[12]3. **Marian Brashear**
v5788.	[12]4. **Lillian Brashear**
v5789.	[12]5. **Allen Brashear**, dec'd bef 1998
v5790.	[11]5. **Philomene Brashear**, b. 14 July 1903, Ponchatoula, Tangipahoa Par, LA, d. 14 Oct 1981, LaFayette, LA; m. ***Denis Hebert***, b. 9 Oct 1899, Milton, LA, d. 19 Oct 1966, both bur LaFayette, LA.
v5791.	[12]1. James B. Hebert
v5792.	[12]2. Jay C. Hebert
v5793.	[12]3. Joseph D. Hebert
v5794.	[12]4. Girlie Hebert, dec'd bef 1998
v5795.	[12]5. John A. Hebert

John A. Hebert, July 1998: "My mother was a Brashear. She identified herself as a Brashear, until her mother died. Then she was a Prejean. A very sick puppy. All olive skin people— Choctaws. I haven't made any attempt to trace the Brashear family, because I am very busy trying to get all the family information on my Dad's side of the family (Hebert). I am sending you the information I have on the Brashear.

SAMUEL BRASHEARS, Creek Warrior:

v5**523.** [8]3. **Samuel Brashears, Jr**, b. June 1792, s/o Samuel Brashears Sr and Rachel Durant; m.1. _____ (Samuel is head of household in the 1815 census of Monroe Co, AL, with a family that consisted of two persons. Samuel and a young wife are in the 1830 Census of Clarke Co, AL: (101001-11001-03). ?m.2. c1833, a white woman.

Under the terms of the Creek Treaty of 1814, ending the Creek War, Samuel was granted Sec 2, T5N R4E, west of the Alabama River, as a "friendly Creek." (ref: *Who Was Who Among the Southern Indians*, by Don Martini, p.61)

In 1832, he wrote from Suggsville, AL, that he had been omitted from that year's Creek census due to "the color of my skin." Apparently, he was too light. (ref: *Who Was Who Among the Southern Indians*, by Don Martini, p.61, citing Creek Reserves, Office of Indian Affairs, Roll 241.)

In 1840 Clarke Co, AL, Census, S. Brashears, aged 40-50, has a wife, 30-40, and 7 children (1010001-121101-??). Samuel apparently died in the 1840s; five Brashears children, apparently his orphans, are living in 1850 (Sumter Co, AL #122-124, p.265) with Thomas and Susan (Brashears) Lanier (names given to the right in the following list of Samuel's children in 1840).

^{v5}796. ^{9}1. son, b. 1810-15, (15-20 in 1830)

^{v5}797. ^{9}2. dau, b. 1820-25, (5-10 in 1830; 15-20 in 1840)

^{v5}798. ^{9}3. dau, b. 1825-30   **?Amanda Brashears**, b. c1831? (19 in 1850)

^{v5}799. ^{9}4. son, b. 1825-30   **?James Brashears**, b. c1833? (17 in 1850)

^{v5}800. ^{9}5. dau, b. 1830-35, (5-10 in 1840), d. young? (not in 1850)

^{v5}801. ^{9}6. dau, b. 1830-35   **?Martha Brashears**, b. c1836? (14 in 1850)

^{v5}802. ^{9}7. dau, b. 1835-40   **?Mallissa Brashears**, b. c1838? (12 in 1850)

^{v5}803. ^{9}8. son, b. 1835-40   **?Jesse Brashears**, b. c1840? (10 in 1850)

After the War of 1812 and the Creek War of 1814, the government decided to sell much of the "public lands" east of the Pearl River. No matter that people, mainly Indians, were living and farming there, the government had decided it would sell the land right out from under them. Samuel Brashear protested and submitted documents to justify his claim to section 2, T5N, R4E, where he had lived for some time. This is about 70 miles south and 30 miles east of the Suk-en-Atcha settlement in Sumter Co, that is, it is in the neighborhood of St. Stephens Trading post and possibly in Clarke County, which is across the river from St. Stephens.

Territorial Papers of the U.S. — Alabama Territory, 1817-1819,
v.18:

Secretary Hitchcock to Josiah Meigs,

> St. Stephens, 13th Jan 1819

Sir, the enclosed affidavits exhibit the grounds of a claim in favor of Mr. Samuel Brashiers to a Section of Land No. 2 in Township No. 5 and Range 4 East of the Basis Meridian, in the District of Public Lands east of Pearl River, by virtue of the treaty of General Andrew Jackson made with the Creek Nation of Indians, dated the 9th day of August 1814 and the acts of Congress passed pursuant thereto.

You will observe that the affidavits substantiate the fact of his being a warrior of the Creek Nation, of his having been friendly to the American Cause, and of his having fought for them during the war which terminated with that treaty, of his having cultivated that section previous to that treaty, of his having continued his possession from that time without intermission, and that he now resides on and cultivates the same, all which bring his claim strictly within the provision of that treaty in favor of friendly Creeks.

The district of Country comprehending this section, by the Proclamation of the President, dated the _____ day of _____ 1818, ordered to be sold at this place, the sale to commence on the 2nd Monday of April next, and, as there is no reservation made in the Proclamation which will save Mr. Brashiers his rights, I have taken the liberty, in his behalf, to forward the enclosed, and have to request, should you deem it proper, that you will take such measures as will enable the Register and Receiver at this place to reserve from sale the section which he claims.

I have the honor to be very respectfully your obedient servant.

> /s/ Henry Hitchcock

Israel Pickens and William Crawford to Josiah Meigs

> Land Office, St. Stephens, 2nd May 1815

Sir, The public sale of lands held here in pursuance of the President's Proclamation have closed after a continuance of 3 weeks. All the Townships advertized have been offered excepting the 4 directed by your letter of 18 Jan to be reserved for the

French Emigrants. The section 2, Township 5, Range 4 East, embracing the claim of S. Brashears was, in consequence of your letter of 3rd Feb last and the accompanying affidavits, not offered. We have understood that several other claims of friendly Creeks are situate somewhere in the 4th, 5th, and 6th Townships of the 4th Range, but we have had no notice from any official source as to the existence or location of these claims. No other tracts were therefore withheld from sale on account of Indian claims.

    [Very long letter, about other things; not copied]
        /s/ Israel Pickens, Register
        /s/ William Crawford, Receiver

If you were an Indian, even a half-breed, and you didn't stand up and protest on paper in the white man's way, you lost your land!

8. ZADOCK BRASHEARS, SR and SUSANNAH VAUGHN

ᵛ⁵231. Zadock Brashears Sr, s/o Jesse Brashear and Elizabeth Prather, was born probably in Orange (now Guilford) County, NC, c1755 (on 13 Jan 1810, he testified in connection with the Succession of David White that he was 54 years old). His father was on the tax list there that year and also received a Granville Land Grant of 637 acres. He died before 11 Nov 1834.

Zadock migrated with his parents to Pensacola about 1773.

Zadock Brashears testified in 1805 that, 24 years before (i.e. about 1781), he was employed by a Mr. Wilson in Pensacola, Florida. (*West Florida Records*, Vol. 10, p.188)

He settled about 1783 on the Tombigbee River, in the vicinity of Fort St. Stephens.

By 1784, Zadock Brashears had land on the Tombigbee River, near its confluence with the Alabama River, about half way between St. Stephens Trading post and Mobile.

In 1788, he was living on the west bank of the Tombigbee River, Mississippi Territory, according to the *American State Papers, Class III, Public Lands*, V.1, 1789-1809. In 1797, he was granted 640 acres of land on the Tombigbee River, presumably the same tract (*Am. St. Pap. Cl. II*, v.1, p.42).

In the late 1790s and early part of the 1800s, he lived on Thompson's Creek (Rio Feliciana in Spanish) in the District of Baton Rouge, Feliciana Parish, Spanish West Florida.

After about 1805-08, he went to live on Suk-en-Atcha Creek, Sumter County, in the old Choctaw Nation, now Alabama. He died there after 1832 and before Nov 1834.

Land and Court Records

Much of Zadock's life can be documented by land and court records.

George Robbins's case No. 37 on the docket of the Board, and No. 26 on the books of the Register. (Thanks to Harley D. Anders for the copy.)

Claim - A donation of six hundred and forty acres, as assignee and legal representative of Zadock Brashear, under the second section of the act.

The claimant presented his claim, together with a surveyor's plot of the land claimed, in the words and figures following, to wit:

To the Commissioners appointed in pursuance of the act of Congress passed the 3d day of March, 1803, for receiving and adjusting the claims to lands south of the Tennessee and east of the Pearl river.

Please to take notice, that the following tract of land, situated on the west side of Tombigbee river, bounded on the southwest by lands claimed by Young Gaines, on the southeast, by vacant land, and on the northeast by the claim of John Cozby; beginning on a large sycamore, and the river bank, and runs south, sixty degrees west, fifty chains, to a red oak; thence, south, thirty degrees east, one hundred and fifteen chains, to a black gum; thence, north, sixty degrees east, sixty chains, to an elm on the river bank; and from thence, the meanders of the river, to the place of beginning; having such marks, natural and artificial, as are represented in the plat annexed, containing six hundred and forty acres; is claimed by George Robbins, legal representative of Zadock Brashear, under and by virtue of a settlement bearing date in the year one

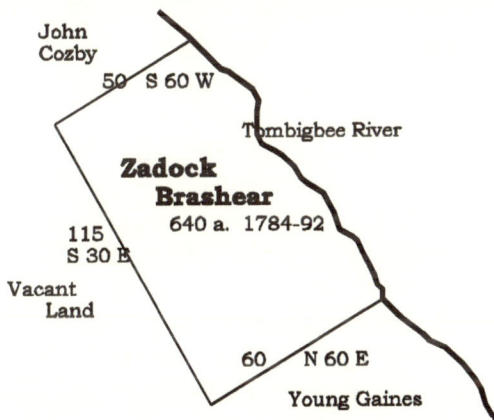

thousand seven hundred and eighty-four, and now exhibited unto the Register of the Land Office established east of the Pearl river, to be recorded as directed by said act. To all which he begs leave to refer, as also to the copy of the plot herewith filed.

GEORGE ROBBINS

(Plat omitted) Entered in record of claims, vol. 1, page 73, by Edward Lloyd Wailes, for

JOSEPH CHAMBERS, Register

Mississippi Territory, Washington County:

Joseph Lawrence and William Shaw came forward and made oath, that they carried the chain for Thomas Bilbo while he was surveying a tract of land for George Robbins, to their best skill and judgment, this tenth day of March, 1804.

JOSEPH LAWRENCE

WILLIAM SHAW

Sworn to before me, John Murrell, J.P.

The claimant exhibited a deed of conveyance from Zadock Brashear, bearing date the 14th date of April, 1799, assigning and conveying to the said Robbins, all the Brashear's rights and title to the improvements which he had made on said tract of land.

Young Gaines, Sen, and Robert Welch were produced as witnesses, and, being duly sworn, the said Gaines deposed, that Zadock Brashear did inhabit and cultivate the land now in question about the years 1791, 1792, and 1793, and then moved out of the territory into the Spanish country, and had lived there ever since; that Brashear's cultivation and improvement was considerably large, and after he went off the place was possessed by the Indians; but how long he could not say.

The said Welch deposes that he agrees with the testimony given by Young Gaines, Senior; and further, that Indians, who were the relations of Zadock Brashear's wife, inhabited and cultivated on the land now claimed, in the years 1797 and 1798; and that Zadock Brashear was in 1797 twenty-one years of age. (Ed. note: The reference to "twenty-one years of age," is interpreted to mean: "Twenty-one years of age, or over.")

The Board ordered that the case be postponed for consideration.

June 2, 1804

George Robbins, representative of Zadock Brashear:

Thomas Eldridge was presented as a witness, and, being duly sworn, deposed, that, in the year 1797, an Indian inhabited and cultivated the land in question, for the use and account of Zadock Brashear; that said Brashear sent him clothing by him, the deponent, which he delivered him for his services in taking care of the houses and plantation of Brashears; that, in the year 1799, said Brashear sent me a letter requesting I would inform the Indian that he might quit the land, as he had sold his right to a man by the name of Robbins; that this Indian lived with Brashear while he resided on said place, and continued to live thereon, from the time Brashear removed therefrom, for account of said Brashear, until the year 1799; that, some time after, he informed the Indian that Brashear had sold it; that said Brashear was, in the year 1799, the head of a family, and more than twenty-one years of age.

On due consideration, the Board is of the opinion that this claim is not supported agreeably to the requirements of law, but that the claimant may be entitled under the third section of the act, to a right of preemption to six hundred and forty acres of land, to be located as follows, to wit:

Beginning at the northwest corner of Matthew Shaw's three hundred and twenty acre tract; thence, with the line of said tract, due east, to the west margin of Tombigbee river; thence, up the same so far as to make ninety-five chains on a due north line; thence, due west, so far that a line therefrom, due south, shall strike the place of beginning. And the Board doth order that a certificate be granted to him accordingly, if requested.

George Robbins, representative of Zadock Brashear:

On further investigation and consideration, the Board is of opinion that this claim be located as follows, viz.: Beginning at a sycamore on the west margin of the Tombigbee river, being also the beginning corner of William William's preemption tract of one hundred and one acres, and the same sycamore described in the claimant's plot, entered in the Register's Office; thence south, sixty degrees west, fifty chains; thence, south, thirty degrees east, to the west margin of the Tombigbee river, and up the said margin to the place of beginning, shall include two hundred and twenty acres of land. (*Early Settlers of*

Mississippi as Taken From Land Claims in the Mississippi Territory, Walter Lowrie, Editor, *The American State Papers*, Vol. 1; *Land Claims in the Mississippi Territory*, p. 616-617, p.717 and p.771.)

(Note: This records leaves out the boundary on the southeast, but is otherwise Zadock's tract of 1784. Say Harley: "The physical description given for this land places it at Nanna Hubba Bluff, near the confluence of the Tombigbee and Alabama rivers. This was part of the Choctaw Nation at this time. This appears to be the same property as is referred to under dates of 6 March 1804 and 14 April 1799.")

On 8 May 1798, Zadock Brashears, a resident of New Feliciana, sold 200 arpents of land on Thompson's Creek to Manuel Monteguado, bounded by land of Zadock Brashears and Thomas Vaughn. (Statement was made in 1806.) (*Archives of Spanish West Florida*, Vol. XIX, p.9) He may have been getting ready for a permanent move to Suk-en-atcha, Sumter Co, AL.

Archives of Spanish West Florida, Vol VII, p.36: Credit sale of a negro boy, by Helene de Grand Pré to Belonie Hebert (Written in Spanish), "I Helene de Grand Pré, authorized by my father, inhabitant of District of Baton Rouge, sell a negro boy called Toby, a native of this colony, 14 years old, which negro I acquired from the inhabitant, ZEDOC BRASHEARS."

Archives of Spanish West Florida, Vol VII, p.?: Auction sale of property of Decedent in the District of Feliciana, Sept 12-17 inclusive. item: another black horse, marked "P" on the left shoulder, was cried out, which was auctioned to John Rhea, for the sum of eight ——, three pesos, and he named ZEDOC BRASHEARS as his bondsman.

3 June 180_: *Archives of Spanish West Florida*, Vol XIV, p.24: Today, June 3rd, I, Pedro Luis Morel notified the preceding decrees to Messrs Edmond Harris, Philip Waltman, and William Meirs who were established on the three thousand arpents included on plan no. 1784, designated by letter "B", and that Pipes from Bayou Sarah had cleared the land near Philip Waltman, who not being present, I could not notify them of the preceding decree, which I certify, and I signed with ZEDOC

BRASHEARS and the aforementioned individuals.

Pedro Luis Morel   Mark [B] of Zedoc Brashears
Mark [X] of Philip Waltman
Edmond Harris
Mark [WA] of William Heirs (prob Ayers)

By 1803, Zadock was living on the Tombigbee River again: 12 May 1803: *Archives of Spanish West Florida*, Vol VIII, p.74, Transfer of power of attorney from Richard Brashears, agent for James Danley, to Zadoc Brashears (Written in Spanish), "Be it known to all who may see this act that I, [p.192] Richard Brashears, a citizen of the settlement of Washington on the Tombigbee River in the territory of Mississippi, as attorney for James Danley of said settlement and territory, that I depose and give my full power and in particular to my cousin and friend Zadoc Brashears, resident of Thompson's Creek in the dominions of His Catholic Majesty, in order that in my name and in the name of the said James Danley, have and pass the sale of the following five head of slaves of the property of said James Danley, named Rosa, thirty-five years old; Amey, fifteen years old; Milley and Comley, eight years of age; and Ana, three years of age, to Christian Bingaman, a resident of New Feliciana in the fourth district, as his property in order that he enjoy them as his slaves and dispose of them as he wishes as his true property, without anyone being able to impede him in any form; and in order that this be evident, I sign with Alcalde John O'Connor and the witnesses of assistance, Solomon Alston and William Barker, New Feliciana, Fourth District, May 12, 1803

Solomon Alston
William Barker   Richd Brashers
Juan O'Connor

On 12 Sept 1803, he was apparently living in New Feliciana: he bought a bolt of linen from the estate of Paul Gardner (*Archives of Spanish West Florida*, v.7, p.127).

On 24 Oct 1805, James Denly, of Washington Co, Mississippi Territory, appointed John Denly of the county aforesaid, his attorney, to demand and receive of and from Zadock Brashears of the Province of New Felianana [sic] in his Catholick Majestys Dominion all money due him from a suit brought by him against Samuel Jones in the Province and dominion aforesaid.

On 7 June 1812, Zadock Brashears of Parish of Feliciana, Territory of Orleans, sold 400 acres of land on Redwood Creek to Anne Lyle, also known as Anne Brashears, daughter of Zadock, in Feliciana Parish. Alexander Vaughn was witness (*West Feliciana Parish Notarial Records*, Bk, A, p.210).

He probably moved about this time to Suk-en-atcha Creek, Sumter Co, AL. On 8 Dec 1816, Zadock Brashears, "late of Feliciana Parish," sold to Elizabeth (Brashears) Buckholtz of Amite Co, MS, she being one of his lawful heirs, for $10.00 and other considerations, a parcel of land, 600 acres, on Redwood Creek. The transaction was recorded in both places: *West Feliciana Parish Notarial Records*, Bk B, p.1; and *Amite Co, MS, Deeds*, Bk 2, p.34-6.

Zadock died before 11 Nov 1834, when Alexander Brashears, Allen Stanton, David W. Wall, and Betsy Buckles made affidavit in Sumter Co, AL, that Zadock was dead. (ref: *Who Was Who Among the Southern Indians*, by Don Martini, p.64)

On 30 April 1837, George S. Gaines made affidavit that Zadock Brashears, deceased, had sold his Choctaw reservation to Green B. Chaney of Mobile, AL, on 30 April 1832.

On 10 Oct 1842, Francis S. Lyon (a local lawyer, who had served in the U.S. House of Representatives) was appointed administrator of the estate of Zadock Brashears, deceased (Sumter Co, AL, Orphans Court Minutes, Bk 3, p.6); John McGrew and William Anderson were bondsmen.

On 26 June 1844, a citation was issued Francis S. Lyons to file his account for settlement of the estate of Zadock Brashears (Orphans Court Minutes, Bk 7, p.585).

The Vaughn Connection

Zadock Brashears married, in 1791, at Jones Bluff (now Epes), Sumter Co, AL, **Susannah Vaughn**, b. c1770, d. c1823, officially d/o Thomas Vaughn, a Scotsman, and a Choctaw woman, Winifred, but possibly (no documentation) a daughter of John Turnbull and Winifred, a Choctaw woman. About 1805-08, they moved to Suk En Atcha Creek, a tributary of the Tombigbee River, and took up land as Choctaws in Sumter Co, Alabama. Zadock was still there in 1831, when a special census was made of Choctaws to determine the beneficiaries of Article 14 of the Treaty of Dancing Rabbit Creek of 1830.

Susannah Vaughn was, officially, the oldest child and only daughter of Thomas Vaughn and "Winifred," his Choctaw wife. Thomas Vaughn was b. c1744, possibly in Georgia. He came from Augusta, GA, to Thompsons Creek, New Feliciana Parish, c1795. That is, it seems highly unlikely that he was in the Choctaw Nation about 1770, when Susannah was born. He was surely in the Choctaw Nation about 1790 when Robert Vaughn was born. He d. in New Orleans, c1804, probably while there on business. Thomas Vaughn's children, named in court proceedings, were Susannah, Robert, James, Louis, Alexander, and George. There was also a Samuel Vaughn, who died young.

The will of Thomas Vaughn, dated Thompsons Creek, 21 Aug 1800, devised all his holdings to Robert and James Vaughn, cutting out Susannah, Louis, Alexander, and George. After a certified copy of the will was proved in New Orleans, Robert and James Vaughn "presented themselves and in the presence of my [i.e. the Alcalde, John Mears] witnesses of assistance, requested permission to protest against the last will and testament of their late father, the certified copy of the certified copy of which had just been read in their presence, because they did not consider it an act of justice in their late father, deceased, to devise to them the whole of his property to the exclusion of their sister, Mrs. Susannah Brashears, the wife of Zadok Brashiers; and their brothers Louis, Alexander, and George, whom the said two legatees Robert and James think ought to participate equally with themselves in the property which may be found belonging to the estate of their father Thomas Vaughn, deceased, in further testimony whereof..." 24 Dec 1804, signed Robt Vaughn and James [X] Vaughn (*Archives of Spanish West Florida*, p.1095-1102, or Vol. 4, p.364-70)

Zadock Brashears was appointed to assess the holdings of Thomas Vaughn. He listed several head of livestock, three negro boys and three negro girls (besides "a negro boy named Stephen about fourteen years old which the late Thomas Vaughn gave to his son Robert when a boy of about five years old, at which time he committed his said son Robert to Zadok Brashiers, his [the boy's] brother-in-law, to be brought up and educated, and delivered at the same time the negro Stephen as son Robert's property, who as well as Robert has been brought up by the said Zadok Brashiers" (pp.1101-02) ... Zadock also mentioned several large tracts of land, some of which were encumbered with debt, some of which had been sold but were in protest and litigation, etc.

The children under fourteen were asked to choose a guardian. Alexander, age about 10, and George, age about 8, chose Zadock Brashears. Catherine Turnbull, David White, and John Downy were called to testify that the four excluded children were children of the same mother, which they did. Then, Robert and James were questioned separately and asked if they really wanted to challenge the will— to which they answered yes. Whereupon the court set aside the will, appointed Edward Hawes as administrator, and proceeded as if the will did not exist.

On 3 March 1805, the administrator brought in an inventory specifying the livestock, negroes, and land that Zadock had enumerated earlier, worth $5369, including debts due the estate from Zadock ($1640) and Samuel Brashears, possibly a cousin ($465). One parcel of land that Thomas had sold was held out of the proceedings as the separate property of Robert Vaughn, the deed having been made some years before and Robert having protested the sale of the land by his father, Thomas. Finally, minors upwards of twelve years of age, Robert and James Vaughn were asked to elect a guardian for themselves; both of them chose Zadock Brashears, "their eldest sister's husband." David White and Edward Hawes were Zadock's bondsmen. But the estate was not, at once, divided equitably among the six children of Thomas Vaughn.

The baptismal certificate for Robert Vaughn, dated 4 May 1794, is extant and identifies his parents as Thomas Vaughn and Winifred, an Indian woman from "Standing Hickory," a Choctaw village in the Oklafalaya District. (Sacramental Records of St. Joseph's Church, Baton Rouge, Item #1, p.33) At the estate proceedings of Thomas Vaughn, Catherine Rucker (widow of John Turnbull) and David White (stepfather of Sylvia Turnbull) testified that all the children mentioned in the will were the children of the same mother, but they never quite say they all had the same father. Susannah is at least 15 years older than Robert, maybe as much as 20 years older, born when Thomas Vaughn was about 26 and probably not in the Choctaw Nation; it is possible, perhaps likely, that Susannah was the daughter of Winifred and some other man, but probably not John Turnbull, as family tradition held, who was probably not in the U.S. when Susannah was born. Some researchers think David White, Catherine Turnbull, and the Vaughn children were engaging in a bit of benevolent perjury, not to say creative lying, in order to allow Susannah to have a share of the Vaughn estate.

From the records, we can infer that (officially) the children of Thomas Vaughn were:

1. Susannah Vaughn, b. c1770 (assuming she was about 15 when her first child was born in 1785); m. 1791, Zadock Brashears Sr
2. Samuel Vaughn, died young.
3. Robert Vaughn, b. bef 1790, bapt. 4 May 1794; under 21 but over 12 in 1805 (in 1811 court records, he was no longer referred to as a minor), d. 1813; m. 11 Aug 1811, Winifred "Winnie" Ford Barrum, (Wilkinson Co, MS, Marriages, Casey's Volume III, p.111). [Bond Bk. B, p.177]). On 23 April 1813, Winny Vaughn petitioned for appointment as curator for the estate of Robert Vaughn, deceased, who died intestate. On 25 Sept 1813, she qualified, with Samuel Clark (?security), to act as and, with no opposition, was appointed curator for Robert Vaughn (her infant son). (Probate Records, West Feliciana Parish, 1811-1819, Book 1, p.68, 79.) Winifred m.2. _____ Gayle; on 7 Dec 1816, Winnifred Gayle, maternal tutor of minor, Robert Vaughn, sold to Llewellen Griffin for $5000 a tract of land on Thompson Creek bounded by lands of Thomas Vaughn and on lower side by lands of Zadock Brashears. (Notarial Bk. AA, p.186, Feliciana Parish, Louisiana)
   1. Robert "Robin" Vaughn, b. 1813, after death of his father.
4. James Vaughn, b. c1791; under 21 but over 12 in 1805; still a minor in 1811.
5. Louis or Lewis Vaughn, b. c1793; "about 12 years old" in 1805
6. Alexander Vaughn, b. c1795; "10 yrs old" in 1805. Under the terms of the Treaty of Dancing Rabbit Creek, Alexander received lot No. 321. SE ¼ of Sec 10, T17, R1W (List of Locations of Choctaw Reservations under the 1830 treaty. Records Relating to Identification of Mississippi Choctaws; Fort Worth Federal Records Center, Microcopy 7RA-116, roll 1). 17 Sept 1841, Title recorded for the NW ¼ and SW ¼ of Sec 10, T17N, R1W, Sumter County, AL, as a reservee under

Choctaw Treaty. (Tract Book II, p.53, Sumter County, Alabama.)
7. George H. Vaughn, b. c1797; "8 yrs old" in 1805

26 July 1811: To the honorable the Judge of Court of Probates for the Parish of Feliciana.

The undersigned executor and heirs of the estate of Thomas Vaughn deceased beg leave to represent that the said heirs having now become of age except the heir George Vaughn who has attained the age of sixteen years and the undersigned executor Zadock Brashears wishing by consent of (these?) heirs to be exonerated from his charge they therefore pray that an examination of this administration of said Brashears may be made by the honourable court for which purpose the Inventory of said estate and the accounts are hereunto annexed. That the said Brashears Be in future exonerated from his administration and that the heir Robert Vaughn be appointed executor and guardian to the minor heir George Vaughn on his giving security for the faithful discharge of his duty. 26th July 1811 ———-

his
Zadock [B] Brashears
mark
Robt. Vaughan
Alexander Vaughan
James Vaughan
George Vaughan
Soosana Brashears

Edmund (—?— Hawes)
Administrator
for the Estate of
Thomas Vaughan
Deced'.

(Probate Records, West Feliciana Parish, Louisiana.)

PETITION #68 [to Feliciana Parish Court]
LEWIS VAUGHAN, et al, THE HEIRS & REP'S. OF THOS. VAUGHAN
Filed November 2, 1812
To the Judge of the Parish Court, Parish of Feliciana:
The petition of Lewis Vaughan, James Vaughan, Alexander and George Vaughan and of Zadock Brashears for his own interest and as guardian of such minors. That Thomas Vaughan, father of the above named Lewis, James, Alexander and George Vaughan, departed this life some eight years past or upward,

leaving a considerable real and personal estate; that your pet'r, Zadock Brashears, was appointed the guardian of the said children, except Lewis who was then of full age as reported - that your pet'r, Zadock, also intermarried with Susan Vaughan, daughter of the said Thomas, by whom he has sundry children called Vaughan, Sophie, Zadock Jr, Turner & others - that your pet'r (—?—) the estimated (—?—) of the Spanish customs as they then were in the settlement of the said Thomas estate & made a division of the estate in (—-?—) manner amongst the heirs by (—-?—-) before an Alcalde which having never become a matter of record & the division not altogether satisfactory.

Showeth that in the lifetime of Thomas Vaughn he permitted a negro boy called Stephen to be called "Robin's Boy", viz: Robert, the oldest son of the said Thomas & at the time of the valuation of the estate by an Alcalde the said boy, Stephen, was not taken into the valuation but remained undivided until the present time - That Robert Vaughn departed this life a short time past leaving a widow and one child called "Robin", born since the death of the said Robert & that altho the heirs of Thomas always contended for the division of the said negro, Stephen, the same has never yet been done and are now desirous that a full division & settlement of the estate may take place with the guardian (—?—) Hon'r. Court.

Your pet'r therefore pray (—?—) as the (—-?—-) is to call all partys before the Hon'r. Court to have their several rights decided & adjudged & settled. That no administration has yet taken place on the estate of the said Robert & that the only child is an infant with the widow may require representation before the Hon'r Court.

Your pet'r therefore submit that your Hon'r will appoint a guardian ad litem if one (—-?—-) to the said child (—?—) to the said Robert's estate who is deceased (—?—) and that (——?——) may be appointed by your Hon'r to divide the estate of the said Thomas the (——?—-) and to settle his estate by making reports (—?—) as in duty bound will ever pray.

Your petitioners further state that Robert Vaughn in his lifetime, by consent of the other heirs, received a valuable negro woman which he sold for his own use to the amount of four hundred and eighty dollars which sum they pray may be deducted out of the share of the heirs of said Robert deceased and your petitioners farther state that other sum, and sums of money are chargeable to the said Robert, deceased, which they beg leave to manifest to your Hon'r and they will pray.

/s/ Lewis Vaughan

Let Winney Vaugan be appointed curator ad litem to represent the estate of Robert Vaughan in the Division of the estate of Thomas Vaughn which is timely ordered to be conducted by L. (?) Griffith, Jno. Stewart & James McGilroy who are (—- ?—-) as soon as convenient to the division of the said estate conformably to the law & make due report to this court.

/s/ John P. Hampton (Judge)

(Petition #68, Probate Records, Feliciana Parish, Louisiana.)

1812 - PETITION #69

VAUGHN BRASHEARS, et al, FOR TUTORSHIP

To the Judge of the Parish Court Parish of Feliciana:
May it be represented to the Hon'r Court that Robert Vaughn, the Tutor and Guardian of the following children, has departed this life some short time past. The said guardianship as will appear by the records of the Hon'r Court - viz:

Vaughn Brashears   Age 14
Sophie "   Age 10
Zadock "   Age 6 (or 8) (documents differ)
Turner "   Age 3

& it is submitted that Vaughn may choose & nominate another Guardian for his (interest?) & that the same may be approved by the Hon'r Court (—-?—-) of the said Sophie, Zadock & Turner Brashears & it is submitted that Zadock Brashears now may be appointed tutor & Guardian, giving bond as may be required.

/s/ (illegible)

Let the prayers of the within petition be granted.
/s/ John P. Hampton, (Judge)
(Petition #69, Parish Court, Parish of Feliciana)

The following Advertisement appeared in a local newspaper, 27 Jan 1816:
PROBATE SALE: WILL be offered for sale to the highest bidder, at the Court House in St. Francisville, on the 10th day of February next, all the estate; real and personal of Thomas Vaughn, deceased, consisting of one Tract of Land, containing

500 arpents, lying near the plantation of Gen. Robert McCausland. One Tract, containing 320 arpents, lying on Thompson's Creek, within two miles of the Court House — One other Tract of Land, containing 400 arpents, lying on the river Amite — Also one pair Horse Mill Stones, of a superior quality. Terms will be made known at the time and place of sale.

J. H. Johnson, J. G. P.

(Court seal dated 10 Feb. 1816)

To the Honorable, the Parish Judge of Parish of Feliciana and exofficio Judge of the Court of Probates in and for the same, the petition of George H. Vaughn of said Parish respectfully shows:

That Thomas Vaughn, late of this Parish, has departed this life leaving a considerable estate; that the said Thomas Vaughn has departed this life leaving as heirs in the direct decendency line Lewis, James, Alexander and George Vaughn, the latter your petitioner; also Robert Vaughn (since dead); all ligitimate children of said Thomas and your petitioner further states that some of the heirs of said Thomas reside out of the state of Louisiana, but all are of full age. Wherefore, your petitioner prays that the Estate of the said Thomas Vaughn may be sold and collection and partition thereof be made among the heirs of said Thomas as directed by law.

/s/ George H. Vaughan

(Probate Records, West Feliciana Parish, Louisiana. No mention of Susannah. Why??)

This following is apparently a fragment from the Estate Sale: One pair Mill Stones adjudged to John Stuart for the sum of fifteen Dollars (-?-) Cash— [NOTE: John Stewart, or Stuart, m. Susanna Brashears, d/o Zadock and Susannah (Vaughn) Brashears.]

And two other Tracts of Land having been repeatedly offered for sale & no bidder appearing to any (—?—) near their (reasonable?) value they was not sold & the sale of Said Estate was concluded at four o'clock in the afternoon - —-

/s/ John H. Johnson, J.C.G.

/s/ J.L. Finlcy

/s/ John Weed

(Probate Records, Feliciana Parish, Louisiana)

10 Feb. 1816,
State of Louisiana)
Parish of Feliciana)

Probate Sale of the Estate of Thomas Vaughn late of this Parish (-?-) made for the purpose of effecting a division of Said Estate amongst the Heirs of Said Vaughn Made under the authority of John H. Johnson, Judge of Said Parish in presence of (Witn'ss ?) John (Weed?), & Joseph L. Finley (——?——) - on a Credit of one, two & three years, the purchasers giving good Security, with Special Mortgage for the Land, done at St. Francis (—-?—-) this 10 day of February, A.D. 1816 - (—? —)

One tract of Land (lot?) of Patrick Tigert of five Hundred Arpents bounded North by land of Robert McCausland & west by Land of Francis Watts (adjudged?) to Robert McCausland for the sum of Two Thousand Dollars, who gives as his Security Alexander Crawford.

                    /s/ Robt McCausland
                    /s/ Alexander Crawford
(Witness) /s/John Weed
          /s/ J.L. Finley
(Probate Records, Feliciana Parish, Louisiana)
(Note: This document contains annotations overwritten across its face relating to payments received, etc.,

12 Feb 1816,

"Know all men by these presents that we George H. Vaughn and John Stuart, of the Parish of Feliciana and State of Louisiana, are held and firmly bound unto Lewis Vaughn, James Vaughn and Alexander Vaughn, heirs of Thomas Vaughn, late of the Parish and State aforesaid in the sum of Six Hundred Sixty Six Dollars, Sixty-six and Two Thirds Cents, lawful money of the United States, to which payment well and truly to be made, we bind ourselves and heirs, executors, administrators and curators, firmly by these presents, sealed with our seals and dated this 12th day of February, in the year of our Lord 1816.

Whereas it has been found necessary to effect a partition of the Estate of the deceased Thomas Vaughn, among his (-?-) heirs, to make Sale thereof, agreeably by the provisions of the Laws governing the case - and whereas, on the 10 day of February 1816, a sale of one tract of land of five hundred arpents, bounded north by lands of Robert W. McCausland, and west by land of Francis Watts, was made by the Honorable John H. Johnson, Parish Judge of the Parish of Feliciana, on the terms following, via: a credit of one two and three years, the purchasers giving good security with special mortgages on the land; at which said Sale Robert W. McCausland became the purchaser of said land - and whereas by a special arrangement made with the purchaser, by the above (bounded?) George Vaughn, one of the heirs of the deceased Thomas Vaughn, the said George H. Vaughn has this day received of the aforesaid Robert W. McCausland the aforesaid sum of Six Hundred Sixty-Six Dollars, Sixty-Six and Two Thirds Cents, the first payment of said purchase -

Now the conditions of the above obligation is such that if the above bound George H. Vaughn shall well and truly account to and with the aforesaid Lewis Vaughn, James Vaughn and Alexander Vaughn (heirs with the said George H. Vaughn, of the estate of the deceased Thomas Vaughn) when thereto required for this partition aforesaid, then the above obligation to be void, else to remain in full force and virtue.

/s/ G.H. Vaughn (seal)
/s/ John Stewart (seal)

Witness:
James M. Bradford

Recd. of Wm. H. Johnson, Judge of the Parish of Feliciana the sum of Six Hundred and Sixty-Seven Dollars, being the amt. of the Second Payment, due from Genl. Robert W. McCausland for the Tract of Land for which the within Bond was given - February 26, 1817.

/s/ G.H. Vaughn

Witness:
Steven Beauchamp
John W. Watts
(Probate Records, Parish of Feliciana, Louisiana, U.S.A.)

On 10 Oct 1818, George Vaughn, acting as agent for: James Vaughn, Lewis Vaughn, and Alexander Vaughn, sold to John Reall of Feliciana Parish for $640, "a tract of land lying and being on River of Feliciana (now Thompsons Creek) bounded by land of Zadock Brashears and below by vacant land, 320 arpents, as appears on figurative plan and Spanish papers hereunto annexed, forming part of this conveyance" (Notarial Record Book A, p.218, West Feliciana Parish) (Note: Above instrument in Spanish on p.631-632 of old Book A and Map on p.632. Map recorded La. Office, Commissioner Land Claims West of Pearl River, East of the Mississippi, in Lib. No. 2, Fol. 42, etc.)

The Turnbull Connection

The relationship of Zadock Brashears and Susannah Vaughn to John Turnbull and his family is uncertain, but they act rather like Susannah was somehow related to the Turnbulls. (Much of the following data is from Chris B. Morgan, for which many thanks.)

John Turnbull, b. 1741, County Dumfries, Scotland, d. 24 Aug 1799, near Baton Rouge and was buried in the Spanish Cemetery, later embraced by the old campus of Louisiana State University, which was destroyed in the early 1930s. John and his brother, Walter Turnbull, came to the Lower Mississippi Valley probably about 1760, certainly by 1763, the year the British took over West Florida from the French. They engaged in the Indian trade, land speculations, and anything else they could turn a buck at.

There is no hard evidence that either participated in the Fort Panmure Rebellion in 1781, but Walter left almost immediately (The Spanish authorities banned him from the colony) and John went into hiding for a while.

Early in 1781, John Turnbull was arrested by the Spanish authorities in Mobile and held prisoner there for a while, until the Chickasaws offered several Spanish prisoners in exchange for him. John Turnbull seems to have sought (or was offered) refuge among the Chickasaw Indians, where his first wife was a member of the tribe. In the Chickasaw Nation, he offered aid to some of the Panmure rebels.

Walter Turnbull removed to the Bahamas, from which he continued to take part in the affairs of the Lower Mississippi. Walter's family is said to have died about this time, though whether in Mississippi or the Bahamas is uncertain. In the Bahamas, Walter married a woman named Mary, who had two daughters by a previous marriage, and they had at least one son, John.

After Walter died (possibly in Georgia while on business), Mary moved to Liverpool, England. Much later, 1801, she wrote John Turnbull's widow, Catherine (Rucker) Turnbull, that she was contemplating a move to New Orleans, and still later, in 1831, trying to figure out some estate matters in England concerning the father of Walter and John Turnbull, who may also have been named Walter.

John Turnbull married at least three times; first to an unknown Chickasaw woman, who was probably close kin to Tuskiatoka, the Chickasaw Chief. They had two sons, William and George Turnbull.

b1. William Turnbull (s/o John Turnbull and a Chickasaw woman), b. c1763, d. c1833; m. Judith "Judy" Perry, d. 1843, d/o Hardy Perry and his Choctaw wife, Anolah. (A few government records render her name as Panola, which is the Choctaw word for "cotton." Many whites were familiar with this word, and, when they heard "Anolah", which means "talker," they quite possibly mistook it for the word they were familiar with.)

A William Turnbull (apparently the same one) lived near Zadock Brashears and Susannah Vaughn in 1787. Oaths of Allegiance to Spain, signed at the Fort of Mobile on the 4th of January 1787, sworn before Señor Don Pedro Favrot, Captain of the Regiment of Louisiana and Commandant of said Fort, includes:

William Turnbull, signed his name

Zadoc Brochire (by mark)

(*Papeles Procendentes de Cuba*, Archivo General de Indias, Seville, Spain, legajo 200:776)

At the time of the Treaty of Dancing Rabbit Creek, 1830, William and Judith lived on land in Section 17, T22N, R4E, on or near the Yalobusha River. The children still at home in 1830, William Jr and Judy Jr, each qualified for a half section of land under Art. 14, Treaty of Dancing Rabbit Creek, and received Sec 18, right next to where their mother, Judy Turnbull, was living in 1830 and had been living for at least a decade (see documents below).

c1. Agnes O. Turnbull, b. c1805, d. 1859; m.1. c1820 (second wife of) Wesley Trahern, who d. 1829 in Hinds Co, MS. See "Delilah Brashears ([v5]837) and Wesley Trahern" for his children by his first wife. After Wesley died, Agnes m.2. Samuel H. Foster. In 1850, Agnes was living with her daughter, Minerva Metcalf, Tallihatchie, MS. Agnes's children included:

d1. Minerva Trahern, b. 1824, Choctaw Nation, MS; m. c1843, in MS, Josiah Metcalf, b. 1818, OH; they had ch: Napolean Metcalf, b. 1844, and Leticia E. Metcalf, b. 1846, both born Tallahatchie Co, MS.

d2. Gilbert Trahern, b. 1825, Choctaw Nation, MS; m. c1856, Laura V. _____. Gilbert was with his sister, Minerva, on the 1850 census, Tallahatchie Co, MS, and in his own right in 1860. He and Laura had a son born c1857, who died before 1860 (mortality schedule), and Louis Trahern, (⅛ Choctaw, Roll #7499, Census Card 2585), b. 12 Nov 1859, Tallahatchie Co, MS, d. 28 Oct 1939, Pauls Valley, OK. Louis Trahern m. Lula E. Eggleston and had children: Willie May; James Walker; Edwin W.; and Gilbert Eggleston Trahern.

d3. Jesse Foster, b. 1830;

d4. Melvina Rebecca Foster, b. 1833;

d5. Agnes O. Foster, b. 1839;

c2. Anthony Turnbull, b. 1807, d. 1849; m. 1829 Hannah Long, b. c1810, d. 1887; their children included Samuel (1831-1857), and Felicity, b. 1847, who m. 1866, in Holmes Co, MS, James Elisha Reynolds.

c3. Robert Turnbull, b. 1808; m. _____ and had at least one son, John F. Turnbull.

c4. Benjamin Turnbull, b. 1811, d. May 1824

c5. Jesse Turnbull, b. c1815, d. 1843; m. 1843, Elizabeth P. _____. Elizabeth m.2. John G. Donley, son of Major John Donley, two of whose daughters m. Greenwood LeFlore.

c6. William Turnbull Jr, b. bef 1820 (over 10 on 27 Sept 1830)

c7. Judith M. Turnbull, b. bef 1820 (over 10 on 27 Sept 1830); m. a cousin, John P. Turnbull.

b2. George W. Turnbull, (s/o John Turnbull and a Chickasaw woman), b. 1760s, d. after 6 Jan 1860, when he made his will in Blue Co, I.T.; m. Sarah _____ (?Apuckshunnubbee), a Choctaw woman. Some circumstantial evidence suggests that Sarah was another "daughter of Taboca" and a blood-daughter of Apuckshunnubbee, Great Medal Chief of the Oklafalaya, or Western District, Choctaws. Turner Brashears, the Choctaw trader who married c1788 "a daughter of Taboca, called Jane Apuckshunnubbee," was very close to George Turnbull, and George Turnbull named his first son, Turner Brashears Turnbull. Perhaps they were double brothers-in-law, having married sisters. George's wife, Sarah, had to be Choctaw, since he was a Choctaw head of family in 1830.

Maybe Sarah d. c1845, because George came to live in 1846 with or near his son Turner Brashears Turnbull Sr, where he had relocated on the Clear Boggy River, near Caddo, OK. In the 1855 Choctaw census, George W. Turnbull was shown as head of a family, living alone. He died after 6 Jan 1860, when he made his will in Blue Co, I.T.

c1. Nancy Turnbull, m. Jesse Bohanon,

c2. Catherine Turnbull, m. Simon Jones,

c3. Sarah Turnbull, may not have married,

c4. Turner Brashears Turnbull Sr, b. 6 April 1816, d. 1877; m. c1840-41, Blue Co, I.T., Angelico "Jerrico" Perkins, b. c1826, d. 1893

    d1. Leroy Brashears Turnbull, b. 1840, killed by outlaws in 1882

    d2. Simeon Turnbull, b. 1843, d. 1881

    d3. Daniel Turnbull, b. c1844, killed in a shoot-out with rustlers in 1871.

    d4. Malvina Turnbull, b. 1849, d. 1855

    d5. Turner Brashears Turnbull Jr, Choctaw Roll #10785, b. 22 Nov 1851, Blue Co, I.T., d. 1908; m. 26 April 1879, Jackson Co, I.T., Adeline Dwight, Choctaw Roll #10786, d. 1941. In the early 1870s, Turner, and his brothers, Simeon and Daniel, were part of "The Turnbull Rangers," a vigilante group dedicated to ridding the area of horse and cattle thieves. He was later a Captain of Lighthorsemen. Frankie James of Tulsa, OK, has written and published an interesting article on "The Turnbull Rangers."

   d6. Mary Ann Turnbull, b. 1856, d. 1917
   d7. Julia Ann Turnbull, b. 1860, d. 1926, ggm/o Frankie James
   d8. Harriet Turnbull, b. 1860, twin to Julia Ann, d. inf.
   d9. Angeline Turnbull, b. 1864, d. 1897
   c5. John P. Turnbull, b. July 1833; m.1. cousin, Judith Turnbull, m.2. Harriet Williard. John P. Turnbull was a baby in arms when the Turnbulls arrived in Indian Territory, 12 Dec 1833, from Mississippi.
   c6. Rebecca Turnbull, m. Reuben Kemp.

John Turnbull married, second, Isabel "Belcie" Perry, d/o Hardy Perry and Anolah, a Choctaw woman. One undocumented source claimed her name was "Elizabeth"; she may have taken the English name, as did many Choctaws who were closely associated with whites. They had at least one daughter, Sylvia.

   b3. Sylvia Turnbull, (d/o John Turnbull and Isabel "Belcie"" Perry), b. 3 Aug 1783, d. 1821; m.1. David Holsten; m.2. William Young.
      On 19 June 1800, Sylvia Turnbull, child of John Turnbull and Isabel Perry, asked that her curator be changed from her maternal grandfather, Hardy Perry, to David White. (*Archives of Spanish West Florida*, v.4, p.226). Isabel "Belcie" Perry, m.2. David White; Sylvia Turnbull was, therefore, a step-daughter of David White of East Feliciana Parish, a very close associate of Zadock Brashears Sr and Susannah Vaughn. David White made Isabel's daughter, Sylvia, his sole heir.
      On 27 July 1809, Polly (White) Brashears, wife of Philip Brashears, and her sister, Nancy (White) Stuart, wife of William Stuart/Stewart, sued to break the will of David White, "uncle of petitioners," because he left his entire estate to Sylvia Turnbull, a half-Indian girl, wife of David Holsten and daughter of John Turnbull and "an unknown Chickasaw woman." Isabel "Belcie" Perry was

half-Choctaw, not Chickasaw, which just goes to show you how much Polly and Nancy knew about their Indian relatives.

John Turnbull married, third, c1784, Catherine Rucker, of Natchez, b. 1769, d. 1832, d/o Peter Rucker and Sarah Wisdom, of Bayou Pierre. Peter Rucker had been an officer in the British Army. He continued living in Mississippi after he left the service. John Turnbull and Catherine Rucker had seven children:

b4. Isabella Turnbull,
b5. Sarah Turnbull,
b6. John Turnbull,
b7. Mary Turnbull,
b8. Susan Turnbull,
b9. Walter Turnbull,
b10. Daniel Turnbull,

As Indian half-breeds, William, George, and Sylvia Turnbull had no legal rights to any part of their father's estate. But John Turnbull left a will in which he named them as his "illegitimate children" and left them a fair legacy.

Will of John Turnbull, 9 June 1798, *Archives of Spanish West Florida*, pp.781-790; also printed in Baton Rouge: W.P.A., 1937 v.3, p.334; [Pages 781 to 785 contain a Spanish translation of the will of John Turnbull, which is written in English on pages 787 to 790.]

In the name of God, Amen. I, John Turnbull formerly of the country of Dumfries in Scotland, but at present of Baton Rouge District in the Province of Louisiana, being now in good health and of sound mind & memory thanks be given unto God, therefore calling unto mind the mortality of my body, knowing that it is appointed unto all men once to die -- Do make and declare this to be my last will & testament - First - I recommend my Soul to Almighty God that gave it and my Body to the Earth to be buried in Christian burial, at the discretion of my Executors, and as touching my worldly Estate wherewith it hath pleased God to bless me in this life, I give demise [devise?] and dispose of the same in the following manner viz: -
I wish that all my just debts should be fully paid, satisfied,

after which I give and bequeath unto George, William & Sylvia, my three illegitimate children, three thousand dollars each, and the remainder or residue of all the property I possess, I give and bequeath unto my lawful and dearly beloved wife, Catherine Rucker, with whatever children may be at my demise, to be equally divided among them, share and share alike. I do hereby nominate and appoint my worthy friends Charles Norwood & John Bisland Executors, and my loving wife Catherine Rucker aforenam'd Executrix and sole Guardian of her Children while unmarried, and afterwards at the discretion of my Executors aforenam'd to whom I give full power and authority, as much as is required by law, extra-judicially to do and perform all and everything necessary according to the intent and meaning of this my last Will and Testament, and without the interference of justice to take an inventory of my property, and making an estimation thereof by persons appointed to their satisfaction, and to do and perform all and every formality necessary to present before any of the justices or tribunals they may think proper for their approbation.

Lastly, I do hereby utterly disallow revoke and disannul all and every other former testaments, legacies & bequests by me heretofore made, ratifying and confirming this and no other to be my last will & testament - In witness whereof I have hereunto set my hand and seal in New Orleans the ninth of June one thousand seven hundred & ninety eight.

/s/ John Turnbull

/s/ Wm. Stephen
/s/ Pedro Rousslau
/s/ Geo. King
/s/ Danl. Hicky
/s/ Joseph McNeil
/s/ Wm. Wikoff, Junr.
/s/ A. Brooks

10 Aug 1799, Gravely ill, but fully conscious, John TURNBULL, broke the seal on his will and re-read the will in presence of witnesses. (*Louisiana Genealogical Register*, Vol. XX, p. 329) (Note: Mr. Duncan Turnbull of Point Clear, Alabama, a great grandson of John Turnbull, stated on April 8, 1983, that his family legend stated John Turnbull was injured while traveling to visit his daughter, Mary, who lived in Mobile. The

injury is said to have occurred when the stage he was riding hit a rut and a plank from the floor struck him in the groin. He is said to have died of this injury. John Turnbull is also said by Duncan Turnbull to have been married to an Indian Princess and that he had three children by that marriage, Mary, George and William.

24 Aug 1799, John Turnbull died. (*Louisiana Genealogical Register*, Vol. XX, p. 330)

From *Archives of Spanish West Florida*, v.4, p.153: William and George Turnbull are placed in possession of the legacy left them by their natural father, John Turnbull. (Written in Spanish). No. 14.

Be it known to all who this act may see how [p.422] I, William Turnbull, a resident of the Yazoo Territory, declare that I have received for my account, as well as for that of my brother, George Turnbull, a resident of the said Yazoo Territory, by virtue of the authority conferred upon me by my said brother, not by special or general power of attorney, due to the impossibility of executing that according to the usual custom, due to the fact that we both live in a territory not inhabited by civilized people and where there is no established jurisdiction, nor residents who could witness to the authority that my said brother has conferred upon me, so as to be able to deal, contract, receive, pay, give releasing receipts, appear in judicial proceedings, and to take all the steps passed, present and future, which in my judgment may be beneficial to his interests, which are common to mine. Therefore, I appear in my [p.423] capacity as partner of my said brother, George Turnbull, to receive as I have already received, from the testamentary executors of the succession of our deceased natural father, John Turnbull, who are his widow, Catherine Rucker, and Charles Norwood, the sum of three thousand hard pesos which our said father bequeathed to each one of us, making the total for both, six thousand hard pesos, the same which they have delivered to me for my account and that of my said brother, George, I remaining responsible to him for his portion, there being no right of action in his favor against the said succession or testamentary executors, given by [p.424] this deed, a formal receipt of the delivery of the six thousand pesos which remain in my possession, with which the last will of our deceased father, John Turnbull, is being complied with.

In testimony of which this deed is made at Baton Rouge on the 14th day of the month of April, 1800.

I, Don Carlos de Grand Pré, Colonel of the Royal Armies, Governor of Natchez with the military and political command of the post of Baton Rouge and its dependencies, certify that I know the grantor, who signed it with Antonio Soler, Captain of the Royal Artillery Regiment, and Second Lieutenant of the Regiment of Louisiana Juan de Mier y Feran, witnesses who were present.

Carlos de Grand Pré   William Turnbull
Antonio Soler   George Turnbull
Juan de Mier y Feran   Brothers and Partners

From *Archives of Spanish West Florida*, v.5, p.36: (Written in Spanish) David Holsten, husband of Sylvia Turnbull, acknowledges that she received the legacy from the succession of her father, John Turnbull, and relieved Catherine Rucker Turnbull and Charles Norwood, executor, from further responsibility for the payment of this legacy.

Be it known to all who this act may see, how I, David Holsten [p.92] in my capacity as husband of Sylvia, natural daughter of the deceased John Turnbull, and with her full authority, declares and says to have received from Catherine Rucker, widow of John Turnbull, and from Charles Norwood, both testamentary executors of the expressed Turnbull, the amount of three thousand pesos, which is the legacy made to my cited wife by her deceased father, John Turnbull, and by this instrument the said testamentory executors are thereby relieved of every responsibility on account of this legacy and dowry of my said wife, of my own free will admitting to have received it for her account for which amount I thereby give formal receipt, [p.93] renouncing to every right and any claims in the future, renouncing further every privilege and the laws in my favor, to all of which I renounce. I empower the Justices of His Majesty to compel me to its performance with the force of a rendered judgment, and likewise I declare that David White is hereby relieved of every responsibility in his capacity as tutor of my said wife, Sylvia, as well as any claim against him now or in the future. In testimony of which this act is made at Baton Rouge on the [p.94] eleventh day of May, 1801.

I, Don Carlos de Grand Pré, Colonel of the Royal Armies,

Governor of Natchez and at present with the military and civil governing command of the post of Baton Rouge and its dependencies, certify that I know the grantor who signed it together with David White, who was previously tutor of Sylvia Turnbull, Francis Poussett and Pedro Goudeau, as witnesses.

Carlos de Grand Pré

Frans. Poussett   David Holsten

Pedro Goudeau   David White

***

Both William and George Turnbull were active in the Indian Trade from about the time of the Revolution onward. They are mentioned in early correspondence as operating the warehouse at Fort St. Etienne, on the upper reaches of the Tombigbee River, in the Chickasaw Nation. In the 1790s, they are mentioned as operating a warehouse at Yazun, the Choctaw village on the Yazoo River, where Turner Brashears lived. With a partner, John Joyce, John Turnbull & Sons was a trading presence in the lower Mississippi Valley until 1795 when Panton, Leslie, & Co of Mobile forced them out of the trade. As we have already seen, the Turnbulls managed to get mixed up considerably with the children of Thomas Vaughn, and both are mixed up with the Brashears families of the lower Mississippi valley, but how they were all related remains a mystery.

The Suk-en-atcha Settlement and Zadock's Family

Susannah (Vaughn) Brashears died some time about 1820-23. On 6 Sept 1824, in Marengo Co, AL, Zadock Brashears Sr married second Rachel (née Durant; wid. Brashears) Walker, the ex-wife of his brother, Samuel Brashears Sr and widow of David Walker (Book A, p.68, Wm. Barton, J.P.; Wm. I. Goodwyn, Bondsman [also summarized by Gandrud as Book 1, May 7, 1818–June 15, 1836]). Rachel had married second Billy McGirth and had one child. She married third, David "Davy" Walker, and had seven children by him; see deed and list above.

In 1830, Zadock was a citizen of the Choctaw Nation (by intermarriage) and head of a Choctaw family on Suk-en-atcha Creek, which included two step children, then under ten, who

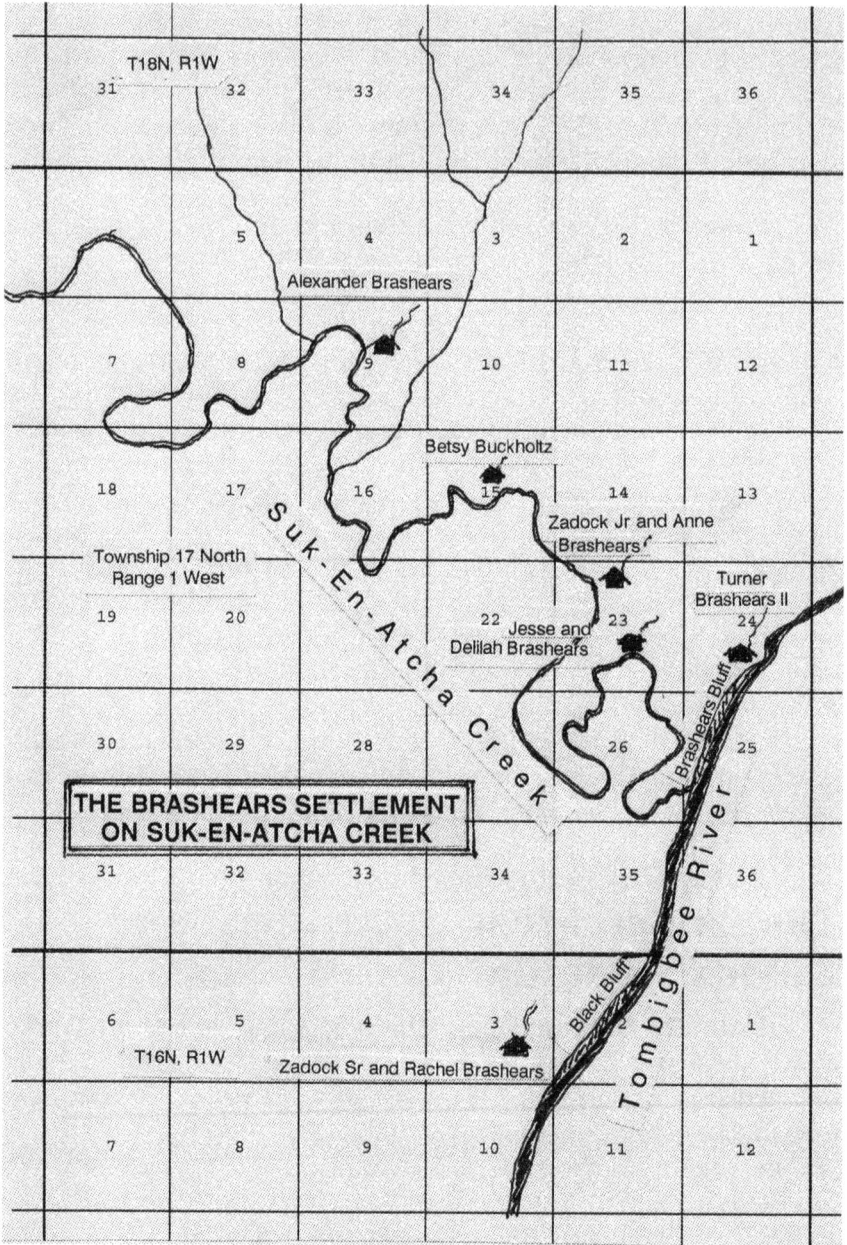

THE BRASHEARS SETTLEMENT
ON SUK-EN-ATCHA CREEK

were in his care: Sophia and David Walker. Zadock was a beneficiary under Clause 19 of the Treaty of Dancing Rabbit Creek and received land: Lot No. 324, the Fractional Sec 20, except SW ¼, T16, R1E, and fractional Sec 21, T16, R1E (List of

Choctaw Reservations under 19th Article... Choctaw Reserve Records, Federal Records Center, Microfilm 7RA-116, Roll 1). This land is five miles south and three and four miles east of the mouth of Suk-en-atcha Creek. It is three miles south and three and four miles east of the Reservation granted to Rachel Brashears, his second wife. A contradictory record, dated 27 Nov 1834, places his land in Fractional Sec 7, Sec 18, and Sec 17, T16, R1E, 612 acres; since the record notes that he had two children in the household over ten, this may have been the children's reservation under Article 14.

On 30 April 1837, George S. Gaines attested to the sale of Zadock Sr's reservation to Greene B. Chaney of Mobile, AL, on 30 April 1832. The affidavit stated that Zadock Brashears was deceased, i.e. before 30 April 1837 (Choctaw Reserve Records, Group 75, Natl Archives). He actually died before 11 Nov 1834.

Family of Zadock Brashears and Susannah Vaughn:

v5831. [8]1. **Maria (or Mary) Brashears**, b. 20 Oct 1785. "On the said day and year [5 July 1789], I baptized solemnly at the said Fort [St. Stephens], Maria who was born the 20th day of the month of October of the year 1785, the illegitimate daughter of Zedeck Beshurs and Susanna Vaughn, Protestants and inhabitants of the Tombigbee River. Her godparent was _____ Mugica, Corporal of the Fort." Signed: Miguel Lamport (ref: The Catholic Center, Archdiocese of Mobile, Mobile, Alabama, *Baptismal Records*, Book 2, p.40. English translation from Spanish; thanks to Harley D. Anders Sr for a copy.)

v5832. [8]2. ***Jesse Brashears**, b. c1791, d. 9 Aug 1827 (his estate was divided in 1837); m. **Delilah Juzan**, a three-quarter-blood Choctaw girl, d/o Charles Juzan and a niece or grand-niece of Pushmataha; lived on the Tombigbee River. Jesse's widow, Delilah, was a beneficiary under Clause 14 of the Treaty of Dancing Rabbit Creek, 1830; she m.2. 10 Jan 1831, David W. Hall, in Marengo Co, AL; m.3. in I.T. _____ Thompson.

v5833. [8]3. ***Elizabeth "Betsy" Brashears**, b. c1792, d. Nov 1837; m. 30 Sept 1811, **William Buckholtz II**. "Betsy Buckley" was a beneficiary under Clause 14 of the Treaty of Dancing Rabbit Creek, 1830.

v5834. 84. **Anne Brashears**, b. c1793; m.1. 11 April 1811, *John Lyles*, (Marriage Index, West Feliciana 1791-1871.);

v5835. 91. Susan Lyles, b. c1811-1814. Anne and John Lyles had at least one daughter, who became a pawn in a political power struggle. See details below.

Anne Brashears m.2. c1815-18, her cousin, *Alexander Brashears* (v5521), son of Samuel Brashears Sr and Rachel Durant. Anne apparently died c1825, for Alexander Brashears m. 15 July 1826, Marengo Co, AL, Emiline Jane Winn.

7 June 1812, Deed of bargain and sale between Zadock Brashears of Parish of Feliciana and Territory of Orleans and Anne Lyle (Alias Anne Brashears), his daughter, of Parish and Territory aforesaid, for $10.00 and considerations of affection and regard for daughter Anne, as his lawful heir, parcel of land 400 A. situate on Redwood Creek. Land bounded by lands of Wesley Trahan and Col. Wm. Kirkland, being remainder of tract cut off by said Trahan's upper line, beginning at Redwood and running West to old lines. To be held in fee simple by Ann.

	His
Wit.: Alexander Vaughan	/s/ Zadock [B] Brashears
William Boyce	Mark
James Trahan	

On 16 Aug 1818, Alexander Brashears and wife, Anne, both of Pearl River in the Choctaw Nation sold 400 a. on Redwood Creek to Thomas Carney of Feliciana Parish. The land was identified as that given to Anne by her father, Zadock Brashears, as her dotal portion (Notarial Records, Feliciana Parish, Bk A, p.208). See Alexander Brashear's listing for their children.

v5836. 85. **Susanna Brashears**, b. c1793, d. MS, 5 May 1850; m.1. 6 May 1805, at New Feliciana, *John Benjamin Stewart*, (4 ch) b. 1784, d. Feliciana Parish bef 28 Sept 1820 (*VA Gazette Genealolgy*, 1959, p.108); m.2. _____ *McNeeley* (no ch); m.3. *George David Graham*, (no ch)

^{v5}837. ^{8}6. ***Delilah "Lila" Brashears**, bap. 4 May 1794, d. c1819-20, possibly in childbirth; m. 24 March 1808, in Hinds Co, MS, **Wesley Trahern**, b. c1779, Pittsylvania, VA, d. 1829, Hinds Co, MS.

^{v5}838. ^{8}7. ***Vaughn Brashears**, b. 1798 (age 33 in Feb 1832); Vaughn died in Indian Territory, about 1853 or 54; m. **Isabella LeFlore**, b. c1804 (28 in 1832), sister to Greenwood LeFlore, the Choctaw Chief who negotiated the Treaty of Dancing Rabbit Creek. Vaughn was a beneficiary under Clause 14 of the Treaty of Dancing Rabbit Creek, 1830, yet was "removed" to Indian Territory in the "Choctaw Trail of Tears."

^{v5}839. ^{8}8. ***Sophia Brashears, I**, b. 7 Feb 1802, bap. 14 Sept 1802, age six months, at St. Francis Church, Point Coupee, LA (Book 7, p.142), d. in Alabama, 21 Oct 1852, bur Belmont Church Cem, Sumter Co, AL; m. **Sampson Moncrief**, in LA. Sampson had nine children when he came to Indian Territory in 1855– Susan, William, Mary Ann, Sarah A., Sampson, Sophia, George, Matthew and Julia.

Daughter Sarah Ann Moncrief (^{v5}1394), b. 30 Jan 1829, d. 14 Dec 1926 kept a diary of family information all her life, and she gave testimony before the Dawes Commission 1896–1904, which corroborates most of this family group.

^{v5}840. ^{8}9. ***Zadock Brashears, Jr**, b. 1804 (age 8 in 1812), d. Aug 1833; m. 22 Aug 1826, **Anne DeCastro**, in Marengo Co, AL (Bk 1, p.128), with Robert Goodwin as Security. Zadock, Jr, was a beneficiary under Clause 14 of the Treaty of Dancing Rabbit Creek, 1830. See below.

^{v5}841. ^{8}10. ***Turner Brashears, II**, b. 1809 (age 3 in 1812; apparently named for his illustrious fourth cousin, R.T. "Turner" Brashear, the Choctaw trader and interpreter); m. 31 Oct 1829, **Ann Holland**, in Marengo Co, AL. Turner Brashears, II, was a beneficiary under Clause 19 of the Treaty of Dancing Rabbit Creek.

The Seduction of Susan Lyles

From Clara Sue Kidwell, *Choctaws and Missionaries in Mississippi, 1818-1918*, p.119:

"In June 1828, Zeddock Brashears, a prominent mixed-blood, accused Stephen Macomber, the teacher at Bethel, of seducing and impregnating his grand-daughter, Susan Lyles, a student at the school. Under questioning, the girl accused both Macomber and Aden Gibbs of seducing her. Missionaries were fallible, despite their moral rectitude, and Macomber was virtually alone in the wilderness with a wife who was a bedridden invalid.

However, [Greenwood] LeFlore seemed less concerned with the morality of the situation than with the question of monetary responsibility for the child. Although traditional Choctaw customs placed no stigma on children born out of wedlock, and the matrilineal kinship system gave the mother's kin responsibility for the child, the Brashears family was mixed-blood. Support had to come from the father, and LeFlore demanded that the missionaries pay five hundred dollars to the nation for the child.

Susan Lyles thus became a pawn in a political power struggle. It gave LeFlore the opportunity to make demands on the missionaries, and to do so on behalf of the nation rather than the girl's family specifically. Kingsbury [of the missionary board] was willing to pay the family, but he refused to recognize any claim by the nation. The incident became a test of wills and also an indication of LeFlore's intent to act as spokesman for the Choctaw Nation. In a sharp exchange of letters with Kingsbury, LeFlore pressed his demands. Macomber was removed from the station at Bethel and ultimately dismissed from missionary service, but Kingsbury never paid the five hundred dollars."

Napoleon B. Brashear's Story

From 1896 to 1908, in testimony before the Dawes Commission, Napoleon B. Brashears claimed to be part of this Choctaw Brashears family ("Napoleon B. Brashears, et al." Dawes Commission No. 877. Commission Nos 7-D-195, 7-D-194, 7-D-187, 7-D-198, 23-929; Government Printing Office, see section called *Five Civilized Tribes in Oklahoma*, pages 315-321;

see esp. p.318, 320). Napoleon B. Brashears, Richard Brashears (ex-slave of Vaughn Brashears), and Josephine Jones, gd/o of a Brashears woman, all three testified that Zadock Brashears had the following sons:

[9]1. **Jesse Brashears,**
[9]2. ***Zadoc Brashears Jr**, called 'Young Zadoc' in the testimony
[9]3. **Vaughn Brashears,**
[9]4. **Turner Brashears,**

Napoleon claimed that Zadock Brashears, Jr, "young Zadoc," had children (Dawes, p.318, 320):
?. ***Joseph Brashears**, [Napoleon said he was sent away young to get an education]
[10]1. **William Brashears**, twin, much younger than Joseph
[10]2. **John Brashears**, twin, may have died in infancy; may have had a small family in Gaines Co, I.T.
[10]3. **Turner Brashears**, d. young, no children.

Trouble is, the probate of Zadock Jr's estate mentions only John, William, and Turner, along with wife, Anne Dicosta [sic: DeCastro]. [There had been another child, James, who died young, and Anne was pregnant with Oleana.] Since Zadock Jr died intestate, the court was doing things and wouldn't care who had decided to disinherit a child; everyone would have been included, and there is no Joseph. Still, it's clear that Napoleon knew these people's history, and probably knew them.

Napoleon Brashears said that Joseph Brashears, s/o young Zadock, was the father of Mortimer Brashears, who was Napoleon's father. However, the 1850 and 1860 censuses indicate that Mortimer Brashears was b. c1809-11; it would have been pretty hard for young Zadock, b. 1804, to have a grandson born c1810. Napoleon was simply lying; his grandfather Joseph Brashears was a son of Ignatius "Nacy" Brashear and Frances Permelia Catheral, of Maryland and Kentucky. For the documents, see my chapter "Mortimer Brashears, of Arkansas" in Vol. 7. See also article, "Napoleon Brashear's Campaign" in "The Dawes Disaster and American Chicanery," last chapter in this book.

Testimony of Sarah Ann (Moncrief) Harlan

Testimony in the case: "Napoleon B. Brashears, et al." Dawes Commission No. 877. Commission Nos 7-D-195, 7-D-194, 7-D-187, 7-D-198, 23-929; Government Printing Office, see section called *Five Civilized Tribes in Oklahoma*, pages 315-321.)

Note by counsel: The following witness was produced by the commissioner for the purpose of contradicting the testimony of the applicant [Napoleon B. Brashears], the affidavit of James D. Coyle and Lucy Jones attached to the original application, and especially for the purpose of impeaching the testimony of the freedman, Richard Brashears, and upon whose testimony the decision of the commission was based.

November 7, 1896. Before the commission at Blocker, Ind. Terr., Sarah Ann (Moncrief) Harlan ([v5]1394) testified as follows (p.319); NOTE: this summarizes her testimony by leaving out the lawyer's questions and giving only the salient points of her testimony:

I was 77 years old last January [her error or the clerk's; she was 67]. My father was Sampson Moncrief. My mother was Sophie Moncrief. I am not sure, but I think my mother died in 1854, in Alabama, Sumter County. Her maiden name was Sophia Brashears. Her father was Zadoc Brashears. Her mother's name was Susan. I recollect seeing grandfather Zadoc Brashears only once. I don't know what county he was in when I saw him. I have never heard when he died. He was not living when I left Alabama to come to the Territory. I was a little girl when I saw him, 5 or 6 years old; just a mere recollection.

Zadoc Brashears possessed no Indian blood. He was a Scotchman. His wife Susan was a half-breed Indian. She died when my mother was a little girl. I came to Indian Territory in 1850. I do not know the name of my great-grandparents on my grandmother's side. I was a beneficiary under the fourteenth article of the treaty of 1830.

I do not know how many children Susan and Zadoc had. I only heard of them through my mother. Jesse Brashears was a brother of my mother. Zadoc Brashears, Jr., was a brother of my mother. Vaughn and Turner Brashears were brothers of my mother. She also had sisters, but don't know that I can name them all— Susan, Elizabeth, Anne, and one more; I don't recollect her name. Jesse died in Mississippi. He never came to the Territory. I do not know what year he died. Anne died in

Alabama— I do not know when. Elizabeth died in Alabama when I was very small. Susan died in Jackson, Miss.; I do not know when, but before I came to the Territory. Turner came to this country and died. I don't know where he settled, but he died out here before I came. He never had any descendants. His wife died in Alabama. Vaughn came to this country and died here. I saw him once after I came here; he died somewhere along in 1852 or 1853. He has one descendant that I know of living now, a boy, named Turner.

Uncle Zadoc died in Alabama after my birth, but I don't recollect anything about it. I was a mere child. I can't say how long before I came to the Territory he died. Zadoc was married at the time of his death. His wife's name was Anne; I do not know the maiden name. He lived near Moscow, on Bigbee River. I visited his home after his death. His children were Turner, John, and William (who were twins), and Oleana. He had no other children. Turner died near Moscow when young. John died when a boy— just a little boy— in Alabama. William died. Oleana moved with her mother to Texas and I lost track of them.

I never heard of Joseph. I never heard of Mortimer Brashears. I never heard of Sarah Vaughn. I have kept up tolerably well with my mother's brothers and sisters. Outside of that I know nothing. When I saw Vaughn Brashears here in the nation he was at Poteau. I have heard it talked of that he brought here a slave by the name of Richard Brashears. If any of the sons of Zadoc lived on Yazoo River, as stated by Richard Brashears, I don't know it. I don't know whether Zadoc Brashears was killed in a horse race, as stated by Richard. He was shot at a horse race, is what my mother told me. His wife's name was Anne.

The two Zadocs, my grandfather and uncle, are the only ones by that name I ever heard of. I got my information from my mother. I didn't know very much about my relatives. Grandfather Zadoc had no Indian blood. He was Scotch. I testified in the case of Joseph Moncrief that Zadoc Brashears married Susan Vaughn. That was her maiden name. I said she was a half-breed Choctaw. That is correct.

Cross examination by attorney for applicants:
I have always heard them say that Dick Brashears was a slave of Vaughn Brashears. In 1853 or 1854, when I went back

to visit my mother, she told me all about her sisters and brothers, and there was no Joseph in her brothers; and if it had been so she would have told it. I did not ask her about a Joseph.

It is correct, as testified by Dick Brashears, that my mother's brother was shot and killed in a horse race. It is correct, as testified by Richard Brashears, that Vaughn Brashears came to the Territory and lived and died here. It is correct, as testified to by Richard Brashears, that Turner Brashears came to the Territory and lived and died here. It is correct, as testified to by Richard Brashears, that Jesse was the oldest child. I never heard of one of the children going away to school, as stated by Richard Brashears. It is correct, as stated by Richard Brashears, that Zadoc Sr, Vaughn, and Jesse Brashears lived in Sumter County, Ala.

All the Brashears who lived there were Indians except the old original Brashears. All that came from there were of Indian descent. I only had two come. It is correct that all that died there and all that came here were of Indian descent. There was only two that came. There were no families living there during my time by the name of Brashears who did not have Indian blood. If Napoleon B. Brashears can connect himself with Turner and Vaughn Brashears he would be an Indian, but I have never been able to connect him.

9. JESSE BRASHEARS
and DELILAH JUZAN,
OF TOMBIGBEE

[v5]**832.** [8]1. **Jesse Brashears**, b. c1788/9, probably on Zadock's first land grant on the Tombigbee River, between St. Stephens and Mobile, Spanish West Florida, d. 9 Aug 1827, Sumter Co, AL, of a paralytic stroke. He was a son of Zadock and Susannah (Vaughn) Brashears and grandson of Jesse and Elizabeth (Prather) Brashears, of Orange Co, NC, Georgia, Pensacola, and Feliciana Parish. He married c1816, **Delilah Juzan**, b. c1800, three-quarter blood daughter of Charles Juzan, half-blood Choctaw, and a full-blood Choctaw, a niece or grand-niece to Pushmataha.

The Juzan and Pushmataha Connection

Charles Juzan, Jesse's father-in-law, is referred to by many contemporary researchers as "John Charles Juzan," but Jennifer Mieirs reports that all the documents pertaining to him say only "Charles Juzan." He was a half-breed Choctaw-French trader who had a stand near the Chickasaw boundary. He was the son of Pierre Francois Juzan, who had been orphaned at one year of age, when his father, Pierre Gabriel Juzan was killed by Chickasaws at the battle of Ackia (near Tupelo, MS), 26 May 1736.

Bienville, the French governor at Mobile, had decided in 1735 to destroy the Chickasaws, because they were hampering French communications with Canada and were urging the Choctaws to join the English for trade and resistance to the French. Bienville ordered a French expedition, led by D'Artaguette, to attack from the Illinois settlements on the Mississippi, while he led an attack up from Mobile. In separate battles, the Chickasaw soundly defeated, first, D'Artaguette, then Bienville himself, forcing the French to retire to the fringes of the land, leaving the Chickasaws more powerful than ever.

Pierre Gabriel Juzan, I, b. 6 June 1697, at Versailles, Siene-et-Oise, France, was Major of Militia for Bienville, who was witness at the wedding of Pierre Gabriel Juzan to Maria Francisca Trudeau, on 29 April 1734, in French Louisiana. Pierre's parents were Pierre Juzan, b. France, 1672, and Michelle Liette, b. France, c1695. Maria Francisca Trudeau, b. 31 Jan 1715, was a daughter of Francois Trudeau and Jeanne Burelle.

Maria Francisca (Trudeau) Juzan died 25 March 1735, in French Louisiana, just five days after giving birth to her son, Pierre Francois Juzan. Her husband, Pierre Gabriel Juzan, I, was killed at Ackia just a year and two months later.

Their son, Pierre Francois Juzan, known as "Don Pedro," b. 20 March 1735, French Louisiana, d. c1802, in Mobile; m.1. 1 Nov 1858, Catherine Parant, b. c1735, in Mobile, d/o Francois Parant and Marianne Arlu, d. c1768, in AL; m.2. about 1765, a Choctaw woman, according to *The Creek War, 1813-1814*, by Hebert and Ball (chap 3.); m.3. 15 March 1794, at Mobile, Pelagie Lorreins, b. c1750, French Louisiana, d/o Jacques Lorreins and Marie Louise Bodin. Pelagie had been married previously to John Baptiste Brazillier.

Children by Pierre Francois Juzan's first marriage were:
1. Pierre Francois Juzan Jr, b. 20 Sept 1759, in Mobile, AL;
2. Daniel Juzan, b. 1760, d. 22 May 1825;
3. Marie (Mary) Josephine Juzan, b. 1766, d. 27 March 1836.

Children by the second marriage to a Choctaw woman (of which there is no French record) were:
4. Charles Juzan, b. c1767, d. c1836
5. Pierre Juzan, (may not have existed. The records of the Creek War and the Indian trade attribute to Pierre Juzan, the same things as are attributed to Charles Juzan. So, was Charles Juzan actually Pierre Charles Juzan, who went by Charles Juzan to avoid being confused with his father? May be confused with Charles Juzan's son, Pierre Gabriel Juzan, II.)

On the other hand, maybe Pierre and Charles Juzan were such close trading partners, having trading houses in a number of towns, including Coosha and Chunky, that it is now impossible to separate the records pertaining to each. They may even have gone off to war together. We do not know what happened to Pierre, if he existed.

Charles Juzan, b. c1767, probably in the Choctaw Nation, d. c1836, in Meridian, MS. He had two wives, probably at the same time— 1st c1787, in Mobile area, "Peggy Trahern," b. c1770-75, sister of Oklahoma and therefore a daughter of Nahomtima, sister to Pushmataha; and 2nd Phoebe Oklahoma, b. c?1800, daughter or sister of Oklahoma, of the Coosha clan, nephew of Pushmataha. These marriages overlapped; polygamy was both accepted and common among the Choctaws, though it appears that Peggy had left Charles Juzan and abandoned her Juzan children at the time he married Phoebe.

Pushmataha had at least two wives, as was the custom. One of them is listed at least three ways on a deed from Holmes County, MS (Book A, p.37; thanks to Jennifer Mieirs for the data). These names are Jamesachikako, Imaghoka, Lunnabaka and Lunnagaka (the last two look like variations of one name; which is correct is unknown.) The children of this marriage that were alive in 1830, are Betsy Moore, Martha Moore, and Haschalahurtibbi, with Rene Logan and Tom Suzara listed as his guardian. Previously, the name Johnson had been associated with Haschalahurtibbi. The girls had apparently taken English names, as was common, and their Indian names have been lost.

Another wife of Pushmataha, according to the testimony of Alexander Favre, was Chamnay, who had a daughter, Pis-tikio-ko-nay, the mother of Alexander Favre.

And according to some sources, Pushmataha and Chamnay also had a daughter, Running Deer, who was the mother of children who went by the name Anderson.

Nahomtima, sister of Pushmataha, had children:
1. Noahtima or Shanke (later called "Peggy Trahern"), b. c?1770-75. She seems to have taken the French name Marguerite, which was converted to the English diminutive, Peggy. She was married to Charles Juzan in 1787 and had eight children by him. She later had two children whose surname was Trahern. Her association with their father is probably

the way she acquired the surname, Trahern.

2. Oka-lah-homa, or Oklahoma, b. c1780-84, d. 1844; he also had two wives: _____, and Anon-Toma (Anon Tooner in 1840 deed). He succeeded Pushmataha as Choctaw chief of the Okla Hunnalli District, in 1825, though he soon lost the chieftainship because of dissipation.

3. Nitakachieubbee, or Nitakechi, Chief of the Southern District, the Okla Hunnalli, at the time of the 1831 Choctaw Census and a Chief in the Choctaw Nation in Indian Territory until 1838. He died in MS in 1845 and is buried in Coosha Cem, Lauderdale Co, MS.

4. Tapenahomma, also said to be a chief, though of what is undetermined; he is buried in Coosha Cem, Lauderdale Co, MS, beside his mother, Nahomtima.

5. (possibly) Phoebe, second wife of Charles Juzan. There is confusion and argument as to whether Phoebe is sister or daughter to Oklahoma.

Family of Charles Juzan: (data from the late Loretta Coppick, of Okmulgee, OK, via Ronald Shawhan, 20 Care Cir, New Providence, NJ 17974-1106; additional data from Jennifer Mieirs. Deed of trust from Oka-lah-homa and wife, Anon-tooner, to Phoebe, wife of Charles Juzan, and the children of Charles Juzan, to Hugh McDonald, Lauderdale Co, MS, 16 March 1840.)

1. Pierre Gabriel Juzan, II, b. 1790, in Choctaw Nation, d. 1841, in Choctaw Nation, I.T. Pierre could speak English, French, and Choctaw with equal ease. He was a prominent trader and leader of Choctaw affairs. When Tecumseh, the great Shawnee leader, came to Mississippi to try to enlist the Choctaws in a Pan-Indian effort to resist white incursion, Pierre opposed the plan and counseled the Choctaw chiefs to reject it, which they did. Pierre led a company of Choctaws in the War of 1812 against the British (see "Juzan's Choctaws Helped Defeat the British," in Winter issue, 1998, *Journal of the War of 1812*.) He removed to Indian Territory, where he was advisor and translator for Nitakechi. Peter James Hudson, reports in *A Story of Choctaw Chiefs*, (Chronicles of Oklahoma, vol. 17, p.13), that he was elected chief of Pushmataha District, I.T., in 1838, for a four-year term.

2. Mary Juzan, b. 1798, Choctaw Nation, d. 29 Sept 1865, in Yakanookany, Ofahoma, MS; m. c1819, in Choctaw Nation, Benjamin LeFlore, s/o Louis LeFlore and Rebecca Cravatt.

Figure 21: Mary Juzan LeFlore

Figure 22:Benjamin LeFlore

3. Delilah Juzan, b. c1800, Mobile area, d. March 1859, Boggy Depot, Atoka Co, I.T.; m.1. 1816, **Jesse Brashears** (^{v5}832), s/o Zadock Brashears and Susannah Vaughn; m.2. 13 Jan 1831, in Sumter Co, AL, David W. Wall; Delilah may have m.3. in I.T. _____ Thompson

4. Rebecca Juzan, b. c1804, Mobile area; m.1. 25 Feb 1825, Marengo Co, AL, John Bond, b. c1800, d. bef 1833; m.2. c1833, George W. Walker, b. c1800, a Creek, s/o Rachel Durant and her third husband, David Walker. Soon after the second marriage, it was discovered that John Bond had numerous debts; Rebecca and George were forced to sell the land. The proceeds only covered about half of the debts.

5. William Juzan, b. c1805; m. 12 Sept 1832, in Sumter Co, AL, "by Canan Pistole, JP," Bondsman: Canan Pistole (Sumter Co, AL, Marriages, Bk 1, p.265), **Harriet Brashears** (^{v5}544), b. before 1820, d/o Alexander Brashears and Anne Brashears

6. Jackson Juzan, b. c1808, Mobile area, d. 1860 at Boggy Depot, Atoka Co, I.T.; m. c1835, Mississippi Allen, b. 18 March 1812, MS, d/o James Allen and Elizabeth Colbert. Mississippi was a Chickasaw; Jackson Juzan ran a small business at Old Boggy Depot, Indian Territory.

7. Lucy Juzan, b. c1809; m.1. 1829, in Marengo Co, AL, <u>Wesley Brashears Trahern</u> (^{v5}1181, s/o Delilah Brashears and Wesley Trahern), b. c1801, d. 1837; m.2. c1838, Amos W. Geary ("Gary" on 1855 Choctaw Rolls); m.3. Charles Smith. Geary and Lucy operated a toll bridge on Boggy River and owned a farm near Red River, OK.

8. Ramona Juzan, b. c1811; m. c1831, Ransom McElroy, b. c1810

9. Narcissa Juzan, b. c1815; m. c1842, William Thomas, b. c1814
10. Eliza Ann Juzan, b. 1819, Lansdale Co, MS; d. 25 July 1890, Atoka, Choctaw Nation, I.T., age 71; m. c1838, Hugh C. Flack, b. 10 March 1817, Bourbon Co, KY, killed in a gunfight over cattle, 6 June 1860, Atoka Co, I.T.
11. Sybil Juzan, b. c1821; m. Benjamin Walker; may also have m. Thomas Lewis.

It is extremely difficult, today, to determine which of these children belong to Phoebe and which to Peggy. Phoebe Juzan claimed dower rights in the estate of Charles Juzan after his death in 1836. The settling of his estate took about 2 years, and the primary beneficiaries were Ramona, Narcissa, and Sybil Juzan, suggesting that those three are Phoebe's children.

Eliza Ann (Juzan) Flack claimed that she was the youngest of the eight children of her mother, Peggy Trahern, whom she also called Shanke. That would make Peggy Trahern the mother of Pierre, Delilah, Rebecca, Lucy, Mary, Jackson, William, and Eliza Ann.

However, Lauderdale Co, MS, Deeds, 16 March 1840, suggests some of these may have belonged to Phoebe: Know all men by these presents that we, Oka-lah-homa and Anon Tooner [Anon-toma], wife of the said Oklahoma, both of the state of Mississippi and County of Lauderdale, for and in consideration of the many acts of friendship shown to us by Charles Juzan, deceased, in his lifetime, and also for the love we have for Phebe, wife of the said Charles Juzan, deceased, and for the following named children of the said Charles Juzan, viz: (maiden and former married names added in parentheses and converted to a list for easier reference):

Delilah (Juzan/Brashears) Wall,
Mary (Juzan) Lafloor (sic: LeFlore),
Rebecca (Juzan) Walker,
Lucy (Juzan/Trahern) Gray,
Subbill (Sybil Juzan) Walker,
Eliza Ann (Juzan) Flack,
Pier Juzan,
Jackson Juzan,

we have made and by these presents give and grant unto our truly trusted friend, Hugh McDonald, of the county of Kemper and State aforesaid, the following tract of land, lying in said county of Lauderdale, and state aforesaid, viz: the west half of section 30 in township eight north of range seventeen east [T8N, R17E] which was located by George W. Martin, by virtue of a right of reservation secured to the said Oklahoma by the Treaty of Dancing Rabbit Creek, to have and to hold the same in trust for the only use and benefit of the said Phebe Juzan for and during her natural life, and then in trust forever for the use of the above named children of Charles Juzan....(After Phoebe's death, the land was to be divided 8 ways, which would have given each of the children 40 acres.)

In order to be mother of many of these children, Phoebe would have to be born c1785 or before, which would make it impossible for her to be a daughter of Oklahoma, b. c1780-84 (he said he was about 60 years old in 1844). If Phoebe were a sister to Oklahoma and Oklahoma were acting in a traditional Choctaw way, the deed would be a means of taking care of his sister's children, his own "clan-children," for which (in the tradition) he was responsible.

On the other hand, Peggy was known to have abandoned her Juzan children, and maybe Oklahoma was making the deed to his daughter, who, as wife of Charles Juzan, was mother and step-mother to all these children. The American legalese of the document suggests that he was not acting in a traditional Choctaw way.

The deed leaves out William, Ramona, and Narcissa, also known to be children of Charles Juzan. Jennifer Mieirs thinks that the inclusion of different children in the will and deed was a way to even out their inheritance, in terms of land.

William and Pierre Juzan were named in the supplement to The Treaty at Dancing Rabbit Creek as persons allotted their own reservations; Lucy had the reservation given to Wesley Brashears Trahern, Rebecca the one given to John Bond; Delilah, widow of Jesse Brashears, had her reservation through her inclusion under Article 14. These circumstances would give some of the children very large allotments and others a mere forty acres in Lauderdale Co, MS.

The niece of Pushmataha who took the name, "Peggy Trahern," also had two children, James Nicholas Trahern, b. 1816 (see below), and Jeremiah "Jerry" Trahern (n.f.i.), between the birth of Lucy and Eliza Ann. They are referred to in the records as Peggy Trahern's "two fatherless children." Peggy seems to have abandoned her Juzan children and may have been living with another man after about 1810, possibly John Donley, the mail carrier. By 1825, Peggy Trahern was living outside the Choctaw Nation, though she returned to get an allotment in Grenada Co, MS, for herself and her "two fatherless children." Since some of these Traherns married into the Brashears and related families, here is some data on them:

[10]1. James Nicholas Trahern, b. 1816, MS, d. 29 March 1883, Indian Territory, bur Trahern Cem, Latham, I.T.; m.1. Sept 1843, in Skullyville Co, I.T., Sarah Hall, b. 1828, MS, d. 28 Dec 1873, Latham, I.T., d/o William Hall and Susan Riddle; m.2. 4 Feb 1877, Ft Smith, AR, Virginia Parelli Clossen; m. by Choctaw law, 11 Aug 1879, Ind. Terr., Virginia Parelli Clossen. Deeds in Grenada Co, MS, show James N. Trahern's mother to be named Peggy and his wife to be named Sarah. An estate proceeding in Skullyville, Choctaw Nation, shows Sarah's surname to be Hall: "To Tandy Walker, heir and legal representative of Mary Walker, b. Riddle, dec'd; Mary Blackburn; heirs of Susan Hall, born Riddle, viz, Catharine Wall, Margerite Moncrief, and heirs of Sarah Trahan, viz, Robert, Lysander, James, Joseph, William, Lavinia, and Catharine; heirs of Jincy Folsom; heirs of Joseph Riddle, viz Moses Riddle, Jesse Riddle, and Betsy Wall; heirs of John Riddle Jr, viz, George, William Douglass, Martha Edmonds, Sarah Cooper, and heirs of Margerite Johnson, grandchildren and heirs of John Riddle Sr...." (Thanks to Jennifer Mieirs for a Xerox copy, via Marlene Mays Clark.)

Family of James Nicholas Trahern and Sarah Hall:

[11]1. Lavinia (Louvinia) Trahern, b. 1844, I.T., d. c1892; ½ Choctaw, #99 on 1885 Roll; m. Willis Henry Daniels ([v5]1261), s/o Mary Ann "Polly" Brashears and Alfred Peter Daniels.

[11]2. Robert S. C. Trahern, b. 1850, Ind. Terr., d. 1899, bur Latham, I.T.; m. c1875, Cornelia _____ (?Gardner) ½ Choctaw, b. 1860. Ch: Admona; Margaret; Loren;

Czarina; Martha; and William Trahern

[11]3. Lysander T. "Don" Trahern, b. 6 Feb 1851, ½ Choctaw, Roll #7684, C.C. 2646, d. 28 Feb 1909, Walls, OK; n.m. Emma Cox ([v5]1231), d/o Charlie Cox and Letha Daniels ([v5]1225, d/o <u>Mary Ann "Polly" Brashears and Alfred Peter Daniels</u>) (1 ch); m.2. 1874, Anna Hardaway (2 ch); m.3. c1880, Sina Colbert, d/o David Colbert (3 ch). Ch: Joseph Cox; Walter; Isabelle; Douglas T.; Martha; and Robert Trahern. Sina Colbert was ½ Choctaw, ½ Chickasaw, and did not speak English.

[11]4. Catherine Trahern, b. 28 March 1852, I.T., ½ Choctaw, Roll #13214, C.C. 4787, d. 6 Feb 1918, Stuart, OK; m. 28 July 1872, Robert Newton, b. 1843, s/o William and Eveline Newton. Ch: James; Robert; Susan; Joseph; Lucinda; Mada; Ernest; Bessie; and Claude V. Newton

[11]5. James D. Trahern, b. 1853, I.T., d. 18 Aug 1900, ½ Choctaw, Roll #8071, C.C. 2755

[11]6. Joseph Hall Trahern, b. 1856, I.T., d. 1897 ½ Choctaw; m. Armantha Holbrook. Ch: Howard; James Harrison Trahern

[11]7. William Trahern, indicated by estate proceedings, n.f.i.

<u>Family of James Nicholas Trahern and Virginia Parelli Clossen:</u>

[11]8. Minnie Trahern, b. 1878, I.T., d. 8 Dec 1900, ¼ Choctaw, Roll #8111, C.C. 2767; m. 1897, Greenwood "Green" Daniels, s/o <u>Turner Brashears Daniels</u> ([v5]1228) and <u>Susan LeFlore</u>. Ch: see Daniels, below

[11]9. Docia Trahern, b. 1881, I.T., ¼ Choctaw, Roll #8072, C.C. 2756; m. 1903, Harvey L. Alford. Ch: Vere; Ophelia; Roy Howard; and four other Alford children, names unknown.

For more on Traherns, Daniels, etc. contact Doug Barkley, P.O. Box 998, Panama, OK 74951 and/or Jennifer Mieirs, 1602 W. 30th Ave, Pine Bluff, AR 71603.

JESSE IN MISSISSIPPI RECORDS

Jesse Brashears served in the War of 1812 alongside several of his mixed-blood relatives, as is indicated by "Rosters of Mississippi Command in the War of 1812." (US Roster 9, TN Lib & Archives.)

[General Thomas] Hind's Battalion of Cavalry, Mississippi Militia:
  Bingaman, Ad, private
  Brashears, Nathan, private
Colonel Claiborne's Regiment of Mississippi Militia:
  Brashears, Benjamin, private
  Brashiers, James, private
  Bucklie, William, private
  Dacosta, Nicholas, private
Major Smoot's Battalion of Mississippi Militia
  Bilbo, James, private
  Brashears, Jesse, private
  Montcreaf, Benjamin, private
  Nail, Joel, private
  Patton, Thomas, Corporal

Jesse also hauled freight for the Choctaw Agency and the Choctaw Trading Post at St. Stephens, Alabama, at about the time of his marriage. *Records of Choctaw Trading Post, St. Stephens, Mississippi Territory, 1816-1824*, Book 2, p.18: "Jesse Brashears account and receipt for $60, Sept 2nd 1816. #1 The Choctaw Trading house to Jesse Brashears for packing four barrels of factory goods from the Choctaw agency house to said trading house (a distance of about 150 miles)... Received from George S. Gaines, agent to the Choctaw Trading house, sixty dollars in full for the above account. /signed triplicates, Sept 2nd, 1816 (signed) Jessee Brashears; witness: Benjamin Everitt."

The Choctaw Agency was about 6 miles west of Turner Brashear's Stand on the Natchez Trace and about 7 miles northwest of Louis LeFleur's Stand at LeFleur's Bluff on Pearl River, site of present-day Jackson, MS. The Choctaw Trading house at St. Stephens was on the Tombigbee River, about 70 miles north of Mobile, in present-day Washington Co, Alabama. Jesse surely stopped to visit with his kinsman, Turner Brashear, when he was on these trading trips. Turner Brashears also appears frequently in the accounts of St. Stephens. This has to be the Turner who married "a daughter of Taboca", for Zadock's son, Turner, II, b. c1804 (and surely named for the older Turner), isn't old enough yet.

A list of accounts paid in 1817, for instance (p.71), shows, among others:

John McGilvary	36.97
Jesse Brashears	106.33
William Hall	59.60
Shophah	1.25
Annuckwyer	10.47
Samuel McGee	510.50
John Wade	126.97
Turner Brashears	51.63
Benjamin LeFleur	17.56

There are also several residents of the Chickasaw Nation on the list: Major George Colbert, James Colbert, James and Levi Perry, Levi Colbert, William Colbert, John McIntosh, and others.

A list of balances due the Choctaw Trading house, 30 June 1817, includes:

Charles Juzan	52.04
Joel Nail	49.78
Jesse Brashears	66.27
William Hall (half-breed)	41.12
Turner Brashears	51.63

A list of payments made, 1 Oct 1818, includes (and I'm going to include some of the Indian names, just for the fun of it):

Turner Brashears	51.63
Pooshtonoporia	32.07
Capt. Tookauneah	93.05
Spanannastubbe	11.07
Benjamin Loftius	26.56
Talking Warrior	543.48
Hopoia Mingo/ Little Leader	34.17
Ogh Eenlah	53.65
Jesse Brashears	50.27
William Hall	104.21

A list of individual's accounts remaining on hand at the Choctaw Trading house, 31 Dec 1819, includes:

Jesse Brashears	320.32
Turner Brashears	119.16
Charles Juzan	25.99
Zedock Brashears	43.13

"Zedock Brashier & son" also appears on a list of balances due individuals, dated 31 March 1821 ($365.20). Turner collected $199.06 on that list, and Vaughn Brashier ($24.25) appears in the Trading House accounts for the first time. Vaughn, s/o Zadock Brashears, was b. c1797-8; so he's about 23-4 years old.

A list of debts due the United States at the Choctaw Trading House, 1 Oct 1822 (rated as to risk), includes:

good	Zadock Brashears & son	$31.26
good	Charles Juzan	413.00
good	Turner Brashears	119.06
good	Greenwood LeFlour	13.88
doubtful	John Walker	242.75
good	Henry Nail	6.88
good	Jesse Brashears	6.75
good	Vaughn Brashears	54.15

About the time of Jesse's death, the land record books of Sumter County were started. The first few entries involve Jesse, possibly post-humously.

Sumter Co AL Deeds, Book A, p.1: Winchester J. Harman to Jesse Brashiers, "a Choctaw Chief, who was part French," a slave. Deed dated 27 July 1825, but not recorded until 19 Aug 1833, probably by Jesse's widow. (See *Pioneer Families of Sumter County, Alabama*, by Nelle Morris Jenkins, p.13)

Sumter Co AL Deeds, Book A, p.3: Zadock Brashears to Jesse Brashears, "I, Zadock Brashears, residing in the Choctaw Nation, for and in consideration of $200.00 paid by Jesse Brashears of the Choctaw Nation, for a Molatto named John," signed Zadock Brashears [odd, because Zadock Brashear Sr customarily made his mark, a capital "B"; had he learned to write his name?]. No date of signing. Witnesses: George Bullock and Vaughn Brashears. [Jesse's brother, Vaughn, b. 1798 (age 33 in Feb 1832)]. Recorded 14 Oct 1833, probably by Jesse's widow.

Jesse Brashears died on 9 Aug 1827. However, there is a report of a deed of certain slaves, Zadock Brashears to Jesse Brashears, 1830, witnessed by William Boyco, Alexander Vaughn, and James Trahern (Marengo Co, AL, Deeds, Book B, p.141). Was this the same transaction as the other?

Delilah (Juzan) Brashears m.2. 10 Jan 1831, in Marengo Co, AL, David W. Wall, a mixed blood who had been a trading associate of Jesse's at St. Stephens. He was a son of Noah Wall and Lucretia Folsom, a Choctaw. The *"Voice of Sumter,"* a newspaper published at Livingston, Sumter Co, reported on 6 June 1837 (p.27) that David W. Wall was administrator in the estate of Jesse Brashear, dec[d]. And the Sumter Co, AL Orphans Minutes (Book I, p.31) reports: David W. Wall, adm for estate of Jesse Brashier, was granted permission to divide estate among legal heirs and representatives of said estate (not named). William Flaker, <u>Alexander Brashier</u>, James Hart, Hardy Abner, and Luke M. Gargsber(?Grigsby) were appointed to divide the estate and make a true report. (See *Marriage and Death Notices in Early Alabama Newspapers, 1819-1893* and *Alabama Genealogical Register, v.8, #4).*

Delilah's Wall children:

Eliza Ann Wall, b. 1833, d. 26 Sept 1836, age 2 yrs 10 mo, bur in Brashers-Wall cem on banks of Tombigbee River, next to Tabitha Brashears; that cemetery has since been destroyed.

Sybil Wall, m. ____ ?Hodges;

Annie Wall;

Joseph Wall; and

Charity Wall.

David W. Wall abandoned Delilah and the children, ran off with her younger sister (Ramona Juzan), went to I.T. and had other relationships, perhaps even marriages. David Wall's estate proceedings in Grayson Co, TX, June term 1857, name three children: Virginia, Zulingka, and David A. Wall, all under age 14 and wards of William S. Burks.

Delilah Brashears is listed in the 1840 Census of Sumter Co, AL (01001-022211). She is next door to Ann Brashears, A. [Augustus] Buckholts, and 4-5 down from Alexander Brashears and Alexander M. Brashears.

Delilah (Juzan) Brashears/Wall removed to Indian Territory, where she died March 1859, Boggy Depot, Atoka Co, I.T. She had apparently married (third) ____ Thompson. On the 1885 Census of Choctaw Freedmen, a black man named Coon Brashears said he had been a slave of Mrs. Delilah Thompson. His wife, Polly Brashears, had been a slave of the heirs of Tom Pitchlynn. Their children on this census were Battice (Battiest); Charles, Emma; Winnie; Richard; and Willie Brashears. (Thanks to Richard A. Greene, of Bakersfield, for a Xerox copy.)

Family of Jesse Brashears and Delilah Juzan

(Sources: Diary of Sarah Ann (née Moncrief, Hawkins) Harlan (^{v5}1394), d. 1925 at Caddo, OK, granddaughter of Zadock Brashears Sr, as reported by Loretta Coppick; data from Patty (Hill) Gambill; family sheets by Alma Mason and James Curtis Ainsworth Jr; Choctaw Census Card of 1902 and Final Dawes Rolls, 1906.)

^{v5}871. ^{9}1. **Tabitha Brashears**, b. 1818, d. 17 Sept 1836, age 18 yrs, 8 mo, bur in Brashers-Wall cem on banks of Tombigbee River; that cemetery has since been destroyed.

^{v5}872. ^{9}2. ***Susan P. Brashears**, b. 1820, bur Skullyville Cem, Indian Territory; m. 9 Oct 1843, *Thomas Lanier*, b. 10 Sept 1810, d. 1859

^{v5}873. ^{9}3. **Charles Juzan Brashears**, b. c1821-22, d. 1853; attended the Choctaw Academy in Great Crossing, Scott Co, Kentucky, 1830-32, according to *Who Was Who Among the Southern Indians*, by Don Martini, p.59. Charles was guardian of his two younger sisters; was removed with his mother to Indian Territory about 1838; married *Czarina Folsom*, (½ Choctaw), b. 5 March 1833, and had a daughter, Lecita, who died in 1853. Charles J. Brashears also died in 1853. Czarina m.2. Pierre Trahern (^{v5}1187); m.3. Dr. Thomas J. Bond (^{v5}526); m.4. D.N. Robb. She was a member of the Baptist Church, "a well-educated, refined Christian lady." (See *Genealogy of the Folsom Family, 1638-1938*)

^{v5}874. ^{10}1. **Lecita Brashears**, b. 1852, d. 1853.

^{v5}875. ^{9}4. **Wesley T. Brashears**, b. c1823, d. 1845 in AL. The "Highland Messenger" reported 7 Nov 1845: "Wesley T. Brashears, a man believed to be aged 22 or 25, found dead Sept 30 or Oct 7, 1845 in the Bigby [Tombigbee] River, Sumter Co, Ala, and believed to have been murdered." (See *Marriage and Death Notices from Extant Asheville NC Newspapers, 1840-1870*.)

^{v5}876. ^{9}5. ***Martha Ann Brashears**, b. 1825, d. 19 May 1875, bur Skullyville Cem; m. 15 Sept 1850, *John Garrett*

Ainsworth, of Mississippi, b. 12 Feb 1818,

v⁵877. ⁹6. *Henrietta Brashears**, b. 1827, d. 19 July 1873; m.1. 17 Dec 1845, *William Patton Bilbo*, b. 1823, d. in 1870s in MS, s/o George S. Bilbo and Elizabeth Martin; m.2. *John Garrett Ainsworth*, her sister's ex-husband.

Susan Brashears and Thomas Lanier

v⁵872. ⁹2. **Susan P. Brashears**, b. 1820, Sumter Co, AL, d/o Jesse Brashears and Delilah Juzan; m. 9 Oct 1843 (Sumter Co, AL, "by William Fluker, J.P.") *Thomas Lanier*, b. 10 Sept 1810, d. 26 June 1859, bur LeFlore Co, OK.

On 25 Sept 1845, Thomas Lanier and wife, Susan (late Susan Brashears) and James Lanier of first part to Hardy Fluker of second part and William Fluker of third part: Thomas and James Lanier indebted to William Fluker, and mortgage slaves (Sumter Co, AL, Deeds, Book H, p.442).

In Thomas Lanier's household in 1850, Sumter Co, AL (#124), there are five Brashears orphans, Amanda, James, Martha, Mallissa, and Jesse.

v⁵798. 1. **Amanda Brashears**, 19, b. c1831

v⁵799. 2. **James Brashears**, 17, b. c1833

v⁵801. 3. **Martha Brashears**, 14, b. 1837 (Choctaw Roll #6339); m. *Thomas H. McMurtrey*, b. _?_, d. Feb 1896, s/o William H. McMurtrey, of KY. Martha and the last two of her family are on Choctaw Census Card #2189, which gives her parents as Tom Linier and Susan Linier. However, *A History of the State of Oklahoma*, by Luther F. Hill, 1909, Vol.1, p.379 (thanks to Frank Shull Needham for a Xerox copy) gives her name as Martha Brashears, b. Alabama, 1837, and also gives some data on her family.
   1. James J. McMurtrey,
   2. John W. McMurtrey, of Hartshorne, OK
   3. Susan R. McMurtrey, m. D. Thomas, of Talihoma
   4. Clyde McMurtrey, b. 18 Oct 1872, LeFlore Co, I.T.; m. in Feb 1897, Della Adams, d/o Thomas H. Adams, who had migrated from TN to KY, to OK. Clyde was President of the Bank of Cameron.
   y. Tom McMurtrey,

5. Nettie McMurtrey (Choctaw Roll #6340), b. c1880 (19 in 1899); m. Enoch Needham, b. c1878 (26 in 1904), (Intermarried Citizen #D767)
    y. Frank Frantz Needham,
      z. Frank Shull Needham,
6. Joseph B. McMurtrey, (Choctaw Roll #6341), b. c1883 (16 in 1899),.

^{v5}802. 4. **Mallissa Brashears**, 12, b. c1838
^{v5}803. 5. **Jesse Brashears**, 10, b. c1840

These Brashears children are probably (no firm documents) children of Samuel Brashears Jr, the "Creek Warrior," (^{v5}523) s/o Samuel Brashears Sr and Rachel Durant. Samuel Jr apparently died in the mid-1840s. These families took care of their own orphans, so it is reasonable to assume that Samuel's orphaned children would have been sent to Suk-en-Atcha, where Samuel's brother, Alexander, was a primary care-giver and where the children's grandmother had married (as her fourth husband) Zadock Brashears, the patriarch of the Suk-en-Atcha settlement. The children were then "given" to a young couple, who had not yet started having children of their own.

Frank Shull Needham writes: "My father was Frank Frantz Needham. His mother was Nettie McMurtrey. Her mother was Martha (Mattie) Brashears. *History of the State of Oklahoma* contains bios of some of the early Oklahomans: "His (Clyde McMurtrey's) father was Thomas H. McMurtrey, a white man, and his mother was formerly Martha Brashears, a Choctaw born in Alabama in 1837, and who is now a resident of Cameron."

Choctaw Census Card #2189 lists "Roll #6339 - McMurtrey, Mattie, 65, F, ¼, Tribal Enrollment 1896, Gaines Co, #9154 - Name of Father: Tom Lineer, Dead, non-citizen - Name of Mother: Susan Lineer, Dead, Skullyville." It looks like Martha "Mattie" (Brashears) McMurtrey claimed her foster parents as her natural parents on census card #2189.

Family of Susan Brashears and Thomas Lanier:
^{v5}878. ^{10}1. Benjamin Lanier, b. 1846, d. 1875; buried at Skully-ville, Indian Territory.
^{v5}879. ^{10}2. Susan Lanier, b. 1848, d. 19—; m.1. Samuel Cooper, m.2. B.B. Shropshire,
^{v5}880. ^{11}1. Henry F. Cooper, b. 1873; was U.S. Marshall

v5881.   11 2. James T. Cooper, b. 1875; m. Tory Forrest,
v5882.   11 3. Stella Cooper, b. 1878; m. Jack Gallagher,
v5883.   11 4. Irene Cooper, b. 1880; m. _____ Robertson,
v5884.   11 5. Frank Cooper, b. 1882
v5885.   11 6. Adolph Shropshire
v5886. 10 3. Edward Lanier, b. 1850; was County Judge of Skullyville Co, OK; m. Rebecca (Krebs) McCurtain, widow of David McCurtain, Sheriff of Skullyville, who was murdered; Rebecca had two children by her first marriage: David Cornelius McCurtain, and Jo Anne McCurtain. Rebecca and Edward Lanier had five children:
v5887.   11 1. Jane Lanier,
v5888.   11 2. Joe Lanier,
v5889.   11 3. David C. Lanier,
v5890.   11 4. Susan P. Lanier,
v5891.   11 5. Edward Lanier Jr,
v5892. 10 4. Joseph Lanier, b. 1855; Sheriff of Skullyville, was killed by a Bill Hughes,

Martha Brashears and John Garrett Ainsworth

v5876. 9 5. **Martha Ann Brashears**, b. 1825, Sumter Co, AL, d. 19 May 1875, at "Oak Lodge," Skullyville Co, I.T., bur Skullyville Indian Cem, Spiro, OK, d/o Jesse Brashears and Delilah Juzan; m. 15 Sept 1850, in Skullyville Co, Indian Territory, *John Garrett Ainsworth*, of Mississippi, b. 12 Feb 1818, Simpson, MS, d. 8 April 1886, Skullyville, I.T., s/o David Ainsworth and Elizabeth Spence. They lived near Skullyville, Indian Territory, near Spiro, OK, where all their children were born. They must have divorced, for John G. Ainsworth m.2. Henrietta (Brashears) Bilbo, Martha's sister. J.G. and Martha Ainsworth are buried in the Skullyville Indian Cemetery. Martha's stone is inscribed: "Wife of J.G. Ainsworth, Born in Ala, Died in Skullyville, IT. An affectionate wife, and indulgent parent. She has gone to her reward." (Data from the late Loretta Coppick.)

Family of Martha Brashears and John Garrett Ainsworth:

[v5]893.   [10]1. Thomas Drennan Ainsworth, b. 19 Oct 1851, Skullyville, I.T., d. 13 May 1917; m. 26 Dec 1875, a cousin, Mrs. Martha Ann (Ainsworth) McCurtain, b. 11 Nov 1846, d. 10 Jan 1904, d/o David Spence Ainsworth and Nancy Pruitt. Martha Ainsworth m.1. Green McCurtain, Chief of the Choctaws.

[v5]894.   [11]1. Martha Jessie Ainsworth, b. 18 Feb 1877 at "Oak Lodge," near Skullyville, I.T.; m. 7 Jan 1897, Edgar Allen Moore, s/o Lyman Moore and Frances Eugenia McClain (gd/o Susan Moncrief).

[v5]895.   [11]2. Frank James Ainsworth, b. 1881, at "Oak Lodge," near Skullyville, I.T., d. age 15 months

[v5]896.   [11]3. Garrett Thomas Ainsworth, b. 28 Sept 1882, at "Oak Lodge," near Skullyville, I.T.; m. Etta Baker,

[v5]897.   [11]4. Ella M. Ainsworth, b. 1884 at "Oak Lodge," near Skullyville, I.T.; m. Frank Tibbitt,

[v5]898.   [10]2. Jesse Brashears Ainsworth, b. 15 Jan 1854, Skullyville, I.T., d. 10 June 1905; m. 1881, Margaret Ainsworth,

[v5]899.   [10]3. Napoleon Breedlove Ainsworth, b. 26 Feb 1856, Skullyville, I.T., d. 20 Aug 1922; m. 1883, Emily K. Thompson,

[v5]900.   [10]4. Johanna (or Johnanna) Faye Ainsworth, b. 26 Feb 1858, Skullyville, I.T., d. 17 March 1920; m. Elijah W. Fannin,

[v5]901.   x. Henry Thomas Fannin, m. Florence Moroni,

[v5]902.   x. Mella Belle Fannin, 1st wife of Cecil Morgan Terrell, step-father of Patty (Hill) Gambill

[v5]903.   x. Martha Pauline Fannin, m. Edwin L. Hickman,

[v5]904.   [10]5. Joseph H. Ainsworth, b. 7 May 1860, Skullyville, I.T., d. 20 Dec 1863

[v5]905.   [10]6. Sibella Ainsworth, (twin), b. 26 Dec 1862, Skullyville, I.T., d. 9 Jan 1863

[v5]906.   [10]7. Isabel Ainsworth, (twin), b. 26 Dec 1862, Skullyville, I.T., d. 9 April 1864

[v5]907.   [10]8. James Thompson Ainsworth, b. 30 Nov 1866, Skullyville, I.T., d. 19 March 1902, Purcell, McClain Co, OK; m. 14 March 1895, in Caddo, Blue Co, I.T., Martha E. Freeny, b. 13 Feb 1880 at Caddo, Blue Co, I.T., d. 2 Aug 1970 at Denver, CO, age 92, d/o Robert

Clay Freeny Jr, of Eagletown, I.T. and Mary Beck,

v5908. [11]x. James Curtis Ainsworth Sr, b. 20 July 1898, Oak Lodge, LeFlore Co, OK, d. 22 Dec 1945, Reno, Washoe Co, NV; m. 28 June 1918, Hazel Griffin, b. 2 Oct 1898, So Bethelehem, NY, d. 16 Jan 1944, Albany, NY, d/o Cornelius Joseph Griffin Jr and Hannah Louise Carkner,

v5909. [12]x. James Curtis Ainsworth Jr, b. 20 July 1921, Albany, NY; m. 14 Jan 1945, in Los Angeles, CA, Ethel Irene McKee, b. 28 Feb 1924, Sargent, Custer Co, NE, d/o Fred McKee and Mary Ethyl Debusk; Irene, who supplied much of the above data, lives (1994) 1756 Sue Way, Sparks, NV 89431. They had seven children:

v5910. [13]1. James Curtis Ainsworth, III; m.1. Lynn Mayo Cusick; m.2. Sandra Lee Taylor

v5911. [13]2. Ronald Eugene Ainsworth; m. Geraldine Pauline Ainsworth,

v5912. [13]3. Mary Ann Ainsworth; m. Rodney Schwendiman Klinger,

v5913. [13]4. John Charles Ainsworth; m. Deborah Elizabeth Fisher,

v5914. [13]5. Patricia Louise Ainsworth; m. Herbert Hall Proctor,

v5915. [13]6. Thomas Edward Ainsworth; m.1. Daureen Lynn Rundle; m.2. Christy Anne Miller; m.3. Jennifer Louise Rimshaw,

v5916. [13]7. Gary Raymond Ainsworth; m. Elizabeth Harris,

Henrietta Brashears and William Patton Bilbo/ John Garrett Ainsworth

v5877. [9]6. **Henrietta Brashears**, b. 1827, Sumter Co, AL, d. 19 July 1873, Carthage, Leake Co, MS, d/o Jesse Brashears and Delilah Juzan; m.1. 17 Dec 1845, *William Patton Bilbo*, b. 1823, d. in 1870s in MS, s/o George S. Bilbo and Elizabeth Martin; m.2. *John Garrett Ainsworth*, her sister's ex-husband. (Data from the late Loretta Coppick.)

Family of Henrietta Brashears and William Patton Bilbo:

v⁵917.   ¹⁰1. Mary Missouri Bilbo, b. 14 July 1848, at Carthage, Miss, d. 5 Jan 1888 at Caddo, OK; m. 10 May 1870, Charles E. Williams, of Carthage

v⁵918.   ¹¹1. Ernestine Williams, b. 1873, Carthage, MS, d. 1949, Kosciusko, MS, bur Stigler, OK; m.1. 30 Dec 1896, James Bower, a descendant of the Moncrief family; m.2. Jim "J.O." Reed. After her mother died, Ernestine "raised" her younger siblings, Annie and Boyd.

v⁵919.   ¹¹2. Royal Cardwell Williams, b. 1879, Carthage, MS, d. 1925, Kosciusko, MS, of pneumonia, bur Williams Plot, Stigler OK Cem; m. Grace Richardson. Royal left five children when he died.

v⁵920.   ¹¹3. Edward Kelsey Williams, b. 1881, Kosciusko, MS, d. 1963, bur Stigler, OK; m. 1904, Mary Eunice "Mamie" Fenton, who spent the last 20 year of her life in a wheel chair.

v⁵921.   ¹²1. Charley Roy Williams, b. 1904, Stigler, I.T., d. Jan 1980; m. 1926, Luthie ___en, (Xerox cut off part of name). Ch: 3 girls, 1 boy.

v⁵922.   ¹²2. Loretta Williams, b. 1906 in Indian Territory, near Stigler, OK; m. June 1928, Lester L. Coppick; Loretta, now dec'd, was a contributor of data to this history.

v⁵923.   ¹²3. Edward Kelsey Williams Jr, b. 1908, d. 1911, diphtheria.

v⁵924.   ¹²4. Mary Pauline Williams, b. 21 Aug 1913, d. of heart attack, Aug 1975, bur Stigler Cem; m. 1940, Everett Culver, who d. 1947; m.2. 1955, Raul Hernandez, who d. 1974

v⁵925.   ¹²5. Gladys Elizabeth Williams, b. 15 Dec 1918; m. 1945, William Wallace; 4 ch.

v⁵926.   ¹¹4. Travis Williams, b. 1883, Kosciusko, MS, d. 1965; m. 1911, Katy Malone, who d. 1914, leaving two ch: Travis Jr and Oscar; Travis m.2. Minnie Duncan.

v⁵927.   ¹¹5. Annie F. Williams, b. 1885, at Caddo, Ind. Terr, d. 1945, CA; m. Mack Stout.

v⁵928.   ¹¹6. Boyd Williams, b. 1888, Caddo, I.T.; d. 1947; m. Sue Bell White v5929. [10]2. Sarah Annie Bilbo, b. 3 July 1850, d. 24 Sept 1893, Ardmore, OK; m. 1 March 1869, John T. Boyd,

v5930. [10]3. Isadora "Dora" Bilbo, b. 14 May 1852, d. 20 June 1911; m. Wyngemund Watkins,

v5931. [10]4. Arlena "Lena" Bilbo, b. 3 Feb 1855, d. 5 Oct 1947 at Ardmore, OK; m. Henry Sutherland,

v5932. [10]5. Charles Abel Bilbo, b. 1858 (age 45 on 25 Sept 1902; Choctaw Roll #10354), d. 12 July 1928; m. Ella Nevada McCoy; 3 ch on Choctaw census card #3662:

v5933. [11]1. Charles C. Bilbo, b. c1891 (11 in 1902)

v5934. [11]2. Cecil A. Bilbo, b. c1893 (9 in 1902)

v5935. [11]3. William W. Bilbo, b. c1895 (7 in 1902)

v5936. [10]6. Ozille or Ozella "Ozzie" Bilbo, b. 29 Oct 1863, d. 31 Dec 1900 at Caddo, OK; m. Robert Travis

10. THE DEBACLE
AT DANCING RABBIT CREEK

Inextricably tied up with the Treaty at Dancing Rabbit Creek and the Brashears family is the name of Greenwood LeFlore, who was rather typical of the mixed bloods who were taking over the tribe. First, a bit of background:

On 20 Oct 1735, *The Prince of Wales* departed from Dornach ?Ireland/ Scotland? with a notable cargo of refugees who were to change southern Indian history. They were all Jacobites, Catholic Highlanders who had tried to replace King George I of Great Britain (i.e. England and Scotland) with James Edward Stuart, son of James II, the Catholic King who was deposed in 1688. Led by Lieutenant William McIntosh, the insurrection failed. The Scots were seriously defeated in 1689 at Killekranke, and thousands sought refuge in Northern Ireland or across the Atlantic. Smaller insurrections (e.g. in 1715) continued until 1745, but many of the best leaders had left from time to time. One of the most notable emigrations of talented Highland Scots was on *The Prince of Wales*, in 1735.

Those arriving at Darien, Georgia, on 10 Jan 1736 included:

John Mohr McIntosh, a direct descendant of Lt. William McIntosh and Chief of the McIntosh Clan;

Lachlan McIntosh, his son, who would become a Brigadier General in the Continental Army;

Roderick McIntosh, later a British Commissary to the Creek Indians and father of the Creek Chief, William McIntosh;

John McIntosh, brother of Roderick, and the first and last British Commissary to the Chickasaw;

Lachlan McGillivray, father of perhaps the most notable of all southern Indian Chiefs, Alexander McGillivray of the Creeks;

Farquar McGillivray, Lachlan's cousin and, in time, a noted minister at Charleston.

Not on the passenger list was James Logan Colbert, but his descendants have claimed since at least 1881 that he was present (perhaps as a stowaway). Actually, he was born in America and was already there when the ship arrived, despite what family tradition says (see "James Logan Colbert of the Chickasaws: The Man and the Myth," by Richard A. Colbert, *The North Carolina Genealogical Society Journal*, May 1994, p. 82). Colbert, about age 15 at the time, had heard glowing stories of personal freedom for those white men who chose to live among the Indians. Sixty and seventy years later, his grandsons, George and Levi Colbert, influential and wealthy Chickasaw Chiefs, were still campaigning for Indian freedom— this time freedom from the encroachment of American immigrants. (See *The Colbert Genealogy*, Indian Archives, Okla. Hist. Soc. Lib, Oklahoma City.)

Already in the country (and more were coming every year) were plenty of lowlander Scots— the Vaughns, Turnbulls, Forbes, Pantons, etc, usually Presbyterian in persuasion. Those who moved into French and Spanish territory soon found they were pressured to become both citizens and Catholics. Both the French and Spanish authorities saw immigration as a way of building their nation's strength, but they wanted loyal citizens. They frequently required loyalty oaths of new-comers and/or citizenship before they would grant them land. And the Catholic church permeated governmental activities by being charged with keeping the official records of baptisms, marriages, successions (probate), oaths and contracts.

Many of these men and others like them entered "The Indian Trade." That is, they bought beads, rum, vermillion, combs, looking glasses, scissors, knives, clothing, strouds (coarse blankets), and, later, guns, powder and lead at the big trading houses in Charles Town (it was still two words in those days), Augusta, Pensacola, Mobile, then transported the goods, usually by horse or mule pack-trains, sometimes by boat and barge, into the Indian country, where they traded the goods for pelts— beaver at first, until they created a "beaver desert," then deerskins and buffalo robes. They soon formed trading companies, commercial partnerships, and found it convenient to leave one of the partners in the Indian country all year, or at least for a good part of the year.

These men who stayed in the Indian country usually took Indian wives. They became "squaw men," as the scoffing idiom of the coastal settlements put it, but most of the trading companies recognized early the security and desirability of their agents in the field having family ties there. Indeed, among some of the tribes, the traders were required to take a wife; were, in fact, often offered the daughters of prominent warriors and chiefs. The Cherokee, for example, thought that a trader would be more trustworthy and more caring for the interest and well-being of the tribe if he had a wife and family among them and at least gave lip-service to some of their customs, including learning a bit of their language and religion.

The dusky half-breed sons and daughters of these men were frequently sent "east" to boarding schools, where they sometimes found wives and husbands, though more frequently they identified as Indian and sought Indian mates. The half-breed sons of these men usually spoke both languages, and their fathers taught them to read, write, and cipher enough to help them in their business.

At first, these literate half-breeds became the secretaries for the tribes. When a traditional chief needed to write a letter ("send a talking paper") to a colonial governor or the king, he usually called on the person who shared some of his blood and genes and also knew both languages from their earliest years. These secretaries soon became envoys or ambassadors, then deputies, and when the older chiefs died away, they became the acknowledged leaders of the tribe, often in the face of opposition and hatred from the more traditional full-bloods.

GREENWOOD LeFLORE

A good example of this new breed of chief was Greenwood LeFlore, grand-nephew of Apuckshunnubbee, one of three principal Choctaws chiefs. CAUTION: It is incorrect that Greenwood LeFlore was a nephew of Pushmataha. That error apparently stems from a mistake made in a charming book, *The Devil's Backbone*, by Jonathan Daniels.

Apuckshunnubbee, b. c1739, became Chief of the Oklafalaya District soon after 1794; he died in Maysville, KY, in 1824, after falling from a retaining wall near the river, while en route to Washington, D.C. on a mission with Pushmataha and Mushulatubbee to protest U.S. failure to live up to the Treaty of 1820.

After his death, the chieftainship of Oklafalaya District passed to Robert Cole, s/o Shumaka (sister to Apuckshunnubbee) and her husband, James? Cole. (NOTE: we are not absolutely sure of his first name, but a James Cole arrived in the Natchez District about 1772 and settled on a creek in the Oklafalaya District, which came to be called Cole's Creek, in present-day Grenada Co, MS. He participated in the ill-fated Fort Panmure Rebellion of 1781 and had to seek refuge in the wilderness afterward. James Cole served as "sworn interpreter" of Choctaw at the negotiations for the Treaty of Hopewell in 1786. No other Cole appears in the records of this time, who both knew Choctaw and was in Mississippi; so we believe that James Cole was the father of Robert Cole.

Shumaka, sister of Apuckshunnubbee, married as her second husband James? Cole and they had the following family (data from Chris Morgan, for which many thanks).

1. Col. Robert Cole, b. ?, d. 1842, Chief of the Oklafalaya District from 1824 to 1826. Robert Cole did not speak English and soon relinquished leadership to his more-educated grand-nephew, Greenwood LeFlore. Robert Cole m. Sallie, a full-blood Choctaw and had at least 13 children: Coleman, b. 1802, Charles, Peter, Malinda, Sampson, Adam, Forbes, Angelica, Betsey, Molly, Susey, Siney (m. Solomon Perry, s/o Isaac Perry), and a daughter who m. Patrick Riley.
2. Nahotima Cole, b. c1760; m. Jean Louis Cravatt and had, at least, daughters, Rebecca, b. 1775, and Nancy, b. 1775, both of whom married Louis LeFlore, father of Greenwood LeFlore. Nahotima may have been d/o Shumaka by her earlier first marriage; considering her birthdate, that is a strong possibility.
3. Hannah Cole, b. 9 Nov 1781; m. c1800, Daniel McCurtain, b. 8 July 1777, MS, and had children Thomas, b. 1801, Cornelius, b. 1803, Daniel, John, Luke, Allen, b. 1810, William, b. 1814 (m. Sawicha), Kennedy, Kemper, Sophia, (m. Hardy Perry Jr), and three daughters, names unknown.
4. Miyahoke Cole, b. c1783; m. c1805, Garrett Enock Belvin, alias Nelson, b. 20 Jan 1781, d. 1838 on Red River in Indian Territory. Miyahokc Cole and Garrett Nelson had children: George, Solomon, Eden, Blount, Mitchell, Chillico, Betsey,

Jenny, and Emahayia Nelson (b. 1806; m. 1829, Cornelius McCurtain).
5. Mishahoya Cole, m. Moses Perry, s/o Levi Perry, and they had at least one daughter, Amy, who m. George Oxberry.

About 1790, Louis LeFleau or Lefleur, b. 29 June 1762 at Mobile, s/o Jean B. Lefleau and Marie Jeanne Girard, set up a Choctaw trading post which came to be called "French Camp" on the Natchez Trace near the Choctaw-Chickasaw boundary and married, not one, but two of Apuckshunnubbee's grand-nieces who went by the English names of Rebecca and Nancy Cravatt. They were daughters of Jean Louis Cravatte and Nahotima Cole, sister to Robert Cole. (Polygamy was both common and legal in Choctaw society.) He was quite successful and built a fairly large and comfortable double house for his double family. A replica of it may be seen today on the Natchez Trace Parkway, near "Line Creek," the ancient Choctaw-Chickasaw boundary.

In 1798, possibly as a result of so much vandalism and robbery on the Trace, Louis LeFleur moved his business and his families to LeFleur's Bluff on the Pearl River, site of present-day Jackson, Mississippi. At LeFleur's Bluff, he was only seven miles southeast of the Choctaw Agency and about nine miles southwest of Turner Brashear's Stand. He remained there until the Treaty of Dancing Rabbit Creek was signed in Sept 1830, then moved to a plantation near the Yalobusha and Yazoo Rivers in Holmes Co, MS, where he died in 1833.

Family of Louis LeFleur and Nancy Cravatt:
1. Louisa LeFleur, b. 1791, French Camp, Choctaw Nation; m. John Harkins,
2. Clarissa LeFleur, b. 1792, French Camp, Choctaw Nation: m.1. James Wilson, m.2. Alfred Leach,
3. Winna LeFleur, b. 1796, French Camp, Choctaw Nation; m. Alex McGahey,
4. Sylvia LeFleur, b. 1798, French Camp, Choctaw Nation; m.1. _____ Moss, m.2. Rubin Harris Sr,
5. Forbes LeFleur, b. 1810, LeFleur's Bluff, Choctaw Nation; m.1. Sinai Hayes, m.2. Rebecca Fisher, d/o Joseph Fisher and Patsy Hayes, a full-blood (Joseph Fisher m.1. Elizabeth Brashear ([v5]203), d/o Turner Brashear and "a daughter of

Taboca"); m.3. Anne Marie Maurier,

Family of Louis LeFleur and Rebecca Cravatt:

1. Benjamin LeFleur, b. 1792, French Camp, Choctaw Nation, d. 1863; m. Mary Juzan, d/o Charles Juzan
2. Felicity LeFleur, b. 1797, French Camp, Choctaw Nation; m. Samuel Long,
3. Greenwood LeFleur, b. 3 June 1800, LeFleur's Bluff, Choctaw Nation, d. 1865; m.1. 1819, Rosa Donley, d/o Major James Donley of Nashville; m.2. Elizabeth Coodey, from the Shorey-Coodey family of the Cherokees; m.3. Priscilla Donley, sister of his first wife.
4. *Isabelle LeFleur*, b. 1803, LeFleur's Bluff, Choctaw Nation; m. **Vaughn Brashears** (ᵛ⁵838), s/o Zadock Brashears and Susannah Vaughn.
5. William LeFleur, b. 1806, LeFleur's Bluff, Choctaw Nation, d. 1844; m. Martha Walker (ᵛ⁵531), d/o Rachel (Durant) Brashears-Walker-Brashears; also m. Cynthia Fisher, d/o Joseph Fisher and Patsy Hayes.
6. Basil LeFleur, b. 1810, LeFleur's Bluff, Choctaw Nation, d. c1860; m. Caroline Goodings; also m. Narcissa Fisher, d/o Joseph Fisher and Patsy Hayes. After the Removal to Indian Territory in 1832, Basil LeFleur became Chief or Governor of his district.
7. Jackson LeFleur, b. 1815, LeFleur's Bluff, Choctaw Nation

In the early years of the 1800s, Pushmataha, Apuckshun-nubbee, and Mushulatubbee were the three Chiefs, or Mingoes, of the Choctaw Nation, each ruling in his own district—Apuckshunnubbee in the Western Division, or Oklafalaya District; Pushmataha in Six Villages, or Okla Hunnalli; Mushulatubbee in the Eastern District, or Ahepat Okla. Jonathan Daniels writes as if Greenwood LeFlore were nephew of Pushmataha, in the passages from his book which follow; but bear in mind that he was a descendant of Apuckshunnubbee's sister, not Pushmataha. At least some of these chiefs favored Greenwood LeFleur from a very early age, and often had him with them at council.

"As a young boy, Greenwood had attracted more than his Choctaw relatives with his charm, wit, and intelligence. A post rider [one who carried U.S. Mail on the Natchez Trace], Major James Donley, of Nashville, asked to take Greenwood to

Nashville, where he could be given a proper education.

"Greenwood got more than that," writes Jonathan Daniels in *The Devil's Backbone, the Story of the Natchez Trace* (p.231). "In Tennessee dialect, his name was corrupted from LeFleur to LeFlore. Also, he fell in love with the major's daughter, Rosa. He was only seventeen then. Rosa was fifteen. Such youthful marriages were not unusual in Tennessee. Major Donley vetoed the match. Greenwood waited. Then, weeks later, young Greenwood spoke casually to his mentor and patron.

"Major, if you were in love with a girl and her parents object to your marrying her, what would you do?

"For once, the major's guard was down. "Why, I should marry her first, and then tell her parents."

"Greenwood did just that."

The elopement took place shortly before Greenwood joined Pushmataha at the council grounds for the Treaty at Doak's Stand in 1820, in which Andrew Jackson got cession of six million acres of Choctaw land, from which nine counties were created within a few years. So strong was white pressure (and greed) on Indian land!

Pushmataha, the Choctaw chief of the Six Villages, or Okla Hunnalli, was described as 50 years old when he returned from leading 600 Choctaw warriors in support of Gen. Andrew Jackson at the Battle of Horseshoe Bend in 1814. That would put his birth in the early 1760's. Pushmataha is buried in the Congressional Cemetery, in Washington, DC, under a sandstone shaft that bears the epitaph: "When I am dead, let the big guns be fired over me." (*The Devil's Backbone*, p.236)

NOTE: The official version is that Pushmataha died of diphtheria in Washington, DC, on Christmas Eve, 1824, while on a diplomatic mission to Washington. The truth is, he died of dissipation. David Folsom (who succeeded Mushulatubbee as Chief of the Eastern District in 1826) was with the delegation and wrote a missionary soon after Pushmataha's death that he died from the effects of alcoholic overindulgence, and that nearly every other headman in Washington with them was so sick from the same cause that he feared most of them would die before reaching home.

Still in his mid 20s, Greenwood LeFlore was chosen to replace Robert Cole as Chief of the Oklafalaya District. "He was persuasive to a great degree in pressing his ideas about adjusting the Choctaws to the civilization of the advancing whites. He divided the Nation for law enforcement purposes, provided for trial by jury, and tried to prevent the bringing of liquor into the Choctaw Nation. The tribal council, which had seen the destructive effects of the white man's liquor on the red man's character, decreed flogging as the punishment for smuggling liquor. And when the first man found guilty turned out to be the husband of one of Greenwood's sisters, he personally applied the lash" (*The Devil's Backbone*, p.236).

THE TREATY AT DANCING RABBIT CREEK

In Sept 1830, Chief Greenwood LeFlore was called to the treaty grounds between the forks of Dancing Rabbit Creek in present-day Oxnubee County (an impressive monument marks the spot today), where, in 1811, Apuckshunnubbee, Mushulatubbee, and Pushmataha had debated whether the Choctaws should or should not join Shawnee Chief Tecumseh in his pan-Indian effort to stop American encroachment on Indian lands. At Dancing Rabbit Creek, in 1830, the American commissioners, General Thomas Hinds and Colonel John Coffee, wanted to negotiate a treaty by which the Choctaws would relinquish their land and accept in return about half of the present state of Oklahoma.

Having lived among and been educated by the whites, Greenwood probably understood their greed and the inevitability that the white glutton was going to devour the Choctaw pie. So he worked out a compromise, for which he has been both praised highly and damned interminably: The Treaty at Dancing Rabbit Creek, 27 Sept 1830.

For those Choctaws who were willing to "sell" their lands east of the Mississippi, he secured fairly decent payment (at least on paper) and the largest reservation granted any tribe in Indian Territory, on land that was reasonably fertile and fairly well watered. For those Choctaws who were unwilling to part with their holdings, he worked out a treaty by which they could be granted "individual reservations" on the land where they lived.

The 14th Article of The Treaty of Dancing Rabbit Creek, provided that "each Choctaw head of a family, being desirous to remain and become a Citizen of the State, shall be permitted to do so, by signifying his intention to the Agent within six months from the ratification of this treaty, and he or she shall thereupon be entitled to a reservation of one Section of six hundred and forty acres of land, to be bounded by sectional lines of survey, in like manner shall be entitled to one half that quantity for each unmarried child which is living with him over ten years of age, and a quarter section to such child as may be under ten years of age, to adjoin the location of the parent." The treaty further provided that, after five years of residence, the reservee would be granted patent to his land in fee simple, like any other citizen of the United States.

In practice, it turned out to be somewhat more complicated: there were dozens of litigations involving squatters on Choctaw reservations, and the President of the United States himself had to approve these "individual reservations."

There can be no doubt that the effects of this treaty on the Choctaws were devastating, both among the full-bloods and the mixed-bloods. While most of his siblings and their families were forcibly removed to Indian Territory, most of them to LeFlore County, Greenwood LeFlore accepted an "individual reservation" in Yazoo Valley and got other lands which some saw as bribes to get him to sign away Choctaw land in Mississippi. Many Choctaws condemned him as a traitor, but he probably got the best deal for the Choctaws that any man could have gotten at the time.

After the removal, his prestige and wealth among white men grew. His plantation prospered. He built a mansion, called "Malmaison," in the French Empire style and filled it with furniture designed in Paris. He was elected to both the House and the Senate of the Mississippi Legislature. One story is told that, irritated by the pompous habit of politicians lacing oratory with Latin phrases which many participants could not have known, Greenwood LeFlore, who spoke Choctaw, French, and English as mother tongues and was probably conversant in Spanish, Chickasaw, Muskogee, and possibly Latin from his school days, gave a one-hour speech entirely in Choctaw, exhorting fairness of proceedings. Granted that the act was audacious, presumptuous, a pompous violation of good sense, exactly like he was objecting to, still (and it's a prejudice on my part) anyone who forces any Mississippi Legislature to listen to a full hour of Choctaw can't be all bad.

THE CHOCTAW CENSUS OF 1831

The terms of the Treaty of Dancing Rabbit Creek required a fairly complete census of the Choctaw Tribe, as well as registers of those wanting to stay on their individual reservations and those willing to accept allotments in Indian Territory.

The Census, reproduced partially on the next page, involves two, distantly related families, on opposite sides of the state. Note, for instance, that there are two Turner Brashears, one in Yazoo Valley on the west side, near Greenwood, MS, one in Kemper Co, which is on the east side, adjacent to Sumter Co, AL; Suk En Atcha Creek runs through both Kemper and Sumter counties, and empties into the Tombigbee River. Delilah (Juzan) Brashears and Turner Brashears, II, owned the land at the mouth of Suk En Atcha Creek. See the map.

The two men— Benjamin and Lewis Brashears— living on the west side of the state, in Yazoo Valley, are sons of R.T. Turner Brashears and "a daughter of Taboca", a Great Medal Chief of the old Choctaw Nation. The Turner in Yazoo City is R. Turner Brashears, the Choctaw trader, interpreter, inn-keeper, s/o Benjamin Brashear and Catherine Belt and brother of Marsham Brashear, of Louisville; also brother of Capt. Richard Brashears, of St. Stephens Trading Post, and Capt. Tobias Brashears, one of the founders of Port Gibson on the Mississippi River. See their chapters.

Turner Brashear in Yazoo Valley is R.T. "Turner" Brashear; Benjamin and Lewis Brashear, also in Yazoo Valley are his sons by his first marriage to "a daughter of Taboca."

Vaughn Brashears at Honey Island is one of the eastern branch, s/o Zadock Brashears, Sr, and Susannah Vaughn. He moved to Honey Island about 1828.

The others in the Census are all on the east side of the state. Zadock Sr at Black Bluff in Alabama is supposed to be married to Rachel (who was Creek, not Choctaw), but Rachel is listed separately. Perhaps they had separated, or were living apart to ensure their separate groups of children got their benefits.

Some extracts from the special 1831 Census of the Choctaw Indian Tribe:

name	# acres	#in fam.	m.16+	ch.0-10	# of slaves	place
Greenwood LeFlore's Company, Miss.--Yazoo City):						
Benjamin Brashears	14	8	3	4	-	Yazoo valley
Lewis Brashears	12	7	1	3	-	Yazoo valley
Turner Brashears	50	7	1	-	-	Yazoo valley
In Humphreys Co, Miss:						
Vaughn Brashears	20	10	2	4	-	Honey Island
In Kemper Co, Miss:						
Alexander Brashears	30	10	2	5	-	Suk En Atcha
Zeddock Brashears, Jr.	25	6	1	4	2	Suk En Atcha
Delila Brashears	50	7	1	4	16	Suk En Atcha
Rachel Brashears	?					
Turner Brashears	?					
On Tom Big Bee River (in Alabama):						
Zeddock Brashears, Sr.	50	2	1	1	14	Black Bluff

<============>

Delilah (Juzan) Brashears is the widow of Jesse, s/o Zadock Brashears Sr and Susannah Vaughn.

Alexander Brashears in the Census is Rachel's son by her first marriage to Samuel Brashears Sr; Alexander had married Anne, d/o Zadock and Susannah. Both were apparently eligible as beneficiaries, though Anne may have been dead by this time.

Turner Brashear [II] in the Kemper Co. Census is the youngest son of Zadock and Susannah Brashears, b. c1809. He's about 22, has no children.

THE CHOCTAW "TRAIL OF TEARS"

Most of the Brashears on the western side of the Choctaw Nation (Holmes and Yazoo Counties), either by choice or force, did not become citizens of Mississippi and the United States, but were removed to Indian Territory:

Harriet (Everidge) Oakes, granddaughter of Turner Brashears and "a daughter of Taboca," called "Jane Apuckshunnubbee", remembered one contingent of the Removal. There were "five or six hundred Indians that came, and cholera struck us at Vicksburg, and many Indians were left on the banks of the Mississippi." [Two of Vaughn Brashear's five children apparently died in this "Choctaw Trail of Tears."] The Indians were taken by boat from Vicksburg to the mouth of the White River, then were marched on foot, first to Little Rock, then to Kiamichi, "landed at Kiamichi River."

Richard Brashears, former slave of Vaughn Brashears, also remembered the Removal and gave the following testimony before the Dawes Commission in 1896-1904: "My old master was in debt to Allen Glover (at Honey Island) and he had to steal us away in the night." They met Ben and Lewis at Vicksburg, where the Indians were assembled on the bank of the Mississippi. The Indians were taken by steamboat from Vicksburg to the mouth of the Arkansas, then by wagons to a place nine miles east of old Fort Towson in the Choctaw Nation.

William S. Colquhon, special agent in charge of part of the Choctaw removal, wrote December 10th 1831: "The weather is colder here than ever known before, and rains have been incessant. The boats which were intended for Little Rock put the Indians out at the Post. This error has thrown together about twenty three hundred. I understand they have no other means of transportation than forty wagons and the roads are impassable. The party is a wretched set of beings nearly naked, and have marched the last twenty hours through sleet and snow barefooted. If I could have done it, I would have given them shoes."

Philena Thacher Hotchkin, wife of Evenezer Hotchkin, two missionaries who journeyed with this contingent said, "Because of the severe weather, scant clothing, and insufficient food, many were sick and numbers perished. Babies were born on the road side, and mother and baby lacking medical attention often perished."

Extract from Vol. 2, *Register of Choctaw Indians* who were moved to Ft. Towson, from Mississippi, 11 Feb 1832:

8. **Brashears, Vaughn**	age 33, b. c1798, 5'1"
9. (Lou?) Gibell	28, b. c1804, 5'4" [garble for Isabella]
10. Eliza	12, b. c1820, 4'; died previous to 1 May 1832
11. Polly	11, b. c1821, 3'10"
12. Deliete	6, b. c1826, 3'5"
13. Vaughn	3, b. c1829, 3'; died previous to April 1832
14. Elmira	½, b. c1832, 2'
15. Frank	21, b. c1811, 5'6"; dropped prev. to April 1832
16. Bolin	29, b. c1803, 5'6"; " " " "
17. Lila	22, b. c1810, 5'4"; " " " "
18. Ned	12, b. c1820, 4'3"; " " " "
19. Nancy	8, b. c1824, 4'; " " " "

20. Dick	5, b. c1826, 3'6"; " " " "
21. Frankey	3, b. c1828, 3'; " " " "
22. **Brashiers, Lewis**	34, b. c1797, 5'10"
23. Nancy	25, b. c1807, 5'6"
24. Jenny	12, b. c1820, 4'6"
25. Sam	9, b. c1823, 4'
26. Washington	7, b. c1825, 3'10"
27. Joseph	1, b. c1831, 2'; died prev. to May 1832
38. **Brashears, Benjamin**	31, b. c1801, 6'1"
39. Illichihana	25, b. c1807, 5'
40. William	13, b. c1819, 4'
41. Lila	7, b. c1825, 3'1"
42. Lou Sukey	3, b. c1829, 3'
43. Anna	1, b. c1831, 2'

Those "dropped prev. to April 1832" were apparently the slaves, who did not qualify as Choctaws by blood. After the Civil War, they were free and expected to leave the Choctaw Nation. They didn't. They were much later enrolled as Freedmen citizens of the Choctaw Nation and allotted as freedmen.

THOSE WISHING TO STAY

Most of the Suk-en-atcha group elected, under the terms of the Treaty of Dancing Rabbit Creek, to remain in Alabama or Mississippi, become citizens of the United States, and accept allotments of land. The *Records of Choctaw Trading Post, St. Stephens, Mississippi Territory (Book 2, p.118)* contains a "register of Choctaws who wish to remain five years & become citizens" (see next page). Note that, on June 13, 1831, several Brashears of the Suk En Atcha group registered:

name	ch 0-10	ch 10+	Remarks
Alexander Brashears	5	2	Indian half breed
Deleley Brashears	2	3	Half breed woman
Zadock Brashears	2	1	Half breed man
Turner Brashears, Jr	0	0	Half breed man
Rachel Brashears	1	0	Half breed woman

Maps filed in the land office at Demopolis, county seat of Sumter Co, in 1837, show where the settlements of several of these Brashears families were located; I have drawn a map (see p. 214) showing the creeks, the bluffs mentioned in many of the records, and the locations of the Brashear "improvements," their houses and barns. These improvements were to be the core of their individual reservations.

```
===========================================================
```
Register of Choctaw names as entered by the agent previous to 24 Aug. 1831, who wish to become citizens, according to a provision of the late Treaty in 1830--

Pack 45
Wards Register
```
===========================================================
```

Date of Entry 1831	Names of persons who wish to remain for five years:	No. of children under 10 years.	No. of Children over 10 years.	Remarks, etc.
Apr. 18 John Moore		4	3	White man, Indian wife.
May 7 Ik-la-nab-bee		-	3	Indian man
" " On-a-tam-be		-	3	Indian man
" " Samuel Byington		-	-	Indian man
" " A-la-ba-che		2	-	Indian man
" " Jack Jenkins		3	-	Indian man
" 17 Samuel Cobb		4	1	Indian half-breed
" " James Pickens		4	2	Indian half-breed
" 20 Hartwell Hardaway		3	4	White man, Indian wife.
23 Henry Garvin		1	-	White man, Indian wife.
" " George Murphy		4	4	White man, Indian wife.
" " Patrick Ryley		2	1	White man, Indian wife.
" " William Christy		4	4	White man, Indian wife.
June 13 **Alexander Brashears**		5	2	Indian half-breed
" " Robert Hancock		3	2	Indian half-breed
" " Arthur Kerney		2	1	Indian half-breed
" " Betsey Beemess		-	-	Half-breed woman
" " Robert McGilvery		2	-	Half-breed man
" " John Walker		3	4	White man, Indian wife.
" " **Deliley Brashears**		2	3	Half-breed woman
" " **Zadock Brashears**		2	1	Half-breed man
" " **Turner Brashears, Jr.**		-	-	Half-breed man
" " Allen Stanton		2	-	White man, Indian wife.
" " Adam James		4	2	Half-breed man
" " **Rachael Brashears**		1	-	Half-breed woman
" " Carvel Howell		2	-	White man Indian wife.
" 14 William Forster		2	-	Half-breed
" 16 O-te-man-sha		-	-	Indian male
" " James Foster		3	-	Half-breed man
" " Hugh Foster		4	-	Half-breed man
" " Jim Tom		4	-	Half-breed man
" " O-ho-you		4	-	Half-breed woman
" 24 Charles Buckhannon		2	-	White man, Indian wife.
" 25 Henry Johnson		-	-	White man, Indian wife.
" " Lewis Bryant		3	2	White man, Indian wife.
Jul 2 Henry Pebworth		4	2	" " "
" 5 John Jones		-	1	" " "
" " Jacob Dannele		4	-	" " "

" " Matthew Sebrush	-	-	" " "
" " Luewe Durant	-	2	Half-breed man
" " William Hall	4	3	Half-breed man
" " Betsy Pinson	2	1	Half-breed woman
" " William Lightfoot	3	-	Half-breed man
" " Antony Parress	3	-	White man, Indian wife.
" " Lewis Robertson	2	-	" " "
" " Lyman C. Collens	-	-	Indian man
" " Jack Tom	4	-	Half-breed man
" 26 Sophia Pitchlynn	1	3	Half-breed woman
Aug. 3 Noah Wall	2	2	White man, Indian wife.
" 13 **Susanna Graham**	-	1	Half-breed woman
" " **Anne V. Lewellyn**	-	1	Half-breed woman

[NOTE: Susanna Graham (^{v5}836) was d/o Zadock Brashears (^{v5}231) and
Susannah Vaughn;
Annie Llewellyn was Susanna Graham's daughter.]

" 23 John McGilvery	2	3	Half-breed man
" " Turner McGilvery	2	-	Half-breed man
" " Little Leader	2	3	Indian man
" " Ho-tah	1	1	Indian man
" " E-ya-tubbee	2	-	Indian man
" " Hia-tubbee	1	-	Indian man
" " O-na-ham-bee	3	1	Indian man
" " O-qua-ho-to-nah	2	1	Indian woman
" " Tu-so-non-sha	2	-	Indian woman
" " A-no-kao-tubbee	3	-	Indian man
" " Sa-lah-ma	3	2	Indian man
" " Ia-nim-tubbee	-	-	Indian man
" " No-a-timah	2	2	Indian woman
" " A-no-la	3	2	Indian woman
" " Is-pia	3	2	Indian woman
" " Tu-way-tu-cha	3	3	Indian woman
" " Na-wah-ho-na	2	3	Indian woman

```
     I do certify that the foregoing persons did apply to me as
Agent, to have their names registered to remain five years,
and become citizens of the State, before the 24th. 1831.
          (Signed) W. Ward
          U. S. Agent, C. N. (Choctaw Nation)
```

===
Ward's Register - supplement
```
     The following persons have produced the certificates of W.
Ward, late Choctaw Agent, to the fact of their having
applied for registration, under the 14th article of the
Treaty of 27th Sept. 1830. On the 20th March last, the
Secretary of War decided that they were sufficient to
entitle them to the benefits of the said Article and
locations have been, or will be made for them.
```
William Simmons
William Thompson
James Oxberry
John Homer

William Turnbull
Sampson Moncrief
Betsey Buckles   Located on W. Cert.
Jubal B. Hancock   Located on W. Cert.

The following persons claim under the 19th Article and also under supplement, viz:
Noah Wall
Little Leader
Lewis Durant
Turner Brashears

So cannot be allowed under the 14th Article.

INDIVIDUAL RESERVATIONS AND SQUATTERS

Col. George W. Martin was appointed as "locating agent" to define individual reservations for the Choctaws. Not long after his appointment, he called them all to Demopolis in neighboring Marengo County and drew up their allotments.

They were hardly home from the trip to Demopolis and the ink hardly dry on the papers, before white squatters began encroaching and settling on their land. The squatters then began complaining that the Indians were on *their* land! I do not have a copy of the map of Col. Martin's allotments, but I have drawn one ("Map No. 1") from the descriptions in the War Department, Office of Indian Affairs, and in the squatters' complaints. The squatters hired a lawyer and sent a petition to their Senator in Washington, William R. King, who forwarded it to Lewis Cass, Secretary of War.

TO THE HONORABLE LEWIS CASS,
SECRETARY OF THE WAR DEPARTMENT OF THE UNITED STATES.
Enclosing the memorial of sundry inhabitants of Sumter County, Alabama relating to the reservations located to Betsey Buckles, Zadock Brashears, Delilah Brashears, Alex. Brashears & Turner Brashears. Papers are also enclosed contending that the locations could have been made without interfering with the Citizens's rights under the Pre-emption law.

The memorial of the undersigned Citizens of the County of Sumter (late Choctaw Territory) State of Alabama respectfully represents;

That your memorialists emigrated to that Section of Country known as the Choctaw Nation, now included in the County of Sumter, after the Treaty was made between the Commissioners of the United States and the Chiefs and Warriors of the Choctaw Nation;

that they selected land, and made settlements, on the North side of the water course known as the Suckanutche, a large Creek emptying into the Tombigbee River, on the West side, about latitude 32, 30;

that in the selection of those lands and settlements, fully aware of the different claims appertaining to the Indian population, under the Treaty of Dancing Rabbit Creek, they set down on land, which it could not be presumed would come in collision with the Indian settlements, or claims, the last being uniformly, without any exception, in their vicinity confined to the water course before-mentioned;

that, in making ample allowance for any species of claims the Indians might prefer, under any of the provisions of said treaty, the undersigned made their selections of settlements miles from the Indian improvements;

that there was a perfect good understanding between the before-mentioned Indians and the undersigned, that the latter would not be disturbed by the former in any locations they might prefer;

that the undersigned felt satisfied if the locations of Indian claims, growing out of the Treaty, were made, agreeable to the spirit, meaning, or plain wording of that instrument. That in any contingency, they could not be disturbed, nor their labor and capital expended on the improvements of the land they had selected, as permanent settlements, be wrested from them;

that the Treaty would be strictly adhered to on the part of the United States, they could not doubt, nor could they anticipate that the Indians would be suffered to deviate from it;

that altho the undersigned, with many others, went on the public lands as trespassers, and into the Nation, somewhat in violation of the Treaty, yet when about to correct their error by a removal therefrom, and when the Indians publicly expressed to the Officer of the Govt. of the United states their wish that the whites should remain, and the Government acquiescing by refraining from a removal of the undersigned and others from the public land, they could not but view themselves as making that kind of removal and settlement justified by the former permission of the general government and that whilst they pursued honorable and useful labor and comported themselves as good citizens, they would find that they had rights, and were under a government, that would protect them in their possession.

Under these impressions, the undersigned expended much capital and labor on the soil, calculating on paying to the general government a fair price for their land when brought into market;

Nor did the Indians express or appear desirous to possess themselves of the capital expended or labor of the undersigned until artful and designing speculators on the public lands and the industry of the country suggested to them the extension of their locations, (altho contrary to the express stipulations of the Treaty) in such a way as to embrace the improvements and plantations of the undersigned and others; and which has been done, unnecessarily, and without any reasonable consideration, except to enable the Reservees under his Treaty to make a more advantageous sale of their claims of land, and the speculators, before mentioned, a more advantageous purchase;

that, in whatever position the undersigned may have stood, before the act passed for granting pre-emptions to settlers on the Public Lands embracing their case, that act, they beg leave to suggest rendered legitimate their claims on the Govt. of the United States and the undersigned would respectfully suggest to the Honorable, the Secretary of War Department, that their rights under the pre-emption act were as good as those of the Savages, after the passage of that Act.

That, if the citizens entitled to the privileges of the pre-emption act had legitimate claims, rendered so by the loss of their country, they were not, they must hope, to be ousted from them by an unlawful compliance with the Treaty on the part, or for the benefit of the Indians; nor by any subordinate officer of the Government of the United States entrusted with the execution of any part of that Treaty.

That, while the undersigned forbears making any reflections as regard the Agent who made the location of the Indian

Reservations, they must, in justice to themselves and in defense of what they believe their sacred right, say, that in the location of the Reservations allowed under the Treaty of Dancing Rabbit Creek, and especially those under the 14th Section, their rights have been outraged by making those locations perfectly contrary to the express provisions of that Treaty, and that, had the Treaty been strictly regarded, no such violations of their rights

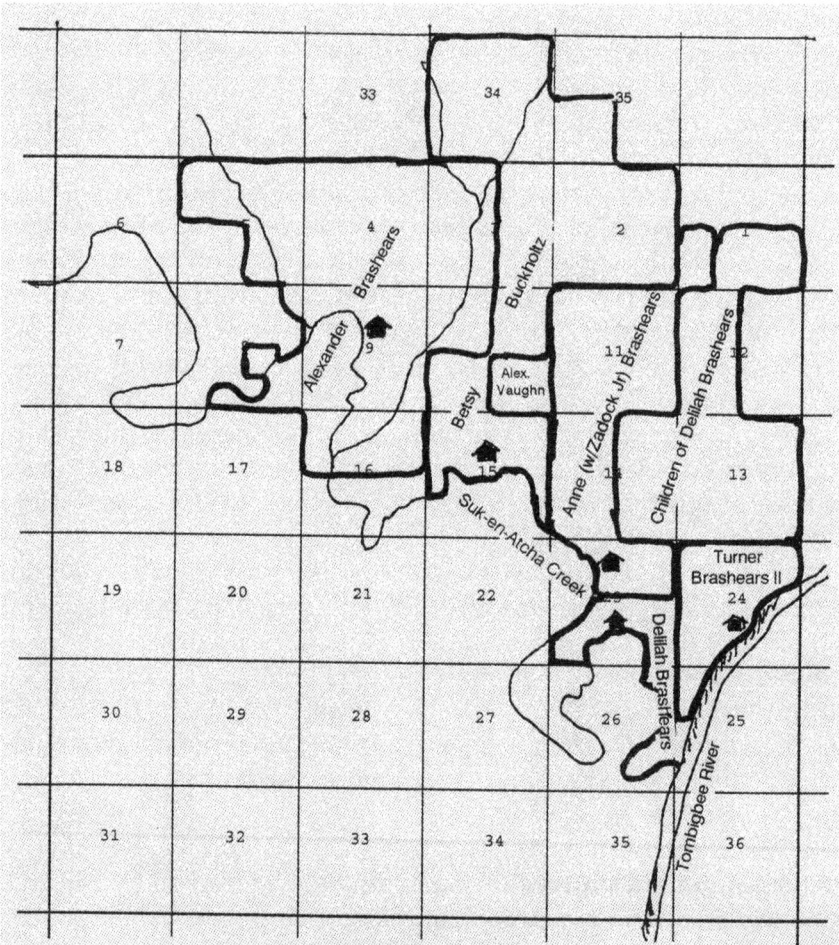

"Map No. 1"
The Brashears Choctaw Reservations
As Recommended by the Commissioner of Indian Affairs and Secretary of War,
and Approved by the President of the United States

(An Approximation of "Map No. 1" Twp 17N, Range 1W, Sumter Co, AL,
Based on land descriptions in War Department Correspondence)

would have taken place.

That, for reasons unknown to the undersigned, the locating agent permitted the Indians to extend their locations entirely on the North side of the Suckanutche which has been called a navigable stream, the undersigned cannot but believe, most erroneously.

That, had the Indian locations have been extended, on both

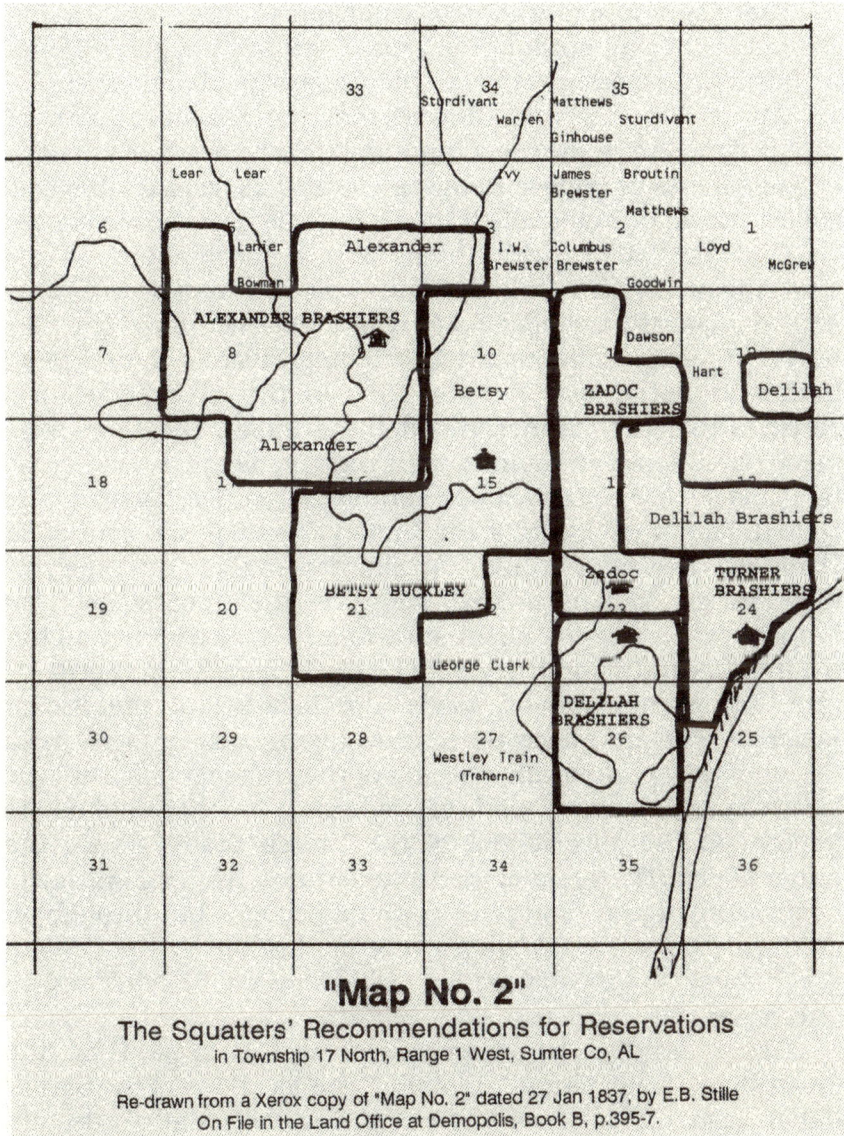

"Map No. 2"

The Squatters' Recommendations for Reservations
in Township 17 North, Range 1 West, Sumter Co, AL

Re-drawn from a Xerox copy of "Map No. 2" dated 27 Jan 1837, by E.B. Stille
On File in the Land Office at Demopolis, Book B, p.395-7.

sides of the Suckanutche creek and, thereby, in the words of the 14th Section of the Treaty "adjoining" the land given for the child, to the "location of the parent," the Treaty would have been complied with and the undersigned would not have been disturbed in the possession of their labor and improvements.

That the lands on both sides of the before-mentioned water course is good land for cultivation, in all respects, and unobjectionable.

That there is and was land sufficient to meet the Indians' Claims in the full spirit of the Treaty without any interference with the pre-emption claims of the undersigned and others.

That it is notoriously known that the Indians who have received those Reservations contemplate, and are daily, making arrangements to remove from the country as soon as they can collect the amount for which they have sold their Reservations.

That the whole, with them, was a speculation, on the Government of the United States, at the instance, and in accordance with the speculations of white men and that they never, in reality, contemplated becoming Citizens of the United States, is notoriously known; nor can the undersigned feel satisfied that the manner in which the Indian Locations were made, that deprived them of their improvements, was such as the Govt. of the United States contemplated. The Agent of the United States for locating the Indian Reservations arrived at Demopolis on Friday evening. An express was sent out the same night to the Indians in the vicinity of the undersigned. On Saturday, the locating Agent shut in a room, excluding all but the Indians and an attorney fee'd by the Indians at an enormous rate, for each claimant, made the location of the Indian Reserves, sweeping away the improvements of the undersigned; the undersigned knowing nothing of the transactions until the locations were made; a mode of processing as well calculated to impose on the government of the United States as on the undersigned. The agent of the United States, availing himself of no means of ascertaining the legitimate claims, but through an individual interested to gain every imposition on the general government in his powers by consideration of fees and of purchase.

That, had the lands improved and cultivated by the undersigned been found "adjoining" the locations of the parent Indian and the necessity of complying with the words and provisions of the Treaty included the improvements of the undersigned, they would have been silent and submitted to a misfortune that appended a just consequence.

For a more perfect understanding of the case of your memorialists, they beg permission to refer the Honorable, the Secy. of the War Department to the accompanying transcript from the records of the Land Office at Demopolis. Number 1 is showing the manner in which the reservations under the 14th Section of the before-mentioned Treaty were located in the 17 and 18 Townships, Range 1 west, BM (Basic Meridian?). No. 2 exhibits the same Townships with also the original or "parent" improvement & residence by virtue of which, the Indians of these Townships, claimed and obtained their Reservations with the improvements of your memorialists on the quarter sections improved by them; also showing how the same reservations allowed in No. 1 might have been located and which locations would have been in perfect conformity with the Treaty and not conflicting with the improvements of your memorialists.

By the first exhibit, or No. 1, it will be seen that the land given to, or for the children, was not "adjoined" to the location of the parent, nor (agreeable to the instructions it was understood the Agent had received) kept in a square or compact form, but scattered over the public land to the great damage, not only of your memorialists, but of the United States.

Your memorialists beg leave to point the attention of the Hon. the Secretary, most particularly, to the several cases of interference;

and first (see exhibit No. 1) it will be seen that in Alexander Brashears (a native Creek Indian) ([v]521) location, instead of the land of the children "adjoining" the location of the parent in section 9, it has been made to extend North from the location of the "parent" to embrace the plantations and improvements and pre-emption claims of Lanier and Bowman.

By confirming the Reserve to the South half of section 4, Section 16 containing the greatest part of his improvement, the NE Qr. of 17 and Section 8 which would have been literally "adjoining" the location of the parent, and on good lands, the improvement of Lanier & Bowman would have escaped and which plantations have been, by the labor and capital of those individuals, highly improved and made valuable.

In the case of Betsey Buckles (^{v5}833), your memorialists unhesitatingly say that the government of the United States has been severely wronged, as well as your memorialists, and to this case, they beg permission most especially to call the pointed attention of the Honorable, the Secretary;

on the books of Col Ward, the enrolling agent, William Buckles, enrolled himself and was recorded as an emigrant, by which he was entitled to 640 acres of land and which the records and returns of that gentleman, to the proper department, will, without doubt exhibit and which the said Mrs. Betsy Buckles has frequently acknowledged, and for a corroboration of which see depositions numbered 3 and which testimony is given by one of the most respectable characters amongst the Reservees and a relative of said Betsy Buckles, and which testimony is fully corroborated by another Reservee and relative -- Wall.

That after the time had expired, allowed by the Treaty, the said Buckles, instigated by the hosts of Land Speculators who have constantly surrounded those reserves, since the date of the confirmation of the Treaty, suggesting every plan they could project, to impose on the government of the United States, through the aid of the Savages, said William Buckles was induced to endeavor to become a five years claimant as the means of acquiring a large body of land.

That, for this purpose, the said Wm. Buckles induced his wife Betsy Buckles to apply to the agent, Col. Ward, and who refused her application on, no doubt, correct grounds.

That, after this, and but a few weeks ago, this said Betsy Buckles appeared before the locating agent, producing a certificate, purporting to be that of Col Ward and supporting it by the depositions of two white men, but who had forgotten the claims of decent society, and correct feelings, had long ago abandoned their connections and country and allied themselves with the Savages.

That, on this showing, the locating Agent gave to Betsy Buckles a Reservation of fifteen quarter sections of land, embracing eleven plantations of your memorialists as will fully appear from the accompanying transcript from the records of the Land Office, and, instead of adjoining the location for the child to that of the parent, the location of the children has been extended from her location and original improvements, in Section 15, unnecessarily, North three miles, sweeping away the improvements and labor of many families of the undersigned and but one location for a child (out of seven provided for) "Adjoining the location of the parent."

That, altho these witnesses testified that they had seen the name of Betsy Buckles down on the register of Col. Ward, for the benefit of the 14th Section of the Treaty, yet the said Wm. Buckles often stated publicly that they had been enrolled as emigrants and had endeavored, but never succeeded in getting a change of register.

That, the whole case of Betsy Buckles location and allowance will not stand the test of investigation, your memorialists are assured.

That, had the claim of Betsy Buckles, improperly allowed as it may be, have been located in strict accordance with the Treaty and 14th section, the labor and improvements and pre-emption rights of your memorialists would not have been swept away and your memorialists cannot hesitate to assess from a knowledge of facts that this whole location of Betsy Buckles, which ought not to have been made, as no change had been allowed in the time called for by the Treaty, or law, from Wm. Buckles' original register, the legal husband of Betsy Buckles and the "Choctaw head of the family" only recognized by the said Treaty, was managed to suit the exorbitant views of avaricious capitalists and land speculators, at whose suggestions the Indian Reservees became mere tools to carry on the projects of those to whose cunning they became dupes in the sale of their lands or Reservations.

That, in the case of Zadock Brashiers [Jr] (^{v5}840), husband of Ann Brashiers, the same departure from the plain words of the Treaty will be observed with additional corrupt processings of misrepresentation of the number of children they possessed, as also, the ages of those they presented, by which, the United States has been wronged, as well as a portion of your memorialists.

That this is corroborated, however astonishing it may appear, by the testimony (accompanying herewith) of Emeline and Alexander Brashiers, Reservees and relatives, Ann Godwin,

Hardy Abney and Robt. Godwin. That as a sample of the course which marks the whole proceeding, the testimony of those persons, as particularly referred to in depositions No. 4, those people, evidently and notoriously, having given in one child not in existence and some over ten years not that age.

To the location of Stanmore Johnston, your memorialists especially beg the attention of the Honorable Secretary. Stanmore Johnston, whose real name is Seth Hazell, a white man, never had any improvement on this Quarter section assigned him, nor had any other person, altho the claim and allowance came under the cultivation Section of the Treaty. The said Johnston, alias Hazell, married the daughter of Mrs. Betsy Buckles after the Treaty and, altho the Reservation stands marked on the official map of the Land office in the name of Stanmore Johnston, he could not have been entitled to a Reservation, in any form. Said Johnston fled from the country under criminal charges, to Texas, in 1833 and this extremely valuable quarter Section, now estimated worth fifteen hundred dollars is now claimed by his representative, a conspicuous claimant of Indian Reservations to whom said Johnston was indebted. By what misrepresentation the locating agent was induced to grant this Reservation is unknown.

In the case of Delilah [Juzan] Brashiers [widow of Jesse Brashears (^{v5}832)], whose improvement lay in Section 23, the same departure from the words of the Treaty as regards locating for the child will be observed. Had her location for the children been put in Section 26 the whole south half of 23, where her improvement is found, and the SE Qr. Section of 12 and Section 13, the improvements and plantations ... [of] ... Loyd, McGrew, Hart, etc., would have escaped; she possessed of good lands, and the Treaty been complied with.

In the case of Turner Brashiers [II] (^{v5}841), your memorialists beg leave to state that his improvement lay in Section 24, that he enrolled himself for five years residence, after some time, went to the agent to have it altered to a cultivation reserve, but in this was refused and, sometime after this, stated to a respectable citizen that he had "got all fixed" by Wm. Armstrong, Esquire, the agent for ascertaining the Indian improvements. A similar reference of "fixture" will be seen in deposition No. 4 (see the testimony of Ann Godwin).

These circumstances and facts your memorialists communicate with painful feelings.

Your memorialists beg leave to point the attention of the Honorable Secretary to Map No. 2 giving an exhibit of the manner in which the foregoing Indian Reservations might have been located on lands unobjectionable and agreeable to the spirit and terms of the Treaty. Your memorialists receiving what the benevolence of the government of their country intended their possession of the fruits of hard and honest labor expended, and the benefits of the pre-emption act of 1834.

Your memorialists beg leave to point the attention of the Honorable Secretary to their situations. After having spent years in the life-wasting labor of clearing and preparing for cultivation, heavily timbered land, some of them at an advanced period of life and after having encountered the privations and hardships, with large families, incident to the first settlement of a new country, they are about to be again driven to the woods; their time wasted, labor and strength expended and their little capital gone; the whole for the advantage, indirectly of those who never intended for a moment to benefit the country by their residence or labors, but directly for the pecuniary advantage of speculators on the public lands and the government of their country.

Feeling the wretchedness of their situation, they most respectfully, but anxiously ask the intervention of the Honorable, the Secretary of War Department as far as his legitimate powers extend in the procurement of that which they are led to believe is their rights and backed by the claims of humanity and justice and as in duty bound, will ever pray.

NW Qr. Sec. 2, T17 R1 west)   /s/ James Bruister
good houses & 44 acres in cultivation)

SW Qr. Sec. 35, T18 R1 west)   /s/ John Matthews
Valuable Gen. house, out houses and open land in cult)

NE Qr. Sec. 2, T17 R1 west)   /s/ James Matthews
Valuable Buildings and 60 acres of land in cultivation)

NE Qr. Sec. 3, T17 R1 west)   /s/ Benjamin Broutin
good dwelling house, cribs cotton houses, barns, stables)
and with 30 acres of land in cultivation.

NE Qr. Sec. 34, T18 R1 west)   /s/ Moses Warren
Out houses, with dwelling house and
about 40 acres of land in cultivation)

SE Qr. Sec. 34, T18 R1 west)   /s/ Dempsey Sturdivant
Valuable house, outhouses and about 30 acres in cultivation.)

SE Qr. Sec. 35, T18 R1 west)   /s/ Elias Sturdivant
dwelling house, outhouses and about 6 acres in cultivation.)

SE Qr. Sec. 2, T17 R1 west)   /s/ Rob't Goodwin
dwelling house, outhouses and 12 acres of land in cultivation)

SE Qr. Sec. 3, T17 R1 west)   /s/ James W. Bruister
Usual improvements and 5 acres in cultivation)

SE Qr. Sec. 5, T17 R1 west)   /s/ John Lanier
Usual improvements and 14 acres fit for cultivation)

SW Qr. Sec. 1, T17 R1 west)   /s/ John Lloyd
Valuable dwelling house & cribs, smoke house & with
60 acres of cleared land)

SE Qr. Sec. 5, T17 R1 west)   /s/ Reubin Bowman
dwelling & outhouses with 12 acres of open land)

NE Qr. Sec. 11, T17 R1 west)   /s/ Peter Dawson
good housing & 60 acres of cleared unimproved land)

SW Qr. Sec. 12, T17 R1 west)   /s/ James N. Hart
Houses and between 40 & 60 acres in cultivation and
between 40 & 60 acres partly cleared)

SW Qr. Sec. 2, T17 R1 west)   /s/ Christopher C. Bruister
houses and 17 acres of open land in cultivation)

NE Qr. Sec. 3, T17 R1 west)   /s/ Charles Ivy

good houses and about 20 acres of open land in cultivation.

SE Qr. Sec. 1, T17 R1 west)   /s/ Clark McGrew
Valuable plantation

Your memorialists would respectfully ask whether the parent Reserve, finding his "present improvement" without interference on a section, is not bound to take that section (altho it may have been surveyed and returned in fractional parts) from the words of the Treaty, as it appears, that in that case, and that only, his section allowed him is "bound by sectional lines of Survey" in the language of the 14 section of the Treaty.

=========

In transmitting the petition to Senator William R. King on 22 Nov 1834, James McGoffin, the squatters' lawyer, commented (innocently):

> As regards the individuals whose names are attached to the memorial, I, with much pleasure, can say, from a long knowledge of most of them, they are worthy and valuable citizens; honest and industrious people. The facts set forth in their memorial, of which they complain, I know to be true. ...
> On an examination of the map. No. 2, it will be seen how carefully those people made their improvements as they thought, and as honorable men would think, out of the range even of the possibility of interfering with the Indian claims.

Another look at the maps and a reading of their descriptions of their own land will tell you that the squatters were trying to grab all the creek bottoms and open fields. The locating agent was apparently trying to save these for the Indians.

Said McGoffin also: "land speculation has poisoned the moral atmosphere amongst us to an extraordinary degree."

11. BETSY BUCKHOLTZ'S BATTLE for her Entitled Land

Elizabeth "Betsy" Buckholtz ([v]5833) (also Buckles and Bucklies in the records), d/o Zadock Brashears and Susannah Vaughn, and wife of William H. Buckholtz, II, attempted to register under the 14th Article of the Treaty of Dancing Rabbit Creek, as a Choctaw resident who wished to remain on her land and become a citizen of the United States, but was refused. Alexander Brashears, always the family care-giver, interceded on her behalf.

The Suk-en-atcha settlement was about 70-80 miles from the St. Stephens trading post; so these following documents indicate a lot of travel and trouble on the part of the Choctaw Brashears, as well as a lot of calculated error and misrepresentation on the part of the whites.

Betsy was finally registered and received a reserve, but not before she died, and not before a gaggle of lawyers, Senators, Congressmen, Commissioners, and even the President of the United States himself were involved.

The State of Alabama
Sumter County

Personally appeared before me, James A. McSwain, an acting Justice of the Peace in and for the Said county, <u>Alexander Brashears</u>, who after being first duly sworn according to the law, to make the following answers to the interrogations propounded to him respecting Betsey Buckholtz's right to a reservation under the Choctaw Treaty concluded at Dancing Rabbit Creek, 27 Sept 1830.

Interrogatory first: Did the said Betsey Buckholts register herself so as to entitle her to a reservation or not?

Answer 1st: I went with the aforesaid Betsey Buckholts to

Col. Ward who was agent for the Choctaws and she made application to register herself under the fourteenth article of the treaty as wishing to become a citizen of the state. But he, Col. Ward, refused to let her be registered for this reason, that her husband, William Buckholtz, had previously registered himself under the nineteenth article of said treaty.

Interrogatory 2nd: Did you not apply in behalf of the aforesaid Betsey Buckholts and try to have her registered in the aforesaid fourteenth article?

Answer 2nd: I did apply to Col. Ward to have Betsey Buckholts, Rachel Brashiers & Zeddock Brashiers, Sen, and he Col. Ward refused to let me register any of them, but said they must be present and do it themselves. I then went with the aforesaid Betsey Buckholts and Rachel Brashiers and Zeddock Brashiers, to the place of Registering and Col. Ward still refused to let her Betsey Buckholts register herself, but the others, that is, Rachel Brashiers and Zeddock Brashiers, Sen. were Registered under the fourteenth article of the aforesaid treaty.

Interrogatory 3rd: Do [you] recollect the time of Betsey Buckholts making her application to be registered?

Answer 3rd: It was the last of June or first of July 1831. I do not recollect precisely.

/s/ Alexander Brashears

State of Alabama
Sumter County
I do hereby certify that the above subscribed Alexander Brashiers is a creditable witness and his statement is entitled to full faith and credit. Oct 27th 1833.

/s/ James A. McSwain (seal)

<============>

Sworn statements by Alexander Brashears and David W. Wall-- 24 Oct 1834.

Evidence respecting the title of Elizabeth Buckles to a reservation which she claims under the fourteenth article of the Choctaw treaty made at Dancing Rabbit on the 27 September 1830. Taken before me, William Bennett, as acting Justice of the

Peace in and for the County of Sumter and State of Alabama on the 24th day of October, 1834.

Interrogatories propounded to Alexander Brashears on the aforesaid subjects.

Interrogatory 1 - Do you or not know of William Buckels enrolling himself as an emigrant for the Arcansaw [Arkansas] Country and of the said Elizabeth or Betsey Buckles going to the Agent, Col. Ward, to get said enrollment altered if you state all you know on that subject?

Answer 1 - I do not know of my own knowledge that William Buckles enrolled himself as an emigrant to go to the Arcansaw. I was in company with the said Elizabeth or Betsey at the agents and heard her make application to be enrolled as a reservee under the 14th Article of the treaty which was refused by the Agent on the ground that her husband, William Buckels had previously enrolled himself as an emigrant.

Interrogatory 2 - Was William Buckels considered by the Choctaw Nation as the head of the family and as such was he entitled to vote and had he all the privileges of a Choctaw?

Answer 2 - I do not know how he was viewed by the Nation whether as head of the family or not. He was entitled to vote and had all the privileges of a Choctaw.

Interrogatory 3 - Was the said William Buckels and the said Elizabeth or Betsey reputed as man and wife and living together as such at the date of said treaty and have they continued to live together as such ever since?

Answer 3 - They have.

Sworn to and subscribed before me on this day and year first above written.

/s/ Wm. Bennett, J. P.   /s/ Alexander Brashears

David W. Wall, after being first duly sworn as to the aforesaid subject deposeth and saith that the facts stated by the said Alexander Brashears are all true to his knowledge excepting the conversation between the said agent and the said Elizabeth or Betsey Buckles detailed above, as he was not present on that occasion.

Sworn to and subscribed before me on this day and year first above written.

/s/ Wm. Bennett, J. P.   /s/ D. W. Wall

I further certify that said Alexander Brashears and the said David W. Wall are credible witnesses and that their statements are entitled to credit.

/s/ Wm. Bennett, J. P.

<============>

BETSY'S FAMILY

Here is the family referred to in the plethora petitions. There were eleven children, not nine; two were born after the date of the treaty. The oldest, Augustus, was attending the Choctaw Academy in Great Crossing, Scott Co, KY, at the time of the Treaty and thus was not "living at home."

[v5]833. [8]2. **Elizabeth "Betsy" Brashears**, b. c1792, Feliciana Parish, Spanish West Florida (now Louisiana), d. Nov 1837, Sumter Co, AL, d/o Zadock Brashears and Susannah Vaughn; m. 30 Sept 1811, *William H. Buckholtz II*, b. c1790, Craven Co, SC, d. 1838, Sumter Co, AL, s/o Jacob Buckholtz and Sarah _____, and gs/o Peter Buckholts, who came from Prussia with brothers Abraham and Jacob to SC in early days.

The will of Jacob Buckholtz, 27 Dec 1824, named wife Sarah, son William H. Buckholtz,
dau Mary Jenkins,
son John C. Buckholtz,
son Abel II. Buckholtz,
dau Sarah Richards,
dau Rebecca McGee,
and the heirs of Elizabeth Miles
(Amite Co, MS, Will, Bk 1, p.65); see also "Grandma Remembers" by Becky Berry, in *The Chronicles of Oklahoma*, Okla. Hist. Soc. Qty., Vol ?, p. ?)

On 31 Aug 1811, Zadock Brashears gave his permission for Betsy's marriage: "Parish of Feliciana, Territory of Orleans: Before me, John Rhea, Judge of the Parish of Feliciana, personally came Zadok Brashear, and by this Instrument gives his consent to the marriage of his daughter, Elizabeth Brashear, to and with William Buckholtz. In witness whereof he now signs with me, and the subscribing witnesses, this 31st day of August, 1811.

/s/ Zadok [B] Brashears

witnesses: Llewellyn C. Griffith,
James McElroy,
John Rhea, Parish Judge."
(Thanks to Mark P. Shuman for the text.)

Elizabeth "Betsy" (Brashears) Buckholtz died in Nov 1837, per correspondence in Choctaw Reserve Records, Group 75, Federal Archives (Thanks to Harley D. Anders, Sr for copies).

On 6 Feb 1838, William Buckholtz applied for and was granted letters of administration on the estate of Betsy Buckholtz (Sumter Co, AL, Orphans Court Minutes, v.1, p.346), and on 22 Feb 1838, he was appointed guardian of the Heirs, who were named and their ages given (same, p.348). Later records include two children, Amanda and Willie Ann, whose relationship is not clear, but who appear to be children born after 1832.

William Buckholtz died before the administration of Betsy (Brashears) Buckholtz's estate was complete, and their son, Augustus Buckholtz, was appointed administrator of both their estates. However, Augustus also died before the completion of the administration, and John C. McGrew was appointed administrator of the estate of Augustus Buckholtz (and presumably took over his duties as administrator of his parents' estates).

Price Williams, Clerk of the Orphan's Court of Sumter Co, AL, was appointed guardian of Zadock, Amanda, and Willie Ann, the minor children of William H. Buckholtz. Celestia, who was still living when Betsy and William died, was deceased by the time Augustus Buckholtz died. On 28 May 1845, the court made distribution of assets, as follows:

From the estate of Betsy Buckholtz: (amounts distributed by Augustus Buckholtz, as administrator of Betsy (Brashears) Buckholtz; each received $305.99)
Augustus Buckholtz,
Rebecca Buckholtz,
Celestia Buckholtz,
Adaline Buckholtz,
Sethfield Hazell, in right of his wife, Caroline,

John Null, in right of his wife, Sarah,
Charley Moran, in right of his wife, Elizabeth,
William P. Buckholtz,
Zadock Buckholtz,
Amanda Buckholtz,
Willie Ann Buckholtz,

From the estate of William Buckholtz: (each received $314.38)
Augustus Buckholtz, to be retained by John C. McGrew
Rebecca Buckholtz,
Celestia Buckholtz,
Adaline Buckholtz,
John Null, in right of wife, Sarah,
Sethfield Hazell, in right of his wife, Caroline
Charley Moran, in right of wife, Elizabeth,
Zadock Buckholtz, to Price Williams, Guardian
Amanda Buckholtz, to Price Williams, Guardian
Willie Ann Buckholtz, to Price Williams, Guardian

These records are followed by a notation that there are no more residuals to be distributed, and an order closing the estate of Celestia Buckholtz, in which Zadock, Amanda, and Willie Ann Buckholtz were declared the legal heirs and each received $1136.27. (Sumter Co, AL, Orphan's Court, Bk 4, p.354-56; thanks to Harley D. Anders, Sr for copies of the texts). There were several claimants, as heirs, including Zadock Buckholts and S. Hazel, J. Goodwyn for his wife, and C. Moran for his. Sarah Buckholts m. 30 April 1831, in Marengo Co, AL, John A. Goodwyn. We believe this is the same Sarah Buckholts who, according to Margie Smith Patterson (g-dau of Jonathan Hazel), married John A. Null on 17 Dec 1832. In fact, it looks like John A. Goodwyn and John A. Null are the same person, under different aliases.

<u>Family of Elizabeth "Betsy" Brashears and William H. Buckholtz II</u>, the first few born in Amite Co, MS, the rest born in the Old Choctaw Nation, Sumter Co, AL.
[v5]961. [9]1. Augustus Buckholtz, b. c1814, Amite Co, MS (23 in Feb 1838), d. bef 28 May 1845; m. 11 Sept 1839, **Letty A.J. Brashears** ([v5]545), b. 1821 (under 10 in

1830; over 18 in 1839), d/o Alexander Brashears and Anne Brashears, (Sumter Marriage Book 1, p.112; "by Robt Goodwyn, JP").

v⁵962. ⁹2. *Sarah H. Buckholtz, b. c1815, Amite Co, MS (21 in Feb 1838); m. 30 April 1831, in Marengo Co, AL, John A. Goodwyn; OR m. 17 Dec 1832, John A. Null, b. c1822 (??error in age. Marry at age 10? He was listed as 48 in 1870, Smith Co, TX; perhaps he was 58). Goodwyn and Null may be the same person.

v⁵963. ⁹3. *Caroline Matilda Buckholtz, b. 7 May 1816, Amite Co, MS (19 in Feb 1838; 44 in 1860, Fayette Co, TX; 52-3 in 1870), d. 1892, I.T.; m. 22 Oct 1830, in AL, Seth Hazel, b. c1800, SC, d. 1867.

v⁵964. ⁹4. *William P. Buckholtz, b. 5 Jan 1818, Amite Co, MS, (18 in Feb 1838), ⅛ Choctaw, Roll #15234, C.C. #3854, d. 17 Oct 1902, Boggy Depot, I.T.; m. 16 Sept 1841 (Sumter Co, AL, Marr Rec, Bk 1, p.33), Matilda Elizabeth Null, b. 11 Dec 1823, LA,

v⁵965. ⁹5. *Elizabeth M. "Betsy" Buckholtz, b. 1821, Amite Co, MS ("Elizabeth I." & 16 in Feb 1838), d. after 1907; m. 22 May 1838, in Sumter Co, AL, Charles H. Moran,

v⁵966. ⁹6. Zadock B. Buckholtz, b. 1824, probably in Amite Co, MS (13 in Feb 1838); m. 3 Nov 1850, Fayette Co, TX, Emaline P. Cleveland. The family moved to Sumter Co, AL, sometimes in 1824, the year of Zadock's birth. Z.B. Buckholtz, aged 37, is in the 1860 census of Fayette Co, TX, Plum Grove P.O. (near the Moran family), with wife, E.P, age 27, b. TX. No ch. in 1860.

v⁵967. ⁹7. Adeline Buckholtz, b. 1826, Sumter Co, AL (11 in Feb 1838)

v⁵968. ⁹8. Rebecca Buckholtz, b. 1828, Sumter Co, AL (9 in Feb 1838)

v⁵969. ⁹9. Celestia Buckholtz, b. 1830, Sumter Co, AL (7 in Feb 1838) d. bef 28 May 1845

v⁵970. ⁹10. Willie Ann Buckholtz, b. c1832, Sumter Co, AL (5 in Feb 1838)

v⁵971. ⁹11. Amanda Buckholtz, b. c1835, Sumter Co, AL; m. _____ Goins,

Sarah H. Buckholtz and John A. Goodwyn/Null

v5**962.** 9. 2. Sarah H. Buckholtz, b. c1815, Amite Co, MS (21 in Feb 1838); m. 30 April 1831, in Marengo Co, AL, John A. Goodwyn; OR m. 17 Dec 1832, John A. Null, b. c1822 (??error in age. Marry at age 10? He was listed as 48 in 1870, Smith Co, TX; perhaps he was 58). Goodwyn and Null may be the same person.

v5972. 10. 1. John Null Jr, b. 1846 (23 in 1870, Smith Co, TX, Garden Valley Beat, with no wife, but father and 5 children); ⅛ Choctaw, Roll #15191, C.C. 284; m. c1870-71, Elizabeth Hamilton,

v5973. 11. 1. Bessie Null,

v5974. 11. 2. Leota Null,

v5975. 11. 3. Mary Estella Null, Choctaw Roll #15196, C.C. #285, with 5 ch; m. 15 Dec 1889, in Blue Co, Ind Terr (by Choctaw Law), William N. Taliaferro, per his testimony 3 Nov 1902, in Tishomingo, I.T.

v5976. 12. 1. Eliza Mabel Taliaferro,

v5977. 12. 2. John Ambrose Taliaferro,

v5978. 12. 3. Janie Madison Taliaferro,

v5979. 12. 4. Henry Buford Taliaferro,

v5980. 12. 5. Robert Dorsey Taliaferro,

v5981. 10. 2. George Null, b. c1855, TX (15 in 1870)

v5982. 10. 3. Rebecca Null, b. c1858, TX (12 in 1870)

v5983. 10. 4. Frances "Fannie" Null, b. c1859, TX (11 in 1870)

v5984. 10. 5. William Null, b. c1866, TX (4 in 1870)

v5985. 10. 6. Robert Henry Null, b. c1867, TX (3 in 1870)

Caroline Matilda Buckholtz and Seth Hazel

v5**963.** 9. 3. Caroline Matilda Buckholtz, b. 7 May 1816 (19 in Feb 1838; 44 in 1860, Fayette Co, TX; 52-3 in 1870), d. 1892, I.T.; m. 22 Oct 1830, in AL, Seth Hazel, (or Seth Field Hazel, according to another branch of the family; he also apparently sometimes used the alias, Stanmore Johnston), b. c1800, SC, d. 1867. After Seth's death, Caroline moved to Indian Territory, where at least some of the family got allotments in 1896 and were on the final Choctaw Rolls in 1907. (data collected by Barbara Schenck <JAS17.aol.com>)

v5986. 10. 1. John Null Hazel, b. 5 Nov 1831, AL; m. Sarah Jane Simpson, v⁵987. ¹⁰2. Walter Columbus Hazel, b. 12 June 1833 (en route to TX)

v⁵988. ¹⁰3. Phillip Buckholts Hazel, b. 7 April 1835, Fayette Co, TX

v⁵989. ¹⁰4. William Henry Hazel, b. 9 Oct 1837

v⁵990. ¹⁰5. Amanda Melvina Hazel, b. 13 Feb 1840; m.1. Jackson Lee, m.2. Charles Simpson. Amanda had 6 ch— a boy and five girls.

v⁵991. ¹⁰6. Zadoc Augustus Hazel, b. 2 Jan 1843

v⁵992. ¹⁰7. Seth Hazel, b. 6 July 1845

v⁵993. ¹⁰8. James Polk Hazel, b. 4 Dec 1848; m. 1871, in TX, Virginia Holt,

v⁵994. ¹¹x. Mary Hazel, m. 1889, in TX, J.L. Jenkins,

v⁵995. ¹²x. Seth Thomas Jenkins, b. 1893; m. 1913, OK, Jewel Johnson,

v⁵996. ¹³1. Seth Perry Jenkins, b. 1914, d. Oct 1995

v⁵997. ¹⁴x. Barbara Jenkins, m. Peter Schenck. Barbara Schenck is a novelist and researcher in this line of the family.

v⁵998. ¹⁴x. Seth Perry Jenkins Jr, b. 1952,

v⁵999. ¹⁵1. Seth Tyler Jenkins, b. 1985

v⁵1000. ¹¹2. Seth Hazel, b. 1875-6; m. Nora Graham,

v⁵1001. ¹³1. Jimmie Hazel,

v⁵1002. ¹⁰9. Caroline Elizabeth Hazel, b. 23 Dec 1849; m.1. W.G. Lane, m.2. George W. Holder,

v⁵1003. ¹⁰10. Jonathan Hazel, b. 3 Feb 1852, Lavaca Co, TX; m. Evaleen Hadley Irwin, b. 10 Dec 1855, Carthage, Panola Co, TX

v⁵1004. ¹¹1. Caroline Matilda Hazel, b. 10 Nov 1876, Blue Co, Ind. Terr.

v⁵1005. ¹¹2. Elizabeth Juanita Hazel, b. 29 Dec 1878, Boggy Depot, Blue Co, I.T.; m. Joseph Pettitt Smith, b. 10 May 1870, Weston, Collin Co, TX

v⁵1006. ¹¹3. Arthur Oscar Hazel, b. 20 Jan 1881, Erin Springs, Garvin, OK; m. Anne Lydia Crosby, b. 15 March 1879, Mason, Mason Co, TX

v⁵1007. ¹¹4. Alberta Evaleen Hazel, b. 1 March 1883, Indian Territory; m. William Blake,

v⁵1008. ¹¹5. Lamar Irwin Hazel, b. 7 June 1885, Erin Springs, Chickasaw Nation, I.T.; m. Pearl Newton Hyer, b. 8 Dec 1884, Providence, RI

v⁵1009.   ¹¹6. Pearl Estelle Hazel, b. 21 Oct 1888, Erin
               Springs, Garvin Co, OK
v⁵1010.   ¹¹7. George Jonathan Hazel, b. 21 Oct 1888, Erin
               Springs, Garvin Co, OK
v⁵1011.   ¹¹8. George Jonathan Hazel, b. 30 July 1890,
               Purcell, McClain Co, OK
v⁵1012.   ¹⁰11. Darlin Augustus Hazel, b. 1 June 1854

William P. Buckholtz and Matilda Elizabeth Null

v⁵964. ⁹4. William P. Buckholtz, b. 5 Jan 1818, Amite Co, MS, (18 in Feb 1838), ⅛ Choctaw, Roll #15234, C.C. #3854, d. 17 Oct 1902, Boggy Depot, I.T.; m. 16 Sept 1841 (Sumter Co, AL, Marr Rec, Bk 1, p.33), Matilda Elizabeth Null, b. 11 Dec 1823, LA, d. 10 Feb 1895, bur Boggy Depot, Atoka Co, I.T., d/o James Null (c1795–1835, Sumter Co, AL) and Mary ____.

In his testimony before the Choctaw Nation, William P. Buckholts says, "I was born in Emit (Amite) County, Mississippi, near the Louisiana line, and when I was about six years old my parents moved to the old Choctaw Nation which is now Sumter County. Lived there until I was twenty-four years old. Started to Texas and stopped in Louisiana." ... stayed there "from the first of May to the first of November when I come back to Mississippi and stayed there eight years and then I started to Texas again."

In 1870 Census, Smith Co, TX, Starrville Beat, William and Matilda are HH #462/462; their son, James, is HH #463/463; across the county are a number of Hazel and Null families. In testimony before the Dawes Commission, William said his family came with him to I.T., "all but one. That was Fate, W.L. Buckholtz."

Family of William P. Buckholtz and Matilda Null
v⁵1013.   ¹⁰1. Lurana (Lura, Lurena) Elizabeth Buckholtz, b. 27
               June 1842, Sumter Co, AL, d. 15 March 1923,
               Wynnewood, Garvin Co, OK, 1/16 Choctaw, Roll
               #15235; m. 11 Dec 1856, at Tyler, Smith Co, TX,
               Rodham Tulloss "R.T." Jones, b. 25 July 1828,
               probably Hall Co, GA, d. 10 Oct 1902,
               Wapanucka, Chickasaw Nation, Indian Territory,
               s/o Benjamin Jones and Mary Hunt. (data
               collected by Hiram Forrest Jones.)
v⁵1014.   ¹¹1. William Tullous Jones, b. 6 Dec 1857, Smith

Co, TX, d. 20 May 1907; m. Mary Jane Shirley,

v[5]1015. [11]2. Francis Marion Jones, b. 25 Sept 1860, Smith Co, TX, d. 6 Dec 1937, Sulphur, Garvin Co, OK; m. Ida M. Melton,

v[5]1016. [11]3. James LaFayette Jones, b. 6 Nov 1862, Smith Co, TX, d. 11 July 1946, Ringland, Murray Co, OK; m. 1888, Martha Ellen Clark,

v[5]1017. [11]4. John Robert Jones, b. 21 Dec 1862, Smith Co, TX, d. 8 Dec 1957, Wynnewood, Garvin Co, OK; m. Martha Shirley,

v[5]1018. [11]5. Perry Washington Jones, b. 9 Jan 1867, Smith Co, TX, d. 30 May 1955, Sulphur, Garvin Co, OK; m. 1889, Martha E. Hinchey,

v[5]1019. [11]6. Matilda Elizabeth Jones, b. 18 Oct 1868, Smith Co, TX, d. 23 Nov 1961, Madill, Marshall Co, OK; m. Nathaniel Simmons,

v[5]1020. [11]7. Lucinda Cordelia Jones, b. 28 May 1971, Smith Co, TX, d. 1 May 1961, Wynnewood, Garvin Co, OK; m. Samuel Oliver Richardson, Five children on C.C. #178

v[5]1021. [12]1. Fannie Elizabeth Richardson,
v[5]1022. [12]2. Panola Richardson,
v[5]1023. [12]3. Niete Jones Richardson,
v[5]1024. [12]4. Lela Buford Richardson,
v[5]1025. [12]5. Robert Devotie Richardson,

v[5]1026. [11]8. Thomas Jefferson Jones, b. 17 Jan 1873, Boggy Depot, Blue Co, Indian Territory, d. 1 Feb 1947, Durant, Bryan Co, OK; m. Rosa _____,

v[5]1027. [11]9. Marcus Alonzo Jones, b. 21 May 1875, Boggy Depot, I.T., d. 26 Jan 1950, Cache, Comanche Co, OK; m. Carrie Gill,

v[5]1028. [11]10. Rodham Forrest Jones, b. 28 Jan 1877, Boggy Depot, I.T., d. 17 Jan 1967, Lawton, Comanche Co, OK; m. 31 May 1903, at Wapanucka, Chickasaw Nation, Indian Territory, Sallie Corrine Epperson, b. 26 June 1885, East Point, Fulton Co, GA, d. 19 March 1974, Lawton, Comanche Co, OK.

v[5]1029. [12]2. Hiram Forrest Jones, b. 17 July 1905, Wapanucka, Johnson Co, I.T.; m. 3 July

1929, Gladys LaGrace Lee. Hiram lived at Crescent City, CA.

v5 1030. 11 11. Elbert Melvin Jones, b. 8 April 1881, Boggy Depot, I.T., d. 15 Dec 1960, Wapanucka, Johnston Co, OK; m. 30 April 1905, Abbye Addie Dumas,

v5 1031. 11 12. Lula Charlotte Jones, b. 17 Jan 1886, Boggy Depot, I.T., d. 28 Dec 1910, Coleman, Atoka Co, OK; m. Charlie Hinchey,

v5 1032. 10 2. Lucinda Diann Buckholtz, b. 15 Sept 1843, Sumter Co, AL, d. Jan 1856, Smith Co, TX

v5 1033. 10 3. James Madison Buckholtz, b. 6 Aug 1845, near Jackson, MS (26 in 1870, Smith Co, TX), 1/16 Choctaw, Roll #15247; m. in Smith Co, TX, Janetta Perryman, b. 8 May 1843 in Tipton Co, MS (24 in 1870). James and Janetta moved in 1872 to Prairie, Indian Territory, 5 miles from Bogey Depot. Eventually, James selected his Choctaw Allotment near Wayne in the Chickasaw Nation, I.T. Children (no order or number):

v5 1034. 11 ? Cora Buckholtz, b. Smith Co, TX; m. Sam P. Robinson, Four ch on C.C. #143

v5 1035. 12 1. Delaney Robinson, (son)

v5 1036. 12 2. Minnie Robinson,

v5 1037. 12 3. Pearl Robinson,

v5 1038. 12 4. Eley Evert Robinson, (son)

v5 1039. 11 ? "Grandma" Becky Buckholtz, b. 23 Feb 1875, Prairie, Ind. Terr.; m. Houston Henry Berry, of Georgia.

v5 1040. 12 ? Rennie Berry; n.m.

v5 1041. 12 ? LeRoy Berry

v5 1042. 12 ? Dr. John Curtis Berry

v5 1043. 12 ? Odell Berry, m.1. Ed Dwight

v5 1044. 12 ? Wayne Berry, b. 24 March 1915, Wayne, OK; d. March 1941, Pearl Harbor, HI.

v5 1045. 10 4. William LaFayette "Fate" Buckholts, b. 8 March 1847, Winston Co, MS, 1/16 Choctaw, Roll #15216, C.C. #410, d. 2 Aug 1929; m. 1870, Annie Watkins,

v5 1046. 11 1. William E. Buckholts, b. 1872, TX, 1/32 Choctaw, Roll #15217

v5 1047.   11 2. Adelbert Lorenzo Buckholtz, m. Carrie Park,
v5 1048.   11 3. Lena Buckholtz, d. young; m. John Cooksey,
v5 1049.   12 1. William Earnest Cooksey, who was raised
            by "Fate" and Annie
v5 1050.   10 5. George Washington Buckholtz, b. 18 May 1849,
            MS, (21 in 1870, Smith Co, TX); m.1. 25 Dec
            1873, at Old Boggy Depot, I.T. Julia Izora Biggers,
            b. 28 July 1857, per family (or 4 May 1857, per
            death certificate), Shelby Co, TX, d. 26 April 1926,
            Spokane, WA, bur Riverside Park Cem, Spokane,
            d/o Robert T. Biggers (or Biggar) and Malisa Jane
            ____. G.W. Buckholtz and Julia Biggers were
            divorced in 1789; m.2. Martha "Mattie" Casey,
    Children of G.W. Buckholtz and Julia Izora Biggers:
            (additional data from Mildred Clarice "Midgie"
            (Smith) Searcy, via a great-nephew, Mark
            Shuman)
v5 1051.   11 1. Anna Caroline Buckholtz, b. 15 Oct 1874,
            Caddo, I.T.; m.1. 21 July 1887, at Ardmore,
            I.T., Everett W. Agee; m.2. 10 April 1900,
            Robert L. "Bob" Smith, brother of her sister
            Nellie's husband; m.3. June 1944, R.L. Edgar.
v5 1052.   11 2. Daisy Buchholtz, b. 23 Sept 1877, d. 5 Dec
            1904; m. John Shelton
v5 1053.   11 3. Rubie Buckholtz, b. 28 Nov 1880, d. 6 April
            1881
v5 1054.   11 4. Ludie Buckholtz, b. 21 Dec 1882, d. 23 June
            1883
v5 1055.   11 5. Nellie May Buckholtz, b. 23 June 1884, d. 12
            Sept 1977, Lawton, OK, bur East Hill Cem,
            Roff, OK; m. 14 July 1901, at Hickory, I.T.,
            Clarence Beauchamp Smith, (he was an M.D.),
            b. 9 March 1876, Honey Grove, Fannin Co,
            TX, d. 2 Dec 1958, Ada, OK, bur East Hill
            Cem, Roff, OK, s/o Napoleon Bonaparte Smith
            and Martha Virginia Beauchamp
v5 1056.   12 1. Martha Virginia "Virgie" Smith, b. 20 July
            1902, Hickory, I.T., d. 27 Nov 1987,
            Oklahoma City, OK; m. 14 June 1925, Mill
            Creek, OK, Milton Keating, b. ?, d. 14 Aug
            1976

v⁵1057.   ¹²2. Anna Zo "Jay" Smith, b. 12 Oct 1905, Selfs, TX, d. 12 May 1986, Summerville, SC; m. 11 March 1927, at Lawton, OK, Velsor "Bill" Barnes, b. ?, d. 26 June 1977

v⁵1058.   ¹²3. Agnes Dorritt Smith, b. 21 Oct 1909, Washington, OK, d. 23 May 1946, St. Petersburg, FL; m.1. 1938, Los Angeles, CA, Marland T. Summers (div. 1945); m.2. 16 April 1949, at Roff, OK, Martin Roy, b. ?, d. 14 Sept 1986

v⁵1059.   ¹²4. Mildred Clarice "Midgie" Smith, b. 27 July 1917, Washington, OK; m. 11 Oct 1941, at Ada, OK, Thurman Clyde Searcy, b. ?, d. 14 March 1991

Children of G.W. Buckholtz and Martha Casey on C.C. #241

v⁵1060.   ¹¹6. Lillie May Buckholtz,

v⁵1061.   ¹¹7. John William Buckholtz,

v⁵1062.   ¹¹8. Willie Ann Buckholtz,

v⁵1063.   ¹⁰6. Joseph Marshall Buckholtz, b. 12 April 1851, d. June 1852, Smith Co, TX

v⁵1064.   ¹⁰7. Napoleon Oliver "N.O." Buckholtz, b. 2 May 1853, Mt. Carmel, Smith Co, TX (17 in 1870, Smith Co, TX), d. 19 April 1898, Boggy Depot, I.T.; m. Linnie ____. Came to I.T. with George W. Buckholtz and R.T. Jones. Listed on the 1896 Choctaw Census with four children

v⁵1065.   ¹¹1. Robert E. Lee Buckholtz, b. c1884 (soon after Oliver's brother with the same name died)

v⁵1066.   ¹²1. Robert Orion Buckholtz, b. 8 Sept 1907, d. 17 Sept 1908, bur Boggy Depot, "son of R.E. and Orpah Buckholtz."

v⁵1067.   ¹¹2. Enos Emmet Buckholtz, b. c1886 (10 in 1896)

v⁵1068.   ¹¹3. Ida Buckholtz, b. c1893 (3 in 1896)

v⁵1069.   ¹¹4. Rhoda Buckholtz, b. c1895 (8/12 in 1896)

v⁵1070.   ¹⁰8. John Monroe Buckholtz, b. 30 Jan 1855, Mt. Carmel, Smith Co, TX; m. 1876, at Boggy Depot, I.T., Frances E. Price, Four ch on C.C. #330

v⁵1071.   ¹¹1. Everitt Buckholtz,

v⁵1072.   ¹¹2. William Lee Buckholtz,

v⁵1073.   ¹¹3. Fannie Olive Buckholtz,

^{v5}1074. ^{11}4. John B. Buckholtz Jr,

^{v5}1075. ^{10}9. Matilda Clementine Buckholtz, b. 1 Aug 1857, Mt. Carmel, Smith Co, TX, d. Chickasha, Grady Co, OK; m. William B. Bailey

^{v5}1076. ^{10}10. Salina Rosanna Buckholtz, b. 6 June 1860, Mt. Carmel, Smith Co, TX, d. Sept 1865, Mt. Carmel, TX

^{v5}1077. ^{10}11. Malissa Buckholtz, b. 14 Jan 1862, Mt. Carmel, Smith Co, TX (8 in 1870, Smith Co, TX), d. 15 June 1894, Chickasha, Grady Co, OK; m. Frank Plato

^{v5}1078. ^{10}11. Robert E. Lee Buckholtz, b. 10 March 1867, Mt. Carmel, Smith Co, TX, d. 5 Aug 1882, age 15 yrs, 4 Mos, 26 days, bur Boggy Depot, Atoka Co, I.T. "son of William and Matilda Buckholtz." This would put his birthdate very late for a child of William and Matilda; perhaps he was a change of life baby, conceived long after the others were almost grown. Matilda was about 44 when he was born.

Elizabeth M. Buckholtz and Charles H. Moran

^{v5}**965.** ^{9}5. Elizabeth M. "Betsy" Buckholtz, b. 1821 ("Elizabeth I." & 16 in Feb 1838), d. after 1907; m. 22 May 1838, in Sumter Co, AL, Charles H. Moran, with John T. Moran as witness (Sumter Co, AL, Marr. Rec, Bk 1, p.75). William H. Buckholtz gave permission for the bride to marry. Charles H. Moran, b. c1813, NC, d. after 1860, TX, s/o Henry Moran and Sarah Young.

Charles and Elizabeth are in the 1850 and 1860 censuses of Fayette Co, TX, Plum Grove P.O. After Charles died, Elizabeth Moran moved to Indian Territory and applied for Choctaw Citizenship for herself and her descendants. It was granted by Choctaw Council, 3 Nov 1879; J.L. Gavin, Principal Chief, signed the order. On the final Dawes Rolls, 1907, Elizabeth (Buckholtz) Moran, 82, is #10445, census card #3692, with her son, Charles H. Moran, age 48. (data mostly from Harley D. Anders Sr)

^{v5}1079. ^{10}1. Henry (or Harvey) Moran, b. c1838, d. after 1895; m. Monetra _____,

^{v5}1080. ^{11}1. John Moran,

$v^5$1081. ^{11}2. Elizabeth Moran,

$v^5$1082. ^{11}3. Sarah Moran,

$v^5$1083. ^{11}4. infant Moran,

$v^5$1084. ^{10}2. Sarah Moran, b. c1841, d. c1880, d. after 1895; m. George Izard,

$v^5$1085. ^{11}1. Mary Izard,

$v^5$1086. ^{11}2. Jane Izard,

$v^5$1087. ^{11}3. Selina Izard,

$v^5$1088. ^{11}4. Silas Izard,

$v^5$1089. ^{11}5. Tabitha Izard,

$v^5$1090. ^{11}6. Georgiana Izard,

$v^5$1091. ^{11}7. _____ Izard,

$v^5$1092. ^{10}3. Salina (or Nancy) Moran, b, c1845 in TX, d. after 1895

$v^5$1093. ^{10}4. Marmaduke Y. Moran, b. Sept 1846, Galveston, TX, d. 17 Nov 1939, Clarita, OK; m. Salina Catherine Watson,

$v^5$1094. ^{11}1. John Moran,

$v^5$1095. ^{11}2. Charley Moran,

$v^5$1096. ^{11}3. Salina Moran,

$v^5$1097. ^{11}4. George Moran,

$v^5$1098. ^{11}5. Maude Moran, b. 3 July 1882, Hayes Co, TX; m. 1899, Oscar Ernest Simmons,

$v^5$1099. ^{12}1. Malsey Fay Simmons, b. 17 Oct 1900, Coal Co, Oklahoma; m. 1915, Harley Anders, s/o William Wallace Andrews/ Anders and Catherine Matilda Lowry,

v^b1100. ^{13}1. Dennis Leo Anders, b. 1915

$v^5$1101. ^{13}2. Harley D. Anders Sr, b. 1918

$v^5$1102. ^{11}6. James Edward Moran; m. Frances Williams

$v^5$1103. ^{12}x. Alton Aline Moran; m. Mamie Brannon

$v^5$1104. ^{13}x. Dorothy Moran; m. Verne Newman (Dorothy Newman is a Moran researcher <dnewman7@earthlink.net>)

$v^5$1105. ^{10}5. Reuben B. Moran, b. c1848, TX, d. after 1896

$v^5$1106. ^{10}6. Charles H. Moran, b. c1848, d. after 1896

$v^5$1107. ^{10}7. John B. Moran, b. c1853, TX, d. after 1895; m. c1885, Mary Ross,

$v^5$1108. ^{11}x. Charles Nathaniel Moran

$v^5$1109. ^{12}x. Ernest Cleo Moran

[v5]1110.   [13]x. Pat Neal Moran, m. Sue _____.

[v5]1111.   [10]8. Daniel Moran, b. c1854, d. after 1895; m. c1888,
                 Willie Agnes Melton,

[v5]1112.   [10]9. Caroline Moran, b. c1856, TX, d. after 1895

THE SQUATTERS' MANEUVERS

Several residents of Sumter Co, AL, filed a number of more or less similar legal briefs to protest the granting of land to Elizabeth "Betsy" (Brashears) Buckholtz and the location and shape of her "individual reserve." Here is a synopsis of their petition:

They [the squatters] represent in an undated petition presented by Hon. Wm. Murphy (probably their lawyer) that, subsequent to the date of the treaty of 27th Sept. 1830, they moved into the Choctaw Country & settled upon lands north of the Sukanutchee Creek, where there were no Indian Claims, with an understanding with the Indians that they should not be disturbed & should pay a fair price for the lands when brought into market. (upon this point, it will be recollected that in March 1832 troops were ordered to the mouth of the Yazoo river to remove white persons who had entered the Choctaw Country. This order was countermanded, upon the representations of Col. Ward & Mr. Plummer, that these persons had been invited to settle there by the Indians themselves, and particularly by [Greenwood] LeFlore. The petitioners may have entered upon these lands on similar invitations)

The petitioners consider that whatever might have been their condition prior to its passage, the preemption law gave them a claim equally good with that of the Indians, against the United States.

The petitioners take exception to the location for Alexander ([v5]521) & Zadock Brashears [Jr] ([v5]840), Betsy Buckles ([v5]833), Stanmore Johnson, Delilah (Juzan) Brashears (see [v5]832) and Turner [II] Brashears ([v5]841). Map No. 1 exhibits these locations. The first objection is that the locations for the children do not adjoin those for the parents agreeably in the provisions of the treaty. The Agent was instructed on the 3d of Sept. '33, that the President considered it "Sufficient that they actually adjoin, whether upon the corners or sides." This objection applies in the cases of Alexander, Zadock [Jr] and Delilah Brashears, & Betsey Buckles. By reference to the map, it will be seen that in each of these cases, but one of the sections adjoined that of the parent, containing the improvements. It may be, that the treaty & the instructions required that each section of the children should adjoin that of the parent. This however is not the ground taken by the petitioners. For in Map. No. 2, in which they show how the location ought, in their judgment, to have been made, this rule is not observed. With one exception, the sections for Delilah Brashears (see ^{v5}832) are disconnected from that on which the improvements are made. The difference between the mode of location, adopted by [Col. George W.] Martin & that proposed by themselves is, that the former confines the location to the North of the Sukanutchee, while the latter crosses it to the South. The former considers this stream to be navigable, the latter asserts that it is not. The treaty contains no provisions upon this subject. But in the instructions of 3d Sept '33, Col. Martin was told that where the streams were of a size to make fractions for the purposes of sale, they would make fractions in the location of reservations. An inspection of the maps will show, that if the locations were made in the manner proposed by the petitioners, they would not only not interfere with their own improvements, but would be more compact.

Another objection to the location for Betsy Buckles (^{v5}833) is, that they were made upon a certification, purporting to be Col. [William] Ward's, that she had signified her intention to remain, whereas her husband, Wm. Buckles, had enrolled for emigration & then sought unsuccessfully, to be enrolled upon the list of cultivators of reserves under the 19th Art.

The following is the entry on Armstrong's register. "Wm. Buckles, 25 acres in cultivation, 10 in family, 1 over 10, six under. On the Sukanutchee. His wife a Choctaw. Whole No. of acres 320." These names are not on Ward's register, nor has Col. [George W.] Martin reported any locations for them. A report from him will be necessary.

In the case of Zadock Brashears [Jr] (^{v5}840), it is alleged that the number and ages of the children are wrongly stated. [William] Armstrong reports 6 in family; 1 over 10, 4 under 10, 2 slaves.

The affidavits, sent in by the petitioners, states that he had none over 10 years, but that his wife was pregnant and 4 were enrolled at the instance of William Armstrong, who it is known was not an Agent at the time.

The petitioners state that Stanmore Johnston is a white man; his true name is Seth Hazell; and that he never had an improvement on the quarter Section located for him; and that he married a daughter of Betsey Buckles after the conclusion of the treaty.

Armstrong reports "Stanmore H. Johnston, 12 acres in cultivation, 2 in family, 1 white, 1 slave; whole no. of acres 160. Married Buckles daughter since the treaty. This place belongs to Alex Vaughan in LeFlore's line."

A report in this case will also be necessary.

An objection is taken to the location for Turner Brashears [II] (^{v5}841). He is entitled to 1½ Sections under the treaty. Colonel Martin has located for him Section 13.16.1 [Sec 13, T16N, R1E] and the North Half of Section 24.16.1. The treaty required 1½ Sections to be so located as to include his residence and improvements. The Sections located are distant from each other and not, it is to be inferred, conformable to the treaty and instructions.

[NOTE: One of the many earlier versions of this petition had Turner's locations erroneously in Sec 13 and Sec 26, which, indeed, do not join. But Sections 13 and 24 share a mile-long boundary. The petitioner is compounding error upon error, perhaps out of his own ignorance of township and range land descriptions, perhaps out of a desire to obfuscate the matter and tie it up in legal shenanigans for years.]

An inquiry will be proper.

The remaining point in the case is that the mode adopted by this Agent did not allow them to know of proceedings that affected their interests. They state that he arrived at Demopolis on Friday evening, assembled the Indians, and on Saturday evening, made the locations when none were present but the Indians and an Attorney fee'd by them.

NOTE: In the instructions of the 3d September 1833, the Agent is directed not to suffer himself "to be influenced by the applications or importunities of white persons." "Arrange your business therefore with the Indians alone."

The petitioners present Map. No. 2 to show that the locations complained of, because they deprive them of their improvements, might have been made without injury to them.

<===========>

Augustus Buckholtz (^{v5}961) was barely 21 when he, too, started trying to get his mother's claim straightened out. Having been educated at the Choctaw Academy in Scott Co, KY, he wrote the following letter to U.S. Senator R.W. Johnson:

November 19, 1835, A. D.
Hon. R.W. Johnson
Dear friend.
I attended at Columbus the first Monday in this month where it was advertised that Col. G.W. Martin would make a final location. Previous to his arrival, I searched Col. Ward's old books and found mother's name and eight children as entitled to land under the 14th Article of the treaty. And when he arrived, I told him that there were a great many assertions by the intruders to overthrow mother's location. He said that if they could not come to him and have the matter settled that they could let it alone.
I told him that they were there at Columbus and would see him concerning it. He said tell your mother that she need not be uneasy, for in a few months it would all be settled right, for, says he, "your mother's name is on record and was in due time." He then took up the book and said "here is your mother's name." Mr. Bruster (one of the intruders that are on mother's location) was present and asked to see it. The book was handed to him and he saw "Betsey Buckles and 8 children." After which, Mr. Bruster asked Col. G.W. Martin a few questions concerning mother's location and Col. G.W. Martin picked up the treaty and read the fourteenth article showing Mr. Bruster that mother's location was agreeable to treaty.
We all left the room and Mr. Bruster then concluded to have nothing more to do with Col. G.W. Martin without having shown a single paper or testamony, but said to me that Col. Martin was not the proper one to settle the business.
Mr. Bruster afterwards said to me "now Buckholts, it is useless for you to expect to get that land, for," says he, "we live

on it and intend there to remain."

I am happy to inform you that I have enjoyed good health since I left the Academy.

If in case this letter should be miscarried, I have written principally the contents of the same to the Hon. F. Lyon [Congressman in the U.S. House of Representatives]. I have nothing more to write than wish these lines may find you enjoying all the blessings that heaven and earth can bestow. If it will not give you too much trouble to answer this, you will confer a favor.

Your obedient and humble servant

/s/ Augustus Buckholts

P.S. If in case it should be doubted that mother's name was found on record, I refer you to Col. G.W. Martin who has it and also to the land office at Columbus on Col. Wards old Books.

<===========>

The squatters were trying every trick they could think of to get Betsy's land, for, as Brewster had said in effect, they lived on the land and they intended to have it, by fair means or foul, by whatever legal maneuver they could pull.

Evidence of the claim of Dempsey Sturdivant to the South East Quarter of Section thirty-four and Township 18, of Range one west in the county of Sumter and state of Alabama, under the preemption law of the 19th June 1834:

Personally came before me, James A. McCain, an acting Justice of the Peace in and for the county of Sumter and state of Alabama, Dempsey Sturdivant of Sumter County and State aforesaid, who, being first duly sworn according to law deposes and answers to the interrogatories propounded by me as follows, to wit:

Interrogatory 1st. Did you or not cultivate any part of the above described land in the year 1835 and continuing thereon? Were you in possession thereof agreeable to the requisitions of the preemption law of the 19th June 1834 and of the instructions given in pursuance thereto?

Ans. 1. I did cultivate corn on said quarter section in the year 1835 and had the same in possession on the 19th June

1834 and had a dwelling house on the same qr. Section and lived in it.

Interrogatory 2. Did any other person in like manner cultivate and hold possession of said land?

Ans. 2nd. No other person did.

/s/ Dempsey (X) Sturdivant

Sworn to and subscribed before me this 20th Nov. 1835.

/s/ James A. McCain, J. P.

State of Alabama)
Sumter County)

Personally came before me, James A. McCain, an acting Justice of the Peace in and for the county and state aforesaid, Hardy Abney and Christopher Columbus Bruister of Sumter County who, being first duly sworn depose and say that they are not interested in the foregoing claim and that the facts testified by Dempsey Sturdivant in the foregoing answers are true.

/s/ Hardy Abney
/s/ Christopher C. Bruister

Sworn to and subscribed before me this 20th Nov. 1835.

/s/ James A. McCain, J.P.

In the records, there are similar interrogations and depositions by

Andrew J. [X] Sturdivant, with supporting affidavits by Dempsey [X] Sturdivant and Christopher Columbus Bruister;
Dempsey [X] Sturdivant, with supporting affidavits by Hardy Abner and Christopher C. Bruister
James W. Bruister, with supporting affidavits by Dempsey [X] Sturdivant and Andrew J. [X] Sturdivant

<============>

State of Alabama)
Marengo County)ss

Before me, John Burwell, a Notary Public in and for the county and state aforesaid, duly commissioned and sworn, personally came and appeared Andrew J. Sturdivant who being duly sworn deposes and says that on the 19th day of June 1834 he resided in the house of Dempsey Sturdivant on a quarter section adjoining the quarter within claimed and cultivated the quarter section claimed by him separately from said Dempsey Sturdivant and for his own use and benefit.

His

/s/ Andrew (X) J. Sturdivant

Mark

Sworn and subscribed before me
this 25th day of November 1835
as witness my hand and Notarial
Seal at Demopolis in said county.

/s/ John Burwell

Notary Public

<=============>

The State of Alabama)
Marengo County)ss

Before me, John Burwell, a Notary Public in and for the State and County aforesaid, duly commissioned and sworn, personally came and appeared James W. Bruister who, being duly sworn, deposes and says that on the 19th day of June 1834 he, being a single man, resided in the house of James Bruister, his father, on the Southeast quarter of Section Three in Township Seventeen of Range one West which said quarter section the said James W. Bruister cultivated as within stated, separately and distinct from the said James Bruister.

/s/ James W. Bruister

Dempsey Sturdivant and Christopher C. Bruister, being also by me duly sworn deposes and say that they have no interest in the above claim of Andrew J. Sturdivant [Sturdivant and Brewster also made an identical statement in support of James W. Bruister] and that the facts testified by him are true.

/s/ Dempsey (X) Sturdivant

/s/ Christopher C. Bruister

Sworn to and subscribed before me this 25th day of November 1835 as witness my hand and Notarial Seal at Demopolis in said county.

/s/ John Burwell, Notary Public

<=============>

LAND OFFICE, DEMOPOLIS
25th November 1835
It is hereby certified that the foregoing proof of Dempsey Sturdivant in support of his right of preemption under the act of 19th June 1834 is deemed satisfactory provided it has been adduced in due time. It is further certified that the quarter section within claimed by said Sturdivant is embraced in the reserve of Betsy Buckles a reservee under the Treaty with the Choctaw Tribe of Indians concluded at Dancing Rabbit Creek on the 27th day of September 1830.

/s/ A.J. Crawford, Register.

In the records are identical certificates regarding the claims of James W. Brewster, Moses Warren, Peter Dawson, Robert Goodwin, Andrew J. Sturdivant, and Charles Ivy.

<=============>
Letter from Congressman F.S. Lyon to Lewis Cass, Secretary of War:

House of Representatives
15 Dec. 1835

Hon. Lewis Cass
    Secretary of War
Sir:
I beg leave to call your attention to a clerical mistake which has occurred in the locations of reservation of land for Betsey Buckles and Stanmore H. Johnson and respectfully do ask its correction. It will be seen by reference to Col. Martin's return that the E ½ of S. 10, T. 17 R. 1 west is included in Betsey Buckles' location and that the SE ¼ of the same section is embraced in Stanmore H. Johnson's thereby giving to both the reserve the same qr. section.
The SW ¼ of Section 10 is the one correctly embraced in his certificate of location now before me. The error would be corrected and each of the reservees secured in the proper quantity of land by attaching to the location of Betsey Buckles the SW ¼ of Section 10 which was by mistake marked as

reserved to Johnson.

The proper quantity of land has been reserved, but a mistake occurred in making the entries by the locating agent in the manner mentioned. I apprised him by letter of the mistake, but having made his return to your department, I presume it was too late for him to correct the error.

I have the honor to be very respectfully

Y obt. servt.

/s/ F.S. Lyon

<===========>

Lyon's letter to Cass transmitted the following memo from Col. G.W. Martin:

I find from examining my return of location under the Chaktaw Treaty that a mistake has occurred as set forth in the foregoing letter and that Alex. Vaughn, whose claim was by mistake located in the name of Stanmore H. Johnson, is entitled to the SE ¼ of Section 10 in Township 17, Range one West embraced in my certificate of location and that the South West qr. Section ten, T. seventeen, R one west ought to be added to the location of Betsey Buckles to make up the quantity to which she is entitled, instead of the South East qr. embraced in her location by mistake.

11 Dec. 1836   /s/ Geo. W. Martin

<===========>

The squatters hired another lawyer, John Erwin, who wrote to Lewis Cass, Secretary of War:

Washington City, 8th Jany. 1836
Hon. Lewis Cass
Secy. of War
Sir.

In opposition to the claim of Betsy Buckholts to a reservation for herself and children under the 14th Art. of the Treaty of Dancing Rabbit Creek, I herewith present the affidavit of Alexander Brashears [he enclosed a copy of Alexander's deposition made 27 Oct 1833, with which I started this chapter, though it was re-dated 27 Oct 1835]. This affidavit, which is properly taken and authenticated, establishes several important facts that deserve to be well considered when a decision comes to be made in this case,

1st.-- That Betsey Buckholts was not the head of her family, but that she had a husband, named William Buckholts, who was the head of the family and who, as I am advised, never did apply himself to be registered under the 14th Art. of the Treaty.

2. -- That William Buckholts was registered and procured a reservation under the 19th Art. of the treaty. The affiant does not specify under what section or provision of the 19th Art. this reservation was claimed, but as I am advised it was under one of the Sections in relation to cultivation claims.

3. -- That the said Brashears applied himself to have the name of Betsy Buckholts registered under the 14th Art. of the Treaty and that Col. Ward, the Agent, refused to register it, because she was not present herself.

4. -- That he afterwards went with Betsy Buckholts to the Agent, for the purpose having her name registered, and that the Agent refused to register it, because her husband, William Buckholts, had registered his name under the 19 Art. of the Treaty, and,

Lastly, that the application of Betsy Buckholts was made the last of June or the first of July 1831.

I need hardly remark that the Tenth Art. of the Treaty requires all applications to obtain the benefits of its provisions to be made by the **head** of the family, nor, that in this instance, that requirement of the Treaty was not complied with. It may, however, possibly be argued that Mrs. Buckholts should be regarded as the agent of her husband in making the application which she did to be registered, if the facts could authorize the argument, but it should be remembered that she did not apply as the agent of, or **in the name of**, or **for the benefit of her husband**, but **in her own name** -- she **having no right whatever.** But an answer to the argument, if it could be made with any semblance of propriety, can readily be produced, which is deemed conclusive. The application was one that could not be made by an agent, and Col. Ward so determined. A man may transact most matters of (___?___) business by an agent, but I apprehend that no man can change his allegiance by agent, or signify, effectively, his intention to do so. The personal presence of the party is always required. In all applications under the naturalization laws of the

United States the presence of the party making it, in court, is deemed essential and indispensable and no court will listen to an application without it. Betsy Buckholts, therefore, could not lawfully signify the intentions of her husband "to become a citizen of the States" (even had she attempted it, (__?__) she did not). It was a personal duty he would have to perform himself.

I also present herewith certificates signed by the Register of the Land Office at Demopolis showing that Charles Ivy, James Bruister, Robert Goodwyn, Peter Dawson, James W. Bruister, Dempsey Sturdivant, Christopher C. Bruister and Andrew J. Sturdivant have, severally, made satisfactory proof entitling them, each, to one quarter section of a part of the lands conditionally reserved for Betsy Buckholts, alias Betsy Buckles, and that the same would have been granted to those persons but for said reservation. If the claim which has been set up to a reservee, in this instance, were established, all the persons whose names I have mentioned would be assured of the (__?__) benefits and advantages which had been extended to other settlers on the Public Lands; and, although that circumstance, of itself, would by no means be sufficient to cause the Department to reject the claim which has been set up to a reservee, it may well be regarded as affording a sufficient motive for a strict and rigid scrutiny into the facts and merits of the claim itself. And, if upon scrutiny, it should be found that the stipulations and conditions of the treaty have not been correctly and faithfully complied with, then the Government will have it completely in its power to do justice to the preemptive claimants; a power which they ought not to hesitate to exercise, when it is for the benefit of a number of men, in moderate circumstances, who are, and always have been American citizens, and when the opposing party consists of a white man, his Indian wife, and their half-breed children, who, no doubt, in this instance, as in almost every other, has been induced to remain in the country by some interested purchasers or speculators until the expiration of five years from the ratification of the treaty, in order to secure a valuable tract of land, without the slightest intention on the part of the individual claimant to become "a citizen of the States," and who will migrate west of the Mississippi the moment a grant shall have been issued by the government.

The Location which has been made of the reserve for Mrs. Buckholts' property, of itself, so strong a ground of interference on the part of the Department, that it is apprehended that it will be difficult to visit it. Had the reserve been made, as it ought to have been, it would not have touched the most of the lands claimed by pre-emption. Instead, however, of the location having been made in a compact form, according to the terms of the treaty, it veers off in a long narrow string, fully three miles long, as I am advised. I have been assured, and am well satisfied of the fact, that several of the persons who claim preemptions on the lands reserved, made it a point, when they made their settlements, to make them so far from where any Indian claimants resided, as in their opinion render it impossible the lands on which they settled could be taken by any Indian reserve, whatever. It would be an extreme hardship on such persons, acting as they did, with they did (which they did with?), most perfect good faith, to have the lands on which they settled taken from them. All the adjacent lands of any value have been sold, and could not now be obtained for five times their original cost. They will, therefore, if they lose the land for which they are now contending, and to which they believe themselves honestly and justly entitled, lose all the labors they have bestowed on those lands, be deprived of the bounty which the Government has extended to others, be compelled to leave their homes and emigrate, or be forced and compelled to pay the most extravagant prices for lands in the section of the country in which they live, which most of them are wholly unable to do.

I have heard it said, since I have been in Washington, that the name of Betsey Buckholts had been found on the register kept by Col Ward, and which is said to be now at Columbus, in Mississippi. If her name is on the register, I have to request a particular examination for the purpose of ascertaining when it was placed there, and by whom it was placed there, I have in my possession some evidence showing that she has, to some few persons, exhibited a certificate of her being registered, with the name of Col. Ward appended to it, and that the whole certificate, including the signature of the name, was in the hand writing of another person than Col. Ward. The persons whom I represent, have repeatedly endeavored to procure a sight of this certificate but it has been studiously withheld from them, lest the fact of its false and spurious character might be made apparent to the

Department. I pretend to know nothing of this matter of my own knowledge, but feel perfectly satisfied in making these suggestions from evidence which I now hold and from communications that have been made to me from sources in which repose confidence. I shall commence as early as I can to collect and complete the evidence on this point and transmit it to the Department and when a determination comes to be made, I request that particular reference may be made to the affidavit of Alex. Brashears as affirming strong corroborative evidence of the facts suggested.

If the whole case should be referred to Congress, I have to request that all the papers filed against the claim to a reserve may be submitted to that body. If the Department should act upon and decide the case, I have to request to be informed of any decision that may be made as early as the convenience of the Department will permit.

I have the honor to be

Your obd. Servt.

/s/ Jno. Erwin

<===========>

Extract from a letter dated June 23d, 1836, from Congressman Lyon to C.A. Harris, Commissioner of Indian Affairs:

"Betsy Buckles relied upon the Certificate of Col. Ward, U.S. Agent for the Choctaws and also upon the testimony of sundry witnesses on file in the Department for a confirmation of her location" also "upon the fact that a list of Reservees under the 14th Article in the hand writing of Col. Ward ... produced by Col. Martin containing her name."

House of Representatives
2 January 1837

C.A. Harris, Esq.
Com. of Indian Affairs
Sir:

In the case of Betsy Buckles who claimed a reservation under the 14th Article of the Treaty of 1830 with the Chaktaws, it is necessary that the patent for such lands as she may be entitled to should issue in order that her heirs or legal representatives may obtain possession of their land granted to her by a resort to suits.

Very respectfully
Yr. Obd. Sert.
/s/ F.S. Lyon

P.S. I received by the last mail a letter from Judge Martin who has purchased a half section of the land located to Betsy Buckles insisting that the patent is necessary to enable him to obtain possession of the part purchased by him.

/s/ F.S. Lyon

<==========>

The State of Alabama)
Marengo County)ss

Before me, Armistead Burwell, a Notary Public in & for the county and state aforesaid, personally comes & appeared Wm. Fluker and J.C. McGrew, who, being duly sworn according to law depose and say that they are acquainted with Betsy Buckles and with Wm. H. Buckles, her husband, citizens of the Chaktaw Nation at the date of the Treaty of Dancing Rabbit of 1830 with the Chaktaws. That the said Betsy & Wm. H. Buckles at the date of said treaty resided where they now do and have (?lived?) on Section 15 in Township 17, Range 1 West and that they have resided on the reservation of land claimed by them under the 14th Article of the Treaty aforesaid for five years since the ratification of said Treaty.

/s/ Wm. Fluker
/s/ J.C. McGrew

Subscribed before me
the 26th day of April 1837.
Witness my hand and seal notarial
/s/ A. Burwell, Notary Public
I hereby certify that William Fluker and J.C. Mcgrew are highly
respectable citizens and that credit is due to any statements
made by them.
/s/ A. Burwell, Notary Public

<===========>

On 7 Sept 1837, Betsy again wrote her Senator, R.M.
Johnson, asking him to use his influence to confirm her
locations under the Treaty of Dancing Rabbit Creek. She asked
for an answer, and asked that her letter be returned to her. On
2 Oct 1837, R.M. Johnson transmitted her request and letter to
C.A. Harris, Commissioner of Indian Affairs.

On 19 Sept 1837, U.S. Senator R.M. Johnson transmitted to
C.A. Harris, Commissioner of Indian Affairs, two letters, one
from Augustus Buckles and one from William Buckles,
requesting that the patents for reserves under the 14th Article
of the Choctaw treaty may be issued to his [Augustus's] mother,
Betsey & the children, & his father's name be excluded.

[to] C.A. Harris, Esq. [Commissioner]
Indian Affairs
You will place me under great obligations to give me your
advice & all the information relative to this case that I may send
your answer to Mr. Buckholts, a favorite student at the Cho.
Academy. (___?___) my friend go to the bottom of it & let me
know if is done (?) & what can be done.
Yours
/s/ R.M. Johnson, 19 Sept. 1837

<===========>

Memorandum from James Whitcomb, Commissioner, General Land Office, to C.A. Harris, Commissioner of Indian Affairs:

General Land Office
January 5, 1838

C.A. Harris, Esq.
Comm. of Ind. Affairs
Sir,

In answer to a verbal inquiry made at this office yesterday in reference to the location for Betsey Buckles under the Choctaw Treaty of 1830, I have to state that on examination of the list that accompanied your letter of the 3d instant, it appears that the N fractional half (North of the Sucarnochee) of Section 15, the E ½ Sec. 10, the E ½ Sec. 3, the whole of Sec. 2 in Township 17 of Range 1 West; the whole of Sec. 34 and the SW ¼, Sec. 35 in Township 18, of Range 1 West, all in the Demopolis District, containing together 2384 & 53/100 acres, were located 29th September 1834 for said Betsey Buckles under the 14th Article of said Treaty.

From the Tract Book for sales in that district posted to the end of July 1837, no interference appears to exist with the above mentioned location except the sale of the NW ¼, 34-18-1 West which was made 30th March 1835.

Very respectfully
Your Obd. Servant
/s/ Jas. Whitcomb
Commissioner

<==========>

War Department, Office of Indian Affairs
Jany. 8, 1838

E.B. Stelle, Esq.
Washington
Sir.

I return the papers received from you on the 4th inst. in relation to the case of Betsey Buckles & Zadock Brashears, and state that the location made for the former under the treaty of Sept. 27, 1830 & the certificate of Col. Ward (now on file in this office & which you can inspect) has been approved by the

President and the Com. of the Genl. Land office informed thereof. Some papers in the case of John Lloyd were received here some months since through (___?___) Henly & Lomax, but none have been received from him direct.

Very re.

(no signature)

<============>

A Memorandum, regarding Reserve. Choctaw J.173

[to] Hon. R.M. Johnson
Senate, 10 Jny. 1838
    Enclosed letter from A. Buckholts inquiring the issuance of the patent for B. Buckholts reserve and wishing, if possible, that the quantity of land to each child may be specified therein.
    Recd. 11 Jny. 1838
    Ans & enclosure returned.
3 Feby. 1838

<============>

Senate Chamber

Jan. 10, 1838

My dear friend, what have you done in the within case. Let the will issue.
patent (_?_) & (_?_) (_?_) is. When will you order the patent ?

Yours

/s/ R.M. Johnson

<============>

Letter from C.A. Harris, Commissioner of Indian Affairs, to Hon. J.R. Poinsette, Secretary of War.

War Department, Office Indian Affairs
January 30, 1838

Hon. J.R. Poinsette
Secretary of War.
Sir,

By the provisions of the 14th Article of the Choctaw treaty of 1830, Betsy Buckles became entitled, in right of herself and children, to 3 ¾ sections of land, which were located on the 29th of September 1834 in the state of Alabama and within the Demopolis Land district as follows:

North fractional half of Section	15,	Twp 17,	Range	1 West
NE & SW quarters of... "	10,	" 17, "	1	"
East half of...... "	3,	" 17, "	1	"
Whole of........ "	2,	" 17, "	1	"
Whole of........ "	34,	" 18, "	1	"
SW quarter of...... "	35,	" 18, "	1	"

The action of this office upon this case has been heretofore suspended that the correct designation of the tracts reserved for her might be reported by the proper agent. This has been done as above indicated. It is stated by the Hon. Mr. Lyon of Alabama, that it is very important in order to enable the heirs or legal representatives of the reserve to obtain possession of the lands assigned her and to remove the intruders who are trespassing upon them, cutting and destroying timber & that the location should be approved without delay, and the patent issue. As some time must elapse before the general list of reserves under that treaty, now preparing, can be completed, and as no claim of the government, or of a reservee will be affected by it, I have deemed it expedient, considering all the circumstances, to submit the case for your consideration; and respectfully recommend that the select(ion) of the tracts of land within designated be laid before the President for his approval, as the reserve of said Betsy Buckles.

Very respectfully
Your Mo. Obt. Svt.,
/s/ C.A. Harris, Com.

<====≡=======>

Memo:

The above mentioned locations are respectfully recommended for approval of the President.

    War Department

    January 30th, 1838

        /s/ J.R. Poinsette

        Secretary of War

Approved: January 30, 1838

        /s/ M. VanBuren [President of the United States]

<=========>

House of Representatives
31 Jany. 1830

C.A. Harris, Esq.

Com. of Indian Affairs.

Sir,

    I am in receipt of your letter of yesterday advising me of the approval of the location for Betsey Buckles, a reservee under the 14th Article of the Treaty of 1830 with the Chaktaws, and informing me that the proof to establish her five years residence upon the land is considered insufficient to act upon at present.

    I was acquainted with Betsey Buckles before the date of the Treaty and up to her death which occurred in Nov. last. My acquaintance with the numbers of the land in her neighborhood does not enable me to identify the particular section she lived upon, but I have no doubt whatever of her having lived upon the land embraced in her location from the date of the treaty and before, up to the time of her death. The proof before you was intended to establish the fact of residence for five years and was believed to be sufficient and in addition to this the fact of residence on the land for the five years was proved before Mr. Brown and will be reported by him. This claim, you are aware, has been warmly contested, but no one within my knowledge has ever questioned or disputed the fact of the five years residence upon the land.

        Very respectfully

        Ur. Obd. Servt.

        /s/ F.S. Lyon

<===========>
War Department, Office of Indian Affairs
Feby 2, 1838

James Whitcomb, Esq.
Comm. Genl. L. O.
Sir,

I have the honor to inform you that on the 30th ultimo, the President approved the selection of the following tracts of land in Alabama, Demopolis Land district, as the reserve of Betsey Buckles, under the 14th Article of the Choctaw treaty of 1830:

```
North fractional half of Section 15, T. 17. R 1 West
NE & SW 1/4. . . . . . .       "    10   "    "    "  "  "
E ½. . . . . . . . . .         "     3   "    "    "  "  "
Whole of . . . . . . . .       "     2   "    "    "  "  "
Whole of . . . . . . . .       "    34   "   18    "  "  "
SW 1/4 . . . . . . . . .       "    35   "   18    "  "  "
```

Satisfactory proof having been addressed to this office that the reservee has complied with the terms of the treaty respecting the five years residence upon said lands, it knows of no objection to the immediate issuing of a patent to the person entitled to receive it.

very res.
(no signature)

<===========>
War Department, Office of Indian Affairs
February 2, 1838

Hon. R.M. Johnson
Washington
Sir,

I return the letters of A. Buckholts, transmitted by you to this office, and have the honor to inform you that the location of the tracts of land reserved for Betsey Buckles, a reserve under the 14th Article of the treaty of 1830, has been approved by the President, and the Commissioner of the Genl. Land Office has, this day, been advised thereof, and informed that this office knows of no objection to the issuing of a patent.

very res.   (no signature)

<====== =>

War Department, Office of Indian Affairs
February 2, 1838

Hon. F.S. Lyon
House of Representatives
Sir,

    I have the honor to acknowledge the receipt of your letter of the 31th ulto., respecting the residence of Betsey Buckles, a reservee under the 14th Article of the Choctaw treaty of 1830 and to acquaint you that the Commissioner of the Genl. Land office has been, this day, advised of the approval of the location made for her and informed that this office knows of no objection to the issuing of a patent to the person entitled to receive it.

Very res.

(no signature)

<====== =>

War Department, Office of Indian Affairs
Feby 13, 1838

James Whitecomb, Esq
  Com. Genl. L. O.
Sir,

    Col. Lyon of Alabama has informed me that an objection exists to the issuing a patent for the reserve of Betsey Buckles as approved by the President on the 30th ultimo, on account of the Agent for location Choctaw reserves, having reported the S.W. ¼ of Sec. 10, T 17, R 1 West for Stanmore H. Johnson. I have to state in relation thereto, that the name of said Johnson was, by order of the Secretary of War, stricken from the list of reservees; that of Alexander Vaughn substituted in its place and the SE ¼ of Section 10, assigned to him in lieu of the SW ¼. It was upon this decision that the action of this office was based and the knowledge of it that induced me to inform you that I know of no objection to the issuing of a patent.

very res.

(no signature)

12. OTHER SQUABBLES WITH SQUATTERS: The Reservations of Alexander Brashears, Delilah (Juzan) Brashears, Zadock Brashears, Jr & Sr, and Turner Brashears, II

ALEXANDER BRASHEARS'S RESERVATION

Alexander Brashears's (^{v5}521) struggle to secure title to his "individual reservation" dragged on and on. Col. F.S. Lyon did not return to Washington as a member of the House of Representatives, but retired to Demopolis where he became an attorney for some of the Choctaws, including Alexander, Delilah (widow of Jesse) and Anne (widow of Zadock, Jr). He also seems to have been commissioner of the land office there.

Alexander's claim to an individual reservation was first messed up by Col. William War, the Agent to theChoctaws, who recorded (incorrectly) two children over ten and five under ten for Alexander. Alexander discovered this error and went to considerable trouble to get it corrected.

The State of Alabama)
Sumter County)

Before me, William Bennett, a Justice of the Peace in and for the County of Sumter and State aforesaid, personally came and appeared Alexander Brashears of said county who, being duly sworn, deposes and says that at the date of the Treaty of Dancing Rabbit Creek with the Choctaw tribe of Indians, and for many years before, he was a citizen of said Choctaw Nation and the head of a Choctaw family residing in said nation. That in the month of June or July, 1831, he, this deponent, applied to Col. William Ward, then U.S. Agent for the Choctaws, and gave notice to him of his intention to remain and become a citizen of the State and that he claimed the benefit of the provision made by the 14 Article of said Treaty, aforesaid, and requested that said William Ward to register his name and the number of his children at that time in conformity with the instructions given said Agent. That the said Ward did accordingly register the name of this affiant and the number of his children at the date of the Treaty— that he had at the date of the Treaty, nine unmarried children living with him, three over ten years of age and six under ten years of age. That all of said children before named are now living. This affiant further says that upon applying to the locating agent, Col. Geo. W. Martin, to locate the lands granted to himself and his children he discovered that two of his children had been omitted on the register of this agent, one over 10 and the other under 10 years of age and in consequence thereof this affiant has by said omission of the agent been deprived of three quarter sections of land granted him under said Treaty and he, therefore, asks that the land granted on account of his two children thus omitted, may be located to him.

/s/ Alexander Brashears

Sworn to and subscribed before
me this fourteenth day of November 1834.

/s/ William Bennett, J. P.

<============>

Before me, William Bennett, Justice of the Peace as aforesaid, personally appeared David W. Wall, Allen Stanton and Betsy Buckles of Sumter County who, being duly sworn say that they are acquainted with Alexander Brashears, named in the foregoing affidavit, that he was a citizen of the Choctaw Nation and the head of a Choctaw family at the date of the Treaty of Dancing Rabbit Creek and that they were present when the said Alexander Brashears gave notice to Col. Ward, the U.S. Agent for the Choctaws of his intention to remain and become a citizen of this state and claimed the benefit of the 14th Article of said

Treaty. That this took place at the Choctaw Agency about the month of June 1831, that this said Brashears had, at the date of the said Treaty, living with him and unmarried, nine children, three of which were at the date of the treaty over ten years of age and six under ten years of age, that he registered with the said agent nine children and that the facts stated in the foregoing affidavit by the said Alexander Brashears are true.

/s/ D.W. Wall
/s/ Allen Stanton
Her
/s/ Betsy (X) Buckles
Mark

Sworn to and subscribed
before me this 14 November 1834.
/s/ William Bennett, J. P.

I William Bennett, Justice of the Peace in and for Sumter County, do hereby certify that I am acquainted with D.W. Wall, Allen Stanton and Betsey Buckles, above, and that they are persons entitled to credit.

Given under my hand this 14 day of November 1834.
/s/ William Bennett, J.P.

I, Daniel Womack, Clerk of the County Court, of the County aforesaid, do hereby certify that William Bennett whose name appears to the foregoing certificate is an acting Justice of the Peace in and for said county and was, at the signing of this the same and that due faith and credit may be given to his official acts as such.

Given under my hand and seal of office at Livingston this 15th day of November, A. D. 1834.
/s/ Dan'l Womack, Clerk.

<===========>

In Aug 1839, F.S. Lyon summarized Alexander's, Delilah's, and Anne's claims for J. Harkey Crawford, Esq., the new Commissioner of Indian Affairs in Washington.

J. Harkey Crawford, Esq.
Comm. Indian Affairs.
Sir:

In the case of Alex. Brashears, a reservee under the 14th Article of the Treaty with the Choctaws, the Agent in his return to the war department showing that the claimant had complied with the terms of the Treaty, omitted a part of his children. Proof was taken to supply the omission and filed with Col. [George W.] Martin, the locating agent, and the proper quantity of land was located. During the last session of Congress, I addressed you a letter bringing to your notice the situation of this case and requested to be informed if the proof filed before and, no doubt, returned by him to the department, was considered sufficient and whether the claim of Brashears to the land located on acct. of the children omitted in the agents return was recognized as valid. The Atty. Gen., in the case of Wm. Buckholtz, expressed the opinion that it was competent for the dept. to receive and act finally upon such proof.

I have not received a reply to my application in relation to his case and, as the children omitted in Col.[William] Ward's return are still with their father in Sumter Co., it is important that the claimant should know whether his testimony is regarded as sufficient in order that he make further proof, if required. The claimant is anxious to have his patent.

In the case of Delila [Juzan] Brashears (the widow of Jesse Brashears (ᵛ⁵832)) a claimant under the same Article and who has sold a portion of her reservation to John W. Foster. I requested, at the instance of Mr. Foster, that the issuance of the patent might be delayed until Mr. Brown or his successor returned the proof taken as to the nature of Foster's contract of purchase, so that the contract might be approved and the patent issued to him as assignee.

A difficulty has arisen about the part of Delila Brashears land not sold to Foster. It is necessary her patent should issue. I have, therefore, to request that you will issue her patent to be issued and forwarded for that part of her reservation not sold and conveyed to Foster as shown by Mr. Brown's return. If there is no objection to the sub-division. If, however, you should deem it best to embrace the entire reservation in one patent, you can cause it to be issued in the name of the reservee, and Mr. Foster can rely upon his deed of conveyance for the part purchased by him.

The part of the reservation not sold and conveyed to Foster has been sold at Sheriff's sale for about 10 cents per acre when the land is, in fact, worth $12 or $15 per acre and my object in requesting the patent is to show the situation of the reservees title and to defeat this sale, if possible.

In the case of Anne Brashears, the widow of Zadock Brashears, Jr. (^{v5}840), my recollection is that you decided last winter that the claimant had in her location, under some mistake made by her husband in his notice to the agent, or by the mistake of Col. Ward in making his return, received one quarter section more than she was entitled to. If so, it is important that this case should be closed. The claimant has sold a part of her land to Messrs. Martin and Alexander. Since she has no agency in the mistake by which a quarter section too much was located to her, it is but just that she should have the right to designate the quarter to be stricken from the location. Without being permitted to make the selection she may be seriously involved by her contract of sale.

Will you have the goodness to advise me of your decision in regard to this matter.

I am the counsel of the several persons named and have been urged to have the claim settled.

Very respectfully
Yr. obdt. Serv.
/s/ F.S. Lyon

<============>

The wheels of Washington grind exceeding slow. Two years later, Lyon was still trying to make Alexander's case heard:

(INTERNAL MEMORANDUM)

Reserve Choctaw L 1234
F. S. Lyon
Demopolis (---?---), July '41

Relative to case of Alex. Brashears, Choctaw Reserve, Issuing Patent to him. Rec'd. 3 July '41.

Statement of Alex. Brashears case under the 14th Article of the Choctaw Treaty.

This individual became entitled to a reservation under the 14th Article of the Choctaw Treaty. His name will be found upon the register. When he applied to Geo. W. Martin to locate his land it was discovered that by some mistake, about half his children had been omitted on the register in possession of Mr. Martin. It will be observed that the treaty does not require the children of a reservee to be registered or returned by the agent. Upon satisfactory proof in writing, of the actual number of children, then and at the date of the Treaty, composing the family of the reservee, the agent located and reserved from sale the quantity of land secured by the treaty.

Brashears' case was, in the first instance, referred to Congress and the Committee of Indian Affairs, in the House of Representatives, reported a bill proposing to confirm his title. The Atty. Gen. Mr. Butler, expressed the opinion in the meantime that it was competent in such a case for the War Department to execute the Treaty, and I had the papers of Mr. Brashears referred to the Commissioner of Indian Affairs and was assured his case should be settled in due time. The Agent, Mr. Martin, as I have lately understood, considered this case very erroneously, as I think, as one of the contingent locations and has at the Land Office here so marked his first location.

Brashears still lives in this neighborhood; is a most respectable man and is at present involved in a law suit on acc't of the mistake of Mr. Martin. He has sold a part of his land and the payment of the purchase money is contested upon the supposed defect in his title. Please examine the return of Mr. Martin. The evidence of the number, names and ages of Brashears children which accompanied it and have his patent issued for the land located to him in the first instance. He is very clearly entitled to it.

/s/ F.S. Lyon
Atty. for Alex. Brashears
Demopolis, 16 July 1841

<=========>

Department of War, Office of Indian Affairs
August 18, 1841

Sir:

Application has been made to this office by Hon. F.S. Lyon for the confirmation of Alex. Brashears location under the 14 Article of the Choctaw Treaty of 1830.

The 14th Article of aforesaid Treaty provided that "each Choctaw head of a family, being desirous to remain and become a citizen of the States, shall be permitted to do so by signifying his intention to the Agent within six months from the ratification of this treaty and he or she shall thereupon be entitled to a reservation of one section of six hundred and forty acres of land to be bounded by sectional lines of survey; in like manner be entitled to one-half that quantity for each minor child which is living with him over ten years of age; and a quarter of section to such child as may be under ten years of age, to adjoin the location of the parent. If they reside upon said lands, intending to become citizens of the States for five years after ratification of this treaty, in that case a grant in fee simple shall issue. Said reservation shall include the present improvement of the head of the family or a portion of it. Reservees who claim under this article shall not lose the privilege of a Choctaw Citizen, but if they ever remove are not to be entitled to any portion of the Choctaw Annuity."

On 21 May 1831, Col. Wm. Ward, Indian Agent for the Choctaws was instructed to be "Careful in keeping a register of the reservations taken under the 14 Article of the treaty, a fair copy of which to be made, duly certified and transmitted for the information of the Department." That register, or a paper purporting to be a "Register of Choctaw names as entered by the Agent previous to the 24th of August 1831, who wish to become citizens according to a provision of the late Treaty of 1830, certified by Col. Ward," was received at the Department on February 1832. Upon that register the name of Alexander Brashears is entered as registered on 13 June 1831, for 5 children under 10 years of age and 2 children over 10 years of age and, of course, entitled to 3¼ sections of land equal to 2080 acres.

On 26 June 1834, Col. George W. Martin was appointed to locate all the reservations granted under aforesaid treaty and on

27 May 1834, he was informed that the President had decided "that he can recognize none as reservees under the 14 Article of the Treaty whose names are not upon that register (Wards).

The first return by Col. Martin of his location under instructions show that on 27 September '34, he selected for claimant the quantity of land called for by the entry above referred to, viz., for the head of the family and for 5 children under, and for two over, ten years of age.

The claimant alleges that the Agent committed an error by the designation above alluded to, and that he had, at the date of application for registration, 6 children under and 3 children over 10 years of age, and that one of the registers kept by Ward sustains him in that assertion and that it is proved to be correct by testimony submitted to Col. Martin and by him forwarded to the War Department.

Anterior to 10 October 1834, several reservees claiming the benefits of the 14 Art., alleged that they had been denied land because their names were not embraced on the register of Ward sent to this office, that the omission to register their names was the result of negligence or carelessness on the part of the Agent and that in some instances they have been enrolled but that the evidence of the fact has been lost or destroyed and on that day, Elbert Herring, Esq., Commissioner of Indian Affairs, submitted a report to Hon. Mahton (?) Dickinson, Acting Secretary of War, of which the following is an extract:

"Applications have been made to this Depart. by many persons claiming reservations under the treaty with the Choctaws of 27 September 1830, that an order may be issued to reserve from public sale the reservations they claim, or where those have been sold, tracts of equal dimensions."

"The applicants have adduced evidence to show, either that they were registered by Mr. Ward and the record has been lost, or that upon his representation, they were led to believe a verbal application, without any record, was a compliance with the treaty; or that they applied to be registered and he refused, in some cases, without sufficient reasons, to record their names; or that he entered their applications erroneously, misstating the number in families."

On 13 October 1834 an order was given by the President, U.S., of which the following are extracts:

"The requisite instructions will be given by the proper Department for the locations and suspensions from sale of reservations of lands in the Choctaw Country, wherever persons claiming reservations under the 14 Article of the Treaty with the Choctaws of 27 September 1830, shall exhibit to Col. George W. Martin, the locating Agent, probable evidence of reliable witnesses of their rights under the provisions of said Article, and that their failure to obtain such reservations, had been caused by the mistakes or neglect of the Agent appointed to make a list of reservees."

"These locations will be contingent, and will be complete only in the event of their being sanctioned by Congress. Until that decision is obtained, the tracts located under this order will be reserved from sale."

Instructions were accordingly issued to the locating agent in accordance with the directions of the President and he was specifically directed to transmit in season for the action of Congress, at its next session (1834-35) detailed reports and all the circumstances in each case.

On February 1838, the President of the U.S. submitted to Congress a report from the Secretary of War, accompanied by the evidence of certain claims to reservations which the locating agent has reserved from sale, in conformity with instructions from the President, who did not consider himself authorized to direct their locations.

With these papers were the evidence adduced by present claimant in regard of the number and ages of his children at date of treaty.

By reference to "Reports of Committee," House document 479, 24 Congress, 1 session, it is ascertained that Mr. Everett, from the Committee on Indian Affairs, made the following report:

"The Committee on Indian Affairs, to which, by resolution of the 1st February, last, was referred a communication of the President of the 6th February 1835, with the accompanying documents, relating to certain claims to reservations under the Choctaw Treaty of 1830, report:

That Zadock Brashears [Jr], Alexander Brashears, Inponah, alias Billy Comnaubbe, and Lisper, the reported wife of George Clark, were, at the date of said treaty, Choctaw Heads of families and that they severally gave notices to the United States Agent, Col. Ward, of their intention to remain and become citizens of the States, and claimed reservations under the 14 Article.

That Alexander Brashears had then living with him nine children, three over ten years of age, unmarried, and six under that age, whose names were registered by the Agent, but that the names of two of said children, one over, and the other under the age of ten years were written in the register returned and he now claims reservations on their account of three fourths of a section of land.

It further appears that, under the direction of the President, conditional reservations, nearly to the extent of the claims have been located, subject to the confirmation of Congress, and that the claimants have resided on their locations since the date of the treaty.

The Committee are of the opinion that those locations ought to be confirmed, and that other locations should be made to satisfy the balance of these claims and they report a bill for that purpose; and also in cases where patents, or patent certificates have issued to others for any part of said locations, and that patents in fee issue for the same, and they report a bill for that purpose."

That report was not reached during the session, and consequently, no action was had upon it, or the bill. It is referred to here, however, to show the view of a prominent committe upon the merits of the claim.

On 3 March 1837, Congress passed "an act for the appointment of Commissioners to adjust the claims to reservations of lands under the 14 Article of the treaty of 1830 with the Choctaw Indians," the 7th Section of which reads as follows:

"And it is further enacted that nothing contained in

this act shall be so construed as to sanction what is calling contingent locations which have been made by George W. Martin for the benefit of such Indians, or were supposed to have been entitled to other lands, which have been sold by the United States, such contingent locations have been made, without any legal authority. It being the true intent of this act to reserve to Congress the power of doing that which may appear just when a correct knowledge of all the facts is obtained."

By reference to a list of claims located by Col. Martin under his instructions of 13 Oct. 1834, I find that Alexander Brashears is registered for the N ½ of Section 16, the SE ¼ of Section 8, in Township 17 of Range 1 West, Demopolis District, Alabama, for two children, one under and one over ten years of age, and as located on 27 Nov. 1834. An examination has been made at the General Land Office in regard of this location and it is found to adjoin that made by Martin in accordance with the treaty as returned by Ward and the examination shows further that no sale has been made of this last location by the U. S., nor does it appear by the books of the Land Office that there is any conflicting claim to said land.

The documents on file in this office connected with the registration of Col. Ward shows that more than one register was kept by him. On a copy taken by this office from the original in 1836, when Col. Martin was in this city, Alexander Brashears is entered for 9 children, 6 under & 3 over ten years of age. The discrepancy between the two registers is not explained by the Agent who made them, but the testimony advanced to this office and submitted to Congress, proves the correctness of that uncertified list.

The brief of the case prepared by Mr. Lyon, attorney for Brashears, accompanies this statement and the facts stated by him are substantially correct.

It appears to me that Alexander Brashears is entitled to lands for 9 children and I should recommend that the additional location made for him be confirmed under an opinion of the Attorney Genl. that evidence might be received other than the register to establish rights and the supplemental register made by Ward, of which we have a copy taken in this office from the original, which seems to take their case out of the operation of President Jackson's decision, in Tim Tom's case, that Col. Ward's register was the only evidence that could be received and conclusive, but my hands are tied, as I conceive, by other acts of the President and the War Department and Congress.

The order of the 13 Oct. 1834, issued by the President, and hereinbefore recited, refers to reservations not made, owing to "the mistakes or neglect of the Agent appointed to make a list of reserves" and adds "These locations will be contingent and will be complete only in the event of their being sanctioned by Congress." The instructions issued by the Acting Secretary of War on the same day to the locating Agent contained this clause: "If they bring themselves within the requisition of the 14th Article, and the evidence induces you to believe that the omission of the names on the register was caused by the mistake or neglect of the Agent, you will make locations for them in the manner pointed out in the instructions heretofore given to you. These locations, it must be understood, are contingent, and will be complete only in the event of their being confirmed by Congress."

Among the papers sent to Congress by the President on the 6 February 1835, this case will be found and, of the whole, the message says "Should Congress consider the claims just, it will be proper to pass a law authorizing their location or satisfying them in some other way." The Committee on Indian Affairs of the House of Representatives (Doc. H.R. 479, 24 Congress, 1 Session) in a report made 24 March 1836, on this subject, refers specifically to this among the other cases, as a claim for ¾ of a section, because of the omission of two of the reservee's children on the register, and speaks of the location made under foregoing instructions, as subject to a confirmation of Congress. On that report no action appears to have been had, probably for want or time. In a subsequent report of 11 May 1836, from the same committee, made by the present Secretary of War, its chairman, it appears both the registers of Col. Ward referred to, were before the Committee and copies are appended. This able paper does not, I believe, speak particularly of errors made by the registering agent in the number of children a claimant had.

From this detail it appears, I think, that the ¾ of a section claimed by Alexander Brashears for the two children omitted on Mr. Wards first register has been regarded as contingent by the

President of the U. S. and the War Department, and the proper committee of the House of Representatives, and I am bound to confine my actions to these views. The decision in this case will affect and control several others.

Very respectfully yours,
Your most Obt. Serv't.
/s/ F. Hartley Crawford

<===========>

State of Alabama)
Sumter County)

    Before me, William Bennett, an acting justice of the peace in & for the County & State aforesaid, personally came and appeared William Flucker and John T. Moran, who, after being duly sworn, deposeth and sayeth that they are acquainted with Alexander Brashiers of said county. That the said Alexander Brashiers, with his family, has, for some years before the treaty of Dancing Rabbit Creek in the year one thousand, eight hundred and thirty and up to this time, lived upon section nine, Township 17, Range one west in Sumter County, the said section being embraced in his reservation under said treaty.

/s/ William Flucker
/s/ John T. Moran

Sworn to and subscribed this
Eighteenth day of March 1836.

/s/ William Bennett, J.P.

The State of Alabama)
Sumter County)

    I, Daniel Womack, Clerk of the County Court of said county, do hereby certify that William Bennett whose signature appears to the above certificate now is and was at the time of signing the same an acting Justice of the Peace in said county and that the signature purporting to be his is genuine.

    Given under my hand and seal of said office this 21st day of March 1836.

/s/ Dan'l. Womack, Clerk
by L. H. Thompson, D.C.

<===========>

Reserve Choctaw L 807
Hon. F.S. Lyon
Demopolis, Aug. 7, 1839

In the agents return, part of Alex. Brashears children was accidentally omitted. Proof of the error was filed with Martin, who made the proper location. Mr. Brashears is anxious to know if any and what further evidence is required. Application was made to this office on the subject last winter, but no answer has been received.

Request that two patents may be issued for Delila [Juzan] Brashears reserve, one to John W. Foster for the part heretofore sold to him and one to the reservee for the balance. If this cannot be done, wants the patent for the whole to Delila Brashears.

It is but right that Anne Brashears, widow of Zadock, Jr., should be allowed to designate the quarter section to be deducted from her reserve because of an error in the agents return, overstating her proper quantity.

Rec'd. Aug. 17, 1839
Ans. 20 Aug. 1839

<===========>

F.S. Lyon, to __?__

The name of Alex. Brashears was returned by Wm. Ward, Agent for the Choctaws, as one of the persons entitled to a reservation of land under the 14th Article of the Choctaw Treaty of 1830. This return of cases admits that Brashears has complied with the provisions of the treaty requiring notice to the agent within six months from its ratification, of his intention to remain in the county (-----?-----) and claim a reservation of land. Brashears had living with him at the date of the treaty nine children, three over and six under ten years of age. The locating agent, G.W. Martin, has located to the claimant the correct quantity of land secured to him by the treaty, but by reference to the return of Mr. Ward, it appears that he committed a mistake in regard to the number of children by stating the number of seven upon his register instead of nine. The proof in the case clearly establishes the current number and ages of the claimants children. This location has been made in conformity with the terms of the Treaty. The location interferes with no other and the correctness of the claim has been acquiesced in by all having a knowledge of the facts. The only question presented in the case is whether or not it is competent for the department to correct the small mistake of the agent as to the No. of children. The Treaty simply requires the claimant to give notice to the agent of his intention to remain and does not require a return to the agent of the No. and ages of the claimants children or that the agent shall make a register of them. No new location is required or floating claim set up, but a confirmation of the location already made in strict conformity with the terms of the Treaty. Under the opinion of the Atty. Gen. of the 27 June 1830, the department is at liberty to receive any credible evidence, documentary or oral, coming from any disinterested source, which may establish the fact of such a mistake as the one committed by the agent in the present case. If claimant should be required to go to Congress for the correction of mistakes such as the one committed in the present case, much unnecessary trouble and delay would be the consequence. In the present case, the right of the Reservee to land is admitted and the only question is as to the correction of the mistake of the agent in stating the No. of children. The proof establishes, beyond doubt, the fact of this mistake and it is respectfully requested that the location be confirmed and the patent issued.

/s/ F.S. Lyon
Atty. for the Claimant

Washington, 22 June 1841

P.S. Since preparing the foregoing brief, it has been discovered that the original book in which Col. Ward entered the names of Claimants under the 14th Article of the Treaty, contains the correct No. and ages of Alexander Brashears' children. A copy of this original list is on file. Compared with the original in Col. Ward's hand-writing by (----?----) whose affidavit of the fact is hereby submitted.

/s/ F.S. Lyon
Atty. for Alexander Brashears

<=========>

As the two children of Brashears, omitted on the attested copy of Ward, the Agent's, register, are embraced on the other, or the original register, kept by him; as there is ample proof that that register is, in this particular, correct and as the position of the land located for them is in conformity with the treaty, and it has not been sold; this case is not, in my opinion, one of those denominated "Contingent Locations" which Congress only can confirm. And, as there is no conflicting claim to the land, I recommend that Brashears' title be now confirmed to the quantity he is entitled to under the treaty, including the three-fourths of a section located for the two children referred to viz., Fraction of Sect. 9, T17, R1 west, North and East of the Suckanochee River, 457 acres., Sec. 4, 639.20. West half Sec. 3, 319.20. East ½ & N.W. ¼ Sect. 5, 479.40, N.W. ¼ of Sec. 10, 160. N ½ Sec. 16 (estimated) 303.60 and the N.W. ¼ of S.E. ¼ and the lots C. F. & H of Sec. 8, all in the same township and range, Demopolis Land district, Alabama.

/s/ Jno. Bell

Sept. 20, 1841
Approved: T. Tyler [President of the United States]

ZADOCK BRASHEARS, SR's RESERVATION

War Department, Office of Indian Affairs
6 May 1842

Hon. B.G. Shields of Fla.
House of Repr., U. S.
Sir:

I have the honor to inform you that I have duly considered the respective claims of Delilah Brashears (widow of Jesse Brashears, [v5]832) and Mr. [Greene B.] Chaney, assignee of Zadock Brashears, Senr., ([v5]231) deceased, and decided to submit them for the favorable action of the Executive. Statements in each case will at once be prepared and presented to the Secretary of War tomorrow. In the case of Zadock Brashears, Senr., I shall recommend that the patent be issued in the name of Mr. Chaney and transmitted to the Register or

Receiver of the proper land office to be delivered only upon the payment by Mr. C. of the balance of the purchase money. The patent for Delilah reservation will, under an opinion of the Attorney General, be issued in her name. You will hear from this office when action of the President has been had on these claims.   Very res.

(no signature)

<===========>

The State of Alabama)
Mobile County)^{ss}

Before me, F.M. Alexander, a Justice of the Peace for said county personally came and appeared George S. Gaines of the city of Mobile who, being duly sworn according to law, deposes and says that Zadock Brashears, Senr., in his lifetime (who was an inhabitant of the Choctaw Nation at the date of the Treaty of 1830 with said tribe of Indians) sold the reservation of land secured to him by said treaty to Greene B. Chaney for the consideration of nineteen hundred and twenty dollars and received in payment therefor three hundred dollars and by his contract in writing dated 10 Apr. 1832 and witnessed by this affiant, D. R. Malone and S.U.U. Schuyler, agreed to receive the remainder of the purchase money whenever he was enabled to make a final and complete title to the land. This affiant further said Zadock Brashears was a male of ordinary intelligence, capable of making a contract and he believes the contract, before mentioned, was fair and without fraud on the part of the purchaser, Greene B. Chaney.

/s/ Geor. S. Gaines

Sworn & subscribed the 30 Apr. 1837

F. M. Alexander, J. P. M. C.

<===========>

War Department, Office of Indian Affairs

Feb. 15, 1842

Hon. B.G. Shields of Ala.

House of Reps.

Sir:

Since the conversation with you this morning in relation to certain claims under Choctaw Treaty of 1830, an examination of all the papers transmitted by Mr. Lyon to you and by you referred to the Commr., Genl. Land office, and by him sent to this Bureau, has been had. That examination shows that Green B. Chaney is not the assignee of Zadock Brashears, Jr., the reservee under 14 article aforesaid treaty, but of Zadock Brashears, Senr., for whom a reservation was located under the 19 article. Consequently, should his title papers be regarded as sufficient to be approved by the President, a patent can issue to him as the assignee of the reservee. I have not to day sufficient time to examine this case with proper care, so as to decide on its character.

The case of Zadock Brashears, Jr., will, at once, be submitted to the Secretary of War for his action. Should he concur in the opinion expressed by me, and the President affirm it, the Genl. Land office will be informed and requested to issue the Patent to the reservee.

The case of Delilah Brashears and that of Jack Tom shall receive as early action as the business (---?---) upon this office will admit.

The letter of Mr. Lyon to you of 20 ultimo is returned herewith; that of 30 Dec., last, in relation to Mr. Chaney's claim is retained.

> Very res.
> (no signature)

<===========>

War Department, Office of Indian Affairs
6 May 1842

Hon. B. G. Shields of Ala.

House of Repr. U. S.

Sir:

I have the honor to inform you that I have duly considered the respective claims of Delilah Brashears (^{v5}832) and Mr. Chaney, assignee of Zadock Brashears, Senr., (^{v5}231) deceased, and decided to submit them for the favorable action of the Executive. Statements in each case will at once be prepared and presented to the Secretary of War to-morrow. In the case of Zadock Brashears, Sr., I shall recommend that the patent be issued in the name of Mr. Chaney and transmitted to the Registrar or Receiver of the proper land office to be delivered only upon the payment by Mr. C. of the balance of the purchase money. The patent for Delilah's reservation will, under an opinion of the Attorney General, be issued in her name.

You will hear from this office when the actions of the President has been had on these claims.

Very res.

(no signature)

<==========>

War Department, Office of Indian Affairs
9 June 1842

Commissioner of the General Land Office,

Washington, D. C.

Sir:

I transmit herewith the copy of a report of (----?----) from this office to the Secretary of War of 6 instant and of the endorsement by the Secretary and President thereon, in relation to the emanation of a patent to Green B. Chaney for the tract of land selected as the reservation of Zadock Brashears, Senr., under 19 Article, Choctaw treaty of 1830. I transmit, also, the agreement between the reservee and Mr. Chaney, that proper (---? ---) herewith letter from your office of 31 January, last.

Very res.

(no signature)

<=============>

War Department, Office of Indian Affairs
9 June 1842

Hon. B.G. Shields of Ala.
  House of Reps., U. S.
Sir:

Referring you to my letter of 4th ultimo, I have the honor now to inform you that the President of the U.S. has approved the suggestion of this office in regard of the emanation of a patent to Green B. Chaney, Esq., for the land selected as the reservation of Zadock Brashears, Senr., under 19 Article, Choctaw treaty of 1830, and that information of the fact has been communicated to the Commissioner of the General Land Office today.

Very res.
(no signature)

<=============>

War Department, Office of Indian Commissioner
28 June 1842

Hon. B.G. Shields of Alabama
  House of Repr., U. S.
Sir:

The patent to Green B. Chaney for the land selected as the reservation of Zadock Brashears, Senr., under the 19th Article, Choctaw treaty 1830, will be sent to the Register of the Land office at Demopolis, Alabama, as an escrow, to-day. The Register will be requested to preserve the control of it and let it remain in his custody until Mr. Chaney shall pay the balance of the purchase money $1620, and the same is applied, according to the law of Alabama, to the payment of Brashears' debits, or received by the legal representative of the estate.

Very res.
(no signature)

<=============>

28 June 1842

Lewis B. McCarty, Esq.,
Register Land Office
Demopolis, Alabama.
Sir:

I transmit herewith, a patent in favor of Green B. Chaney for the land selected as the reservation of Zadock Brashears, Senr., under 19 article of Choctaw treaty of 1830, and a copy of a communication from this office to the Secretary of War of 6 instant, and the endorsement upon it by the said Secretary and the President, which was the basis for the emanation of the Patent.

The Patent is sent to you as an escrow on the suggestion of Hon. F. S. Lyon. You will please preserve control of it and let it remain in your custody until Mr. Chaney shall pay the balance of the purchase money, $1620, and the same is applied according to the law of Alabama to the payment of Brashears debts, or received by the legal representative of his estate.

You will please acknowledge the receipt of the accompanying document and when the conditions precedent to the delivery of the Patent to Mr. Chaney have been complied with, please acquaint this office thereof.

Very res.
(no signature)

DELILAH (JUZAN) BRASHEARS' RESERVATION

Demopolis, Alabama
7 Aug. 1839

J. Harkey Crawford, Esq.
Comm. Indian Affairs.
Sir:

In the case of Delila (Juzan) Brashears (the widow of Jesse Brashears (^{v5}832)) a claimant under the same Article and who has sold a portion of her reservation to John W. Foster, I requested, at the instance of Mr. Foster, that the issuance of the patent might be delayed until Mr. Brown or his successor returned the proof taken as to the nature of Foster's contract of purchase so that the contract might be approved and the patent issued to him as assignee.

A difficulty has arisen about the part of Delila Brashears land not sold to Foster. It is necessary her patent should issue. I have, therefore, to request that you will issue her patent to be issued and forwarded for that part of her reservation not sold and conveyed to Foster as shown by Mrs. Brown's return. If there is no objection to the sub-division. If, however, you should deem it best to embrace the entire reservation in one patent, you can cause it to be issued in the name of the reservee and Mr. Foster can rely upon his deed of conveyance for the part purchased by him.

The part of the reservation not sold and conveyed to Foster has been sold at Sheriff's sale for about 10 cents per acre when the land is, in fact, worth $12 or $15 per acre and my object in requesting the patent is to show the situation of the reservees title and to defeat this sale, if possible.

Very respectfully
Yr. obdt. Serv.
/s/ F.S. Lyon

<============>

August 20, 1839

His Excellency
The Secretary of War
Sir:

About twelve months since we transmitted to the War Department certain depositions in behalf of John Lloyd, an applicant for pre-emption to the S.W. ¼ of Sect. 1 of Township 17 in Range 1 West, and in opposition to the claim of the heirs of Zadoc Brashirs reserve under the 14th Article of the treaty of Dancing Rabbit Creek to a part of said land, and also submitted an application to have the location made to Delilah Brashiers so changed as to embrace that land which it would have included had the reservation for the heirs of Zadoc Brashiers not been made. And have since been awaiting your excellency's decision upon the testimony and application. We would now respectfully ask leave to call your excellency's attention to the matter and beg that some action may be had upon it and that we may be informed accordingly.

Respectfully
Yr. Obt. Servts.
Henly & Lomax

ZADOCK BRASHEARS, Jr and ANNE DeCASTRO'S RESERVATION

Zadock Brashears Jr (^{v5} 840)apparently tried to cheat on his application for an "individual reservation" by claiming more children than he was father of. He married Anne DeCastro about 1826, and they had three children at the time of the Treaty of Dancing Rabbit Creek, but Anne was also pregnant. That fourth child was born before Zadock Jr registered with Col. Ward as wanting to remain on his land and become a citizen. Zadock registered at St. Stephens in 1831 as having four children, one of them over ten years of age, but that was later shown to be in error.

In the 1831 Census, however, Zadock Jr is listed correctly with 6 in his household; four children, himself and wife, though none of the children were over ten.

Zadock Jr was shot and killed at a horse race in Aug 1833, under circumstances that smack of murder. Richard Brashears, Vaughn Brashears' ex-slave, testified in Dawes hearings that Turner Brashears, II, Zadock Jr's younger brother, told him that he was responsible for Zadock's death.

Sumter Co, AL Orphan's Settlement Book 1, p.3, 19 Aug 1833: Ann Brashears, relict, and George W. Harper, sheriff, appointed administrators in estate of Zadock Brashears. Appraisers of the property were David W. Wall, Green Berry Chaney, Benjamin Walker, Wesley B. Trahern, and Hardy Abner.

On 13 Sept 1833, an inventory of the property of Zedick Brasiers was made by G.B. Chaney, D.W. Wall, and B. Walker. The value of property was $525.62. On 22 Jan 1834, a sale of the estate was conducted (Sumter Co, AL Orphans Minutes, Book I, p.34-37); purchasers included:

Robert Goodwin	Abel Wilson
Robert Williams	W.B. Graham

Elizabeth Buckhold	C.H. Vaughn
B. Walker	W.C. Pistole
Gideon Webb	D.W. Wall
Rachael Brashiers	Lucy Graham
John Null	Samuel Webb
Joshua Neston	Hardy Abner
Ann Brashiers	

Orphan's Settlement, Book 1, p.9, 3 Oct 1833: Ann Brashears, relict of Zadock Brashears, was appointed guardian of minor heirs of said deceased, to wit: <u>John, William, and Turner Brashears</u>.

From 1896 to 1906, Napoleon B. Brashears claimed there was another heir: Joseph, from which he was descended. See the story of his hoax and fraudulent claim in separate chapter. Sarah Ann (Moncrief) Harlan ([v5]1394) testified that there was no Joseph, but there was a daughter, Oleana, who moved to Texas with her mother. But why wasn't she mentioned in the Orphan's Settlement— Anne was pregnant when Zadock was shot; so Oleana wasn't yet born.

Ann Brashears is in the 1840 Census, Sumter Co, AL: (02100-100001), between Delilah Brashears and A. Buckholts. This listing would support the existence of Oleana. The twins and Oleana are listed too young; perhaps the census taker came early, or the children were small.

Sumter Co, AL Deed Book H, p.379: Zadock Brashears received two sections of land from the U.S. Government by virtue of the 14th clause of the Treaty of Dancing Rabbit Creek, 1830. It was not recorded until 1845, probably by his wife.

The description of the land received in the Treaty of Dancing Rabbit Creek is the same as part of the land later owned by William Brashears, s/o Zadock, Jr. William d. 1848. Turner Brashears, who resided out of the state (possibly Texas), is said to have inherited William's share. We have found no record of his disposing of the land. If Sarah Ann (Moncrief) Harlan was right, the heir may have been Oleana, not Turner.

[v5]**840.** [8]8. **Zadock Brashears Jr**, b. 1804; d. Aug 1833 in a horse race; m. 24/25 Aug 1826, **Ann DeCastro**, "Dicosta" in some records. The birth dates of their four sons were recorded

in a family Bible (whereabouts unknown) and in a letter in the War Department, Office of Indian Affairs (see Choctaw Reserve Records Group 75).

[v5]1151. [9]1. **Turner Brashears, III**, b. 11 June 1827. Died near Moscow, AL, when young, according to testimony of Sarah Ann (Moncrief) Harlan, but he may have been William's heir.

[v5]1152. [9]2. **John Brashears**, (twin), b. 23 Feb 1829, said in some testimony to have died when a little boy, in other testimony to have married and had one child; see chapter on "Woes in Oklahoma."

[v5]1153. [9]3. **William M. Brashears**, (twin), b. 23 Feb 1829, said to have lived on Zadock Jr's land, and died 1848. Richard D. Shackelford was administrator of the estate of William M. Brashear, decd (*Sumter Democrat*, 17 July 1852).

[v5]1154. [9]4. **James Brashears**, b. 2 May 1831, d. 1833

[v5]1155. [9]5. **Oleana Brashears**, b. c1833-34. Ann was pregnant when Zadock was killed and Oleana was born after Oct 1833. Sarah Ann (Moncrief) Harlan testified that Oleana moved to Texas with her mother. The family lost track of them.

Draft of a letter written in behalf of Zadock Jr's heirs: Zadock Brashears Jr, at the date of the Treaty of Dancing Rabbit Creek, 27 Sept 1830, was an inhabitant of the Choctaw Nation, was the head of a Choctaw family and entitled to the benefits of the treaty.

The report of Wm. Ward, the Choctaw agent to the War Department, shows that Brashears gave the notice of his intention to remain in the country ceded, required by the treaty, that he claimed the benefit of the provision made by the 14th Article and was registered as the head of a family with <u>one child over ten and two under ten years of age.</u> The precise date of the notice to the agent is unknown, but was, of course, between the 24 Feb. 1831, and the date of the ratification, the 24th Aug. of the same year, the time within which the notice was required to be given. A mistake was evidently committed, either by Brashears or the agent, as to the <u>number and ages of his children,</u> but not as is believed of such character as will diminish or increase the quantity or land secured to the head of the family by the Treaty.

The Treaty was agreed upon in Council on the 27th September, 1830 and ratified on the part of the U.S. on the 24th Feb. 1831.

The family of Brashears consisted of his wife and four children of the following names and ages as appears by an extract from the family bible

Turner Brashears, [III] born 11 June 1827
William and John, twins, 23rd Feb. 1829
James, born 2 May 1831

Under the return of the agent, one Section of land was located to the head of the family and one section on account of his children (½ Section for the child supposed to be over ten and ¼ Section each for the two children under ten).

Now if, for the four children named, the claimant is entitled to one qr. section each as provided by the treaty, the proper quantity of land has been located, but it is contended that the claimant has received one qr. section too much, the child James having been born after the date of the treaty. The 14th Article provides that each head of a family being desirous to remain shall be permitted to do so by signifying his intention to the agent within six months from the ratification of this treaty and he or she shall thereupon be entitled to a reservation of survey; in like manner shall be entitled to one half that quantity for each unmarried child which is living with him over ten years of age to adjoin the location of the parent.

From this claim, it is evident that the right to the land on account of the children accrued from the date of the notice. Upon giving the notice of intention to remain "he or she shall thereupon be entitled." The claimant was allowed until the 24 Aug. 1831 to give this notice. His fourth child was born on the 2d day of May 1831 and if between that period and the 23 Aug, the claimant gave the notice required and had living with him four children under ten years of age he was thereupon entitled by the express terms of the Treaty to one Section for himself as the head of the family and to one qr. section for each of his children. Whether the notice was in fact given before or after the birth of the 4th child cannot now be ascertained as the claimant who gave the notice has since died — but this cannot be material. The agent by making the return has admitted that the notice was given within the six months and it would be competent even now for the claimant or his representative to show by proof the number and ages of his children. The Treaty requires notice from the head of the family of his intention to remain, but does not require notice within the six months of the No. & age of his children. Proof now the notice and the return of the Agent is conclusive, with satisfactory evidence that at the time of the notice the claimant had four children under ten years of age would perfect the right to four qr. sections on account of the children.

But suppose the notice of intention to remain was in fact given between the 24 Feb., the date of the ratification and the 2nd May, the date of the birth of the fourth child, the law regulating and protecting the right of infant in <u>Ventra va mere</u> is considered as born for all purposes which are for his benefit and so far as this principle that if land to be devised to B for life, remainder to such child or children of B as shall be living at the time of his decease, a posthumous child will take equally with those who were born at the time of B's death. (See Dee vs Clarke, 2d. Hon. Black, 399.)

If ever a doubt could be created as to the right of the claimant to the section as the head of the family and one qr. section for each of the four children under ten years of age, the quantity already located to satisfy the claim, such doubt is expressly required by the treaty to be construed most favorably for the claimant.

The widow is unable to explain the return of the agent giving her one child over ten and but two under ten years of age. If it was the mistake of the Agent she is not responsible. If the act of her husband, now dec'd., she had no agency in it. She has furnished an extract from her family Bible of the ages of her children and claims only such quantity of land as the Treaty secures to her.

(EDITORIAL NOTE: The foregoing apparently is a preliminary opinion and precedes the following in the order of filing in the record. It is undated and unsigned.)

<===========>

Evidence respecting the title of Ann Brashears to a Reservation which she claims under the 14th Article of the Choctaw treaty made at Dancing Rabbit on the 27th day of September 1830. Taken before me, William Bennett, an acting Justice of the

Peace, in and for the County of Sumter and State of Alabama on the 24th day of October 1834, who after being first duly sworn according to law depose and say as follows, to wit:

Interrogatories propounded to Emeline Brashears on the aforesaid subject:

Interrogatory 1— Do you or not know how many children Zadock Brashears [Jr] and the said Ann Brashears had at the time he, Zadock Brashears, enrolled himself as a reservee? If you tell, tell how many there was and what their ages was at the time as near as you can.

Answer 1— I do not know at what time he enrolled himself. He had but three children at the time of the treaty, none of whom are ten years old at this time and all are living.

Sworn to and subscribed before me the day and year first above written.

/s/ Wm. Bennett   /s/ Emeline Brashears

Alexander Brashears, deposing upon the above subject, says that the statement above is true.

/s/ Wm. Bennett   /s/ Alexander Brashears

Ann Goodwyn, deposing upon the above subject, says that the above statement is true to the best of her knowledge and she further states that the said Ann Brashears told her some time in the Summer of 1831 that when William Armstrong, the present agent, came 'round he told her if she could slip the fourth and youngest child in as a reservee and get land for it it would be a fine quantity of land and further stated that the said agent was a-going to try to do it.

Sworn to and subscribed before me the day and year first aforesaid.

/s/ Wm. Bennett   /s/ Ann Goodwyn

Interrogatories propounded to Hardy Abney on the above subject:

Interrogatory 1— What did Zadock Brashears [Jr] tell you on the subject of his children being entitled to reservations?

Answer 1— Said Brashears told this affiant in his lifetime that when he enrolled himself as a reservee, he had but three children, but his (wife) was pregnant and he enrolled four.

Sworn to and subscribed before me the day and year first aforesaid.

/s/ Wm Bennett   /s/ Hardy Abney

Interrogatories propounded to William C. Pistole on the above subject:

Interrogatory 1— Tell all you know about the number of children Zadock Brashears had at the time of the treaty; what their ages was as near as you can, and how many he had at the time of his death.

Answer 1— I do not know any thing about it of my own knowledge.

/s/ Wm. Bennett   /s/ Wm. C. Pistole

<============>

Washington
26 April 1836

The Hon.
The Secretary of War
Sir,

A person entitled to a reservation under the 14th Article of the Treaty of 1830 with the Chaktaws, after giving the requisite notice of his intention to remain in the country ceded and become a citizen and, after having his name with the No. and ages of his children registered by the Agent, died before the expiration of the five years from the ratification of the treaty during which he was required to reside upon the land before a grant in fee simple could issue. In the case referred to, the widow has continued the residence for the five years and I have been requested to inquire whether the grant in fee simple will issue to the widow who became the head of the family by the death of the husband.

It is insisted by the person at whose insistence I make this inquiry, that the reservation secured by the 14th Article of the Treaty is to the reservee in the character of representative of her family and that, by his death, the widow was substituted as the surviving head of the family, to his rights and entitled to the Patent. I make this inquiry at the instance of a constituent and must ask the favor of you to furnish me with the information he desires. I have reference to the case of Zadock Brashears whose widow requests that the patent may issue in her name if she is entitled to it.

Very respectfully
Yr. Obt. Servt.
/s/ F.S. Lyon

<===========>

War Department, Office of Indian Commissioner

Dec. 12 '36

Messrs: Bliss & Scott
  Gainsville, Sumter Co.
Gentlemen:

You were advised on the 12th of July, last, that your application to have additional lands located for Jim Tom under the Choctaw Treaty of 1830, would be submitted to the President.

I have now to inform you that he has decided that the register kept by Col. Ward is the only evidence that can be recd. of the rights of claimants under the 14th Art. of the treaty and that no float can be allowed under it; and, of course, this application cannot be granted.

Very res.
(no signature)

<===========>

War Department, Office of Indian Affairs

Dec. 30 '36

James Whitecomb, Esq.
Comm. C. L. C.
Sir,

I return the papers enclosed in your communication of the 30th, ultimo, respecting the claim of J. Lloyd under the preemption law.

In reply, I have to state that Z. Brashears, a part of whose reserve is claimed by Lloyd, having had assigned to him only the quantity to which, according to the official register of the Indian

Agent, which register, the President has directed, shall be the sole guide, he was entitled under the treaty, the affidavits forwarded by Lloyd, which do not preclude the possibility of Brashears having been married prior to 1826, cannot be admitted as sufficient to warrant an alteration in the quantity of land set apart for him. If no other objections be made, the location will be submitted for approval.

Very res.

(no signature)

<===========>

Washington City
February 4th 1837

Hon. B.F. Butler
  Secretary of War.
Sir,

I respectfully request the suspension of the decision of the Department and of the President of the United States, in the case of John Lloyd vs Zadock Brashears [Jr], claiming land under the Treaty between the United States and the Choctaw Nation of Indians, concluded at Dancing Rabbit Creek on 27th Sept. 1830; for the following reasons --

1. That Z. Brashears married Anne DeCastro on the 24th or 25th August 1826, and therefore it is more than probable could not have had more than two, or three children at fartherest.

2. That said Brashears has had located to him two sections of land, when in fact he is entitled to but one and three quarters.

3. That John Lloyd placed in the hands of Col. Martin, the locating Agent, to be transmitted by him to the Department, evidence and documents having an important bearing in this case, and going immediately to prove the fact that Brashears is not entitled to the quantity of land located to him (as may be seen by an examination of Lloyd's letter to the Hon. D.H. Lewis, on file, I presume, in the Department) by the Government's locating Agent. None of said evidence or documents have yet arrived at either the General Land Office, or the War Department.

We pray that the Department will grant us sufficient time, before its final decision in this case to enable us either to procure the original papers placed in the hands of Col. Martin, or a certified copy of them.

I have the honor to be
Very Respectfully
Yr. Obt. Servt.
/s/ Edw. B. Stelle
for Hon. D.H. Lewis

<===========>

I, the within named Anne Brashears, widow of Zadock Brashears, Jr., deceased, do hereby acknowledge to have sold and conveyed to Luke H. Grigsby the west half of the South West quarter of Section one in Township Seventeen, Range one West, embraced in the reservation allowed and secured to me under the 14th Article of the Treaty of Dancing Rabbit, which said sale and conveyance was for the consideration of one thousand dollars and I hereby request that the patent may issue to the said Luke M. Grigsby for the half quarter section above described. Witness my hand and seal this 26th April 1837.

/s/ Anne Brashears

Witness:
 F.S. Lyon
A.V. Brown, Commr., L. O. [Land Office]

<===========>

The State of Alabama)
Morengo County   )ss
Before me, Armestead Burwill, a Notary Public in and for the county and state aforesaid, personally came and appeared John C. McGrew and John Null, who, being duly sworn, depose and say that they knew Zadock Brashears, Jr., in his lifetime who died shortly after the treaty of Dancing Rabbit of 1830 with the Chaktaws and who was at the date of said Treaty a citizen of the Chacktaw Nation; that the said Zadock at the time of his death

lived on section 23, in township 17, Range 1 West. That Anne Brashears, the widow of the said Zadock, with her family has lived on said Section from the date of the Treaty aforesaid 'till the present time.

/s/ J.C. McGrew
/s/ John Null

Sworn & subscribed before me this
26th day of April AD 1837.
  Witness my hand & seal notarial -
  H. Burwill, Notary Public
(Attest - H. Burwill, Notary Public)

<============>

The State of Alabama)
Sumter County)[ss]
    Personally came and appeared before me, Philip S. Glover, an Acting Justice of the Peace, duly elected, commissioned and qualified in and for the county above mentioned, John McGrew, who being first duly sworn the truth to tell deposes and says - that he was well acquainted with Zadock Brashiers and his family at the date of the Treaty of Dancing Rabbit Creek between the U.S. Government with the Choctaw tribe of Indians, and that from the best of his recollection, the said Zadock Brashier had not, either at the date or ratification of said treaty, more than three children, all of whom he believes were under the age of ten years and that to satisfy himself as to the correctness of his recollection in this particular he some time since made inquiry of Ann Brashiers, the widow of the said Zadock Brashiers as to the ages and number of her children at the date and ratification of the said treaty and that she, the said Ann Brashiers for this purpose, informing this affiant in relation therewith, gave him an extract as she said and then as written from her family bible, from which this affiant took a memorandum as follows:
    "Ages of Ann Brashear's children:
        Turner [III]was born June 1827
        William and John were born 23 Feby. 1829
        James was born on 2nd May 1831"

/s/ J.C. McGrew

Subscribed and sworn to before me
this 9th day of January AD 1838.
    (Attest - Price Williams, Clerk,
    County Court, Sumter County, Ala.)

<=============>

The State of Alabama)
Sumter County ss

    Personally came and appeared before me, Philip S. Glover, an Acting Justice of the Peace, duly elected, commissioned and qualified in and for the county above written, William Fluker who, being first duly sworn the truth to tell, deposes and says:

    That he was well acquainted with Zadock Brashiers, Junr., for many years before his death; that he (this affiant) moved into the neighborhood of the residence of the family of the said Zadoc Brashiers in the month of December 1832; that he lived within a mile of them and this affiant was and has been ever since his removal into their neighborhood, the constant attending physician in the family of the said Brashiers; that in December 1832 Ann Brashiers, the widow to the said Zadock, had four children, none of whom this affiant would, at that period (1832) have supposed to be as much as ten years of age. In the course of the year 1833, the youngest of these four children died, but this affiant cannot say at this distance of time what was the probable age of the child last mentioned.

               /s/ Wm Fluker

Sworn to and subscribed before
me this 9th day of January AD 1838.
    /s/ Philip B. Glover, J. P.
(Attest: Price Williams, Clerk, County Court, Sumter County)

<=============>

Demopolis, Alabama
February 13, 1838

To His Excellency
  The Secretary of War
Sir,

As the attornies of John Lloyd, an applicant for a pre-emption on the South West quarter of Section No. 1 of To. 17 of Range 1 West, we are now engaged in procuring testimony to defeat the title of the heirs of Zadoc Brashiers [Jr], a reservee under the 14th Article of the Treaty of Dancing Rabbit Creek to the West half of the said quarter Section, which is a part of the land embraced by the said reservation, upon the ground that at the time the said Zadoc Brashiers registered his name as applicant for a reservation, he had **no child over ten years of age**; instead, as would appear from the certificate of allotment, **two children under and one over ten years of age.**

Should we succeed in establishing this fact, as from conversations with the witnesses we have the best reason to believe we will, we shall contend that the location should be changed as to embrace only such land as would have been originally allotted to the said Zadoc Brashiers had the ages of his children have been property registered. And we shall, at the same time, require the location of the land to **Delilah Brashiers, the adjoining reserve,** to be so altered as to embrace only such land as would have been allotted her had the location to Zadock Brashiers been properly made in the first instance, which would allow the pre-emptor his full quota under the act.

We would, therefore, in the name and on behalf of the said John Lloyd respectfully **protest** against the issuance of a patent to the heirs of the said Zadoc Brashiers or to Delilah Brashiers for any portion of the quarter section now claimed by the said John Lloyd under the pre-emption act of the 15th June 1834, until the merits of the present controversy can be finally adjudicated and determined by a proper officer of the Government.

Respectfully
Henley & Lomax
Attys. of Jno. Lloyd

<==========>

War Department, Office of Indian Affairs
March 26, 1838

Hon. J.R. Poinsette
  Secty. of War.
Sir,

In compliance with your direction to report upon the letter of Messrs. Henley & Lomax, respecting the claim of Zadock Brashears [Jr], to state that the attention of the Department was called to this case by the Commr. of the Genl. Land Office on the 30 Nov. 1836. That officer was informed on the 30th December, following, that Brashears, a part of whose reserve is claimed by Lloyd, having had assigned to him only the quantity to which, according to the official register of the Indian Agent, which register the President had directed should be the sole guide, he was entitled under the treaty. The affidavits forwarded by Lloyd, which did not preclude the possibility of Brashears having been married prior to 1826, could not be admitted as sufficient to warrant an alteration in the quantity of land set apart for him. Subsequently, on the 4th February 1837, the Hon. Mr. Lewis, requested the suspension of the decision of the Department on this case, to enable him to procure evidence. He was informed on the 8th of the same month, that a reasonable time would be allowed for that purpose. And it was recommended that the evidence should be taken either before Col. Martin, the locating agent, or Mr. A.D. Brown, the certifying agent, and, that reasonable notice of the time and place should be given to the opposing party. Since this last date no information respecting this case has been received from Mr. Lewis. But, on the 27th ulto, there was referred by you to this office a communication from Messrs. Simpson and Moore of the 10th ulto, enclosing, at the request of Messrs. Henley & Lomax, certain papers, purporting to be affidavits adverse to the claim of Brashears, and of the character they are now engaged in procuring. This case, with others under the same treaty, will be prepared, as early as practicable, for your action and that of the President. But should you deem it expedient to allow Messrs. Henley & Lomax a further time to provide testimony, they can be informed of your decision, and the further consideration of the case be suspended for the present. Their letter is herewith returned.

Very resp.
(no signature)

<===========>

War Department, Office of Indian Affairs
March 27, 1838

Messrs. Simpson & Moore
  Demopolis, Alabama
Gentlemen,
The Secretary of War has referred to this office your letter of the 10th ulto. with the papers accompanying it, respecting the loction made for Zadock Brashears [Jr], under the 14th article of the Choctaw Treaty of 1830.
Very Resp.
(no signature)

(EDITORIAL NOTE: - Only the last two pages of the following document are available. The date of this document is unknown; however, the affidavits which it transmitted are all dated in April, 1838.)
The letter continues -
then supposed to be pregnant.

It appears however from the return of the agent that in addition to the section located to Brashiers himself, he obtained a half section for a child over ten and a quarter section each for two children under ten; making, in amount, the same quantity he would have been entitled to if he had four children under ten. It, therefore, clearly appears that Zadoc Brashiers [Jr] reservation included a full quarter section more then he was legally entitled to either from the ages or the number of his children. Had a true statement of facts then been made to the Agent at the time of the Registration, Brashiers would only have obtained Section 11 in which was his residence, and four hundred and eighty acres (being one quarter for each child in Sects. 14 & 23, which would be the land more immediately adjacent to the Section allotted to him. And under the provisions of the treaty, his reservation could not then have embraced any part of the South-West quarter of Sec. (_?_), the land claimed by Lloyd, the pre-emptor.

It is contended, however, that although Brashiers had no child over ten years of age, nor more than three children in epe. at the time of his registration, that he was legally entitled, under a liberal construction of the treaty, to an additional allotment of one quarter for the child in ventra va mere, and that had not, therefore, obtained more land than he was legally entitled to. The principle of law, that a child in ventra va mere can only claim by inheritance or devisee is too well established to be now contested, and the terms of the treaty too obviously refer to children in epe to admit a doubt as to the proper application, and the Government cannot, in justice, by indulging in a liberal construction of this Article of the Treaty, disregard the established rights of conflicting claimants.

The pre-emptor is perfectly willing to submit his case to the decision of the Department upon a fair statement of the facts, which would have been long since forwarded but for the difficulty in obtaining the affidavits of the several witnesses, some of whom now reside at an inconvenient distance, and it will no doubt be ascertained by references to the proper depository in the Department, that the same facts now set forth, were proved in affidavits, transmitted to the Department some years since.

Respectfully
Henley & Lomax
Attys. of Thos. Lloyd

<============>

The State of Alabama)
Sumter County   )ss

Personally came and appeared before me, Samuel B. Boyd, an acting Justice of the Peace, duly elected, commissioned and qualified in and for the county above written, Hardy Abney, who, being first duly sworn the truth to tell, deposes and says that he was well acquainted with Zadoc Brashiers, Junr., a reservee under the 14th Article of the Treaty of Dancing Rabbit Creek between the U.S. Government and the Choctaw tribe of Indians. At the date of said treaty and afterwards till the time of his death which occurred some time in the year 1832. That he, this deponent, does not himself know how many or the ages of the children the said Zadoc had at the date of ratification of the said treaty, but that some time in January or February 1832, he, this deponent, had a conversation with the said Zadoc Brashiers who then informed this deponent that he, the said Zadoc, was registered as a reservee under the 14th Article of the said treaty and that, at the time he, the said Zadoc, so registered himself as a reservee, that for the purpose of obtaining a larger portion of land than he would be otherwise entitled to, he, the said Zadoc, had given in to the agent of the Government a larger number of children than he really had at the time of such registration, in-as-much as he, the said Zadoc, as he then admitted to this deponent, had included in the number of his children so given in to the Agent, a child of which his then, said Zadoc's wife, was at the date of his registration, supposed to be pregnant and that he, the said Zadoc, then expected to obtain for this child the same quantity of land to which the child would have been entitled had the said child been born before the date of his registration as aforesaid.

/s/ Hardy Abney

Sworn to and subscribed before me
this 4th day of April, A.D. 1838
  /s/ James B. Boyd
   Justice of the Peace
Attest.: Price Williams, Clerk, County Court,
      Sumter County, Alabama.

<===========>

The State of Alabama)
Sumter County)[ss]
    Before me, Joseph Arrington, an acting Justice of the Peace in and for the county, aforesaid, personally came Sarah Leah, wife of James Leah, known to me as a resident of Maringo, and to be of good character for truth and veracity, who being by me first duly sworn, deposes and says that she was well acquainted with Zadoc Brashears, Junr., deceased, in his life time, who was a reservee under the 14th Article of the Treaty of Dancing Rabbit Creek, and also, with the family of the said Zadoc Brashears, Junr. She further sayeth that at the date of the said treaty of Dancing Rabbit Creek the said Zadoc Brashears, Junr., had but three children, all of whom were under ten years of age by several years. The said Zadoc Brashears, Junr., was married about they year 1826 or 1827 and all of his children were

borned after that time. She further saith that she is not interested in any manner what-so-ever, either to establish or defeat the claim of the said Zadoc Brashears, to any part of his reservation.

Her
/s/ Sarah X Leah
Mark

Sworn to and subscribed before me
this 7th day of April, A. D. 1838
  /s/ Joseph S. Arrignton
  Justice of the Peace
  Attest: Price Williams, Clerk, County Court,
      Sumter County, Alabama.

<===========>

The State of Alabama)
Sumter County)^{ss}

Before me, J. Pennington, an acting Justice of the Peace in and for the county aforesaid, personally came Emeline Brashears, wife of Alexander Brashears, known to me as a resident of said county and to be of good character for truth and veracity, who, being by me first duly sworn deposes and says that she was well acquainted with Zadoc Brashears, Junr., deceased, in his life time, who was a reservee under the 14th Article of the treaty of Dancing Rabbit Creek, and also, with the family of the said Zadoc Brashears, Junr. She further saith that at the date of the said Treaty of Dancing Rabbit Creek the said Zadoc Brashears, Junr., had but three children, all of whom were under ten years of age by several years. The said Zadoc Brashears, Junr., was married about the year 1826-1827 and all of his children were born after that time. She further saith that she is not interested in any manner what-so-ever either to establish or defeat the claim of the said Zadoc Brashears, Junr., to any part of his reservation.

/s/ Emeline Brashears

Sworn to and subscribed before me
this (-?--) day of April, A.D. 1838.
  J. Pennington
  Justice of the Peace.
  Attest: Price Williams, Clerk, County Court,
      Sumter County, Alabama.

<=============>

The State of Alabama)
Maringo County)^{ss}

Before me, A.R. Manning, a Justice of the Peace in and for the county and state aforesaid, personally appeared Luke M. Grigsby who is personally well known to me, and on oath duly administered, deposes and says that he resided in Sumter County, in the State aforesaid, and in the immediate vicinity of John Loyd of said county during the years 1833, 1834 and 1835. That he was well acquainted with the location and condition of the tracts of land thereabout and that the said John Loyd did not cultivate and had no improvement of any sort on the half-quarter, or eighth of a section which was located for and granted to Ann Brashiers, relic. of the late Zaddock Brashiers, as her reservation, under the treaty entered into and contracted by the Choctaw Tribe of Indians on the one part and the United States on the other part at Dancing Rabbit Creek in the year 1830, which half-quarter, aforesaid, is the west half of the southwest quarter of Section No. one, in Township No. seventeen in Range No. one West in the district of lands for sale at the Land Office at Demopolis in the State aforesaid.

/s/ Luke M. Grigsby

Sworn to and subscribed
before me this seventeenth day
of May anno domini 1838 -
/s/ A. R. Manning
Justice of the Peace
Attest: Ann Robinson, Clerk, County Court,
Marengo County, Alabama.

<=============>

The State of Alabama)
Sumter County)^{ss}

Personally came before me, Jno. R. Larkins, an acting Justice of the Peace in and for said county, Wm. Fluker who says on oath duly administered that he resides in the above named county in the state, aforesaid and in the immediate vicinity of John Loyd of said county during the years 1833, 1834 and

1835. That he was well acquainted with the location and condition of the tracts of land thereabout and that the said John Loyd did not cultivate and had no improvement of any sort on the half quarter or eighth of a section which was located for and granted to Ann Brashears, relic. of the late Zadock Brashears [Jr] as her reservation under the treaty entered into and contracted by the Choctaw Tribe of Indians, on the one part, and by the United States, of the other part, at Dancing Rabbit Creek in the year 1830, which half quarter is the west half of the southwest quarter of Section one, Township seventeen, Range one West in the district of Land Sale at Demopolis in the state aforesaid.

/s/ Wm. Fluker

Subscribed to and sworn
before me this 22nd May 1838.
/s/ Jno. R. Larkins, J. P.
Attest: Price Williams, Clerk, County Court,
      Sumter County, Alabama.

<=========>

F. Hartley Crawford, the Commissioner of Indian Affairs, summarized the case as follows, and recommended it to the Secretary of War and the President:

The controversy between Zadock Brashears' heirs and John Lloyd and Peter Dawson seems to present the following facts. By the 14th Section of the treaty of Dancing Rabbit Creek, of September 1830, with the Choctaw Nation "each Choctaw head of a family, being desirous to remain and become a Citizen of the States, shall be permitted to do so, by signifying his intention to the Agent within six months from the ratification of this treaty, and he or she shall thereupon be entitled to a reservation of one Section of six hundred and forty acres of land, to be bounded by sectional lines of survey, in like manner shall be entitled to one half that quantity for each unmarried child which is living with him over ten years of age, and a quarter section to such child as may be under ten years of age, to adjoin the location of the parent."

Under this provision, Col. William Ward was appointed an Agent to ascertain who were entitled and to how much — to receive their notices of intention and to register their claims accordingly. He made a report to this Office on the 11th of February 1832, by which it appears that he, on the 13th June 1831, registered Zadock Brashears as entitled to a Section in his own right, a half section for one child over ten years of age and a quarter section for each of two children under ten years.

On the 26th day of June 1833, George W. Martin, Esq., was appointed to locate the land to which Choctaw heads of families were entitled under this and other articles of the treaty. On the 3d of September, 1833, he was instructed as follows - "in locating the reservations of children, which are to adjoin the tracts of their parents, it is not necessary that the reservations of a parent and child should adjoin each other along the whole extent of one of their lines. It is sufficient that they actually adjoin, whether upon the corners or the sides." The rights of Zadock Brashears under these instructions were located on the 29th September, 1834 on the west half of section 14, the west half of the south west quarter of section 1, north fractional section 23 (that part of 23 known as N.E. (--?--)(illegible) and section 11, Township 17, Range 1 west. This is the title of Z. Brashears.

In an argument submitted by his counselor, Hon. F.S. Lyon, it is, however, stated that instead of three children, one of whom was over ten years of age, he had four under ten, one of whom was born on 2d May, 1831, that is, after the making and ratification (24th February 1831) of the treaty, and before the notice was given to the Agent, Mr. Ward. Mr. Lyon insists that Brashears is entitled for the child of (February?).

It is unnecessary to decide this question, for the President, United States, on an appeal to him to correct an alleged error in Ward's register, on the 16th November, 1836, made this decision. "The register of Indian claims under the 14th Section of the Choctaw treaty, is the only testimony that can be received, the records kept by him (Col. Ward, Indian Agent) is the only evidence that we can receive, therefore, the claim of Jim Tom, for more land than he and his family are entitled to agreeably to this register, cannot be allowed. No float under the 14th Section can be allowed — They must include and be adjoining to the improvement. This determination, I conceive, is binding on me, and makes the register conclusive.

Another difficulty suggests itself to my mind. The tracts in right of the children must adjoin that in the parents name. It was a question whether each child's reservation must adjoin the parents - or whether if one of the former touches the latter it was sufficient. It was found often impracticable to carry out the former idea by reason of contiguous improvements. Besides as all the reservations in fact belonged to this parent, it has been thought that if one joined his improvement, the next bounded that and so on, it would be a compliance with the treaty; the object of which was to give the reservee a compact body and to prevent him from running over this district after the best land. The practice has been in accordance and the rights of Z. Brashears have been so located. Betsy Buckles was similarly located, and the President has approved the assignment to her, which seems to fit the construction of the treaty. The title of Zadock Brashears would then appear to be good, if there is not a better one in Lloyd or Dawson.

John Lloyd claims south west quarter of Section 1, Township 17, Range 1 west, and Peter Dawson North east quarter of Section 11, same Township and Range with the claim of the former, it will be seen that Zadock Brashears' location conflicts to the extent of one half, and with the whole of the claim of Dawson.

It appears that Messrs. Lloyd and Dawson made their settlements after the treaty of Dancing Rabbit Creek was concluded — and the former represents that he has "dwelling houses and cribs, smoke house, etc., with 60 acres of cleared and improved land." By the treaty (18th Art.) no settlements were to be permitted until the Choctaws would remove, that is, it is conceived until the time of their removal, as arranged in the treaty, should come round, which by the third article is fixed for one half of them in the falls of 1831 & 1832, and for the residue, in the Autumn of 1833. The preemption law of 1834 (19th June) enables Lloyd & Dawson to enter the lands they now claim if they belonged to the United States.

There is on file a certificate from the Register and Receiver at Demopolis, setting forth that Peter Dawson, on the 12th December 1835, adduced satisfactory evidence of his right to preemption under the act of 19th June 1834, on the North East quarter of Section 11, Township 17, Range 1, West. It is stated in a letter from the General Land Office on file, of 30th November 1836, that a similar application was made by John

Lloyd, but Luke M. Grigsby & William Fluker testify that they lived in Sumter County in the immediate vicinity of John Lloyd during the years 1833, 1834 & 1835, and that they were well acquainted with the locations & condition of the tracts of land thereabouts and that the said Lloyd did not cultivate and had no improvement of any sort on the West half of the South West quarter of Section 1, Township 17, Range 1 West, which was located for and granted to Ann Brashears, widow of Zadock Brashears [Jr]. This testimony is not contradicted.

Messrs. Dawson & Lloyd assail the title in right of Zadock Brashears by proving that he had but 3 children when the treaty was made, all under ten years of age, and that he was married in 1826 or 1827. One of the witnesses testifies that Mrs. Ann Brashears allowed him an inspection of her family Bible, from which he gives an extract, that shows she had three children before the treaty and a fourth born after, viz., 2nd May 1831 - which is in accordance with the admission of her counsel, Mr. Lyon. The youngest of the four, Mr. Fluker proves, died in the year 1833, and Hardy Abney testifies that Zadock told him he had given in to the Agent four children, altho he had only three born, his wife being then pregnant with the fourth. This relation is inconsistent with the register of Col. Ward, and with the fact that at the time that register was made and when Zadock Brashears made his return to the Agent on 13 June 1831, the four children were in actual being, the youngest having been born on 2nd May. The complainants object further to the location for Zadock Brashears because it would seem, every part of it does not adjoin the tract in the parent's name and because they say the Agent should have gone South of Sucknatache.

In relation to streams, the 5th paragraph of the instructions of 3d September 1833 to George W. Martin, says "all streams, which by the return of the Surveyors, made fractional Sections and sub-divisions will be considered as making fractions in all cases of Indian locations. When the stream is not of such a size as to make fractions for the purpose of sale it will not make them in the case of Indian locations. On this subject some testimony is adduced, but in the view taken, it does not appear to be very material.

The claim of Brashears was consummated by the ratification of the treaty, which vested in him an indisputable right to land under the 14th Article. He would be entitled to more or less as his family might consist of more or fewer children. It has been proved and is admitted, that the reservee had 3 children under ten years of age at the making of the treaty, that a fourth was born to him after the ratification of it and before he applied to the Agent to be registered, and that in the year 1833, the last child died. It has been contended strenuously that the infant in *ventra va mere*, both at the making and ratifying of the treaty, gave as much claim to a quarter section of land as any of the others, because it is said it had existence in legal contemplation — and because it was born before the notice was given to Col. Ward.

Much might be said on the other side — it was not living with its father within the probable meaning of the treaty, either when made or ratified, and it would seem that it was not returned to the Register, for he returns only three children. But it is unnecessary to dwell upon the question for the register in regarded as decisive of it. It has been so determined by the President, United States, in the case of Jim Tom already referred to. By this register he is entitled to the quantity of land located for him.

Was it rightly placed, or is the manner and form of the location such as to require that it be disapproved? As already stated, the course pursued in this case is the one which has been approved by the Executive and the objection urged against it is thought to be untenable. In point of fact, the location was made on the 29th September, 1834, and the application of Peter Dawson was made for entry at the Land Office, at Demopolis, on the 12th December 1835. When Lloyd's was made is not known precisely. Here is a period of upwards of 14 months, within which it is not known that any steps were taken to correct the location for Brashears. There is no testimony of the precise time when either Dawson or Lloyd came into the Choctaw Country. They settled there with a full knowledge of Indian rights. When the improvements of either of them were made is no where proved, and there is positive evidence that Mr. Lloyd had no improvements of any sort on the West half of South West quarter of Section 1, Township 17, Range 1, West in 1833, 1834 or 1835. These cases may be and I dare say are hard, but taking the whole circumstances into view it appears to me the location made in right of Zadock Brashears [Jr] should be approved.

/s/ F. Hartley Crawford

4 March 1842
I concur in the opinion of the Commissioner,
     /s/ (illegible; prob Commr, Land Office)
     Approved 8 March 1842
     /s/ T. Tyler [President of the United States]

<============>

War Department, Office of Indian Commissioner
9 March 1842

Hon. Shields of Ala.
 House of Reps., U. S.
Sir:
     I have the honor to inform you that the President of the United States has approved the report of this office in relation to the location under the 14th Article of the Choctaw treaty of 1830, of the reservation of Zadock Brashears, [Jr] dec'd., (now occupied by his widow, Anne Brashears) and that the Commissioner of the General Land office will be informed to-morrow that this office knows of no objection to the emanation of the Patent.
          /s/ (illegible)

<============>

War Department, Office of Indian Commissioner
10 March 1842

E. M. Huntington, Esq.
 Commr. Genl. Land office
Sir:
     The President of the United States approved on 8 instant, the location made under 14 Article Choctaw treaty of 1830, for Zadock Brashears, usually called Zadock Brashears, Jr., in his own right and that of two children under and one child over ten years of age. The tracts of land selected as his reservation are being noted by the locating agent as the W ½ of Section 14, the West half of the South West quarter of Section 1, that part of fractional Section 23, known as N.E. ¼, and Lot A, and Section 11, all in Township 17, of Range 1, West, Demopolis land Dist.,

Alabama and containing 1262 88/100 acres, according to map of survey in your office.

This department is satisfied that the stipulation in the treaty, in regard of five years residence on the reservation has been complied with; the proof on file here showing that, after the reservee died shortly after the treaty was concluded, his widow, Anne Brashears, with her family continued in the occupancy of the land. No objection is now known to the emanation of a Patent.

Hon. B.G. Shields of Alabama has been informed of this approval by the President and that you would be apprised that no objection exists on the part of this office to the issuing of a patent.

/s/ (illegible)

<===========>

General Land Office
March 18, 1842

F. Hartley Crawford, Esq.
  Comr. of Ind. Affs.
Sir:

In your letter to me of the 10th Inst., referring to the approval on the 8th Inst, of the "location made under the 14th Article Choctaw Treaty of 1830, for Zadock Brashears, usually called Zadock Brashears, Jr., you state that "the tracts of lands selected as his reservation are designated by the locating Agent as the (1) w ½ of Section 14, (2) the W ½ of the SW ¼ of Section 1, (3) that part of fractional Section 23 known as N. E. ¼ and Lot a, and (4) Section 11, all in Township 17 of Range 1 West, Demopolis Land District, Alabama, and containing 1262 88/100 acres according to map of Survey in this Office."

It is as to the 3rd tract, above alluded to, that I desire an explanation, and, in order to be clearly understood, I send a diagram of the N part of fract'd. Sect. 23 and request that you will inform me whether under the description given in your letter, I am to treat all the land East of the "Su can no chee" and in the North part of the fractional section, viz., Lot A, 53 acres, the two 40 acres lots immediately East and contiguous thereto, Lot B, 50 acres, and the 40 acre lot immediately East and contiguous thereto, as embraced in this location. The aggregate of these lots is 22 acres, and the other lands described by you, make up the quantity of 1262 88/100 acres stated in your letter.

You will perceive from the diagram that there is no such subdivision as the N.E. ¼ of Sec. 23 and that if ordered the quantity with that of Lot A of said section, and the other tracts represented by you as embraced in the location would reduce the whole quantity 10 acres.

You will find a yellow shade around the lots in Sec. 23, which it is presumed are intended to be embraced as the location, but which, under the description in your letter would not, strictly speaking, be included in said location.

Very respectfully

Your Ob. Servt.

/s/ E.M. Huntington, Commissioner

=========================

The description proposed to be given so as to embrace these lots is as follows: The Fraction, East of the Sucanochee River, of the North fractional half or part of fractional section 23, T17N R1W, contg. 223 acres.

EMR

<============>

War Department, Office of Indian Commissioner

Mar 26 1842

E. M. Huntington, Esq.

  Commr. G. L. Office

Sir:

In reply to your letter of 18th instant, relative to the approved location made for Zadock Brashears, Jr., under the 14th Art. Choctaw Treaty of 1830, I have to state that said approval is intended to cover all of the N ½ of Fractional Section 23, 17. 1 W lying East of the Sucanuchee to wit Lots A & B and the three 40 acre lots contiguous thereto making in all 223 acres.

Very res.   (no signature)

THE RESERVATION OF
TURNER BRASHEARS, II

v5841. 810. **Turner Brashears II**, b. 1809, s/o Zadock Brashears and Susannah Vaughn; m. 31 Oct 1829, *Ann Holland*, in Marengo Co, AL. Sarah Ann (Moncrief) Harlan (v51394) testified that he went away to school at Johnson Institute in Kentucky.

Take care not to confuse this Turner Brashears, II, with Turner Brashears, IV (v51222), a son of Vaughn Brashears, who was born in Indian Territory.

Turner is listed in the 1831 Choctaw census as having 40 acres in cultivation, 2 in family, 7 slaves, i.e., he apparently had only a wife, no children. He also registered in June 1831 at the Choctaw Trading post as having no children. He died without descendants, according to Sarah Ann (Moncrief) Harlan (v51394).

Turner was a beneficiary under Clause 19 of the Treaty of Dancing Rabbit Creek, 1830. The records show he received Lot No. 71 in Sec 13, T16N, R1E, and the north ½ of Sec 24, T1N, R1E (List of locations of Choctaw Reserves, Microfilm 7RA-116, roll 1, Federal Records Center).

In 1832, Turner is mentioned in Indian Commissioner's minutes as running a ferry across the Tombigbee River at Moscow, AL.

In 1834, he sold his allotment under the Treaty and moved to Oklahoma. In Indian Territory, he told Richard Brashears, ex-slave of Vaughn Brashears, that he was the cause of Zadock Jr's death. He may have been selling out and moving from bad conscience or to avoid reprisals.

Turner, II, left Alabama rather hastily, perhaps to escape reprisal or guilt in connection with his brother, Zaddock Jr's, death. But he may have had more on his conscience:

From Sarah Ann (Moncrief) Harlan's testimony before the Dawes Commission: "Well, gentlemen, I will tell you more now. This brother of my mother, Turner Brashears, was a rich, young, foolish man. He went to Mobile and married a woman of not the nicest character. My mother's people wouldn't allow him to bring her home, and he was mother's youngest brother, so he brought her to our house. She [the wife] tired of my uncle and started to leave; she was horseback. He started to follow her. This was told me by my mother.

She started back to Mobile horse-back, and he followed her and killed her. He came to tell mother good-bye, and his lawyer bonded him and he left here, and where he stopped I couldn't tell, but my uncle said he came here, but didn't state at what time. I don't know whether he stopped on the way or not. You know I have held that tragedy back in my accounts. My mother has told me about these things."

From *Territorial Papers of Alabama, National Archives*, v.3, p.78:
Turner Brashears, a reservee under the 19th [sic] Article of the Treaty of Dancing Rabbit Creek is registered and located for the ___?___ described tract of land — the register of land office at Demopolis is requested to reserve the same from sale and to make the map of lines accordingly.
September 27, 1834   /s/ Geo ___?___

I, Turner Brashears,[II], do hereby apply to locate the three quarter sections of four hundred and eighty acres of land allowed me under the 19th Article of the Treaty of Dancing Rabbit Creek upon the following described tract of land, fractional section 24 in Township seventeen, range one west, containing 432 50/100 acres [and] a lot [of] 37 acres in section twenty five, same township and range.
September 27, 1834   /s/ Turner Brashears

DEED OF CONVEYANCE
Know all men by these presents that I, Turner Brasher, of the Chaktaw Nation, resident in the Chartered limit of the State of Alabama, and entitled under deed by the provision of a Treaty made and concluded between the Chaktaw Nation of Indians and the United States of America to a reserve of three quarter sections of land, being four hundred and eighty acres commonly called Brashier Bluff, and located (? — It ran along the river just above the mouth of Suk En Atcha Creek; see "Map #2") reserve by cultivation to include the place and improvements; occupied by the said Turner Brashier at the time of the signing and execution of said Treaty; which said treaty was made and signed at a place called Dancing Rabbit Creek in said Chaktaw Nation in the month of September in the year 1830 by John T.C. Eaton,

and John Coffee, Commissioners, on the part of the United States and the Cheefs head men and warriors of said Nation. Now for and in consideration of the sum of seven hundred and fifty dollars to me, the said Turner Brashier, in hand paid by John C. McGrew and Daniel Womack of the State of Alabama ... I, have bargained and sold ... my rights, title, interest, and claim in and to the said four hundred and eighty acres of land commonly called Brasheirs Bluff ... In witness whereof I have hereunto set my hand and seal this 27th day of March 1832

/s/ Turner Brashiers (Seal)

Test: William Craig

Demopolis, Ala, 27 Oct 1835

I hereby certify that the purchase (?price, which) owners mention in the written deed of seven hundred fifty dollars was paid by John C. McGrew to Glover Gaines at the request of Turner Brashears, and that the said Turner Brashears was an intelligent half-breed, entirely capable of making his own contracts— and I am satisfied that there was no unfairness in the contract between him and John C. McGrew, as I never heard the least complaint on the part of Brashears. I further certify that the said Turner Brashears offered me the same land at the same price it was sold to McGrew.

/s/ Allen Glover

Turner Brashears was apparently selling out, preparatory to moving to Choctaw Territory in Oklahoma.

Richard Brashears, ex-slave of Vaughn Brashears, testified in Dawes hearings that Turner Brashears, son of Old Zadock, "died here at Tuskahoma," Indian Territory.

13. THE LOST AND FOUND RESERVATION OF Susanna (Brashears) Stewart-Graham

The case of Susanna Brashears, daughter of Zadock Brashears Sr and Susannah Vaughn, illustrates another aspect of Col. William Ward's ineptitude, chicanery, or at least his penchant for making errors where Choctaws were concerned. This is not to say that Susanna and her children were without their share of chicanery in the exercise of their greed.

Some time after 1829, Susanna left her long-time home in Feliciana Parish, LA, and moved to Holmes Co, MS, where she took up land near Rankin within the old Choctaw Nation, apparently so she would qualify for benefits under Article 14 of the Treaty of Dancing Rabbit Creek.

The names of Susanna Graham, a half-breed woman, and her daughter, Anne V. Llewellyn, appear on Ward's register, dated 13 Aug 1831, of Choctaws who wished to become citizens according to the provision of the treaty of 1830. Susanna had one child over ten [John Brashears Stewart; he was actually just over 16. Her three daughters were all married.] (see register in a separate chapter; also evidence offered in a Dawes hearing in 1901, with reference to *American State Papers*, v.7, p.133).

In the 1831 census of Choctaws to determine the beneficiaries of the Treaty of Dancing Rabbit Creek, Susanna Graham was cultivating 110 acres near Rankin, Holmes Co, MS, in Greenwood LeFlore's District, valued at $640. She listed five in the family, 1 male over 16, which would be her son, John Brashears Stewart. She was entitled to a section in her own right and a half section in right of her son.

However, her claim to her own land was mishandled and her

property was sold to H.C. Adams, Esq, on 11 Nov 1833. (See case No. 325, by Wm. Medill, Commissioner of Indian Affairs, Bk A, p.573.)

Correspondence from the Dawes hearings gives us a clue as to what happened: "In accordance with the provision of the 14th article of the treaty of 1830, the Government directed an agent of the Choctaws in Mississippi to register the names of those Choctaws who might desire to remain and become citizens of the States. The records of the Government show that this agent failed to register and report to the Government the names of many Choctaws who did really signify to him their intention to remain in Mississippi and take advantage of the provision of the 14th article of the treaty of 1830.

"On this account, in many instances, the land upon which the Indians had improvements, and which they desired reserved for them under said 14th article, was sold by the Government at public land sales, and the Choctaw Indians were deprived of their land.

"This action of the Government caused many complaints by the Choctaws, and Congress passed an Act approved on March 3, 1837, providing for the appointment of a Commission whose duty it should be to come to Mississippi and hear evidence in cases where Choctaws might claim that they had complied with the provision of the treaty, but had not received land thereunder. By the Act of Congress approved February 22, 1838, this commission was continued until August 1st, 1838. A commission was appointed by the President and the Commissioners came to Mississippi and heard a few of the applications for right under the 14th article of the treaty of 1830, but in the time allowed by the Act of Congress under which they were appointed, they were able to hear only a comparatively small number of the cases.

"Prior to August 1, 1838, this commission made a report of their work; later Congress provided for another commission by an Act of Congress approved August 23, 1842. This second commission also was to hear cases of Choctaws who claimed they had complied with the provisions of article 14 of the treaty of 1830, but had not received any benefits thereunder. This second commission was duly appointed by the President and the Commissioners came to Mississippi and heard a large number of cases.

"The Act of Congress of August 23, 1842, provided that in case it should be finally determined that a Choctaw had complied in all respects with the provisions of article 14 of the treaty of 1830, but that his land had been sold by the Government, he should be entitled to select land from the public domain in the States of Mississippi, Alabama, Louisiana, or Arkansas, and that a certificate to that effect should be given him. These certificates were called scrip."

When her land was sold, Susanna apparently moved across the county line into Carroll Co (or the boundary lines moved) and she appealed through her attorney, F.E. Plummer, who was a lawyer and a member of the U.S. House of Representatives. On 26 Jan 1846, her claim was finally recommended for approval, and approved by the President of the U.S. on 2 Feb

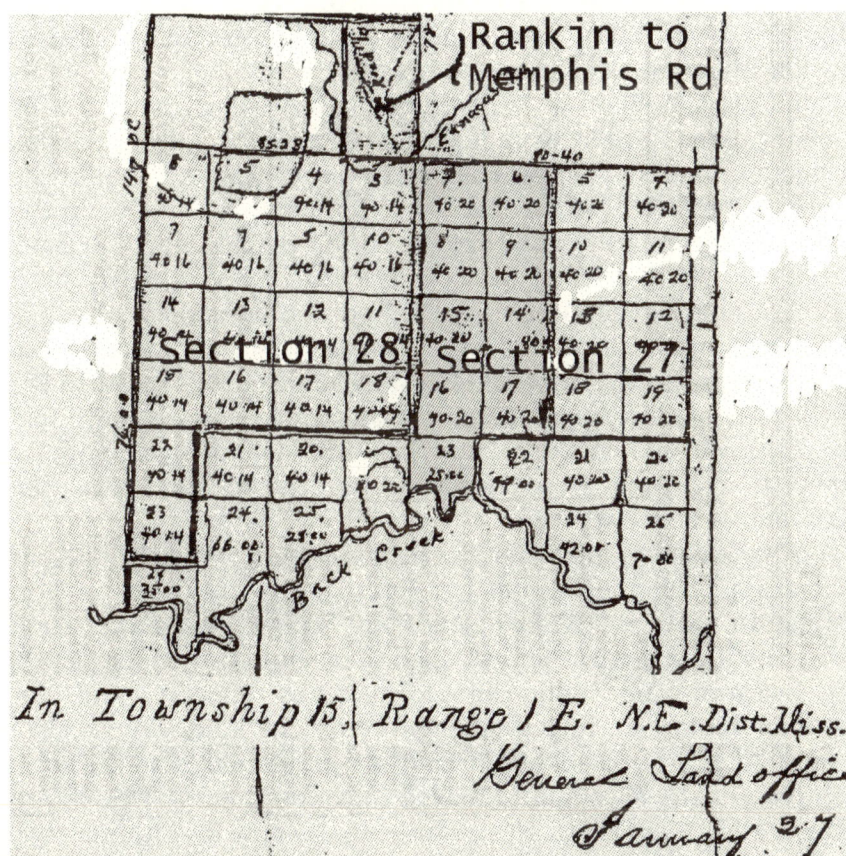

Figure 25: Susanna (Brashears) Stewart-Graham's Reservation in Holmes Co, MS, under Article 14, Treaty of Dancing Rabbit Creek

1846. Her reservation was "laid out on the following described land: viz, Lots 6, 7, 8, 9, 14, 15, 16, 17, and 23 of Section 27, Township 15, Range 1 East, all in the North Eastern Land District of Mississippi. Proof of residence as required by the Treaty has been recently submitted to this office (Secretary of War, Department of Indian Affairs), and the location, as above designated, does not appear to interfere with any other Reservation, I, therefore respectfully recommend that the location of the said reservation be approved by the President of the United States." Wm. Medill, General Land Office, January 27, 1846.

Anne V. Llewellyn was allotted land adjoining, but Annie died about 1833; presumably her claim went to her son, Joseph R. Plummer, who was hardly two months old and in the care of his grandmother, Susanna (Brashears) Stewart-Graham. The east ½ of Sec 27, T15 R1E, was reserved for John Brashears Stewart, son of Susanna Graham.

In 1836, William W. Walton, being duly sworn, said that he was well acquainted with Susanna Graham, a mixed blooded Choctaw woman, that he knew her ever since 1829, that at the date of the late Choctaw Treaty of Dancing Rabbit Creek, the 30th day of Sept 1830, the said Susanna resided north of Back Creek in the district of the county ceded by said treaty on a tract of land designated on the map of the published survey of said land made since said treaty, on Sect. No. 27, in Township 15, Range one East, in what is now called Holmes County in the said state of Mississippi. That said Susanna Graham continued to reside on said section of land from the date of said treaty for more than 5 years from the ratification thereof until after the 24th day of February 1836.

(One might doubt this sworn statement, considering that Susanna was possibly off her land during this time and in litigation over it. White men were known to make such statements to create clear title, so they could buy Indian land!)

Susanna, her son, John Brashears Stewart, and her grandson, Joseph R. Plummer, lived on the land a number of years. After John died, about 1845-47, Susannah sold the land, rented out the slaves, and moved to Hinds County, MS, where she died 5 May 1850. Her grandson, Joseph R. Plummer Jr, moved to Indian Territory and was recognized as a Choctaw by blood in 1883. (For more, see "The Burton Grab" in chapter 17.)

Family of Susanna Brashears
and John Benjamin Stewart

[8]5. ***Susanna Brashears**, (d/o Zadock Brashears Sr and Susannah Vaughn), b. c1793, probably in AL, on Zadock's land grant on the Tombigbee River, d. Hinds Co, MS, 5 May 1850; m.1. 6 May 1805, at New Feliciana, (St. Joseph's Church, file 5, folder 6, Vol. 3, Diocese of Baton Rouge), **John Benjamin Stewart**, (4 ch) b. 1784, d. Feliciana Parish bef 28 Sept 1820 (*VA Gazette Genealolgy*, 1959, p.108), s/o Guillermo (William) Stewart and Anne Brand; m.2. _____ **McKneely** (no ch); m.3. **George _David_ Graham**, (no ch).

The area was not served regularly by the Catholic Church, so John Benjamin Stewart and Susanna Brashears were first married in a protestant civil ceremony in March, 1804. Then a Declaration of Marriage between John Benjamin Stewart and Susannah Brashears was registered (in Spanish) in St Joseph's Cathedral, Diocese of Baton Rouge, 6 May 1805.

We know nothing at all about Susanna's second marriage; just that when she married George David Graham in a protestant, civil ceremony on 18 Sept 1827, she was called Susan McNeely.

"To the Judge of the Parish of St Tammany: The petition of David Graham of said Parish represents that he is about to enter into a contract of marriage with Susannah McKneely, and that he has charge of a Schooner, which must necessarily remain idle until said marriage takes place. He therefore ask that the notices required by law may be dispensed with and license may issue."   David Graham

State of Louisiana
Parish of St. Tammany

We the under signers do certify that David Graham and Susannah McKneely was married agreeable to the rules and regulations of the state the 18 of September in the year of our lord 1827, by

John Crawford, J.P.	David Graham
Daniel Cujec (?)	Susan McKneely
Elias Wilson	
E. Singeltary	

We do not know what happened to George David Graham; almost immediately, Susanna was acting as head of the family. Not long after the marriage, she moved (apparently with only her son, John Brashears Stewart, and her daughter, Anne V. (Stewart) Llewellyn) to Holmes Co, MS.

Family of Susanna Brashears and John Benjamin Stewart: (re: Testimony in 1901 and 1906 before Dawes Commission by Joseph R. Plummer, Susan C. Marshall, Susan S. Burton, Lillie Fountain, and Laura McPhail in reference to the application of Susan S. Burton and others for recognition as Choctaws by blood.)

v5 1161.   9 1. Mary Brashears Stewart, b. c1809, d. 1833; m. 27 Sep 1827, Hardy S. Crump, b. c1800, AL, d. after 1850

v5 1162.   10 1. *Susan Stewart Crump, b. 6 Jul 1828 (73 in 1901), Feliciana Parish, LA, d. 4 Mar 1921, Duncan, OK; m. 10 Dec 1851, Henry David Burton, b. 25 Oct 1826, Jackson, MS, d. 17 Sep 1892, Hazlehurst, MS. See "The Burton Grab" in the last chapter for their children.

v5 1163.   10 2. John B. Crump; m. 7 April 1853, Ann Trawick
v5 1164.   10 3. James Crump,
v5 1165.   10 4. Cornelius Crump,
v5 1166.   10 5. Laurie Crump,
v5 1167.   10 6. Emily Crump,

v5 1168.   9 2. Susan P. Stewart, b. c1811, Feliciana Parish, LA, d. bef 13 Feb 1854; m. 5 Oct 1828, East Feliciana Parish, LA, Dr. Ephraim Loyd.

v5 1169.   10 1. Susannah Loyd; m. Dr. _____ Fisher, of Carroll Co, MS

v5 1170.   10 2. _____ Loyd, minor heir in 1854
v5 1171.   10 3. _____ Loyd, minor heir in 1854

v5 1172.   9 3. Anne Vaughn Stewart, b. c1813, d. c1833; m.1. Samuel J. Llewellyn, m.2. Joseph R. Plummer Sr, Annie V. Llewellyn registered as a Choctaw in 1831.

v5 1173.   10 1. Joseph R. Plummer Jr, b. 1833, only child; said he was raised by his grandmother, Susanna (Brashears) Stewart-Graham, from

the age of two months; registered by council
as Choctaw citizen, 1883.

[v5]1174. [9]4. John Brashears Stewart, b. c1814 (minor over 16
at time of Treaty of Dancing Rabbit Creek, 27
Sept 1830; over 16 in 1831), d. c1845-47, Holmes
Co, MS, bur Carroll Co, MS. John lived with his
mother on her Choctaw allotment in Carroll or
Holmes Co, MS. He was apparently unmarried;
his mother and his siblings were his heirs.

Descent of Lois (Tigert) Belk from Susanna, d/o Zadock and
Susannah (Vaughn) Brashears:

[8]4. Susanna Brashears, b. c1793, d. MS, 5 May 1850; m.1. 6
May 1805, at New Feliciana, John Benjamin Stuart or
Stewart, b. 1784

[9]1. Mary Brashears Stewart, b. c1809, d. 1833; m. 27 Sep 1827,
Hardy S. Crump, b. 1800 in Ala, d. after 1850

[10]1. Susan Stewart Crump, b. 6 July 1829, Feliciana Parish, d.
4 Mar 1921, Duncan, OK; m. Henry David Burton, b. 25 Oct
1821, Jackson, MS, d. 17 Sep 1892, Hazlehurst, MS

[11]1. John Ezra Burton, b. 30 Sep 1852, MS, d. 20 Feb 1899,
Indian Territory; m. Virginia Prestridge, b. 6 Oct 1855

[12]1. Sallie Virginia Burton, b. 24 Oct 1875, MS, d. 18 Sep 1952,
Ardmore, OK; m. Walter Marx, b. 12 Oct 1871

[13]x. Miriam Alberta Marx, b. 13 Jun 1898, Ms, d. 22 Aug 1940,
OK; m. Claude Allen Tigert, b. 1891

[14]x. Lois Tigert, m. Ensley Belk. Lois Belk used the wrong
Zadock Brashears in her application for membership in the
D.A.R. She erroneously used Zadock Brashears, s/o John
Brashears and Mary Dowell, of Anne Arundel Co, MD.

Some researchers have claimed four other children for
Susanna (Brashears) Stewart, among them: Joseph Wooten
Stewart, 26, m. 7 April 1831, in Hinds Co, MS, Matilda Pullen,
16, d/o Henry Pullen and Margaret Looney. Witness to this
marriage was John B. Stewart.

Since John Brashears Stewart was over 16 that year, but
still a minor, it is impossible for this witness to be him, as some
have claimed. And, of course, John Benjamin Stewart had been
dead a number of years. This witness was from some other
Stewart family. This branch of Stewarts (and the Pullens) moved

before 1840 to Scott and Newton Co, MS.

Still others claim that Susanna Brashear and David Graham had a son, Galant Graham. This claim also seems to be a hoax, an attempt to claim Choctaw citizenship. For details and proof, see "The Burton Grab," in the last chapter.

William Stewart (Stuart) Sr, and his sons, William Jr, David B., James, and John Benjamin, were all living in the Thompsons Creek community and had accounts with the Chochan/Rheas General Store. In Spanish, Thompson's Creek was called Rio de la Feliciana; it separates East Feliciana from West Feliciana.

At the auction of the property of Paul Gardner, a bolt of Irish linen was cried out on the conditions that the bid must have secure bondsmen and be paid within fifteen months. Zedack Brashears offered seventeen pesos for the cloth, and he named his son-in-law, John B. Stewart as his bondsman. (East Feliciana Parish, Probate Records, Book ?, p.127)

In 1833, Susanna made her nephew, Wesley Brashears Trahern, her attorney to claim any part of Jesse Brashear's estate she could get. (which seems to me a little greedy.)

"For good and sufficient consideration, etc, placing full and entire confidence in my relative and friend, Wesley B. Trahan of Sumpter County, I, Susannah Brashears of E. Feliciana Parish, State of LA, appoint Wesley B. Trahan of Sumter County, State of Ala, my true and lawful attorney to sue, demand, etc, for all estate real and personal as I may have become entitled to in the State of Ala, as one of the legal heirs of Jesse Brashears, dec'd, late of the State of Alabama, whether by will and testament or by legal inheritance or any other manner whatsoever, etc."

19 Feb 1833 /s/ Susannah Brashears
Wits: George Lucas
John Freeland
East Feliciana Parish, Book C, p.309

The Squabble over Zadock's Land

On 28 Nov 1812, Zadock Brashears deeded to John and Susannah Stewart "a certain tract or parcel of land lying on Thompsons Creek, containing Eight Hundred Acres, adjoining the survey of Robert Vaughn on the North side, beginning at a

Laurel on said Thompson's Creek and running North seventy-one degrees East, two hundred and Ninety-five and one-third poles to the corner, thence North Nineteen degrees East, to the corner of a survey made for Manuel Monteguado, thence with the line of said survey to the corner on Thompson's Creek, thence running with the meanders of Thompson's Creek to the beginning, ..." (East Feliciana, Book A, p.45). Proved by Witnesses William Stewart and Alexander Pickard, 7 June 1813, before Llewellyn C. Griffith, Parish Judge.

The consideration for this "sale" was $6,000, but no money seems to have changed hands. A good number of people later testified that the deed was supposed to be a gift to Zadock's daughter, Susannah, and was to be considered her separate property. Zaddock made similar gifts to daughters Anne Lyles and Betsy Buckholtz.

However, on 19 Nov 1817, John Stuart and _____, his wife, transferred this property (this *may* have been a mortgage, since the family seems to continue to have control of the property later) to John C. Boon, for $3,000. "land situated and lying on the East side of Thompson's Creek, whereon Zadock Brashears formerly lived." (East Feliciana, Book A, p.175). John Stuart signed for himself AND wife.

After John Benjamin Stewart died, some of his descendants claimed rights to this property:

H.S. Crump
   vs.
Susanna Graham
The counsel for H.S. Crump and wife, contended that the land mentioned in plaintiff's petition is community property and that the deed of transfer from Zadock Brashear to John Stewart and his wife, Susanna, is evidence of an act of donation...
L. Andideas, attorney for Susanna Graham
A. Hartson, attorney for H.S. Crump and wife, Mary
        and for Ephraim Loyd and wife, Susan.

William Trahan testified that the transaction was intended to be an act of donation instead of a deed of transfer.

James Trahan (he called William Trahan his brother): "Colonel Kirkland was requested by Mr. Brashears to write a deed of conveyance from Zadock Brashears to his daughter,

Susanna Stewart, now Susanna Graham. Colonel Kirkland allowed he had no form, nor could he write a deed of conveyance of the kind warranted...."

[Zadock then apparently applied to James Trahan] "whether I could write such an instrument. My copy [apparently of a legal manual of some sort] has that I could write a conveyance in the usual form made use of in the state of Virginia, and consequently undertook to write one and wrote the deed above mentioned. Mr. Brashears made a calculation of the value of the land to be conveyed in the deed: which amount is put down in the deed, as he valued the land. ... was intended by the party as an act of donation from Zadock Brashears to his daughter, Susanna Stewart, now Susanna Graham, as cash in said deed and John Stewart was put in the deed as a matter of form ... [Stewart was supposed to understand] that the land was given as an act of donation to his wife by her father, Zadock Brashears" (East Feliciana Probate Court, Case No. 304, 13 April 1829).

The Estate of John Benjamin Stewart

The will of John B. Stewart, filed 29 Sept 1820, first in Feliciana Parish (Box 94), then, after the split of the parish, in East Feliciana Parish. The inventory of real and personal property, made by William Wade, Parish Judge, with assistants, Charles Elliott and William Stewart, included:

- 23 slaves, listed by name: William, Sally, Leah, Moses, Phoebe, Gregory, Ace, Chary, Judy, Febe, Rachel, Lucy, Carolyn, Lewis, Milky, Eliza, Stephen, Harriet, Routh, Frank, Masaih, Phaton, and George;
- tract of 500 acres, whereupon is situated the plantation house where the deceased late resided, estimated worth $6,000;
- 40 head of cattle, 5 horses, 5 beds, rifle, misc farming utensils;
- a deed from Zadock Brashears to John Stewart and Susanna Stewart for a tract of 50 arpents, lying in Feliciana Parish, 3 May 1811. (The land description: "beginning at a bay tree on Redwood Creek, North 71° W, 550 perches to a corner white oak, North 19° E, 120 Perches to Wesley Trahan's corner

with Haley, then Tra-
han's line North 71° E,
400 perches to his
corner Laurel on
Redwood, thence down
Redwood to the begin-
ning." (Feliciana Parish,
Book A, p.25-26,
witnesses John Scott,
James Trahan);

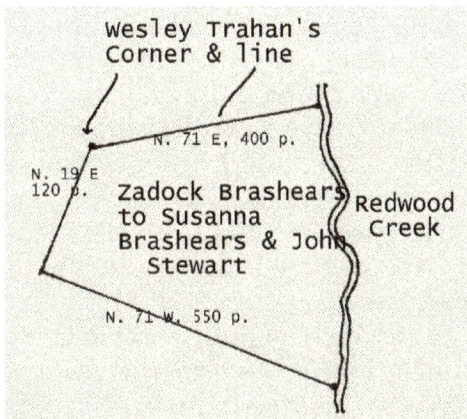

Figure 26: My drawing of Zadock's land on Redwood Creek. In earlier deeds, Wesley Trahan's corner and line were the corner and line of Manuel Monteguado.

- ▸ a C.L. Cosby and Feelor Skipworth Certificate of confirmation of a patent for 2370 acres of land, in favor of Zadock Brashear, Claim No. 52, dated 2 March 1819; (see text below)

- ▸ a number of notes due John Stewart and a number of bills outstanding, e.g. to Huken and Fletcher, for merchandise.

On 11 Nov 1820, Susanna Stewart, wife of John Stewart, dec'd, requested letters of tutorship to her children. William Culade, Parish Judge, named her tutor of the minor children, Mary B., Anne V., Susan P., and John Brashears Stewart. (Probate Records of Feliciana Parish, Book 2, p.106).

In 1821, Samuel McCaleb appeared before Judge Culade and asked for a letter of under tutorship to the minor Stewart children. The letter was granted 18 Jan 1821. (Probate Records of Feliciana Parish, Book 2, p.119).

Thomas U. Scott, Parish Judge, appointed Benjamin Kendrick and Thomas Scott (himself) to examine the tract of land in East Feliciana "whereon the said John Stewart did reside at the time of his death" and report "whether the said tract of land can be conveniently partitioned in kind between the said Susanna Graham and the heirs of John Stewart... in the following manner, one half (1/2) to Mrs. Graham and the remaining one half (1/2) between the heirs of John Stewart, dec'd, in equal portions, there being four heirs. (East Feliciana Probate Court, Case No. 304, 20 Oct 1830).

However, Susanna agreed to take "a child's portion of said community, in lieu of the one half of Jany 5th, 1829." (East Feliciana Probate Court, Case No. 304).

The estate amounted to $8,173.50. Each of the five heirs got slaves, land, and livestock equal to $1,634.70. The heirs were Susanna Graham, Mrs. Mary B. Crump, Mrs. Anne V. Llewellyn, Mrs. Susan P. Loyd, and John Brashears Stewart, a minor over 14 years of age, represented by his curator, Samuel McCaleb, Esq.

The heirs of John Benjamin Stewart tried also to claim the Cosby and Skipworth certificate of survey that was made to Zadock Brashears:

Land Office, ST. HELENA

Z. BRASHEARS)   PETITION NO. ____ (LEFT BLANK)
CERTIFICATE NO. 28)   Feliciana
dated 2[d] Nov[r] 1819)   April 26th, 1825

The heirs of Z. Brashears claim twenty three hundred and Seventy Arpens of land situate in the Parish of East Feliciana in Virtue of Certificate No 28, dated 2[d] Nobember 1819 and signed Charles S. Cosby, Reg[r], and Fulwar Skipwith, Rec[r], this claim being founded on a Survey executed by P. Tygart on the 9th day of September 1792. It is therefore ordered that said Claim be located and Surveyed in Strict conformity to the said original Survey of P. Tygart so as to include said quantity of twenty three hundred and Seventy aprens of land.

> Given under our hands this
> 26th Day of April, 1825
> (signed)   Saml J. Rannels, Regr
> Will Kinchen, Recr

(On the back are the following endorsements):
Principal Deputy Surveyors Office
Baton Rouge, 5th November 1829

I certify the within ~~Certificate~~ (struck out) Order of Survey to be a true copy of the Original order of Survey deposited in this office,
> Wm. Brown, Principal Deputy Surveyor

Received of William Brown, Principal Deputy Surveyor, the Order of Survey of which this is a Copy, the 5th day of Nov[r] 1819,
> James Trahern

(On the four-fold (outside) are the following clerk's notations):
Order of Survey for
    2370 Arps
Zadoc Brashears
    Cosby, 1813, B, 52
    Cert 28
S 46, T2S, R1E, &
S 40, T3S, R1E

The certificate is apparently filed in Book B, p.52. Zadock, of course, was far from dead, but Susanna and her children seem to be making a claim on the land here in the early 1820s.

The Squabble over Susanna's Estate

<u>Will of Susanna Graham</u>: 30 April 1850. In the name of God, amen. I, Susanna Graham, residing in the county of Hinds in the State of Mississippi, being of sound mind and disposing mind and memory, do hereby make and constitute this, my last will and testament, in manner and form as following:

First, I give and bequeath unto my daughter, Mary B. Crump, in addition to which I have heretofore given her during her natural life and after her death, to her children, one Negro woman, named Hannah, and her child, Lucinda, and one Negro boy named Jackson.

Second, I give and bequeath to my daughter Susan P. Loyd, in addition to what I have heretofore given her during her natural life and after her death to her children, one Negro man, named Morris, and a Negro woman, named Floras and her child, Lizzy.

Third, I give and bequeath to my grandson, Joseph R. Plummer, Junior, the following: Negro man named Stephen, one named Zachariah, one boy named Lance, one boy named Abram, one boy named William, and one Negro woman named Martha, known and called by the name Patsy, one Negro named Rachel and her son Cyrus, and also one Negro girl named Betsy, during his natural life, and then to the lawful heirs of his body. But, should the said Joseph R. Plummer, Junior, die without heirs of his body, then it is my will and desire that the Negroes herein given to him, shall go/belong to in equally valuable portions, my daughters, Mary B. Crump and Susan P. Loyd, if living during their natural lives and then to their children: but if dead at the time of death of said Joseph R. Plummer, Jr, without heirs of his body, given to him, to go to and be divided among the children of my daughters above named.

I do hereby further give and bequeath unto my grandson, Joseph R. Plummer, Junior, all my household furniture, whatever it may be.

I do further ordain, and hereby appoint my nephew, William Trahan, the guardian of the property given above to Joseph R. Plummer, Jr, until he shall be of lawful age to transact and manage the same. [Joseph was 17 at the time.]

I do hereby constitute and appoint my nephew, William Trahan, my executor, to execute this my last will and testament.

Given under my hand and seal this 13th day of April, A.D. 1850,
/s/ Susanna Graham
Wits: Thos. J. McCarroll
Hugh Campbell, Jr

Codicil: I give my grandson, Joseph R. Plummer, the old woman Milke in addition to this, or Negroes already given in the body of my will. I wish my administrator to sell the old man, William, his wife, Selly, her daughter, Zlea, and her three children, to pay the debts of the Estate, and if any more is left from their sale after the payments of said debts to divide it equally among the heirs. My buggy I wish disposed of in the same manner and for the same purpose.
/s/ Susanna Graham
wits: Geo. G. Banks   Thos. J. McCarroll
Hugh Campbell   on 30 April 1850.

State of Mississippi
Hinds County

In the Probate Court of said County, May term, A.D. 1850.

Personally appeared ... Thomas J. McCarroll and Hugh Campbell Jr, ...[swore] that said testatrix subsequently after making of said will ...[on] the 5 day of May, A.D. 1850, departed this life without revoking or amending..."
16th May 1850.

On 17 May 1850, an inventory and appraisal of her estate was filed. She owned 22 slaves, valued at $8075, and goods and chattels valued at $333.35, for a total estate of $8408.35.

On 13 Aug 1850, William Trahan gave notice that "by virtue of an order of the Probate Court of Hinds County, Mississippi, made at the August Term, 1850, the undersigned executor of the estate of Susanna Graham, deceased, will on Monday, the 16th day of September next, between the hours prescribed by law at Clinton in said County expose for sale at public auction, to the biggest bidders, on credit of six months from the day of sale, the following, to wit: Old William, his wife Salley, one grandchild, a boy, Aaron, one chest of irons, one lot of trucks and books, one side saddle, one Barouch and harness. The purchasers of said personal estate will be required to give bonds with good and ample security and payable in six months for the purchase money."

/s/ William Trahan

Judging from her estate sale, I would say that Susanna was a cultured, well-read, and well-to-do woman. The estate sale took place on 4 Nov 1850. Items sold included:

Rollin, *History*, 8 vols	to S.P. Loyd	1.00
G. Newton, *Theology*, 5 vol	to P.W. Charton	1.00
Scott, *Works*, 1 vol	to J. McKay	.50
Bucke, *Dictionary*	cash	.50
Smollett, *Works*, 2 vols	to H. Campbell	.75
Six vols, different works	to S.P. Loyd	.75
Shakespeare, 2 vols	cash	.75
Five vols, miscellaneous	to S.P. Loyd	.30
Four vols.	to Thomas McCarroll	.30
1 lot of books	to S.P. Loyd	.30
1 trunk	to C. Parish	.20
1 plow and gear	to Wm. J. Brown	3.10
1 box and contents	to C. Parish	5.10
1 side saddle	to S.P. Loyd	13.00
1 churn and dumaham	to S. Smith (cash)	.90
2 trunks	to W. Trahan	.25
1 Baruch & harness	to L. Lawrence	60.00
Billy, Sally, & infant	to S.P. Loyd	300.00
Boy, Aaron	to P.W. Charlton	215.00
total		603.70

On 5 Nov 1850, William Trahan, Executor, delivered slaves valued at $1600 to Susan P. Loyd; slaves valued at $1200 to Mary B. Crump; and slaves valued at about $5000 to Joseph R. Plummer. However, the estate just would not close. Money kept trickling in and trickling out.

On 14 June 1852, William Trahan was notified to appear in court and give cause why he had not made his annual statement regarding Susanna's estate. On 10 July 1852, he was again ordered to appear and give a statement. At the Sept term of the Probate Court, he presented bills that he had paid, amounting to $312.50. The notes from the estate sale kept trickling in, some of them late, so that William had to again and again answer in court. He also had trouble getting his sums to add up correctly.

On 2 Jan 1854, Mary B. Crump and her husband, H.S. Crump, submitted a petition to the probate court: "respectfully represents that said petitioner, Mary B. Crump, is a daughter 0and heir at law of Mrs. Susannah Graham, late of said county of Hinds, deceased, that Mrs. Susannah Graham made her last will and testament in which certain specific legacies are detailed of, which will property, and recorded in your Honorable Court in the month of May 1850, at which time or soon thereafter, William Trahern (who is now a citizen of Holmes County) took out letters of executorship on said estate, in your Honor's Court, and is still acting as such executor—

Your petitioner states that the time for entering claims against said estate has long since passed; that all the valid debts of said estate have been paid; and that there is no longer any necessity for continuing the administration of said estate; and the same should now be closed. Petitioners are advised from the knowledge of the affairs of said estate and the face of the records that there will be in the hands of said Executor for distribution under the said will, to you petitioner, Mary B. Crump, and the other heirs of said Testatrix, a sum of money amounting probably to about the sum of twelve or fourteen hundred dollars. When the said estate is properly and lawfully settled, one third of which will belong to said Mary B. Crump.

Your petitioner therefore prays that a citation issue to said William Trehan, commanding him to appear before your Honorable Court, on a day ...xxxx... named, and answer the delegation of the petition, and show cause if any he can, why he shall not be ordered by your honor to make final settlement of said estates and distribute the fund remaining in his hand according to law, mercifully submitted this 2nd January 1854.

/s/ Mary B. Crump
/s/ H.S. Crump

William Trahern responded that he saw no reason why the estate could not be settled, and he enumerated the heirs, as of 13 Feb 1854:

Mary B. Crump, of Simpson Co, MS; Joseph R. Plummer, of Holmes Co, MS; Susan P. Loyd, the other legatee under the will is dead, leaving three heirs, Susannah Fisher, wife of Doct. Fisher who resides in Carroll Co, MS, also two infant heirs of Susan P. Loyd, who are in Carroll Co, MS with E. Loyd, their lawful guardian. "Petitioner prays that they may all be cited to appear and show cause if they can why his final .... should not be allowed."

In March, 1854, William Trahern filed what he called a final account:

1st: slaves delivered to legatees under the will .... $ 8075.00
2nd: cash paid creditors, as of 7 Sept 1852 .... 274.50
3rd: Cash paid Creditor as of 14 Nov 1853 .... 597.32
4th: Cash paid to acct of W.H. Allen 43.93
5th: Cash paid Brooks & Anderson 10.00
6th: my commission [plus something I don't understand] ... 475.88
7th: cash paid W.J. Brown 50.00
8th: cash paid Daniel N. Wilkerson as help as Executor 179.30
sub-total 9707.93
deducted amount of estate 9517.70
Balance due the executor 188.23
9th: cash paid John & Guine as counsel retained to Probate and sustain the will of Susannah Graham and for service during the administration of the estate 500.00
total (due Trahern) 688.23

He charged himself with the following receipts:
1. Slave delivered to legatees 8075.00
2. Inventory of money on hand and due the estate .. 839.00
3. Amount of sales of personal estate 603.70

On 6 June 1854, William Trahern filed a report in the Probate Court of Hinds County, to be taken up in the July term. He reviewed the legal maneuvering: "....had appeared in person this court to make his final settlement, but upon inquiring into the condition of the estate it appeared that there was one suit still pending ... in Holmes County Circuit Court....

In the meantime, Crump and wife filed their petition for a final account, knowing that this deponent was willing and anxious to settle the account at the earliest possible moment, and, further, in answer to said petition, deponent denies that there is any sum of money in the hands of this deponent to be distributed and, if there were any such sum, deponent denies that said Crump and wife would be entitled to the same or any share of it.

Respondent further states on information and belief that said Crump and wife are largely in debt to the estate of John B. (Brashears) Stewart, having purchased property at the sale of said estate far beyond the share that would be due to the wife of said Crump and they had not paid the same.

That Susanna Graham at the time of her death was also indebted to the estate of John B. Stewart in the sum of six hundred and seventy nine dollars, seventeen cents ($679.17).... said Susanna Graham had set aside the sum of six hundred, seventy one dollars and placed the sum in the hands of Wm. J. Brown, to be paid by him to the heirs of said estate of John B. Stewart, but at the time of the death of Susanna, said Brown had not paid over said sum of money....

upon representing these facts to Judge John Sims, who was then Judge of the Honorable Court, respondent was advised that it was the duty of the respondent to collect said sum of money from said Brown and pay the same as directed by the said Susanna in her lifetime to the estate of or heirs of said John B. Stewart... Respondent then collected [the money] and upon examination of the matter, found that the sum of six hundred and seventy nine dollars and 17/100 and probably more was due said estate and that the sum was payable to the heirs of Susan P. Loyd, dec'd, of whom E. Loyd was the legal guardian, and whom receipts for said sum is on file as a voucher in this court...

After the death of Susannah Graham, the said Crump and wife and the said Susan P. Loyd and E. Loyd... [filed a]

proceeding in the court to set aside the will of the said Susannah Graham, deceased, and informed this respondent that they had employed Anderson Counsel, to wit: George S. __?__ and Trotter....

Respondent was therefore compelled to retain counsel to aid him in probating ... said will... and so respondent retained John and V. Freeman as his counsel and agreed to give a fee of five hundred dollars for his service in said case, which sum of money he has since paid and which sum included all the service of said Freeman under and about the administration of the said estate, for which this respondent claims an allowance by the court.

Respondent states that this course pursued by said Crump and wife and said E. Loyd and Susan P. Loyd in threatening to brake said will forced this respondent to employ said counsel, and he therefore says that they may be compelled to share a proportion of the expense which they made it necessary to incur in the proper administration of said estate. Respondent files herewith his final account and prays to be allowed therein stated.

/s/ William Trahern

Sworn to in court, 6 July 1854, before G.B. Downey, Clerk

On 24 Oct 1854, William Trahern appeared in Holmes County court and stated that he was unable to make a final settlement in the estate of John Brashears Stewart, of which he was administrator, having taken the place of Susanna Graham as administrator. He had employed Chas. Sheppard as his attorney "to make said settlement, but owing to the sickness of the said Sheppard's infant, has been unable to get the settlement made out in time for the Nov term, 1854 of the Carroll County Probate Court and consequently he is unable to make his settlement at the Nov Term 1854 Hinds Probate court as administrator of Susannah Graham, dec'd.

May 1855, Hinds County court: "now come H.S. Crump and Mary B., his wife, and insisting upon their right to the exhibition at this time of all the values of said executor (William Trahern) for all payments made by him.... they will insist upon the following exemptions to the various settlements and proceeding of said executor:

1. They except because he has not anywhere or in any of his settlements, [charged] himself with any sums of money, one of hire of Negroes before the death of Testatrix and afterwards, and before the sale as delivery thereof to the respective devisees;

2. Because he appropriated to the payment of general debts of Testatrix the sum of six hundred and seventy one dollars, received by him of William J. Brown, who it had been left by Testatrix in her lifetime and by her (as admitted in the Inventory of money and debts) in her lifetime appropriated to the payment of a debt due by her to the estate of John B. Stewart, instead of distribution of said sum to Stewart's heirs, this exemptor Mary B. Crump, the children of Susan P. Loyd, and Joseph R. Plummer, the said Mary and Susan being sisters, Joseph, a nephew of said John B. Stewart, as he legally ought to have done.

3. Because he has paid without authority of law ... said five hundred seventy nine 17/100 dollars to E. Loyd, guardian of the heirs of S.P. Loyd, dec'd, and claimed credit therefore in his annual settlement at November Term, 1853, and to which credit they insist he is not entitled.

4. Because the rate of commissions charged is said final statement at five per cent is altogether too large and unreasonable, and ought to be redeemed.

5. Because the allowance claimed of $500 attorneys fees is not a lawful and proper charge, ... [This claim was apparently reduced by the Judge to $350.]

At the June, 1855, term of the Hinds Co, MS Probate Court, William Trahern petitioned for permission to sell some left-over items: "represents to your Honor that the last will and testament of said Susanna Graham requested that the old man William, his wife, Sally, her daughter, Lea and her three children should be sold to pay the debt of her estate. Lea and two of her children have died since the death of the testator, your petitioner therefore prays your Honor to make an order to sell ... Negroes such as ... Ann? and Alice to carry out the provision of said will.... In addition ... wishes to sell 1 chest of sundries, 1 lot of trunks and books, 1 side saddle, and 1 barouche and harness."

Finally, at the July Term, 1855, of Hinds County Probate Court, William Trahern filed his final accounts in the estate of Susanna Graham; it was examined, audited, and acknowledged. The accounts were pretty much as given previously, and there was $632.99 left to divide among the heirs, in addition to what they had already received. "Exor discharged from further accounting to this court."

14. THE TRAIL OF WOE TO OKLAHOMA: The Families of Delilah "Lila" Brashears and Wesley Trahern & Vaughn Brashears and Isabella LeFlore

Trouble, trouble, trouble; you'd think there'd be an end to it. The immensely complicated terms of the Treaty of Dancing Rabbit Creek ensured that plenty of lawyers, bureaucrats, politicians, and even the President of the United States himself would sooner or later be involved. No doubt, those who wrote the Treaty thought they were protecting the Indians from avaricious Americans, who (the commissioners knew) would certainly cheat the Indians out of their lands, if they were not put under such complicated restraints. But the lengthy law suits on the Suk-en-Atcha were just as effective, though slower; they tied up the Choctaws' assets, while their expenses kept growing and growing, up and up. Several of them found it necessary to sell a portion of their holdings, presumably to pay expenses. Delilah (Juzan) Brashears, widow of Jesse Brashears, may even have lost her land to taxes (I don't know how that hassle came out). What is clear is that, by the middle of the century, there was not one Brashears family left in the Suk-en-Atcha settlement. The squatters had taken over every parcel. Alexander moved his family to Mobile, Anne took her little family to Texas, Delilah disappeared (and was reported in Indian Territory), all of Zadock's children and grandchildren ended up in Indian Territory, west of the Mississippi, i.e. in Oklahoma.

Brewster was right, when he told young Augustus Buckholtz, in effect: 'To hell with the authorities; it is useless for you to contend for your land, because we are living on it, and we intend to have it.' It reminds me of Red Cloud's comment: The whites "made us many promises, but they never kept but one. They promised to take our land, and they took it."

None of the Choctaws, so far as I know, left Mississippi or Alabama with hope in their hearts; yet that must have been so. They must have thought of Oklahoma as a kind of haven— a place where they would be left at peace, a place where they could raise their families, perpetuate their language and culture; a place where they could get away, safely away, from the Americans. The winters were much more severe in Indian Territory than they were used to, and the summers were much more dry, but many of them trudged west with a determination to start over, to carve out of that unwanted wilderness a place, not just to survive, but to prosper.

But, over and over, it was a trail of pain. And every family that traveled had a different kind or degree of woe.

SARAH MONCRIEF'S TRIP WEST

One of Zadock and Susannah Brashears' granddaughters, Sarah Ann Moncrief (^{v5}1394), m.1. a white man, Erasmus B. Hawkins, m.2. in Indian Territory, another white man, Aaron Harlan. She and Erasmus lived prosperously with the help of their slaves for some years at peace in Mississippi and had two children. But by the middle of the century, there was social (and legal) pressure to get rid of the "half-breeds." No matter that Sarah Moncrief Hawkins was only 1/16 Choctaw, no matter that she looked white, could read and write well, and was the wife of a prosperous slave-holder, she spoke the Choctaw language and she was Indian. One iota of Indian blood made you Indian. Why didn't one iota of white blood make you white? "Get rid of her!"

In the very dead of winter, 1849-50, she and some of her siblings were forced to move to Indian Territory. Why, why do authorities repeatedly pick the dumbest, worst time of year to travel? Much later, when she was an old woman of 84 in 1913, she dictated her memoirs, which were even later collected in the W.P.A. *Oklahoma Indian-Pioneer Interviews*, "Sarah Ann Harlan," 24 Aug 1837. The opening passage of those memoirs tells of the trip west in 1850:

From "Biography of Sarah Ann Harlan"

There was a great opening in the west, and this being about the time the pale faces were wanting to get the Indians all out of Mississippi and Alabama, a bill was passed to have the Government move us. The Government made appropriations to move us all west, paying our expenses and furnishing one year's rations, issued as the soldiers were issued, every three months. This applied to our Negroes as well as to ourselves. We began to make preparations. There were men who contracted for this work. They went around among the Indians enrolling their names, ages, etc.; and then set the date to leave, traveling by boat. The emigration agents sent the Indians by deck passage.

We emigrated under Lewis and Bridges. We had always traveled by boat, but never by deck passage. We made arrangements with the agent to let us travel our usual way and we would apply the difference ourselves between that and deck passage. We did not think it wise to take deck passage; we had never been used to such a way of traveling. The agent knew that such Indians as we were, and many others just like us, could not stand deck passage. This was in January, 1850.

We took the boat at McDowell's landing. When we got there we found pale faced Indians there, too. We then made our start for the west down Tom Bigbee Bayou River, to Mobile, Alabama. There we crossed Lake Ponchartrain between Mobile and New Orleans.

Cholera was raging in New Orleans and we were anxious to take the first boat out. It was an old boat and not a very safe one, by the name of "Alvardo." We had not gone up the Mississippi very far, when we found we were not in a first-class boat. Never the less, we would have taken anything to get away from the cholera. We found that nearly all the officers and hands were thieves. We had a single brother along, and they broke into his trunk and stole a number of articles. After this, he brought his money and gave it to one of my sisters saying, "I sleep so soundly I am afraid I'll be robbed."

"We sleep so soundly I am afraid I'll be robbed." We kept this very quiet, and kept a watch out. One night we saw one of the captain's boys with a little fancy hat that my mother had sent to my brother's little boy who lived in the west. Then my husband and my sister's husband went to the captain and said, "Here is the one who has broken into our brother's trunk." So, the captain made the boy produce all the little trinkets and things that belonged to my brother. We had very great fear, for we knew we were among a den of thieves. We traveled on; and in a night or two Mr. [Robert Smith] McCarty, my brother-in-law, found that his state room was being broken into. We tried to keep good watch; and when this fellow reached in to grab the trunk, my brother-in-law struck out at him with a pocket knife and cut his arm, so that stopped him. Then he awoke all the rest of us, and notified us of what was going on.

We expected to be murdered. We traveled on a little farther, and one very foggy night, the river being very high and the levee breaking in some places, our boat ran upon the levee and tied us up for two days. We signaled every boat that passed, but no one would come to our aid. We learned in after years that steamboats were like everything else: they had a monopoly, and they would not pull us off. Finally, a White River boat came to our rescue.

This boat being loaded with salt in sacks, the officers pressed passengers and all into service, carrying sacks, the officers had them to carry sacks from the prow to the stern of the boat. They were a half a day getting us off; but we were glad to get off, for we thought our boat would sink.

In those days, we did not pay our passage until we got to the end of the journey. So the captain had to beg the passengers to help him out by paying half of their fare in order that he might pay the captain of the White River boat to pull him off, and we did so. I was the only one of my sisters who was anxious to see and know everything that was being done, and I know this to be so.

There was not much sleeping done by the men from there to the mouth of the Arkansas River. We found we were in another den of thieves. Where the Mississippi backed up into the Arkansas River there was a sea of water: nothing but water as far as the eye could penetrate. An old steamboat was tied up on the wharf to receive passengers and freight, and it was a dismal looking place. Napolion was the name of this place at the mouth of the Arkansas River. Finding that we were among thieves and cut throats, none of us slept that night but the children. None of us undressed. We landed about dark, and had to stay all night. The next morning, an Arkansas boat came along, the "Western Water Lady," it was called, so we took passage on her.

There were so many drifts and so much danger on the Arkansas River that we made slow progress. It took us a whole week to get up to Ft. Smith.

My oldest sister [Susan (Moncrief) McClain]'s baby was very sick with congestion of the brain. There was a French doctor on the boat who took care of it, and he finally told me it would not recover. So just as we pushed off from Van Buren, the babe drew its last breath.

On this boat I saw, for the first time, a drunken woman. I thought we had struck the other world. She was really boisterous and as we were distressed over the baby's death, I undertook to command her and quiet her down. She was a well dressed woman, about half breed Cherokee, and very large. She brought out an oath, and grabbed me and said, "I'll throw you overboard." My husband and brother-in-law caught her; the captain came running, and told her if he heard another word out of her he would put her out. They locked her up, but she got out; so the captain stopped about a mile above Ft. Smith and shoved her right out in the timbers and left her. I said, "No, don't do that, there are no houses near; she will get lost." But he said, "She will find a place."

We ran on to Ft. Smith, landed there, and while the cargo was being unloaded, we had a coffin made. There were no undertakers in those days, we had to have a little rough coffin made as quickly as possible.

About ten miles above Ft. Smith, the boat landed at Ft. Coffee; this was late in the afternoon. Captain White remarked to us at dinner, "You must not drink too much spring and well water; you have been drinking Mississippi and Arkansas water so long, it will make you sick." I thought of the good well of water at Ft. Coffee that my mother told me about. I had my husband buy me a pitcher and tin cup to take up there with me. Fort Coffee was an old abandoned fort which had been turned over to the Choctaws for a school. We camped in what was known as the old guard house, right on the bank of the Arkansas River, and our brothers went to bury the infant.

While they were gone, my niece, Helen [Marr McClain], and myself went up on the high bluff to the fort, and asked permission to get a pitcher of water. The old minister, Reverend William McAlester, greeted us very pleasantly. "Get all the water you want," he said, asking if we were immigrants. "Oh! yes, we are Indians," I said, and we entered into conversation. He asked where we were from, and when we told him, he shook hands with us. He was an old Mississippi missionary who had followed the Indians west, always as a missionary from the Methodist Church. Well, we did as the captain had requested; did not even drink as much as a half pint of the water. We went back under the hill to our camping place. Just as I stepped into the hall, I held out the pitcher, saying to my sister, "Take it"; and I fell, knowing nothing for many days. [She was stricken with Cholera, and was extremely ill, but recovered.]

DELILAH BRASHEARS
and WESLEY TRAHERN

[v5]837. [8]5. **Delilah "Lila" Brashears**, (d/o Zadock Brashears and Susannah Vaughn), bap. 4 May 1794, St. Joseph's Catholic Church, Diocese of Baton Rouge (sponsors: Jersey Bishears (Jesse? almost certainly a Spanish mis-pronunciation of Asa) and Rush (Ruth) Bishears; recorded St. Joseph's Parish of Baton Rouge, Book 1, p.35). Delilah died about 1820.

On 24 March 1808, Delilah Brashear married **Wesley Trahern**, in Hinds Co, MS. The Wilkerson Co, MS, marriage records contain an entry: "Westrum Traham to Lila Brashears" 23 March 1808. Perhaps they were actually married in Wilkerson and also registered the marriage the following day in Hinds? Wesley Trahern m.2. c1820, Agnes Turnbull, d/o William Turnbull and Judith Perry. (See "The Turnbull Connection" in Chapter 8 for details.)

Wesley Trahern was born c1779, in Pittsylvania Co, VA, s/o Nehemiah and Amelia Trahern. Nehemiah Trahern's will in Pittsylvania Co, PA, probated 17 Sept 1804, names nine children: (Thanks to Jennifer Mieirs for data.)

To my daughter, Mary Ann, a negro woman, Cas;
To my son, James, a negro boy, George;
To my daughter, Elizabeth Hester, a negro, Hannah;
To my son, Samuel, a negro, Stepney;
To my daughter, Serena, a negro, Bob;
To my son, Wesley, a negro called Gilbert;
To my daughter, Milley, a negro girl, Little Lucy;
To my son, William, a negro girl, Mary.

I desire my daughter, Polley, to have as much money to make equal with the value of the negros given to the others. I gave Hester a negro earlier (probably is son-in-law, Samuel Hester). To my beloved wife, Amelia, during her natural life, the tract of land where upon I now live, with all the stock, furniture, and negros, Harry, Watt, Lucy, Cloe, and Jenny. At her decease, the negros to be divided between my children above named. I desire the children under age remain with their mother until lawful age. I appoint my son, James, and Samuel Hester, executors.

Of these children, at least James, Wesley, and William moved to the Thompson's Creek settlement, LA, before 1812, possibly before 1808, when Wesley married Delilah, and all had dealings with Brashears. James was b. c1769, in Maryland or Virginia; he was old enough in 1797 to witness a deed. Wesley was born about 1779 in Pittsylvania Co, PA, and William was born there c1783.

In 1812, Wesley Trahan (yet another misspelling of the name) owned land on Redwood Creek, bordering a parcel which Zadock Brashears gave to his daughter, Anne (Brashears) Lyles. The deed was witnessed by Alexander Vaughn, William Boyce, and James Trahan. (See Anne (Brashears) Lyles/Brashear's entry for text of the deed.)

In 1824 and 1825, Wesley Trahern was on the Tax Lists of Hinds Co, MS. In 1825, he was mentioned in the obituary of a nephew. His daughters, Amelia and Letha, were discussed at length in American State Papers, because the agents responsible for taking the Choctaw Census decided that orphans had no rights. See below.

Wesley Trahern died in Hinds Co, MS, before 1829, when his probate was opened. His brother, William Trahern, was executor; his brother, James, disputed his will. (MS court records, High court of error and appeals 1799-1859, drawer 67 case #66 Hinds Co. MS (Info from Doug Barkley, via Jennifer Mieirs).

Family of Delilah "Lila" Brashears and Wesley Trahern:
[v5]1181.   [9]1. *Wesley Brashears Trahern, b. 1808, Choctaw
        Nation, MS, d. 29 March 1839, MS; m. c1829 in
        AL, Lucy Juzan, b. c1809, Choctaw Territory, d/o
        Charles Juzan and a niece or grand-niece of

Pushmataha.

v5 1182.   9 2. Mary Trahern, b. 1810, Choctaw Nation, MS; m. 11 April 1826, Hinds Co, MS, J.W.J. Minor, b. Choctaw Nation, MS.

v5 1183.   9 3. *William Trahern, b. 1812, Alabama, d. c1890, MS, bur near Lexington, Holmes Co, MS; m.1. 1834, (no return) Lucy Lee; m.2. 1835, Mariah B. Trahern, b. c1820, VA or MS (she is from a different Trahern family of Loudon Co, VA, originally Quakers); m.3. Rebecca Long, b. c1828, MS, d. c1895, in I.T.

v5 1184.   9 4. Amelia Trahern, b. 1814, d. after 1835; m. Richard C. West, b. c1814,

v5 1185.   9 5. Letha Trahern, b. c1818, d. after 1835; m. Columbus Lane, b. c1816,

v5 1186.   9 6. *George Washington Trahern, b. 15 April 1825, Choctaw Nation, MS, d. in California. [May be listed as Jesse Trahern on 1841 emigration from Old Nation.]

Family of Wesley Trahern and Agnes Turnbull: (see "The Turnbull Connection" for more details.)

7. Minerva Trahern, b. 1824, Choctaw Nation, MS; m. c1843, in MS, Josiah Metcalf, b. 1818, OH

8. Gilbert Trahern, b. 1825, Choctaw Nation, MS; m. c1856, Laura V. _____.

At the time of the Treaty of Dancing Rabbit Creek, Amelia, Letha, and George Washington Trahern were orphans between the ages of 10 and 16, both their parents having died. They were supposed to be enrolled in accordance with the portion of Article 19 of the Treaty that dealt with orphans, but Col. William Ward, with his usual ineptitude (or malevolence, when it came to Choctaws) really messed up their applications. It took almost a ton of correspondence to get their case straightened out. (Thanks to Jennifer Mieirs for the following quotes from the Records of the Choctaw Reserves, Federal Records MicroFilm 7RA-116, Office of Indian Affairs, roll 188, frame 623; roll 189, frame 418; roll 190, frames 383, 387-88, 1125.)

The girls, or one of the girls and George Washington Trahern, are often confused with "Peggy Trahern and her two fatherless children." Other records show that Peggy Trahern's children were James Nicholas Trahern and Jeremiah Trahern. Peggy was a d/o Nahomtima, Pushmataha's sister.

A letter from William Ward dated October 19, 1932 states that "Peggy Trahern is in no way connected with Wesley Trahern, deceased, nor with his two wives, Delilah, deceased, or Agnes, who survived him." (American State Papers, "Public Lands", 1834, p. 37)

House of Representatives
January 4, 1832

Lewis Cass,
Secretary of War.
 Dear Sir:

Misses Amelia and Letha Trahern, natives and citizens of the Choctaw nation, Mississippi, request to know whether their names have been forwarded to the War Department for the purpose of obtaining a quarter section of land each, under, and by virtue of, the 19th article of the treaty of Dancing Rabbit creek, held September 27, 1830. They are both minors and orphans. Please to address me on the subject. Most respectfully, your obedient servant.

/s/ F.E. Plummer

(Source: American State Papers, no. 1230 - 1834, pg. 35) [NOTE: F.E. Plummer was serving in the U.S. House of Representatives and also as Commissioner of Public Lands.]

Department of War, Office of Indian Affairs
January 11, 1832

 Sir:

In reply to your several communications, I beg leave to state that the agent, Col. Ward, has not forwarded to this department the names of those persons who have, in due time, signified their intention of citizenship under the 14th article of the treaty of Dancing Rabbit creek. He will be instructed to forward to this office the names of all those who have signified such intention; and it is highly probable, from the representations of those persons of whose behalf you have addressed the Secretary of War, that their names will be among the number.

With respect to your inquiries as to Amelia and Letha

Trahern, minors and orphans, I find that, in a supplement to the said treaty, the following provision was made for them: "And there is given a quarter section of land each to Peggy Trahern, an Indian woman residing out of the nation, and her two fatherless children."

It is believed that to entitle a person to a conveyance in fee simple under that treaty on the expiration of five years after its ratification, he must not only have signified his intention of citizenship, but must also have actually resided upon the land during that period. With great respect, & c.

/s/ Elbert Herring

Washington City
April 5, 1832

Hon. Lewis Cass,
Secty of War.
Dear Sir:

I take the liberty of requesting you to inform me whether the agent of the Choctaws has forwarded to the War Department any returns of the application of Amelia and Letha Trahern to obtain a reservation of land, as orphans, under the treaty of Dancing Rabbit creek. Peggy Trahern and her two fatherless children, who are provided for in the supplement to said treaty, and referred to in the letter of Mr. Herring (of the War Dept., under date of January 11), are not the persons to whom I refer. Most respectfully, your obedient servant,

/s/ F.E. Plummer,
Comm. of Public Lands

Department of War, Office of Indian Affairs
April 7, 1832

the Hon. Lewis Cass,
Secty of War.
Sir:

In reply to the inquiry of the Honorable F. E. Plummer, I have the honor to state that the register of the names of orphan Choctaw children to be provided for by the Choctaw treaty of 1830, transmitted to the department by the Choctaw agent, Col.

William Ward, contains the name of Letha Trahern, but does not contain the name of Amelia Trahern. I have, &c

/s/ Elbert Herring (p. 33)

Department of War
April 9, 1832

Hon. F. E. Plummer,
House Representatives, United States.
Sir:

Your letter of the 5th instant in relation to reservations of Choctaw lands in favor of Amelia and Letha Trahern has been received, and, in answer, I have the honor to enclose a report of the officer in charge of the Indian Bureau, which furnishes the information requested.

/s/ Lewis Cass (p. 33)

Washington City
June 24, 1832

Lewis Cass,
Secty of War.
Sir:

On the 5th of April last, I addressed you on the subject of the business of Amelia and Letha Trahern, who claim one quarter section of land each, under and by virtue of the nineteenth article of the treaty of Dancing Rabbit Creek held on the 27th day of September, 1830, with the Choctaws. By the report of the officer in charge of the Indian Bureau, enclosed in your reply of the 9th same month, I learn that the register of the names forwarded to the War Department by Col. Ward, agent for the Choctaws, contains the name of Letha, but not the name of Amelia Trahern.

I now take the liberty of enclosing to you a correspondence on the subject between Col. Ward and myself, and request that the name of Amelia Trahern may be placed on the register, or on file in the War Department, as an orphan, under the article of the treaty before referred to, entitled to a quarter section of land. You will discover from the letter of Col. Ward that Amelia Trahern comes within the provisions of the 19th article of the treaty, and that she filed her application within the time specified. The agent had no authority to strike her name from the list, nor had he, Mackay, any authority to decide that she was not an orphan, and did not come within the provisions of the treaty because 16 or 17 years of age. I presume that it is unnecessary to say anything more upon the subject.

/s/ F.E. Plummer

(Source: American State Papers, no. 1230, 1834, p. 33)

Department of War, Office of Indian Affairs
June 27, 1832.

Sir:

In obedience to your direction to report upon the case of Amelia Trahern, presented by the Hon. F.E. Plummer, I have the honor to state that, although the register of names of orphan Choctaw children to be provided for by the Choctaw treaty of 1830, forwarded to the department by Gen. W. Ward, does not contain the name of Amelia Trahern, yet there is reason to believe, from the letter of Gen. W. Ward, of the 24th of May last, to the Hon. Mr. Plummer, and herein enclosed that the name of Amelia Trahern ought to have been inserted in that register.

It appears from the letter of Gen. Ward that he was requested to enter the names of three orphans of the name of Trahern, one male and two females, which he did on his memorandum book; that Mackay, an interpreter, went afterwards through the nation, by Gen. Ward's order, to take down the names of parents and children, and their ages, and that he reported only two orphans of the name of Trahern; and, being asked why the name of Amelia was not on his register, he replied that she was sixteen or seventeen years of age, and that he did not think her entitled to the provision of the treaty. It further appears that Gen. Ward was told that both her parents were dead, and that he, Ward, knew that her father had a wife when he died, who was not the mother of Amelia; and that he was acquainted with Wesley Trahern, the father of the three children named in Mr. Plummer's letter, of whom Amelia was one.

I am of opinion, from this explanatory letter of Gen. Ward, that the name of Amelia Trahern was improperly omitted, and ought to have been inserted in the aforesaid register transmitted to the department. I am of opinion that Peggy Trahern was the second or subsequent wife of Wesley Trahern; and that provision for her and her two fatherless children, Letha and the boy, was made by the second article of the supplement to the aforesaid treaty, and that Amelia was the daughter of the said Wesley Trahern by a former wife, that both her parents were dead; and that she is entitled to a quarter section of land under the nineteenth article of the said treaty.

The name of Amelia Trahern ought, however, to appear on the aforesaid register, or there should be a certificate by Gen. Ward that the name was omitted, and ought to have been inserted in said register. Gen. Ward should, therefore, be written to for such a certificate. I have the honor to be, &c

/s/ Elbert Herring (p.32)

Department of War
June 28, 1832

Hon. F.E. Plummer,
House of Representatives, United States:
Sir:

In answer to your letter of the 24th inst., I have the honor to enclose you a copy of the report of the officer in charge of the Indian Bureau, and to state that the instructions have been given to place the name of Amelia Trahern on the register, on the production of the certificate referred to in the report. I have, &c,

/s/ Lewis Cass (Secty of War)

(Source: American State Papers, no. 1834, "Location under the Choctaw Treaty," p.31.

Choctaw Agency
October 19, 1832

Elbert Herring, Esq.,
Washington City.
Sir:

Your letter of the 28th June I had the honor to receive some time since, respecting the claim of Amelia Trahern to a reserve

---

of land as an orphan under a provision of a treaty with the Choctaws in the year 1830. I have to observe that Wesley Trahern had two wives. He, Wesley, is dead; and his first wife, by the name of Delilah ["Lila" Brashears], is also dead. They had, at the time of the making of the late treaty of 1830, several children living: the three youngest was by the names of Amelia, Letha, and [George] Washington: the oldest, Amelia, was about sixteen or seventeen years of age when the interpreters registered the names of the Choctaw orphan children; and he supposed her, (as he has since told me,) not to come under the class of orphans, is the reason that her name is not found on the book returned by me to the Office of Indian Affairs. These children of Trahern are all yet single, and dependent upon their friends for support in a great measure. Wesley Trahern, the deceased father of Amelia, Letha, and Washington, before his death, intermarried with the second wife, whose name was Agnes [Turnbull], who since has married a man by the name of Foster.

William Ward

Department of War, Office Indian Affairs
November 3, 1832

Col. William Ward,
Choctaw Agency, Miss.
Sir:

Your letter of the 19th Ultimo, mentioning the reason why the name of Emelia Trahern was not inserted in the list of Choctaw orphans transmitted to the department has been received.

The application for reservations of land by Tubbee and other, whose names are mentioned in your letter, cannot be granted. The treaty requires that each head of a family, being desirous to remain and be a citizen of the States, should be permitted to do so by signifying his intention to the agent within six months from the ratification of the treaty, and that he should therefore be entitled, &c.

This appears to have been omitted. They represent that they signified such intention. You say that the books of your office make no mention of the fact; nor have you expressed any opinion or belief of the truth of their assertion. No good reason is perceived for the interposition of the department in their behalf. With much respect, &c.

/s/ Elbert Herring

Amelia and Letha Trahern each claimed a quarter section in the E½, Sec27, T25, R2E in a letter dated October 15, 1833. By then, Amelia was married to Richard C. West.

On April 3, 1838?, (can't read the exact day) F.E. Plummer of Tchula in Holmes County wrote regarding Amelia West and Letha H. Lane (wife of Columbus Lane), both of Holmes County.

Wesley Brashears Trahern and Lucy Juzan

[v5]1181. [9]1. Wesley Brashears Trahern, (s/o Wesley Trahern and Delilah "Lila" Brashears), b. 1808, Choctaw Nation, MS, d. 29 March 1839, MS; m. c1829 in AL, Lucy Juzan, b. c1809, Choctaw Territory, d/o Charles Juzan and either Peggy Trahern, a daughter of Pushmataha's sister, Nahomtima, or Phoebe Oklahoma, a daughter of Oklahoma, son of Nahomtima.

Wesley B. Train [another misspelling; the Irish "Trahan" apparently rimes with "crayon"] is on the 1831 William Armstrong rolls of persons in Natachachi's [Nitakechi's] District, who wished to remain on their land and become citizens. There were six persons in his household, including one child over 16 (probably his sister, Amelia), one under 10, and three slaves. They lived on the west side of the Tombigbee River, adjoining the homestead of Delilah (Juzan) Brashears, widow of Jesse Brashears. He was named in Supplement 2 of the Treaty of Dancing Rabbit Creek to receive one section of land, apparently Sec 27, T17N, R1W. (See Map.)

After Wesley Brashears Trahern died in 1839, Lucy (Juzan) m.2. Amos W. Gary (Geary). Lucy and Amos are listed as "self emigration from the old Nation" in 1841, with children:

Charles Gary, [s/o Amos W. Gary and Lucy Juzan]

Amelia Trahern, [sister of Wesley B. Trahern, d/o Wesley Trahern and Delilah Brashears]

Jesse Trahern, [may be same as George Washington Trahern, s/o Wesley Trahern and Delilah Brashears]

Pierre Trahern, [s/o Wesley B. Trahern and Lucy Juzan]

William Trahern, [s/o Wesley B. Trahern and Lucy Juzan]

slaves Eliza, Elizabeth, Silla, [apparently the slaves of Wesley Trahern and Delilah Brashears]

Amos and Lucy Gary are found on the 1855/56 Census/payment rolls of Choctaws in Indian Territory.

Pushmataha District, Atoka Co.

A.W. Gary

Lucy [Juzan/Trahern] Gary

Amelia Gary [Amelia Trahern, sister of Wesley B. Trahern, d/o Wesley Trahern and Delilah Brashears]

Pierse Trahern [s/o Wesley Brashears Trahern and Lucy Juzan]

Charles Gary [s/o A.W. Gary and Lucy Juzan]

Lucrecia Gary [d/o A.W. Gary and Lucy Juzan]

Jackson Wall [unidentified]

Charles Juzan [unidentified]

Washington [??Trahern? possibly brother of Wesley B. Trahern, s/o Wesley Trahern and Delilah Brashears]

Family of Wesley Brashears Trahern and Lucy Juzan:

v51187.   101. Pier (Pierre, Piers, Pierce) Trahern, b. after 1829; m. Czarina Folsom, b. c1833

v51188.   102. William Trahern, b. after 1829; m. _____?,

v51189.   111. Sallie (or Mary) Trahern, b. ___, d. 1881, Blue Co, Choctaw Nation, I.T.; m.1. Anolatubbee, b. c1825, Choctaw Nation, MS; m.2. Oliver Thomas, b. c1830, IN; m.3. _____ Walters

v51190.   121. dau Anolatubbee, b. c1880

v51191.   122. Jack Anolatubbee,

v51192.   123. James Anolatubbee, b. 1845; m. Sallie _____

v51193.   124. Soloman Anolatubbee; m. _____

v51194.   131. Selina Anolatubbee (¾ Chickasaw, Roll #14; C.C. #4), b. 1858; m.1. _____ Hamilton; m.2. 1885, Humphrey Colbert, ¾ Chickasaw, Roll #13)

v51195.   125. Eliza Anolatubbee, m. c1875, Ellis Carnes, b. April 1856

v51196.   126. George W. Walters, (Choctaw-Chickasaw mix); m. _____ (Cherokee)

v51197.   131. William S. Walters,

Counties of the Choctaw Nation in the Nineteenth Century

(The dotted lines and small numbers indicate the counties of Oklahoma after 1906: 1. Hughes, 2. Pittsburg, 3. Haskell, 4. LeFlore, 5. Coal, 6. Latimer, 7. Atoka, 8. Pushmataha, 9. McCurtain 10. Bryan, 11. Choctaw)

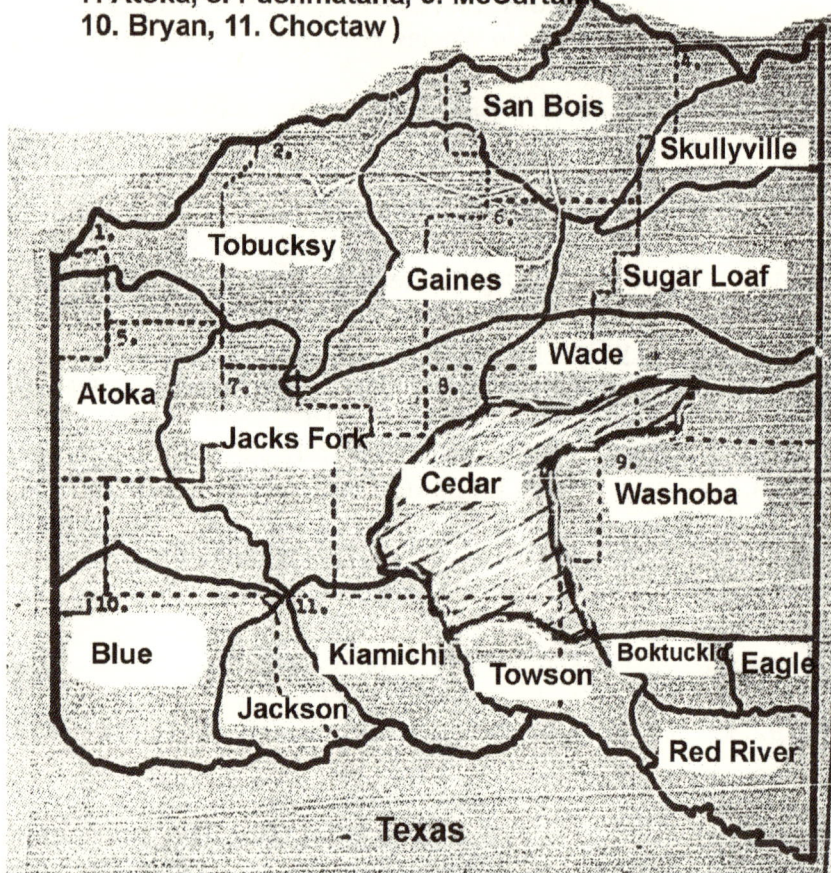

San Bois

Skullyville

Tobucksy

Gaines

Sugar Loaf

Wade

Atoka

Jacks Fork

Cedar

Washoba

Blue

Kiamichi

Towson

Boktuckl Eagle

Jackson

Red River

Texas

Family of Lucy Juzan and Amos W. Gary:
1. Charles Gary, b. before 1841
2. Lucretia Gary, b. 1841-1855
3. Eliza Ann Gary, b. c1849 [1/16 Choctaw; C.C. 4809; Roll #13260], d. after 1905; m.1. James C.M. McClain, Jr (^{v5}1407; see his entry); m.2. c?1875, Elisha Heskett, b. c1849 (36 in 1885); m.3. before 1902, Charles Smith (intermarried Citizen

#1140)
1. William Alexander McClain (^{v5}1429), b. 16 Jan 1861
2. Eliza Ann Heskett, b. 1876
3. Henry F. Heskett, b. 1880 [1/32 Choctaw, C.C. 4809; Roll #13261]
4. Amos Wesley Heskett, b. 1881 [1/32 Choctaw, C.C. 4809; Roll #13262]
5. Elizabeth Heskett, b. 1884; m. _____ Hammons, b. c1880, d. before 1902. ch: Cecil Emory Hammons, b. c1900. Choctaw Census Card #4812
6. Inez O. Heskett, b. 1885 [1/32 Choctaw, C.C. 4809; Roll #13268]

Choctaw Census of 1885, Tobucksy Co:
679. Heskett, Elisha E., 36, M/W, Farmer, 60 acres
680. Heskett, Eliza A., 36 [b. c1849; Eliza Ann Gary, d/o Lucy Juzan and Amos W. Gary; Dawes Roll #13260]
681. McClean, Wm., 18 [Eliza Ann's son from her first marriage to James C.M. McClain, Jr]
682. Heskett, Annie, 7 [b. c1878],
683. Heskett, Henry F., 5 [b. c1880; Dawes Roll #13261
684. Heskett, Amos W. [Wesley], 4 [b. c1881; Dawes Roll #13262]
685. Heskett, Elizabath, 1 [b. c1884],
...born after census of 1885:
    Inez O. Heskett, b. c1886 [16 in 1902; Dawes Roll #13268]

William Trahern and Rebecca Long
^{v5}**1183.** ^{9}3. William Trahern, (s/o Wesley Trahern and Delilah Brashears), b. 1812, Alabama, d. c1890, MS, bur near Lexington, Holmes Co, MS; m.1. 1834, (no return and no further info) Lucy Lee; m.2. 1835, Mariah B. Trahern, b. c1820, VA or MS (she is from a different Trahern family from Loudon Co, VA, originally Quakers); m.3. Rebecca Long, b. c1828, MS, d. c1895, Skullyville Co, Indian Territory.
    William Trahern signed the Treaty of Dancing Rabbit Creek as William Trahorn. He was listed in Supplement 2 as William Train, to receive ½ section of land. He attended the Choctaw Academy in Great Crossing, KY, and also taught there as well. Listed in 1831 and 1834. He is on the Armstrong Rolls of 1831 as a person who intended to remain on his land and become a

citizen.

When Susanna (Brashears) Stewart-Graham died in 1850, she made her nephew, William Trahern, her executor. See Susanna's entry for the considerable family fighting over her estate.

<u>Family of William Trahern and Rebecca Long:</u>

v5 1198.   10 1. William Trahern, Jr, b. c1848, Holmes Co, MS, d. before 1860, Holmes Co, MS.

v5 1199.   10 2. Joseph W. Trahern, b. 1853, Holmes Co, MS, ¼ Choctaw, Roll #7435, C.C. 2559, d. after 1907

v5 1200.   10 3. Laura Trahern, b. April 1855, Holmes Co, MS, d. 1941, bur Greenhill Cem, near Cameron, OK, ¼ Choctaw, Roll #7487, C.C. 2560; m. 1880, in Jackson, MS, Samuel S. Walker, b. June 1852, MS, d. after 1895, s/o Frederick and Lucy Walker. Laura's father was ⅛ Choctaw, so for her to be ¼, her mother, Rebecca, had to be about ½. Their children are on Choctaw Census Card #2560.

v5 1201.   11 1. Beatrice Ann Walker, (Choctaw Roll #7438), b. Aug 1885.

v5 1202.   11 2. Rosa B. Walker, (Choctaw Roll #7439), b. 3 April 1888, Cameron, OK, d. there, 8 April 1971; m. 1909, in Cameron, OK, Booker A. Wilemon.

v5 1203.   11 3. Edgar Edward Walker, (Choctaw Roll #7440), b. 11 Oct 1891, Cameron, OK, d. there 8 Nov 1976; m. c1915, Leavie _____

v5 1204.   11 4. Pauline Walker, (Choctaw Roll #14762), b. Oct 1895, Cameron, OK

v5 1205.   10 4. Hannah Trahern, b. March 1858, Holmes Co, MS, ¼ Choctaw, Roll #8026, C.C. 2743; m.1. c1879, in Jackson, MS, Joseph Deloach, b. c1850, MS, d. bef 1898, MS; m.2. 21 Jan 1898, in Skullyville Co, I.T., Reddick Cartwright, b. May 1840, IL, d. after 1910

v5 1206.   11 1. Maud Deloach, (Choctaw Roll #8030, C.C. 2744), b. Dec 1880, MS; m. c1897, Jefferson Johnson, b. March 1875. Two ch: Ola Johnson, (Choctaw Roll #8031), b. 1898; and Sarah Johnson (Choctaw Roll #8032)

v5 1207.   11 2. Carrie Deloach, b. Dec 1883, ⅛ Choctaw, Roll
            #8027, as "Annie"
v5 1208.   11 3. William M. Deloach, b. 1888, ⅛ Choctaw, Roll
            #8028
v5 1209.   11 4. Josephine Deloach, (⅛ Choctaw, Roll #8029,
            C.C. 1743), b. May 1893, Indian Territory; m.
            c1910, Marcus Nelson Hedges, b. c1895. Ch:
            Mosell; Anne Norene; Marcus Nelson Jr;
            Marion; Juanita; Oleta; and Leon Hedges.
v5 1210.   10 5. Wirt Breckenridge Trahern, b. 1863, MS, d. 1897,
            Indian Territory; m. c1893, in Skullyville Co, I.T.,
            Clara L. Cowden, b. May 1870, IL
v5 1211.   11 1. Roy D. Trahern, b. May 1894, I.T., ⅛
            Choctaw, Roll #7356, C.C. 2533
v5 1212.   10 6. Joel P. Trahern, b. 1865, MS, ¼ Choctaw, Roll
            #7436, C.C. 2559

George Washington Trahern

v5 1186. 9 6. George Washington Trahern, (s/o Wesley Trahern
and Delilah Brashears), b. 15 April 1825, Choctaw Nation, MS,
d. in California; m. 1 March 1860, Henrietta B. Childers, b.
1842, MO, d/o Johnson Childers and Margaret Blair. George
Washington Trahern attended the Choctaw Academy in KY,
1831-1834. He was in the Mexican War, and later in the
California gold fields, but he made his career as a cattleraiser
near Stockton, CA. A biographical sketch of him appears in
History of San Joaquin County [CA], and he was written up in
Gold and Sunshine, Reminiscences of Early California, by Ayers.

From *History of San Joaquin Co*, [CA], c1890, pp. 650-651:

George Washington Trahern, a rancher, residing in Stockton,
was born in Mississippi, April 15, 1825, a son of Wesley and
Delilah (Brashear) Trahern. The father, a native of Virginia,
moved to Mississippi, where be became owner of a plantation on
Pearl River, seven miles below Jackson, the State capital. There
he raised cotton and corn chiefly, besides dealing in stock. He
was married at the home of his bride, on the Tombigbee, in
Alabama. They had three sons and two daughters, the latter still
living in Texas; of the sons, only the subject of this sketch
survives.

In his youth, he acquired some knowledge of cattle on his
father's place, and afterward from a brother-in-law in Texas,

where he also handled some cattle on his own account. He joined the Texas rangers in the struggle for separation from Mexico, and with them enlisted for the Mexican War, serving to the end, and is a pensioner of that war.

With fourteen others, he set out for California in 1849, coming by way of Chihuahua, Mexico, and arriving in Wood's Diggings, near Sonora, he gathered a little gold in a brief trial of that industry. He then pushed on for the plains [of California], and in the fall settled in this county, near what is now Linden and engaged in the cattle business.

In 1850, he was joined by John McMullen, one of his companions on the trip from Texas, and they located 160 acres each on the Calaveras, about three miles north of Linden. In 1851, they formed a partnership, and in 1852 bought 400 acres adjoining the 320, making a compact body, which they made headquarters for their stock business. In 1852, Mr. Trahern went East [to the mining country] and drove 1,000 cattle across the plains.

They had free range of large tracts in those days, reaching sixteen miles south to the Stanislaus and as far to the east, to the limits of the county, shared in, however, by other cattle dealers. At the death of his partner, in 1868, they owned 21,000 acres in different parts of the county, which were divided between himself and the McMullen heirs in the spring of 1869.

Mr. Trahern has continued in the stock business right along, being thus engaged in the county for forty years. He owns 8,600 acres in Castoria Township, at the mouth of the Stanislaus, and 3,342 acres on "the west side" of Tulare Township. Of the former tract, he farms 3,300 acres, and of the latter, 1,500, raising wheat chiefly, but also considerable barley and rye.

Mr. Trahern was married March 1, 1860, to Miss Henrietta B. Childers, born in Missouri in 1842, a daughter of Johnson and Margaret (Blair) Childers. The father, a native of Kentucky, had moved to Missouri, and thence to California in 1852. He mined for a time at Volcano, in Amador County, and afterward settled in Calavers County, where he carried on a Half-way House on the Mokelumne Hill Road for a few years. About 1855, he settled in this county, where he died at the age of forty-seven, leave six children, of whom five are living.

Mr. and Mrs. Trahern are the parents of five living children: Laura Trahern; Rachel O., the wife of N.C. Farnam, a merchant of Bantas, in this county, has one child, Henrietta Hazel [Farnam], born June 19, 1887; Bessie Lee, now Mrs. Percy Williams, of Union Island, has one child, Thomas Hansford Williams, born in November, 1889; Lydia Trahern and David Douglas Trahern.

Mr. G.W. Trahern is a member of the San Joaquin Valley Society of California Pioneers since 1868. (Thanks to Jennifer Mieirs for the copy.)

From Chapter VII, p.70, of *Gold and Sunshine*:

It was at this camp [in the California mine fields] that I first met George W. Trahern. He was in the cattle business, and had driven in several herds of beeves which he sold readily at the rate of six ounces ($96) a head. I had heard a good deal about "Wash Trahern" before, and felt interested in him. He was dressed in a buckskin suit, with a wide-brimmed sombrero, from which depended a wealth of black hair falling over his shoulders. He had a keen black eye and a wary look. He had been a Texas ranger, conspicuous for his bravery during the war of independence of the Lone Star state, and had been in the forefront of all the thrilling exploits of that daring band of partisan warriors. He came to California, soon after the close of the Mexican war, with his partner, John McMullin, a kindred spirit, who has long since passed over to the majority.

"Wash Trahern" was one of the famous castle of Pirote prisoners during the war for Texas independence, and successfully ran the terrible gauntlet of drawing the black bean. This awful lottery was resorted to whenever the Mexicans desired to shoot a number of their unhappy prisoners. The devilish process pursued was to range their captives in line, when a Mexican officer [p.69] would make each man draw a bean from a vessel containing one for every prisoner. As many black beans as the number of men they had doomed to death were placed in the urn. When a poor fellow drew the black bean he was set aside for execution; the others were returned to their loathsome dungeons with the terrible knowledge that the infernal lottery would soon be repeated. Could the refinement of cruelty go farther?

I remember that A.B. Laforge, a noble fellow, who was Treasurer of Calaveras County in the early fifties, and who made his escape from Pirote, told me that the intense agony the prisoners suffered after each of these horrible ordeals, was worse than death, and that they envied the good fortune of their comrades who drew from the urn the black prize which doomed them to certain, speedy and welcome death.[p.70]

Family of George Washington Trahern and Henrietta B. Childers:

v51212a. [10]1. Laura Trahern, b. c1861
v51213. [10]2. Rachel O. Trahern, b. c1863; m. N.C. Farnum
v51213a. [11]1. Henrietta Hazel Farnum, b. 10 June 1887
v51214. [10]3. Bessie Lee Trahern, m. Percy Williams
v51214a. [11]1. Thomas Hansford Williams, b. Nov 1889
v51215. [10]3. Lydia Trahern, b. c1867
v51216. [10]4. David Douglas Trahern, b. 11 April 1873, California, d. 23 April 1849, San Joaquin, CA

VAUGHN BRASHEARS and ISABELLA LeFLORE

v5838. [8]6. **Vaughn Brashears**, (s/o Zadock Brashears and Susannah Vaughn), b. 1798 (age 33 in Feb 1832); Vaughn is reported to have died in Indian Territory, about 1853 or 54, though there is a Vaughn Breshay in Gaines Co, I.T., on the 1855 census; m. 1819, at Brashears Landing, Mississippi, *Isabella LeFlore*, b. c1803 (28 in Feb 1832), at LeFleur's Bluff, on the Pearl River, MS, d/o Louis LeFleur and Rebecca Cravatt. Isabelle was sister to Greenwood LeFlore, the Choctaw Chief who negotiated the Treaty of Dancing Rabbit Creek. Rebecca Cravatt was a granddaughter of Shumaka, sister to Apuckshunnubbee.

Another version of the allotment reads all of Sec 31, T16, R1E and Lots 1, 2, 3, 4, 5, 6, 7, 8, 10, 11, in Sec 6, T15, R1E. However, he seems to have lost his land, for he and his family are among those Choctaws forcibly removed to Indian Territory. At least two of his children died in this "Choctaw Trail of Tears."

Richard Brashears, Vaughn's ex-slave, testified in 1906 that Vaughn left Alabama, "come to Honey Island, Yazoo River, Mississippi, and made three crops. Left MS in 1830 and arrived in Oklahoma Territory in 1831." But he was still in Yazoo for the special Choctaw Census of 1831, when he had 10 in fam, 2 males 16+, 4 m. & 4 fem under 10; no slaves.

(NOTE: There is surely a mistake there, for Vaughn and Isabella are not old enough to have sons over 16; some of those in this census must have been slaves. Vaughn's slave, Richard Brashears, was originally on the Chickasaw Freedmen Roll, card #912, but was transferred to Choctaw Census Card #1179, Choctaw Freedmen Roll. He was a son of Lila, another of Vaughn's slaves. Richard m. Harriett _____, and they had at least one son, Edward Brashears, #4267, Choctaw Freedmen Roll.)

Extract from Vol. 2, *Register of Choctaw Indians* who were moved to Ft. Towson, from Mississippi, 11 Feb 1832, in the company of Capt Edward McKenny:

8. **Brashears, Vaughn**   age 33, b. c1798, 5'1"
9.   (Lou?) Gibell   28, b. c1804, 5'4" [garble for Isabella]
10. Eliza   12, b. c1820, 4'; died previous to 1 May 1832
11. Polly   11, b. c1821, 3'10"
12. Deliete   6, b. c1826, 3'5"
13. Vaughn   3, b. c1829, 3'; died previous to April 1832
14. Elmira   ½, b. c1832, 2'
15. Frank   21, b. c1811, 5'6"; dropped prev. to April 1832
16. Bolin   29, b. c1803, 5'6"; " " " "
17. Lila   22, b. c1810, 5'4"; " " " "
18. Ned   12, b. c1820, 4'3"; " " " "
19. Nancy   8, b. c1824, 4'; " " " "
20. Dick   5, b. c1826, 3'6"; " " " "
21. Frankey   3, b. c1828, 3'; " " " "

Vaughn was listed as having one son under 10, two daughters under ten, two daughters 10-25, and seven slaves, 3 males and four females, for a total of 14 in the family (Arrivals, Red River Distrist, Choctaw Muster Rolls, Microfilm, Shreve Memorial Library, Shreveport, LA). Vaughn was listed as 5' 6" tall, while Isabella was 5' 4". His slave, Dick Brashears, was listed as five years old, b. c1826, though he claimed he was born in 1821 (he claimed he was 79 in 1899); perhaps he was small for his age and the census enumerator made a mistake? Richard's testimony says that Vaughn's son, Turner, "was grown about two years after we got here" i.e. to Indian Territory. I believe that is a clerical error for "born about two years after...."

Vaughn was fairly literate and well-regarded, as is evidenced by letters in the Choctaw Agency files (Office of Indian Affairs: Choctaw Files A21-23-34-63-80. Agency A23. Thanks to Jim Karlos for copies):

Choctaw Nation, 7th July 1836

To Capt W. Armstrong, Choctaw Agent,

Dear Sir: It becomes my duty to inform you as our Agent, that I have been badly treated by Mr. Little, mail rider on the route to Fort Towson, who takes advantage of his being U.S. mail rider, and has taken the liberty, to ride up to my house, and in my own yard, setting on his horse, abuse me, more than ever I was abused by a man in my life, and even threatened me with his horse whip, all of which, I had to submit to, on account of his being U.S. mail rider. And now sir; I apply to you for redress; However all that I ask is that he be removed from the limits of my country, as soon as possible; or otherwise I shall be under the necessity of seeking satisfaction with my own hands, at all hazzards. He has fell out with me, because I stated to Mr. Clarke (Post master at the Agency) the facts in relation to the two faileurs, he made on this route last Winter. He is a man of no respectability, as he has publickly taken up with a slave negro in the nation for his wife; I do not conceive that such a white man ought to be countinenced in the Indian country; In conclusion I respectfully request that you adopt such means as to have him forthwith removed from the Nation.

I am verry respectfully your
friend and obdt Servant
Vaughn Brashears

Choctaw Agency, 8th July 1836

Elbert Herring Esqr,
Comr of Ind Affairs
Sir

The enclosed communication from Vaughn Brashears was received this day; and I have felt it my duty to forward it to the Department, with a request that it be laid before the Postmaster Genl. Brashears is a Half breed Choctaw, lives on Kiamechee about half way between this and Towson, is a respectable Indian of a numerous connection; and knowing him as well as I do, I am astonished that he has submitted to the insult, complained of. If the mail rider should be killed with the present excited state of the public mind in the country, about Indian wars, it would no doubt be magnified into an open act of hostility against the Government, and perhaps troops sent out to inquire into it.

I have heard of Little the rider between this and Towson, making the attack on Brashears; and to avoid any difficulty, I would request the Post Office Dept to have him dismissed as a mail rider, by Caffrey & Holoway, the present contractors.

Respectfully
Your Obt Servt
Wm Armstrong, Choct Agent

On 17 Jan 1837, Vaughn boarded Choctaw and Chickasaw delegates to the meeting at Doaksville, I.T. to negotiate a treaty. (ref: *Who Was Who Among the Southern Indians*, by Don Martini, p.63, citing "payments from the Chickasaw Fund, Office of Indian Affairs.")

Family of Vaughn Brashears and Isabella LeFlore:

v51217.   91. **Eliza Brashears**, b. c1820, d. prev. to 1 May 1832 (i.e. during the removal.)

v51218.   92. ***Mary Ann "Polly" Brashears***, b. c1820; m. ***Alfred Peter Daniels***,

v51219.   93. ***Deliete Brashears***, b. c1826; m. ***Robert L. Cochran***, b. 15 Aug 1815,

v51220.   94. **Vaughn Brashears Jr**, b. c1829; died previous to April 1832 (i.e. during the removal.)

v51221.   95. **Elmira Brashears**, b. c1832; m. ***John Pursley***, according to testimony in hearings before the Commission to the Five Civilized Tribes (The Dawes Commission) at Spiro, I.T., 13 June 1899, related to Choctaw Freedmen Roll Application #730. Ed Brashears and his father, Dick Brashears (former slave of Vaughn Brashears), testified that Vaughn had given Ed to his daughter, Elmira Pursley. Richard Wilson testified that John Pursley and Elmira lived near Tobuskey, Cole Co, "on the other side of Brushy, this side of Old McAlester."

v51222.   96. ***Turner Brashears IV***, b. 1 March 1835 in Indian Territory, d. 3 Nov 1884, bur Latham, OK, ½

Choctaw on Rolls. The testimony of Sarah Ann (Moncrief) Harlan ([v5]1394) before the Dawes Commission that he was still living in 1896 is obviously in error, though his son, Turner Brashears V, was still living.

Mary Ann "Polly" Brashears and Alfred Peter Daniels

[v5]1218. [9]2. **Mary Ann "Polly" Brashears**, b. c1820 (11 in Feb 1832, d/o Vaughn Brashears and Isabella LeFlore), d. c1876, Indian Territory; m. c1837, in Choctaw Nation, I.T. (second wife of) *Alfred Peter Daniels*, b. c1813, Kentucky, d. Texas. His first wife was Mary LeFlore.

Family of Mary Ann "Polly" Brashears and Alfred Peter Daniels: (for more, contact James P. Karlos, 2030 Settlers Trail, Vandalia, OH 45377-3228, or Doug Barkley, P.O.Box 889, Panama, OK 74951. Additional data from Jennifer Mieirs <jenniferhsrn@ cablelynx.com>

[v5]1223. [10]1. Catherine Daniels, b. after 1837, I.T.; n.f.i.

[v5]1224. [10]2. Louisa Daniels, b. c1839

[v5]1225. [10]3. *Letha Daniels, b. 23 Feb 1841, I.T., d. 4 Jan 1916, Shadypoint, OK; m.1. c1862, Charley Cox, b. c1830, TN, d. c1890, I.T.; m.2. c1884, _____ Smith, b. c1840

[v5]1226. [10]4. *Lucinda Daniels, b. 1846, I.T., d. 1 Jan 1875; m.1. c1860, Albert Kee Folsom, b. 14 July 1841, d. 1872, Skullyville, I.T.; m.2. c1872, David Robert Welch.

[v5]1227. [10]5. *Mary A. Daniels, b. 1847, I.T., d. 8 Oct 1876; m. Feb 1869, Miles Standish Collins, b. May 1833, TN, d. 5 Dec 1919, I.T.

[v5]1228. [10]6. *Turner Brashears Daniels, ¼ Choctaw, Roll #7771, C.C. 2672, b. 11 June 1849, Jacks Fork Co, I.T., d. 5 Jan 1911, Stuart, OK; m.1. c1869, Susan LeFlore, b. c1855, d. 1885, I.T.; m.2. 29 Dec 1886, *Joanna (Brashears) Lilly* ([v5]1289), b. c1860; m.3. 26 Aug 1892, I.T., Louvenia Safronia Allen, b. 1871, d. 1950, Stuart, OK.

[v5]1229. [10]6. *Willis Henry Daniels, ¼ Choctaw, Roll #7535, C.C. 2601, b. c1853, Jacks Forks Co, I.T., d. 15

state of the public mind in the country, about Indian wars, it would no doubt be magnified into an open act of hostility against the Government, and perhaps troops sent out to inquire into it.

I have heard of Little the rider between this and Towson, making the attack on Brashears; and to avoid any difficulty, I would request the Post Office Dept to have him dismissed as a mail rider, by Caffrey & Holoway, the present contractors.

Respectfully
Your Obt Servt
Wm Armstrong, Choct Agent

On 17 Jan 1837, Vaughn boarded Choctaw and Chickasaw delegates to the meeting at Doaksville, I.T. to negotiate a treaty. (ref: *Who Was Who Among the Southern Indians*, by Don Martini, p.63, citing "payments from the Chickasaw Fund, Office of Indian Affairs.")

<u>Family of Vaughn Brashears and Isabella LeFlore:</u>

v5 1217.   9 1. **Eliza Brashears**, b. c1820, d. prev. to 1 May 1832 (i.e. during the removal.)

v5 1218.   9 2. ***Mary Ann "Polly" Brashears***, b. c1820; m. ***Alfred Peter Daniels***,

v5 1219.   9 3. ***Deliete Brashears***, b. c1826; m. ***Robert L. Cochran***, b. 15 Aug 1815,

v5 1220.   9 4. **Vaughn Brashears Jr**, b. c1829; died previous to April 1832 (i.e. during the removal.)

v5 1221.   9 5. **Elmira Brashears**, b. c1832; m. ***John Pursley***, according to testimony in hearings before the Commission to the Five Civilized Tribes (The Dawes Commission) at Spiro, I.T., 13 June 1899, related to Choctaw Freedmen Roll Application #730. Ed Brashears and his father, Dick Brashears (former slave of Vaughn Brashears), testified that Vaughn had given Ed to his daughter, Elmira Pursley. Richard Wilson testified that John Pursley and Elmira lived near Tobuskey, Cole Co, "on the other side of Brushy, this side of Old McAlester."

v5 1222.   9 6. ***Turner Brashears IV***, b. 1 March 1835 in Indian Territory, d. 3 Nov 1884, bur Latham, OK, ½

Choctaw on Rolls. The testimony of Sarah Ann (Moncrief) Harlan ([v5]1394) before the Dawes Commission that he was still living in 1896 is obviously in error, though his son, Turner Brashears V, was still living.

Mary Ann "Polly" Brashears and Alfred Peter Daniels

[v5]1218. [9]2. **Mary Ann "Polly" Brashears**, b. c1820 (11 in Feb 1832, d/o Vaughn Brashears and Isabella LeFlore), d. c1876, Indian Territory; m. c1837, in Choctaw Nation, I.T. (second wife of) *Alfred Peter Daniels*, b. c1813, Kentucky, d. Texas. His first wife was Mary LeFlore.

Family of Mary Ann "Polly" Brashears and Alfred Peter Daniels: (for more, contact James P. Karlos, 2030 Settlers Trail, Vandalia, OH 45377-3228, or Doug Barkley, P.O.Box 889, Panama, OK 74951. Additional data from Jennifer Mieirs <jenniferhsrn@ cablelynx.com>

[v5]1223. [10]1. Catherine Daniels, b. after 1837, I.T.; n.f.i.

[v5]1224. [10]2. Louisa Daniels, b. c1839

[v5]1225. [10]3. *Letha Daniels, b. 23 Feb 1841, I.T., d. 4 Jan 1916, Shadypoint, OK; m.1. c1862, Charley Cox, b. c1830, TN, d. c1890, I.T.; m.2. c1884, _____ Smith, b. c1840

[v5]1226. [10]4. *Lucinda Daniels, b. 1846, I.T., d. 1 Jan 1875; m.1. c1860, Albert Kee Folsom, b. 14 July 1841, d. 1872, Skullyville, I.T.; m.2. c1872, David Robert Welch.

[v5]1227. [10]5. *Mary A. Daniels, b. 1847, I.T., d. 8 Oct 1876; m. Feb 1869, Miles Standish Collins, b. May 1833, TN, d. 5 Dec 1919, I.T.

[v5]1228. [10]6. *Turner Brashears Daniels, ¼ Choctaw, Roll #7771, C.C. 2672, b. 11 June 1849, Jacks Fork Co, I.T., d. 5 Jan 1911, Stuart, OK; m.1. c1869, Susan LeFlore, b. c1855, d. 1885, I.T.; m.2. 29 Dec 1886, *Joanna (Brashears) Lilly* ([v5]1289), b. c1860; m.3. 26 Aug 1892, I.T., Louvenia Safronia Allen, b. 1871, d. 1950, Stuart, OK.

[v5]1229. [10]6. *Willis Henry Daniels, ¼ Choctaw, Roll #7535, C.C. 2601, b. c1853, Jacks Forks Co, I.T., d. 15

May 1902, McCurtain, OK; m.1. c1876, Ellen Hudlow; m.2. c1885, Mary B. Riley; ?met3.(?) c1885, Lavina (or Louvenia) Trahern, (½ Choctaw) b. c1855, Skullyville Co, I.T., d. there, c1892; ?met4.(?) c1878, Jane Overton,

v51230.   107. Peter Alfred Daniels, b. 20 Feb 1856, d. 6 April 1878, Latham, OK (Trahern Station), bur Aykni Achukma.

Letha Daniels and Charley Cox

v51225. 103. Letha Daniels, (d/o Mary Ann "Polly" Brashears and Alfred Peter Daniels), b. 23 Feb 1841, Jacks Fork Co, Indian Territory, d. 4 Jan 1916, Shadypoint, OK, bur Dog Creek Cem, LeFlore Co, OK; m.1. c1862, Charley Cox, b. c1830, TN, d. c1890, I.T.; m.2. c1884, _____ Smith, b. c1840

v51231.   111. Emma Cox, b. 1864, Skullyville, I.T., d. there, 1890; met Lysander T. "Don" Trahern, b. 6 Feb 1851, Skullyville Co, I.T., d. 28 Feb 1909, Walls, OK, s/o James Nicholas Trahern and Sarah Hall. Lysander Trahern was ½ Choctaw, Roll #8216, C.C. 2802. Son, Joseph Cox, was not registered on Dawes Rolls.

v51232.   122. Joseph Cox, b. 1886, Walls, OK, d. 1925, Milton, OK, m. 4 Sept 1907, Alice Herron, b. 1894, AR. ch: Bessie A., Josie, Ruby, Cecil, and Edna Cox.

v51233.   113. Charles Cox, b. 1867

v51234.   114. Joseph Rufus Cox, b. 1877, Skullyville Co, I.T.; m. c1895, _____ Bush, b. c1877; ch: Charles, 1895; John, 1897; and Mary Mazona Cox, 1901.

v51235.   115. Maggie Etta Cox, b. 23 March 1880, Skullyville, I.T., d. 11 Jan 1961, Poteau, LeFlore Co, OK; m. 12 March 1894, in Red Oak, I.T. David E. Davis, b. 23 Oct 1863, Rapides Parish, LA, d. 20 Nov 1934, Shadypoint, LeFlore Co, OK; ch: Letha, Lennie, Bertie Lorena, Eva, Sue, Julia Josephine, Lessie Leona, Vancil, and Elvis E. Davis.

v51236.   125. Sue Davis, b. 26 Feb 1904, Shadypoint, LeFlore Co, I.T., d. 11 March 1968, Waukegan, Lake Co, IL; m. 3 July 1924, Waukegan, IL,

James P. Karlos Sr, b. 9 Nov 1889, Peania, Greece, d. 2 Nov 1978, Bellbrook, Greene Co, OH

v51237.   132. James "Jim" Peter Karlos Jr, b. 28 May 1925, Waukegan, IL; m. 8 Feb 1948, Waukegan, IL, Ruth A. Schaefer, b. 17 April 1925, Waukegan, IL. Jim is a researcher in this line of the family. Ch: Gregg J., Joanne, Karen S., and Bradley W. Karlos.

v51238.   116. Letha A. "Coonie" Cox, b. 11 Oct 1882, Skullyville, I.T., d. 31 Jan 1964, Rosedale, LeFlore Co, OK; m. 9 Aug 1908, Wallace Belt, b. AR, d. 1918, LeFlore Co, OK; ch: Susie J., Charley, Mary M., Willie, Maggie, and Mattie Belt.

Lucinda Daniels and Albert Kee Folsom

v51226. 104. Lucinda Daniels, (d/o Mary Ann "Polly" Brashears and Alfred Peter Daniels), b. 1846, Jacks Fork Co, Indian Territory, d. 1 Jan 1875, bur Welch Cem, Brazil Station, Choctaw Nation, Ind. Terr.; m.1. c1860, Albert Kee Folsom, b. 14 July 1841, d. 1872, Skullyville, I.T., s/o Col. David Folsom and Jane Hall; m.2. c1872, David Robert Welch.

According to Allie Mae Folsom, granddaughter of Albert Kee Folsom, family oral tradition stated that Albert Kee was shot and killed by Green McCurtain. Later, at the time of the final rolls of the Choctaw, Green McCurtain was to become Principal Chief of the Choctaw Nation.

v51239.   111. George Folsom, b. c1860, d. 1875, bur Brazil Station, Choctaw Nation, I.T.

v51240.   112. Joseph Folsom, b. 1864, I.T.

v51241.   113. Albert Peter Folsom, ¼ Choctaw, Roll #8115, C.C. 2770, b. 13 Dec 1866,Council House, Skullyville, OK, d. 11 Nov 1937 (or 1939), Latham, OK, bur Folsom Cem, LeFlore Co, OK; m. 18 July 1887, **Susie Katherine Brashears** (v51299), d/o Judge Turner Brashears and Kate McSweeney. See her entry, below.

v51242.   114. David Crockett Folsom, b. 7 Oct 1868, ⅜ Choctaw, Roll #7518, C.C. 2590, d. 25 June 1945, bur Old Panther Cem, McCurtain, Haskell Co, OK;

m. 12 March 1894, in Skullyville Co, I.T., Mary Jane Daniels, (^{v5}1264) b. 15 March 1879, Skullyville Co, I.T., d. McCurtain, Haskell Co, OK, his cousin, d/o Willis Henry Daniels and Ellen Hudlow; no ch.

^{v5}1243. [11]5. George Folsom, b. 1870, I.T., d. there, 1875

Mary A. Daniels and Miles S. Collins

^{v5}**1227.** [10]5. Mary A. Daniels, (d/o Mary Ann "Polly" Brashears and Alfred Peter Daniels), b. 1847, I.T., d. 8 Oct 1876, Spiro, OK, bur Skullyville Cem, Spiro, OK; m. Feb 1869, Miles Standish Collins, b. May 1833, TN, d. 5 Dec 1919, I.T., s/o John and Minerva Collins;

^{v5}1244. [11]1. Miles Standish Collins Jr, b. Aug 1870 ⅛ Choctaw, Roll #8221; m. 16 Aug 1893, Gracie A. Jones, b. 1875, Iowa, d/o J.R. and Ann Jones. Ch: Stella M., Dennis Owen, Mary A., Miles Ricker, Henry Monroe, Ollie Belle, Myrtle, Gracie, Beatrice and Rachel Collins.

^{v5}1245. [11]2. Andrew Collins, b. 22 Dec 1872, ¼ Choctaw, Roll #7972, d. 5 Feb 1905, bur Short Mountain Cem; m. 3 April 1895, Claudie L. Kersh, b. c1880, d/o Sam and Alice Kersh. Ch: Claudie C., Andrew Lee, Thomas Hugh, and Lilly Collins.

^{v5}1246. [11]3. John Foley Collins, b. March 1875, ⅛ Choctaw, Roll #8230, d. 1944, bur Skullyville Cem; m. 14 May 1894, Daisy L. Bishop, b. Sept 1877, d. 1946, d/o David and Myrah Bishop. Ch: Foley D., Andrew Elijah, Clara May, Clarence Cole, Viola, and Joseph E. Collins.

Turner Brashears Daniels and his Three Wives

^{v5}**1228.** [10]6. Turner <u>Brashears</u> Daniels, (s/o Mary Ann "Polly" Brashears and Alfred Peter Daniels), ¼ Choctaw, Roll #7771, C.C. 2672, b. 11 June 1849, Jacks Fork Co, Choctaw Nation, Ind. Terr., d. 5 Jan 1911, Stuart, OK, bur Pryor Cem; m.1. c. 1869, Susan LeFlore, b. c1855, d. 1885, I.T.; m.2. 29 Dec 1886, *Joanna (Brashears) Lilly* (^{v5}1289), b. c1860, d/o Judge Turner Brashears, IV, and Catherine "Kate" McSweeney; m.3. 26 Aug 1892, I.T., Louvenia Safronia Allen, b. 1871, d. 1950, Stuart, OK.

Family of Turner Brashears Daniels and Susan LeFlore:

v5 1247.   11 1. Mary Ann Daniels, b. 1870 (#92 on 1885 Skullyville Co, I.T. census), d. 18/28 March 1892, d/o Turner Brashears Daniels and Susan LeFlore, m. 5 Oct 1890, Thomas Foster. Ch: Mary A. Foster, m. Thomas Lee Shirley,

v5 1248.   11 2. Greenwood Daniels, b. Oct 1874, Skullyville Co, I.T., ½ Choctaw, Roll #8110, C.C. 2767, d. 1915, Phoenix, AZ; m.1. c1895, Minnie Trahern, (½ Choctaw) d/o James Nicholas Trahern and Virginia P. Clossen, b. 1878, Skullyville Co, I.T., d. there, 8 Dec 1900; m.2. 5 Nov 1905, May Ferguson, m.3. 15 Feb 1915, Alice Wilson. Ch: Thelma (⅜ Choctaw, Roll #8112, C.C. 2767); William W.; and Edmond Daniels.

v5 1249.   11 3. Napoleon B. Daniels, b. 1881, I.T., d. 1897 at Spencer Academy, I.T.

v5 1250.   11 4. Lucy C. Daniels, b. 1883, I.T., d. 30 April 1901, ⅜ Choctaw, Roll #7772

v5 1251.   11 5. Susan Rebecca Daniels, b. 8 April 1885, I.T., ⅜ Choctaw, Roll #7773. d. 20 March 1907, Stuart, OK; m. Z.R. Harlow,

Family of Turner Brashears Daniels and Joanna Brashears:

v5 1252.   11 6. Turner Brashears Daniels Jr, b. 3 Dec 1888, ¼ Choctaw, Roll #7774, d. 6 Feb 1971, bur Pryor Cem; m. Bessie Newton, (¼ Choctaw, Roll #13221), b. 27 July 1892, Skullyville, LeFlore Co, I.T., d. 27 Oct 1980, Stuart, OK, d/o Robert Newton and Catherine Trahern. Ch: both b. after 1905: Jessie; and Howard Daniels

v5 1253.   11 7. Zeno Daniels, b. c1890. n.f.i.

Family of Turner Brashears Daniels and Louvenia Allen:

v5 1254.   11 8. Ida Daniels, b. Nov 1893, ⅛ Choctaw, Roll #7775; m. Arthur Shirley,

v5 1255.   11 9. Otto Daniels, b. 17 March 1895, ⅛ Choctaw, Roll #7776, d. 31 Oct 1987, bur Pryor Cem; m.1. Audie Crain, m.2. 23 Nov 1905, Thelma _____. Ch: Clyde, Alfred Lee, Betty Lou, and Otto, Jr Daniels.

v5 1256.   11 10. Lottie Daniels, b. July 1899, ⅛ Choctaw, Roll #7777; m. Hugh Loftis,

v5 1257.   11 11. Mattie Daniels, b. 6 Feb 1901, ⅛ Choctaw, Roll

	#7778, d. 8 Nov 1973; m. J.W. McNally,
^{v5}1258.	^{11}12. Minnie Daniels, b. 6 Feb 1902, ⅛ Choctaw, Roll #7779; m. John David Bennett, b. 20 May 1902, d. 24 Sept 1924
^{v5}1259.	^{11}13. Willie T. Daniels, b. 13 Feb 1903, I.T., d. 5 Feb 1915, Stuart, OK
^{v5}1260.	^{11}14. Robert E. Lee Daniels, b. 10 May 1905, ⅛ Choctaw, Roll #NB 495, d. 22 May 1982, bur Pryor Cem; m. Jimmie L. June, b. 11 Jan 1905, d. 18 July 1987
^{v5}1261.	^{11}15. Letha Lou Ella Daniels, b. 4 July 1907,
^{v5}1262.	^{11}16. Isabel Daniels, b. 1 March 1909, d. 3 April 1909

Willis Henry Daniels and his Four Wives

^{v5}1229. ^{10}6. Willis Henry Daniels, (s/o Mary Ann "Polly" Brashears and Alfred Peter Daniels), ¼ Choctaw, Roll #7535, C.C. 2601, b. c1853, Jacks Forks Co, Choctaw Nation, I.T., d. 15 May 1902, McCurtain, OK, bur Old Panther Cem, San Bois Co, Choctaw Nation, Ind. Terr; m.1. c1876, Ellen Hudlow, m.2. c1885, Mary B. Riley, d/o Jesse and Elizabeth Riley; ?met3.(?) c1885, Lavina (or Louvenia) Trahern, (½ Choctaw) b. c1855, Skullyville Co, I.T., d. there, c1892, d/o James Nicholas Trahern and Sarah Hall; ?met4.(?) c1878, Jane Overton,

Family of Willis Henry Daniels and Ellen Hudlow:

^{v5}1263.	^{11}1. Rutha Agnes Daniels, b. 1877 in MO, ⅛ Choctaw, Roll #7540; m. 22 Dec 1892, Henry Blaylock. Ch: Louella, Willis Henry, David Solomon, George Washington, Isaac, and Joseph Francis Blaylock.
^{v5}1264.	^{11}2. Mary Jane Daniels, b. 16 March 1879, Skullyville, I.T. ⅛ Choctaw, Roll #7519; m. 12 March 1894, in Skullyville Co, I.T., David Crockett Folsom, her cousin, (^{v5}1242) b. 7 Oct 1868, I.T., d. 25 June 1945, McCurtain, OK, s/o Albert Kee Folsom and Lucinda Daniels,
^{v5}1265.	^{11}3. Agnes "Annie" Daniels, b. 1881; m. 25 June 1899, Charles A. Brown, Ch: Turner Brown.
^{v5}1266.	^{11}4. Charlie Daniels, b. 1883
^{v5}1267.	^{11}5. Mahaley Daniels, b. 1885

Family of Willis Henry Daniels and Amanda Jane Overton:

| ^{v5}1268. | ^{11}6. Mary Ellen Daniels, b. c1880, illegitimate d/o Willis Daniels and Amanda Jane Hudlow; m. 7 |

Oct 1901, George B. Petty, b. April 1871, MO, s/o Enoch and Matilda Petty. Ch: David Petty

Family of Willis Henry Daniels and Louvina Trahern:

v5 1269. [11]7. Susan Gertrude Daniels, b. 9 June 1885, d. 5 Jan 1946, OKCity, bur Dog Creek Cem, LeFlore Co, OK, ⅛ Choctaw, Roll #7684, C.C. 2646 (actually ⅜ Choctaw); m.1. 16 July 1889, in Milton, I.T., Sam W. Fout. (Great-grandparents of Douglas R. "Doug" Barkley, P.O.Box 998, Panama, OK 74951, who collected much of this data), s/o Joun Fout and Amanda Kinard; m.2. Frank Johns (an escaped prisoner from Missouri, who took the name Frank Johns from a tombstone).

v5 1270. [12]1. Luevina Elizabeth Fout, (Choctaw Roll #7685; 1/16 Choctaw) b. c1900, Skullyville, Mushatabbee Dist, I.T.; m. c1920, Elmer Watts, b. c1900. Ch: Raymond; Opal; Willis; L.V.; June; and Donnie Joe Watts.

v5 1271. [12]2. Sallie Jane Fout, (Choctaw Roll #7686; 1/16 Choctaw) b. 12 Nov 1901, Milton, OK, d. 4 Nov 1981, OK; m. c1902, Eli Fayette Mize, b. 30 Oct 1905, d. Feb 1972, OK

v5 1272. [12]3. Turner Fout, b. c1901-1905

v5 1273. [12]4. Nelson Fout, b. 30 Oct 1905, d. Feb 1972, OK; m. c1925, Alice Allen, b. c1905

v5 1274. [12]5. Samuel Fout, b. 25 July 1905, OK, d. 26 Aug 1905, OK

v5 1275. [12]6. Rosie Bell Fout, b. 1908, OK, d. 1969, OK; m. Robert Lee Lovell, b. c1908, OK

Family of Willis Henry Daniels and Mary A. Riley:

v5 1276. [11]8. Joseph David Daniels, b. 28 Jan 1892, d. 20 Aug 1966, Milton, OK, bur Milton Cem, LeFlore Co, OK; m. Willie Ann Seay,

v5 1277. [11]9. Alfred Peter Daniels, b. 18 March 1895; m. Alice M. Derry Berry,

Deliete Brashears and Robert L. Cochran

v5 1219. [9]3. **Deliete Brashears**, (d/o Vaughn Brashears and Isabella LeFlore), b. c1826; m. **Robert L. Cochran**, b. 15 Aug 1815, d. 1864, Stonewall, OK. After death of Deliete, Robert married Jincy Bohannon. Robert L. and Deliete had at least one child (data from descendant Pam Caplan <lcaplan@oklahoma. net>):

v5 1278.   10 1. Mary Isabella Cochran, b. 16 July 1847, d. 21 Feb 1916; m. 1865 (second wife of), Tandy C. Walker, b. 14 July 1839, d. 23 Oct 1910. They moved to Stonewall, OK, and lived there until their deaths. They are buried in the cemetery in Frisco. Tandy was a well to do farmer, stockman, Senator, lawman, etc. He was #1 on the final Dawes Chickasaw Indian Rolls. He was on the Dawes Commission. Tandy m.1. Adeline Wade and they had two children, Annie Walker (who m. George Perry, brother to Alice Perry, Mrs. Robert T. Walker, below), and Theodore Walker.

v5 1279.   11 1. Robert T. Walker, b. 1870, #10 on Final Chickasaw Rolls; m. Alice Perry, b. 1875, d. 1919 (#3998 on Chickasaw Rolls)

v5 1280.   12 1. William Douglas Walker, b. 28 Feb 1898, d. 2 Dec 1950, OkCity, (#3999 on Chickasaw Rolls). (Pam Caplan's grandfather)

v5 1281.   11 2. J.T. Walker, b. 1873, #2 on Chickasaw Rolls

v5 1282.   11 3. J. Cent Walker, b. 1876, #3 on Chickasaw Rolls, d. 1965. He was a lawman in Ada, OK; m. 26 Sept 1900, Lucy Blackwell, b. 1880

v5 1283.   11 4. Ida Mary Walker, b. 1884, #4 on Chickasaw Rolls; m. 20 May 1897, J.M. Byrd

v5 1284.   11 5. G. Cleveland Walker, b. 1885

v5 1285.   11 6. Minnie Walker, b. 11 June 1887

v5 1286.   11 7. Catherine Walker, d. inf?

v5 1287.   11 8. Mary Cornelia Walker, b. 1880; m. Bruno Mayer

Judge Turner Brashears IV and Kate McSweeney

v5 **1222.** 9 6. **Turner Brashears IV**, (s/o Vaughn Brashears and Isabelle LeFlore), b. 1 March 1835, in Indian Territory, d. 3 Nov 1884, ½ Choctaw on Rolls; bur near Latham, OH, at Trahern Station, located about 7¾ miles west of Shady Point, about 20 yards off the Latham Road, south of the old Trahern Station site, on Leon Watson's property. A historical marker beside the road designates the location of Trahern Station on the Butterfield Stage Overland Mail route. The plot is fenced. Others buried there, beside Brashears, are Daniels and Traherns.

Judge Turner Brashears, IV, m. **Catherine "Kate" McSweeney**, b. 22 Feb 1840, d. 22 Dec 1886, a non-citizen, in one record; ¼ Choctaw, Roll #8116 in another. The Ancestral File in Salt Lake City says she was named Kate or Catherine McSweeney (their son's death certificate says "Cathaleen"), and that she was born in Cork Co, Ireland; on the other hand, one of her daughters, Mary Irena (Brashears) Wyers, believed she was born in Fort Smith, AR.

Richard Brashears testified in "J.W. Hyden vs. Choctaw Nation" that Turner had at least three children: "one who married Joes Moore, one who married John Wise (Mississippi black pronunciation of Wyers), and one who married Albert Folsom."

Turner Brashears seems to have been married previously. On the 1855 Choctaw Census/payment record, he has a wife, Per-ma-laye, and a daughter, Ellen. No further record on either of them.

This was also apparently Kate's second marriage. Testimony of Simon E. Lewis, Dawes file 2900, shows that Kate Daniels, a non-Choctaw, m.2. Turner Brashears and they were the parents of Mattie (Brashears) Moore. Kate apparently had one child by her first marriage: Peter Alfred Daniels, b. 20 Feb 1856, d. 6 April 1878, bur Latham, Skullyville Co, Choctaw Nation, Ind. Terr. Inscription: "son of C. & K. born in Choctaw Nation, died at Council House, No Cross, No Crown." Several lists of the children of Turner Brashears, IV, and Kate McSweeney include him, including Bible records of Judge Turner Brashears, sent me by Helen Wyers.

Kate Brashears, age 40, is on the 1885 Census of Skullyville, with children, John, 19; Irena, 15; Susie, 13; Allie, 10; and Tod, 8. Judge Turner Brashears had died in 1884; Kate died in 1886.

Family of Turner Brashears IV and Per-ma-laye:
v5 1288.   10 1. **Ellen Brashears**, on 1855 Choctaw census; n.f.i.
Family of Turner Brashears IV and Kate McSweeney:
v5 1289.   10 2. **Joanna Isabella Brashears**, b. 1 Oct 1858, d. c1891-2, ¼ Choctaw; m.1. 26 Dec 1878, **I.H.**

Lilly, m.2. 29 Dec 1886, (2nd wife of) **Turner Brashears Daniels, Sr** (v⁵1228), ¼ Choctaw, Roll #7771, C.C. 2672, b. June 1849, Jacks Fork Co, Choctaw Nation, Ind. Terr., s/o Alfred Daniels and Mary "Polly" Ann Brashears. Turner Brashears Daniels m.1. Susan LeFlore and had a daughter, Mary Daniels, who m. Thomas Foster.

v⁵1290.   ¹¹1. Lela Lilly, b. 1878
v⁵1291.   ¹¹2. Kate Lilly, b. 1879

See Turner Brashears Daniels, Sr, above, for Joanna Isabella's Daniels children.

v⁵1292.   ¹⁰3. **William T. Brashears**, b. 18 Feb 1861 d. 1 Jan 1884, per Bible; b. 18 Feb 1865, d. 2 Jan 1884, per stone; bur Trahern Station, Latham, OK

v⁵1293.   ¹⁰4. **Mattie Lorena Brashears**, b. 15 Feb 1864, Ind. Terr, ¼ Choctaw, (Census Card #2900); m. 10 Jan 1885, at New Hope, I.T., **Joseph J. Moore**, b. c1853, a non-Choctaw, s/o Levi and Ann Moore.

v⁵1294.   ¹¹1. Levi Moore, b. 1886, ⅛ Choctaw
v⁵1295.   ¹¹2. Joe J. Moore, b. 1888, ⅛ Choctaw
v⁵1296.   ¹¹3. Susie O. Moore, b. 1889, ⅛ Choctaw

v⁵1297.   ¹⁰5. **John H.T. Brashears**, b. 2 Feb 1866, ¼ Choctaw, Roll #8856, C.C. 2021 (listed as age 35 on the "final rolls" of 25 Sept 1902); m. 16 June 1889, **Minnie Moore**, b. c1866 (36 in 1902), non-citizen, d/o Levi and Amy Moore. Minnie was admitted in 1896 as a Choctaw Citizen by marriage (Case #883). No children listed on final rolls, 1906; John was identified as s/o Turner Brashears of Skullyville and Kate Brashears of Thon City [?Towson?] Co?? Marriage of parents verified by testimony of R.O. Edmonds, Choctaw case #883.)

v⁵1298.   ¹⁰6. *****Mary Irena Brashears**, b. 5 Nov 1868, Spiro, Leflore Co, OK, ¼ Choctaw, Roll #7808 C.C. 2711, d. 28 May 1940 of diabetes; m. 23 March 1887, **John William Wyers**, b. 5 Nov 1869, Clarksville, Johnson Co, AR, d. 25 Jan 1922.

v⁵1299.   ¹⁰7. *****Susie Katherine Brashears**, b. 5 Dec 1872, d. 30 Dec 1935, bur Folsom Cem, LeFlore Co, OK, ¼ Choctaw, Roll #8117; m. 18 July 1887, **Albert Peter Folsom** (v⁵1241), b. 13 Dec 1866, v5 1300.   10 8. **Allie Wishus Brashears**, b. 5 Aug 1875, ¼ Choctaw, Roll #14345 C.C. 3112; m. 1893, *James S. Latimer*, b. c1856. James gave testimony on 17 Dec 1902, in Dawes case #3112, that he had married Allie Brashears twice, once by U.S. law in 1893, and secondly by Choctaw law in 1897, in order to comply with Choctaw laws.

v5 1301.   11 1. Winifred Latimer, b. 1895, ⅛ Choctaw, Roll #14346

v5 1302.   11 2. Alvin Latimer, b. 1897, ⅛ Choctaw, Roll #14347

v5 1303.   10 9. **Turner "Todd" Brashears Jr [V]**, b. 27 Oct 1879 (per Bible), or 29 Oct 1879 (per death certificate; age 21 in 1902), d. 22 Oct 1939, bur Fairview Cem, near Panama, OK, ¼ Choctaw, Roll #8961, C.C. 3066; m. _____

v5 1304.   11 1. **Turner Brashears VI**, b. 1906, d. 1962, bur Fairview Cem, near Panama, OK

v5 1305.   10 10. **Oscar Brashears**, b. 19 Oct 1881, d. 31 March 1884, age 2½, bur Trahern Station, Latham, OK

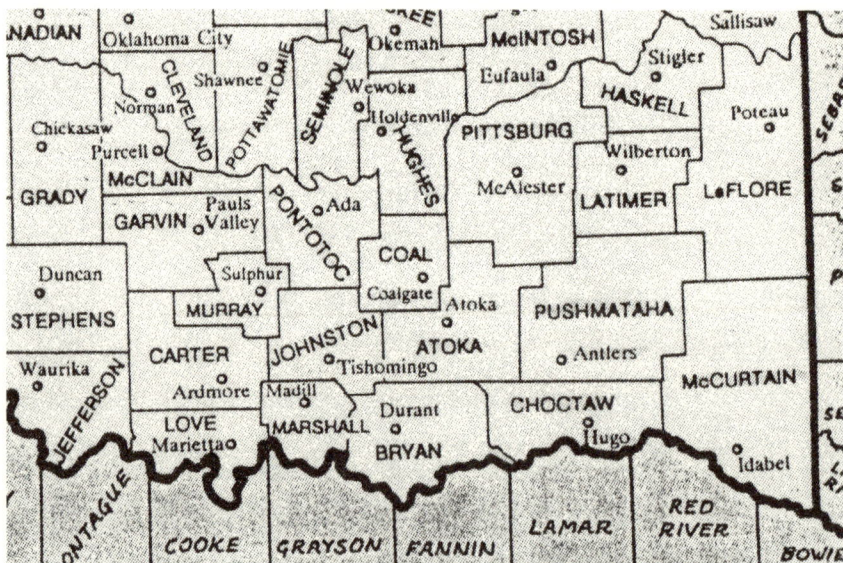

Figure 28: Counties of Southeast Oklahoma, after statehood

Mary Irena Brashears and John William Wyers

v5 1298. [10]6. **Mary Irena Brashears**, (d/o Turner Brashears, IV, and Catherine "Kate" McSweeney), b. 5 Nov 1868 (per Bible; or 1870, per *Oklahoma Indian-Pioneer Interviews*; or 1872, per tombstone), Spiro, Leflore Co, OK, ¼ Choctaw, Roll #7808 C.C. 2711, d. 28 May 1940 of diabetes; m. 23 March 1887, **John William Wyers**, b. 5 Nov 1869, Clarksville, Johnson Co, AR, d. 25 Jan 1922. (data from Helen Wyers (Mrs. Sampson Wyers Jr), Ancestral File, SLC, and Final Dawes Rolls)

Helen Wyers writes: "William Wyers, John W.'s father, was born in New York in 1827. He was in the Civil War in Missouri and settled in Clarksville, AR after that. He bought land there and established a mill; in fact, the stone he used is supposed to be on the courthouse lawn in Clarksville. He married Ellen Trotter Higgins in 1866 or 1867 and they had 8 children. Ellen had been married before, but Mr. Higgins had been killed by bushwackers during the war. William had been married previously, but his wife had died.

"Irene Brashears was considered an educated woman for her time. She went to a Catholic School known as Saint Edwards in Fort Smith, AR and also a Baptist Seminary. She taught school before she married (at age 15, 17, or 19). John was illiterate, and she taught him to read and write. He learned to be a government surveyor, and he served as a field Deputy U.S. Marshall with the Indians, a Pinkerton railroad security officer on the Fort Smith and Western Railroad, plus was sheriff. He also ran a ranch. He learned to speak the Choctaw language, and according to Lorena, his daughter, the Wyers children were raised to have great pride in their Choctaw heritage." John Wyers was sheriff of Haskell Co from 1917 until his death (in 1922); then his son Sampson was sheriff for three years.

v5 1306. [11]1. Bessie Belle Wyers, b. 27 July 1888, Leguire, Haskell Co, OK, ⅛ Choctaw, Roll #7909; m. William Savage. From Helen Wyers: "They had 2 sons, Ed Savage and John Savage. They have both passed away. John's wife's name was Mary, and they lived in Cement, OK. Ed's wife's name was Sara, and they lived in Duncan, OK. We heard that Sara also died and that their son lives in the house they did. Ed and Sara had the original of the photograph of the family. John had diabetes and had lost a leg."

[v5]1307.   [11]2. Bailey W. Wyers, b. 10 Nov 1889, Leguire, Haskell Co, OK, ⅛ Choctaw, Roll #7910. "Bailey was living in Denver, CO in 1965. He had no children and he had passed away before Edna died. He had had one or both legs amputated from diabetes."

[v5]1308.   [11]3. Effie E. Wyers, b. 9 Aug 1891, Leguire, Haskell Co, OK, ⅛ Choctaw, Roll #7911; m. _____ Calmes. Helen Wyers: "Sam has always pronounced it like "Clamenes", but on the records for the estate, it is spelled Calmes. Effie had 3 children. John Calmes was one, but the names of the other two are unknown; their children participated in Edna's estate. The children of one were Carole Calmes Brewnce and Janis E. Calmes. The other's children were Dr. Robert Calmes, Paul Calmes and Darlene Calmes Mason."

[v5]1309.   [11]4. John Norman Wyers, b. 10 June 1894 Leguire, Haskell Co, OK, ⅛ Choctaw, Roll #7912; m. Martha Ersula Wilson, b. 5 Oct 1885, Morris, IL

[v5]1310.   [12]1. Norman A. Wyers, b. 4 Sept 1922, McCurtain, Haskell Co, OK

[v5]1311.   [12]2. Robert Austin Wyers, b. 12 Aug 1923, McCurtain, Haskell Co, OK, d. bef estate settlement of Edna (Wyers) Kirkwood, 1972.

[v5]1312.   [12]3. Edna Wyers; m. Charles Ray Adams,

[v5]1313.   [12]4. Paul Ernest Wyers,

[v5]1314.   [11]5. Paul E. Wyers, b. 7 June 1896, Leguire, Haskell Co, OK, ⅛ Choctaw, Roll #7913; wife's name unknown. He had 4 children: Frances Wyers, Marie Wyers Baker, Normal Wyers, and Terrel Wyers.

[v5]1315.   [11]6. Sampson (B.) Wyers, b. 13 May 1898 Leguire, Haskell Co, OK, ⅛ Choctaw, Roll #7914, d. Oct 1965, bur Fr. Gibson, AR; m. Oteka Ruth Oliphant, ⅛ Chickasaw. (in 1997, she was in a nursing home.) Sampson claimed he had no middle initial, but when he joined the Navy in WWI, they insisted he choose one; he picked "B" to reflect his mother's maiden name.

v5 1316.   12 1. Oteka Johnese Wyers, b. 15 March 1922, Stigler, OK, d. 1972; m. Paul Mastrangelo, and had four children.

v5 1317.   12 2. Sampson Wyers Jr, b. 10 Jan 1925, Stigler, OK; m. Helen Patricia Buske, who has sent a great deal of Wyers info, for which many thanks.

v5 1318.   12 3. Paul Tecumseh Wyers, b. 13 July 1931; m. Charlotte Belle Warren; 3 ch. "Paul just found out that he has diabetes."

v5 1319.   12 4. Patrick Zane Wyers, b. 8 June 1934; m. Mary Ellen Abell, a Ph.D. in Nursing who teaches at a university in Fort Worth.

v5 1320.   12 5. Scotty Wyers b 28 March 1937, married Becky Huggett and they had 4 children.

v5 1321.   12 6. LaQuita Francell Wyers b 16 March 1942, married James Patrick Yatsik, they had 2 sons. Jim passed away and LaQuita still runs their business enterprises in Kodiak, Alaska.

v5 1322.   11 7. Lorena Wyers, b. 22 April 1900, ⅛ Choctaw, Roll #7915, d. 23 April 1995; m.1. Robert Marion Furry (1 ch); m.2. L.M. Laughlin.

v5 1323.   12 1. Marcella Furry, m. Frank Regan; 3 ch

v5 1324.   11 8. Edna Wyers, b. 7 Feb 1902, McCurtain, Haskell Co, OK, ⅛ Choctaw, Roll #7916; m. _____ Kirkwood, no ch. Helen Wyers: "In the late 1970's, Edna (Wyers) Kirkwood died and, since her husband had died and she had no children, her estate was divided among her siblings or their issue. There were 2 wills, so the judge threw them both out. We have the list of people who participated in the estate; consequently, I am able to give you more information on the descendants. At that time, two sisters, Lorena and Juanita were still living."

v5 1325.   11 9. Juanita Wyers, b. 28 July 1904, McCurtain, Haskell Co, OK; m. Bob Thompson (2 ch: Mary Ann Thompson and William Thompson).

v5 1326.   11 10. Fritz Wyers, b. 3 Sept 1910, McCurtain, Haskell Co, OK; m. _____; 2 ch: Susan Wyers and Greg Wyers.

In spite of being on the final Dawes Rolls as ¼ Choctaw and eight of her children being registered Choctaws (things she could hardly be unaware of), Mary Irena (Brashears) Wyers denied she had any Indian blood. In the *Oklahoma Indian-Pioneer Interviews*, v.101, p.17-19, she gave this account of her family:

Mrs. John Wyers, b. 5 Nov 1870, Skullyville
Father, Turner Breashears, b. MS
Mother, Kate McSweeney, b. Fort Smith, AR

My father, Turner Breashears, was of English descent. He ran away from home coming to MS. Later he came to the Indian Terr and settled in LeFlore Co.

My mother, also of English descent, was born in Ft Smith, Ark. This is where she met my father and they married in Ft Smith, coming to Skullyville where they made their home. After settling and building here my father went into business. He had a merchandise store located one mile from the coach stop. His place of business was known as the Brazil Station. In order to keep his store stocked up with merchandise, he would make one trip a year to Ft Smith, Ark, in wagons. It took several days to make a trip.

My mother was well thought of by the Indians, who came to her when they were ill. She would go to their homes to nurse them through their pains and grief. Most of the people who lived in Skullyville at this time farmed. They would have big get-togethers, bring dinner and work on one farm all day. Then when they finished one farm they would go to another place. They kept this up until all farms were cared for. There were eight children in our family of whom I was the oldest. I was born in 1870, in Skullyville, LeFlore Co., was married to Mr. John Wyers of Mulberry, Ark, later coming to McCurtain, OK and making this our home.

Mr. Wyers was elected sheriff of Haskell County, in 1917. He served five years until his death in 1922, on Jan 25. It was then that our son Sampson took his place and served three years. Mr. Wyers and I had five girls and five boys, who are all living at this time.

Susie Katherine Brashears and Albert Peter Folsom

ᵛ⁵1299. ¹⁰7. **Susie Katherine Brashears**, (d/o Turner Brashears, IV, and Catherine "Kate" McSweeney), b. 5 Dec 1872, d. 30 Dec 1935, bur Folsom Cem, LeFlore Co, OK, ¼ Choctaw, Roll #8117; m. 18 July 1887, **Albert Peter Folsom** (ᵛ⁵1241), b. 13 Dec 1866, in Council House, Skullyville, OK, ¼ Choctaw, Roll #8115, C.C. 2770, s/o Albert Kee Folsom and Lucinda Daniels.

Albert was a grandson of Turner's sister, Mary Ann "Polly" (Brashears) Daniels (ᵛ⁵1218); also grandson of Chief David Folsom and Jane Hall and great-grandson of Chief Nathaniel Folsom. At age 21, Albert was the youngest senator in the Choctaw Senate. He was also a farmer and stock-raiser in McCurtain, OK. Family from *Genealogy of the Folsom Family, 1638-1938*, Oklahoma Families, with added data from Douglas Barkley.

Will of Albert P. Folsom (Thanks to Don Johnson, of Emporia, KS, for the copy and additional data on Folsom descendants): I, Albert Folsom, of Milton, LeFlore County, OK, being of sound mind and memory and in possession of all of my faculties, do hereby make, publish, and declare the following to be my last will and testament, hereby revoking and canceling all other and former wills by me made at any time.

First. I direct the payment of all my just debts and expenses of my last sickness.

Second. I give and devise to my children named as follows: Claud C. Folsom, Dave Folsom, Allie Folsom Statham, Ollie Folsom Allen, Joe S. Folsom, Susie Folsom Parker, Pike Folsom and Lucy J. Folsom the Northwest Quarter of the Northeast Quarter of Section Thirty-four (34), Township Eight (8) North, Range Twenty-three (23) East, LeFlore County, OK. Said children to hold the above described real estate jointly, conditioned, however, as follows: On said real estate is located the old home of the testator and family and it is the desire, wish and direction of the testator that said home and real estate shall be held as the home and gathering place of his children where each of them has the right and privilege to come and go at any time. That said real estate shall not be sold by his children until three-fourths (3/4) of them shall agree to sell same; but if at any time as many as three-fourths (3/4) in the number of my then living children shall agree that the reasons and purposes for which the testator restricted the sale and conveyance of said real estate no longer exists, then they have the legal right to sell and convey the same. And I also give and devise to my said children the following personal property to be held by them with and under the same conditions as they shall hold the above described real estate: All the household goods and furniture of whatsoever kind, located and being in our home at the time of my death; also the old family mule, known by the name of Kate, and one milch cow and calf to be selected from my cattle by my executors; said household goods, mule and cattle shall be kept at and on the old home place. My executors are directed to place one of my children in charge of said home and real estate shall at all times extend a welcome to my other children and my grandchildren to come and visit the old home. My executors shall in some way they think best, provide for the paying of the taxes on said old home and real estate.

Third. All the rest and residue of my property, real and personal, of every kind and wherever situated, whether vested or contingent at the time of my death, I give and devise to my said children, they to share equal in said property.

Fourth. It is my desire and wish that my said children shall reserve the title to the family burying ground situate and being on the homestead allotment of my deceased wife, Susie K. Folsom.

Fifth. I appoint and designate Joe S. Folsom, Claud C. Folsom and Lucy J. Folsom, three of my children, to be my executors without bond, of my last will and testament.

In Witness whereof I, Albert Folsom. have to this my last will and testament, consisting of 1 sheet of paper, subscribe my name this 23rd day of May, 1936.

/s/ Albert Folsom

Signed by Albert Folsom in the presence of each of us, the undersigned, and at the same time declared by him to be his last will and testament and we thereupon at the request of Albert Folsom, in his presence and in the presence of each other, sign out names hereto as witness this the 23 day of May, 1936.

/s/ F.J. White   /s/ Arthur Davies
Address, Bokoshe, OK   Address, Bokoshe, OK

Family of Albert Peter Folsom and Susan Katherine Brashears:
(additional data from Vickie Ludiker <vcludiker@msn.com>)
v5 1327.   11 1. Claudius Condren Folsom, b. 8 Feb 1890, Milton, Choctaw Nation, I.T., d. 27 July 1959, ¼ Choctaw, Roll #8117 (named for cousin Czarina Claudia (Colbert) Condren, authoress of many articles on "Chacotaws" and Chickasaws in *The Chronicles of Oklahoma*); m. 7 May 1910, Altha

Magby, b. ?, d. 17 Feb 1953

v⁵1328. ¹²1. Opal A. Folsom, b. 22 Jan 1911, d. 22 Jan 1911, bur Folsom Cem, LeFlore Co, OK

v⁵1329. ¹²2. Zola Marie Folsom, b. 12 Nov 1911

v⁵1330. ¹²3. Francis P. Polsom, b. 25 July 1913, d. 19 May 1919; bur Folsom Cem, LeFlore Co, OK

v⁵1331. ¹²4. Victor Wayland Folsom, b. Jan 1918, d. 10 Aug 1919; bur Folsom Cem, LeFlore Co, OK

v⁵1332. ¹¹2. David William Folsom, b. 26 Dec 1891, d. 21 Dec 1957, ¼ Choctaw, Roll #8118; m.1. Myrtle Nixon (1 ch); m.2. Bertha Horton, (1 ch)

v⁵1333. ¹²1. Myrtle L. Folsom, b. 4 Dec 1914, d. 6 May 1917, bur Folsom Cem, LeFlore Co, OK

v⁵1334. ¹²2. Wrenetta Folsom, b. 14 Aug 1919, Milton, OK

v⁵1335. ¹¹3. Allie May Folsom, b. 18 April 1894, ¼ Choctaw, Roll #8119, d. 22 Aug 1989, Spiro, OK; m. 2 Aug 1913, in Ft. Smith, AR, Frank Statham, b. 19 Dec 1894, Hartford, AR, d. 2 Aug 1962, Spiro, OK, s/o George Statham and Marsaleat Hinton

v⁵1336. ¹²1. Dora Ella Statham, b. 28 Feb 1914, Spiro, OK; m. 24 Feb 1938, Dale King Davies, b. 22 Feb 1911, d. 24 Feb 1987, s/o William Davies and Ellen Ramage. Ch: Dorothy Gene Davies; Frank William Davies

v⁵1337. ¹²2. Joe Frank "Bill" Statham, b. 28 Sept 1915, Spiro, OK (he was a Greyhound Bus driver); m. 25 Dec 1936, Mildred Olivia Joyce, b. 22 Sept 1915, Lexington, AL, d/o Emit Joyce and Rose Newton. Ch: Larry Wayne; Joyce Ann; and Betsy Lynn Statham.

v⁵1338. ¹²3. George Albert Statham, b. 2 Dec 1920,; m.1. Bess James, b. 2 Sept 1900(?), d. 24 Dec 1940, Spiro, OK, d/o Sam James and Loanie Henley (1 ch: Barry George Statham); m.2. 3 July 1941, Clara Forrestor, b. 9 Feb 1921, d/o Ray Forrestor and Flora Bickform (1 ch: Larry Joe Statham)

v⁵1339. ¹²4. Virginia Jo Statham, b. 25 Oct 1925, Spiro, OK; m. 9 May 1942, in Spiro, OK, Edward Anthony Remer. b. 26 Dec 1920, Lawton, OK, d. 2 Aug 1985, Fort Smith, AR, s/o Samuel

Remer and Callidonia Gilpatrick. ch: Eady Joann; Sharron Kay; Kerry Nan; and (Dr.) Samuel Thomas Remer.

v5 1340. [11]4. Ollie Ella Folsom, b. 29 March 1896, d. 31 Aug 1970, ¼ Choctaw, Roll #8120; m. Charles Frank "Dick" Allen,

v5 1341. [11]5. Joseph Schley Folsom, b. 12 June 1898, ¼ Choctaw, Roll #8121; m.1. 1917, Buela Gladys Roberson, (no ch); m.2. 21 June 1926, Sarah Ruby Moseley, b. 7 Aug 1906

v5 1342. [12]1. Joe Alford Folsom, b. 4 April 1927

v5 1343. [12]2. Ruby Jean Folsom, b. 29 Aug 1930

v5 1344. [11]6. Susie Irene Folsom, b. 27 Jan 1902, ¼ Choctaw, Roll #8122; m. 29 Jan 1920, Guy Parker,

v5 1345. [12]1. James Albert Parker, b. 10 Nov 1922

v5 1346. [12]2. William Norman Parker, b. 1 Nov 1924

v5 1347. [12]3. Betty Sue Parker, b. 31 Oct 1931

v5 1348. [12]4. Robert Eugene Parker, b. 11 April 1934

v5 1349. [11]7. Albert Pike Folsom, b. 15 March 1905, d. Dec 1992, Poteau, OK, ¼ Choctaw, Newborn Roll; m. 7 June 1925, Myrtle Goforth,

v5 1350. [12]1. Albert William Folsom, b. 22 March 1926, d. 21 Nov 1993, Wister, OK

v5 1351. [12]2. Arthur Wayne Folsom, b. 5 Oct 1927

v5 1352. [12]3. David Allen Folsom, b. 19 March 1934

v5 1353. [11]8. Francis Warren Folsom, b. 22 July 1908, d. 9 April 1909, bur Folsom Cem, LeFlore Co, OK

v5 1354. [11]9. Nellie Lucinda Folsom, b. 1 Sept 1910, unm. in 1937, d. 20 Jan 1981, bur Charleston, AR; m. Bud Cooper

15. GOOD TIMES IN INDIAN TERRITORY: Descendants of Sophia Brashears, I, and Sampson Moncrief

[v5]**839.** [8]7. **Sophia Brashears, I**, (d/o Zadock Brashears and Susannah Vaughn), b. 7 Feb 1802, bap. 14 Sept 1802, age six months, at St. Francis Church, Point Coupee (Book 7, p.142; sponsors: Patrique Tigre and Patience Bourg, later Patrick's wife), d. Belmont, Alabama, 21 Oct 1852, bur Belmont Church Cem, Sumter Co, AL; m. 1818, LA, **Sampson Moncrief**, b. 1793, NC, d. Jan 1856, Choctaw Nation, Indian Territory. (Take care not to confuse this Sophia Brashears with another Sophia Brashears, Sampson's second wife, d/o Alexander Brashears and Anne Brashears, b. c1820-25; this Sophia, II, m.1. John L. Jones; m.2. Amos Goins; m.3. Sampson Moncrief, b. 1793, d. 1856, who lived from c1853 to Jan 1856 on the Poteau River, near Skullyville, I.T., near where the second Sophia Brashears lived.)

Sampson knew little about his family, he being an orphan, b. NC. Sophia and he met while she was attending a boarding school in Louisiana, probably a Catholic convent, since she was Catholic. Sampson was apprenticed at the time to a Mr. Shiply, who had extensive land holdings and many slaves. Sampson acquired one slave, Tom; together they worked, saved their money, and when Sampson was 21, set out on their own. They went to Louisiana, where Sampson went to school and Tom worked. Sampson and Sophia were married in Louisiana, and later moved to the Alabama and Mississippi Territories to take up Sophia's land claim "east of the Pearl River"—the land was actually on the Tombigbee River, where Sampson qualified as an intermarried head of a Choctaw family.

Their plantation prospered and was known as "Mulberry

Grove"; it was a stop on the government stage line, called "The Military Road." Sarah Ann (Moncrief) Harlan (^{v5}1394) gave testimony in the Dawes hearing concerning Joseph C. Moncrief's application for recognition as a Choctaw by blood (thanks to Marlene Mays Clark for copies) that Sampson's land in Sumter Co, AL, consisted of a section of land three miles west of Demopolis and three miles east of Belmont, lying about a mile west of the Tombigbee River.

She said Sampson was about five ft. five inches tall, black hair, blue eyes, stocky and heavy-set. Sophia was tall and very dark; black eyes and black hair. When asked what improvements were located on this land, Sarah answered, "Story and a half building, out houses and barns, nigger quarters, little houses all around, and about six or seven hundred acres in cultivation: that's as far back as I can recollect."

Neither her mother nor her father were known by any Indian name. She was not sure, but thought maybe they lived in Mush-u-la-tubbee District. The patent to Sampson's land was printed on sheepskin. He sold the land to a man by the name of May. When Sampson died, he still had forty acres at Sulphur Springs, MS.

Sarah Ann testified that she was born and raised on the land that is described above and she lived there until she was about 21. She was 19 when she was married and moved to her own allotment adjoining Sampson's on the northeast. Her father had four children at the time of her birth— Susan, William, Mary Ann, and Sarah Ann. At the time of the Dancing Rabbit Treaty of 1830, Susan was over twelve; William, probably two or three years younger— under ten; and Mary Ann two years older than Sarah Ann; Sampson probably 2½ years younger than Sarah A., probably born 1831 or 32;

When asked about their neighbors, she first named Viceroy Tut, who was a white man and a farmer. Then, they asked her about Indian neighbors. She named William Hall and Tandy Walker— "not the younger Tandy Walker, but the one that had been dead for a good many years— the back ancestor of all these Walkers"— the one that had been governor of the Choctaw Nation, I.T. The only other Indian neighbors she could remember were the Jackson Riddles.

She knew Alex and Annie Brashears and they lived about 15 miles from them in the same county, probably southeast on the

Sucarnoochee Creek near Moscow post office. Alex had land, but she does not believe he lived on it, but on the land of his father-in-law, Zedek Brashears (who was a Scotchman with no Indian blood). Annie Brashears' mother was Susan Vaughn, who was Choctaw.

Marengo Co, AL, Deeds, Book B, p.55: Deed of gift, Zadock Brashiers Sr, gives certain slaves to his daughter, Sophia Moncrief, wife of Sampson Moncrief. Witness: Turner Brashiers [II]. Recorded 22 May 1829. [It states Zadock signed his name; he habitually made his mark, a capital "B"]

Marengo Co, AL, Deeds, Book B. p.142: Sampson Moncrief and Zadock Brashears make a friendly compromise to recover one undivided one-third interest in right of wife to a Negro slave, Jude, and her 7 children, dated 6 Jan 1830, recorded 13 May 1830. Zadock made his mark, a capital "B".

Marengo Co, AL, Deeds, Book B, p.43: Zadock Brashears to Sampson Moncrief, deed for a Negro girl, ?dated 21 Jan 1830. recorded? witnesses? signature?

In 1853, after the first Sophia (Brashears) Moncrief died in Alabama, Sampson Moncrief decided to sell his plantation in Alabama and move to Indian Territory. He settled on land at the junction of the Arkansas and Poteau Rivers. With his many slaves, his plantation prospered. About 1854-55, he married the second Sophia Brashears, niece of his first wife, widow of John L. Jones and Amos Goins, and d/o Alexander Brashears (^{v5}521) and Anne Brashears (^{v5}834), sister of Sohpia Brashears, I.

Sampson Moncrief was known to have a bad habit: he carried large quantities of gold on his person. In Jan 1856, he disappeared and was never found, assumed to have been killed for the $20,000 he was reputed to be carrying. A reward of $10,000 was offered for information leading to the apprehension of the murderers, but, though the country was full of searchers, nothing helpful ever turned up.

Another account of his death is given by great grandson, Edgar Moore. In an interview (WPA interviews, the *Oklahoma Indian-Pioneer Interviews*), Edgar said that his grandfather Moncrief (he had to mean g.grandfather) "was tragically killed and his body burned at the time of a negro uprising which occurred near Skullyville about 1860 or 1861. This uprising was instigated by an overseer, who in reality was a northern sympathizer, but in the employ of Mr. Moncrief. After the uprising, with its tragic result, the overseer took the slaves out of the Choctaw Nation, disposed of them and never returned." [Thanks to Marlene Mays Clark for the data. Edgar may have been mistaken about the year, since it's pretty clear that Sampson died in 1856; or Edgar may have been confusing Sampson with someone else. He was relating incidents that happened a dozen years or more before his birth; so he was relying on the hearsay of others.]

Family of Sophia Brashears, I, and Sampson Moncrief:

[v5]1391. [9]1. *Susan Moncrief, b. 10 Feb 1819, Sumter Co, AL, d. 31 Aug 1860, bur Leard Cem, near Cavanaugh, AR; m.1. 26 Jan 1834, AL, James C. Monroe McClain, d. 1855; m.2. c1857, in Choctaw Nation, I.T., Francis Marion Monk.

[v5]1392. [9]2. *William L. Moncrief, b. 20 April 1820, Sumter Co, AL, d. 15 Feb 1872, bur in Chickasaw Nation; m. 1839, in LeFlore Co, OK, Margaret "Mahala" Hall, b. 6 Oct 1820, d. 26 Jan 1915

[v5]1393. [9]3. *Mary Ann Moncrief, b. 24 Oct 1826, Sumter Co, AL, d. 16 April 1911, bur McAlester, OK; m. 23 Dec 1844, in Sumter Co, AL, Robert Smith McCarty.

[v5]1394. [9]4. *Sarah Ann Moncrief, b. 30 Jan 1829, Sumter Co, AL, d. 14 Dec 1926, Caddo, OK; m.1. 2 May 1847, in Sumter Co, AL, Erasmus Bryant Hawkins, d. 1851; m.2. in 1855, at Ft. Smith, AR, Aaron Harlan, b. 18 Dec 1811, d. 3 March 1876

[v5]1395. [9]5. Sampson <u>Brashears</u> Moncrief, b. 7 March (or 3 July) 1831, Sumter Co, AL, d. 31 March 1857, AL, bur Belmont Church Cem, Sumter Co, AL; m. 1854, Penelope White

[v5]1396. [9]6. Sophia Moncrief, b. 1833, Sumter Co, AL, d. in OK before 1854; m. 13 Nov 1850, at Mulberry Grove, Sumter Co, AL, Francis Eubanks, d. before Oct 1852.

[v5]1397. [9]7. George W. Moncrief, b. 1835, Sumter Co, AL; m.1. Mary J. _____, who d. 1876 (2 ch); m.2. 19 Sept 1878, Alice McDougal, b. 1857 (2 ch). George moved to Indian Territory in 1850 along with his sisters, Mary Ann (Moncrief) McCarty ([v5]1393) and

Sarah Ann (Moncrief) Hawkins (^{v5}1394).

^{v5}1398. ^{10}1. Byron Moncrief, b. c1867, Choctaw Census Card #4797; m. 18 Oct 1903, Coalgate, OK, Mrs. Lettie Johnson.

^{v5}1399. ^{10}2. Captain R. "Cap" Moncrief, b. c1868, Choctaw Roll #4566; m. 9 Oct 1894, at Krebs, OK, Annie Green, d/o Elijah Green and Kate _____ (ch: Ester Moncrief, b. 1896)

^{v5}1400. ^{10}3. George Washington Moncrief, b. 29 Jan 1881, Canadian, I.T., d. 1957; m. 27 Jan 1909, in Canadian, OK, Bevie Knapp, b. 26 March 1888, Enterprise, I.T., d/o James Knapp and Callis Lewallen. Choctaw Census Card #4793.

^{v5}1401. ^{10}4. Renolds Moncrief,

^{v5}1402. ^{9}8. Francis M. "Frank" Moncrief, b. 16 Dec 1836, Sumter Co, AL, d. 18 Dec 1852, age 16, bur Belmont Church Cem, Sumter Co, AL; n.m.

^{v5}1403. ^{9}9. Julia Ann Moncrief, b. 5 Feb 1839, Sumter Co, AL, d. 4 Feb 1864, bur Leard Cem, near Cavanaugh, AR; m. 17 Nov 1853 in Sumter Co, AL, James M. Coleman, b. c1835. In 1854, Julia Ann and James Coleman migrated to Indian Territory and took up land about 8 miles south of Fort Smith, AR, at a place called "Cherry Grove," one mile south and one-half mile west of Cavanaugh, AR, just inside Indian Territory. Julia died there about eleven years later.

^{v5}1404. ^{10}1. Eliphlit "Liff" L. Coleman, (adopted son) b. 15 Nov 1858, d. 24 Oct 1941, at Fort Smith, AR; m. 25 Dec 1879, Mary Denny. Their children (thanks to Diana Pratt): Lorenzo, 1884; Evy, 1885 (Diana's ggrandmother); Mattie, 1887; Nova 1890; Brockett, 1892; Noah, 1893; Gus Coleman, b. 9 Feb 1896, d. 20 Nov 1966 (Bill & Jim Coleman's father). Billy G. Coleman, (s/o Gus), b. 1926, lived at Spiro, OK.

Statement by Noah Coleman given when he was 79 years old in 1972 (thanks to Diana Pratt for a copy): "Liff, known as Eliphlit Coleman, was born Nov 15, 1858 in Savannah, Georgia... His parents were from Holland, of Dutch decent, their surname unknown. Liff's father was a buyer for a large textile company. Since Georgia was a cotton county, it was believed he'd come to the United States to purchase cotton... Liff's parents were killed, the reason unknown, but thought the reason was because he carried large sums of money. Some woman brought Liff to Fort Smith Arkansas and put him up for adoption. A family named James Coleman adopted & raised him."

^{v5}1405.   ⁹10. Matthew L. Moncrief, b. 5 Feb 1841, d. 24 Nov 1861, Skullyville, OK. In the 1855 census of Choctaws, Matthew was living with his sister, Mary Ann (Moncrief) McCarty. He came west with Sampson Moncrief in 1854-55.

Child of Sampson Moncrief and Sophia Brashears, II:

^{v5}1406.   ⁹11. Joseph C. Moncrief, b. c1854, at a place later called Oak Lodge, near Skullyville, I.T.; m. 12 Aug 1888, Lulu Self, b. 1878 (?58), d/o Pleasant and Arta Self. In an *Oklahoma Indian-Pioneer Interview*, he gave his birth year as 1857. Since he was on the 1855 Census of Choctaws, completed in Dec 1856, we think someone mis-read 1854 as 1857. Joseph may not have known accurately when he was born.

Some of the slaves of Sampson Moncrief:

Tom, owner listed as "Biddy Hall," [Margaret (Hall) Moncrief, Sampson's daughter-in-law]

Nancy, [wife of Tom]

Lizzie Rogers, d/o Tom and Nancy

Jesse [Moncrief]

Nelson Coleman, b. 1851, slave of Julia Coleman and s/o of Jesse Moncrief and Olivia Coleman; Choctaw Freedman Roll #5121. Julia Coleman was Sampson Moncrief's youngest daughter.

In the 1830s, the U.S. Government, responding to white needs for land, encouraged Indians to move west to Indian Territory. In 1839, James C. Monroe McClain responded to this pressure and went west to take a look, along with his family and Susan's oldest brother, William L. Moncrief. At Skullyville, the Choctaw Agent placed their names on the roll and filed their claim on land near the Poteau River. The slaves soon erected a home for the McClains, as well as quarters for themselves.

The farm and ranch flourished, but Susan was so unhappy away from her mother and family that, a year later, they returned to Sumter Co, AL, where James M. McClain began the practice of law.

In 1849, with pressure on Congress increasing, the Government made Indian Removal mandatory, instead of voluntary. The Government promised to pay expenses for the move and furnish a year's rations for those who moved west. The only other choice remaining for the Indians was to cede their property to the Government and enter the Indian Reservations set up for them in Alabama.

After Sampson and Sophia Moncrief visited their son, William, who had remained in I.T., they were impressed by what they saw and encouraged their other children to migrate. As a result, their daughters and their families— Susan and James M. McClain, Mary Ann and Robert Smith McCarty, and Sarah Ann and Erasmus Bryant Hawkins— enrolled with the emigration agent and booked steamboat passage, along with their brother, Robert Moncrief. (See Sarah Ann's account above).

In spite of their precautions, Cholera struck their party, and they were quarantined at Fort Coffee. When they believed the danger had passed, William L. Moncrief, their brother, came to Ft. Coffee and took them to his home until they would be able to travel again. However, the danger of the disease was not passed: William's baby and Mary Ann's baby died at the same time.

When their health returned, the immigrant families went to Skullyville, enrolled with the Choctaw Agent, and were issued their year's rations. The three families went three directions, James and Susan McClain settling on their 1839 plantation on the Poteau River. Mary Ann and Robert McCarty settled in Skullyville County, near the Arkansas line. Sarah Ann (Moncrief) and E.B. Hawkins settled on land near Tishomingo, I.T., where they prospered. Hawkins died in 1851, and Sarah's brothers-in-law, Robert McCarty and James M. McClain, helped to supervise the plantation, though with a dozen or so devoted slaves, she had no real troubles.

About 1855, Aaron Harlan, a merchant of Fort Smith, AR, moved his business to Tishomingo, and soon after, he and Sarah Ann were married. They soon became quite wealthy.

Susan Moncrief and
James C. M. McClain/ Francis M. Monk

[v5]**1391.** [9]1. Susan Moncrief, (d/o Sampson Moncrief and Sophia Brashears), b. 10 Feb 1819, Sumter Co, AL, d. 31 Aug 1860, bur Leard Cem, near Cavanaugh, AR; m.1. 31 Jan 1834, Mulberry Grove, Sumter Co, AL, James C. Monroe McClain, Sr, b. __?__, d. 1855; m.2. c1857, in Choctaw Nation, I.T., Francis Marion Monk.

Susan was educated by a private tutor, whom her father had hired to teach his children. James M. McClain was a surveyor, who stopped at Mulberry Grove while surveying for a railroad. He was a handsome, well-educated young man who practiced law as well as surveying; they were married a year later and took up Susan's Choctaw claim "on the Pearl River," as the official documents said; actually the land was near the Tombigbee River.

Family of Susan Moncrief and James C. Monroe McClain:
(Thanks to Sandi Carter, 2416 Pierce Court, Simi Valley, CA 93065-4910 for data.)

[v5]1407.　　[10]1. James C. Monroe McClain Jr, b. 1840, Sumter Co, AL, was robbed and murdered at Fort Smith, Sebastian Co, AR, by Amos McCurtain; m. Eliza Ann Gary, b. 1849 [1/16 Choctaw; C.C. 4809; Roll #13260], d. after 1905, d/o Lucy Juzan and Amos W. Gary. They had only one child, William Alexander McClain, who founded a dynasty of sorts; see below. After James McClain, Jr, was killed, Eliza Ann Gary m.2. c?1875, Elisha Heskett; m.3. before 1902, Charles Smith (intermarried Citizen #1140). See under Wesley Brashears Trahern for her other children.

[v5]1407a.　　[11]1. *William Alexander McClain, b. 16 Jan 1861, Spiro, I.T.; m.1. Susan A. Weimer; m.2. Lillie Mae Hutcheson. See below.

[v5]1408.　　[10]2. Helen Marr McClain, b. 1842, Sumter Co, AL, d. 1849 (error? Helen was living in 1850, went with her aunt, Sarah Ann, to get water; see Sarah Ann (Moncrief) Harlan's account). Other documents list Helen as dying of typhoid, in 1850, at Fort

Coffee, I.T.

v⁵1409.　¹⁰3. Sophia McClain, (Choctaw Roll #7411; C.C. #2549), b. Aug 1843, Sumter Co, AL, d. 1914, Spiro, OK. Sophia McClain was born blind.

v⁵1410.　¹⁰4. *Frances "Fannie" Eugenia McClain, b. 25 Aug 1844, Sumter Co, AL, d. 31 Jan 1933; m. 21 Dec 1869, Lyman Richard Moore, Sr, b. 1837, Washington Co, AL, d. 11 Dec 1881. Lyman Moore was ¾ Creek Indian.

v⁵1411.　¹⁰5. Mary Ann McClain, b. 1846, Sumter Co, AL; m.1. Dr. William G.R. Kayser Sr, b. 1842, Prussia (2 ch); m.2. James Bowers (5 ch)

v⁵1412.　¹¹1. William G.R. Kayser, Jr, b. 15 March 1861, Ft Smith, Sebastian Co, AR; m. Lula Watkins

v⁵1413.　¹²1. Nola Alverda Kayser, b. 4 Sept 1887, d. 22 May 1943; m. Clyde C. Goodner

v⁵1414.　¹²2. Viola Lucille Kayser, b. 29 Sept 1893, d. 18 Dec 1918; m. Stearl J. Slack, Sr

v⁵1415.　¹³1. Alverda Slack,

v⁵1416.　¹³2. Roda Marie Slack; m. Dr. _____ Woodson,

v⁵1417.　¹³3. Stearl J. Slack, Jr; m. Melba Whittacher (4 sons)

v⁵1418.　¹²3. William G. Kayser,

v⁵1419.　¹¹2. Henry Kayser,

v⁵1420.　¹¹3. James "Jimmie" Bowers, m. Ernestine Williams (ch: Mary and Bessie Bowers)

v⁵1421.　¹¹4. Mamie Bowers, m. Josiah E. Foster, Sr (ch: Josiah E. Foster, Jr)

v⁵1422.　¹¹5. Lillie Bowers; m. _____ LeFlore

v⁵1423.　¹¹6. Walter Bowers, b. 6 July 1863, d. 17 April 1899

v⁵1424.　¹¹7. Emma Bowers, b. 1866, Ft Smith, Sebastian Co, AR, d. 17 Feb 1884

v⁵1425.　¹⁰6. Louis Oliver McClain, b. 1850, MS, d. 1850, Ft. Coffee, Choctaw Nation, I.T. (Sarah Ann (Moncrief) Harlan describes this death and the infant's burial in her "biography," *Oklahoma Indian-Pioneer Interviews*, dictated in 1913.)

v⁵1426.　¹⁰7. Lila McClain, (Choctaw Roll #7419; C.C. #2552), b. 1851, Skullyville, I.T., d. Ft Smith, AR; m.1.

William Shawl, m.2. 18 March 1899, John Quinn. No ch. She was about nine years old when her mother died. She lived with her aunt, Sarah Ann (Moncrief) Hawkins/Harlan a good part of her life.

v51427.   108. *George Washington McClain, (Choctaw Roll #7402; C.C. #2548), b. 1 April 1856, Skullyville, I.T.; m. Laura Belle Boyd, b. Pattio Co, MO

Child of Susan Moncrief and Francis M. Monk:

v51428.   109. Susan Monk, m. Frank Battles.

William Alexander McClain and Susan Weimer/ Lillie Hutcheson

v51407a. 111. *William Alexander McClain, (s/o James C. Monroe McClain, Jr, and Eliza Ann Gary), b. 16 Jan 1861, Spiro, I.T.; m.1. 11 Jan 1891, Susan A. Weimer, b. 16 Jan 1871, Spiro, I.T. (3 ch); m.2. Lillie Mae Hutcheson, (5 ch). Many of his descendants spelled the surname McLain.

Family of William Alexander McClain and Susan A. Weimer:

v51429.   121. Addie McLain, b. 1892; m. Bill Wood. Ch: Arvin; Susan; and Jessie Wood

v51430.   122. George William McLain, b. 10 June 1894, d. 28 Jan 1965, Fresno, CA; m. c1911, Bessie Tolbert (1 ch); m.2. c1913, Anna _____ (1 ch); m.3. c1915, Lizzie White (2 ch); m.4. Winnie Bradshaw (1 ch)

v51431.   131. Joy McLain, b. 11 Sept 1911; m.1. Maysel Laverne "Pat" Ficher

v51432.   132. Mildred Francis McLain, b. 12 April 1914, d. 22 Dec 1990, San Leandro, Alameda Co, CA; m. _____ Kelso

v51433.   133. Pocahontas McLain, b. 1916; m.1. in Michigan, Lucas Ramazetti (ch: Richard; Sylvia; Gary Sr {ch: Gary Jr and Dino}; and Louise Ramazetti); m.2. _____ Harrington (ch: Catherine; Bridgette; and two sons Harrington)

v51434.   134. George Walter McLain, Sr, b. 12 Jan 1922, Stigler, OK; m.1. c1940, Gloria Jean Wood (2 ch); m.2. 1947, Marjorie Louise Fink, b. 1 April 1928, Knoawa, Pottawatomie Co, OK, d. 7 July 1988, Modesto, Stanislaus Co, CA (1 ch); m.3.

4 July 1948, Fresno, Fresno Co, CA, Roena Mae Ramsey, b. 30 May 1929, Sulphur, Murray Co, OK (4 ch)

v⁵1435.   ¹⁴1. Elizabeth McLain,

v⁵1436.   ¹⁴2. Paulette McLain,

v⁵1437.   ¹⁴3. Pamela Jane McLain, b. 6 March 1948, Modesto, Stanislaus Co, CA; m.1. 3 July 1965, Santa Rosa, Sonoma Co, CA, Michael Jay Shafer, b. 31 July 1947, Berkeley, Alameda Co, CA; m.2. 25 May 1974, Oreal Lee Keys, b. 4 March 1950, Noel McDonald Co, MO; m.3. 26 Dec 1987, James Roderick Kennon, b. 1 Dec 1940, San Francisco, CA

v⁵1438.   ¹⁵1. Michael Parrish "Mickey" Shafer, b. 18 June 1966, Santa Rosa, CA, d. 15 Nov 1967, Santa Rosa, CA

v⁵1439.   ¹⁵2. Jonathan Ray "Jon" Shafer, b. 17 Sept 1968, Santa Rosa, CA; m. Nov 1991, Krista Lynn Berry, b. 20 July 1970, Modesto, Stanislaus Co, CA

v⁵1440.   ¹⁶1. Micky Ray Shafer, b. 12 March 1988, Modesto, CA

v⁵1441.   ¹⁶2. Miranda Shafer, b. 5 March 1992, Springfield, Lane Co, OR, d. there, 5 March 1992

v⁵1442.   ¹⁶3. Mariah Shafer, b. 10 Feb 1993, Modesto, CA

v⁵1443.   ¹⁵3. Leeann Renee Keys, b. 4 March 1972, Modesto, Stanislaus Co, CA; m. Nov 1988, Floyd Thomas Forsythe, b. 7 Sept 1966, Turlock, Stanislaus Co, CA

v⁵1444.   ¹⁶1. Jenna Larie Forsythe, b. 30 March 1988, Modesto, CA

v⁵1445.   ¹⁶2. Charles Lee Ray Forsythe, b. 16 Sep 1989, Modesto, CA

v⁵1446.   ¹⁶3. Thomas James Forsythe, b. 22 May 1992, Modesto, CA

v⁵1447.   ¹⁶4. Kayla Nicole Forsythe, b. 17 April 1995, Modesto, CA

v⁵1448.   ¹⁵4. James Ray Keys, b. 11 June 1976,

Modesto, Stanislaus Co, CA

v5 1449.   14 4. Cheryl Lynne McLain, b. 27 Oct 1948, Madera, Madera Co, CA; m. 14 Jan 1967, Kerman, Fresno Co, CA, Rich Wayne Dowd, b. 17 Nov 1946, Fresno, CA

v5 1450.   15 1. Richard Glenn Dowd, b. 14 Jan 1970, Modesto, CA; m. 3 July 1992, Modesto, Stanislaus Co, CA, Madga K. Ibraham, b. 26 March 1970

v5 1451.   16 1. Natasha Noel Dowd, b. 8 July 1992, Modesto, CA

v5 1452.   16 2. Victoria Nicole Dowd, b. 20 Jan 1997, Modesto, CA

v5 1453.   16 3. Sara Noel Dowd, b. 26 Dec 1998, Modesto, CA

v5 1454.   15 2. Angela Lynne Dowd, b. 17 Sep 1972, Modesto, CA; m. c1991, Jerry Dale Remides, b. 1 Dec 1967; met, Michael La Shon Douglas "Tioga" Bettle, b. 18 April 1972

v5 1455.   16 1. Cody Blake Remides, b. 17 July 1992, Modesto, CA

v5 1456.   16 2. Zane Pierce Remides, b. 26 Sept 1996

v5 1457.   16 3. Lucas Andrew Bettle, b. 12 Jan 1999

v5 1458.   15 3. Lori Anne Dowd, b. 13 July 1977, Modesto, CA; met, c1991, Luis Manuel Maldonado, b. 19 July 1976, Santa Ana, Orange Co, CA; m.1. 16 Sept 1995, Hughson, Stanislaus Co, CA, Jose Cruz Campos, b. 1 June 1974; m.2. 10 Dec 1999, Atwater, CA, Guillermo "Randy" Campos, b. 25 May 1967, Ventura, Ventura Co, CA

v5 1459.   16 1. Anthony Glenn Maldonado, b. 21 April 1992, Modesto, CA

v5 1460.   16 2. Monique Evette Campos, b. 15 Dec 1994, Modesto, CA

v5 1461.   14 5. Susan Marie McLain, b. 20 Sept 1951, Brawley, CA; m. Michael Brady

v5 1462.	15 1. Misty Jenel Brady. Ch: Nikita Brady,
v5 1463.	14 6. Gayle Denise McLain, b. 17 Jan 1952, Brawley, CA; met c1969, Butch Silva, a.k.a. Butch Baker; m. c1971, Alie Cabarlic, b. Feb 1972, San Jose, Santa Clara Co, CA
v5 1464.	15 1. Lisa Rene (McLain) Baker, b. April 1970
v5 1465.	15 2. Aaron Gabriel (Cabarlic) Baker, b. Feb 1972, San Jose, CA
v5 1466.	14 7. George Walter McLain, Jr, b. 12 July 1972, Brawley, CA; m.1. 1972, San Jose, Santa Clara Co, CA, Marilyn _____ (2 ch); m.2. c1982, Darla _____ (1 ch); m.3. c1989, Becky _____ (2 ch)
v5 1467.	15 1. Clinton George (McLain) LeBein, b. 3 April 1972, Santa Clara, CA
v5 1468.	15 2. Jarrod (McLain) LeBein, b. 3 April 1972, Santa Clara, CA
v5 1469.	15 3. Natilie Roena McLain, b. c1983, Fresno, CA
v5 1470.	15 4. George Walter McLain, III, b. c1990
v5 1471.	15 5. Shannan McLain, b. c1995
v5 1472.	13 5. Clara June McLain, b. 1928; m. Lonnie L. Rolen (ch: Janice Elaine and Timothy McLain Rolen)
v5 1473.	12 3. Wilma Zola McLain, b. 26 Nov 1901; m.1. _____ (ch: Dude; June; Bernice {ch: Nelson and Teddy _____}; and Vivian _____); m.2. Ceb Phillips

Family of William Alexander McClain and Lillie Mae Hutcheson:

v5 1474.	12 4. Lillie V. "Flossie" McLain, b. 1 Aug 1906, I.T.; m.1. Albert Shelton; m.2. Orville Mays,
v5 1475.	13 1. Dealous Wayne Shelton, b. 10 Aug 1922, OK; m. _____
v5 1476.	13 2. Billy Joe Shelton, Sr, b. 24 April 1924, d. 1944; m. _____
v5 1477.	14 1. Billy Joe Shelton, Jr,
v5 1478.	13 3. Thelma Lorrine Shelton, b. 27 Oct 1925, OK
v5 1479.	13 4. Mary Lois Mays,
v5 1480.	12 5. Mary Lou McLain, b. 5 Oct 1980, OK; m.1. Ralph

v5 1481.   13 1. Thurman Ralph Lester, b. 12 Jan 1925, OK; m. _____

Lester; m.2. Arville Taylor

v5 1481.   13 1. Thurman Ralph Lester, b. 12 Jan 1925, OK; m. _____

v5 1482.   13 2. Doris Marie Lester, b. 22 Feb 1927, OK; m. _____ Elton,

v5 1483.   12 6. Letha Mae McLain, b. 22 Feb 1910, OK; m. W. Miles Campbell

v5 1484.   13 1. Muriel Louise Campbell, b. 30 May 1931, OK; m. _____ Logue,

v5 1485.   13 2. Betty Jo Campbell, b. 9 Aug 1935, OK, m. _____ Hall

v5 1486.   12 7. Aaron McLain, b. 16 Nov 1911, OK; m. Billie Ratliff

v5 1487.   13 1. Aaron Carlos McLain, b. 10 July 1937, McCamey, TX

v5 1488.   13 2. Terry Don McLain, b. 21 Jan 1941, Raton, Colfax Co, NM

v5 1489.   13 3. Billie Jean McLain, b. 13 Dec 1943, Raton, Colfax Co, NM; m. _____ Aderhalt

v5 1490.   12 8. Eugene V. "Gene" McLain, b. 15 April 1920, OK; m. Estelle Barnes

v5 1491.   13 1. Gary Gene McLain, b. 24 Jan 1944, Roswell, Chaves Co, NM

v5 1492.   13 2. Marcus Wayne McLain, b. 9 Aug 1949

v5 1493.   13 3. Billy Earl McLain, b. 31 Aug 1954

Frances Eugenia McClain and Lyman Richard Moore

v5 **1410.** 10 4. Frances "Fannie" Eugenia McClain, (d/o James C. Monroe McClain and Susan Moncrief), b. 25 Aug 1844, Sumter Co, AL, d. 31 Jan 1933, bur Skullyville Indian Cem, Spiro, OK; m. 21 Dec 1869, (second wife of) Lyman Richard Moore, Sr, b. 1837, Washington Co, AL, d. 11 Dec 1881, bur Skullyville Indian Cem, Spiro, OK. Lyman was ¾ Creek. Their son, Edgar Moore, gave information about the family in a WPA interview, now part of "The Oklahoma Indian-Pioneer Interviews."

Figure 29: The Moore Family in 1889

Family of Frances Eugenia McClain and Lyman Richard Moore:

v⁵1494. ¹¹1. Gertrude Moore, b. 11 Oct 1871, d. 1961; m. Edward Spencer Bowman

v⁵1495. ¹²1. Euwela Bowman, b. 20 Nov 1894, Skullyville, I.T.; m. William C. Pratt, b. 1885

v⁵1496. ¹³2. William C. "Billy" Pratt, Jr, b. 4 Sep 1919, Spiro, LeFlore Co, OK, d. 1945

v⁵1497. ¹²2. Edward Granville Bowman, b. 1902; m. Kathryn _____

v⁵1498. ¹³1. George P. "Mickey" Bowman,

v⁵1499. ¹³2. Margaret Bowman,

v⁵1500. ¹³3. _____ Bowman

v⁵1501. ¹²3. Lois Annie Bowman, b. 1905; m. Phillip Lee Manke. ch: Robert Manke,

v⁵1502. ¹²4. Lucille L. Bowman, b. 1906; m. Dave Holloway

v⁵1503. ¹¹2. Edgar Allen Moore, b. 7 Jan 1873, Skullyville, I.T., d. 7 Jan 1945, bur Skullyville Indian Cem, Spiro, OK; m. 7 Jan 1897, Jessie Martha Ainsworth, b. 1877, d. 1955, bur Skullyville Indian Cem. Edgar Allen Moore was elected to the Choctaw Council in 1898, 1900, 1904, 1906. He was Skullyville Co Judge in 1902, member Oklahoma State Legislature, 1907-08; delegate of Choctaw Convention, 1934; Choctaw Advisory Council, 1934 to death. Cemetery records name children:

v⁵1504. ¹²1. Pauline Allen Moore, b. 28 Aug 1898, Skullyville, I.T., d. 22 Nov 1969; m. Oliver Lee Gentry, b. 22 June 1895, d. 23 Dec 1950

v⁵1505. ¹³1. David Allen Gentry, b. Nov 1923, d. 12 May 1997

v⁵1506. ¹³2. Oliver Wendell "Zub" Gentry, b. 4 Nov 1926, d. 1 Oct 1975; m. Kathryn "Kathy" Schuster, b. 1927

v⁵1507. ¹⁴1. Edgar Allan Gentry, b. 1949; m.1. Theresa _____; m.2. Brenda Kay Underwood (1 ch).

v⁵1508. ¹⁵1. Shawn Allan Gentry, b. 1971

v⁵1509. ¹⁵2. Cale Gentry, b. 1973

v⁵1510. ¹⁵3. Wendy Gentry, b. 1979

v⁵1511.

¹⁴2. Eric Steven Gentry, b. 1954; m. Debbie _____

v⁵1512.

¹⁴3. Oliver Mark Gentry, b. 1963; m. Marsheilah Dawn Clark, b. 1964

v⁵1513.

¹⁵1. Christopher Mark Gentry, b. 1986

v⁵1514.

¹⁵2. Blake Tyler Gentry, b. 1989

v⁵1515.

¹⁵3. Kaitlyn Breann Gentry, b. 1996

v⁵1516.

¹³3. Martha Ellen Gentry, b. 1931, d. 1991; m. Joe Arley Johnson, b. 1930

v⁵1517.

¹⁴1. Joe David Johnson, b. 1951; m. Diana Linn Judy, b. 1953. ch: Sarah Elizabeth Johnson,

v⁵1518.

¹⁴2. Martha Ann Johnson, b. 1951; m. Glenn A. Mead, b. 1952. Ch: Glenn Scott and Heather Ann Mead

v⁵1519.

¹⁴3. Carolyn Lee Johnson, b. 1953; m.1. Joseph John Reinke; m.2. Kenneth Ray Lewallen. Ch: Jared Michael and Christopher George Lewallen. Lee Lewallen sent data, for which many thanks.

v⁵1520.

¹⁴4. William Marvin "Bill" Johnson, b. 1954; m. Karen Rae Baublit, b. 1957. Ch: William Dustin; Timothy Allan; Megan Alissa; and Kayla Nicole Johnson

v⁵1521.

¹⁴5. George Robert Johnson, b. 1956, d. 1983

v⁵1522.

¹²2. Alvin Custer Moore, b. 25 Nov 1899, Skullyville, I.T.; m. Kathleen Moore

v⁵1523.

¹²3. Thomas Ellena "Thomallena" Moore, b. 1902, d. 1906

v⁵1524.

¹²4. Lyman Southard Moore, b. 18 April 1904, Skullyville, I.T., d. 1983; m. Freida Isabelle Ward, b. 1903, d. 2002

v⁵1525.

¹²5. Edgar Ainsworth Moore, b. 23 May 1907, Skullyville, OK, d. 11 May 1985, bur Skullyville Indian Cem; m. 5 Jan 1931, Marcella Patricia Fitzgerald, b. 1911, d. 1990.

v⁵1526.

¹³1. Jean Paul Moore, b. 25 Nov 1935; m.1. Kay Sollars (2 ch); m.2. Laraine Murphy, b.

	1967
v51527.	141. Paul Ainsworth Moore, b. 16 April 1960
v51528.	142. Frank Southard Moore, b. 13 June 1963
v51529.	132. Tod Allen Moore, b. 1938; m. Wyneth Harwell
v51530.	141. Tod Allen Moore, Jr, b. 1966
v51531.	113. Lyman Richard Moore, Jr, b. 1874; m. Ida Noah McCurtain, b. 1880
v51532.	121. Ethan Allen Moore, b. 1903, d. 1981; m. Bertha Mae _____, b. 1913, d. 1998
v51533.	122. Jessie Irene "Dolly" Moore, b. 1906, d. 1997; m.1. Floyd A. Vanderwall, b. ?, d. 1965; m.2. Lloyd Barker
v51534.	123. Frances Eugenia Moore, b. 1909, d. 1999; m. Dr. Clifford W. Moore, b. ?, d. 1991
v51535.	131. George Clifford Moore, b. ?, d. 1991; m. Sylvia R. _____
v51536.	114. Louis Oliver Moore, b. 1876, Skullyville, I.T., d. 1903; m. Dora McDevett
v51537.	115. Herbert McClain Moore, Sr, b. 2 July 1878, Skullyville, I.T., d. 3 Dec 1943, bur Skullyville Indian Cem, Spiro, OK; m. Lena McCurtain, b. 1881, d. 1966
v51538.	121. Corrine Moore, b. 1904, d. 2000; m. Otway Thomas Rabon, b. 1905
v51539.	131. Nancy Ann Rabon, b. 1934; m. Bob Lewis, d. 2000
v51540.	132. Carol Rabon, b. 1939; m. Stanley Ray Shelton. ch: Mark Shelton
v51541.	133. James Wesley Rabon,
v51542.	134. Philip Rabon,
v51543.	122. Inez Moore, b. 26 April 1906, d. 18 Nov 1983; m.1. Herbert C. Bookhardt; m.2. Paul Von Derau
v51544.	131. Patricia Lee Bookhardt, b. 1929
v51545.	132. Catherine Frances Bookhardt, b. 1932
v51546.	123. Greenwood McCurtain Moore, b. 24 Aug 1908, d. 15 Nov 1909, bur Skullyville Indian Cem, Spiro, OK, "Son of Herbert and Lena."

v⁵1547.   ¹²4. Herbert McClain Moore, Jr, b. 1911, d. 1986; m.1. Nine Buchannon; m.2. Shirley Fulton (2 ch)

v⁵1548.   ¹³1. Herbert McClain Moore, III, b. 1953

v⁵1549.   ¹³2. Peggy Lyn Moore, b. 1955; m. _____ Hollis,

v⁵1550.   ¹²5. Betty Patricia Moore, b. 1924; m. John William Ward, b. ?, d. 2000

v⁵1551.   ¹³1. Frances Eugenia "Dena" Ward, b. 1941; m. Ronald D. Pitchford

v⁵1552.   ¹⁴1. Ronald D. Pitchford, Jr, b. 1966

v⁵1553.   ¹⁴2. David Lee Pitchford, b. 1968

v⁵1554.   ¹³2. John William Ward, Jr, b. 1943; m. Dee Palmquist

v⁵1555.   ¹¹6. Napoleon B. Moore, b. 11 March 1880, Skullyville I.T., d. 1950, bur Skullyville Indian Cem, Spiro, OK; m. Mary Lawthers, b. 1879

v⁵1556.   ¹¹7. Lena Belle Moore, b. 1882, Skullyville I.T., d. 1974; m. Ree V. Smith

v⁵1557.   ¹²1. Jessie Louise Smith, b. 24 May 1905, d. 13 Feb 1906

v⁵1558.   ¹²2. Louis V. Smith, b. 7 Aug 1906, Spiro, Skullyville Co, I.T.; m. Vera Jo Glenn (ch: Glenn V.; Eleanor; and Ann Smith)

v⁵1559.   ¹²3. Vivian Smith, b. 6 Jul 1909, Spiro, LeFlore Co, OK; m. James P. Crow (ch: William Seldon; Michael; and Richard Crow)

George Washington McClain and Laura Belle Boyd

v⁵**1427.** ¹⁰8. George Washington McClain, (s/o James C. Monroe McClain, and Susan Moncrief), b. 1 April 1856, Skullyville, I.T.; m. Laura Belle Boyd, b. Pattio Co, MO, d/o John Boyd and Sarah Ellis. George's children are listed on Choctaw Census Card 2548; he is Roll #7402, ⅛ Choctaw.

Family of George Washington McClain and Laura Belle Boyd:

v⁵1560.   ¹¹1. James Thomas McClain, (Choctaw Roll #7403), b. 25 Sept 1880, Skullyville, I.T., d. 1972; m. Susan Lanier, b. 1880, d. 1960

v⁵1561.   ¹²1. Edward George McClain, b. 1903, Skullyville, I.T.; m. Beulah Blackmon

v⁵1562.	¹³1. Ella Sue McClain, b. 24 Dec 1923, Spiro, OK; m. Larry Burton Young
v⁵1563.	¹⁴1. Larry Burton Young, Jr, b. 30 Oct 1949
v⁵1564.	¹⁴2. Edward Thomas Young, b. 28 Feb 1957
v⁵1565.	¹⁴3. John Lance Young, b. 15 Dec 1958
v⁵1566.	¹³2. Alyce Jayne McClain, b. 19 Aug 1935, Sprio, OK; m. Garland Rogers,
v⁵1567.	¹⁴1. Leah Kay Rogers, b. 2 April 1957
v⁵1568.	¹²2. James Thomas McClain, Jr, b. 8 March 1905, Skullyville, I.T.; m. Jewel Robertson
v⁵1569.	¹³1. Bobbie Joe McClain, b. 2 Sept 1926, Spiro, OK; m. Jean Kritz (ch: Gregory Ray and Deborah Jewel McClain
v⁵1570.	¹³2. Patricia Jewel McClain, b. 26 Aug 1931, Spiro, OK; m. Murphy Moore (ch: Philip Lee and Gatha Jean Moore)
v⁵1571.	¹³3. Donna Sue McClain, b. 7 Oct 1933, Spiro, OK; m. Eugene Goforth (ch: James Steven and Donna Mechell Goforth)
v⁵1572.	¹²3. Felix McClain, b. 29 Jan 1907, d. 27 Sep 1928
v⁵1573.	¹²4. John McClain, b. 28 Dec 1909, Skullyville, LeFlore Co, OK, d. there, 12 Nov 1929
v⁵1574.	¹²5. Sallie McClain, b. Skullyville, LeFlore Co, OK; m. Fred Imbush
v⁵1575.	¹³1. Susan J. Imbush; m. James Earl Christian
v⁵1576.	¹⁴1. James Earl Christian, Jr,
v⁵1577.	¹³2. Sallie Jane Imbush; m. William E. Howard,
v⁵1578.	¹⁴1. Malissa Susan Howard,
v⁵1579.	¹³3. James Fred Imbush,
v⁵1580.	¹²6. Jack McClain, b. 1919, Skullyville, I.T.; m. Donna Smith
v⁵1581.	¹¹2. Susan Leona McClain, (Choctaw Roll #7404), b. 17 April 1882, Skullyville, I.T., d. 8 Dec 1963; m. Lon Evans
v⁵1582.	¹²1. Girl Evans, b. 8 May 1901, d. 18 May 1901
v⁵1583.	¹²2. Agnes L. Evans, (Choctaw Roll #7410), b. 24 June 1902; m. Bland Mayfield

v⁵1584. ¹³1. George Robert Mayfield, b. 11 Sept 1926; m. Mary Louise Knox

v⁵1585. ¹⁴1. Sammy Ray Mayfield, b. 14 Sept 1960

v⁵1586. ¹⁴2. Randy Lee Mayfield, b. 18 April 1965

v⁵1587. ¹³2. Eugene Evans Mayfield, b. 25 Sept 1928

v⁵1588. ¹³3. Theresa Alois Mayfield, b. 7 March 1928; m.1. Wilburn Johnson; m.2. Charles Gatlin

v⁵1589. ¹⁴1. Kenneth Johnson, b. 23 Oct 1947

v⁵1590. ¹⁴2. Richard B. Johnson, b. 19 March 1950

v⁵1591. ¹⁴3. Roberta Sue Johnson, b. 11 Sept 1953

v⁵1592. ¹⁴4. Charles Vernon Gatlin, b. 21 Jan 1958

v⁵1593. ¹⁴5. Terri Y. Gatlin, b. 19 Sept 1960

v⁵1594. ¹⁴6. Gary Gatlin, b. 4 April 1962

v⁵1595. ¹²3. Ethel O. Evans, b. 2 Feb 1904; m. Joe Truitt

v⁵1596. ¹³1. George Walter Truitt, b. 14 Jan 1932; m. Mary Ethel McKimmey

v⁵1597. ¹⁴1. George Austin Truitt, b. 16 April 1954

v⁵1598. ¹⁴2. Julie Prentice Truitt, b. 26 Feb 1961

v⁵1599. ¹⁴3. Laura Carol Truitt, b. 10 June 1962

v⁵1600. ¹²4. Clarence M. Evans, b. 5 Sept 1906, Skullyville, I.T.; m. Golda Gibson

v⁵1601. ¹²5. Mary S. Evans, b. 22 March 1909, McCurtain Co, OK; m. B. Lewis Webb

v⁵1602. ¹²6. Hope D. Evans, b. 2 Jan 1911, Millerton, McCurtain Co, OK; m. William Stanley LaShier

v⁵1603. ¹³1. William Stanley LaShier, Jr, b. 6 Aug 1933, Amarillo, Potter Co, TX; m. Patricia Sue Stooksberry

v⁵1604. ¹⁴1. William Scott LaShier,

v⁵1605. ¹⁴2. Cathryn Hope LaShier,

v⁵1606. ¹²7. Woodrow A. Evans, b. 3 Feb 1913, McCurtain Co, OK; m.1. Dessie Christian (1 ch); m.2. Marie Cole (1 ch)

v⁵1607. ¹³1. Linda Jay Evans, b. 16 Dec 1942

v⁵1608. ¹³2. Vickie Lynn Evans, b. 1 Jan 1954

v⁵1609. ¹²8. boy Evans, b. & d. 16 Dec 1914

v⁵1610. ¹²9. Juanita Sue Evans, b. 17 March 1918, Millerton, McCurtain Co, OK; m. Harry Keaton, Sr

v⁵1611. ¹³1. Harry Keaton, Jr, b. 22 Dec 1942

v⁵1612.   ¹¹3. Annie Eliza McClain, (Choctaw Roll #7405), b. 21 Jan 1884, Skullyville, I.T., d. 15 Oct 1957; m. Albert Tobler, b. 1884

v⁵1613.   ¹²1. Emmitt Albert "Bill" Tobler, b. 9 Feb 1905, Oak Lodge, OK; m. Alice Swafford

v⁵1614.   ¹³1. Billie Jean Tobler, b. 12 Sept 1930, Sprio, OK; m. James Wrenn

v⁵1615.   ¹⁴1. Aleta Jean Wrenn, b. 22 Nov 1953

v⁵1616.   ¹⁴2. Jacqueline Wrenn, b. 29 Jan 1959

v⁵1617.   ¹³2. Tom Tobler, b. 27 Aug 1938, Spiro, OK; m. Anita Means

v⁵1618.   ¹⁴1. Ernest Alan Tobler, b. 23 Nov 1962

v⁵1619.   ¹²2. Annie Lila Tobler, b. 15 Oct 1907, Spiro, OK, d. 2 July 1958; m. Claude Burl Blackmon

v⁵1620.   ¹³1. Anna Carolyn Blackmon, b. 11 Feb 1934, Spiro, OK; m. Vernon Underwood

v⁵1621.   ¹⁴1. Marie Ann Underwood, b. 5 July 1957

v⁵1622.   ¹⁴2. Mark Vernon Underwood, b. 9 Nov 1959

v⁵1623.   ¹²3. Vivian Catherine Tobler, b. 23 Jan 1919, Spiro, OK; m. Edward C. Robinson, b. Lebanon, Wilson Co, TN

v⁵1624.   ¹³1. Edward Leon Robinson, b. 7 April 1931, Lebanon, TN, d. 1940

v⁵1625.   ¹³2. Elizabeth Jane Robinson, b. 18 July 1933, Lebanon, TN; m. Gene E. Hale

v⁵1626.   ¹⁴1. David Alan Hale, b. 23 July 1956

v⁵1627.   ¹⁴2. James Michael Hale, b. 28 Dec 1959

v⁵1628.   ¹³3. James Porter Robinson, b. 12 May 1940, Lebanon, TN; m. Elaine Bastion

v⁵1629.   ¹²4. Leon Nolen Tobler, b. 23 Jan 1913, Spiro, OK, d. 23 Sept 1965; m. Theresa Ainsworth

v⁵1630.   ¹²5. Roy Joe Tobler, b. 10 Dec 1916, Spiro, OK; m. Lyna Mae Blackwell

v⁵1631.   ¹³1. Roy Gene Tobler, b. 28 Dec 1942, Ft Smith, Sebastian Co, AR; m. Beverly Byrd

v⁵1632.   ¹⁴1. Wesley Gene Tobler, b. 5 Dec 1962

v⁵1633.   ¹⁴2. Christopher Martin Tobler, b. 2 Oct 1964

v⁵1634.   ¹²6. Mattie Belle Tobler, b. 4 Sept 1919, Oak Lodge, OK; m. James E. Richardson

^{v5}1635.   ¹²7. Charles Gilliam Tobler, b. 14 Aug 1922, Oak Lodge, OK; m. Gladys Couch

^{v5}1636.   ¹³1. Charles Leon Tobler, b. 7 April 1953

^{v5}1637.   ¹³2. James Randal Tobler, b. 13 March 1954

^{v5}1638. ¹¹4. Sallie Frances McClain, (Choctaw Roll #7406), b. 26 March 1886, Skullyville, I.T., d. 25 June 1955; m. James Hamilton Tibbitts

^{v5}1639.   ¹²1. James Yeager Tibbitts, b. 31 May 1910, Spiro, OK; m. Irene Greenwood

^{v5}1640.   ¹³1. Frances Irene Tibbitts, b. 7 March 1933, Spiro, OK; m. Sid Henry, Jr

^{v5}1641.   ¹³2. James Harden Tibbitts, b. 11 June 1934, Spiro, OK; m. Kathryn Kuykendall (ch: Debra Kay; Karen Sue; and Jimmy Don Tibbitts)

^{v5}1642.   ¹²2. George McClain Tibbitts, b. 30 April 1914, Spiro, OK; m. Lucille Vivian Frye

^{v5}1643.   ¹³1. Barbara Jean Tibbitts, b. 21 Nov 1934; m. Louie G. Conte

^{v5}1644.   ¹⁴1. Denise Marie Conte, b. 21 Feb 1954; m. Carl David Borgdon

^{v5}1645.   ¹³2. George Hamilton Tibbitts, b. 3 March 1938, Ft Smith, AR; m. Carol Jean Parker

^{v5}1646.   ¹⁴1. George Craig Tibbitts, b. 11 March 1965, Modesto, Stanislaus Co, CA

^{v5}1647.   ¹³3. Jerry Wayne Tibbits, b. 12 Sep 1939, Spiro, OK

^{v5}1648.   ¹²3. Nellie Louise Tibbitts, b. 27 Nov 1917; m.1. Harold Cottingim; m.2. J.D. Fleming

^{v5}1649.   ¹³1. Harold Lynn Cottingim, b. 27 Dec 1939

^{v5}1650.   ¹²4. Mary Lucille Tibbitts, b. 25 Jan 1921, Spiro, OK; m. Cecil Jack Adams

^{v5}1651.   ¹³1. Ronald Cecil Adams, b. 16 May 1949

^{v5}1652. ¹¹5. Georgia Belle McClain, (Choctaw Roll #7407), b. 4 Dec 1888, Skullyville, I.T.; m. David Spence Ainsworth, Sr, b. 1880, d. 1960

^{v5}1653.   ¹²1. Bessie M. Ainsworth, b. 16 July 1910, Oak Lodge, OK; m. George Watterson Jones

^{v5}1654.   ¹³1. Georgann Jones, b. 30 May 1941; m. Charles Roy Campbell

^{v5}1655.   ¹⁴1. George Ray Campbell, b. 16 Oct 1960

v5 1656.   12 2. David Spence Ainsworth, Jr, b. 30 July 1914, Oak Lodge, OK; m. Susan Ona Gill

v5 1657.   13 1. Ona Bess Ainsworth, b. 2 Sep 1933, Spiro, OK; m.1. Harold Watson; m.2. Roy Gould

v5 1658.   14 1. Angelia Watson, b. & d. 28 March 1953

v5 1659.   14 2. Harold Lloyd Watson, b. 26 Feb 1954

v5 1660.   14 3. Patricia Ann Watson, b. 16 May 1955

v5 1661.   14 4. Susan Renee Watson, b. 6 March 1958

v5 1662.   14 5. John David Watson, b. 21 Feb 1960

v5 1663.   13 2. Georgie Sue Ainsworth, b. 28 April 1935, Spiro, OK; m. Jerry Nichols

v5 1664.   14 1. Penny Ann Nichols, b. 21 Feb 1961, d. 24 Feb 1961

v5 1665.   13 3. David Spence Ainsworth, III, b. 4 Feb 1937, Spiro, OK; m. Shelva Fesperman

v5 1666.   14 1. Sherri Sue Ainsworth, b. 16 Sept 1957

v5 1667.   14 2. David William Ainsworth, b. 1 April 1959

v5 1668.   14 3. James Edward Ainsworth, b. 19 July 1961

v5 1669.   13 4. Johnnie Margarette Ainsworth, b. 2 Jan 1949, Spiro, OK; m. _____ Harrison

v5 1670.   12 3. Johnnie McClain Ainsworth, b. 24 March 1918, Oak Lodge, OK; m. Georgia Belle Snawder,

v5 1671.   13 1. Jane Ann Ainsworth, b. 27 Feb 1952

v5 1672.   11 6. John Quinn McClain, (Choctaw Roll #7408), b. 1891, Skullyville, I.T., d. 1963; m.1. Jean Wilson (no ch); m.2. Mary Gossett (1 ch)

v5 1673.   12 1. Buddy Gilliam McClain, b. 1943

v5 1674.   11 7. Jessie Juanita "Warneta" McClain, (Choctaw Roll #7409), b. 18 April 1895, Skyullyville, I.T.; m.1. Howard Brady; m.2. Edgar J. Woodruff

v5 1675.   12 1. Lois Lavenia Brady, m.1. Paul Champion, Sr; m.2. Herman E. Davenport

v5 1676.   13 1. Paul James Champion,

v5 1677.   13 2. William George Champion,

William L. Moncrief and Margaret Hall

[v5]**1392.** [9]2. William L. Moncrief, (s/o Sampson Moncrief and Sophia Brashears, I), b. 20 April 1820, Sumter Co, AL, d. 15 Feb 1872, bur Moncrief Cem, near Ninnekah, Grady Co, OK, said to be the first person buried there; m. 1839, in LeFlore Co, OK, Margaret "Mahala" Hall, b. 6 Oct 1820, d. 26 Jan 1915, Rush Springs, OK, bur Moncrief Cem, near Ninnekah, Grady Co, OK, d/o William Hall and Susan Riddle, d/o John Riddle Sr.

On the Choctaw Roll of 1902, Margaret "Mahala" (Hall) Moncrief (⅜ Choctaw, Census Card #14548; Roll #431) was 70 years old. "Mahala" was said to be her Indian name, while Margaret was an English near-equivalent. In the 1910 census, she was 98 [mistake for 88], living with her daughter and son-in-law, the Slatons; her tombstone says she died 26 Jan 1915, age 94 yrs, 8 mo, 26 days.

"William Moncrief, a native of Alabama, was of mixed white and Choctaw extraction, born about 1830. He came to Indian Terr. in 1851, settling near Skullyville. Some fifteen years later, he settled in the western part of the Chickasaw country. Seemingly, being far out of reach of the tribal school, he had established a temporary residence at or near the Comanche-Kiowa Indian Agency in order to give some of his younger children the opportunity to attend the new academy which was as yet but sparsely attended by children of the tribes for which it had been established. His widow survived him for many years, dying but a few years ago. His numerous descendants mostly live within the limits of the old Chickasaw country, some of them being prominent and influential citizens." (ref: *Chronicles of Oklahoma*, v.6 (1928) p.513; thanks to Marlene Mays Clark for the copy.)

AGED CHOCTAW WOMAN PRESENT WHEN TREATY SIGNED
Rush Springs, [OK], Feb. 13, 1915 (news clipping)

Mrs. Margaret Moncrief, aged 95 years, whose funeral occurred here two weeks ago, was one of the most widely known of the Choctaw Indians in Okla. She was born in Cherokee Co., Alabama, Oct. 6, 1820: was present with relatives when the Treaty of Dancing Rabbit was signed in 1830, giving to the Choctaws all of the land west of the Arkansas and north of the Red River, south of the So. Canadian and west to the limits of the U. S. in 1834.

In 1834, she with her father, William Hall, moved to what is now La Flore Co., Okla. and 5 years later married William [L.] Moncrief. The newly married couple, two years later moved to Fort Arbuckle to assist in the establishment of the fort, and in 1870 moved to a farm on the Little Washita River about 7 miles S/E of the present site of Chickasha.

About that time a stage coach line was placed in operation from Caddo to Anadarko and following the death of her husband two years later, Mrs. Moncrief supported her 5 sons and 6 daughters by conducting eating houses along the route. "The Widow Moncrief Places" became a familiar phrase among Okla. women during the early days.

In 1892, Mrs. Moncrief went to Rush Springs, Okla. where she made her home with her daughter, Mrs. James A. Slaton, where she resided until her death, Jan. 26 of the year (1915). During the last 12 years of her life, Mrs. Moncrief was bedfast, due to a fall.

During her young days, she assisted her husband in erecting the first house in what is now Murray Co., Okla. and the first house in what is now known as Grady Co., Okla. Both counties at that time being known as Pickens Co., Indian Territory.

During her time she saw the ox wagon give way to the modern stage coach and the stage coach give way to the steam railroad and automobile. (Thanks to Marlene Clark for the copy.)

Family of William L. Moncrief and Margaret "Mahala" Hall : (data from gggdau, Marlene Mays Clark, additional data from Sandi Carter):

v5 1678. 10 1. Martha Moncrief, b. c1840; m. 24 July 1868, Pickens Co, OK, J.R. (?Robert) Garner
v5 1679. 10 2. Sophia Moncrief, b. 17 Sept 1841, d. 28 July, 1889; m. before 1860, Willis Martin (1 ch); m.2. 1863, Charles Winter, b. 1834, d. 1889 (3 ch)
v5 1680. 11 1. Sam Martin, b. 186?
v5 1681. 11 2. William Henry Winter, b. 16 Sept 1864
v5 1682. 11 3. Joseph Egbert Winter, b. 1 July 1865, d. 1880
v5 1683. 11 4. Clifton Elmer Winter (son: Charles Thomas Winter)
v5 1684. 10 3. *William Hall "Bill" Moncrief, b. 26 Jan 1846, d. 17 March 1921, Chickasha, Grady Co, OK; m. 20 Sept 1877, Pauline Lina Maupin, b. 17 Sept 1857,

          d. 9 April 1948,

v⁵1685.   ¹⁰4. Sam Moncrief, (name may have been Sampson or Samuel; it appears as "Sam" on all the documents), b. 28 Jan 1849, Skullyville, Indian Terr., d. 24 Aug 1933, Sulphur, OK; m.1. Margaret Hall [no mistake; both Sam and his father married women named Margaret Hall], b. 1852, d. 1883 (3 ch); m.2. Josephine Moss, d. 1889 (1 ch); m.3. 1892, Virginia "Jennie" Dodson, b. 1856, d. 1943 (3 ch).Sam was a rancher in Purcell, OK. He was 52 in 1902, when part of his family was listed on Choctaw Census Card #128; he was listed as ⅛, Roll #267.

v⁵1686.   ¹¹1. Florence Moncrief, b. 1870, d. 1879

v⁵1687.   ¹¹2. Mary Jane Moncrief, b. c1873

v⁵1688.   ¹¹3. Walter Lee Moncrief, (1/16 Choctaw, Roll #268), b. 23 Dec 1879, Ninnekah, I.T.; m. 1901, Olivia "Olive" Clouney (ch: Clinton Moncrief)

v⁵1689.   ¹¹4. Georgia Henrietta Moncrief, (1/16 Choctaw, Roll #269), b. 1882, d. 1959; m. Charles Edgar Anderson (ch: Murray Moncrief; Wilbur Duane; Phillis Elizabeth; and Arthur Gale Anderson)

v⁵1690.   ¹¹5. Sammie Myrtle Moncrief, (1/16 Choctaw, Roll #270), b. 1888, d. 1954; m. John R. Law, of Ardmore, OK. (ch: Jot; Vivian; and Josephine Law. Jot Law, served 30 years in the U.S. Air Force.)

v⁵1691.   ¹¹6. Infant Moncrief, b. & d. 1892

v⁵1692.   ¹¹7. Lennye "Inez" Moncrief, b. 1894, d. 1989; m.1. 1911, Horace Clinton Pool, b. 1891, d. 1966; m.2. after 1966, Walter Bergman

v⁵1693.   ¹²1. Jack Horace Pool, b. 1912

v⁵1694.   ¹²2. Norma Pool, b. 1915; m. 1940, Nash Phillip Truss, Jr, b. 1914, d. 1989

v⁵1695.   ¹³1. Nash Phillip Truss, III, b. 1942; m. Mary Alice Clarkson, b. 1943

v⁵1696.   ¹⁴1. Holly Elizabeth Truss, b. 1970; m. Mark William Carlin. b. 1970 (ch: McKenzie Ann, 1998; and Bryce

Sumter Carlin, 2002)

v⁵1697.   ¹⁴2. Bradley Butler Truss, b. 1975

v⁵1698.   ¹³2. James Alton Truss, b. 1947

v⁵1699.   ¹¹8. Grace "Gracie" Moncrief, b. 1895, d. 1977;
            m.1. John Summey (ch: S.M. Summey); m.2.
            Sam Ben White (ch: Sam Ben, Jr; and Harry
            Wesley White)

v⁵1700.   ¹⁰5. Robert Moncrief, b. 17 Feb 1852, d. 18 Feb 1862,
            bur Fort Arbuckle, but when the family moved,
            his body was exhumed and reburied in the
            Moncrief cem then at Fred, OK, which has since
            disappeared.

v⁵1701.   ¹⁰6. *Susan Moncrief, b. 15 July 1854, Fort Arbuckle,
            OK, d. 26 June 1943, Pauls Valley, Garvin Co,
            OK; ¼ Choctaw, Roll #250; m. Samuel Johnson
            Garvin, intermarried white #784.

v⁵1702.   ¹⁰7. Mary Jane Moncrief, b. June 1857, I.T.; m.1.
            1879, A. McDonald; m.2. 1898, James A. Slaton,

v⁵1703.   ¹¹1. Canales McDonald, b. c1883

v⁵1704.   ¹¹2. Muir McDonald, b. c1894

v⁵1705.   ¹⁰8. Margaret Moncrief, b. 6 April 1852, Ft Arbuckle,
            OK, d. 3 Dec 1913, Chickasha, Grady Co, OK; m.
            1873, Wallis Bennett; m.2. c1881, Joseph B.
            Anderson, b. c1852

v⁵1706.   ¹¹1. Walter Lee Bennett, b. 1881; m. Georgia

————

v⁵1707.   ¹¹2. Albert Loray "Ray" Anderson, b. 1882

v⁵1708.   ¹¹3. Willis Elliot Anderson, b. 1884

v⁵1709.   ¹¹4. Burney Etta "Verna" Anderson, b. 1886; m.
            Charles Beaver Pruner, Sr, b. 1879, d. 1965

v⁵1710.   ¹¹5. Manly Manlin Anderson, b. 1888

v⁵1711.   ¹¹6. Joseph Kyle "Joe" Anderson, b. 1890

v⁵1712.   ¹¹7. Cynthia Payne Anderson, b. 1892, d. 1974; m.
            Charles Beaver Pruner, Sr, b. 1879, d. 1965

v⁵1713.   ¹²1. Charles Beaver Pruner, Jr, b. 1912, d.
            2000; m. 1940 Richanda M. _____

v⁵1714.   ¹²2. Norma Pruner, m. Gaylord Knowles

v⁵1715.   ¹²3. Robert Pruner, m. _____

v⁵1716.   ¹³1. Nancy Jane Pruner; m. Roy Lee
              Jarnigan

v⁵1717.   ¹¹8. Maxey Overton Anderson, b. 1894

WPA Project; *Oklahoma Indian-Pioneer Interviews*
WALTER L. MONCRIEF, INTERVIEW, 14 Jan 1938

I was born at Ninnekah, December 23, 1879, and was raised in Garvin County, where I went to school. I received most of my education by reading, as school terms in those days were short, and inherited from my father a gift of memory which has been a great help to me during my life.

My grand-parents, Wm. and Margaret Moncrief, moved from Alabama, where both were born and raised, to Skullyville. The trip was made by wagon and steamboat on the Arkansas River. They moved their household goods, farming tools, which were few and crude, also livestock.

My grand-parents were considered well-to-do in those days, as they were able to pay their way on the steamship. Some friends who moved at the same time made the long tiresome trek by wagons, alone. Even with the help of a steamboat, it took months for the trip. My grand-parents lived at Skullyville until 1849. Then moved to what is now Fort Arbuckle. They built their first house, a log one, on the west side of Washita River. They lived there until the Civil War, then moved to where Tishomingo now stands. At the close of the Civil War they moved back to Fort Arbuckle and lived there until 1869. My grandpa was one-eighth Choctaw, my grandma was one-fourth Choctaw. I suppose the Indian blood in them gave them their roving disposition. The first land in Oklahoma to be given Indians who lived east of the Mississippi River was ceded by treaty, October 18, 1820, to the Choctaws. The next move my grand-parents made was to the mouth of the Little Washita River.

Grandpa died at Fort Sill in 1872, and was buried at Moncrief Cemetery, where, for years no other person was buried except a member of the Moncrief family. This burial ground was about six miles southeast of what is now Chickasha.

The plains Indians would raid my grandpa's farm and steal horses, cattle and grain about once or twice a year. Grandpa killed three Indians on one of these raids. He was given a contract from the Government to furnish beef to soldiers at Fort Cobb and Fort Arbuckle. He had a large herd of cattle.

One time Grandfather was sent on a scouting expedition

with Captain Marcy to Salt Lake but at Santa Fe, New Mexico, he became too ill to go on and lay for weeks with fever.

At another time he was taken with soldiers to a Wichita Indian village, east of Rush Springs, on Rush Creek because he knew so many of the Indians at the village and could talk the language. An Indian from the village had killed a soldier at Fort Arbuckle and an uprising was feared because friends of the soldier were on the way to the village to kill the Indians. Excitement was running high, and soldiers were sent to keep down trouble but reached the village in time to see the head of the Indian, who had killed the soldier, brought in to white friends. Further trouble was avoided by the presence for several weeks of the soldiers at the village.

My father, Sam Moncrief, was born at Skullyville, January 28, 1849. Here his boyhood was spent. He did not receive much education but was a great reader. After his marriage, he began to follow in the footsteps of his father, farming and raising cattle and horses. Life was hard in those days; some seasons they had plenty to eat and other times food was scarce. Father moved to Ninnekah and lived there until 1881, then moved near what is now Maysville, in 1903, on a creek near Maysville, then called Beef Creek. He lived there until 1918, then moved to Sulpher where he died August 24, 1933. When he was farming and raising cattle, he would take herds of cattle up the Chisholm Trail to Caldwell and Dodge City, Kansas, on trading expeditions. He would trade what cattle he could not sell for groceries, buffalo hides or any other articles that they could use. One time he brought home a cook-stove, the first one in that part of the country, and people came from miles around to see it. Father would take cattle to Fort Arbuckle, too, and barter for buffalo hides from Indians. He helped drive the first herd of cattle that ever crossed Washita River.

The old Chisholm Trail ran east of the Cheyenne-Arapaho Reservation and the Cherokee outlet to Dodge City. As pasture became scarce in Texas, Chisholm started to Western Indian Territory with great herds of cattle to find new grazing lands; and then on to Wichita and Dodge City, Kansas, where the cattle were sold. Thus, he established a new trail, which bears his name today. At one time when he had stopped to graze for several days, the cattle stampeded and my father with the help of neighbors rounded them up and got the bunch back together.

The old trail runs from Red River in Texas to Wichita, Kansas.

A Delaware Indian scout named Red Blanket helped Chisholm with the first bunch of cattle taken through Indian Territory. A chuck-wagon and supplies were always taken along as towns were few and far between. Herds consisted of from two thousand to twenty-five hundred cattle. From twenty to thirty cowboys would be taken along as helpers. Red Blanket and my father became fast friends. The Chisholm Trail in later years was divided to seek more and newer grazing lands, the first fork being near Waurika. Today the old trail in places has washed, sometimes fifteen or twenty feet deep and formed creeks.

BIOGRAPHY AND REMINISCENCES OF
Edgar Moore, Spiro, Okla. July 20, 1937

Mr. Moore, the subject of this sketch, was born at Skullyville on January 7th 1873, of parents, who, when quite young, were brought from Alabama to the Indian Territory in compliance with the terms of the treaty made with the Federal Government at Dancing Rabbit Creek council grounds on September 27th, 1830, on the part of the Choctaw Indians and the treaty made on March 24, 1832, on the part of the Creek Indians at Washington, D. C. [His father, Lyman Moore, was listed as ¾ Creek Indian.]

He attended the community school at Skullyville until he reached the age of fourteen years. Afterwards he was a pupil at Spencer Academy, near Goodland, and then he was selected as one of a group of fifteen young men to attend Roanoke College at Salem, Virginia, where after one year, he was transferred to the Kemper Military Academy at Booneville, Missouri, and where Judge D.C. McCurtain, now in legal department of the Indian Service at Washington, D.C.; Reford Bond, now Chairman of the State Corporation Commission, and J.B. McAlester, attended at the same time.

This, indeed is a remarkable accomplishment when it is considered his father, Lyman Moore, died when he was scarcely eight years of age, and reflects honor and credit upon his mother who was, before her marriage, a member of the Moncrief family, for her maternal solicitation for the education of her children in the absence through death, of her life mate. She was permitted by Divine Providence to live to the ripe old age of eighty nine years, and was the mother of seven children, Edgar

A., Lyman R., Louis C., (now [1937] dead), Herbert H., Napoleon B., Gertrude (now [1937] Mrs. Bowman), and Lena (now [1937] Mrs. Smith).

He was a member of the first legislature and served as a member by appointment of William H. Murray, who was then Speaker of the House, of the Squirrel Rifle Brigade.

With the exception of the years 1903-1904, he has been a member, and still is, of the Choctaw Council. A membership which he has enjoyed since its institution and of which he feels justly proud.

The land holdings of the Moore family, before allotments were made, embraced the area now occupied by the city of Spiro. With rare foresight the two brothers had a townsite platted on this land and sold lot, contingent upon the approval of the Townsite Commission. The location of the townsite together with its provision for streets of adequate width as shown by the plat was quickly approved by the Townsite Commission, and the contingent sales were made bonafide and in conformity with the townsite regulations. Thus the beautiful little city of Spiro was born, and although it has not attained note as an industrial centre, it has enjoyed a brisk agricultural trade due to its location in an exceedingly rich farming and stockraising area.

Mr. Moore, aside from his activities in State and Tribal affairs, has devoted his life to stockraising and overseeing of his vast farm interests.

His [great]grandfather Moncrief was tragically killed and his body burned at the time of a negro uprising with occurred near Skullyville about 1860 or 1861. This uprising was instigated by an overseer, in the employ of Mr. Moncrief, who in reality was a northern sympathizer. After the uprising, with its tragic result, the overseer took the slaves out of the Choctaw Nation, disposed of them and never returned. In another uprising which occurred about the same time, three brothers, Joseph, Robert and Dave Hall, were brutally murdered by the slaves owned by them, under the leadership of another faithless overseer employed by the Hall family. However in this case, the traitorous overseer was in turn killed by a surviving brother who was assisted by one of the slaves who had heroically refused to join in the uprising.

During the turbulent years of the Civil War many of the

families who owned slaves and plantations in Skullyville County went as refugees to Doaksville, and in some instances to Clarksville, Texas, taking the slaves with them.

At the close of the Civil War, the negroes who had been scattered in the confusing conditions attendant on the prosecution of the war, in many instances returned to the homes of their former owners and insisted on being cared for in the same manner as that in which they had been cared for before their freedom.

It is significant that most, if not all, of the slaves in all the area lying north of the Kiamichi Mountains and south of the Arkansas River were owned by plantation owners having possessions in the Arkansas and Poteau River bottoms, and that these slaves were owned in the main by intermarried whites or mixed blood Indians, while the full blood Indians selected their home sites on the vast prairies where game was more plentiful. Jonico Prairie, so called by reason of its first settler being John Jonico, a full blood Choctaw Indian, was noted for its abundance of game and excellent fishing streams. The Poteau River is its eastern boundary, while on its south side Brazil Creek traverses it for several miles.

What a paradise for the nimrod and the angler. The present village of Panama is located on its eastern side, while it extends westward into Haskell County. Its north and south extent is approximately fifteen miles. Small wonder the full blood Choctaws saw in this a realization of their dreams; a return to the life of their forefathers in which for unnumbered centuries they had lived by the chase. One can mentally picture their extreme happiness and contentment amid such surroundings, and which they could still be enjoying had the whites not thrust their unwelcome presence into their midst.

As a relic of those bygone days, Mr. Moore has in his possession a treasure in the form of a letter which was written by his paternal grandmother, dated at Micco Creek Nation, West of Arkansas to her son, (his father) Lyman Moore, while he attended school at Cane Hill, Arkansas, admonishing and pleading with him to shun evil companions while he was thus unavoidably deprived of her personal care and direction. Time has obliterated the date, however since he was born in 1837, it may reasonably be presumed it was written somewhere between the years 1850 and 1855.

A perusal of this letter will set at ease all misgivings we may have as to the intellectual attainments of the Indians of that period who had been favored with educational advantages. It fairly breathes maternal love; couched in language so beautiful and expressive that one is led to believe that the communion of the Most High was very, very near when it was written. The chirography, too, is excellent and attractive, having a similarity to both the Old English Script and the Spencerian types of handwriting. A copy of this letter may possibly be in the archives of the Historical Society, as the original was sent to it as historical matter and afterwards it was returned to Mr. Moore, who doubtless receives much inspiration from the angelic thoughts expressed by its author.

Mr. Moore, entering upon young manhood in the early nineties, has not only personally experienced the epochal changes which have been brought about since that period, but has been highly instrumental in directing the course of those changes on through the years. Truly a type of citizen of which Oklahoma, his native state, may well feel proud.

William Hall Moncrief and Pauline Maupin

[v5]1685. [10]3. William Hall "Bill" Moncrief, (s/o William L. Moncrief and Margaret "Mahala" Hall), b. 26 Jan 1846, d. 17 March 1921, Chickasha, Grady Co, OK; m. 20 Sept 1877, Pauline Lina Maupin, b. 17 Sept 1857, d. 9 April 1948, d/o John Maupin and Mary Williams. (For data, thanks to Marlene Mays Clark and Sandi Carter.) William Muncrief, 56, and his family are on Choctaw Census Card #433; he is Roll #835 on the final rolls, dated 25 Sept 1902.

[v5]1719.   [11]1.   Jefferson "Jeff" "Bump" "Bunk" Moncrief, (3/32 Choctaw, Roll #836), b. 1879, d. 1962

[v5]1720.   [11]2.   James Valentine

Figure 30: Bill Moncrief and Lina Maupin

"Jim" Moncrief, (3/32 Choctaw, Roll #837), b. 1881, d. 1962; m. 1907, Hattie A. Nunn, b. 1891, d. 1963 (Marlene Mays Clark writes: Jim was born on Valentine's Day. That is how he got his middle name.)

[v5]1721.   [12]1. John William Moncrief, b. 1908, d. 1975; m. 1932, Zuma Mary Sitterding, b. 1909, d. 1985

[v5]1722.   [13]1. Kay Johnna Moncrief, b. 1936; m. 1955, Jerrell Dean "Jerry" Strange,

[v5]1723.   [14]1. Brenda Kaye Strange, b. 1956

[v5]1724.   [14]2. Terri Gaye Strange, b. 1957

[v5]1725.   [14]3. Sherri Raye Strange, b. 1960

[v5]1726.   [14]4. Kerri Renee Strange, b. 1962

[v5]1727.   [13]2. James Robert "J.R." Moncrief, b. 1942; m. 1967, Patricia Yvette "Pat" Crumper

[v5]1728.   [14]1. John Mark Moncrief, b. 1974

[v5]1729.   [12]2. LeRoy "Buster" Moncrief, b. 1912, d. 1994; m. 1935, Loletta "Leta" Holt, b. 1913, d. 1986

[v5]1730.   [13]1. Jerry Dean Moncrief, b. 1951

[v5]1731.   [11]3. Wallace "Wally" Moncrief, (3/32 Choctaw, Roll #838), b. 1885, d. 1952; m. Alice Ogden, b. 1887, d. 1950

[v5]1732.   [11]4. Luetta "Lula" Moncrief, (3/32 Choctaw, Roll #839), b. 1887, d. 1964; m. Charles J. "Charley" Baker, b. 1882, d. 1962

[v5]1733.   [12]1. Juanita Baker, b. 1910, d. 1983; m. Daniel C. McCormick

[v5]1734.   [13]1. Danita McCormick, b. 1939, d. 1956

[v5]1735.   [13]2. Pete McCormick, b. 1942

[v5]1736.   [11]5. John Moncrief, (3/32 Choctaw, Roll #840), b. 1889, d. 1968

[v5]1737.   [11]6. William Hall "Jigs" Moncrief, Jr, (3/32 Choctaw, Roll #841), b. 1892, d. 1963

[v5]1738.   [11]7. Tolbert Baine "Tollie" Moncrief, (3/32 Choctaw, Roll #842), b. 1894, d. 1979; m. Gertrude B. Shafer, b. 1908

[v5]1739.   [11]8. Mary Margaret Moncrief,

Mary Moncrief

(3/32 Choctaw, Roll #843), b. 1899, d. 2001; m. 1917, Seamon James Wheelock, b. 1895, d. 1950

v5 1740.   12 1. Tollie Bain Wheelock, b. 1918, d. 1918
v5 1741.   12 2. Charles William Wheelock, b. 1919, d. 1996; m.1. c1943, Marjorie Lee McCrory, b. 1922 (1 ch); m.2. c1948, Amalda Eleana Tamagnini, b. 1923, d. 1994 (3 ch); m.3. Takeko Shigyo
v5 1742.   13 1. Lawrence Michael (Wheelock) Herrell [adopted by a step-father], b. 1944; m. Lourdes Zapata
v5 1743.   13 2. Sonia Marie Wheelock, b. 1949; m.1. 1968, William Charles Golden, b. 1948; m.2. 1987, James Vincent Zeik, b. 1948
v5 1744.   14 1. Mark Allen Golden, b. 1976
v5 1745.   13 3. Veda Lynn Wheelock, b. 1949; m.1. 1970, Virgil Robert Reeves; n.m.2. (friend) George Allen Harris
v5 1746.   14 1. Alisha Estelle Reeves, b. 1972; m. Albert David "Al" Miller, b. 1975
v5 1747.   15 1. Alec David Miller, b. 1998
v5 1748.   15 2. Kylie Lynn Miller, b. 2001
v5 1749.   14 2. Randy Allen Harris, b. 1973; m. Jennifer ____
v5 1750.   15 1. Randy Allen Harris, Jr,
v5 1751.   15 2. Jordan Allen Harris,
v5 1752.   13 4. Richard Carl Wheelock, b. 1955
v5 1753.   12 3. Katherine Wheelock, b. 1921; m. 1940, Sealy Leroy Waller, Sr, b. 1916
v5 1754.   13 1. Sandra Sue "Sandy" Waller, b. 1942; m. 1960, James R. Dowlen
v5 1755.   14 1. Jill A. Dowlen, b. 1961; m. Daniel T. Ferguson
v5 1756.   15 1. Tiffany Nacole Ferguson,
v5 1757.   15 2. Ashley Ann Ferguson,
v5 1758.   15 3. Jacob Todd Ferguson,
v5 1759.   14 2. Jeffery S. Dowlen, b. 1964
v5 1760.   13 2. Patricia Ann Waller, b. 1943; m.1. 1960, Mark L. Boykin; m.2. 1972, Larry Clark, b. 1944
v5 1761.   14 1. Buddy Mark Boykin, b. 1961; m. Sharyn Burley

v5 1762.   151. Kandis Jean Boykin,
v5 1763.   152. Colton Wade Boykin,
v5 1764.   153. Jace Dakota Boykin,
v5 1765.   142. Katherin Jan Boykin, b. 1962
v5 1766.   143. J.R. Clark, b. 1979
v5 1767.   133. Sealy Leroy Waller, Jr, b. 1945; m. 1967,
                              Phyllis Gale Wheat
v5 1768.   134. Charles Steven Waller, b. 1953; m. 1975,
                              Connie Jean Melton

Oklahoma Indian-Pioneer Interview with Mrs. Bill Moncrief (Pauline <u>Lina</u> Maupin), Chickasha, Grady Co, Oklahoma (Thanks to Marlene Mays Clark for the copy.)

My folks and I came by train to Caddo in 1874. From there we traveled by covered wagon to Pauls Valley, in the Chickasaw Nation, where my father rented a farm and farmed for three years. He raised between forty and fifty bushels of corn to the acre and sold it for 15 cents a bushel.

Mr. Miller and Mr. Green each had a general mercantile store in Pauls Valley. George Laughlin did the freighting for both stores from Caddo.

There were no schools or churches at Pauls Valley in 1874 that I remember: but there was a Chickasaw Indian preacher south of Pauls Valley named Star.

In 1875, the Masons sponsored a Fourth of July Celebration at Erin Springs. A barbecued beef dinner was enjoyed by all. That night there was a dance at the home of Frank Murray, near Erin Springs.

In 1877, I married Bill Moncrief, a quarter-blood Choctaw Indian. We drove to a place near Ardmore in a hack and were married by Judge Boyd. We then made our home for some time on the Little Washita River. We did our trading at Erin Springs. The Store was owned by Doctor Ryan, and Church was held in the Masonic Hall.

Our home was a log house covered with slabs chipped off of logs that had been sawed into two shirt lengths and then covered with dirt.

There were all kinds of wild game with the exception of buffalo. We dried lots of beef by cutting it in strips, and salting it, then putting it in the sunshine.

I have seen thousands of Texas Longhorn cattle come up the Chisholm Trail. They usually crossed the Washita at what was called Rock Crossing, southeast of Chickasha, then trailed in a northerly direction toward Silver City, (now a ghost town) where they crossed the Canadian River.

In 1882, my husband and I moved to a place four miles northwest of where Chickasha now is. We crossed the river at the Maupin Crossing, near Pensee, then a store and post office run by Jacob Descombus. Meek Smith had one of the largest herds of cattle near Chickasha. His brand was called "Long O."

I used to wash clothes for some of the cowboys, and nearly all of them wore flannel shirts the year around. They also wore high top boots that reached to their knees. Not many of the cowboys in those days had razors and their whiskers and mustaches would grow out long. I have seen some of the cowboys cut their whiskers with a small pair of scissors. They could cut their whiskers so short that they would look like it hadn't been over two days since they had been shaved.

Frank Fred had a store north of the Indian agency, between the agency and the river, and he was a mighty fine man. Dr. Hume was the Government doctor at Anadarko. Colonel F. H. Hunt was the Indian Agent and Mr. Slagle was the Government blacksmith.

I have seen the Government men issue cattle to the Indians for beef purposes. They would call out the Indian's name and then turn his beef out and the Indian would run it out a little way and shoot it down and have it dressed in a very short time.

Oklahoma Indian-Pioneer Interview with Bunk Moncrief, Chickasha, Oklahoma:

I was born in the Chickasaw Nation, on Roaring Creek, in 1879. My father was a farmer and trader. He raised corn to feed his cows, horses, hogs and chickens. He bought his supplies at Pauls Valley.

In 1886, when I was seven years old, I went to stay with my Grandmother Moncrief, who lived on the Little Washita River, about three miles south of where the Fred post office was. My grandmother had one of the first herds of Durham cattle that there was in the country and her brand was M+. The country was all open, but her cattle never strayed far.

My grandmother was a widow, and the cowboys were kind

enough to keep a watch over her cattle, even though they never worked for her. If they would find one of her cows several miles from home, they would bring or send it back. That is one outstanding thing about the frontier men; they would all help, and respect women.

Dave and Scott Cook had the post office at Fred, and they ran a general merchandise store. Mail was delivered at Fred about once a week, being carried in a stage coach or hack. From Fred, the stage coach went to Anadarko, and then back on its way to Pauls Valley and Caddo.

I went to school in a little one-room cottonwood box house in Fred. The benches we sat on and the tables we used for desks were made of cottonwood; the lumber used to build our school house and desks came from Bitter Creek, where there was a sawmill.

There were about twenty five school children going to school at Fred and most all of them rode to school horseback. Our teacher's name was Bud Gibbs. Our school books were made by McGuffey, and we used a slate instead of pencil and paper. All of the children brought their lunches, which consisted mostly of biscuits and meat.

After going to school at Fred several terms, I was sent to Sacred Heart, a Catholic Missionary School in the Pottawatomie county. I was treated very nice there, and they fed us good. After going to school there one term, I quit school.

In 1895, when I was sixteen years old, I saddled my horse and made a trip to Texas by myself, hunting work. The people along the way whom I stayed overnight with treated me nice, fed me and my horse and never charged me anything.

I got a job in Texas working on a big cattle ranch, and stayed there one year then returned to my parent's home on the north side of the Washita river, just north of Chickasha. I was allotted five miles northwest of Chickasha. I am one-eighth Chickasaw [should be "Choctaw"].

News article from *AMARILLO SUNDAY NEWS-GLOBE*, Amarillo, Texas, Sunday Morning, September 25, 1955 (Thanks to Marlene Mays Clark for the copy.)

HIS GRANDCHILDREN HEAR
TRUE STORIES OF COWBOYS, INDIANS

James V. Moncrief Recalls Tribal History of Family
By Edith B. Underwood

In this day of space ships, men from Mars and other such things, it is somewhat of a relief to meet a grandfather who can entertain the 'small fry' in his family with old-fashioned cowboy and Indian stories. Such tales will never grow old to the grandchildren of James V. (Jim) Moncrief, 83. They are entirely true and the very fabric of his life because he is part Indian and grew up in Indian Territory on land allotted to members of the Choctaw tribe by the government.

His story begins before the Civil war when his French grandfather, a major in the U. S. Cavalry, married a Mississippi Choctaw maiden whose name was Margaret, English version of the Indian name "Mahala." When the government made a treaty with the Choctaws and began moving them to the Indian Territory, Maj. William Moncrief, his wife, a son and a daughter made the trip from Mississippi in an ox wagon. The exact date of the journey is not known but probably not before 1850 when a group of 500 or more came at one time. The trip through Southern Arkansas and up the Ouachita river was made under great hardship. They had seen floods and drought and suffered smallpox and other diseases. The miles seemed long, indeed, before they reached the land allotted to them about 40 miles from Fort Sill. The Choctaw tribe had been allotted the southern portion of the territory from the Arkansas line westward, but other groups that came earlier had settled in the eastern portion.

The son, William, who had been born in Mississippi, was the father of Jim Moncrief. Another son, "Uncle Sam," had been born in the ox wagon en route to Indian Territory, and five other children were born after they settled there. Major Moncrief continued in the employ of the government until he was killed by the Indians in one of their raids. Grandmother Margaret lived 98 years, dying in 1913. She was buried beside her husband in the old Moncrief Cemetery near Chickasha.

When her husband was killed, Mrs. Moncrief continued to live with her family at a place called "Old Fred." Her home was a half-way stop for government riders between Pauls Valley and

Anadarko. She had a small store and post office where mail for the entire district was left twice a week. It was 70 or 80 miles on the stage route between the two places and the dispatch riders pastured their horses at her place. If a tired pony was left and the rider failed to pick it up on the return trip, a government man soon arrived to claim the U. S. property. Everything issued to the Indians, from clothing to livestock had the U. S. brand placed upon it.

Being postmaster was no great chore, as there was only seven or eight families in the district at that time. There was constant danger from the marauding Indians, because the Apaches and other wild tribes were still making raids on the white settlers.

When the oldest son, William, grew up he became a dispatch rider for the government, carrying messages from Fort Sill to Fort Reno (now El Reno) and thence to Fort Riley, Kans. Although he could neither read nor write, his wife did all the book work and he was able to carry on his duties with her help. Their home was on the old Chisholm Trail and it was there, in the small community then known as Pence, that James Moncrief was born, Feb. 14, 1881.

Although the grandmother had been the only one with Indian blood in her family none of her children or grandchildren married Indians— the family had all of the inherited rights of the Choctaw tribe. When a white person married an Indian, he could be enrolled as a member of the tribe upon the payment of $500 to the government. William Moncrief, Jr, had paid that amount to have his wife's name placed upon the Indian rolls. She was Lina Maupin, whose family had come to Indian Territory from Kentucky when she was quite small.

Upon payment of $500, the person was given a roll number or headright which is his right to vote in all tribal affairs. The grandmother's number was 14,548. William Moncrief and his wife, Lina, had numbers 834 and 835. James, who was the second of their eight children, now has roll number 837. No roll numbers have been issued since 1906. Because she was enrolled as a member of the tribe, James' mother received the same allotment as his father each time one was made, but she did not inherit any of his estate upon his death. The government is guardian, and an Indian agent always divides the estate, which goes to the children.

When Jim was a small child, the family did not farm. They had some cattle and hogs which were allowed to run wild. They always had a small patch of corn which they called their "Tom Fuller" patch. Tom Fuller was their name for a favorite food which the Indians called pishofa. The corn was made into hominy and then ground into a sort of meal, which they cooked with beef or pork, preferably pork, to make pishofa. It is still cooked and served today at all Indian pow wows, and Moncrief still recalls the delicious goodness of the "Tom Fuller" he ate as a child.

He also remembers with less pleasure the times of terror when the Apaches of Geronimo's bunch, broke loose and went on the warpath. On one such occasion, they came to the Moncrief home while his father was away. His mother had seen them on a hillside near the house and realized the impending danger to her children playing in the yard. As the band rode toward them, she warned the children that they must go ahead with their play and, above all, they were not to act frightened or run from the Indians.

Two of the braves separated from the band and rode on toward their home, demanding "waha"— Indian word for beef. Mrs. Moncrief dared not refuse and she pointed to their small herd grazing about half a mile away. They rode off and killed a calf before a band of soldiers, who were trailing them, could prevent it. They were soon taken into custody, and that was the last time the Apaches escaped from the reservation.

Because of his lack of education, William Moncrief wanted his children to have the advantages he had not known. James first attended Fate's Mission school near Anadarko. A Mr. and Mrs. Fate acted as superintendent and principal in this school, established by the Methodist church. A Methodist preacher made periodical visits to the school, and held services for the pupils.

When he was about 11 James was sent to the Carlyle Indian School for boys. When he had been there about a year the children were vaccinated against smallpox and when he tells his grandchildren about the crude unsanitary way he was vaccinated, they only have to look at the scar he still bears today to realize what a painful experience that was. The arm was slashed three or four times with a penknife and the serum applied with a dirty quill. James nearly lost his arm and, when the pain became unbearable, he ran away from school and made his way home. Perhaps he was a little homesick, but no doubt his mother's nursing helped to make things right. Later, he attended a subscription school in a log cabin on the banks of the Washita river. The tuition was a dollar a month. It was during this time that he knew Quanah Parker and became friends with Quanah's daughters, Lucy and Mary.

Another pleasant experience of Jim's boyhood occurred when the Rock Island built a new line which passed about 300 yards from the Moncrief home. There was no sale for eggs in those days and Jim would gather a large bucketful and take them over to the engineer on the work train. These he swapped for rides on the work engine. It was quite a treat in two ways. After riding up and down on the slow-moving engine until he got his fill, the engineer would send him over to the mess camp where the cook would fill him with pie and cake. The crew had fared well on the quail and other game which was plentiful and the boy came in for his share on the egg-swapping trips.

Always as a child he had watched the cattle being driven to market on the Chisholm Trail in front of their home and it was no wonder that the young boy developed a yearning for the life of a cowboy. In later years, he was to make that same trip with his uncles when they would ride the train back as far as they could and then take their horses back to the ranch. His first experience was on the Waggoner spread near Lawton in old Indian Territory. Dan and Tom Waggoner had leased 2,000 acres of Indian land which was called the Big Pasture. Jim Moncrief started his life as a cowboy when he was about 16.

It was while he was working on the Big Pasture that Jim came in contact with the notorious Geronimo, who had been captured in Arizona and taken to Fort Sill to spend the rest of his life in the guardhouse on the reservation. After he had apparently become reconciled to captivity, he was allowed to go about the grounds but always with heavy ball and chain shackles.

When the cowboys from the Big Pasture rode in to buy tobacco and other things from the commissary at Fort Sill they often saw Geronimo. One time, he saw Geronimo pick up his shackles and dart for the mess hall, where he tried to get a butcher knife. Upon several occasions, he nearly killed soldiers and had to be kept under heavier guard for many months.

In 1900, the Waggoners lost their Big Pasture lease, and it was opened up for settlers. Many people are familiar with the opening of the Cherokee strip in 1892, but the Big Pasture run in 1900 was quite real to Jim Moncrief. He saw the prospective settlers come in and camp for two months before the day of the run. Many of them lived off the Indians and white people nearby, killing their cattle and taking other things to meet their daily needs, after they had used their own supplies.

Back in 1896, Jim had made a trip to Texas and New Mexico with an uncle, and he liked what he had seen well enough to strike out on his own in 1901. His experience with the Waggoners had been a happy one, and he went next to XIT, where he worked about a year and a half. His entire time with them was spent in the Yellowhouse Canyon division. He had done some bronc busting, but he began to get more experience there. When a cowboy went to a ranch and hired out, he rode his own horse, but he never rode it again as long as he worked there, unless he just wanted to. It was turned loose on the range until he chose to ride it again. The first day, the boss took his new cowpuncher to the corral, he picked out seven horses—one for each day of the week. These, he had to break himself, and it didn't take the boss long to find out the sort of man he had hired. Twenty-five dollars a month was top wages at that time.

When he was about 21, Jim went to the LFD Cattle Co. at Roswell, N. M. and hired out to George and Bill Littlefield. It was while he was working for them that he had the one serious accident of his life. He had been thrown, kicked, run over and knocked down many times, but, in roping a bull, he had his horse jerked from under him. The horse fell on him and, before the other men could cut the bull loose and get the horse off him, Jim was bruised and lacerated. Not knowing the extent of his injuries, Bill Littlefield put him in the buckboard and started on the journey to the hospital in El Paso. They left the LFD headquarters near Roswell late one afternoon and drove all night by way of Carlsbad to Van Horn, arriving there about noon the following day. There they took the train to El Paso and Jim spent 30 days in the hospital. Littlefield had stayed only long enough to see that his cowboy was not going to die and returned on the next train.

Once or twice a year Jim would saddle his horse and make

the trip back to Indian Territory for a visit with his family. In 1906, he made such a trip and on that visit he was to meet a girl who had moved into the community since his last visit. Perhaps the girl had something to do with it, but, after another visit in 1907, he decided to give up broncbusting and cowpunching to marry Hattie Nunn.

Hattie had lived through some exciting experiences during the 16 years before her marriage. She had been born in Kentucky and upon the death of her father, when she was nearly 8, her mother took her three children to Decator to make her home near her father-in-law. The family lived there for several years until her mother remarried. The stepfather took them to Potawatomi County in the eastern part of what was soon to be Oklahoma. In 1905, the family moved to the community near Chickasha.

This trip was made in a covered wagon, and Mrs. Moncrief recalls many of the dangers of the trip. Near Purcell, they had to ford the Canadian river, where guides were stationed to lead the wagons across the dangerous quicksand. Their fee was $5 for each wagon, and the stepfather was determined not to pay that much. He watched as other wagons were guided across and thought he could follow in their tracks. The Canadian is a treacherous river, and it wasn't long before the horses floundered and, for awhile, it looked as though all would be lost. The guides rescued the family by horseback from the wagon and then roped the horses to pull them and the wagon to safety. Their best horse died soon after from the experience.

Soon after their marriage, Jim bought a claim near Ima, N.M., and the young couple made the trip out there in a covered wagon in the summer of 1908. The altitude proved too high for Mrs. Moncrief and, in October, the doctor ordered her to return to Chickasha. After accompanying his wife to her mother's home, Jim returned to the place in New Mexico and stayed until January of 1909. Their oldest son, John was born during his absence and another son, LeRoy "Buster," also was born at Chickasha.

The family moved over to Wapanucka in 1912, to stay three years, but both sons started to school and graduated in Chickasha. Both married there.

John, who has a son and daughter, still lives there, although he lived in Amarillo for a number of years during the war. L. R., who has two sons, lives at 205 N. Belleview.

Since 1943, the Moncriefs have lived in Amarillo where he was employed by the city and later at the Amarillo Country Club for four years. As long as his health would permit, he enjoyed the outdoor work but, in recent years, the care of his lawn and garden and the raising of prize dahlias has occupied his time.

There are always old friends to visit with and talk of days upon the trail and nights around the campfire and times when a man might be called up before a tribal court, but wasn't. Although the Indians are governed by the white man's laws now, there was a time when an Indian trial was enough to make a cowpuncher keep on the straight and narrow trail. Life for Jim Moncrief will still be pleasant as long as there are little boys to sit in openmouthed wonder while grandfather tells another yarn about cowboys and Indians.

Susan Moncrief and Samuel J. Garvin

[v5]1702. [10]6. Susan Moncrief, (d/o William L. Moncrief and Margaret "Mahala" Hall), b. 15 July 1854, Fort Arbuckle, OK, d. 3 Dec 1943, Pauls Valley, Garvin Co, OK; ¼ Choctaw, Roll #250, C.C. #122; m. Samuel Johnson Garvin, Intermarried cit. #784 (gp/o Marlene Mays Clark). The Garvins lived in Paul's Valley, OK. Susan Moncrief Garvin is #209 on the Census of Choctaw Nation, taken 1896, with five children; she and her children after John Garvin are on Choctaw Census Card #122, dated 25 Sept 1902.

[v5]1769.   [11]1. Lizzie Garvin, b. 1872, d. 1895; m. J.E. Burch, Jr, b. 1867, d. 1911

[v5]1770.   [11]2. Robert H. "Bud" Garvin, b. 24 Nov 1874, 1/16 Choctaw, Roll #9426, C.C. #3266, d. 6 Aug 1903; m. Mercades "Mattie" Fleming, b. 13 Feb 1879, Austin, TX, d. before 4 April 1957, Maysville, Garvin Co, OK, d/o J.T. Fleming.

[v5]1771.   [12]1. Vashti Garvin, b. c1899 (3 in 1902), Choctaw Roll #9427; m. Joe Camp, b. c1898 (4 in 1902), Choctaw Roll #248, C.C. #121

[v5]1772.   [13]1. Jim Garvin Camp,

[v5]1773.   [13]2. Patricia Camp, m. V.C. Springfield

[v5]1774.   [12]2. Robert H. Garvin, Jr, b. 14 July 1901, Choctaw Roll #9428, C.C. 3266, d. 20 Sept 1965

v5 1775.   11 3. John B. Garvin, b. c1877, Choctaw Roll #251, C.C. #122; m.1. 14 Sept 1908, Martha Elizabeth Brewington (no ch); m.2. after 1910, Isoletter Devere Garrison

v5 1776.   12 1. Dorothy Sue Garvin,

v5 1777.   12 2. Samuel Franklin Garvin; m. Juanita ____

v5 1778.   12 3. John B. Garvin, Jr

v5 1779.   11 4. Margaret Garvin, b. 23 Oct 1879, d. 4 Nov 1879

v5 1780.   11 5. Birdie Garvin, (Choctaw Roll #252, C.C. #122), b. 1882, I.T., d. 28 Sept 1910; m. 30 April 1899, Thomas Gardner Mays, (Chickasaw Roll #4441, C.C. #415), b. 8 April 1877, d. 19 Nov 1958, s/o David Mays and Susan Mitchell (Chickasaw Roll #4439, C.C. 415). Thomas told Marlene Mays Clark that, when David and Susan were married, they were married in the Indian ceremony, as well as a civil ceremony; that is, by cutting the wrists and mixing the blood, so that David Mays would be accepted as an Indian.

v5 1781.   12 1. Samuel Johnson "S.J." "J." Mays, b. 1901, Pauls Valley, OK, Choctaw Roll #254, C.C. #122, d. 16 April 1969, Maysville, OK; m. 10 Aug 1922, Julia Houghlin, b. 3 May 1900, d/o Fletcher Houglin and Mary Heady

v5 1782.   12 2. Thomas Gardner Mays, Jr, b. 1902 (Newborn Chickasaw Roll #302, C.C. #334), d. 1932; m. Mary Sadler

v5 1783.   13 1. Marilyn Mays; m. John Beard

v5 1784.   12 3. Clarence Elmo Mays, (Newborn Chickasaw Roll #86, C.C. #136) b. 12 March 1905, Maysville, Garvin Co, OK, d. 19 Feb 1937, Pauls Valley, OK; m.1. 22 Feb 1930, Ruby Elizabeth Dugas, b. 22 Nov 1907, Houston, Harris Co, TX, d. there 4 Feb 1969, d/o David Dugas and Elizabeth Simoneaux.

v5 1785.   13 1. Marlene Mary Mays, b. 24 Aug 1931, Oklahoma City, OK; m. 12 Aug 1950, in OK City, Siburn Jefferson "Jeff" Clark, Jr, b. 18 July 1930, Corpus Christi, TX, s/o Siburn Clark Sr and Gussie McLendon

v5 1786.   14 1. Siburn Jefferson Clark, III, b. 21 Dec

	1956, Port Lavaca, Calhoun Co, TX, d. 29 Oct 1990, Houston, TX
v⁵1787.	¹⁴2. Clarence Robert Clark, b. 31 July 1958, Ganado, Jackson Co, TX; m. 16 Oct 1982, in Lake Jackson, Brazoria Co, TX, Rhonda Kay Weber, b. 2 Sept 1962, Houston, Harris Co, TX, d. 12 Dec 1996, LaPorte, Harris Co, TX
v⁵1788.	¹⁵1. Clarence Robert Clark, Jr, b. 7 Aug 1984
v⁵1789.	¹⁴3. Teresa Marlene Clark, b. 9 Dec 1960, Ganado, Jackson Co, TX; m. 14 Feb 1987, in Houston, Harris Co, TX, William Crissman Shipman, b. 19 July 1955, Camp LeJeunne, NC, s/o Jack Shipman and F. Jean Crissman
v⁵1790.	¹⁵1. Christine Denise Shipman, b. 28 March 1989, Houston, Harris Co, TX
v⁵1791.	¹⁴4. Charles Duane Clark, b. 5 Sept 1964, Victoria, Victoria Co, TX; n.m. Christine Marie Wallace, b. 17 Jan 1969, Houston, Harris Co, TX
v⁵1792.	¹⁵1. Kayla Nicole Clark, b. 13 Feb 1993, Houston, Harris Co, TX
v⁵1793.	¹²4. Sue Bernice Mays, b. 1906, d. 1907
v⁵1794.	¹²5. Jack Mays, b. 1908, d. 7 March 1969, Pauls Valley, OK
v⁵1795.	¹¹6. Vivian Garvin, b. 1891, Choctaw Roll #253, C.C. #122, d. 1916
v⁵1796.	¹¹7. Garvin baby, (male) age 2 in 1896, b. c1894
v⁵1797.	¹¹8. Mercedes F. Garvin, b. 24 Aug 1903, d. 24 Aug 1904

From the Garvin County History book dated 1957; thanks to Marlene Mays Clark for the copy:

Mrs. Susan Garvin, wife of Samuel Garvin and daughter of Mr. and Mrs. William Moncrief, was born at Fort Arbuckle but established a residence at Pauls Valley after her marriage in 1870 to Mr. Garvin. She platted and dedicated 'Garvin Addition to Pauls Valley.' She remembered as a child her parents defending their homestead against attacking Kiowa Indians who succeeded in burning a portion of their property and driving off their livestock. Mrs. Garvin was a true pioneer and her influence in Pauls Valley was wholesome and progressive. She stood on the high red bluff at Purcell, Okla., and witnessed the opening of old Oklahoma and the run from that point on April 22, 1889. She gained state-wide publicity and prominence after the first World War for encouraging aviation and as often as she could, she made airplane rides with Earl Witten, son of Cody Witten, a lifelong friend of Mr. and Mrs. Garvin.

Things that Marlene Mays Clark was told:

A daughter of Susan and Samuel was to marry Wiley Post, but the girl (it must have been Lizzie) died before she was married. Susan often flew with Wiley Post and Will Rogers.

I find it hard to believe, but Mrs. Katie Grant said Susan had a scalp hanging on the head of her bed. Susan loved to travel and sometimes she would return home only to change trunks for the season's clothing.

From *History of Indian Territory*

"A brilliant example of a self-made American citizen is found in Samuel J. Garvin. His singular success is due to his own energy and to the high ideals which his laudable ambition placed before him, and his success in all the walks of life is an indication that untiring energy, persistent effort, executive ability and strict integrity were characteristics which Mr. Garvin possessed in an eminent degree. He is now the vice-president of the First National Bank of Paul's Valley and the owner of extensive realty interest, and has also been actively identified with mercantile affairs in his section of the Indian Territory.

Mr. Garvin was born in Fleming County, Kentucky, January 28, 1846, and when eleven years of age accompanied his parents on their removal to Missouri, where he acquired his education. He was in Denver, Colorado at the time of the inauguration of the Civil War; at Bent's Fort he joined the Confederate army, but was captured at Big Bend, while on his way to Fort Smith with A.B. Miller, who had organized a company for service with southern troops. After being taken prisoner, he went with the quartermaster's department of the Union army, worked for the government and after the close of hostilities continued in the government service.

In 1867, he was sent to Fort Arbuckle and since that time has resided in the Indian Territory. Here he became interested in the live-stock business and his efforts in that direction were crowned with a high degree of success. He gradually extended the field of his operations, becoming the owner of a large herd, and upon the market his cattle found a ready sale, bringing to him a handsome income.

His resourceful business ability prompted him to embark in other enterprises and today he is a leading stockholder and vice-president of the First National Bank in Paul's Valley. In connection with C.J. Grant and W.G. Kimberlin, he erected the courthouse in Paul's Valley and rented it to the United States. He engaged in merchandising at Whitebead, Paul's Valley, Rush Springs, Paoli, Purdy, and Beef Creek, his operations along that line of business until March 1, 1899, when he sold out to the Hart Drug Company, being very extensive, but at the present time he is not associated with mercantile affairs.

In the year 1870, Mr. Garvin was united in marriage to Miss Susan Moncrief, of Choctaw blood, a daughter of William Moncrief, who was a delegate to establish the meridian line, is a government contractor and a prominent stock man. Unto Mr. and Mrs. Garvin have been born five children, but Lizzie, the eldest, is now deceased. The others are Robert, John B., Birdie and Vivian. Mr. Garvin was made a Mason at Erin Springs, Indian Territory, and now belongs to Whitebead Lodge, No. 73, F. & A.M. He has attained the thirty-second degree in the Scottish rite of Masonry, his membership being with Wichita Consistory, No.2. He also belongs to Whitebead Lodge, No.3, I.O.O.F., and Crescent Lodge, No. 15, K.of P.

Mr. Garvin has had a creditable business career, while he has met with some difficulties and obstacles, and the tide of prosperity with him has been largely uninterrupted, and he is today in control of several business interests and investments. He is very approachable, showing courtesy to all with whom he comes in contact, and is a conspicuous young man, having a host of warm friends. He acts from honest motives and in all relations of business affairs, and in social life he has maintained a character and standing that has impressed all with his sincere and manly purpose to do by others as he would have others do by him."

From the Garvin County History book dated 1957:

Samuel J. Garvin was born Jan. 28, 1844 or 1846 in Kentucky, the son of John and Mary (Stithe/Smoot). At the outbreak of the Civil War, he migrated to Colorado. He joined a freighting caravan headed for the Southwest. There were seven wagons loaded with merchandise, each pulled by five or six teams of oxen. They were owned by Henry Myers. Experience gained on this trip from Colorado east down the Santa Fe Trail fitted him for his years as a freighter in the Indian Territory.

At Fort Arbuckle, he met and married an Indian girl, Susan Muncrief, and by so doing became an adopted member of the Chickasaw (this should be Choctaw) tribe. He gained control of large blocks of land, which were later relinquished when allotment by severalty was enacted.

He moved to Pauls Valley and operated a mercantile business. One of his employees was Walter J. Harris, who provides some clear impressions of the character of the namesake of Garvin County. Mr. Harris regards Samuel Garvin as one of the best judges of character he has ever known— a man who could size up a customer's honesty, credit rating and future potentials with a glance. In the many years he worked for Garvin in his store and banks, he does not recall this judgment ever causing his boss a loss.

Hard life as a freighter had been a good teacher. Mr. Garvin became widely identified with the banking institutions of the area. With Calvin J. Grant, he first organized a private bank, which was followed by the First National Bank of Pauls Valley, of which he was president at the time of his death on July 20, 1908. He was also president of the First National Bank of Maysville and a director and vice president of the State Bank of Elmore City. He was president of the Pauls Valley Mill and Elevator Company also, and retained extensive ranching interests.

He married Susan Muncrief in 1870. Their children were Lizzie, Robert, John, Birdie and Vivian. Samuel Garvin was a Mason, 32nd degree, Scottish Rite, Odd Fellow and a member of the Knights of Pythias.

From *Historical and Biographical Record of the Cattle Industry and the Cattlemen of Texas and Adjacent Territory*, published by Woodward & Tiernan Printing Co., Saint Louis 1895.; thanks to Marlene Mays Clark for the copy.

"Kentucky is Samuel J. Garvin's native state, and his father, John Garvin, was also a Kentuckian. The mother, whose maiden name was Mary Smoot, was born in Virginia. John Garvin was a farmer, and the greater part of his life was spent in that occupation in Kentucky, but before his death, which occurred in 1855, he had removed with his family to Missouri. His wife survived him only a year.

Our subject was born in 1846, and was therefore but ten years old when the death of his parents left him to make his way in the world as best he might. His boyhood was passed in various portions of the West, and as there was no one to make his education their special care, it may readily be supposed that his school days were of brief duration.

He eventually drifted into the Indian Territory, and as the cattle business was about the only one followed there, he took it up as a matter of course and his first engagement of consequence was in the capacity of cowboy. In 1866, a herd of cattle started from Old Cherokee Town in the Chickasaw Nation, bound for Fort Union, New Mexico, where it was to be delivered to the United States commissary officials, and Mr. Garvin hired to accompany it, receiving $60 a month for his services. Nearly all of the other hands employed were "blanket" Indians, a wild and unruly crowd, but capable herders for all that.

The trip consumed several weeks, and Mr. Garvin remained in New Mexico until the following fall. Returning then to the Indian Territory, he commenced the next year to work for a Mr. Harlan (note by Marlene — this is probably William Moncrief's brother-in-law, husband of Sarah Ann Moncrief), who had a great many cattle on the range and was in need of a steady and efficient hand. Mr. Garvin only remained with him one season, however, though the wages paid were the same as he had received on the range.

Giving up his position he went to Fort Arbuckle, and there arranged to take and hold a herd of about 3,500 cattle on shares. Mumford [Montford T.] Johnson was the owner of this herd, and being a man of experience and sagacity, he was quick to recognize the sterling qualities of this new aspirant to the title of cattleman, while young Garvin fully appreciated the chance given him to work his own advancement, and applied himself zealously to the task of watching over and caring for the herd which had been intrusted to his care.

His aim in life was now to get a start of cattle of his own, and with this end in view he invested every spare dollar in stock, and was continually making trades, each of which added to the size of his herd. Luckily, cattle were cheap at that time, and their owners were generally glad to dispose of them for almost any consideration. On one occasion, Mr. Garvin traded a saddle pony for twenty head of cattle, and similar exchanges were of frequent occurrence.

Managing as described above, Mr. Garvin soon acquired quite a nice little herd, and under his attentive care it prospered and grew in numbers. He kept the Johnson cattle two years and returned them to their owner and bought 1,000 head from J.C. Loving. This herd was purchased on credit, and was delivered to him by Lee Dyer, at a point on the Little Washita, near where the "Western Trail" afterward crossed it, though at the time of which we write, the idea of driving cattle across the Indian Territory that far west had not yet been evolved.

Mr. Garvin had already become quite well known as a cattleman and in 1869 he commenced handling the cattle furnished by McKee & McDonald, the beef contractors, to the different forts and Indian agencies. In those days, the holder of a government contract in the Indian country had a fat thing of it, to use a slang phrase, and Mr. Garvin's salary was high in proportion. While receiving and delivering government cattle, he was receiving $150 a month, and consequently was enabled to pay up for his own cattle and purchase enough more to bring his holding up to 2,000 head, all good cattle and free from debt. This was not a period of idleness to him, however, for he was continually in the saddle, almost night and day.

While his prospects were the brightest, an added ray of sunlight was cast upon his life through his marriage with Miss Susan Moncrief, daughter of a prominent citizen of the Chickasaw Nation, who had been the largest cattleman in all that region prior to the war. Miss Moncrief was born in 1855, and was raised and educated at old Fort Arbuckle, which had been in its time the most important trading post in that entire section of the West. She was a young lady noted for her beauty and mental qualities, and she has made Mr. Garvin a most estimable helpmate, sharing, as a good wife should, in his joys and sorrows, and lending her smiles and sympathy to cheer him over the rough places of the pathway of life.

After his marriage, Mr. Garvin located his home on the Little Washita, and resided there continuously until 1881, holding his cattle on the adjacent ranges. He then moved his family to Kansas, in order that they might have the benefit of better educational facilities, but finding that he could not well conduct his business at a point so remote from his home without losing too much time in traveling back and forth, he brought his family back to the Indian Territory after the end of the first year, and settled at White Bead Hill, where he still resides.

His children were not the losers by this change of location, since there are excellent schools at the place last named; as good, in fact, as any that they had attended in Kansas. Mr. Garvin's eldest child, Lizzie, is now married to a Mr. Burch; the other children— Robert, John, Bird and Vivian— are living at home with their parents. The sons are in the cattle business, for which they have a pronounced fondness, and they will hardly turn to any other occupation so long as this continues profitable.

Mr. Garvin's cattle interests have occupied the greater portion of his time, and have added greatly to his prosperity. In 1884, he bought the Murray stock of cattle, one of the oldest and best herds in the Territory, for $96,000, and two years later he became the owner of the "Triangle" brand, which was then worn by about 2,700 cattle. He bought them from their original owner, Jim Rennie, of White Bead Hill, at $20 a head, all counted.

He has since been raising cattle, and fattening a good many annually for the spring market, and while he has made a good deal of money, he has suffered some severe losses. At one time, he sold a herd to some parties on credit, and lost $52,000 on one note, but his profits from the business have since made this loss good.

He has frequently driven cattle to markets further north, buying them in Texas and localities in the Indian Territory, and it is a rare thing to find him without some enterprise on foot calculated to increase his prosperity. He uses cotton seed largely in fattening his stock, and has found it better adapted for that purpose than anything previously tried. His cattle are invariably placed on the market in good condition, and bring the top prices. During the past winter (1894-'95) he fed 500 head of beef steers, which brought him $40.50 each, sold and delivered at his pens. He has now about 3,000 head of cattle, all told, and he carries on his ranch about 100 head of horses and a great many hogs. A good number of fine porkers are slaughtered for market each year, and his sales of mules are also a considerable source of income.

A life passed amid the wild surroundings of the Indian country must naturally be an eventful one, and it is to be regretted that Mr. Garvin can not be induced to relate some of the incidents and adventures through which he has passed. He has always been a bitter enemy of lawlessness in all its forms, and the horse-thieves, whisky peddlers, and others of that class which have overrun the Chickasaw Nation in the past, quickly learned to regard him as their foe and to shun him as such. He is a man who has earned and possesses the respect and esteem of every right-minded citizen of his section, and not a blur can be found upon his reputation for honesty and fair dealing.

Stories told in the WPA Indian-Pioneer Interviews.
"I remember in 1884 that the people had built a big brush arbor near the cemetery at Whitebead and a young preacher came from Missouri to hold a big meeting. The meeting had been going on for three or four nights, and my father and mother had been attending it every night. As we were on our way to church one night, I remember hearing my father tell Mother not to be alarmed at what she would see that night, as some of the boys were going to introduce the new preacher into their circle. Of course, we children didn't know what was going to take place, but after the preacher was through preaching and everyone was getting ready to start home, a gang of cowboys from the Sam Garvin ranch and, I believe, some from the Jack Florence ranch, began shooting. They shot out the lights, and everything was in an uproar. I remember children were crying and women screaming. I have heard my father talk about it, and he said after things quieted down, they went out looking for the preacher, and it was about three hours before they found him and, when they did find him, he was about a half a mile from the arbor, hidden under a brush pile. The preacher

wanted to leave town the next day." *Interview with Dr. Thos. Peter Howell*

"I went to work for Mr. Sam Garvin, who owned a large ranch. His brand was the Coffee Pot brand ... Mr. Garvin and Mr. Burk had under their control the range from Pauls Valley to Story, and near Elmore City." *Interview with Jim F. Davis*

"I also dealt in cattle. I borrowed thirteen hundred dollars at the bank from Mr. Garvin. At that time, it was easy to borrow money if you were using it to buy cattle. In that time, people tried to help each other." *Interview with W.R. Campbell*

"The first money I ever borrowed was from Sam Garvin, President of the First National Bank at Pauls Valley. I borrowed $100.00, paying 20% interest and had to put up $500.00 worth of stock for security. We didn't have cheaper interest until after Statehood and the usury law passed." *Interview with Benjamin H. Blackwell*

"In 1893 White Bead Hill was a small inland town located about fourteen miles west of Pauls Valley.... Mr. Garvin was a big cowman. He owned the first general merchandise store in this little town. He built a nice home and was considered the wealthiest man in this locality. He would lend the farmers money, taking mortgages on their crops in time of need, and would carry the mortgages for several years. George Shull, a German, rented land from Sam Garvin. They bought and traded cattle together, being very close friends. One night the German dreamed that he and Sam Garvin were in Purgatory. Here he saw the devil and a big black kettle turned upside down. The German wanted to see what was under this kettle, so he tried to peep under it and the Bad Man caught him, saying, "Don't look under there, you'll see Sam Garvin, and he'll have a mortgage on this place in fifteen minutes." When the dreamer told Mr. Garvin of his dream, Mr. Garvin laughed and took it very good naturedly. He was a very good man and was liked by everyone." *Interview with Mrs. George Bundy*

Mary Ann Moncrief and Robert S. McCarty

[v5]**1393.** [9]3. Mary Ann Moncrief, (d/o Sampson Moncrief and Sophia Brashears, I), b. 24 Oct 1826, Sumter Co, AL, d. 16 April 1911, bur McAlester, OK; m. 23 Dec 1844, in Sumter Co, AL, Robert Smith McCarty. They moved to Indian Territory when Nancy Ann was 3 and lived near Skullyville on the Arkansas

line. In the 1855 Choctaw census, they have three children: Helen, Lelah E., John W., and Mary Ann's brother, Matthew L. Moncrief, in their household. Mary Ann listed as ¼ Choctaw, Roll #7521; C.C. #2592.

Doug Barkley says that Mary Ann had three illegitimate children by John Johnston, Sr, before marrying Robert S. McCarty: William Worth Moncrief, Franklin Pierce Moncrief, and Douglas H. Cooper Moncrief. On 4 Nov 1857, these children were given the Johnston surname.

[v5]1798.   [10]1. Nancy Ann McCarty, (⅛ Choctaw, Roll #13048), b. 13 March 1846, Demopolis, Sumter Co, AL; m.1. William Chunn, m.2. Eugene Hill. Nancy A. Hill gave testimony in the application for enrollment of Joseph Moncrief, her uncle, as a Choctaw by blood.

[v5]1799.   [11]1. Mattie Chunn,

[v5]1800.   [11]2. Ida Chunn,

[v5]1801.   [11]3. Ada Chunn,

[v5]1802.   [11]4. William R. Chunn,

[v5]1803.   [11]5. Oscar Chunn,

[v5]1804.   [11]6. Eugene Hill, d. as a child

[v5]1805.   [11]7. Edward Hill,

[v5]1806.   [11]8. Nancy A. Hill,

[v5]1807.   [10]2. Mary Elizabeth McCarty, b. 29 Dec 1847, d. 22 April 1850, bur Skullyville Indian Cem, "Dau of R.S. & M.A. — 2y 3m 23d"

[v5]1808.   [10]3. Helen Marr McCarty, (1/16 Choctaw, Roll #12809, C.C. 4633), b. 25 Aug 1850, d. 15 Feb 1924; m. Dr. Daniel Morris Hailley, b. 1841, d. 1919.

[v5]1809.   [11]1. Edward S. Hailley,

[v5]1810.   [11]2. Lutie Hailley, m. _____ Walcott

[v5]1811.   [11]3. Mattie Hailley, m. _____ Little

[v5]1812.   [11]4. William E. Hailey, b. 21 April 1871, d. 1945, was a municipal judge; he had a dau, Mrs. M.O. Ruppert.

[v5]1813.   [10]4. Lela McCarty, b. 2 Oct 1852, d. May 1909; m. A.E. Dobson,

[v5]1814.   [10]5. John Wesley McCarty, (⅛ Choctaw, Roll #7696; C.C. #2652), b. 24 April 1854.

[v5]1815.   [11]1. Malichia McCarty, (1/16 Choctaw, Roll #7697)

[v5]1816.   [11]2. Robert McCarty, (1/16 Choctaw, Roll #7698)

v5 1817. 113. Oscar McCarty, (1/16 choctaw, Roll #7699)

v5 1818. 114. Artie McCarty, (1/16 Choctaw, Roll #7700)

v5 1819. 106. Susan McCarty, b. 25 Nov 1855

v5 1820. 107. Laura E. McCarty, (⅛ Choctaw, Roll #7394; C.C. 2546), b. after 1856; m. _____ McHan

v5 1821. 108. Cora McCarty, b. 21 Aug 1857; m. James Thomas Leard,

v5 1822. 111. James Norman Leard, b. 23 March 1875

v5 1823. 112. Idona Leard, b. 1876, d. 1880

v5 1824. 113. Minnie M. Leard, b. 25 Oct 1878, d. 19 Dec 1894

v5 1825. 114. Annie T. Leard, b. 13 July 1880, d. 1902; m. Charles Overstreet,

v5 1826. 115. Walter F. Leard, b. 1 April 1882, d. 11 July 1948; m. Wynemia Ross

v5 1827. 116. James Andrew Leard, b. 27 April 1884, d. 31 Dec 1938; m. Celia Panther

v5 1828. 117. Cora Helen Leard, b. 1876, d. 1972; m. Raymond B. Davis

v5 1829. 118. Terry T. Leard, b. 7 Jan 1889, d. 1918

v5 1830. 119. Mary Leard, b. 29 March 1892, d. 1893

v5 1831. 1110. Robert Rainey Leard, b. 16 Jan 18__

v5 1832. 1111. Laura A. Leard, b. 29 Aug 1896

v5 1833. 1112. Wheeler R. Leard, b. 15 March 1899,

v5 1834. 109. Cordelia McCarty, (¼ Choctaw, Roll #7008; C.C. 2425), b. after 1856; m. 17 Sept 1879, Samuel Lowery

v5 1835. 111. Goldie L. Lowery (⅛ Choctaw, Roll #7009), b. 1881

v5 1836. 112. Samuel S. Lowery (⅛ Choctaw, Roll #7010), b. 1884

v5 1837. 1010. Robert E. Lee McCarty, (⅛ Choctaw, Roll #7825; C.C. 2685) b. 21 Dec 1863, d. 18 May 1939; m.1. Nanny _____, b. 29 Jan 1877, d. 1898 (3 ch); m.2. 1 Jan 1902, Elizabeth V. Young, b. 1 Sep 1881, d. 12 June 1967 (8 ch, but I only have two).

v5 1838. 111. Claude A. McCarty, (1/16 Choctaw, Roll #7826), b. 1892, I.T.

v5 1839. 112. Floyd S. McCarty, (1/16 Choctaw, Roll #7827), b. 1896, I.T., (adopted Marie Horton, child of his half-sister

v5 1840.	11 3. Leroy McCarty,
v5 1841.	11 4. Myrtle Lee McCarty, (1/16 Choctaw), b. 2 Oct 1905; m. 5 Dec 1924, Crayton Thomas Hendrix, b. 29 Oct 1903, d. 2 June 1992
v5 1842.	12 1. Thomas Lee Hendrix, b. 31 March 1930, McAlester, OK; m. 26 June 1954, Patsy Ruth Horn
v5 1843.	11 5. Bobbie Marie McCarty, m. _____ Horton
v5 1844.	1. Marie Horton

Sarah Ann Moncrief and
E.B. Hawkins/ Aaron Harlan

v5 1394. 9 4. Sarah Ann Moncrief, (d/o Sampson Moncrief and Sophia Brashears, I), b. 30 Jan 1829, Sumter Co, AL, d. 14 Dec 1926, Caddo, OK; m.1. 2 May 1847, in Sumter Co, AL, Erasmus Bryant Hawkins, d. 1851, and had 2 ch; m.2. in 1855, at Ft. Smith, AR, Aaron Harlan, b. 18 Dec 1811, d. 3 March 1876, a widower with 6 ch, and had at least two more. Sarah Ann Harlan, age 73, 1/8 Choctaw, is on Census Card #4611.

Sarah Ann Moncrief received 160 acres in Sumter Co, AL under the 1830 Treaty of Dancing Rabbit Creek. The land adjoined her father's (NE of Sampson's), and her patent (like her father's) was on sheepskin. She lived on her allotment after she was married. She sold the land to Viceroy Tut and migrated to Indian Territory in 1850. After her first husband died, she and a son, Sampson Hawkins, visited her father in AL. In the 1855 Choctaw Census, she is married to Aaron Harlan and has two Hawkins children at home.

During the Civil War, while Aaron was away in service of the Confederacy, Sarah Ann and her family lived a part of the time at Bonham, TX, where her children and step-children attended school. Foreseeing that the War would last for several years and that supplies of all kinds would be scarce before it ended, Sarah laid in stocks of dry goods, coffee, etc. to tide her household through to the end of the struggle. At last, peace was restored and the home life was resumed at Tishomingo.

Although the slaves were free, they refused to leave; so Sarah Ann made them partners of sorts in the plantation, each receiving a portion of the proceeds of the land. Aaron's business had been destroyed by the war, but was soon on the repair.

Prosperity and wealth were returning.

But Aaron died soon after, in an attempt to extend his business into the western areas of I.T., and Sarah Ann was left to fend for herself. She moved to Caddo, where she was recognized as a positive factor in the life of the community. In her later years, Sarah Ann traveled from child to child, including the household of her niece, Lila (McClain) Quinn, whom Sarah Ann had raised from the age of seven.

About a year before her death, she expressed a desire to go to the Confederate widows home in Ardmore, OK, where she died on

Figure 32: Sarah Ann (Moncrief) Harlan in 1914

December 19, 1926. Her body was taken back to her old home at Caddo, and she was buried in the family cemetery, next to her husband, Aaron Harlan, who had passed away more than a half century before.

Family of Sarah Ann (Moncrief) Hawkins/ Harlan:

^{v5}1845. ^{10}1. Julia Vermelle Hawkins, d. age 36, before the 1885 Choctaw Census of Skullyville; m. William C. Falconer, (or Faulkner), b. c1841 (44 on 1885 Choctaw Census). Choctaw Census Card #2485 lists children, Henry Falconer, age 32, 1/32; William C. Falconer, age 26, 1/32; and Julia V. Underwood, age 22, 1/32.

^{v5}1846. ^{11}1. Henry Falconer, b. c1870 (15 in 1885; 32 in 1902)

^{v5}1847. ^{11}2. Mary Belle Falconer, b. c1872 (13 in 1885)

^{v5}1848. ^{11}3. Susan E. Falconer, b. c1875 (10 in 1885)

^{v5}1849. ^{11}4. William C. Falconer, Jr, b. c1876 (8 in 1885; 26 in 1902)

^{v5}1850. ^{11}5. Julia Vermelle Falconer, b. c1880 (6 in 1885; 22 in 1902); m. _____ Underwood. Julia V. Underwood, of Oklahoma City, owned a 97-

page manuscript "Biography of Sarah Ann Harlan," which Sarah Ann dictated in 1913, and which became part of the "*Oklahoma Indian-Pioneer Interviews*," 24 Aug 1937.

v5 1851.   11 6. Erasmus Bryant Falconer, apparently died young, perhaps when his mother, Julia V. Hawkins, died.

v5 1852.   10 2. Sampson Philanders Hawkins, b. 4 March 1851, d. age 6 yrs, 8 mos.

v5 1853.   10 3. Lorena Harlan, m. W.F. Kelly,

v5 1854.   10 4. Aaron Harlan, Jr, b. c1870 (32 on Choctaw Census Card #4808, with one daughter). We aren't absolutely certain this is Sarah Ann's son, but the name and dates sure fit!

v5 1855.   11 1. Willie Louisa Harlan, b. c1900 (age 2 in 1902)

v5 1856.   10 5. Juanita H. Harlan, b. c1872 (30 on Choctaw Census Card #4772, with two children), d. c1905, age 33; m. Dr. W.E. Crowder,

v5 1857.   11 1. Robert S. Crowder, b. c1894 (age 8 in 1902)

v5 1858.   11 2. Edwin McC. Crowder, b. c1901 (age 1 in 1902)

16. THE CHOCTAW CHILDREN OF R.T. "TURNER" BRASHEAR

"Some of these mixed and full blood Choctaw Indians were as fine people as the lord ever let live. I went to the home of Captain Joe Everidge. He was a US Marshal and was away from home a great deal, and wanted me to stay there with his wife for protection and to do the chores while he would be away. I made myself generally useful to the Oakes, and the Everidges.

In this Choctaw Nation, we had an awful time getting our girls to school at Skullyville at New Hope Seminary for young ladies. By our girls, I mean daughters of the Everidges and Oakes, and any of the young ladies of the country. ...

It was a long trip to Skullyville up near Fort Smith. We would load up the girls and their trunks in wagons, and maybe take two or three wagons at a time, and start out. We would take our axes and camping outfits. We had to cut our road a lot of the way. The road was just an old line cattle trail from Texas to Fort Smith, but it was so seldom traveled that we had to make our roads as we would go. Maybe trees would have fallen across the trail previously cut. No bridges either; we would have to hunt crossing on streams and get across the best way we could. Some times we would miscalculate the depth and be in swimming water the first thing we would know. And we camped just wherever night overtook us. We would usually try to find a stream or spring. And believe me, those girls never came home for Christmas holidays either. They stayed once they were there.

It would take us usually six days to go up to Fort Smith, but we could return quicker, because we would have our way cut and mapped out and our loads would be lighter. The boys all went to Spencer Academy and to the States to colleges. (From Robert Allison interview, Hugo, OK, 26 June 1937, interviewer: Hazel B. Greene, *Oklahoma Indian-Pioneer Interviews*, v.2, p.73.)

EVA (Illiapotubbe) BRASHEAR
and THOMAS WILLIE EVERIDGE

[v5]**201.** [8]1. **Illiapotubbe, or Eva Brashear**, (d/o R.T. "Turner" Brashear and "a daughter of Taboca," called "Jane Apuckshunnubbee"), b. c1789, d. 1879 "about 90 years old," according to testimony of her daughter, Harriet Oakes; m. c1814 (had been married 19 years in 1832), *Thomas Willie Everidge*, b. 28 Aug 1788, West Va (just VA in those days; Thomas Everidge was ostracized by his family for marrying an Indian). Eva and Thomas removed to Indian Territory on the "Choctaw Trail of Tears" in 1832, with two children, Harriet and Joel; the older children were either dead or already married. Thomas died about 1863 and Eva in 1879.

Thomas Everidge was a wheelwright— "made wheels and looms and all that, besides farming"— testified his daughter, Harriet. Thomas received a section and a half of land in Mississippi under Article 14 of The Treaty of Dancing Rabbit Creek, the right of his wife and children, but still moved the family to Indian Territory in 1832, then went back to Mississippi in 1833 to settle Turner Brashear's estate, of which he was administrator.

Figure 33: Illiapotubbe (Eva Brashears)

Oca-ye-mitta, the full-blood Choctaw second wife of R.T. "Turner" Brashear, deeded her interest in Turner's estate to Thomas W. Everidge, in return for him taking care of her and her three very small sons. Oca-ye-mitta and her children moved to Indian Territory with the Everidges.

"The Everidge House" (*Smoke Signals,* Chapter 6)

Choctaw county's oldest continuously occupied house, believed to be the only area house in continuous ownership of the same family for more than 100 years, is the Everidge home southeast of Hugo on a 10-acre tract of land not far from Frogville.

This rough log house is the home of Mr. and Mrs. Henry Everidge. The former is a descendant of Thomas Willie Everidge, a full blood Englishman born August 28, 1788, and Eve (Brashears) Everidge, a full blood [error: she was half-blood] Choctaw girl, to whom he had been married 19 years when they came to Indian territory. They came to the wild Indian country from Kentucky [should be Alabama!] in 1833 and acquired the land. One year later, he began construction of the home that still stands 142 years later and houses another Everidge family.

Thomas Willie Everidge, a carpenter-farmer back in Kentucky, worked alongside slaves on "the big house," while his Choctaw wife and children lived in another log structure nearby. The original portion of the home consists of two rooms, built of hand-hewn logs, notched and fitted at all corners. In between the two rooms, the builder left a wide, open-at-each-end hallway, known as a dog rot. A deep front porch extended the width of the structure on the south, toward which it faces. Between the flat-sided logs of both outer and inner walls, one still may find bits of the original mud and straw material used for chinking.

Originally, both rooms had fireplaces, but the one on the west side "fell in," according to the present occupants, after only about a hundred years of service. The east wall in the same room had a stairway which led to a small opening in the low ceiling and an attic.

An interesting feature—although not original to the structure—still is considered in its youth. The so-called "Masonic chimney" bears the date of its construction, 1891, which is only 85 years ago. Built of native rock, the Masonic chimney dominates the outer east wall of the east room, topped with a sharp, mortar imprint of the familiar blue square and compass of the Masonic lodge, and the date, 1891. Many visitors assume this was the year the house was built. But this particular chimney was built by Henry Everidge's grandfather, Joel W. Everidge, a noted figure in the Choctaw Nation before the turn of this century.

Joel Everidge was a member of the old Doaksvillie Lodge No. 2, A.F. and A.M., Indian Territory's first Masonic body. The present occupant's grandfather was proud of that affiliation and placed the emblem above his hearthstone in tribute to York Rite Masonry.

A few yards from the home is the Everidge family cemetery in which Thomas and Eve Everidge are buried along with approximately 60 of their descendants, collateral kin and, in a special section, their slaves. That latter is the only known marked slave burial section in Oklahoma, though many elsewhere can be recognized as such by the custom of placing large, plain, sandstone rocks at the heads of the graves.

Above Thomas Willie Everidge's grave is a marble marker bearing the date of his birth, Aug. 28, 1788, the earliest known to appear on a gravestone in Choctaw County. Since it is only 15 years later than the state's claimed earliest grave marker date (in the Samuel Garland cemetery at Tom, Oklahoma), the Everidge marker is credited with bearing the state's second earliest gravestone date—a claim still undisputed in 1976.

Family of Eva Brashear and Thomas Willie Everidge (data from various records, Harriet Newell Everidge, and fgs by Phil Payne):

[v5]1881.   [9]1. Eden B. Everidge, b. 29 July 1815, d. 11 Feb 1825. (I'll bet his middle name was "Brashear.")

[v5]1882.   [9]2. Sarah "Sally" Everidge, b. 27 Nov 1817, d. 21 Feb 1834 [??how can she die years before her children are born? that's probably a marriage date]; m. Samuel B. Marshall (a white man)

[v5]1883.   [10]1. Mary Jane Marshall, b. 27 Nov 1835

[v5]1884.   [10]2. Rosanna B. Marshall, b. 11 Feb 1837

[v5]1885.   [9]3. Edward M. Everidge, b. MS, 20 Aug 1820, d. 4 Nov 1839, says Phil Payne; d. c1865 of consumption, at Doaksville, said Harriet; m. 27 Dec 1837, Betsey Graves,

[v5]1886.   [9]4. *Harriet Newell Everidge, b. Mississippi, 10 Dec 1824, d. 4 Dec 1906, Oklahoma Ind. Terr; m. 5 Dec 1839, Thomas Wilson Oakes Jr, b. NC, 14 Feb 1814, d. 12 Nov 1890, and had 11 children.

[v5]1887.   [9]5. S.E. Everidge, inf. b. c1826: "one between us (Harriet and Joel) that died when I was very

small," said Harriet.

^{v5}1888. ^{9}6. *Joel W. Everidge Sr, b. Mississippi, 29 Aug 1828 (listed as 4 yrs old at time of Removal in 1832), d. 5 June 1901; m. 3 Aug 1848, Sophia C.A. Folsom, b. 1832, d. 10 Oct 1894

^{v5}1889. ^{9}7. Elizabeth W. Everidge, b. 7 Feb 1833, d. 27 Jan 1841, "age 12"

^{v5}1890. ^{9}8. Abraham H. Everidge, b. 25 Nov 1835, in Indian Territory, d. 6 Aug 1839, age 3 yrs, 9 mos.

Harriet Newell Everidge and Thomas Wilson Oakes

^{v5}**1886.** ^{9}4. Harriet Newell Everidge, (d/o Eva "Illiapotubbe" Brashear and Thomas Willie Everidge), b. Mississippi, 10 Dec 1824, d. 4 Dec 1906, Oklahoma Ind. Terr; m. 5 Dec 1839, Thomas Wilson Oakes Jr, b. NC, 14 Feb 1814, d. 12 Nov 1890, and had 11 children.

Harriet and the family are on Choctaw Census Card #1469; she is Choctaw Roll #4105. They are on the 1855 and 1860 censuses of Kiamitia County, Indian Territory.

Figure 35: Harriet Newell Everidge

Figure 34: Thomas Wilson Oakes

From the *Oklahoma Indian-Pioneer Interview* with Sophia (Hibben) Payne: "Grandfather Oakes [that is, Thomas Wilson Oakes] was a carpenter, cabinet and furniture maker, and his house was full of those old treasures, but they are all gone or scattered. One of the old hickory, split bottomed rocking chairs that Grandfather made is being exhibited at the Pan American Exposition in Dallas now. The reason Grandfather did not go into service in the Civil War was because he was needed at home to make looms, spinning wheels, and furniture for his people. The Government had sent him out here to do work like that and to build homes for the Indians and to build their Council Houses when they were first coming out here in the 1830's. Grandfather came along with some of the first immigrants.

In our home were home-made corded bedsteads, trundle beds, bureaus, candle stands, tables, chairs, wardrobes and desks. Grandfather was also a shoemaker. He tanned hides and made shoes for his own family and for half the people for miles around.

People freighted their cotton by ox-wagons to Shreveport and returned with such supplies as they could not produce at home such as salt, sugar, coffee, yam and lumber. However, they made some salt, not very much. They decided it was not worth the effort it took. It took two months to make the trip to Shreveport and to return loaded with supplies. Grandfather brought back the first jars for the canning of fruit that most of the settlers had ever seen. The jar I have is a half gallon size of crockery ware. A lid fits into a groove all around the top and this groove is filled with hot sealing wax. But very little food was canned then. Much fruit was preserved when we could get the sugar and a big lot of it was dried. Preserves were put up in crocks and some of them would hold five gallons. But when there were large families it took lots of sweetening. I can remember the water buckets, tubs and churns of cedar with brass hoops. I know that Grandmother Oakes old cedar churn held ten gallons. A woman could hardly handle a churn with milk in it. Our smoke house was a sight. I say ours, because we lived with my grandparents for a many years after Grandfather went blind.

The smoke house was built of logs and was about 20 x 22

feet and high enough for a double row of joists running each way with wooden pegs eighteen inches apart on them to hang meat upon. When their family was growing up and they had slaves, Granny said they never killed less than twenty hogs each winter. They rendered lard in immense wash pots and put it up in two hogsheads and used the cracklings to make soap which they made by the barrel. This soap was made of lye dripped from ashes that were saved and put up in an ash hopper out behind the smoke house.

Some of the soap would be firm enough to cut out in blocks that were carefully dried and put away in a container and saved for the washing of the nicer clothes. The soap that was in the bottom of the pot was soft soap, jelly like. I imagine it was soft because of the lean meat. There were usually three barrels of soap made in the Springtime, when the moon was right to do the washing for the whole family and for the slaves.

Along each side and along the back of the smoke house were box-shaped troughs, hewn out of big trees, which were used to salt the meat down in until it was ready to be hung and smoked with hickory chips to give it the right flavor. An immense meat block stood just outside the door. It was a section of a giant oak tree. A ladder stood against the clapboard roof, which we climbed wearily several times daily in summer to spread and turn over fruit that was put there to dry for winter consumption. Jars were too scarce to can much fruit. A few were brought from Shreveport along with nails, wire, little brass lamps, lumber, yam, etc.

My Grandparents were staunch Presbyterians.

Family of Harriet Newell Everidge and Thomas Wilson Oakes Jr:

v5 1891. 10 1. *Charles D. Oakes, b. 15 April 1841, d. 14 Jan 1925; m.1. 19 Feb 1862, Judith E. Belvin, d. c1877; m.2. c1879, Margaret Ann (née Buchanan) Phillips

v5 1892. 10 2. Jane "Jincy" Oakes, b. 15 Jan (or April) 1843, d. 1 Dec 1857, age 14

v5 1893. 10 3. Elizabeth E. "Bessie" "Beth" Oakes, b. 10 Feb 1845, "a cripple, lived at Hugo, OK, 1904", d. 25 Dec 1913; m. 3 Feb 1870, Richmond Landford

v5 1894. 10 4. *Thomas E. Oakes, b. 24 Dec 1846, d. 16 Jan 1929, Atlas, OK; m. 23 April 1867, Mary Amney

Baxter (née Duncan) (no ch?); m.2. 10 April 1870, Rock Creek, OK, Margaret J. Ervin (½ Choctaw, Roll #4098).

[v5]1895. [10]5. Henry W. Oakes, b. 5 Dec 1848, d. 10 Dec 1850, age 2.

[v5]1896. [10]6. George Wellington Oakes, b. 20 July 1851; m. 1872, Frances A.E. Baxter, m.2. Aurilia G. Folsom, d/o Simpson Folsom

[v5]1897. [11]1. George Wellington Oakes, Jr, b. 1 Feb 1890; m. 25 Dec 1896, in Frogville, I.T. (married by Judge Ed Everidge), Rosa E. Buchanan. In 1903, Rosa testified before the Dawes Commission that George had deserted her about 1900, and she had not lived with him since. At that time, Beulah was her only child.

[v5]1898. [12]1. Beulah Belle Oakes, b. 17 Dec 1897 (per certificate to Dept of Interior)

[v5]1899. [12]2??. Chester D. Oakes, b. 7 Sept 1908, Hugo, OK, d. 26 July 1998, Paris, TX; m. 11 March 1930, in Hugo, OK Ester Young. Ch: Mickie Harold; Winford; Boyce; Larry; Karon; and Donna Oakes.

[v5]1900. [10]7. Samuel Lorenzo Oakes, b. 24 Dec 1853, d. 8 Oct 1926; m. 17 Nov 1899, in Lamar Co, TX, Cleora Grant, d/o James Wilson Grant. He voted at the Choctaw elections in 1872, and at Goodwater in 1883. Samuel was elected Judge of Kiamichi Co, in 1890. "Judge Oakes is one of the sons of Thos. W. Oakes. He was born at Goodwater, Choctaw Nation, in December, 1853, and was sent to the neighborhood schools until 1870, after when he was placed at Shilo, west of Paris, Texas, until 1872. He returned to his home that year and there remained for two years, after when he resumed his studies at Shilo in 1875. In 1885, he was appointed clerk of the supreme court, serving creditably and without intermission until August, 1890, when he was elected judge of Kiamichi county by a good majority over Nolan Hensen, John Fowler, and A.T. Stephens. Mr. Oakes is a descendant of the Hyak-pah-tuk-kalo clan

through his mother, Harriet Everidge. (*Leaders and Leading Men of the Indian Territory*, by H.F. O'Bierne, 1891, p.281). Three children:

[v5]1901. [11]1. Tommie Ophelia Oakes, b. 23 Oct 1900, d. 2 Feb 1945; m. John L. Welborn

[v5]1902. [11]2. James Grant Oakes, b. 30 Aug 1902, d. 7 Nov 1961; m. Ruby Rosson

[v5]1903. [11]3. Harriet Eliza Oakes, b. 1905; m. Charlie Polk Cross

[v5]1904. [10]8. *Lemuel Wellington Oakes, b. 3 Jan 1857, d. 1 Jan 1930, Hugo, OK; m. 25 Dec 1879, Goodwater, OK, Lucy E. Smith, b. c1862

[v5]1905. [10]9. *Joel Everidge "Dock" Oakes, b. 1 Jan 1859, d. 5 Dec 1937, Hugo, OK; m. 1878, at Goodwater, I.T., Josephine Eunice Kronk, b. c1862

[v5]1906. [10]10. *Sarah Evelyn Oakes, b. 5 June 1861, d. 14 April 1947, Stamford, TX; m. 7 Nov 1877, Joshua Billings Jeter, b. c1852

[v5]1907. [10]11. *Mary Hester Ann Oakes, b. 1 Jan 1864, d. 12 Nov 1931; m. 10 Aug 1884, at Frogville, Kiamitia Dist, Ind. Terr., Thomas Dickerson Hibben, b. c1860

Charles D. Oakes and Judith Belvin/ Margaret Buchanan

[v5]1891. [10]1. Charles D. Oakes, (s/o Thomas Wilson Oakes Jr and Harriet Newell Everidge), b. 15 April 1841, d. 14 Jan 1925; m.1. 19 Feb 1862, Judith E. Belvin, d. c1877; m.2. c1879, Margaret Ann (née Buchanan) Phillips.

Family of Charles D. Oakes and Judith Belvin:

[v5]1908. [11]1. Henryetta Oakes, m. Bill Cody

[v5]1909. [12]1. Gene Cody, b. 4 Jan 1933, d. 29 June 1989

[v5]1910. [11]2. Sue Oakes,

[v5]1911. [11]3. John Oakes,

[v5]1912. [11]4. Ruth Oakes,

[v5]1913. [11]5. Fannie Lavenia Oakes, b. 24 June 1865 (Choctaw Census Card #1424; Roll #3052); m. Albert Nelson,

[v5]1914. [12]1. Albert J. Nelson, b. c1892 (Choctaw Roll #3053)

^{v5}1915.   ¹²2. Louise B. Nelson, b. c1895 (Choctaw Roll #3054)

^{v5}1916.   ¹²3. Florence Nelson, b. 1897 (Choctaw Roll #3055)

^{v5}1917.   ¹²4. William D. Nelson, b. c1901 (Choctaw Roll #3056)

^{v5}1918.   ¹¹6. Christopher Oakes, b. c1884 (18 on C.C. 1588; Choctaw Roll #4503)

^{v5}1919.   ¹¹7. Annie M. Oakes, b. c1886 (16 on C.C. 1588; Choctaw Roll #4504

Family of Charles D. Oakes and Margaret Buchanon: (their children through 1903 are listed on Choctaw Census Card #1588)

^{v5}1920.   ¹¹8. William W. Oakes, b. 12 May 1890 (Choctaw Roll #4505); m. Pearl Thomas

^{v5}1921.   ¹¹9. Henry Frank Oakes, b. 31 Dec 1892 (Choctaw Roll #4506

^{v5}1922.   ¹¹10. Lavenia Frances Oakes, b. 25 Aug 1894, d. 16 Oct 1973, (Choctaw Roll #4507); m. 13 Feb 1916, Malcolm Newton McFarland, b. 5 Sept 1889, d. 31 Oct 1969 (data from Cathy McFarland, of San Pablo, CA)

^{v5}1923.   ¹²x. Ezra Lee McFarland, b. 5 Aug 1923, d. 1 July 1990; m. 28 Sept 1946, Alice Luanna May Stjepovich

^{v5}1924.   ¹³x. E.L. Craig McFarland, b. 30 Nov 1955; m. 28 March 1981, Cathy Lynne Schoonover, b. 4 March 1960

^{v5}1925.   ¹⁴1. Christopher Craig McFarland, b. 2 July 1983

^{v5}1926.   ¹⁴2. Cody Patrick McFarland, b. 21 Nov 1990

^{v5}1927.   ¹¹11. Laura Bell Oakes, b. 25 Jan 1897 (Choctaw Roll #4508); m. Dan Bennett

^{v5}1928.   ¹¹12. Harriet Oakes, b. 28 June 1900 (Choctaw Roll #4509); m. Bill Cody

^{v5}1929.   ¹¹13. Albert Osward Oakes, b. 12 Dec 1901 (Choctaw Roll #4510); m. Elsie _____

^{v5}1930.   ¹¹14. Martha Oakes, b. 3 Sept 1903; m. Leslie Smith

^{v5}1931.   ¹¹15. Florence Oakes, b. 12 June 1906; m. George Dodson

Thomas E. Oakes and Margaret J. Ervin

[v5]**1894.** [10]4. Thomas E. Oakes, (s/o Thomas Wilson Oakes Jr and Harriet Newell Everidge), b. 24 Dec 1846, d. 16 Jan 1929, Atlas, OK (Census Card #1467; Choctaw Roll #4097); m. 23 April 1867, Emily Duncan, (died in childbirth), d/o Rev. H.A. Duncan, of Tahlequah, Cherokee Nation, I.T.); m.2. 10 April 1870, Rock Creek, OK, Margaret J. Ervin (½ Choctaw, Roll #4098), d/o Calvin Ervin and Sally Gibson.

"The first public office held by Thos. E. Oakes was that of supreme [court] clerk, which he filled for six years. In 1882, he was elected county judge, occupying the bench until his election to the House of Representatives in 1884. In 1885, he became county judge and served two years. In 1888, he was appointed district collector of the third district, a position which he now [1891] holds. Thomas E. became a member of the Masonic order in 1883—Doaksville Lodge No. 2, and was made worshipful master in 1885. He is the owner of two farms containing three hundred and fifty acres under cultivation, and a small herd of cattle. (*Leaders and Leading Men of Indian Territory*, by H.F. O'Bierne, 1891, p.142)

Figure 36: A day working at the Oakes Cemetery:
left to right: Mary Hibben, Gertrude Jeter, Joel Everidge Oakes,
Samuel Lorenzo Oakes, Charles D. Oakes, and Judge Lemuel W. Oakes

From *History of Indian Territory* by Gaines, pp. 594-595.

"Judge [Thomas E.] Oakes is one of the distinguished citizens of the Indian Territory, having been prominently connected with the public affairs of the Choctaw Nation through many years. He has had marked influence molding public policy and his efforts have ever been characterized by an unswerving devotion to duty. His entire life has been spent in the territory, his birth having occurred in Kiamichi County, in the Choctaw Nation, December 24, 1846.

His father, Thomas W. Oakes, was a white man, born in North Carolina, and his death occurred in the Territory in 1893. He married Harriet Everidge, a half [should be quarter] Choctaw, who was born in the Choctaw Nation and is now living there. She is a member of the noted Everidge family that has become so prominent in the affairs of the Nation. Mr. Oakes was one of the pioneer settlers of this portion of the country, having come to the west at a very early epoch in the development of this region.

Thomas E. Oakes was reared in the usual manner of farmer lads, pursued his education in the neighborhood schools and, on entering upon his business career, became identified with agricultural pursuits. Throughout the period of his manhood, he has engaged in the tilling of the soil and the raising of stock and has also operated a cotton gin. He lives on a fine farm of about three hundred acres, ten miles northwest of Goodland, and, in addition to his extensive farming interests, he is well known as a cattle-raiser, and he also operates a cotton gin, carrying on that line of business on an extensive scale. He is one of the most prominent and prosperous citizens of Kiamichi County.

His sterling traits of character have enabled him to advance steadily to a prominent position in both the business and political world. He has occupied several very important places in public life, being first made clerk of the Choctaw Supreme Court, in which capacity he served for eight years. After that time, was elected County Judge of Kiamichi County and discharged the duties of the office so acceptably through the first term that he was then re-elected. On the expiration of his second term, he resigned from the office, but at a later period he was again called to the same position and once more served for two terms.

In 1884 he was elected a representative to the National Council for one year, and following this he was chosen District Collector for two years. On the expiration of that time, he was elected National Auditor, occupying that position for one term.

The lady who bears the name of Mrs. Oakes was in her maidenhood Miss Margaret Irvin (sic Ervin), who was born in Towson County of Choctaw parentage. They now have five children— Daniel W., Thomas J., Susan K., Rosa and Edgar O.

Socially, Mr. Oakes is a very prominent Mason, an exemplary representative of the fraternity which throughout many ages has been a potent factor for good among men. His membership is with the lodge at Goodland, and he has there served as worshipful master for two terms, while at the present time he is acting as its treasurer. He and his wife are members of the old Scotch Presbyterian Church, and their lives are in harmony with their professions. Judge Oakes is regarded as one of the leaders in this portion of the territory in business, political, social and church life. His opinions having marked influence over public thought and action, he has ever been found on the side of progress and improvement.

From *Oklahoma Indian-Pioneer Interviews*, Vol 68, p.3; interview with Dan W. Oakes, Soper, OK (son of Thomas E. Oakes):

I have a ledger which my father kept while operating the store and the Oakes ferry across Red River. This ledger was the means of saving a young man's life. Late one evening, a young man stopped at my father's place and asked for work. Father told him there was no work just then, but if he wanted to stay awhile, maybe he could use him in a few days. The young man stayed and father put him to work doing odd things around and, when the boy had earned some money, he bought a shirt and some pants from father. After this young man had been there a month, a marshal from Texas arrested him and said he was wanted for murder in Texas. The day he made the purchase from father's store was the day on which he was charged with having committed the murder. So my father showed the entry in the ledger, proving that the young man was in Indian Territory that day, and he was cleared of the murder charge. I have the old wooden lock and key used by my father to lock the store at Oakes ferry.

From *Oklahoma Indian-Pioneer Interviews*, Vol 68, p.35; interview with Margaret (Ervin) Oakes. Mrs. Margaret Oakes is the daughter of Calvin Ervin, a white man, and Sally Gibson, not quite a full blood Choctaw (also of French blood). Her parents were married in Mississippi, and, to quote her, "migrated to this God-forsaken country" when the other Indians were brought here about 1833 or 34.

Father [Calvin Ervin], a native of North Carolina, had taught school in Mississippi. Sally Gibson went to school to him, and when they began moving the Indians to this country, they got married and came here with her family. He engaged in carpenter work out here, and was rebuilding old Spencer Academy, [when Margaret and Thomas E. Oakes got married]. There were several buildings, and they had been torn down by soldiers in time of the war. They had camped in them and as nearly demolished them as they could without burning them to the ground.

So father took a contract to rebuild them, and took his family up there and resided till he had the work completed. It took him a year or more. They were large two-story buildings, and the rest of them were frame. "I remember," Mrs. Oakes said, "there were a lot of skeletons, bones, and skulls in one of them. We were told that that was the medical department, and the skulls, bones, etc, might have been used in classes. I knew that we children were scared to death to go near that particular building after night. I was sixteen years old, then.

Father and mother first settled a place about four miles northwest of old Doaksville. That was our home, mother died there and was buried in the garden. No tombstone was ever put over her grave. [Calvin Ervin re-married after Sally Gibson died, and moved to Hartshorne, where he died and was buried. Margaret apparently did not know whom he married or when.]

I went to school some, to neighborhood schools, then to Pine Ridge Academy. It was not a boarding school when I went there. It had gotten broken up in time of the war.

"I remember when all west and northwest of old Doaksville was a vast rolling prairie. One could see for miles. Now, they tell me that is timbered country. There were a few red clay hills around Doaksville proper."

Margaret Ervin was one of the youngest children of the family, a little past sixteen when she married Thomas E. Oakes. They were married at the old Methodist church ground on Rock

Creek, northwest of what is called Spencerville now. "That was where old Spencer Academy was being built by my father. A protracted meeting had been going on and, at the close of it, we got married and stayed up there at my father's home about two weeks. Then we came on over here and settled at Atlas. Twelve children were born to us. Four died very young, five are living now: Mrs. Howard Morris, that is Sue; Mrs. Rosa Huff; Dan, and Ed Oakes, all of Soper, Oklahoma; Thomas of Dallas, Texas.

My husband surely did like to dance, and we would to go dances. Finally, we had been to a dance when our second child was a baby, and we got to talking it over and decided that folks who were raising a family should settle down. So that was our last dance. We quit and both joined the Presbyterian church.

Thomas E. Oakes lived to be 82 years old, had all of his teeth, and they were sound and he was getting his second sight. As the children married off and left us, lots of folks tried to get him to break up our home out there in the country and move to town. "Never," said he, "till they take me feet foremost." And that is the way he went.

He said that he wanted to stay where he could be raising things as long as he lived. Thomas E. Oakes always tried to raise twice as much produce, garden vegetables and hogs, as his family would use; because, he said, there were always unfortunates, who didn't have so much and would be glad to get some of the things he raised. Sometimes, they would work for foodstuffs. But if they could not work, they never left Tom Oakes' house empty-handed. We raised just everything that was good to eat. In addition to our twelve children, we never turned away an orphan. We partly raised several.

Then we gave our children all the education they would take. When they finished in our neighborhood schools, we sent them to colleges. The girls went to New Hope, and O.P.C. at Durant, and the boys went to Spencer, Stillwater, and Muskogee. We sent them to colleges as long as they would go, and always gave them their choice of going and finishing college or settling down and marrying. They all preferred to marry and not finish college. We even sent some of them to Missouri and some to Sherman, just everywhere they preferred to go, because we wanted to make refined men and women of them. One daughter, Mary, who died two years after she married C.L. Harris, was especially refined. She and Sue went to Mary Conner College in Paris,

Texas.

The Oakes were usually buried at the Oakes family burial plot at old Goodwater, but Thomas preferred to be buried at Soper. He died and was buried at Soper in January, 1928, and just in the fall before that expressed a wish to be buried at Soper. He was about one-eighth Choctaw Indian.

Family of Thomas E. Oakes and Margaret J. Ervin: (ref: Choctaw Census Card #1467)

[v5]1932.   [11]1. Robert L. Oakes, b. 15 July 1871, d. 15 Aug 1874

[v5]1933.   [11]2. Harriet A. Oakes, b. 26 Jan 1873, d. 11 Oct 1877

[v5]1934.   [11]3. Daniel W. Oakes, b. 16 Feb 1874 (Choctaw Roll #4099)

[v5]1935.   [11]4. Mary Josephine Oakes, b. 10 Feb 1876; m. C.L. Harris

[v5]1936.   [11]5. Christopher C. Oakes, b. 22 Nov 1877, d. Dec 1878

[v5]1937.   [11]6. Thomas J. Oakes, b. 31 July 1880 (Choctaw Roll #4100)

[v5]1938.   [11]7. Susan K. Oakes, b. 28 June 1882 (Choctaw Roll #4101); m. Howard Morris

[v5]1939.   [11]8. William Oakes, b. 3 Feb 1884

[v5]1940.   [11]9. Jake Oakes, b. 6 Jan 1888

[v5]1941.   [11]10. Rosa Oakes, b. 2 Aug 1889 (Choctaw Roll #4102); m. _____ Huff. Rosie Oakes was present at the burning of Spencer Academy and told about it in an *Oklahoma Indian-Pioneer Interview* on 26 April 1937. See below.

[v5]1942.   [11]11. Edgar Omega Oakes, b. 27 Feb 1891 (Choctaw Roll #4103)

WHAT I REMEMBER ABOUT
"NEW" SPENCER ACADEMY BURNING
(*Oklahoma Indian-Pioneer Interview*, with Rosa (Oakes) Huff, Soper, OK, 26 April 1937)

I am nearly forty-eight years old, will be in August. I was six years old in August before Spencer Academy burned in the fall. My father, Thomas Oakes, owned a store at our home, at what is, or was later, named Atlas. There was a Post Office in his store, and I believe it was called Oaksville. We lived about three miles south of the academy. It was a school for boys only. My

Uncle, J.B. Jeter, was Superintendent. It was Friday afternoon, and he had bought my brother, Thomas, home for the weekend [and] to make some purchases at the store. He took me home with him for the weekend to visit with my aunt and cousins.

That day, Uncle had whipped some big untidy boys, and Saturday midnight they saturated both the back and front stairs of the Main building with coal oil, and set fire to them. I don't know the boys' names; there were three of them, and they were sent to prison for the crime they had committed and died there years later.

Uncle and family and the teachers lived upstairs in this building, and it was supposed that they wanted to burn up Uncle's family out of a spirit of revenge for having been whipped. The dining room and kitchen were in this building too.

Upstairs was a ward for little boys, aged from about six to twelve years. A big boy, about 20 years old, took care of these smaller boys, saw that they were up and dressed and ready for breakfast, and all such. He slept up there with them. There were about fourteen in his charge. When that building was burning, I saw the most heroic and most tragic sight I ever witnessed. These little boys were afraid to jump from the windows to the ground. So another big boy— I don't know his name, but I can still see him in my mind's eye as he placed a mattress on the ground, and called to the boy up in the ward to pitch the children down to him. He caught them in his arms, and slid them to the mattresses until he could no longer hold his arms up, and then stood there and permitted himself to break their way downward to the mattress till he was bleeding from nose, ears and mouth from those little fellows hitting him so hard on the chest. He fell from exhaustion and died before morning from loss of blood. He just gave his life for those children.

When the fire drove the boy-nurse from the ward upstairs, he slid down the drain pipe.

Of course, the poor children were frightened almost to death, and nearly crazy. They scattered in every direction in an effort to get as far away from that horror as possible. Neighbors gathered them in and cared for them. They took a number of them to my father's home. Several were so badly burned that they died a few days later. Among them was poor Pat Springs, son of Mr. and Mrs. Joel Springs, at Goodland. I'll never forget his screams and groans as he lay on a mattress out in our yard for a while. In the emergency, all beds were full and we were making room for all as fast as possible. It was about three o'clock in the morning when they got some of them there, and of course they kept on bringing them in. Pat had gotten out safely, but he returned to his room for some money his folks had sent him that day, I believe. As he came running out through the fire, his clothes caught on fire and they say he inhaled the flames.

There were no telephones in those days. The only way to send a message was by a runner, so runners were sent out to the parents of the unfortunate children all over the country. They came, mostly horseback, as that was the quickest way. No good roads then. It was 12 or 14 miles to Goodland, where Pat's parents lived. They got there about noon, with a hack, covered the back of it with bows and a sheet, and loaded him in. Dr. Johnson, or another doctor there, gave him a shot in the arm to alleviate the pain, but even then his screams were heart-rending. He died in a day or so. Dr. W.B. Johnson, now of Hugo, was the house physician at the Academy.

I don't remember the names of any of the others who were burned to death. Some were burned to ashes. They were picked up in shoe boxes and given to the heart broken parents who carried them, usually on horseback, sorrowfully to their homes for burial. Some of them were many miles away, away back in the mountains. Sometimes, it would be just a few handfuls of little bones, and ashes, that would be all they could find of one.

It was due to the watchfulness of Professor Appleton that I did not burn, too. That night, my uncle had given me some chewing gum he had bought at the store. It was while I was standing out on the hot roof, waiting to be helped down, when I thought of my gum and began to climb though the window. When Professor Appleton saw me, he caught me by my little gown and pulled me back. The roof of the porch was of sheet iron and was so hot that some one had stood me on a pillow. I caught on fire and my feet were blistered before we got off of the roof.

Green "Tubby" Walker, who lives out near Kent, spliced two ladders together and brought them around there and Professor Appleton started down with me in his arms. When nearly down, the building began to collapse, and he had to jump. We were the last ones out. He had used a small grass rope, the kind that was used to tie around trunks, to let the women down with till his hands were cut to the bones. His own wife and daughter happened to be away for a visit.

My father went to his store and passed out flour, sugar, coffee, and just anything that the neighbors needed to take care of the refugees till they could be taken to their homes. And of course [he cared] for a lot of them himself.

Some one had told my mother that everybody had burned, and she had gone from one faint into another, till father placed me in bed beside her. She had thought her "Baby" was among the dead.

It was horrible, I can still see those little boys clinging to the larger boy, afraid to jump, and he'd have to tear them loose from him to pitch them down. But he saved all in his ward, and then slid down the drain pipe. I dream of it often, even yet after 42 years.

My sister's son has a lovely home on the old site. Sometimes I visit there, but believe me I do not sleep much and not up stairs at all.

The old barn is still standing. Just like it was. The land was allotted to my sister, Mrs. Howard Morris, of Soper, OK.

The dormitory for the big boys, the laundry house, nor out houses did not burn. That was about 1895. The Academy was re-built and ready for use the next fall, and I believe Gave E. Parker took it over, as Superintendent, but it burned again and was never re-built.

It might have been several years from the time it burned the first time, but anyway, they were fumigating things, preparatory to beginning school and it caught fire by accident.

Lemuel W. Oakes and Lucy E. Smith

[v5]**1904.** [10]8. Lemuel Wellington Oakes, (s/o Thomas Wilson Oakes Jr and Harriet Newell Everidge), b. 3 Jan 1857, d. 1 Jan 1930, Hugo, OK (Choctaw Roll #4071); was Judge of Choctaw Co, I.T.; m. 25 Dec 1879, Goodwater, OK, Lucy E. Smith, b. c1862 (40 at testimony in 1902 before Dawes Commission), d/o Henry Smith.

"L. W. Oakes received about two years' education at Springfield, Mo. In 1879, he engaged in farming and married

Lucy Smith, daughter of Henry Smith, living close to Paris. [six children, not copied; see below). In 1883, he was appointed third district collector, and held the office for three years. In 1888, he was elected member of the Senate. Mr. Oakes has a comfortable home, two hundred acres of land under fence, one hundred of which is under cultivation, besides a small herd of cattle and two hundred head of hogs. This gentleman is pleasant and congenial and very popular wherever he is known. He has been a member of the Masonic order since 1884, and an Odd Fellow since 1882. (*Leaders and Leading Men of the Indian Territory*, by H.F. O'Bierne, 1891. p.184-85)

Lemuel W. Oakes (from *History of Oklahoma*, early 1900's):

Under the terms of the Treaty of 1866 the Choctaws were compelled to grant land or its equivalent to negroes who had been their slaves before the Civil War. This class of negroes were termed Freedmen. Allotments were made in due time, but in the early 80's new claimants for land or money arose among negroes of Arkansas, Texas, Mississippi, and probably some other Southern states, to the number of several hundred. It was a demand for enrollment similar to that which has been made insistently during recent years by members of the Choctaw Tribe in Mississippi. The principal chief of the Choctaw Nation appointed a commission to hear and pass upon these claims. The commission was composed of Lemuel W. Oakes, now of Hugo; R.J. Ward, now of Spiro; and the late Ben Watkins, an intermarried citizen and educator. Cole E. Nelson, a prominent full blood minister, educator, merchant and lawyer, was at that time Attorney General and he counseled with and advised the commission. The result of the commission's labors was that only twenty-one of the negro applicants were given their demands. Under the law an applicant whose claim was valid had a choice of forty acres of land or one hundred dollars in money, the money to satisfy in full all claims the applicant possessed. Some of the successful ones took land and others the money and left the territory.

This was not the only public service rendered by Lemuel W. Oakes as a Choctaw citizen. For ten years, he was a member of the Senate of the Choctaw Nation, serving under the administrations of Principal Chief Jackson McCurtain and J.M. Smallwood. He was a member of the McCurtain faction in one of the heated contests provoked by Victor M. Locke, a leader of the full blood element. While he was a member of the Senate, Henry Ward and Joe Bryant occupied the position of President of the Senate, and Senator Oakes was filling his seat at the death of Chief Jackson McCurtain. At one time, he also held the office of revenue collector of the Third Judicial District of the Nation.

Lemuel W. Oakes was born at the old town of Goodwater, situated twelve miles east of the present site of Hugo. His parents were Thomas W. and Harriet N. (Everidge) Oakes... [duplicate information, not copied].

The first school attended by Lemuel W. Oakes was the Goodwater Mission, when it was taught by the Rev. Theodore Jones, a Presbyterian missionary, who came into the nation before the Civil War from Wisconsin. Later, in another school, Mr. Oakes was a schoolmate of Peter J. Hudson, now of Tuskahoma, who has been one of the leading men of the Nation for a number of years. Farming has been the principal occupation of Mr. Oakes. He moved to Hugo a few years ago, and for six years has been Justice of the Peace having been elected on the democratic ticket. He has taken an active and important part in politics since statehood, and has been one of the real factors in the agricultural development of the county. He is a member of the Methodist Episcopal Church South. Fraternally, he belongs to the Masonic Lodge at Grant, which originally was Lodge No. 2, Ancient Free and Accepted Masons, of Indian Territory.

In 1879, he married Miss Lucy E. Smith at Goodwater. They are the parents of seven children: Mrs. Bessie Beardon, wife of a farmer near Hugo; Mrs. Lillie Spring, wife of a farmer near Hugo; Clarence A. Oakes, deputy treasurer of Choctaw County; Frank Oakes, who lives at home with his parents; Mrs. Mattie Collins, and Mrs. Nola Tibbett, wives of farmers near Hugo; Mrs. Nona Baird, wife of a laundryman at Hugo.

Mr. Oakes has five brothers and two sisters: Charles Oakes, a farmer living eight miles east of Hugo; Thomas E., whose farm is near Soper and he is president of the bank of that place; George, a farmer near Hugo; Samuel, a farmer, ginner, merchant, Justice of Peace, and Postmaster at Frogville; Mrs. Sarah Jeter, wife of a farmer living near Soper; and Mrs. Mary Hibben, wife a farmer living near Frogville.

From *Oklahoma Indian-Pioneer Interviews*, Vol. 68, p.27:
Interview with Lem W. Oakes, Justice of the Peace in Hugo:

My father's name was Thomas W. Oakes. He was a white man. His birth place was North Carolina, but he left there young and went to Mississippi, from there he came to the Indian Territory about 1837, to a place on Red River called Pine Bluff Ferry, about twenty-three miles from what is now Hugo. Pine Bluff Ferry was a landing place for steamboats, which came up Red River. There was a warehouse there, that the people of the country had built to store goods that had been shipped by steamboat. Then merchants from all over the country, some of them a hundred miles away, could come there and get the goods. People close around who had money would meet the merchants there and buy some of the goods. Or it they had anything that they could trade for them, they would do that.

Steamboats sometimes went up the river as far as Denison, Texas. Small steamboats. And sometimes, they entered the mouth of Kiamichi River. My father was very much interested in this warehouse, when he first saw it, because he was a carpenter. It was built of split logs, or half logs with the ends sunken in the ground, and covered with boards that were riven by hand. Riving boards was done by cutting a piece of timber the desired length of board, then they would quarter that, lengthwise, and proceed to split off pieces of the desired thickness with a froe and mallet.

He met and married my mother, Harriet N. Everidge, soon after they both came here. She was born in Mississippi. They settled on a farm that they cleared about four miles northwest of Frogville, but there was no Frogville then. There was a school called Goodwater. Presbyterian Missionaries from up north had built it. And those Missionaries tilled the soil, and made their livings just like everybody else did. There were several buildings at Goodwater, but in time of the war the Confederate soldiers were stationed in them and just tore them up, destroyed them, and the buildings they put up after that were never so good.

There were nine of us children, four of whom are still living.... We hadn't much time to go to school; we all had to work, big, little and young. We had hogs, cattle and horses, chickens, etc. and had those to attend to, because we raised everything we had to eat and almost everything we had to wear. We raised cotton for our cotton clothes and wool for our wool ones. Mother spun, wove, and carded and made our clothes.

For years, we had only corn bread; of course [she] cooked it different ways. Then we got to raising wheat, and father put in a little grist mill, kinda like a sorghum mill. Then we ground wheat, and would eat the whole wheat flour. We had biscuits on Sunday mornings only. Then a man put in a mill that would grind the wheat and separate the shorts, etc. We'd take our wheat over there and swap it for so much first grade flour and so much shorts, or seconds, but we ate it all. None of it was wasted. This mill was located just over in Texas on the road to what is now Paris. But I remember when there was no Paris, Texas. They put oxen on an immense wheel, and they kept walking to turn it, and operated the mill that ground the meal and flour.

There were no post offices in the country. We had to go over in Texas to get mail. The post office was called Tamaha. Then it was changed to something else. It was in Travis Wright's store, across the river from Goodwater. Then years later, a post office was established at Doaksville, I don't remember just when. We didn't pay any attention to those changes, we were too busy trying to make a living to remember these changes. I don't even remember when the railroad was put through here.

When I was growing up, there were no doctors in the country. I was half grown before I ever heard of one. Everybody those days went out in the woods and gathered roots, herbs, and barks for remedies, gathered them when they were at the proper stage of maturity, and hung them up in the house, for winter use just the same as we hung our meat in the smoke house. We'd kill enough meat to do us from one year to the next. And I believe that was one reason we were so healthy. We lived mostly on hog meat and corn bread and molasses. I attribute the most of the present day ills to modern food. We never heard of appendicitis. Perhaps they had it and didn't know what it was. Anyway, when one got sick, they sent for the neighbor women, and they generally knew just what herb to brew to bring about the recovery of the patient. If people would live on things produced at home more now, they would be better off. ...

Then I sold my farm and moved to town, and have held the office of Justice of the Peace ever since. I own my home, and make a garden all the time. I always keep something growing in my garden. I make enough stuff on it to feed two families. We have always canned the surplus that we have not given to our less fortunate neighbors.

Men who were good prosperous farmers have quit their farms and quit trying to make a living, and come to town to live on a little old government job. The government did nothing for us. We didn't want it to do anything for us. There is a living for every able-bodied man, right in the earth, and he can have a bounteous one by digging and working for it. Too much help has ruined many good men. It is making outlaws of them too. I've been Justice of the Peace here in Hugo continuously for 26 years, and if I live I have two more years to serve and am certainly in a position to know what I am talking about.

Family of Lemuel Wellington Oakes and Lucy E. Smith:

[v5]1943.   [11]1. Bessie Oakes, b. 2 Nov 1880 (Choctaw Census card #1441; Roll #4020); m. Charles Edward Bearden (Choctaw Intermarried Citizen #233)

[v5]1944.   [12]1. Flora O. Bearden, b. c1898 (Choctaw Roll #4021)

[v5]1945.   [12]2. Oscar Payton Bearden, b. c1900 (Choctaw Roll #4022)

[v5]1946.   [12]3. Florence Esther Bearden, b. c1901 (Choctaw Roll #4023)

[v5]1947.   [12]4. Beulah Bell Bearden, b. c1902 (New Born Choctaw Roll #978)

[v5]1948.   [11]2. Lillie Oakes, b. 15 March 1882, d. 17 July 1966 (Choctaw Census Card #1444; Roll #4029); m. Louis Spring,

[v5]1949.   [12]1. Clarence Edward Spring, b. 1 Nov 1899 (Choctaw Roll #4031)

[v5]1950.   [12]2. Etha May Spring, b. 1 Jan 1900, d. 16 Aug 1948 (Choctaw Roll #4032); m. William Henry Robison. Ch: Dorothea Lee; Bill Don Robison.

[v5]1951.   [12]3. Essie M. Spring, b. 18 June 1902 (Choctaw Roll #4033)

[v5]1952.   [11]3. Clarence E. Oakes, b. 23 Aug 1883, b. 1944, Hugo, OK (Choctaw Roll #4072); m. Harriet Gibbons

[v5]1953.   [11]4. Frank Oakes, b. 25 July 1885, d. 1 Aug 1939, Hugo, OK (Choctaw Roll #4073)

v⁵1954. ¹¹5. Mattie Oakes, b. 16 Aug 1887, d. 23 Dec 1972
(Choctaw Roll #4074); m. Cephus Collins

v⁵1955. ¹¹6. Nola Oakes, b. 20 May 1889, d. 31 March 1978
(Choctaw Roll #4075); m. _____ Tippit,

v⁵1956. ¹¹7. Nona M. Oakes, b. 21 May 1891, d. 8 Oct 1963
(Choctaw Roll #4076); m. 17 Oct 1906, William W.
Baird,

Joel E. Oakes and Josephine Kronk

v⁵**1905.** ¹⁰9. Joel Everidge "Dock" Oakes, (s/o Thomas Wilson
Oakes Jr and Harriet Newell Everidge; "named for my brother,
Joe," said Harriet), b. 1 Jan 1859 (Choctaw Roll #4328); living in
1904 at Hugo; d. 5 Dec 1937, Hugo, OK; m. 1878, at Goodwater,
I.T., Josephine Eunice Kronk, b. c1862 (age 40 in 1902, at
testimony before Dawes Commission), d/o John Cronk and
Emiline _____.

From *Oklahoma Indian-Pioneer Interviews*, Vol 68, p.15:
interview with Joel E. Oakes, 27 April 1937: [The interviewer
first made a number of comments]: Joel E. Oakes lives 3½ miles
NE of Hugo, Oklahoma. He was born January 15, 1859 at the
old Oakes place at Goodwater Mission School, right in hollering
distance of the church and school. ... In spite of his many years,
he is fairly erect and moves about quickly and alertly, has never
used eyeglasses and reads the Dallas News or any other
newspaper without aid of glasses, although he admits that his
eyes are beginning to fail now.

The house is built in a square, with porches all around. All
the usable space in the attic was just the same as the hall below
and that was where they bed the hay hands and on the roof of
the back porch. It was built about 1885.

The parlor has an old fashioned straw matting on the floor,
the center table with family pictures on it and the swinging lamp
hanging from the ceiling above the table. An organ in one
corner, an old fashioned sofa in another corner. Some hats
which were stylish 40 years ago were in the closet, also an old
cap-and-ball hand-made rifle.

Out in the yard stood an old split-log wash bench. The old
grindstone stood nearby, both under an immense oak tree.
Years ago, the old man decided to go modern and bought a car.
It stood in the barn nineteen years without being driven, after
the first few times. Then a progressive grandson came along and

traded it in on a pickup to be used around the farm. The first radio was brought into the house since the first of this, 1937. In speaking of the days when they were settling this country, Mr. Oakes said, "Them was the good old happy days. I wish it were like that now. Everybody was happier.

"My father was sent by the Government, I mean the U.S. Government, to the Choctaw Nation to build Capitols, or Council houses. He was a carpenter. The first council house he built was at Tuskahoma. It was built entirely of pine logs, and was located about one quarter or one half mile east of the old Council house that stands there now, the old plastered one. He built others, but I don't know just where. I've forgotten.

When his contracts were completed, he came down in this country near Hugo and married mother, Harriet N. Everidge. Built his home right there at Old Goodwater Mission School. We went to school there, then we moved to near Frogville, and had to walk four miles to school. I finished the eighth grade at Goodwater, then father sent me to Paris to school one term. A Mr. Stock was superintendent of schools at Paris.

It was no uncommon thing to find boys and girls out in the hills far away from the schools who did not know their A.B.C.'s, but they were gathered up and sent to the Government school and taught to speak English. Lots of them could not speak a word of English.

After a while, the Choctaw Nation took over the mission schools. Goodwater was a Presbyterian Mission School, as was also Goodland; and Skullyville, 15 miles this side of Ft. Smith, was a Methodist school for girls. We sent three of our kids to Skullyville: Cora, Virgie, and Lizzie all graduated there.

After the schools were taken out of the hands of Missionaries, my boy, Bert, went to Goodland to school. When he got through there, I sent him to Business College in Hugo, Oklahoma. Then he married and died. He left two daughters: Lois Oakes, now Harris, and Naomi Oakes.

About two miles east of my place there are some salt springs from which Salt Creek gets its name. In time of the Civil War, my father and old Bob Jones, a wealthy full blood Indian who lived at Rose Hill, decided that they would make salt there, instead of going with ox wagons to "Jordan" Saline, Texas, for it. It would take them a week or two to make the trip, and all that time they would be afraid that soldiers of the Northern Army would catch them and take it away from them. So they made a kettle or two and quit, deciding it took too much boiling, and they went back to the ox team and wagon route.

Merchants over here in the Indian Territory used to freight their goods and supplies by ox wagons and teams, from Jefferson, Texas. Sometimes, steamboats would come up the river and bring goods and supplies, and we most always shipped cotton back down the river by steamers to New Orleans. We used a lot of it though.

My mother's mother brought her loom and spinning wheel and a part of her dishes, but not many, from Mississippi. They brought everything they were permitted to bring. My daddy, being a carpenter, made a spinning wheel and loom for mother, and many were the nights and days, too, that I have kept the fire going in the loom house while mother wove the cloth. She had slaves to do her housework, but she preferred to do the weaving herself. Two of these negro slave women never left us, said they didn't know where to go, and wanted to stay as long as "old massa" would let them.

When I was a lad, I spent three years on a ranch out in Arizona. When I went out there, I took my four horses, but I hired to a ranch owner who would have no horses on his ranch except his own. So I had to sell my horses. He paid me good wages and furnished horses for me to ride, but I didn't like it out there. It was too cold and windy. It would get cold out there in October and not thaw out till late Spring; so I quit and came home. I bought, at auction in Tucson, a horse and buggy for $65 and started home Sunday morning. Snow was 12 inches deep that November Sunday morning when I left, and the nearer to old Goodwater I got, the warmer I got, and the better I liked it. I got there about ten o'clock Saturday night. There was a big meeting there next day at Goodwater.

That day I met the girl I afterwards married. Her folks came from Michigan, their name was Cronk. The old man was a sufferer of erysipelis, and was advised to go to a warmer climate or "peg out." They arrived in Texas near Clarksville in the springtime, and all land was rented. They went to Paris. Dr. White had a hundred acres in the river bottom not rented, so let them have it. The old man had fine teams. Old timers here advised him to sell the horses, that they would die here, not being acclimated. He thought it was because people abused their horses and he would not dispose of them, and sure enough they died.

Dr. White, of course, wanted good crops and wanted him to buy enough teams to farm the hundred acres. They disagreed about that, so Mr. Cronk moved over into Indian country, thinking he'd get rich, but he didn't. In a few months, Josephine Cronk and I married, and I tried to make three crops on a little place I settled down there. Then in 1881, the third overflow came and ruined the crops and drowned lots of cattle. Father had me to bring out of the river bottoms 600 head of cattle to this high ground, and we settled on this place.

The first winter, we lived in a camp, cooked out of doors, and slept in the one 16 x 16 foot room I built. We sat by the camp fire till bed time each night and went to bed. Then the next winter, I built the chimney you see standing there. As my family increased, my house was too small, so I built this larger one. We had eight children, four are now living.

I hauled water for five years; folks said you could not strike water in this rocky dry land. One day, I noticed crawfish holes in the yard, so I called me a buck negro and we begun digging and struck good sweet water at 20 feet. Later, I dug the cistern that is there in the kitchen. Cistern water was supposed to be more healthy and I did not want my wife to have to go out of her kitchen for water.

I've been here 58 years and this place is never left alone. It has been left alone once in 58 years. Someone always stays at home. Our old home place at Goodwater was a double log house with a hall between the two rooms, side rooms made of boxing plank and porches along back and front. But one could not see the place now. It is all grown up with trees and underbrush. One might see a mound where the chimney stood. Same at old Goodwater. There was a cemetery at Goodwater for the Missionaries, but it is doubtful if one could ever find the tombstones in it; they are all fallen and broken down. The Oakes cemetery about a half mile away is kept in good shape and worked.

I served two years as deputy sheriff under a full blood sheriff of Kiamichi County, named Wesley Sunny. Things were pretty "squally" here sometimes. One woman was married six times and every husband was killed but one; he was smart and ran away. Her son was murdered and had been dead so long when they found him that he had stiffened. He had on some fine hand-made, square-toed boots, and they buried him in those boots. He was Dock Willis.

One son of a prominent citizen took up with some negroes and was living with them. His brother went over to the negro house to persuade his brother to leave them. He found the brother lying across the bed. He walked in and slapped him on the back; the brother on the bed had his gun beside him, grabbed it and fired, killing his brother instantly.

Little Britt Willis killed Jim Willis, a half-brother. Their father kept fine racing horses and lots of carousing took place around his place. Another son of his was drunk, a friend undertook to take him home. He drew a gun and attempted to kill the friend, but the friend killed him. Sim M. Folsom was the friend who killed Hamp Willis.

Colonel Sim H. Folsom is supposed to have killed 19 men. Once at his gin at the mouth of Kiamichi River, a fellow by the name of Nance who sometimes asked questions when he should have been quiet, asked him how many he had killed. He replied that he had killed eight that he knew of, and had stood trial at Fort Smith for only one, and came clear of that. But he said, "Young man, don't ever kill a man. Run if you must, but don't ever kill one. You can see them every time you close your eyes to sleep."

Family of Joel Everdige "Dock" Oakes and Josephine Eunice Kronk: (Choctaw Census Card #1543.)

^{v5}1957. ^{11}1. Cora Lee Oakes, b. 31 July 1879; m. Jim Law

^{v5}1958. ^{11}2. Florence Virginia "Virgie" Oakes, b. 23 Jan 1882, d. 14 July 1954 (Choctaw Roll #4329); m.1. George A. Lovett; m.2. 11 June 1901 ("by J.P. Gibbons, M.G."), Thomas Lee McBride, b. c1870 (31 at time of testimony in 1901)

^{v5}1959. ^{11}3. Elizabeth "Lizzie" Oakes, b. 6 Feb 1883, d. 22 Nov 1948 (Choctaw Roll #4330); m. Edward Grant,

^{v5}1960. ^{11}4. Bert Oakes, b. 22 Dec 1885, d. 22 March 1925, Plainview, TX (Choctaw Census Card #1543; Roll #4331); m. 16 July 1911, Alma Frances Hamm. Ch: Lois and Naomi Oakes.

^{v5}1961. ^{11}5. Maybell Oakes, b. 15 Aug 1886, d. 18 June 1887

^{v5}1962. ^{11}6. Effie Oakes, b. 8 April 1888, d. 25 June 1962

(Choctaw Roll #4332); m. Melton E. Flemming,
v5 1963.   117. Sarah Evaline Oakes, b. 18 Aug 1889, d. 22 May
1933 (Choctaw Roll #4333); m. Lewis Mills Bevan,

Sarah Evelyn Oakes and Joshua B. Jeter

v5 1906. 1010. Sarah Evelyn Oakes, (d/o Thomas Wilson
Oakes Jr and Harriet Newell Everidge), b. 5 June 1861, d. 14
April 1947, Stamford, TX; m. 7 Nov 1877 "by Rev. J.B. Lloyd" per
J.B. Jeter's testimony in 1902), Joshua Billings Jeter, b. c1852
(fifty at time of testimony before Dawes Commission, in 1902).

Joshua Billings Jeter, of Choctaw. This gentleman was born
at Wetumka, Alabama, in August, 1852, and was educated at
Central Institute, Alabama, and Shilo Academy, near Paris,
Texas. He came to Kiamichi County, Choctaw Nation in 1872
and there commenced teaching public school. In that year, he
was elected district trustee of the Third district, and held the
office for two years. In 1886, when Thompson McKinney was a
candidate for principal chief, J.B. Jeter was elected to the
senate from Kiamichi county. He was the second white citizen
who had ever been elected to the Choctaw legislature; but no
sooner had he taken his seat than they forced him to retire,
appointing John Martin, from the same county in his place. Mr.
Jeter had voted the wrong ticket that year. Two years later, he
might have taken his seat without a majority opposition. [He]
obtained his citizenship through marriage with Sarah E. Oakes,
second daughter of T.W. Oakes. The issue of their marriage [as
below]. Mr. Jeter owns one hundred acres in farm, fifty head of
cattle, one hundred and fifty hogs, and an interest in three
undeveloped coal mines. His is a young man of excellent
education, intelligent, bright, and of good moral character, a
Mason and a member of the Presbyterian church. He was
appointed coal weigher for the Nation on the Choctaw Coal and
Railway Co." (*Leaders and Leading Men of the Indian Territory*, by
H.F. O'Bierne, 1891. p.182-3)
v5 1964.   111. Gertrude F. Jeter, b. 8 Sept 1878, d. 1907; m.
George A. Lovett,
v5 1965.   112. Harriet Selena Jeter, b. 11 June 1880, d. 4 March
1976; m. 3 Dec 1903, John F. Larcey,
v5 1966.   113. Samuel Tilden Jeter, b. 20 Feb 1882, d. 3 Dec
1885
v5 1967.   114. James Thomas Jeter, b. 1884, d. 1912; m. Jessie

French,

v5 1968.   11 5. Fanny Belle Jeter, b. 12 Feb 1886, d. 7 Dec 1895
v5 1969.   11 6. William Whitney Jeter, b. 19 July 1888, d. 4 Dec
           1944; m. Katherine Suggs
v5 1970.   11 7. Bonnie Beatrice Jeter, b. 11 Aug 1890, d. 3 July
           1891
v5 1971.   11 8. Olive Mae Jeter, b. 6 Oct 1895, d. 21 Oct 1976;
           m. Grover Barton,

Mary Oakes and Thomas D. Hibben

v5 **1907.** 10 11. Mary Hester Ann Oakes, (d/o Thomas Wilson
Oakes Jr and Harriet Newell Everidge), "youngest of 11
children," (Choctaw Roll #231), b. 1 Jan 1864, d. 12 Nov 1931;
m. 10 Aug 1884, at Frogville, Kiamitia Dist (County), Ind. Terr.,
Thomas Dickerson Hibben, b. c1860 (age 42 in 1902 at Dawes
hearings), s/o William Hibben and Eliza Lusk,

Oklahoma Indian-Pioneer Interview with Mrs. Ethel Hibben
Carter: "My father was Thomas Dickerson Hibben, a white man
from Arkansas. He was clerk of the Supreme Court of the
Choctaw Nation till the tribal laws were abolished. Then he was
a County Commissioner of Choctaw County for years.
Sometimes he would be gone from home for months at Supreme
Court. He died Feb 1st, 1916.

"My mother was Mary Oakes, daughter of Thomas W. Oakes
and Harriet Everidge Oakes. Mother was a sister to Lem, Dock
(Joel E.), George, Tom, and S.L. Oakes. [NOTE: she neglected to
mention Charles Oakes, Sarah Jeter, and Bess Landford, her
mother's other siblings.] She died November 13, 1932 in Hugo.
Father and mother are both buried at the Oakes family cemetery
near Goodwater.

"I was born August 21, 1885, at the old Oakes home place.
Father and mother lived with Grandfather and Grandmother
Oakes at this old home place until after grandfather died; then
grandmother broke up housekeeping and went to live with her
son, S.L. Oakes, at Frogville, where she died fourteen years or
more after grandfather did. Mother was born in that old house,
so was I and my daughter, now Mrs. Beatrice Mathis, of Hugo,
Oklahoma— three generations.

"In 1902, Dr. M.L. Carter had just graduated from Medical
school at Tulane University at New Orleans, LA, and had located

on "The Big Farm" that was owned by some wealthy Texans..." [page cut off; interview by Hazel B. Greene, not dated.]

From *Oklahoma Indian-Pioneer Interview* with Sophia (Hibben) Payne: "Thomas Hibben was just three years old at the time his parents died and he was shifted from one relative to another the balance of his boyhood. Nobody wanted him and nobody cared where he went. He was never sent to school a day in his life. Thomas D. Hibben was just tolerated by his relatives. They didn't care what he did, though he never did anybody a wrong. He was deeply religious and religiously kept the Sabbath Day Holy.

In his wanderings, he came to the Indian Territory, Choctaw Nation, and worked as "snipe" on the new railroad that was being built through here. Later, he went to work for and lived at my uncle's, Thomas Oakes, who was then County Judge of Kiamichi County, Indian Territory, Choctaw Nation. They lived down near Frogville, not very far from the house of my grandfather, Thomas W. Oakes, who was the father of Lem W., Joel E. and George Oakes. My mother was teaching school when she fell in love with and married my father, Thomas D. Hibben. Uncle Thomas, in the capacity of County Judge, performed the ceremony.

Father was twenty-three years old then and could not write his name nor read a word. Mother taught him after they were married. Each night, she carefully and faithfully taught him his lessons. Then, when we children came along and were going to school, we brought our books home with us to study and Father could work problems for us that we could not work and that Mother could not work. Father was just naturally above the average man in intelligence.

I can remember when he was Clerk of the Supreme Court of the Choctaw Nation and stayed at Tuskahoma a lot of the time. After statehood, he became one of the first county commissioners of Choctaw County. My uncle, Thomas Oakes, and Lee W. Ratliffe were the other two commissioners. R.M. Connell was Sheriff; W.J. Milam was County Attorney.

My father was a Methodist, so Mother became one too. We went to Sunday School every Sunday if we were not sick abed, then home to dinner, which was always cooked the day before. There was never any cooking or churning on Sunday.

We lived right close to Goodwater Church site for a number of years. Then, we built a home about a mile away. Of course, I do not remember when it was a mission school. There are plenty of histories to tell when it was founded and discontinued as a mission school. But there was a frame building on the site, and we went to school there until I was fifteen. I started to school at five. Then I went to Tuskahoma a year and started back another year, but they were so crowded up there that my sister and I and a lot of others had to go home in order to make room for less fortunate children, for there were some who had no school at all within reasonable distance of their homes.

I believe the Goodwater Mission School and church was established before 1848 because two tombstones there were erected over graves that were made in 1848. They were all moss grown, but I scratched the moss off and copied the inscriptions in a little notebook and have carried it in my purse for years. One reads, "L.C. Downer, Missionary. Died Oct. 1st, 1848." The other was "C.M. Belden. Nove. 5, 1848, Missionary." There were a lot of old sandstone tombstones from which the inscriptions were worn off by the weather and were very likely older than the two which were inscribed, because they looked older, but the inscriptions on them were indecipherable.

There were many lost graves in that old cemetery. As far back as I can remember, graves were occasionally dug into when new ones were being dug. There would be no sign of one until the spades would turn out some bones or jewelry or buttons and a few coffin nails, the coffins having rotted away.

Grandmother Oakes was Harriet E. Everidge, daughter of Thomas William Everidge and his wife, Sophia [NOTE: There are some errors in Sophia Payne's memory; her great-grandmother was Eva Brashear, d/o R.T. "Turner" Brashear]. She and my grandfather, Thomas Oakes, built their home right close to the Goodwater Church in Choctaw Co., about eighteen miles southeast of Hugo and, when my parents married, they lived there with Grandfather Oakes for a number of years, then they built a home about a mile from the church and that was where I was born.

Even though they were near the Goodwater Cemetery they never buried any of their folks there. They buried them right there a few steps from the house, their children, grandchildren, and slaves who died. Grandmother said that a lot of Confederate Soldiers were also buried in their family cemetery and that many of the soldiers were buried in the Goodwater Cemetery and also many full blood Choctaw Indians. Some of those inscriptions showed that graves were made there forty years before I was born in 1887, and it is reasonable to suppose that in view of the fact that tombstones were not very common in those days, over the first graves in this cemetery there might not have been any tombstones. Hence, the large number of lost graves that would be dug into and not a sign of a coffin left, only nails. The coffins would be entirely rotted away.

The Confederate Soldiers were stationed in camp about the mouth of the Kiamichi River between Grandfather's place and Ft. Towson, but on the west side of the river I believe, hence, the burial of those who died in camp at the Oakes Cemetery and at Goodwater and every grave in their cemetery was marked by a stone but there were no inscriptions on these stones.

One corner of this cemetery was set aside for the slaves. The bodies of the soldiers were buried in another place, and the bodies of those belonging to the Oakes family at another in the Oakes Cemetery. My mother was the last one to be buried there in 1931. We laid her beside my father who died 1915.

We used to have the grandest camp meeting, Union meetings, Methodists, Presbyterian, and sometimes Baptists would come and camp for two and three weeks. We lived so close to the camp meeting ground that we stayed at home and attended services regularly and we had as good a time as those who were camping. Relatives met there yearly who seldom ever saw each other any other time. Distance and slow and poor transportation prevented.

New dresses and new hats were always in evidence at those camp meetings. It didn't matter so much about new clothes the balance of the year, just so they had new ones for the camp meeting. Our mothers began in the winter tucking our voluminous under skirts, chemises and drawers. They all had yards and yards of lace, tucks, and embroidery, and we had to have lots underclothing for the summer. We wore two, three and four petticoats at the time, depending upon the thinness of our dresses. Those girls who lived ten or fifteen miles away brought trunks full of clothes, with Negroes, to the camp meeting to do the cooking and take care of their clothes, but a girl would wear a new summer dress all summer without washing it. We prided ourselves our keeping our dresses clean and nice. My grandmother had clothes packed in her trunk that she had had for thirty years, that had never been wet in water. Some of them she had had even thirty-five and forty years, and when we did get new dresses, pieces of them were sent to relatives and friends in letters for them to admire and put in their quilts and pincushions. Granny Oakes said that when she was young they made pretty buttons by covering acorns with material like the garment they wanted to put them on or covered with contrasting colors for trimmings.

I remember one Spring when a shipment of hats for girls and women came to Joel Spring's store from some commission house. They were very pretty too, even if sometimes a half dozen were alike, except as to color. They were all just $1.50 apiece. The girls and women knew for weeks ahead that these hats were expected and saved their money for them. Some of them chopped cotton for their $1.50 and some dug snakeroot for theirs, and some had picked cotton the fall before, and some had sold hickory nuts in Paris, TX, the fall before, and had saved their money in anticipation of the Spring hats being brought in.

A lot of the mothers made the boy's shirts too. I recall one mother who made her boy's shirts with straight brands for collars and buttoned all the way down the back until the boys got the courage to protest when they were nearly grown; even then, she gave up pretty hard. She was one of the kind of women who never even changed the style of dressing their hair.

Family of Thomas Dickerson Hibben and Mary Hester Ann Oakes:

^{v5}1972. ^{11}1. Ethel Hibben, b. 21 Aug 1885, d. 21 May 1972, Hugo, OK; m. 28 Feb 1904, Madison L. Carter,

^{v5}1973. ^{12}1. Alma Carter, m. _____ Massengale,

^{v5}1974. ^{12}2. Lois Carter, b. 21 Feb 1916, Hugo, OK, d. 20 Jan 1997, Shawnee, OK; m. _____ Billingsley. Ch: Danny Billingsley.

^{v5}1975. ^{11}2. Sophia Minnie Hibben, b. 19 Jan 1887, d. 7 Oct 1957; m. 9 Nov 1904, Charles Francis Payne. Grandparents of Phil Payne, who sent data and pictures.

^{v5}1976. ^{11}3. Samuel Lorenzo Hibben, b. 13 Sept 1889, d. 4

Aug 1958, Hugo, OK; m. 30 Oct 1913, Rosetta Collins,

v⁵1977.   ¹²1. Hubert Henry Hibben, b. 7 Oct 1914, d. Aug 1985; m. Mary Evelene Latta. Ch: Samuel Lee Hibben.

v⁵1978.   ¹¹4. Eliza Wilson Hibben, b. 5 March 1892, Paris, TX (Choctaw Roll #3934), d. 25 Feb 1972, Paris, TX; m.1. 16 June 1910, Carroll Napoleon Frazier, M.D.; m.2. 30 Sept 1917, in Paris, TX, George E. Parr,

v⁵1979.   ¹²1. Vivian Frazier, b. c1901, m. James Gentry. The late Vivie (Frazier) Gentry was a family researcher.

v⁵1980.   ¹¹5. William Thomas Hibben, b. 11 March 1894, d. 29 July 1973, Shawnee, OK; m. 12 Oct 1912, Lillie Mae Cannon, b. 1886, d. 1968, d/o Wylie Cannon and Rena Lantrip

v⁵1981.   ¹²1. Thomas Dickson Hibben, b. 1915, Frogville, OK; m. 19 June 1936, Beulah Leoma Trimble. Ch: Joann; Thomas Dixon; Patsy Ruth; and Mary Susan Hibben.

v⁵1982.   ¹²2. Imogene Fay Hibben, b. 22 Aug 1918, Frogville, OK, d. 17 Jan 1981, Lodi, CA; m.1. Earl Johnson, s/o James Johnson and Mary Lund; m.2. James Julius Kirkland. Ch: William Glen; James Ray; and Earlene Sue Johnson; and Addie May; Abbey Kay; and Michael Benjamin Kirkland.

v⁵1983.   ¹²3. William Theodore Hibben, b. 24 March 1920, Paris, TX, d. July 1976; m. Eloise Roberts,

v⁵1984.   ¹²4. Willey Wayne Hibben, b. 14 Sep 1923, Frogville, OK; m. 11 Jan 1946, in Hugo, OK, Orville Ethel Bryant. Ch: Sharon Lee; Wayne Thomas; Michael Dennis; and James Edward Hibben.

v⁵1985.   ¹¹6. Frances Harriet "Mit" Hibben, b. 20 Oct 1896; m. Randolph D. Carter,

v⁵1986.   ¹¹7. George Wellington Hibben, b. 5 Nov 1899, Hugo, OK, d. 27 Feb 1992, at Longview, TX, bur Shoals cem, Choctaw Co, OK (see obituary, below); m. 20 Sept 1925, Golden Collins. ch: Thomas S. and

Kenneth Gordon Hibben (who m. Jan Vinson and had ch: Timothy George; Kenneth Gordon Jr; and Lynn Hibben.

[v5]1987.   [11]8. Mary Gertrude Hibben, b. 19 April 1903, Hugo, OK, d. 17 July 1925, Goodwater, OK; m. 22 Dec 1928, Charles T. Watts (either death or marriage date is wrong!)

Obit, George Wellington Hibben (27 Feb 1992, Longview [TX] *News-Journal*). Services for George W. Hibben, 92, of Longview, will be 10 a.m. Friday at Welch Funeral home in Longview with the Rev. Dewayne Beaty officiating. Graveside service will be 3 p.m. Friday at Shoals Cemetery, in Choctaw Co, Oklahoma.

He died Tuesday. A Choctaw Indian, he was a product of the "Trail of Tears," his grandparents having been removed from their homeland in Mississippi. He was born in Indian Territory in 1899 and was on the original roll of the Choctaw Nation. He lived in Longview since 1933, coming from Oklahoma. He was a member of the First Baptist Church since 1934, former teacher of Business Men's Bible Class and member of the Longview Masonic Lodge no. 404 & Knights Templar No. 086. He worked for Humble Pipeline from 1933 until retirement in 1964. He was preceded in death by a son, Thomas S.

Survivors include wife, Golden, son and daughter-in-law, Ken and Jan of Hugo, Okla; grandsons Ken Jr of Dallas and T. George of Atlanta, GA; granddaughter, Lynn of Greenville; and great grandchildren, J.T. and Becky, both of Dallas, and Hillary of Atlanta, GA.

Joel W. Everidge and Sophia Folsom

[v5]1888.   [9]6. Joel W. Everidge Sr, (s/o Eva "Illiapotubbe" Brashears and Thomas Willie Everidge), b. Mississippi, 29 Aug 1828 (listed as 4 yrs old at time of Removal in 1832), d. 5 June 1901, bur in Everidge cem, Goodwater, OK; m. 3 Aug 1848, Sophia C.A. Folsom, b. 1832, d. 10 Oct 1894, d/o John Folsom. For 30 years, Joel was Chief Judge of the Choctaw Supreme Court. His son, Joel, testified on 31 June 1904 that his father died "3 years ago, 5th of this month."

In hearings connected with J.W. Hyden's claim for recognition as a Choctaw by blood, Edward Mitchell Everidge testified that he was fifty-five years of age and the son of Joel W. Everidge, a Choctaw by blood, who died in 1901, at the age of seventy-three, and Sophia Everidge, also a Choctaw by blood, who was born in the year 1830; that Joel W. Everidge was the son of Thomas Everidge, a white man, and Eve Brashears, a one-half Choctaw Indian, who died between the years 1870 and 1873; and that said Eve Brashears was the daughter of ___R. Turner Brashears, a white man. Said witness further testified that Eve Breashears had two full brothers and two full sisters, whose names were Elizabeth, Lewis, Ben, and Isabelle; that he had been acquainted with the principal (Hyden) applicants herein only a few years, and that only information he had relative to the question whether or not the applicants are possessed of Choctaw blood was a statement made to him by his father to the effect that they were related to him, witness's "grandmother being a full sister to the grandmother of the principal applicants herein." [This relation proved to be false.]

Family of Joel W. Everidge Sr and Sophia C.A. Folsom:

[v5]1988.　　[10]1. Elizabeth "Lizzie" H. Everidge, b. 1849; m. Christopher Columbus Ervin, s/o Calvin Ervin and Sally Gibson; C.C. was a brother to Margaret, Mrs. Thomas E. Oakes and to Susan, Mrs. Joel Everidge Jr. 10 ch: Viola, Myrtle, Hattie, Pauline, W.P., Emmitt, M.H., A.A., Roy, and T.L. Ervin.

[v5]1989.　　[10]2. Edward Mitchell Everidge, b. 15 Sept 1851, age 53 in June 1904, per his own testimony, d. 6 Feb 1916; m.1. Siney Gibson (3 ch); m.2. 1899, Lula Williams (2 ch). (Lula was admitted as an intermarried citizen, Roll #642. The last part of the family is on Census Card #1769.) Edward was elected District Judge in 1896 and lived at Grant in 1901.

[v5]1990.　　[11]1. Florence Everidge,
[v5]1991.　　[11]2. Inez Everidge
[v5]1992.　　[11]3. Jackson F. Everidge
[v5]1993.　　[11]4. Ezra Dora Everidge, b. c1899 (Roll #5018)
[v5]1994.　　[11]5. Joel Everidge, b. c1900, (Choctaw Roll #5019)
[v5]1995.　　[10]3. *Joel W. "Joe" Everidge Jr, b. 3 June 1853, in Kiamichi Co, I.T., d. 29 July 1911; m. 1871, Susan Ervin,

v⁵1996.   ¹⁰4. Robert Turner Everidge, b. 19 Nov 1856, d. 6
            April 1921; m. 22 June 1890, Lula Hulen
            Tarrence, 10 ch: Edward M., Clara W., Thomas H.,
            D.M. Hailey, Effie, Eva Laura, Sophia Ann, Minte
            L., Clarence, and Daisy Everidge. Daisy, b. 20
            Sept 1909, was the oldest living Everidge in 1995.
v⁵1997.   ¹⁰5. Martin Van Buren Everidge, b. 20 July 1860, d.
            16 Jan 1922; m. Minto L. Goswick,
v⁵1998.   ¹⁰6. Arabea "Bee" Everidge, b. 23 Dec 1863, d. 18
            March 1938; m. Robert Raulston,
v⁵1999.   ¹⁰7. Laura Everidge, b. 2 May 1869, d. 23 March
            1932; m. Bee Nation,

Joel W. Everidge, Jr and Susan Ervin

v⁵1995. ¹⁰3. Joel W. "Joe" Everidge Jr, b. 3 June 1853, in
Kiamichi Co, I.T. (52 years old in 1904), d. 29 July 1911; m.
1871, Susan Ervin, d/o Calvin Ervin and Sally Gibson, of
Doaksville, Towsen Co, I.T. Susan was a sister to Margaret J.
Ervin, Mrs. Thomas E. Oakes, and to Lizzie Everidge's husband,
Christopher Columbus Ervin.

From notes of Daisy Everidge: "Joseph" was Capt in Light
Horse, 1878, Sheriff of Kiamitia Co, 1882, served in House of
Representatives, Choctaw Nation, 1884, Senator, Choctaw
Nation, 1884, District Collector, 3rd Dist, 1885-1888. Testimony
in "J.W. Hyden v. Choctaw Nation" reveals that Joel was
Attorney General of Choctaw Nation in 1904.

"Like his father, he is tall of stature and powerfully built, fair
complexioned and intelligent-looking. He is descended from the
Hyah-pah-tuk-kalo clan." (*Leaders and Leading Men of the
Indian Territory*, by H.F. O'Bierne, 1891, p. 120-21)

Family of Joel W. Everidge, Jr, and Susan Ervin (six children
before 1891, per *Leaders and Leading Men of the Indian
Territory*)
v⁵2000.   ¹¹1. Willie Everidge,
v⁵2001.   ¹¹2. Emma Everidge,
v⁵2002.   ¹¹3. Joseph H. Everidge, b. 1877 (Choctaw Census
            Card #5356; Roll #13571); m. Mabel O. _____
            (Intermarried Citizen #601)
v⁵2003.   ¹²1. Helen Blanche Everidge, b. c1901
            (Choctaw Roll #13572)

^{v5}2004. ^{11}4. Ella Everidge,
^{v5}2005. ^{11}5. Robert Everidge,
^{v5}2006. ^{11}6. Mary Everidge
^{v5}2007. ^{11}7. Henry Everidge; m. Edna McLemore,

Family, according to other sources:
  14 ch: Thomas W., Emma, Joseph H., Rosey Ella Florence, James Stanley, Robert E. Lee, Eddie, Frankie, May, Governor Jones, Pala Sophelia, Gertrude, Tommy, and Robbie Everidge.

LUCY (BRASHEAR) PATTON/STANDLEY

^{v5}**202.** ^{8}2. **Lucy Brashear**, (d/o R.T. "Turner" Brashear and "a daughter of Taboca," called "Jane Apuckshunnubbee"), b. c1792-3, d. 1825, bur Standley Plantation, Carroll Co, MS; m.1. c1809, **William? Patton**, and had three children; m.2. 1816, **Capt. James S. Standley**, and had another family.

For much of this data on Standleys, thanks go to descendant Jane Proctor Smith, 7543 East 28th St, Tulsa, OK 74129, who compiled it from the book, *Captain J.S. Standley, Ancestors and Descendants*, by Mrs. B.S. Smiser, (1933). Jane also had access to a family bible, marriage, birth, and death certificates, and her personal knowledge of the people.

James S. Standley, b. 22 June 1792, TN, d. 12 Nov 1862, Standley Plantation, Carroll Co, MS, bur "Ridgeway," Standley Plantation, s/o Abraham Standley, s/o Alfred Standley, s/o John Standley, the English immigrant to New York Colony. James Standley's plantation was four miles west of Black Hawk, Carroll Co, MS. Many of the family were born there, died there, and are buried in the family cemetery there. In the Standley book, the plantation is described as being in the Yazoo River bottom. "The county lines of three counties ran through the plantation, viz: Yazoo, Holmes, and Carroll, and the final survey put the place in LeFlore County."

After Lucy Brashear Standley's death, James S. Standley, m.2. 1829, Eve Cochenaur, and had children Ephriam Foster;

Jane; Abram; Ben Franklin; Amanda; George Washington; and Cornelia Carraway Standley.

Family of Lucy Brashear and ?William Patton:

v5^{v5}2008.   91. Melinda Patton, b. 1806; m. Hiram Vinson

v5^{v5}2009.   92. Sylvia Patton, b. 1807; m. Edmund McKenney

v5^{v5}2010.   93. *Turner S. Patton, b. 1808, MS, d. 1857; m. 22 Oct 1835, Susan Standley, b. c1817, d. c1844.

Family of Lucy Brashear and Capt. James S. Standley:

v5^{v5}2011.   94. Eliza Standley, b. c1817; m. c1831, Freeman J. Smith (a white man), b. 10 April 1808, Massachusetts, d. 15 Nov 1842, Yalobusha Co, MS, s/o John Smith, Jr and Hannah Putney, of Goshen, Mass. (Data from Jane Proctor Smith, a descendant)

v5^{v5}2012.   101. Adeliza Fidelia Smith, b. 23 Aug 1835, MS, d. 22 Feb 1893, Tobucksy Co, I.T., bur Canadian Masonic Cem, Pittsburg Co, OK; m.1. 14 July 1851, Robert Freeman Turner, Sr, b. c1800, d. 7 June 1854 (will), Carroll Co, MS; m.2. 31 Oct 1854, in Carroll Co, MS, John T. Nicholson; m.3. 10 Sept 1857, in Carroll Co, MS, Albert C. Jackson; m.4. 29 April 1868, in Yalobusha Co, MS, A.H. Howden. The *History of Carroll Co,* by William Franklin Hamilton, gives (p.51) Adeliza as "Mrs. Aldridge Houdon" whose two children "were Medora and Robert Turner." After Adeliza died, A.F. Howden m. 19 March 1884, in Choctaw Nation, I.T., J. R. Forster.

v5^{v5}2013.   111. Eliza Medora Almeda Turner, b. April 1852, MS, d. 6 Feb 1909, Indianola, OK; m. 1874, Benjamin F. Hightower,

v5^{v5}2014.   112. *Robert Freeman Turner, Jr, b. 28 June 1854, Carroll Co, MS, d. 27 Feb 1926, Norman, OK; m. 30 July 1876, Olga Theresa Standley, a cousin, once removed, d/o James Standley, Jr.

v⁵2015.   ⁹5. James Standley, Jr, b. 17 April 1819, MS, d. 10
Oct 1872, Tobucksy Co, I.T.; m. 11 June 1840,
in Carroll Co, MS, Margaret Irvin Tadlock, b. 17
Sep 1820, near Hopkinsville, Christian Co, KY,
d. 7 June 1867, Carroll Co, MS, d/o John H.
Tadlock and _____ Irvin. Children all born at
Standley Plantation, 4 miles west of Black
Hawk, Carroll Co, MS. James Standley Jr was
educated at the Choctaw Academy near Great
Crossing, Scott Co, KY.

v⁵2016.   ¹⁰1. James Stirman Standley, III, b. 8 March
1841, d. 20 Oct 1904, Atoka, I.T.; m.1. 10
June 1863, Alice Robinson Posey, b. ?, d. 4
April 1881, Atoka, I.T., d/o Humphrey
Marshall Posey and Sarah McDougal; m.2.
29 Nov 1882, in Leesburg, VA, Mrs. Lizzie C.
(Edwards) Harris. James Standley graduated
from Kentucky Military Institute and was
elected Lieutenant upon the formation of
"The Carroll Rifles," which became Co. K,
11ᵗʰ Mississippi Regiment, CSA. He served
as Adjutant under three generals during the
Civil War and was promoted to Captain. He
was severely wounded in the right arm at
the battle of "Seven Pines," near Richmond,
VA, 31 May 1862. The wound forced his
retirement. In 1872, he accompanied his
father and brother, William, to I.T., where
the father died. In 1874, he moved to I.T.
and located a farm on the South Canadian
River. In Jan 1881, he removed from South
Canadian to Atoka, where three months
later his wife died. Ten ch: the first six born
in MS, the last four in I.T.

v⁵2017.   ¹¹1. Blanche Standley, d. young in MS
v⁵2018.   ¹¹2. Norma Earl Standley, b. 15 July 1865,
MS; m. B.S. Smiser. Norma, Mrs. B.S.
Smiser, was author of the book, *Captain
James S. Standley, Ancestors and*

^{v5}2019.　^{11}3. Lillian Standley, d. young in MS

^{v5}2020.　^{11}4. Mary (or Jennie) Standley, drowned in Boggy Creek, 3 July 1886, near Atoka, I.T.

^{v5}2021.　^{11}5. Kate Standley, d. young in MS

^{v5}2022.　^{11}6. James S. Standley IV, b. 3 July 1873, Winona, Montgormery Co, MS, d. in Atoka, I.T., 31 March 1896; m. 3 Jan 1895, Betha Salmon, d/o J.B. Salmon, of Atoka

^{v5}2023.　^{11}7. Eva A. Standley, b. 10 Jan 1875, Canadian, I.T.; m. 9 Feb 1893, at Atoka, Judge J.G. Ralls, Sr, a U.S. Commissioner and native of IL.

^{v5}2024.　^{11}8. Claude Money Standley, (fem), b. 23 Sept 1877, Canadian, I.T.; m. Rev. J.O. Catlin, of St. Louis, MO.

^{v5}2025.　^{11}9. Lonna Spann Standley, (twin), b. 28 Aug 1879, Canadian, I.T.; m. J.D. Fulton, a pharmacist of Van Alstyne, TX. He owned drug stores in Atoka and Canadian, and was a surveyor for the Dawes Commission.

^{v5}2026.　^{11}10. Anna Posey Standley, (twin), b. 28 Aug 1879, Canadian, I.T., d. in Atoka, I.T., 5 Sept 1884

^{v5}2027.　^{10}2. John Tadlock Standley, b. 26 Oct 1843, Carroll Co, MS, d. 10 Oct 1886, I.T. bur Savanna, I.T.; m. Margaret O'Harro. John moved to I.T. in 1875 and was a coal weigher for J.J. McAlester. He and Margaret had two daughters Nannie and Gertrude Standley.

^{v5}2028.　^{10}3. Leona Standley, b. 24 Jan 1847, d. 9 Dec 1891, Brooken, I.T., m.1. 12 Nov 1867, in MS, John Spann, who moved to I.T. in 1873 and operated a general merchandise business in Canadian, I.T., d. at Canadian,

	I.T., 29 March 1877; Leona m.2. July 1879, at Brooken, I.T., John Sanders. Two Spann sons died in infancy in Mississippi.
v[5]2029.	[11]1. Freeman R. Spann, b. 7 March 1874; m. 5 Nov 1905, at Norman, OK, Dixie Vincent
v[5]2030.	[11]2. Harry Spann, b. 10 May 1876
v[5]2031.	[11]3. Pitt Sanders, d. quite young
v[5]2032.	[11]4. Newt Sanders, b. c1882; m. 1907, Ida Brassfield
v[5]2033.	[11]5. Nona Sanders, m.1. William H. Burris; m.2. _____ Snell.
v[5]2034.	[10]4. William Pitt Standley, b. 6 June 1849, d. Nov 1872, Standley Plantation, Carroll Co, MS; m. 30 Aug 1868, Mary H. Pate. Ch: Maggie and J.W. Standley. In Fall, 1872, Pitt and his brother, James, accompanied their father to I.T., where the father died; Pitt died a few weeks after returning to MS.
v[5]2035.	[10]5. Eva Standley, b. 25 Nov 1852, d. 31 Jan 1876, Winona, MS; m. 1 Oct 1873, Edward N. May. No children.
v[5]2036.	[10]6. *Olga Theresa Standley, b. 29 Nov 1855, at Standley Plantation, Black Hawk, Carroll Co, MS, d. 3 March 1926, Norman, OK; m. 30 July 1876, Robert Freeman Turner, grandson of Eliza Standley. Since her mother died when she was 12, she lived with her brother, James, and her sister Leona Spann. In Fall 1873, she came to I.T. with her sister, where in 1876 she married a cousin once removed.
v[5]2037.	[9]6. Amelia Standley, b. c1822; she attended school at Eliot Mission; m. 31 March 1842, Nathaniel A. Clarke. Amelia married a doctor in New Orleans, according to Harriet Oakes's testimony in 1904.
v[5]2038.	[9]7. Lucy Standley (?) n.f.i.
v[5]2039.	[9]8. Alex Standley (?) n.f.i.

Robert Freeman Turner, Jr
and Olga Theresa Standley

[v5]2014. [11]2. Robert Freeman Turner, Jr, (Choctaw Roll #13167, s/o Robert Freeman Turner, Sr and Adeliza Fidelia Smith), b. 28 June 1854, Carroll Co, MS, d. 27 Feb 1926, Norman, OK; m. 30 July 1876, Olga Theresa Standley ([v5]2036), (Choctaw Roll #13168), b. 29 Nov 1855, at Standley Plantation, Black Hawk, Carroll Co, MS, d. 3 March 1926, Norman, OK, a cousin, once removed, d/o James Standley, Jr and Margaret Irvin Tadlock. They were both descendants of Lucy Brashear and Capt. James S. Standley, Sr.

Robert F. and Olga Turner (and five of their children: Apuckshunnubbee, Benjamin, James, Leona, and Nora R. Turner) are listed in Hastain's *Index to Choctaw and Chickasaw Deeds and Allotments*, published by the Oklahoma Historical Society, pp.1284-85.

[v5]2040. [11]1. Robert Standley Turner, (Choctaw Roll #13169), b. 4 Jan 1878, Tobucksy Co, I.T., d. 28 Nov 1967, Dallas, TX; m. 22 Jan 1899, Lena May Terrell, b. 28 Dec 1879, Farmington, MO. Robert S. Turner was in the hotel business in OkCity.

[v5]2041. [12]1. Harold Van Turner, b. 30 Sept 1903, Indianola, I.T.; m. 22 April 1925, Dorothy Wage. Harold was a star athlete (track) at OkCity High School and U.OK. Ch: Norma Jene Turner, b. 19 Jan 1926, Norman, OK.

[v5]2042. [12]2. Mildred Turner, b. 10 Feb 1909, Indianola, OK; m. 9 June 1927, J. Otis Gossett. Mildred receive a B.A. from U. OK, and was very active in the American Association of University Women.

[v5]2043. [11]2. Eva Almeda Turner, b. 14 Dec 1879, Canadian, I.T., d. 6 Aug 1903, Indianola, I.T.; m. 1 May 1901, Thomas Edgar Manners

[v5]2044. [11]3. Leona Theresa Turner, (Choctaw Roll #13170), b. 4 Sept 1882, Indianola, I.T., d. 6 March 1978, Kansas City, KS; m. 25 Dec 1910, John

Greene Terrell

v⁵2045.   ¹²1. Maxine Almerta Terrell, b. 13 June 1909; m. 30 Dec 1933, James Neal Miller,

v⁵2046.   ¹²2. Norma Artelle Terrell, b. 29 Aug 1912, Indianola, OK; m. 30 Dec 1933, Edgar G. Gerth,

v⁵2047.   ¹²3. John Robert Terrell, b. 22 Dec 1915, Indianola, OK; m. 13 June 1936, Harriet Rice,

v⁵2048.   ¹¹4. James Irvin "Jim" Turner, (Choctaw Roll #13171), b. 30 Jan 1885, Canadian, I.T., d. 12 June 1912, Hot Springs, AR; m. 17 April 1910, Laura B. "Dottie" Pearson

v⁵2049.   ¹¹5. John Benjamin "Ben" Turner, (Choctaw Roll #13172), b. 8 July 1887, Indianola, I.T., d. 16 May 1968, Indianola, I.T.; m. 7 Oct 1906, Maude Dill. Ben stayed in Indianola and was a rancher and farmer.

v⁵2050.   ¹²1. John Gerald Turner, b. 14 July 1907

v⁵2051.   ¹¹6. William Foster Turner, b. 27 Oct 1889, Tobucksy Co, I.T., d. there, 1 Jan 1891,

v⁵2052.   ¹¹7. Albert Apuckshunnubbee "Puck" Turner, (Choctaw Roll #13173), b. 17 July 1892, Indianola, I.T., d. 26 July 1964, McAlester, OK; m.1. 10 Oct 1910, Abby Mays; m.2. 1 June 1913, Ola Harper. Puck was a rancher and farmer in Indianola. no ch.

v⁵2053.   ¹¹8. Nora Fidelia "Pat" Turner, (Choctaw Roll #13174), b. 17 Sept 1895, Indianola, I.T., d. 12 April 1978, Tulsa, OK; m. 7 Sept 1913, Oliver Pope Proctor, b. 30 May 1890, Scottsboro, AL, d. 9 April 1956, McAlester, OK, s/o Hugh Alexander Proctor and Laura Jane Selby.

v⁵2054.   ¹²1. Olga _Jane_ Proctor, b. 5 July 1917, Indianola, OK, m. 2 Oct 1937, Jack Thomas Smith, b. 12 March 1913, d. 29 Aug 2000, receive a B.S. from OU in June 1937. Jane Proctor Smith gathered much of the data on this line.

v⁵2055.   ¹³1. Joan Carol Smith, b. 1 March 1942, OkCity; m. 17 June 1965, Charles Phillips Cotton

v⁵2056.   ¹³2. John Proctor Smith, b. 1 April 1946, Lawton, OK; m. 4 March 1967, Jeanne Elaine Trimble

v⁵2057.   ¹²2. Oliver Pope Proctor, Jr, b. 2 Aug 1921, Indianola, OK; m. 27 Sep 1943, Alverna Ray McAlpine, b. 24 Dec 1925, McAlester, OK, d/o John Clark McApline and Ester Lou Daniels.

v⁵2058.   ¹³1. Pamela Lynn Proctor, b. 29 July 1944, McAlester, OK

v⁵2059.   ¹³2. Robert Wayne Proctor, b. 18 Feb 1947, Borger, TX; m. 30 May 1969, Janice Kay Diedrich

v⁵2060.   ¹²3. Baby Proctor, b. & d. 3 Aug 1930, McAlester, OK

Turner S. Patton and Lucy Standley

v⁵2010. ⁹1. Turner S. Patton, (s/o Lucy Brashear and William? Patton), b. 1808, d. 1857; m. 22 Oct 1835, in MS, Susan Standley, b. c1817, d/o David (or John) Standley of Davidson Co, TN and Matilda Harlin of Virginia. Turner and Susan are in the 1840 Census of Carroll Co, MS, with 3 sons, aged 0-5. Harvey, Robert B. and William S. Patton all three enlisted in the U.S. Army, 29 Sept 1863, at Ft. Smith, AR. (refs: 1855 Census, Skullyville Co, Choctaw Nation, I.T., Payment Roll 7RA-09; Military records of Harvey, Robert, and William Patton.

v⁵2061.   ¹⁰1. William S. Patton, b. 3 Nov 1836, Carroll Co, MS, d. 27 May 1926, Choctaw Nation, OK; m. Elizabeth (Richardson) Dougherty, b. 1836, ⅛ Cherokee, d/o William Richardson and Annie Sanders. Wm. S. Patton served as a representative of Union Choctaws in 1865. (ref: *History of Sequoyah Co*; Newspaper obits; family data collected by Bob and Ann Condren.)

v5 2062.   11 1. Emaline Patton, m. 10 June 1889, Seymour (or Raymond) Drake,

v5 2063.   12 1. Emma Drake,

v5 2064.   12 2. Seymore Drake,

v5 2065.   11 2. Dumont D.M. Patton, b. 21 Sept 1870, d. 6 Sept 1957, 1/8 Cherokee, Roll #4056, C.C. 1498; m. Anna Turner, b. 9 Oct 1879, d. 28 Dec 1959, bur Garden of Memories, Muldrow, OK.

v5 2066.   12 1. Roy G. Patton,

v5 2067.   12 2. William Dewey Patton, b. 9 Sept 1898, d. 9 July 1959, 1/16 Cherokee, Roll #4057

v5 2068.   12 3. Helen L. Patton, b. 1900, 1/16 Cherokee, Roll #4058

v5 2069.   12 4. Richard Patton,

v5 2070.   11 3. Gideon Jay Patton, b. 1875, d. 1967, 1/16 Cherokee, Roll #27296, C.C. 1501; m. Nora Blackard. Children: Moody; Joe Butler; Marie; Patsy; Elizabeth; Dorothea; and Nadine Patton. Two children are on the final Rolls of the Cherokee Nation:

v5 2071.   12 1. Marie Patton, b. 1898, 1/32 Cherokee, Roll #27296

v5 2072.   12 2. William M. Patton, b. 1900, 1/32 Cherokee, Roll #27297

v5 2073.   10 2. *Robert Brashears Patton, b. 24 Dec 1837, Carroll Co, MS, 1/8 Cherokee, Roll #4150; C.C. 1544, d. 13 July 1913, Paw Paw, Sequoyah Co, OK; m.1. 8 Feb 1866, Ruth A. Thompson, an enrolled Cherokee, b. 1 Dec 1849; m.2. c1880, Charlotte Whitfield, 1/2 Cherokee.

v5 2074.   10 3. Harvey C. Patton, b. c1839-40, d. 1 Jan 1864 in General Hospital, Springfield, MO, a Civil War casualty.

v5 2075.   10 4. Lucy Patton, on 1855 Choctaw Census, Skullyville Co, Ind. Terr.

v5 2076.   10 5. Ellen Patton, on 1855 Choctaw Census, Skullyville Co, Ind. Terr.

Robert Brashears Patton and
Ruth Thompson/ Charlotte Whitfield

v⁵2073. ¹⁰2. Robert Brashears Patton, (s/o Turner S. Patton and Susan Standley), b. 24 Dec 1837, Black Hawk, Carroll Co, MS; d. 13 July 1913, Paw Paw, Sequoyah Co, OK, bur Ft. Smith National Cem, Ft Smith, AR, grave 2220; ⅛ Cherokee, Roll #4150; C.C. 1544; m.1. 8 Feb 1866, Sequoyah Dist, Cherokee Nation, I.T., Ruth A. Thompson, an enrolled Cherokee, b. 1 Dec 1849, Dwight Mission, I.T., d. 6 Jan 1879, Paw Paw, I.T., d/o John "Jack" Thompson and Nancy Sanders, both enrolled Cherokees; m.2. 5 July 1881, at Camp Creek, Sequoyah District, Cherokee Nation, I.T., Charlotte Whitfield, ½ Cherokee, d/o George Whitfield.

From a biography by Louise Humphrey (source unknown; Xerox sent me by Faye Dunham). "Robert B. Patton was a resident of Skullyville County Choctaw Nation after his removal from Mississippi. On September 29, 1863, he enlisted as a private in Co. I, 2nd Regt, Ark Cav, to fight for the Union Army. He became ill on January 1, 1864, in Cassville, Missouri, due to exposure to the elements, but returned to active duty on February 29, 1864. He served as Private, Corporal, and Sergeant with Co. I.

"On September 2, 1864, Sgt. Patton transferred to Co. C, of 2d Cav and on September 20, 1864, was promoted to 2ⁿᵈ Lieutenant. He again was ill due to an injury to his leg on February 2, 1865, and returned to duty on March 18. He was honorably discharged at Memphis, Tennessee on August 20, 1865.

"Mr. Patton then returned to the Choctaw Nation and with his brother, William S. Patton, was appointed to represent the Choctaws at a council between the Choctaws and Chickasaws held in Fort Smith, Arkansas, on September 8, 1865.

"Robert Patton moved from the Choctaw Nation to the Cherokee Nation on August 26, 1866 and his nearest post office was Fort Smith until about 1876, where he received his mail from Camp Creek, Indian Territory. He gave farming as his occupation.

"He married Ruth Thompson, a Cherokee full blood, and three children were born to this union: September 7, 1867, Turner B. Patton, d. August 13, 1909; November 4, 1870, Charles F. Patton; and 1874, John T.A. Patton.

"Ruth Thompson Patton died at Paw Paw, Indian Territory, on January 6, 1879. On January 1, 1870, Mr. Patton requested that Tribal Annuities be paid to the loyal Choctaws instead of the regular Choctaw government and that he be made their representative.

"On July 5, 1881, at Camp Creek, Indian Territory, Judge Franklin Faulkner married Robert Patton and his second wife, Charlotte Whitfield. Witnesses to this marriage were Isaac Jacobs and Mr. and Mrs. Robert Dougherty. To this marriage these children were born: June 28, 1882, William S. Patton; September 7, 1885, Susan J. Patton; December 16, 1889, Robert Edward Patton; January 5, 1895, Lucy M. Patton.

"Robert B. Patton was appointed the first postmaster of the Breedlove Station on March 7, 1891. He also taught school in the Paw Paw area. Throughout his lifetime, he was active in Indian affairs and worked for both the Cherokees and the Choctaws in negotiating with the Federal Government on land and Indian rights.

"Turner B. Patton married Emma Jane Kennedy and they had three children: Delta Patton, who married Oshea Lemley; Robert Isom Patton, died as a child, and Grace Lea Patton, who married Leonard A. Condren.

"William S. Patton [Robert's brother, not his son] and Elizabeth Patton had three children: Emiline Patton, Dumont Patton, and Gideon Jay Patton. Many descendants of Robert B. and William S. Patton still reside in Sequoyah County."

Robert served in 1865 as a representative of the Union Choctaws, along with his brother, William S. Patton.

Both of Robert Brashears Patton's wives were Cherokee, he was adopted into the Cherokee Tribe, and his children were enrolled Cherokees. He was the only Choctaw Commissioned Officer in the U.S. Army in the Civil War. (ref: Civil War pension records for Robert Brashears Patton; correspondence with Interior Department relative to treatment of Choctaws in the Union Army; Death certificates of William Sunkum Patton, Lucy May Patton; and Indian Records for Susan J. and Robert Edward Patton, researched by Ann and Bob Condren, of Oklahoma City, for which many thanks.)

<u>Family of Robert Brashears Patton and Ruth A. Thompson</u>:

v5 2077. [11]1. Turner Brashears Patton, b. 7 Sept 1867, Paw Paw, I.T., ¼ Cherokee, Roll #4040, C.C. 1489, d. 12 Aug 1909, Sequoyah Co, OK; m. 26 May 1895, Emma Jane Kennedy, b. 1874, d. c1906, Sequoyah Dist, I.T., d/o Isom Kennedy and Celesta A. Northam.

v5 2078. [12]1. Audie Patton, b. 1897, d. c1901

v5 2079. [12]2. Delta C. Patton, b. 3 March 1898, ⅛ Cherokee, Roll #4041, d. 26 Dec 1981; m. Oshea Lemley

v5 2080. [12]3. Robert Isom Patton, b. 17 Nov 1901, ⅛ Cherokee, Roll #4042, d. c1904

v5 2081. [12]3. Grace Lea Patton, b. 15 Nov 1903, d. 9 June 1955; m. 24 Dec 1919, at Fort Smith, AR, Leonard A. Condren, d. 28 Oct 1978, Ft. Smith, AR, s/o Robert Lee Condren and Kitty King.

v5 2082. [13]1. Robert W. Condren, b. 13 Nov 1920; m. Ann W. Griffin. Bob and Ann Condren have done considerable research in family history.

v5 2083. [13]2. Gracia Louise Condren, b. 3 Jan 1923, d. 3 Oct 1986

v5 2084. [13]3. Robbie Sue Condren, b. 8 Feb 1925

v5 2085. [13]4. L. Patton Condren, b. 8 March 1927

v5 2086. [13]5. Emma Lou Condren, b. 18 Oct 1930

v5 2087. [13]6. Billy Ed Condren, b. 22 Feb 1937

v5 2088. [13]7. JoNell Condren, b. 16 April 1939, d. 24 May 1991

v5 2089. [13]8. Glen Paige Condren, b. 10 June 1942

v5 2090. [13]9. Gary Lee Condren, b. 7 April 1946

v5 2091. [11]2. Nancy E. Patton, b. 16 July 1869, d. 27 Oct 1869 v⁵2092.   ¹¹3. Charles Frederick (or Franklin) Patton, b. 4 Nov 1870, Paw Paw, I.T., ⅛ Cherokee, Roll #4156, C.C. 1545, d. 10 Feb 1913, Sallisaw, OK; m. 2 Sept 1984, in Paw Paw, I.T., Nancy Ellender Hood, b. 26 Nov 1879, Sebastian Co, AR, d. 1966, Sallisaw, OK, d/o Solomon Hood and Melissa Gardenhire,

v⁵2093.   ¹²1. Caleb Franklin Patton, b. 19 Jan 1897, 1/16 Cherokee, Roll #4157, d. 25 Dec 1982, Bristow, OK, bur Oaklawn Cem, Bristow, OK; m. Jan 1924, Renna Flowers, b. 15 Aug 1900, d. 21 Aug 1964, bur Oaklawn Cem, Bristow, OK, d/o Andrew Paul Flowers and Lenora Tennessee Whitlock,

v⁵2094.   ¹³1. Carlos Quinton Patton, b. 30 Aug 1924, d. of heart attack, 1989; was on Cherokee and Choctaw Rolls; m. 20 March 1943, Delores Giddeon, b. 5 July 1925, Drumright, OK, d/o Charles Raymond Giddeon and Nannie Lee Morgan

v⁵2095.   ¹⁴1. Jerri Ruth Patton, b. 12 Nov 1945, m. 1973, Richard A. Harmon, b. 4 April 1946

v⁵2096.   ¹⁴2. Jimmy Wayne Patton, b. 11 Jan 1948, m. 1971, Sandra K. Crane, b. 31 Jan 1951

v⁵2097.   ¹³2. Cash Kenneth Patton, b. 24 Feb 1926, Sallisaw, OK, d. 25 April 1939, Shamrock, OK, bur Oaklawn Cem, Bristow, OK; n.m.

v⁵2098.   ¹³3. Charles Curtis Patton, b. 29 Oct 1928, Shamrock, OK; m. Gussie _____,

v⁵2099.   ¹³4. Glenna Carolyn Patton, b. 4 Dec 1939, Drunright, OK; m.1. _____ Sorrells, m.2. Charles Norman,

v⁵2100.   ¹²2. Minnie Mae Patton, b. 15 Feb 1899, Sallisaw, OK, 1/16 Cherokee, Roll #4158; m. Willard Tuggle,

[v5]2101.   [13]1. Jack Charles Tuggle, b. 17 Feb 1918, Sallisaw, OK, d. Nov 1991, CA

[v5]2102.   [12]3. Robert Solomon Patton, b. 31 May 1903, d. 27 March 1965, bur City cem, Sallisaw, OK; m. Iva Rhodes. Ch: Max Patton.

[v5]2103.   [12]4. Charles William Patton, b. 24 Aug 1907, Sallisaw, OK, d. 20 Oct 1932, McAlester, OK; m. Trixie Stevens. Ch: Dempsey Patton.

[v5]2104.   [12]5. Floyd Arthur Patton, b. 6 Aug 1911, Sallisaw, OK, d. 28 Sept 1984, Shreveport, LA; m. 17 June 1933, Sallisaw, OK, Mary Magdalene Remy, d/o Anderson Remy and Julia Wright

[v5]2105.   [13]1. Charles Ray Patton, b. 16 Jan 1935,

[v5]2106.   [13]2. Mary Joan Patton, b. 16 Jan 1935,

[v5]2107.   [13]3. Arthur Loyd Patton, b. 6 Nov 1940

[v5]2108.   [13]4. Henry Floyd Patton, b. 6 Nov 1940

[v5]2109.   [11]4. John T.A. Patton, b. 20 Dec 1878, d. 7 Oct 1888

[v5]2110.   [11]5. William Thomas Patton, b. 20 Dec 1878, d. 21 March 1879

Family of Robert Brashears Patton and Charlotte Whitfield:

[v5]2111.   [11]6. William Sunkum Patton, b. 28 June 1882, 5/16 Cherokee, Roll #4152, C.C. 1544, d. 1956

[v5]2112.   [11]7. Susan J. Patton, b. 7 Sept 1885, 5/16 Cherokee, Roll #4153, d. 21 March 1905

[v5]2113.   [11]8. Robert Edward Patton, b. 16 Dec 1889, 5/16 Cherokee, Roll #4154, d. 26 March 1907

[v5]2114.   [11]9. Lucy May Patton, b. 5 Jan 1895, Paw Paw, I.T., 5/16 Cherokee, Roll #4155, d. 24 Feb 1985; m. Robert Clifton Bailey

ELIZABETH BRASHEAR
and JOSEPH FISHER

ᵛ⁵203. ⁸3. **Elizabeth Brashear**, (d/o R.T. "Turner" Brashear and "a daughter of Taboca," called "Jane Apuckshunnubbee"), b. c?1795; in order to have her second child by c1810-13, Elizabeth would have to be born about 1795. Harriet Oakes testified that Elizabeth and her husband "lived right there in the neighborhood, where we all lived," i.e. the Rankin area, 12 miles from the Pearl River. Elizabeth d. in MS before 1832, i.e. before the Choctaw Removal, per Harriet Oakes; m. in MS, *Joseph Fisher*, (a white man). Joseph Fisher d. in 1852 or 1853 at age 96, according to a grandson, Joseph R. Lawrence (see Choctaw Enrollment Card #5187).

Joseph Fisher and his second wife, Martha "Patsy" Hayes, a full-blood, moved with the Everidges to Indian Territory in 1832, and "lived down beyond Doaksville." Eva (Brashear) Everidge continued to think of Joe Fisher as a brother-in-law and often went to visit him, occasionally taking Harriet and/or Joel with her. Fisher's children by his second wife included:

    Narcissa Fisher, m. Gov. Basil LeFlore;
    Rebecca Fisher, m. Forbes LeFlore;
    Cynthia Fisher, m. William LeFlore;
    Sarah Effie Fisher, d. c1862; m. Dr. Davis;
    D. Osborn Fisher; and
    Sidney Fisher.

Harriet (Everidge) Oakes described Joe Fisher as "a small man, raw boned, just like he had been sick and fallen off to nothing but skin and bones. He was a diseased man, (had a kidney and bladder disease) and he wilted away to nothing." It took him a while, though: he had at least eight children by two wives. Grandson Joseph R. Lawrence, who lived with Joe Fisher when a child, testified on 30 Jan 1907 that his grandfather died when he was 14, i.e. c1848.

Family of Elizabeth Brashear and Joseph Fisher:

v5️⃣2115.   9️⃣1. Silas D. (or G.D., per his family bible) Fisher, d. bef. Civil War; m. Polly or Molly Kelley. They had 2 children:

v5️⃣2116.   10️⃣1. "a little boy; got stung by a centipede; crawled across him; the mark rotted and he died" (per Harriet Oakes)

v5️⃣2117.   10️⃣2. "a little girl; caught fire and died" (per Harriet Oakes)

v5️⃣2118.   9️⃣2. Mary L. "Polly" Fisher, b. ?; to have her 3rd child in 1833, Polly would have to be b. c1810-13; d. bef Civil War; m.1. Jim Campbell, a white man, m.2. David Lawrence, a white man

v5️⃣2119.   10️⃣1. Jim Campbell, died at Spencer Academy, Ind. Terr; n.m.

v5️⃣2120.   10️⃣2. Lavinia Campbell; m. Johnson Frasier, an Indian, and lived in Chickasaw Nation.

v5️⃣2121.   10️⃣3. John R. Lawrence, b. 1833, Kiamitia, per his own testimony in "J.W. Hyden vs. Choctaw Nation"

v5️⃣2122.   10️⃣4. Joseph R. Lawrence, b. 1834. On Choctaw Enrollment Card #5187, he identified his grandparents as Joseph Fisher and Elizabeth Brashears, d/o R.T. "Turner" Brashears.

v5️⃣2123.   10️⃣5. Silas Lawrence,

v5️⃣2124.   10️⃣6. Sidney Lawrence, b. 31 May 1847, per his testimony in "J.W. Hyden vs. Choctaw Nation." Sidney testified that his grandmother's name was recorded as Isabella Brashear in the G.D. Fisher family bible.

v5️⃣2125.   10️⃣7. Cordelia Lawrence, m. c1861-68, John McCoy, part Choctaw. They separated during the Civil War.

v5️⃣2126.   11️⃣1. Louise McCoy,

From "Interview with Clemmie Davis Sacra," d/o Effie Fisher, b. MS, *Oklahoma Indian-Pioneer Interviews*, v.80, p.6: "My mother died when I was three years old and I went to live with my uncle." (Clemmie was born in 1859.) "I will try to tell you about an old Bible that came over the [Choctaw] "Trail of Tears" with my grandparents from Mississippi. This Bible was fifty years old when it was brought from Mississippi to the Indian Territory with my great-grandmother, Martha (Brashears) Fisher [Clemmie seems to have her ancestral eggs scrambled: her great-grandmother was probably Martha "Patsy" Hayes, not Brashears]. In this old Bible was recorded the births, marriages, and deaths of four generations and it was handed down until it was in the hands of Rebecca Fisher, Osborne Fisher's oldest daughter, who married Ed Bounds. They moved out on a farm near Glassess Creek, Chickasaw Nation. After Rebecca's death, Ed Bounds moved to Sherman, Texas, leaving the old Bible stored with some other books in the barn. Later, the Dawes Commission offered five hundred dollars for this precious book of records. My cousin, Joe Lawrence, went out to the farm to get it for them—too late—the rats had eaten it and destroyed all the records."

LEWIS BRASHEAR

[v5]204. [8]4. **Lewis Brashear**, (half-blood Choctaw; s/o R.T. "Turner" Brashear and "a daughter of Taboca," called "Jane Apuckshunnubbee"), b. c1797 (age 34 in Feb 1832); m.1. in MS, _____, a full-blood Choctaw (mother of 1st 4 ch); m.2. in MS, **Nancy** _____, a mixed-blood Chickasaw, b. c1806 (25 in 1832), (mother of 3 ch). When Lewis died, Nancy's relatives came and took her and the children back to the Chickasaw Nation, according to Harriet (Everidge) Oakes. After about 1832, an "s" is added to the surname.

Lewis was one of the participants in treaty negotiations at Doak's Stand in 1820, and signed the proceedings.

Lewis was a U.S. Mail carrier in 1830, on the route from Vicksburg to New Mexico, a village in Washington Co, MS, where a very distant cousin, Lomax Brasher, was postmaster.

(Frances Brasher Coorpender, a great-granddaughter of Lomax, said that Lewis was b. 1794, the 8th child of Turner Brashear, and that he d. 1832. But that doesn't agree with the documents we have: he served 17 Jan 1837 as a member of the commission to sell the western part of the old Choctaw Nation to the Chickasaw Nation for $530,000.

Lewis Brashears, received lot No. 34 under the provisions of Article 19, Treaty of Dancing Rabbit Creek: the W ½ of SE ¼ of Sec 12, T16, R12E, and E ½ of SW ¼ of Sec 12, T16, R12E. (Federal Records Center, Microfilm 7RA-116, roll 1). That would indicate that he had chosen to accept an "agricultural reserve" for himself in the Old Choctaw Nation in Mississippi.

Still, he was removed to Indian Territory on the "Choctaw Trail of Tears." He and his family (up to 1832) are on a *Register of Choctaw Indians who were moved to Ft. Towson, from Mississippi, 11 Feb 1832*, Vol 2:

22.	Brashiers, Lewis	34, b. c1797, 5'10"
23.	Nancy	25, b. c1806, 5'6"
24.	Jenny	12, b. c1819, 4'6"
25.	Sam	9, b. c1822, 4'
26.	Washington	7, b. c1824, 3'10"
27.	Joseph	1, b. c1830, 2'; died prev. to May 1832

Family of Lewis Brashears and 1st wife, a full blood Choctaw:

v5 2127. 9 1. **Rebecca Brashears**, (¾ Choctaw), m. bef 1832, in MS, **David McCoy**, ½ Choctaw

v5 2128. 9 2. **Jenny Brashears**, (¾ Choctaw), b. c1819 (12 in Feb 1832); m. **Jim Cedar**, a full blood Choctaw, s/o Old Red Cedar

v5 2129. 9 3. **Sampson "Sam" Brashears**, (¾ Choctaw), b. c1822 (9 in Feb 1832)

v5 2130. 9 4. **Washington Brashears**, (¾ Choctaw), b. c1824 (7 in Feb 1832). According to *Who Was Who Among the Southern Indians*, by Don Martini, p.63, Washington Brashears lived in Kiamitia Co, in 1855, with family Visa, Ginny, Richmond, Lewis, and Lizzie. **Visa** ____ was probably his wife.

v5 2131. 10 1. **Ginny Brashears**,

v⁵2132.	¹⁰2. **Richmond Brashears**,
v⁵2133.	¹⁰3. **Lewis Brashears**,
v⁵2134.	¹⁰4. **Lizzie Brashears**,

Family of Lewis Brashears and Nancy_____, part Chickasaw:

v⁵2135.	⁹5. **Joseph Brashears**, b. c1830 (1 in Feb 1832); d. young bef May 1832 in Choctaw Trail of Tears.
v⁵2136.	⁹6. **George Brashears**, d. young
v⁵2137.	⁹7. **Patsy Brashears**, m. in Chickasaw Nation. After her mother died, some of her Chickasaw relatives came and got her. She then married and lived in the Chickasaw Nation.

Lewis *may* have married a third time, a much younger woman named Jincey Homer (or Homma):

Louis Brashears, b. ?, d. bef 1885; m. *Jincey Homer*, b. c1860 (42 in 1902), d/o Edward Homer and unknown, both full-bloods of Kiamitia District. Jincey (Homer) Brashears m.2. Sam Gardner, b. c1832 (70 in 1902), full-blood, d. 8 Jan 1900. Also ward in Sam Gardner's household: Solomon Homer, 10, full blood, s/o Edward and Maggie Homer, apparently at least a half-brother to Jincey. "Homer" is probably supposed to be Homma. Census Card #3477 of 1902 says Louis and Jincey had a son, Joseph. Jincey, 28, and Joseph, 7, are on the 1885 Choctaw census in Atoka Co, I.T., but Louis was apparently dead. He *may* have named this son for the son who died on the Choctaw Trail of Tears. (Louis *may* be the "L.E. Brashears" who was witness for Alfred Brashears in his marriage to Martha Grissom.)

v⁵2137a.　**Joseph Brashears**, b. c1878 (7 in 1885; 21 on 1899 application; age 24 on 1902 rolls, #9908, C.C. 3477), full blood of Blue Co. Census Card #3477 says he is <u>the son of Louis Brashears (dec'd) and Jincey Homer</u>, b. c1860 (45 in 1902).

Whether this is him is undocumented: Joseph H. Brashear, age 28, m. 24 Feb 1904, Della M. Benton, age 15, at Springer, I.T., *Chickasaw Nation Marriage Index, 1895-1907*, Bk H, p.84.

BENJAMIN BRASHEAR and ILLICHIHANA

v⁵205. ⁸5. **Benjamin Brashear**, (s/o R.T. "Turner" Brashear and "a daughter of Taboca," called "Jane Apuckshunnubbee"), b. c1800-01 (age 31 in Feb 1832); m. **Illichihana**, b. c1806-07 (25 in 1832). Benjamin's wife, Illichihana, was a full blood Chickasaw, according to Harriet (Everidge) Oakes.

Benjamin and his family to 1832 are on a *Register of Choctaw Indians who were moved to Ft. Towson, from Mississippi, 11 Feb 1832*, Vol 2:

38. Brashears, Benjamin	31, b. c1801, 6'1"	
39. Illichihana	25, b. c1807, 5'	
40. William	13, b. c1819, 4'	
41. Lila	7, b. c1825, 3'1"	
42. Lou Sukey	3, b. c1829, 3'	
43. Anna	1, b. c1831, 2'	

Family of Benjamin and Illichihana Brashear:

v⁵2138. ⁹1. ***William W. Brashear***, b. 1819 (13 in 1832); removed with family in Choctaw "Trail of Tears" to Indian Territory; lived near Skullyville, LeFlore Co, OK; m.1. *Caroline* _____, m.2. *Mary Jane Collins*,

v⁵2139. ⁹2. **Delila "Lila" Brashears**, b. c1825 (7 in 1832); m. a full-blood Choctaw

v⁵2140. ⁹3. **Lou Sukey Brashears**, b. c1829 (3 in 1832), n.m.

v⁵2141. ⁹4. **Anna Brashears**, b. c1831 (1 in 1832), n.m.

William W. Brashears and Mary Jane Collins

v⁵2138. ⁹1. **William W. Brashears**, (s/o Benjamin Brashears and Illichihana), b. 1819, in Old Choctaw Nation in present-day Mississippi, (13 in 1832) ½ Choctaw (actually, he was ¾ Indian since his father was half-blood Choctaw and his mother was full-blood Chickasaw); removed with father's family in Choctaw "Trail of Tears" to Indian Territory; lived near Skullyville, LeFlore Co, OK. He d. 19 March 1892, age 73, near Panama, Indian Territory, bur Fairview Cem,

Panama, OK. William served as a private, Co. D, 2nd Battalion, Choctaw Mounted Rifles, Confederate States Army. We know his middle initial from descendants of daughter, Letha Ann.

William W. Brashears m.1. **Caroline** _____, ½ Choctaw, of Kiamitia District, and had one child; m.2. **Mary Jane Collins**, ¾ Choctaw, Roll #7357, C.C. 2536, b. July 1839, Choctaw Nation, MS, d. 25 May 1908, age 67 near Panama, Indian Territory; bur Fairview Cem, Panama, OK, d/o Gilbert and Cynthia Collins. Mary Jane's mother, Cynthia, was an enrolled Cherokee, on 1896 Old Settlers Cherokee Roll, #1300; on 1851 Cherokee Roll from Flint Dist, #58.

In 1885, Census of Skullyville, George [sic: William], 60, wife, Mary J., 45, are listed with some of the younger children: Lee, 15 (Letha?); B.F., 13; Mary, 9; and Lucinda, 3.

Family of William W. Brashears and Caroline _____:

v5²142.   ¹⁰1. **George Washington Brashears**, b. c1845 (death cert. 1930 says 85 years old), (listed as 41 in 1902) ½ Choctaw, Roll #4170, C.C. 1491, b. 1858, d. 31 Dec 1930, age 85; m.1. **Mary Homma**, b. c1878 (24 in 1902), d. 11 Oct 1900, d/o Ompsion and Sophia Homma, both full-bloods of Kiamitia District; m.2. **Susan McCoy**, Freedman Roll #1346, C.C. 615 (no ch). Two children by first marriage reported on Choctaw Census Card #1491 of 1902.

v5²143.   ¹¹1. **Betsy Brashears**, b. c1899 (4/12 in census taken 1899), d. 15 Aug 1899, as noted in census of 1902. Choctaw Roll #4171; stricken from Rolls because of death.

v5²144.   ¹¹2. **Edward Brashears**, b. c1900 (2 in 1902) ¾ Choctaw, Roll #4172

Family of William W. Brashears and Mary Jane Collins:

v5²145.   ¹⁰2. ***Tobias Brashears**, ⅝ Choctaw, Census Card #2536, Roll #7358, b. 3 Jan 1861, Choctaw Nation, I.T., d. 8 Nov 1922, bur Lona Cem, near Kinta, OK; m.1. **Mrs. Alice Garland**, (no ch);

m.2. 22 Oct 1899 in Spiro, I.T., **Bessie Dean Howard**,

v⁵2146.   ¹⁰3. **Emma Jane Brashears**, ¾ Choctaw, Roll #7497, b. 11 Oct 1866 (1868 on death cert), Choctaw Nation, I.T., d. 19 Nov 1956, age 88, Panama, OK, bur Oakland Cem, Poteau, OK; m. **John H. Goodnight**, b. 1 Nov 1858, d. 8 Dec 1930, bur Poteau, OK, s/o Luke Goodnight,

v⁵2147.   ¹¹1. Edmond G. Goodnight, ⅜ Choctaw, Roll #4657, b. 31 Oct 1883, d. 22 Jan 1940; m. **Isabel** _____, b. 6 March 1885, d. Sept 1962

v⁵2148.   ¹⁰4. **Letha Ann Brashears**, ¾ Choctaw, Roll #7328, b. 4 July 1867 (1863 says death cert), Choctaw Nation, I.T., d. 12 July 1942, age 79, Hughes Co, OK; m.1. 1880, in Lamar Co, TX, **Dr. John Henry Rowe**, (at least two ch); m.2. 5 Aug 1897, **James R. Mote**, d. 17 Aug 1903, s/o Drury Mote (James R. Mote's application for Choctaw citizenship by marriage was approved 25 July 1903; he died less than a month later, 17 Aug 1903. For more Mote information, c o n t a c t   T o m   M o o n e y <tmooney@mindspring.com>); Letha Ann m.3. 14 Jan 1904, McCurtain, I.T., **Arthur Alcorn**, no children. Letha A. Mote is #7336 on Dawes Rolls.

v⁵2149.   ¹¹1. Mary Ann Rowe, b. 1882, ⅜ Choctaw, Roll #7441; m. John R. Ingram (grandparents of R. Ann (Ingram) Wright <annw@whidbey. com>. Ch: John Sullivan; Claud H.; Annie; and Lille E. Ingram

v⁵2150.   ¹¹2. Charles Henry Rowe, b. 1895, ⅜ Choctaw, Roll #7337

v⁵2151.   ¹⁰5. **Frances "Fannie" Brashears**, ⅝ Choctaw, Census Card #2537, Roll #7362, b. 8 Feb 1869 (says death cert), (23 Feb 1871, says Fitzer write-up in *History of Oklahoma*, p.279)

Choctaw Nation, I.T., d. 9 Dec 1938; m. 6 June 1895, in Kinta, San Bois Co, I.T., **James H. Fitzer**, b. 20 Oct 1873, d. 25 June 1955. Ch, all b. Indian Territory:

v⁵2152. ¹¹1. Pearl B. Fitzer, 5/16 Choctaw, Roll #7363, b. c1897 (age 2 in 1899 Choctaw census)

v⁵2153. ¹¹2. Jewell L.B. Fitzer, 5/16 Choctaw, Roll #7364, b. c1898-99 (age 8 mos in 1899 Choctaw census)

v⁵2154. ¹¹3. Jack Harvey Preston Fitzer, 5/16 Choctaw, Roll #7365, b. Sept 1900 (1 mo old when enrolled, 20 Oct 1900)

v⁵2155. ¹¹4. Ivory Ellen Fitzer, b. 1903

v⁵2156. ¹¹5. Raymond W. "Judge" Fitzer, b. 28 Feb 1904, d. 22 Oct 1992. Obit: R.W. "Judge" Fitzer, 88, passes away October 22, 1992 in a Stigler Hospital. He was born Feb 28, 1904 in Calconda, I.T., to J.H. and Frances (Brashers) Fitzer. Mr. Fitzer was a retired Postmaster. He was the owner of a store in Kinta and also a carpenter. He was an original enrollee in the Choctaw Tribe.

v⁵2157. ¹²1. Sybil Fitzer; m. _____ Brown, living Okmulgee in 1992

v⁵2158. ¹²2. Shirley Fitzer; m. _____ Cumming, living Kinta in 1992

v⁵2159. ¹¹6. Ruby Ellen May Fitzer, b. 1906

v⁵2160. ¹¹7. James Sherman H. Fitzer, b. 6 Oct 1907, Brooken, Haskell Co, OK, d. 29 Jan 1991; m. Annie Pulse, b. ?, d. 27 Nov 1994

v⁵2161. ¹⁰6. **Benjamin Franklin Brashears**, ¼ Choctaw, Roll #7450, b. 21 April 1872, d. 17 May 1919, Panama, OK, bur Fairview Cem. Ben was Marshall of Panama, OK; he was killed accidentally by Frank Massey, when answering a burglary call at Frank Massey's store (see article below). Ben m. 1 Jan 1899, **Myrtle Lipsey**. Three children on Choctaw Census

Card #2564; others from other sources:

v⁵2162.	[11]1. **Mary Estella Brashears**, b. 22 Nov 1900, ⅛ Choctaw, Roll #7451, d. 2 March 1996, Poteau, OK; m. 31 Oct 1922, *Clyde F. Bates*,
v⁵2163.	[11]2. **Johnny Tobias Brashears**, (twin) b. 19 Feb 1902, ⅛ Choctaw, Roll #7452, d. 30 Dec 1902
v⁵2164.	[11]3. **Tola Brashears**, (twin, fem) b. 19 Feb 1902, ⅛ Choctaw, Roll #7453, d. 19 Dec 1920
v⁵2165.	[11]4. **Ira May Brashears**, b. 12 Nov 1903, d. 16 July 1905; Newborn Choctaw #711.
v⁵2166.	[11]5. **Evelyn Brashears**, b. 1906; m. _____ Duke.
v⁵2167.	[12]1. Myrtle Ann Duke, b. 1 Sept 1926, Panama, LeFlore Co, OK; m. 31 July 1945, Robert H. Whitaker. ch: Bobby Duke and Bradley Whitaker
v⁵2168.	[11]6. **Clarence Brashears**, (twin) b. 10 April 1910, d. 20 April 1910
v⁵2169.	[11]7. **Lawrence Brashears** (twin), b. 10 April 1910, d. 20 April 1910
v⁵2170.	[11]8. **Madge Marie Brashears**, b. 11 Dec 1912, d. 5 March 1991; m. 1931, *Clarence W. Kiger*, b. 1 April 1906, d. 20 Oct 1990, age 84, per obituary. Five children, all b. Panama, LeFlore Co, OK.
v⁵2171.	[12]1. Bennie Bob Kiger, b. 1932,
v⁵2172.	[12]2. Ronnie Gene Kiger. b. 1934,
v⁵2173.	[12]3. Nancy Sue Kiger, b. 1936,
v⁵2174.	[12]4. Larry Joe Kiger, b. 1938,
v⁵2175.	[12]5. Davey Jon Kiger, b. 1949,
v⁵2176.	[11]9. **Margaret Brashears**, b. 1919, Panama, OK; m. 6 Oct 1940, *Millard J. Rowley*,
v⁵2177.	[12]1. Max Ben Rowley, b. 27 April 1947, Panama, LeFlore Co, OK; m. Lynn _____. ch: Butch and Christy Rowley

v⁵2178. ¹⁰7. **Mary Madeleine Brashears**, ½ Choctaw, Roll #9527, b. 19 Jan 1877, d. 21 Sept 1967, age 90; m.26 Feb 1896, at Ft Smith, AR, **J. Goldman Ingram,**

v⁵2179. ¹¹1. Lulu M. Ingram, ¼ Choctaw, Roll #9528, b. 12 Aug 1897 (age 2 when enrolled in 1899), d. 12 April 1979; m. R. Floyd Hightower,

v⁵2180. ¹¹2. James Hall Ingram, ¼ Choctaw, Roll #9529, b. c1899 (age 6 mos when enrolled)

v⁵2181. ¹⁰8. **Lucinda Ann Brashears**, ⅝ Choctaw Census card #2636, Roll #7359, b. 1 Oct 1881, d. 2 Dec 1956, Shafter, CA; m. 1900, **William W. Fitzer**, b. 26 June 1873, d. 14 Aug 1956. "Lourinda" Fitzer, 20, and Benjamin F. Fitzer, 1, are in her father, Tobias's household on the final Choctaw Rolls, 1906, but there were several other children.

v⁵2182. ¹¹1. Benjamin F. Fitzer, 5/16 Choctaw, Roll #7360, b. 11 Oct 1901 (6 weeks old when enrolled, 29 Nov 1901)

v⁵2183. ¹¹2. Grace M. Fitzer, b. 8 Aug 1903, d. 19 June 1960; m. Jasper Johnson,

v⁵2184. ¹¹3. Tobias "Tobe" Fitzer, b. 18 Nov 1905, d. 18 Aug 1994, Stigler, OK; m. Annie F. Trollinger, b. 4 Aug 1910, d. 26 July 1975. ch: Juanita (m. Townley); Nioma (m. Cox); Ramona (m. Mitchell); Virginia (m. Spears); Sam; Joe; James; Bill; John; and Mary F. Fitzer (m.1. Melvin Neal; ch: Lavada Jo; Tweela; Kathy; and Anna Neal; m.2. _____ Watts. ch: Jimmy Watts)

v⁵2185. ¹¹4. Starlie Fitzer, b. 1909; m. _____ Smith

v⁵2186. ¹¹5. Olga M. Fitzer, b. 1915; m. _____ Stark

v⁵2187. ¹¹6. Naoma R. Fitzer, b. 1916; m. _____ Brewer

v⁵2188. ¹¹7. Jack Fitzer, b. 1917; m. Viola Lowrimore

v⁵2189. ¹¹8. Josephine "Josie" Fitzer, m. _____ Webb

v⁵2190. ¹¹9. Eva L. Fitzer, b. Jan 1920

CHOCTAW MARSHALL INDUCTED INTO NATIONAL LAW ENFORCEMENT HALL OF FAME

(*Bishinik*, June 1994, p.5) A former town Marshall of Panama, Oklahoma, has been inducted into the National Law Enforcement Hall of Fame in Washington, D.C., as of May 17, 1994. Benjamin Franklin Brashears, a Choctaw, was shot and killed in the line of duty on May 17th, 1919, while answering a burglary call. A newspaper clipping regarding the incident reads:

FATAL ACCIDENT AT PANAMA. Last Monday morning about four o'clock, Frank Massey shot and killed Ben Brashears of Panama. A shot gun was the weapon used. Mr. Brashears was city marshall of the town and had been called to look after a man who was supposed to be a burglar. At the same time, Mr. Massey was called and told that a man was attempting to break into his store. Both men responded and met at the store, and both thought the other was the man they were looking for, and both shot with the result mentioned above. They are both highly respected citizens of the town and the fatal affair is greatly regretted by their friends all over the country. They were good friends and both were in the line of duty as good citizens when the killing occurred.

The National Law Enforcement Hall of Fame Memorial Fund wrote to the current Chief of Police in Panama, to announce they were proud to recognize and honor Brashears. The memorial's purpose is to perpetuate the memory of fallen officers. In conjunction with the recognition of Brashears at the monument of May 17th, the town of Panama was also issued a proclamation by Mayor Jerry Ammons naming May 17, 1994, Benjamin Brashears Day.

On June 12th of the year Brashears died, the Woodmen of the World signed and adopted a Resolution of Respect. Brashears, born April 21, 1872, was 1/4 Choctaw, the son of William and Mary Jane (Collins) Brashears. He married Myrtle Lipsey the first day of January, 1898, and became Panama Town Marshall, November 12, 1912.

Figure 37: Benjamin Franklin Brashears, Choctaw Marshall

Although Brashears always claimed to be one-fourth Choctaw, his brothers and sisters claimed a higher degree of Indian blood, according to his grandson, Max Rowley. "The story is told that the purpose of this was that he had future plans to hold public office and his dealing in business and banking affairs would be affected if he claimed a higher degree of Indian blood heritage," writes Rowley. Rowley added that the Brashears descendants are all very proud of their Indian heritage and especially proud of Benjamin Brashears, who gave his life for the protection of others.

Tobias Brashears and Bessie Dean Howard

ᵛ⁵2145. ¹⁰2. **Tobias Brashears**, (s/o William W. Brashear and Mary Jane Collins), ⅝ Choctaw, Census Card #2536, Roll #7358, b. 3 Jan 1861, Choctaw Nation, I.T., d. 8 Nov 1922, bur Lona Cem, near Kinta, OK; m.1. **Mrs. Alice Garland**, (no ch); m.2. 22 Oct 1899 in Spiro, I.T., **Bessie Dean Howard**, Choctaw Citizen by intermarriage #1528, b. 19 Aug 1880, d. 25 Oct 1957 at Kinta, OK, d/o David Howard and Louise True, non-citizens.

ᵛ⁵2191.　¹¹1. **William Jennings Brashears**, 5/16 Choctaw, Census Card #2536, Roll #7361, b. 27 Jan 1901, at Spiro, LeFlore Co, I.T., d. 9 June 1982, Santa Ana, CA, bur Fairhaven Mem Park, Orange Co, CA; m. 25 July 1920, **Lula King**, b. ?, d. 16 June 1982, Santa Ana, Orange Co, CA, d/o W.P. "Parker" King and Mary Molly,

ᵛ⁵2192.　¹²1. **Irene Brashears**, b. 11 Nov 1921, Kinta, Haskell Co, OK, d. 18 March 1991, Mission Viejo, Orange Co, CA; m. 8 March 1940, **John West**, b. ?, d. 6 Oct 1965; m.2. 7 May 1966, **Adrianus Maaskant**, b. 14 June 1916, in Holland.

ᵛ⁵2193.　¹³1. Patricia Lee West, b. 11 Nov 1941, Bakersfield, CA; m. 25 Aug 1962, Jesse H. Marr Jr,

ᵛ⁵2194.　¹⁴1. John Christopher Marr, b. 1 Sept 1967, Santa Ana, CA (adopted)

ᵛ⁵2195.　¹⁴2. Rebecca Lee Marr, b. 18 Aug 1969,

Santa Ana, CA (adopted)

v⁵2196.
⁴³. David Patrick Marr, b. 3 June 1975, Santa Ana, Orange Co, CA

v⁵2197.
¹²2. **Pearl Lee Brashears**, b. 15 Sept 1928, Kinta, Haskell Co, OK; m. 15 June 1946, **Boyd Porter West**, b. 9 April 1926, Stigler, OK

v⁵2198.
¹³1. Linda Lee West, b. 15 April 1946; m. 19 Aug 1967, Frank Sauso,

v⁵2199.
¹⁴1. Robert Francis Sauso, b. 16 May 1970, San Francisco, CA

v⁵2200.
¹⁴2. Kimberly Deanne Sauso, b. 27 Feb 1975, Bakersfield, Kern Co, CA

v⁵2201.
¹³2. Boyd Michael West, b. 22 March 1947; m. 7 Dec 1974, Sharon Blake,

v⁵2202.
¹¹2. **Buster Brashears**, (Choctaw Newborn Roll #677), b. 8 Jan 1903, Spiro, I.T., d. bef 1994; m. 5 June 1923, at Stigler, OK, **Jimmie Vaught**, b. 26 March 1899, Whitefield, I.T., d. 18 May 1978, Stigler, OK, d/o Jim Vaught and Hattie B. England,

v⁵2203.
¹²1. **Betty Jo Brashears**, b. 20 Dec 1924, Kinta, OK; m. 22 Dec 1942, **J.D. Haggard**,

v⁵2204.
¹³1. James Clark Haggard, b. 20 April 1945, Pryor, OK; m. 17 May 1964, Carole Bergant,

v⁵2205.
¹⁴1. Kelly Jay Haggard, b. 27 Oct 1965, Pittsburg, Crawford Co, KS

v⁵2206.
¹⁴2. Jon Frank Haggard, b. 13 Oct 1966, Pittsburg, KS

v⁵2207.
¹⁴3. Michael Todd Haggard, b. 22 June 1970, Pittsburg, KS, killed in motorcycle accident in KS, 1 Oct 199? (Xerox cut off one number)

v⁵2208.
¹³2. Barbara Jo Haggard, b. 15 June 1946, Muskogee, OK; m. 10 April 1970, William Novero, b. 22 Aug 1948

v⁵2209.
¹⁴1. Andrew Joseph Novero, b. 11 Aug

1975, Tulsa, OK

v⁵2210.   ¹³3. Jerald David Haggard, b. 9 Oct 1960, Pittsburg, Crawford Co, KS, d. 13 March 1982 (accidental electrocution)

v⁵2211.   ¹²2. **Jackie Thomas Brashears**, b. 20 Dec 1928, Kinta, OK; m. 4 June 1953, at Las Vegas, NV, *Yvonne Clepper*, b. 19 March 1933, Strawn, TX, d/o Alfred Clepper and Oza Boggus,

v⁵2212.   ¹³1. **Linda Brashears**, b. 14 March 1956, Henderson, Clark Co, NV; m. 16 Aug 1975, *Wendell Roy Welch*, b. 1 Jan 1956, Johnson City, TN, s/o William Roy Welch, and Thelma Thompson,

v⁵2213.   ¹⁴1. Erick Roy Welch, b. 25 June 1980, Albuquerque, NM

v⁵2214.   ¹⁴2. Danielle Marie Welch, b. 27 Aug 1984, Tacoma, WA

v⁵2215.   ¹⁴3. Jana Rose-Lynn Welch, b. 1 May 1986, Tacoma, WA

v⁵2216.   ¹³2. **Michelle Brashears**, b. 8 Nov 1961, Santa Barbara, CA; m.1. 20 June 1981, Glenn Kevin Nagel, b. 23 Oct 1961

v⁵2217.   ¹⁴1. Andrew Kevin Nagel, b. 27 Feb 1983, Palm Springs, San Bernardino Co, CA

v⁵2218.   ¹⁴2. Kile Philip Nagel, b. 16 Sept 1986, King City, Monterrey Co, CA

v⁵2219.   ¹³3. **John Carl Brashears**, b. 31 Aug 1965, Santa Barbara, CA; m. _____,

v⁵2220.   ¹⁴1. **Tyler Buster Brashears**, b. 1994

v⁵2221.   ¹¹3. **Viola Brashears**, (Choctaw Newborn Roll #678), b. 29 Oct 1904, Spiro, I.T., celebrated her 90th birthday in 1994, which was written up in the Oct 94 issue of *Bishinik*, the official Newsletter of the Choctaw Nation, d. 29 July 1998; m. 11 July 1924, *Henry W. Lowrimore*, b. 19 April 1903, and they lived in Lona Valley until his death on June 6, 1988. He was s/o

Jasper Lowrimore and Mattie S. Mathews,

v⁵2222.   [12]1. Sybil Juanita Lowrimore, b. 10 March 1926, Kinta, OK; m. 21 Feb 1946, George W. Foster, and lives in Norman, OK.

v⁵2223.   [13]1. Johnnie Mae Foster, b. 10 June 1947, Montgomery, AL; m. Earl Keith Parman, b. 28 Dec 1946, Cordell, OK

v⁵2224.   [14]1. James Douglas Parman, b. 20 Jan 1968, Oklahoma City, OK

v⁵2225.   [14]2. Nicole Christina Parman, b. 26 Nov 1972, Oklahoma City, OK

v⁵2226.   [13]2. Naomi Foster, b. 27 Dec 1950, Montgomery, AL; m. Harry Eugene Williams, b. 9 Feb 1938, Mulhall, OK, d. 30 May 1990

v⁵2227.   [14]1. Oteka Lynn Williams, b. 20 Aug 1976, Norman, OK

v⁵2228.   [13]3. Michael Ray Foster, b. 28 Feb 1953, Denver, CO; m. 2 June 1973, Mone Lynn McGhee, b. 10 Oct 1954, Valliant, OK

v⁵2229.   [14]1. Michelle Lynn Foster, b. 10 Sept 1973, Durant, Bryan Co, OK,

v⁵2230.   [12]2. Leo Jay Lowrimore, b. 11 Feb 1929, Kinta, OK; m. 16 July 1948, Naomi Louise Bullard, b. 2 Aug 1929, d/o Granville A. Bullard and Tretty Thompson. Leo lives in La Quinta, CA

v⁵2231.   [13]1. Billy Leo Lowrimore, b. 16 March 1950, McAlester, OK, d. 16 March 1950

v⁵2232.   [13]2. Toni Lynn Lowrimore, b. 6 Aug 1952, Muskogee, OK; m. 9 Jan 1980, Josef Fritz, b. 23 Oct 1958, Bad St. Leonard, Karten, Austria

v⁵2233.   [13]3. Patti Jouise Lowrimore, b. 24 July 1954, Muskogee, OK

v⁵2234.   [11]4. infant son, b. 8 Sept 1906, Lona Community, near Quinton, Haskell Co, I.T., d. 10 Oct 1906

v⁵2235.   [11]5. infant son, b. 29 July 1908, Quinton, OK, d. 17 Oct 1908 v⁵2236.   ¹¹6. infant daughter, b. 22 March 1913, Quinton, OK, d. 12 April 1913

v⁵2237.   ¹¹7. **Bertie Brashears**, b. 10 Aug 1915; m. 18 June 1933, *Thomas Carl Mitchell*, b. 15 Nov 1909, Arnett, OK, d. 29 May 1977, Quinton, OK, s/o Thomas Calhoun Mitchell and Louticia Emmaline Stewart,

v⁵2238.   ¹²1. Vestal Juanita Mitchell, b. 5 April 1934, Kinta, OK, d. 4 Jan 1941

v⁵2239.   ¹²2. Ramona June Mitchell, b. 8 March 1936, Kinta, OK; m. 18 April 1959, Raymond LeRoy Etris, b. 20 Nov 1933, Decatur, AR, s/o LeRoy Austin Etris and Eby Philpott,

v⁵2240.   ¹³1. Karen Jean Etris, b. 21 Jan 1960, Oklahoma City, OK; m. 21 Feb 1986, Ricc Bo Lightfoot, b. 8 May 1964, El Paso, TX

v⁵2241.   ¹⁴1. Levi Lightfoot, b. 25 Nov 1987, Oklahoma City, OK

v⁵2242.   ¹³2. Darrell Lee Etris, b. 29 Oct 1961, USAF Hosp, Fukuoka, Japan,

v⁵2243.   ¹³3. David Kenneth Etris, b. 21 Sept 1963, Oklahoma City, OK; m. 24 June 1991, Debbie (Oberg) Robertson, b. 9 July 1970, Midwest City, OK

v⁵2244.   ¹⁴1. Kristen Kay Robertson, b. 25 March 1988, Ok city, OK

v⁵2245.   ¹⁴2. Amanda Diane Etris, b. 7 March 1993, Ok city, OK

Enoch Brashears and Luclihoma

v⁵2246.   ⁹x. **Enoch Brashears** **may** (no documents) be a son of Lewis or Benjamin Brashears, born after 1832, when the brothers were removed to Fort Towson, Indian Territory. Enoch Brashears is on the 1855 Choctaw Census/payment rolls in Kiamitia Co, with a family consisting of *Luclihoma* (or Licki-hona), Mary, and Alfred Brashears, according to *Who Was Who Among the Southern Indians*, by Don Martini, p.59. Luclihoma *may* have been called "Louisa" in later years; Amanda A. (or R.) Brashears, a daughter of Enoch and Louisa, was enrolled as a Choctaw. Enoch and family are not on the 1885 Census; Amanda is listed alone, age 11, in Kiamitia Co.

Family of Enoch Brashears and Luclihoma:

^{v5}2247. ^{10}1. **Mary Brashears**, b. c1850, n.f.i.

^{v5}2248. ^{10}2. **Alfred (or Albert) Brashears**, b. 1852, Skullyville, Leflore Co, I.T., d. c1891; m. 5 March 1885, at Savanna, I.T., ***Martha Helen Grissom***, b. 1861, d. 10 Dec 1929, Coalgate, OK. His name is Albert on the marriage certificate, Alfred on the Indian papers; his brother, George, said his name was Alfred.

(from *Who was Who Among the Southern Indians, A Genealogical Notebook*, p.58) — "Albert Brashear, Choctaw, married Martha A. Grissom (born 1860), a white, at Savanna, I.T. He died at his home six miles from Savanna in 1890 or 1891. He was a brother to George Brashears, born in 1865 and a resident of Hartshorne. Application for enrollment, Choctaw Nation, Case 5862."

Marriage certificate dated 5 March 1885 in Savanna, I.T., of Albert Brashears to a Martha Grissom, witnessed by L.E. Brashears (unidentified). Martha (Grissom) Brashears (enrollment #1234) and son, Ira Brashears, received land. Ira Brashears is listed as Indian on WPA census. Contact: Corky <lrharmon@pacbell.net>.

Albert Brashears, 33, is on the 1885 Choctaw Census, Atoka Co, I.T.

^{v5}2249. ^{11}1. **Ira Brashears**, (s/o Albert Brashears and Martha Grissom), b. 27 Jan 1896, Sandridge, OK, d. 25 June 1953, Los

Angeles, CA; m.1. 17 July 1916, in Coalgate, OK, **Viola "Belle" Maybelle Purdy**, b. 6 April 1881, Dallas Co, AR, d. 5 March 1939, Coalgate, OK (mother of the child); m.2. 1939, in Atoka, OK, **Nan (Carlisle) Faulconer**; m.3. 7 Aug 1941, Yuma, AZ, **Pearl Kelso**

v⁵2250.   ¹²1. **Dorothy Marie Brashears**, b. 28 Nov 1921, McAlester, OK, d. 16 March 1991, Salinas, CA; m.1. 12 Nov 1940, in Reno, NV, **Virgil Kenneth Harmon**, b. 1 Aug 1918, Sallisaw, OK, d. 27 Jan 1967, Fresno, CA; m.2. 28 April 1967, in Reno, NV, **Raymond Earl Hicks**, b. 1 May 1928, Sayre, OK,

v⁵2251.   ¹³1. Larry Ronald Harmon, b. 1942, CA; m. in California, Cora Elizabeth "Corky" Myers

v⁵2252.   ¹³2. Deanna Carole Harmon, b. 1950, CA; m.1. in Nevada, Keith O'Mara; m.2. in California, Gordon Arthur Spence; m.3. in Hawaii, Richard Belding

v⁵2253.   ¹⁰3. **George W. Brashears**, b. 1865 (40 at time of marriage in Sept 1904); m. 4 Sep 1904, in Ada, Chickasaw Nation, Bk H, p.321), **Blanche Wilburn**, b. c1884 (20 at time of marriage), Census Card #2319, Choctaw Roll #6704, [do not confuse him with the George William Brashears on Choctaw Census Card #3172, Choctaw Roll #9171].

(from *Who was Who Among the Southern Indians, A Genealogical Notebook*, p.58)— "George Brashears was possibly the George who voted at Sugar Creek in 1883. He was a candidate for sheriff in Gaines Co in 1896, voted at Hartshorne in Gaines Co, in 1897 and was a resident there in 1903. His brother,

Albert, died in 1890 or 1891. Applications for enrollment, Choctaw Nation, Case 5862."

George and Blanche had a son before the rolls were closed (they may have had more later),

v⁵2254.   ¹¹1. **Lovel Sumner Brashears**, 7/16 Choctaw, b. 29 Aug 1905, and enrolled as a minor Choctaw on Card #518, d. Dec 6, 1908, "s/o G.W. & Blanche", bur Hickory Cem, Murray Co, OK.

v⁵2255.   ¹⁰4. **Jane Brashears** (d/o Enoch Brashears), b. c1875 (if about 15 when marrying), d. May 1893; m. 14 Nov 1890, in Paris, Lamar Co, TX (TX Marr Recs online) (first wife of) *John William Wood*, b. 1866, son of William Wood and Nannie _____. They had one child:

v⁵2256.   ¹¹1. William Edgar Wood, b. 29 Aug 1891. (11 in 1902; Choctaw Roll #4458)

v⁵2257.   ¹⁰5. **Amanda A. (or R.) Brashears** (½ Choctaw, Roll #4457; d/o Enoch Brashears), b. c1875 (10 on 1885 census). Libby Nations <vnations@gte. net>, writes: "Amanda Brashears was already on the Choctaw roll when she married John W. Wood. And he applied and was listed on the roll because his wife Amanda was. So I would think that Amanda's parents would be on the roll also. Maybe what I need to do is find Enoch on the roll and see if he has an application." [Enoch is NOT on the rolls; was apparently dead before 1885.] Amanda, age 10, is alone on the 1885 Census, Kiamitia Co, I.T. Amanda married 6 July 1894 in Paris, Lamar Co, TX (per data in Choctaw application) (2nd wife of) *John William Wood*, (widower of her sister), b. 1866 (per data in Choctaw application), son of William Wood and Nannie _____. Four children were enrolled on Choctaw Census Card #1578. The oldest, Edgar, is s/o Jane Brashears

(Amanda's sister) and John William Wood.

^{v5}2258. ^{11}1. George Henry Wood, b. c1895 (7 in 1902; Choctaw Roll #4459)

^{v5}2259. ^{11}2. Thomas L. " Tommy" Wood, b. 6 Jan 1897 (6 in 1902; Choctaw Roll #4460), (Dept Interior affidavit says 3 Jan 1897); d. August 1984, Dallas, TX (SS death records)

^{v5}2260. ^{11}3. Robert Dewey Wood, b. 5 Dec 1899, Hugo, OK (SS death records) (3 in 1902; Choctaw Roll #4461); d. Oct 1971, Dallas, TX (SS death records); m. Eunice Rozanna Harris; b. 2 July 1899, Paris, TX (SS death records); d. August 1994, Dallas , TX (SS death records).

Amanda Brashears and John W. Wood *may* have had several other children, after the Choctaw Rolls were closed. Some researchers accredit them with children named: Arthur; Florence; Ina; Ivey; Naomi; Rosie; and Ruth Wood. (No documents.)

George William Brashears

^{v5}2261. ^{10}1. **George William (or Washington) Brashears**, b. c1866 (35 in 1902), ½ Choctaw, Roll #9171; Census Card #3172 says he was s/o <u>John and Julia Brashears</u>, both dec'd, of Gaines Co, I.T. George's father has not been identified, but George *may* be a son of John Brashears (^{v5}1152), b. 23 Feb 1829, s/o Zadock Brashears Jr (^{v5}840) and Anne DeCastro (no documents).

One circumstance that tends to support this ancestry is the testimony of Napoleon Bonaparte Brashears before the Dawes Commission. He claimed (fraudulently) to be a descendant of Zadock Brashear Jr, through a son, Joseph, who never existed. Napoleon said: "I know the Brashears people in the Choctaw Nation. Some of them recognize me as their relative. George and John Brashears both recognize me as a relative. George lives near Ada. John lives in Chickasaw Nation." Napoleon seems to be implying that George and John Brashears were descendants of Zadock Brashears Jr.

George William Brashears had an uncle, William Stanton (see below). In order for this relationship to work, his mother, Julia, would have to have been Julia Stanton. An unidentified Allen Stanton, who had an Indian wife, was a close associate of Alexander Brashears in the Suk-en-Atcha settlement in the 1830s. Julia Stanton, b. c1830s, *may* be a d/o Allen Stanton.

George William Brashears was a resident of Roff in 1907, according to *Who Was Who Among the Southern Indians*, by Don Martini, p.59, who may be confusing him with George W. Brashears, s/o Enoch Brashears and Luclihoma (Case 5862).

George Washington Brashears, 38, is ½ Choctaw, Roll #9171, with children Julia F., and Ivey on Census Card #3066. George William Brashears, his parents (John and Julia Brashears), and two of his children, Julia and Ivey, are listed on Census Card 3172.

George William Brashears n.m. **Martha Ann Stepp**, b. 1856 and had one daughter; m.1. **Lizzie _____**, a non-citizen and had one daughter; m.2. 29 Dec 1893, at Fort Smith, AR, **Lida B. Bridges**, non-citizen, d/o L.S. Bridges. They lived at Hartshorne, OK, close to McAlester.

v5 2262. [11]1. **George Ann "Annie" Brashears**, b. c1876, McAlester, I.T., d/o Martha Ann Stepp and George William Brashears; m. **Charlie Evans**, (see below)

v5 2263. [11]2. **Julia F. Brashears**, b. c1885 (17 in 1902), ¼ Choctaw, Roll #9172, d/o the first wife, Lizzie _____.

v5 2264. [11]3. **Ivy Brashears**, b. c1902 ("Ivey"; 2/12 in 1902) ¼ Choctaw, Roll #9173, d/o Lida B. Bridges.

Martha Ann Stepp, b. 6 Jan 1856, MS, d/o Ivey and Frances Stepp; m. 25 April 1869 (at age 13) at South McAlester, OK, Alexander Burns, a citizen of the Choctaw Nation. She lived with him approximately seven months; then her parents came and took her home. Alexander Burns later sent the Sheriff, asked for a divorce, and remarried.

Frances Stepp, apparently a widow by that time, took in boarders in South McAlester, among them George William Brashears. During the time he was boarding with the Stepps, Martha became pregnant with his child, George Ann Brashears. Martha claimed she could not marry George William Brashears, because she was still married to Alexander Burns. George stayed in the area and always claimed George Ann as his daughter.

On 20 July 1879, Martha Ann (Stepp) Burns m. William Stanton, uncle of George William Brashears, *possibly* a son of Allen Stanton of Suk-en-atcha and his Indian wife. Bill Stanton (b. c1835-40) was 15-20 years older than Martha and had several children by a previous marriage. Martha and Bill lived together about seven years, until he was killed. She then married a white man by the name of E. Edwards.

George Ann (Brashears) is listed on the census as Annie Stanton, though she used the surname Brashears on her school work. At the time of her first marriage, her mother told her she should go by the name of Burns, since that was her mother's name at the time of her birth; so on her wedding license, she is listed as George Ann Burns. She m. 2 March 1895, Charlie Evans. Her mother did not want her to marry Charlie; so there was a riff between them.

Annie Evans applied to the Dawes Commission for recognition as a Choctaw by blood. (Case 5892) She lived in Troy, IL, in 1907.

TOBIAS BESHIRS

[v5]**208.** [8]8. **Tobias Beshirs**, (s/o R.T. "Turner" Brashear and Oca-ye-mitta), b. c1830, d. early 1880s; m. *Susan* _____, a Chickasaw (their descendants are on the Chickasaw Rolls, not the Choctaw). Tobias was described by Harriet (Everidge) Oakes as "still sucking at the breast" when they were removed to Indian Territory in Feb, 1832. Oca-ye-mitta, widow of R.T. "Turner" Brashear, and her three small sons, Jefferson, William, and Tobias, moved with the Everidges. Illiapotubbe, Eva (Brashears) Everidge, "took care of them," along with her own small children.

Tobias Brashears lived in Kiamitia District in 1855 and was an election judge in 1866. After Tobias died, Susan m.2. G.W. Thompson, a Choctaw, and had one son, Greenwood Thompson, age 17 in 1897, who is a half-brother of Aaron Cub Beshirs on his Chickasaw Census Card (un-numbered).

[v5]2265.   [9]1. **Aaron Cub Beshirs Sr**, b. 21 April 1861, Mississippi, d. 15 Dec 1925, Yuba, Bryan Co, OK, bur Yarnaby, OK, s/o Tobias and Susan Beshirs; m. Dec 1887, *Laura Belle Thompson*, b. 20 Feb 1868, Savannah, I.T., d. 15 June 1938, Yuba, OK, bur Yarnaby cem, Yarnaby, OK, d/o Tom Thompson, a white man, and Marriah Sheco, a Chickasaw (d/o Charlie Sheco and Amelia Wolfe). Aaron, Laura, and seven of their children are on Chickasaw enrollment cards dated 12 Dec 1902 and 5 May 1903; they are listed as living in Panola Co, I.T.

[v5]2266.   [10]1. **William Edward Beshirs**, b. 25 Oct 1888, Yuba, I.T., d. 22 Jan 1952; m. *Elizabeth Maguire*,

[v5]2267.   [10]2. *****James Alexander Beshirs Sr**, b. 2 Jan 1890, Yuba, I.T.,

[v5]2268.   [10]3. **baby Beshirs**, b. 20 Oct 1892, d. 20 Oct 1892, "s/o A.C. & L.B." Yarnaby Cem.

[v5]2269.   [10]4. **Joel Everige Beshirs**, b. 14 Jan 1894, Yuba, I.T.; m. *Willie Mae Purvis*,

v⁵2270.   ¹⁰5. **Ella Beshirs**, (twin) b. 11 Jan 1895, Yuba, I.T., d. 22 Sept 1895.

v⁵2271.   ¹⁰6. **Elbert Beshirs**, (twin) b. 11 Jan 1895, Yuba, I.T., d. 24 April 1899, "s/o A.C. & L.B." bur Yarnaby Cem.

v⁵2272.   ¹⁰7. **Aaron Cub Beshirs, Jr**, b. 10 Oct 1896, d. 28 May 1929.

v⁵2273.   ¹⁰8. **Ada Belle Beshirs**, b. 12 Nov 1898; m. *Cecil Turnbull*,

v⁵2274.   ¹⁰9. **Frances Mary Beshirs**, b. 27 Jan 1901; m. *Joe Ashmore*,

v⁵2275.   ¹⁰10. **Lee Ora Beshirs**, b. 1 July 1904, Bryan Co, I.T.; m. *George Brady*,

The Sheco Connection:

x1. Charlie Sheco, b. 1800, d. 1883, Yarnaby, Bryan Co, I.T.; m. Amelia Wolfe, b. c1813, d. c1848, Yarnaby, Bryan Co, OK;

    y1. Marriah Sheco, d. 1851; m. Tom Thompson,

        z1. Laura (Belle or Louise) Thompson, b. 20 Feb 1868, Savannah, I.T., d. 15 June 1938, Yuba, OK, bur Yarnaby cem, Yarnaby, OK; m. **Aaron Cub Beshirs Sr**.

    y2. Sarah Sheco, b. Yarnaby, Bryan Co, I.T.; m. Charlie Camden.

    y3. Ellen Sheco, b. Yarnaby, Bryan Co, I.T.; m. _____ Porter.

    y4. "Bud" Sheco, b. Yarnaby, Bryan Co, I.T.

    y5. Fannie Sheco, m. Ed Potts.

    y6. Mary Sheco, b. 20 Feb 1848 in Bryan Co, I.T., d. 12 March 1907; m. 1866, John James Cravens,

    y7. Rob H. Sheco, b. 24 Nov 1872 in Yarnaby, Bryan Co, I.T., d. 1 Feb 1899.

    y8. Tom Sheco, b. 11 March 1883 in Yarnaby, Bryan Co, I.T., d. in Yarnaby, Bryan Co, Okla. He married Betty Powell.

v⁵2269. ¹⁰2. **James Alexander Beshirs, Sr**, b. 2 Jan 1890, Yuba, I.T., Indian Territory, d. 15 Sept 1966, or 1955, s/o Aaron Cub Beshirs Sr and Laura Belle Thompson; m. *Isadora Lyda Gannon*, b. 19 Sept 1894, Indian Territory, d. 5 Sept 1966, Durant, OK.

v⁵2276. ¹¹1. **Unis (Eunice?) Beshirs**, (twin) died as child.
v⁵2277. ¹¹2. **Anderson Beshirs**, (twin), died as child ?.
v⁵2278. ¹¹3. **Maudie May "Soodie" Beshirs**,
v⁵2279. ¹¹4. **John Beshirs**, b. (twin), d. 1994.
v⁵2280. ¹¹5. **Leora Beshirs**, b. (twin), d. ?? Murdered?.
v⁵2281. ¹¹6. **A.J. "Joe" Beshirs**,
v⁵2282. ¹¹7. **O.C. Beshirs**, b. ? male or female?
v⁵2283. ¹¹8. **Wanda Oleata Beshirs**, d. 1992.
v⁵2284. ¹¹9. **James Alexander Beshirs, Jr**, b. 1915.
v⁵2285. ¹¹10. ***Ruel Emmanuel "Buster" Beshirs**, b. 7 July 1917, m. *Nettie Freeman*,
v⁵2286. ¹¹11. **Andrew Beshirs**, b. 9 March 1920, Yuba, OK, killed 25 April 1967, in a pool hall in Lorenzo, Texas; m. 3 Aug 1940, *Louise Dunham*, b. 14 March 1921, Powerly, Texas, d. 19 April 1995, Bakersfield, California.
v⁵2287. ¹²1. **Steve Beshirs**, b. 20 Nov 1943, Santa Paula, California.

v⁵2287. ¹¹10. **Ruel Emmanuel "Buster" Beshirs**, b. 7 July 1917, d. 28 Sept 1994, s/o James Alexander Beshirs, Sr and Isadora Lyda Gannon; m. *Nettie Freeman*,

v⁵2288. ¹²1. ***J.M. Beshirs**,
v⁵2289. ¹²2. ***Norma Jean Beshirs**,
v⁵2290. ¹²3. ***R.A. Beshirs**,
v⁵2291. ¹²4. ***Nelda Beshirs**,
v⁵2292. ¹²5. ***Billy Randell Beshirs**,
v⁵2293. ¹²6. ***Bobby Granville Beshirs**,
v⁵2294. ¹²7. ***Carolyn Ann Beshirs**,
v⁵2295. ¹²8. ***Joe Dee Beshirs**,
v⁵2296. ¹²9. ***Ruel Emmanuel Beshirs Jr**,
v⁵2297. ¹²10. **Jimmy Waydell Beshirs**, b. 2 Dec 1952.
v⁵2298. ¹²11. ***Michael Lynn Beshirs**,

^{v5}2299. ¹²12. ***Paul Andrew Beshirs**,

^{v5}2290. ¹²1. **J.M. Beshirs**, b. 7 Oct 1935, s/o Ruel Emmanuel "Buster" Beshirs and Nettie Freeman; m. *Alice Starks*,

^{v5}2300. ¹³1. **Jerell Wayne Beshirs**, m. *Jo Ann* _____,
^{v5}2301. ¹⁴1. **Jerell Wayne Beshirs Jr**,
^{v5}2302. ¹⁴2. **Angie Beshirs**,
^{v5}2303. ¹⁴3. **Amanda Beshirs**,
^{v5}2304. ¹³2. **Samuel David Beshirs**, m. _____,
^{v5}2305. ¹⁴1. **Samuel David Beshirs Jr**,
^{v5}2306. ¹⁴2. **Jeremy Beshirs**,
^{v5}2307. ¹⁴3. **Elizabeth Beshirs**,
^{v5}2308. ¹³3. **Billy Ray Beshirs**, m. *Tressa* _____,
^{v5}2309. ¹⁴1. **Lona Beshirs**,
^{v5}2310. ¹⁴2. **Billy Ray Beshirs Jr**,
^{v5}2311. ¹⁴3. **Stephanie Beshirs**,
^{v5}2312. ¹³4. **Glen Edwin Beshirs**, m.1. *Susan* _____, (2 ch); m.2. *Cathy* _____,
^{v5}2313. ¹⁴1. **Tuesday Beshirs**,
^{v5}2314. ¹⁴2. **Christopher Beshirs**,

^{v5}2291. ¹²2. **Norma Jean Beshirs**, b. 5 Sept 1938, d/o Ruel Emmanuel "Buster" Beshirs and Nettie Freeman; m.1. *A.D. Purvis*, (2 ch); m.2. *Orville Trammel*,

^{v5}2315. ¹³1. Nettie Ilene Purvis; m. Dewayne Stephens.
^{v5}2316. ¹⁴1. Cloid Dewayne Stephens
^{v5}2317. ¹⁴2. Sondra Melissa Stephens
^{v5}2318. ¹³2. Robert Emanuel Purvis; m. Laura _____, (1 ch); m.2. Paula _____, (1 ch)
^{v5}2319. ¹⁴1. Amber Deann Purvis
^{v5}2320. ¹⁴1. Amelia Jo Purvis

^{v5}2292. ¹²3. **R.A. Beshirs**, b. 22 Dec 1939, s/o Ruel Emmanuel "Buster" Beshirs and Nettie Freeman; m. *Katherine Farmer*,

^{v5}2321. ¹³1. **Katherine Jenice Beshirs**, m. _____,
^{v5}2322. ¹⁴1. Michael _____, died, car accident.

v⁵2323.   ¹⁴2. Addell _____,
v⁵2324.   ¹⁴3. Mirandy _____,
v⁵2325.   ¹³2. **Lawana Beshirs**, m. _____,
v⁵2326.   ¹⁴1. Robert _____,
v⁵2327.   ¹⁴2. Alvin _____,
v⁵2328.   ¹⁴3. Samuel R A _____,
v⁵2329.   ¹³3. **Terry Jo Beshirs**, m. _____,
v⁵2330.   ¹⁴1. child one
v⁵2331.   ¹⁴2. child two
v⁵2332.   ¹³4. **R.A. Beshirs Jr**,

v⁵2293. ¹²4. **Nelda Beshirs**, b. 31 Jan 1941, d/o Ruel Emmanuel "Buster" Beshirs and Nettie Freeman; m. ***Wayne Farmer***,

v⁵2333.   ¹³1. Loretta Merril Farmer; m.1. _____ Dunnagan; m.2. _____ Davis; m.3. _____ Wakefield,
v⁵2334.   ¹⁴1. David Wayne Dunnagan
v⁵2335.   ¹⁴1. Katrina Renee Davis
v⁵2336.   ¹³2. Retha Renita Farmer; m. Darrel Dickerson.
v⁵2337.   ¹⁴1. Misty Dawn Dickerson
v⁵2338.   ¹⁴2. Jennifer Lynn Dickerson
v⁵2339.   ¹³3. Norma Lee Farmer; m. Mike Freeman.
v⁵2340.   ¹⁴1. Eric Lee Freeman
v⁵2341.   ¹⁴2. Tawania Diane Freeman
v⁵2342.   ¹³4. Sebrina Marie Farmer; m. Danny Osmer,
v⁵2343.   ¹⁴1. Daniel Osmer
v⁵2344.   ¹⁴2. Stephen Osmer
v⁵2345.   ¹⁴3. Devon Osmer

v⁵2294. ¹²5. **Billy Randell Beshirs**, b. 2 Sept 1942, s/o Ruel Emmanuel "Buster" Beshirs and Nettie Freeman; m.1. ***Lynn*** _____, (3 ch); m.2. ***Bonnie*** _____, (2 ch).

v⁵2346.   ¹³1. **Virginia Beshirs**, was christened, has 2 boys, one girl; m. _____,
v⁵2347.   ¹⁴1. boy 1
v⁵2348.   ¹⁴2. boy 2
v⁵2349.   ¹⁴3. girl 1
v⁵2350.   ¹³2. **Debra Beshirs**, was christened, has, one son;

m. _____,
^{v5}2351.   ¹⁴1. son
^{v5}2352.   ¹³3. **Billy Randell Beshirs Jr**, was christened, has 2 girls; m. _____,
^{v5}2353.   ¹⁴1. girl 1 **Beshirs**,
^{v5}2354.   ¹⁴2. girl 2 **Beshirs**,
^{v5}2355.   ¹³4. **Shannon Beshirs**, b. c1984.

^{v5}2295. ¹²6. **Bobby Granville Beshirs**, b. 2 Sept 1942, s/o Ruel Emmanuel "Buster" Beshirs and Nettie Freeman; m. *Dorthy* _____, now divorced.
^{v5}2356.   ¹³1. **Barbara Sue Beshirs**, was christened, has 2 children; m.
^{v5}2357.   ¹⁴1. child 1
^{v5}2358.   ¹⁴2. child 2
^{v5}2359.   ¹³2. **Ramona Kay Beshirs**, was christened, has 2 children; m.
^{v5}2360.   ¹⁴1. child 1
^{v5}2361.   ¹⁴2. child 2

^{v5}2296. ¹²7. **Carolyn Ann Beshirs**, b. 30 June 1945, d/o Ruel Emmanuel "Buster" Beshirs and Nettie Freeman; m. *Thomas Barnett*, d. Oct 1994, of cancer.
^{v5}2362.   ¹³1. Tammy Ann Barnett; m. Gary Karr,
^{v5}2363.   ¹⁴1. Brandon Scott Karr
^{v5}2364.   ¹⁴2. Angel Beth Karr
^{v5}2365.   ¹⁴3. Calvin Tyrell Karr
^{v5}2366.   ¹³2. Ricky Leon Barnett; m.1. Dawn _____, d. 31 Oct 1989, car train wreck (2 ch); m.2. Angel _____, (1 ch).
^{v5}2367.   ¹⁴1. Micha Barnett, died, 31 Oct 1989, car train wreck.
^{v5}2368.   ¹⁴2. Chamilla Barnett, died, 31 Oct 1989, car train wreck.
^{v5}2369.   ¹⁴3. Tyler Barnett,
^{v5}2370.   ¹³3. Danny Lee Barnett; m. Oct 1994, _____,
^{v5}2371.   ¹³4. Bradly Ray Barnett; m. Dawn _____,
^{v5}2372.   ¹⁴1. Kustin Barnett,

^{v5}2373.   ¹⁴2. ? girl Barnett,
^{v5}2374.   ¹³5. Robert Carl Barnett; m. Tandy _____.
^{v5}2375.   ¹⁴1. Collin Barnett,

^{v5}2297. ¹²8. **Joe Dee Beshirs**, b. 13 April 1948, s/o Ruel Emmanuel "Buster" Beshirs and Nettie Freeman; m. *Margaret Davis*, (5 ch); m.2. *Carolyn Dailey*, (3 ch)
^{v5}2376.   ¹³1. **Pamala Tyann Beshirs**, was christened, has two boys; m. _____,
^{v5}2377.   ¹⁴1. boy 1
^{v5}2378.   ¹⁴2. boy 2
^{v5}2379.   ¹³2. **Rodney Joe Beshirs**, was christened, one boy, one girl; m. _____,
^{v5}2380.   ¹⁴1. girl **Beshirs**,
^{v5}2381.   ¹⁴2. boy **Beshirs**,
^{v5}2382.   ¹³3. **Lisa Ilene Beshirs**, was christened, 2 girls, one boy; m. _____,
^{v5}2383.   ¹⁴1. girl 1
^{v5}2384.   ¹⁴2. girl 2
^{v5}2385.   ¹⁴3. boy
^{v5}2386.   ¹³4. **Joe Dee Beshirs Jr**,
^{v5}2387.   ¹³5. **Sammy Jean Beshirs**, was christened, 2 children; m. _____,
^{v5}2388.   ¹⁴1. child 1 **Beshirs**,
^{v5}2389.   ¹⁴2. child 2 **Beshirs**,
^{v5}2390.   ¹³6. **Christopher Dee Beshirs**,
^{v5}2391.   ¹³7. **Joel Daniel Beshirs**,
^{v5}2392.   ¹³8. **Deritha Jane Beshirs**,

^{v5}2298. ¹²9. **Ruel Emmanuel Beshirs, Jr**, b. 30 Nov 1950, s/o Ruel Emmanuel "Buster" Beshirs and Nettie Freeman; m. *Nancy Farmer*,
^{v5}2393.   ¹³1. **Laura Ann Beshirs**, m. *James Smith*, Now divorced.
^{v5}2394.   ¹⁴1. Tiffany Smith,
^{v5}2395.   ¹³2. **Joseph Aaron Beshirs**, m. *Shawna* _____,
^{v5}2396.   ¹⁴1. **Brittany Beshirs**,
^{v5}2397.   ¹³3. **Kytonia Delene Beshirs**,

ᵛ⁵2300. ¹²11. **Michael Lynn Beshirs**, b. 4 Aug 1954, s/o Ruel Emmanuel "Buster" Beshirs and Nettie Freeman; m. *Debra Dunnagan*,

ᵛ⁵2398.   ¹³1. **Michael Jo Beshirs**,
ᵛ⁵2399.   ¹³2. **Nirita Beshirs**,
ᵛ⁵2400.   ¹³3. **Tashia Lynn Beshirs**,

ᵛ⁵2301. ¹²12. **Paul Andrew Beshirs**, b. 19 Aug 1958, Paris, TX, s/o Ruel Emmanuel "Buster" Beshirs and Nettie Freeman; m. 20 Aug 1975, Garretts Bluff, Tx, *Deborah Louise Dawes*, b. 25 Sept 1957, Paris, TX.

ᵛ⁵2401.   ¹³1. **Brock Andrew Beshirs**, b. 21 Dec 1976, Hugo, OK.
ᵛ⁵2402.   ¹³2. **Candace Lucinda Beshirs**, b. 30 June 1980, Talinina OK Indian Hospital.

17. THE DAWES DISASTER AND AMERICAN CHICANERY

First, a little background:

In 1893, Congress passed an act establishing "The Commission to the Five Civilized Tribes," usually called simply "The Dawes Commission," after its sponsor, Senator Edward Dawes of Connecticut. The purpose of this commission was "removal of the Indians" east of the Mississippi River and termination of their separate-nation status, by taking lands belonging to the five civilized tribes— Cherokee, Chickasaw, Choctaw, Creek, and Seminole, including their lands in Indian Territory— and granting allotments to individuals in fee simple in Indian Territory and to compensate individuals for surrender of their lands. Each Indian head of a household was to get an allotment in Oklahoma, and (guess what!) all the land left over was to be opened to white settlement. No matter that the sun hadn't quit shining, nor had the rivers stopped flowing, no matter that everyone could still see as far as the eye could see, no matter that Indians had always held land in common and did not understand individual or fee simple ownership ... it was all an elaborate and fairly malevolent effort to dispossess the Indians of their lands. And no one, least of all Senator Ed Dawes, doubted that it would work.

The assigning of allotments required a fairly complete census of the five civilized tribes, and the tribal leaders set about at once to compile such a census. Then they discovered problems. The most conservative members of the tribes, those who had been cheated most and most severely by the U.S. Government, hesitated to enroll themselves in the census, fearing that it was another white trick to gyp them out of whatever they had. And they were right, of course. Many of them hid in the hills when the census was being taken. These tended to be the full bloods and mixed bloods who could not speak much, if any, English. The tribes extended the enrollment period and commissioned special enumerators to go among the people and convince hold-outs that it was in their best interest to be on the lists. In 1896, Chief Greenwood McCurtain of the Choctaws wrote the Secretary of War that he thought his tribal census was fairly complete ... that there were perhaps 50 people who deserved to be on the rolls who weren't, and perhaps 50 who were on the rolls unjustly. For a tribal roll of about 14,000, he thought that was pretty good.

But Congress is capable of grinding the dots on the "i" exceeding small. And they wanted the rolls to be "perfect." Against the frantic protest of the tribes, Congress re-opened the enrollment process in 1896 and provided that <u>everyone</u> who applied was to be given a hearing in a U.S. District Court.

Suddenly, there were literally thousands of applicants.

Suddenly, every person who could convince him/herself that he/she had a dark-complected ancestor, who shared a name with a known Choctaw (or other tribal) family, were "Indians" and entitled to grab a piece of the land and get a pocket-full of the annuities.

The District Court hearings were conducted by pro-tem judges, who were the lawyers who were advocating the claims of these sudden Indians. Often, a lawyer who one day argued for a client, was the next day the temporary judge, passing judgment on claims represented by the other lawyers. Tribal enrollment and fraud became synonymous.

Even Congress can't ignore such flagrant abuse forever. Finally, on 17 Dec 1902, at the request of the Choctaw and Chickasaw Councils, Congress set aside all the District Court decisions since 1898 and created a three-judge panel of the U.S. Court of Claims to hear appeals. From 1904 to 1906, this "Choctaw and Chickasaw Citizenship Court" heard 256 appeals, of which it approved 161. About 200 legitimate Indians were added to the census rolls in those 161 cases, but nearly 2,000 fraudulent Indians were turned down in the 105 cases that were denied.

The three judges of the U.S. Court of Claims were (as far as I can tell) scrupulously honest, meticulously thorough, and they made a record of almost everything that was said in the hearings. These "Records of the Commissioner to the Five Civilized Tribes: The Choctaw and Chickasaw Citizenship Court" have been microfilmed and are available at the Federal Records Centers as Microfilm Series 7RA27. The census that resulted is generally known as "The Dawes Rolls," which are published in book form and are detailed on Microfilm series 1186, "Enrollment Cards of the Five Civilized Tribes." The "Applications for Enrollment" were also kept (and filmed), whether the claim was successful or not. These three records comprise hundreds of individual microfilms and contain a great deal of information: spouses, siblings, children, wards, sometimes parents and/or grandchildren, sometimes relatives who are applying separately on their own.

These hearings and rolls were intended to establish citizenship, not "blood." Citizens were the ones getting allotments and annuities, not Indians. To be enrolled as a citizen, one had to have some degree of Indian blood and have lived in an Indian community and have been recognized as a member of that community, or be "intermarried" with such a citizen. Being on one of the earlier rolls or having an ancestor on an earlier roll was taken as evidence of habitual residence with the tribe. Even full-bloods who had left the tribe and were living as "white men" (and yes, there were a number of them; the Sizemore family is perhaps the largest and most noted) were not eligible for enrollment as citizens for purposes of the allotment of lands and the distribution of annuities under the Dawes Act.

As one might imagine, this opportunity brought out about every variety of American chicanery known— and probably invented a few.

THE BURTON GRAB

Susanna (Brashears) Stewart-Graham (^{v5}836), d/o Zadock Brashears and Susannah Vaughn, registered on 13 Aug 1831 (eleven days before the cut-off date) for benefits under Article 14 of the Treaty of Dancing Rabbit Creek. Susanna had one child over ten at home (her son, John Brashears Stewart). Her married daughter, Annie V. (Stewart) Llewellyn, registered at the same time. Though Susanna was quarter-blood at most and Annie was one-eighth, they are both listed as "half-breeds." Apparently any quantum of Indian blood made you a half-breed to Col. William Ward, the Choctaw Agent at the time. Both the Choctaw Council and the Dawes Commission took this registration as impeccable evidence of Susanna's Choctaw ancestry.

Later testimony strongly suggests that Susanna was living in Feliciana Parish, Louisiana, at the time, and thus had no land and improvements in the old Choctaw Nation to "remain on" and become a citizen of the United States. That is, she was committing a certain amount of fraud: she was born in Feliciana Parish, LA; married there, had her children there, was listed in the census there; married a second and third time there; she had never lived in Choctaw territory. As a non-resident, she was not eligible for benefits under the Treaty of 1830. She and Annie traveled up to St. Stephens specifically for the purpose to getting their chompers into the Choctaw pie.

She apparently had a farm near Rankin, Holmes Co, MS, where she lived at the time of the 1831 census of Choctaws. Her claim to this land was ignored and the land sold to a white man. Later, she was treated as one of those Choctaws whose claim had been sold out from under them by the U.S. Government in one of its "mistakes."

"That's the way she drawed land," testified her granddaughter, Susan S. Burton, in 1901. When asked where Susanna's allotment was located, Susan Burton was uncertain: "I think she drawed it in LeFlore County or Carroll County [Mississippi]; she lived in Carroll a long time; she drawed and three of her children."

I doubt that <u>three</u> of Susanna's children were recipients of treaty benefits, but the idea that one was left out was the basis of Susan Burton's claims to land and citizenship some seventy years later. The family seems to have fabricated a story that some sort of family squabble before the treaty had caused Hardy S. and Mary (Stewart) Crump, Susan Burton's parents, to remove from Mississippi to Louisiana, and that they could not afford to travel back to the Choctaw Nation to claim benefits under the treaty of 1830.

<u>Family of Susan Stewart Crump and Henry David Burton:</u>

[10]1. Susan Stewart Crump, (d/o Mary Brashears Stewart and Hardy S. Crump), b. 6 July 1828 (73 in 1901), Feliciana Parish, LA, d. 4 March 1921, Duncan, OK; m. 10 Dec 1851, Henry David Burton, b. 25 Oct 1826, Jackson, MS, d. 17 Sept 1892, Hazlehurst, MS

[v5]2431.   [11]1. John Ezra Burton, b. 30 Sept 1852, MS, admitted as Choctaw Citizen by Choctaw Council, 1883, d. 20 Feb 1899, Indian Territory; m. 27 Jan 1875, Virginia Prestridge, b. 6 Oct 1855.

[v5]2432.   [11]2. Fannie Ester Burton, b. 26 Sept 1854; m. 3 Nov 1892, Steven F. Wiltshire, no ch.

[v5]2433.   [11]3. Laura Kate Burton, b. 14 March 1858 (48 in 1906); m. 30 Dec 1880, Frank Marion McPhail, ch: Frank M., b. 1881; Myra, b. 1883; Fannie, b. 1885; Grace, b. 1887; Gates, b. 1889; Preston, b. 1891; Virgil, b. 1896, and Homer McPhail, b. 1898.

[v5]2434.   [11]4. Mary Emily Burton, b. 31 Oct 1859, d. 22 April 1937, Durant, OK; m. 7 Aug 1877, William Hill Dees, b. 17 Feb 1850, Copiah Co, MS, d. 18 Feb 1918, Ft. Worth, TX

[v5]2435.   [12]1. Henry Hill Dees, b. 1 July 1879, d. 1956; He was a Policeman in Ft Worth. (ch: Thomas and Herbert Dees)

[v5]2436.   [12]2. Mary Estelle Dees, b. 10 July 1881, Copiah Co, MS, d. 11 Aug 1962; m. 10 Jan 1900,

William Carleton "Carry" Wood, b. 22 Aug 1879, Hazlehurst, MS, d. 3 Nov 1958, both bur Tishomingo, OK. (4 ch:

v⁵2437.   ¹³1. Mary Jane Wood, b. & d. 10 June 1901, Hazelhurst, MS

v⁵2438.   ¹³2. Mattie Hazel Wood, b. 4 July 1902, d. 1 May 1904, Hazlehurst, MS

v⁵2439.   ¹³3. Sammy Dees Wood. b. 18 July 1904, Hazlehurst, MS, d. 14 Oct 1974; m. 15 April 1925, Beulah May Berger, b. 26 June 1906, Midland twp, I.T., d. 2 July 1995. (great-grandparents of Clarissa, who sent data)

v⁵2440.   ¹³4. Henry Hugh Wood, b. 25 Oct 1908; m.1. Ruth Coon, (1 ch: Patsy Ruth Wood); m.2. Minnie Golden (1 ch: Mary Elizabeth Wood)

v⁵2441.   ¹²3. Walter Dees, was a painter and decorator; lived in Los Angeles

v⁵2442.   ¹²4. George Dees, Tulsa Railroad man; died of cancer

v⁵2443.   ¹²5. Edgar Dees, lived in Durant, Oklahoma

v⁵2444.   ¹²6. Oscar Eugene Dees, died in late 1920's of appendicitis; buried in California

v⁵2445.   ¹²7. Fannie Esther Dees, b. 21 June 1897, d. 9 Oct 1973, Tucson, AZ; m. Jack Orin Weaver

v⁵2446.   ¹²8. Katie Belle Dees, b. 29 June 1899

v⁵2447.   ¹²9. Willie Wirt Dees, Spent about 25 years in prison in Texas and McAlester, Oklahoma (Maximum security prison is in McAlester) Shot guard in one penitentiary and someone cut his throat in Ada. Last living in Ft. Worth.

v⁵2448.   ¹²x. Other possible children: Austin Dees, Tommie Dees,

v⁵2449.   ¹¹5. Henry David Burton Jr, b. 6 Sept 1861 (39 in 1901); m. Lucy J. _____, ch: Austin G., b. 1890; Susan O., b. 1892; Florence A., b. 1894;

and Jewel A. Burton, b. 1896

v5 2450. [11]6. Hardy Crump Burton, b. 13 Nov 1863, killed on a bridge in Cleveland, OH, 1898; no ch

v5 2451. [11]7. Susan Cornelia Burton, b. 2 Sept 1865 (34 in 1901); m. _____ Marshall, ch: Valentine and John Henry Marshall.

v5 2452. [11]8. Margaret Lillie Burton, b. 30 June 1868 (38 in 1906); m. Alec Fountain, no ch.

v5 2453. [11]9. George Wyche Burton, (fem), b. 21 April 1871 (26 in 1906); m. Frank Morrison, Ch: Emma Z., b. 1896; Anna, b. 1898; Henry Burton, b. March 1901; Frank Wert, b. 1902; and Fannie Hazel Morrison, b. 1905.

On 13 Sept 1901, Susan S. (Crump) Burton, age 73, testified before a Dawes Commission hearing at Meridian, Mississippi, that she was a resident of Hazlehurst, Copiah Co, MS, and had lived there since the age of 5. She was born 6 July 1828, in Feliciana Parish, LA, "five miles from Jackson." Her mother, Mary (Stewart) Crump, had "never lived in Mississippi" before Susan was born, and the family moved to Copiah County when she was five years old.

In 1892, and again in 1893, Susan S. (Crump) Burton, d/o Mary Brashears (Stewart) Crump and gd/o Susanna (Brashears) Stewart-Graham, applied to the Choctaw Council at Tuskahoma, Indian Territory, for recognition as a Choctaw Citizen by blood. Her cousin, Joseph R. Plummer Jr, and her son, John E. Burton, had been recognized by the Choctaw Council in 1883 and registered as Choctaw citizens by blood; so she was assured her application would be a shoo-in. But nothing happened. The Council failed to take up the matter. And after 1893— the Dawes Act had passed Congress— "the Chief told me they had changed the laws, that anyone who wasn't living there couldn't draw land, but that if I would come and live there and locate my land, my petition would go through. It didn't go through." Her application was neither approved nor denied.

On 13 Sept 1901, Susan S. Burton applied to the Dawes

Commission in Meridian, Mississippi, for recognition as a Mississippi Choctaw who had been denied her benefits under Article 14 of the treaty of 1830. A part of the Act of Congress of 27 June 1898 provided that "said Commission shall have the authority to determine the identity of Choctaw Indians claiming rights in the Choctaw lands under article fourteen of the treaty between the United States and the Choctaw Nation, concluded September 27th, eighteen hundred and thirty, and to that end may administer oaths, examine witnesses, and perform all other acts necessary thereto, and make report to the Secretary of the Interior."

From questioning of Susan S. Burton by the Dawes Commission, 13 Sept 1901, at Meridian, MS: "Did she [Mary (Stewart) Crump, Susan's mother] signify her intention to the United States Indian Agent of the Choctaws here in Mississippi to remain and become a citizen of the States under this article? Answer: She never did. Q: Why didn't she? A: It was like I told you. Pa had bought a place in Mississippi, and he didn't have the money to go. Q: Now, wait a minute! To go where? Answer my question: did your mother, at the time this treaty was made— according to your statements, she had a family of her own and was a grown woman; the fourteenth article provides that each head of a family, that is, each man or woman who was married and had children of their own, should signify to the United States agent their intention, within six months after the ratification of the treaty, their desire to remain and become citizens of the States and take land under that article of the treaty. Did your mother do that? A: She didn't. Q: Why didn't she? A: She couldn't do it. Q: Why couldn't she? A: Didn't do it. Q: Why didn't she? A: I don't know; she told me she wasn't able to go. Q: Go where? A: Wherever the treaty was. Q: Yes; why didn't she go? A: It was so she couldn't. Q: She never made any application then? A: No sir, she didn't. I never heard of it; she herself told me she never did; she always wished she had."

In addition to Susan S. Burton, (M.C.R. 3547, i.e, Mississippi Choctaw Rejected,[claim] #3547), her son, Henry D. Burton, et al. (M.C.R. 1556), and her daughter, Susan

Cornelia Marshall, et al. (M.C.R. 3181) applied. So did Bettie Robinson, et al. (M.C.R. 338) and Jim Pittman, et al. (M.C.R. 379), claiming descent from Susanna (Brashears) Stewart-Graham through a son, Galant Graham. These five cases were consolidated in 1901.

Jim Pittman and Bettie Robinson's claims were based on their being children of Mattie Graham and Samuel Pittman, Mattie Graham being a daughter of Galant Graham, who was said to be a son of Susanna (Brashears) Graham. Robinson and Pittman failed to appear at the hearing held at Muskogee, I.T., 19 Dec 1901. Joseph R. Plummer Jr, b. 1833, s/o Annie V. (Stewart) Llewellyn-Plummer, testified that his mother had died young and he had been raised by his grandmother Graham from his infancy to her death, 5 May 1850. He identified Susanna (Brashears) Stewart-Graham's four children by her first marriage to John Benjamin Stewart, but emphatically denied that she had any children by her last marriage to David Graham. The attorney for the Burtons commented: "these parties that claim through Galant Graham, if they claim through this particular Susanna Graham who was his [Plummer's] grandmother, their claim is not well founded." Essentially, the Commission threw out the Robinson and Pittman claims as being fraudulent. They had a lot of practice at that; thousands of the Choctaw Citizenship claims were pure fraud.

Summary statement read into the record by the attorney: "[The records show] that Susanna Graham was a half breed Choctaw woman; now his mother, the mother of the applicant [Henry David Burton], was a daughter of Susanna Graham, but the record does not show the mother of this applicant, but it does show the applicant's mother's sister, another daughter of Susanna Graham, that is Anne V. Llewellyn; and then she had a brother by the name of John B. Stewart who died a good many years ago. ... at the time of the treaty of 1830 when the squabble came up about the treaty, that family became dissatisfied and removed off down into Louisiana or the southern portion of the then Mississippi country and made no application whatever as far as we can find out as Mississippi Choctaws, and after the matter was settled, why they came back to Mississippi and consequently his mother's name does not appear on the record that shows directly the status of those parties, the descendants of Susanna Graham."

It's obvious to me that Henry David Burton, s/o Susan S. Burton, moved to Indian Territory, purely and simply to make himself eligible for an allotment under the Dawes Act.

Dawes Commission Hearing at Atoka, I.T., 28 March 1901:

Examination of Henry D. Burton, age 39, by the Commission

Q: What is your post office address?
A: Durant, Indian Territory.
Q: How long have you lived at Durant?
A: Since the first of February.
Q: Where did you live before that?
A: In Dallas County, Texas.
Q: How long have you lived in Texas?
A: ... since '82.
Q: Where were you born?
A: Copiah Co, Mississippi.
Q: How long did you live in Mississippi?
A: ... till I was twenty one years old.
Q: Where did you remove to from Mississippi?
A: to Dallas Co, TX.
Q: And have lived there until you removed to Durant?
A: Yes, well I have been backwards and forwards around through the country to other places, but that has been my home.

"Can you speak the Choctaw language?" asked the Dawes Commissioner of Susan S. (Crump) Burton, on 13 Sept 1901, at Meridian, MS.
A: No sir.
Q: Did your mother?
A: No. I don't know that grandma could either."

The Commissioner then made a notation in the record: "The applicant is apparently white, and has none of the appearances or characteristics of a Choctaw Indian; she is unable to speak the Choctaw language, nor has she any knowledge of the same. She claims her rights as a Mississippi Choctaw as a descendant of Susan Graham. It does appear from the records in possession of the Commission that a woman by that name did receive benefits under the 14th article of the treaty of 1830. At the time of the making and the ratification of the treaty of 1830, it appears that both this applicant and her mother, through whom she claims her Choctaw blood, were residents of the State of Louisiana, and that her mother, Mary B. Crump, never complied or attempted to comply with the provisions of the 14th article of the treaty of 1830."

Her petition was denied, though it was later changed to "Identified" status.

In 1903, Susan S. (Crump) Burton tried again, and this time her other children filed for recognition: George W. Morrison (fem), Laura K. "Ella" McPhail, Lillie Margaret Fountain, Mary E. Dees, and Fannie E. Wiltshire. Most of them testified in a Dawes hearing at Muskogee, 6 July 1906, Susan's 78th birthday. How old are you? asked the Commissioner.

A: I am 78 today.

Q: What is your post office address?

A: Durant, Indian Territory.

Q: Are you the identical Susan S. Burton who made application to the Commission to the Five Civilized Tribes at Meridian, Mississippi, September 13, 1901, for identification as a Mississippi Choctaw?

A: Yes.

Q: Received and selected an allotment as a duly identified Mississippi Choctaw?

A: Yes sir.

If we take that testimony at face value, Susan got land in Mississippi. But I've never seen any document on it. For this testimony, she was in Indian Territory to help her children get theirs. That's the theme that runs through all their application and testimony: we've come to get land, to "draw" land. When asked about her daughter, George Wyche Morrison, Susan said George was living in Durant, had lived there since November two years ago, had lived before that in McComb City, Mississippi, had moved to become eligible for an allotment. When Susan's son, John Ezra Burton, had filed his application, he didn't even know which tribe they "belonged" to, and Susan had to tell him.

Laura McPhail testified that she lived in Beaumont, TX, had lived there more or less continuously since leaving Hazlehurst, MS. Her mother, Susan Burton, had passed through Beaumont, on the way to Indian Territory "to see about this land." "I understood that she tried to get the land." "Well, she come through Beaumont and said she was coming to the Territory to my sister's and brother's, and they was going to try again for the land."

Lillie Fountain admitted that she "moved to Durant the 15th day of November, 1904, for the purpose of getting my claim to property and make my application here at Durant," but she was not living in Durant at the time of the testimony; she was living at Humble, TX. When asked about allotments and claims, she said, "We spoke of that, that my brother John E. Burton had his claim, that is he had land. We supposed he had it and settled on it. And she [Susan Burton] thought we would all get our land here through her application." "We have talked often about getting us a home, and when we would meet. We thought if Mother received her land, we would get ours, too."

The lawyer for the Choctaw and Chickasaw Nations asked Lillie: "When did you authorize her [Susan Burton] to apply for you?

A: When she came through going— I think about 13 years ago when she made application, it was understood that she applied for all her children. ...

Q: When was the first time you authorized her to apply for you?

A: When she came through Sour Lake in August, 1903, on her way to Durant to make application.

Q: That was the first time?

A: Yes, next time.

Q: Mrs. Fountain—is that your name?— Don't you know that 13 years ago the Dawes Commission was not hearing applications of any kind?

A: I don't know what Commission it was.

Q: I asked you, if you don't know of your own knowledge, that the Dawes Commission did not receive applications of any character 13 years ago?

A: I don't know.

Q: why did you say that your mother appeared 13 years ago and applied to the Dawes Commission for your identification?

A: Did I say that I authorized her to apply to the Dawes Commission?

Q: Yes.

A: If I did, I said that she made application about 13 years ago, and I don't know whether it was to the Dawes Commission or not, or what Commission it was."

Questions by counsel for the Nations make it clear that none of the Burtons had any idea at all of citizenship, or that they were applying for citizenship before the Choctaw Council; they wanted land. "I understood that she [Susan Burton] tried to get the land," said Laura McPhail. "That was a separate and distinct matter," snapped the lawyer. "That has nothing to do with applying to the Dawes Commission for identification as a Mississippi Choctaw."

THE J.W. HYDEN HOAX

From 1895 through 1904, James W. Hyden and several of his siblings and their children tried to get enrolled as Choctaw citizens by blood, claiming that they were descended from Elizabeth Brashears, d/o R.T. "Turner" Brashears and "a daughter of Taboca." At first, their application was approved, but in the long run, their attempt all proved a hoax.

The Hyden scenario went like this:

Whit W. Hyden had moved from Falls Co, TX, to Ardmore,

Ind.Terr., about 1892 and contacted Judge Joel W. Everidge Sr to see if Hyden's grandmother, Elizabeth (Brashears) Hyden, was the same as the Elizabeth Brashear who was a sister of Judge Joel's mother, Eva (Brashear) Everidge, d/o R.T. "Turner" Brashear and "a daughter of Taboca," called Jane Apuckshunnubbee. They concluded on the basis of names and hearsay that the two Elizabeth Brashears were one and the same. On the basis of Judge Everidge's testimony (he had been Chief Justice of the Choctaw Supreme Court for about 30 years, so his testimony was considered with great weight), the Choctaw Council enrolled Whit W. Hyden and his son, Frank S. Hyden, as Choctaw Citizens by blood, on 31 Oct 1895.

Immediately, J.W. Hyden, Whit's brother, and their other siblings applied for enrollment, and the Choctaw Council temporarily admitted them on 1 Nov 1896, except those members who were not residents of Indian Territory. Their application of 17 Aug 1896 included:

J.W. Hyden and Mrs. Mollie Hyden, his wife
> George Hyden, 14, their son
> Cleveland Hyden, 12, their son
> Maude Hyden, 8, their daughter
> Mollie Hyden, 5, their daughter

Mrs. Sallie Jackson (sister of J.W. Hyden) and her husband, A.M. Jackson
> Mrs. Nancy Pruitt, d/o Mrs. Sallie Jackson, and Henry Pruitt, her husband, and their children: John Henry, age 8, Evan A., age 6, and Eula Irene, age 4
> Sam Jackson, 22, s/o Mrs. Sallie Jackson
> Maude Jackson Smith, 19, wife of Cecil Smith
> Oscar Jackson, 17
> Willie Jackson, 15
> Albert Jackson, 13
> Bessie Jackson, 10

D.M. Hyden (brother of J.W. Hyden) and his wife, Dicey Hyden
> Sallie Hyden, 14 their daughter
> Pearl Hyden, 12, their daughter [m. _____ Wilcox]

Sam Hyden, 10, their son
Garnett Hyden, 6, their son
Mrs. Nancy J. Hood (sis/o J.W. Hyden)
Edward Hood, 20, her son
Willie Mapes, 8, her grandson
Alberta Evans Connelly (d/o Virginia Hyden, dec'd sis/o J.W. Hyden) and James Connelly, her husband
William Wesley Connelly, their son
Eva Margaret Hyden, d/o Frank S. & Georgia Hyden
Martha Hyden, wife of Whit W. Hyden
Georgia Hyden, wife of Frank S. Hyden
Nancy D. Hyden, mother, grandmother, and great-grandmother of the above named parties.

On 23 June 1897, Mrs. Nancy D. Hyden and Mrs. Nancy Hood were reported as residents of the Chickasaw Nation, I.T., and were entitled to enrollment, as were Cecil Smith, Henry Pruitt, and A.M. Jackson, who were recommended as "intermarried citizens."

But the tribe was not satisfied with certain irregularities. On 21 Jan 1898, the Choctaw Nation filed for a new trial. The case was heard at Ardmore, I.T., on 9 March 1903 (case #141), where the Hydens' applications were approved, and they were enrolled. If you read the record only this far, you will conclude that the Hyden claim is legitimate. Our past family sheets have been based on the data so far. But it all proves to be false.

In 1902, when, at the request of the Choctaw and Chickasaw Nations, all cases heard since 1898 were set aside by Act of Congress, the Hydens and others like them were forced to appeal if they wanted to be enrolled. A panel of three judges of the U.S. Court of Claims was appointed to hear the appeals. At the June Term, 1904, The Choctaw Nation requested the appeals court to open the Hyden case in Lee Co, VA, in order to hear testimony there of Henry T. Ferguson and other descendants of James and Nancy Brashears. The case was then heard by the Choctaw and Chickasaw Citizenship Court (CCCC) at Tishomingo, I.T., in 1904 (CCCC case #48T).

The transcript of the case is hundreds of pages long (it took me 17 hours to read it on microfilm at the Federal Records Center in Fort Worth), and it includes testimony by just about everyone the court could find, including 33 pages by Harriet (Everidge) Oakes, d/o Eva (Brashear) Everidge. In addition, various depositions taken earlier were admitted to consideration. The court was trying to be absolutely thorough and absolutely honest.

A <u>deposition of Nancy D. Hyden</u>, taken 25 Feb 1899, was admitted. She swore that she was 82 years old, the widow of Samuel Hyden, who died Sept 1880. She was formerly Nancy Lockheart, and she and Sam were married on 25 Dec 1842. Whit W. Hyden, she swore, was a son of Sam and herself. Sam's parents, said Nancy, were John and Elizabeth Hyden, and Elizabeth was formerly Elizabeth Brashears, daughter of Turner Brashears and Nancy Vaughn of Pontotoc Co, Mississippi, who were Choctaws. She had first known Elizabeth (Brashears) Hyden in Lee Co, VA, about 1825 and lived near them until about 1845. Some of Elizabeth's siblings were John Brashears, called "Lightfoot Jack," Martin Brashears, and Dicey Brashears [Mrs. Henry T. Ferguson Sr]. Elizabeth's hair was very dark and very coarse, and her skin very dark, testified Nancy, and "the Brashears were known as Indians... passed as Indians, were known as Indians." However, "the people I knew during the time I knew the Brashears and Elizabeth Hyden are all dead or moved out of the country." The statement was sworn to before J.B. Thompson, Notary, but ample testimony proves that Nancy was twisting the truth to make a simple, no, an elaborate lie.

In a deposition taken in Falls Co, TX, 14 Aug 1896, Nancy testified that her and Sam's children were:

1. Nancy J. Hyden, b. 17 Sept 1843, now Mrs. Nancy Hood
2. Whit W. Hyden, b. 7 July 1845
3. Virginia Hyden, b. 25 Oct 1847; m. _____ Evans
4. Sarah L. "Sallie" Hyden, b. 31 July 1851; m. A.M. Jackson

5. James W. Hyden, b. 11 Aug 1852
6. David M. Hyden, b. 12 March 1856

The underline deposition of Harriet (Everidge) Oakes, d/o Eva
(Brashear) Everidge, was taken by H.S. Foote, Judge of
CCCC, on 10 and 11 June 1904, at the home of Judge S.F.
Oakes (?her son). She swore that she was 79 on 10 Dec 1903
(b. 10 Dec 1824), that she was a granddaughter of Turner
Brashear, a white man. Her grandmother, she said, was a
full-blood Choctaw. The children of Turner Brashears
included Lewis Brashears, who m. twice, once in MS, once in
I.T., to full-bloods both times; Benjamin Brashears, who m.
a full Chickasaw; Lucy Brashears, who m.1. a [?William]
Patton and m.2. Capt. James S. Standley; Eve Brashears (her
mother), who m. Thomas Everidge; and Elizabeth Brashears,
who m. Joseph Fisher. After her grandmother died, Turner
m.2. a full-blood whose name Harriet did not recall [the
estate papers establish it as Oca-ye-mitta], and they had
three little boys, Jefferson, William, and Tobias Brashears,
"all younger than I was. Their mother was incapable of taking
care of them and my mother [Eva] took care of them and
carried them with us" to I.T. "Their mother came too. One of
the boys married a Turnbull."

Harriet had an excellent memory and could recite the
names of the children of all these children of Turner Brashear
and "a daughter of Taboca," called "Jane Apuckshunnubbee"
(see family groups for details). When questioned about her
information, she replied, somewhat testily: "I do not know
dates, when they married, dates or months, but then I know
the people."

She was about 8 years old at the time of the Removal. She
could remember her grandfather, R.T. "Turner" Brashear: "a
short man, hair had been dark, but was gray" when Harriet
was a child. He lived in a double log house, with a hall
between and side rooms, "at a place we called Checopa, near
Rankin." 12 miles up from the Pearl River. "We had to cross
Big Black [River] to get to Rankin." Turner had brothers

named Eden and Tobias. Turner died in his own house at Checopa.

Her grandfather Turner had once bought a colored man, William Glover, and said he had belonged to Zadock Brashears in Alabama. He also had two old slaves, "too old for hard service, just kept house for my grandfather," one named Lewis and "one old nigger woman, Teena." The Everidges brought these slaves with them to I.T., as well as an old black man named Joe Standley, b. 1828.

Harriet remembered the Removal itself. There were "five or six hundred Indians that came, and cholera struck us at Vicksburg, and many Indians were left on the banks of the Mississippi." [Two of Vaughn Brashear's five children apparently died in this "Choctaw Trail of Tears."] The Indians were taken by boat from Vicksburg to the mouth of the White River, then were marched on foot, first to Little Rock, then to Kiamichi, "landed at Kiamichi River."

Her father, Thomas Everidge, came with them to I.T., then returned to Mississippi in 1833 to settle the estate of Turner Brashears, of which he was the executor. Harriet had no doubt in her mind: the Elizabeth Brashears who was daughter of R.T. "Turner" Brashears had married Joseph Fisher; she knew and had played with her Fisher cousins ("they moved to I.T. at the same time as we did. They married and lived at Cosoma.") and she knew their children and some of their grandchildren.

Testimony by John R. Lawrence and Sidney Lawrence, sons of Mary (Fisher) Campbell-Lawrence, who was daughter of Elizabeth Brashears and Joseph Fisher, corroborated her testimony and the family groups.

The other witnesses repeatedly confused three or four Elizabeth Brashears:
1. Elizabeth Brashears (^{v5}203), d/o R.T. "Turner" Brashear and "a daughter of Taboca," of Yazoo Co, MS; she married Joseph Fisher;
2. Elizabeth Brashears (^{v2}881), d/o James Brashears and Nancy ?Bolling, of Lee Co, VA; she married John C. "Jack"

Hyden Sr; and sometimes

3. Elizabeth Brashears (^{v5}239), d/o Jesse Brashears and Elizabeth Prather, of Pensacola, FL; she married William Taylor of Feliciana Parish, LA;

4. Elizabeth Brashears (^{v5}833), d/o Zadock Brashears and Susannah Vaughn, of Suk-en-atcha Creek, Sumter Co, AL; she married William Buckholtz.

Testimony of Richard Brashears, b. 1821, ex-slave of Vaughn Brashears. He said the children of Turner Brashears were Lewis, Ben, Miss Evy, Lizzie, and Kaziah (I wonder if Lucy's middle name was Keziah). Lizzie, he said, married John Hyden, but he proved to be mistaken. More than once, his testimony seemed to be "for hire."

"Old Man Turner," he said, had a wife, a full-blood, and 3 boys, and [he died, but] she came when we did (in 1832, during the Choctaw Removal). Richard does not seem to realize that the Turner, father of Lewis, etc, and "Old Man Turner" are the same person. In another case, he named the three sons of Old Man Turner as Jefferson, William, and Tobias.

Turner Brashears, [II] s/o Zadock, he said "died here at Tuskahoma."

Turner Brashears, [IV] s/o Vaughn, was grown [I think this word is a mistake for "born"] "two years after we got here" and died in Skullyville.

Turner, s/o Vaughn, had children: one m. Joes Moore, one m. John Wise [Wyers], one m. Albert Folsom. "That young one (Turner Brashears, V) living near Wilburton, that boy makes the fourth Turner Brashears" that Richard knew about.

Richard remembered the Removal: "My old master was in debt to Allen Glover (at Honey Island) and he had to steal us away in the night." They met Ben and Lewis at Vicksburg, where the Indians were assembled on the bank of the Mississippi. The Indians were taken by steamboat from Vicksburg to the mouth of the Arkansas, then by wagons to a place nine miles east of old Fort Towson in the Choctaw Nation.

Beginning on 30 Aug 1904, testimony in the Hyden case was taken at Jonesville, Lee Co, VA, from a wide variety of witnesses, the descendants of James Brashears and Nancy ?Bowling. See Vol 2 for details and documentation on this branch of the family.

Testimony of Mrs. Malinda Hall, age 84, b. 21 Oct 1820 on Wallin's Creek and raised there. She had known John and Elizabeth (Brashears) Hyden until about 1832 ("John Hyden lived on the main big road on Wallin's Creek"). Elizabeth Brashears's mother was Nancy Brashears, called "Grannie Brashears." Elizabeth (Brashears) Hyden's children were Jack, Sam, Wis, and "I knowed the girls, one was Jennie." Sam Hyden m.1. [Eliza] Carter. "Sam Hyden family lived at Swercum Flat, 2-3 miles from Wallin's Creek." "He left here with another woman. I don't know whether they were married or not. Left here with a Lockheart woman, Nancy Lockheart." [Other testimony establishes that Sam abandoned his first wife and six children.]

Elizabeth (Brashears) Hyden had a brother, Martin ("he had fits, that's why I remember him"), and a brother, John, who lived with Grannie Brashears ("wasn't more than a mile from where Daddy lived to where Nancy Brashears lived away up on the mountain"). A sister, Dicey (Brashears) Ferguson, was Mrs. Hall's mother.

Testimony of John R. Hyden, age 68, b. 23 March 1837, Lee Co, VA, s/o James Hyden and Katie Ritter, gs/o Billy Hyden and Nancy Brashears [a d/o "Grannie Nancy Brashears"]. He understood that his grandmother and Elizabeth (Brashears) Hyden were sisters, because his uncle John Hyden and his father had said so. "John and Wilse Hyden," sons of John and Elizabeth (Brashears) Hyden, "always stopped at my father James Hyden's place on Wallin's Creek when they went to court. Spent the night. Uncle John, when he lost his wife, came to live with James a year or two, then moved to MO, that was Sam Hyden's father."

John R. Hyden had been in the Confederate Army during

the Civil War. He was captured and sent to Chicago where he was guarded by a Regiment of Indians. "Tall, red-complected, straight— wasn't much good looking."

The judge questioned: "You considered it a kind of disgrace to be related to the Indians? not much of an honor?"

"Didn't consider it much, but if I happened to be that and I couldn't help it, I wouldn't deny it."

Testimony of Mrs. Elvira Ball, age 64, b. c1841, Lee Co, VA, d/o Daniel Lockheart and his second wife, Charity Brashears, d/o "Grannie Brashears" and sister to Elizabeth (Brashears) Hyden. She named the children of Grannie Brashears and the girls' husbands:

1. Charity Brashears, m. Daniel Lockheart, parents of Mrs. Elvira Ball. Charity d. when Elvira was young.
2. Elizabeth Brashears, m. John Hyden
3. Berthenia Brashears, m. Hiram Hyden
4. Nancy Brashears, m. William Hyden
5. Dicey Brashears, m. Henry T. Ferguson
6. John Brashears,
7. Martin Brashears,

Elizabeth Brashears and John Hyden had children, John (who later moved to Kentucky), Wilson, Sam, Elizabeth, James, and Nancy.

Sam Hyden m.1. Eliza Carter and had children: John, Granville, Rice, Mary, Texas, and Sallie. Sam abandoned this family and ran away with Nancy Lockheart, Elvira's half-sister, d/o Daniel Lockheart and his first wife. Nancy Lockheart had m.1. Dan Jones and had one child, Polly Jones, about the same age as Elvira. Nancy and Dan were separated. Nancy then had two children by Sam Hyden, Nannie and Whit, before the two decided to run away. Whit was "a little chunk of a boy, 3-4 years old" when Nancy came by and told Elvira's family in the yard that Sam Hyden was taking her to Whitley Co, KY.

Elizabeth Brashears and John Hyden lived about two miles above Elvira's father's place. They came by to say goodbye as they were moving.

"Grannie Brashears was very old, lived with uncle Henry Ferguson, but would come to father's to stay a few days." Elvira thought her grandparents may have come from the eastern part of the state, "around James River."

Testimony of Granville Hyden, age past 65, b. 30 Jan 1840 on Wallin's Creek, Lee Co, VA, s/o Sam Hyden and Eliza Carter, gs/o John Hyden and Elizabeth (Brashears). He testified that the siblings of Elizabeth Brashears were Charity (Brashears) Lockheart, Dicey (Brashears) Ferguson, but he didn't remember the brothers.

He named the children of Sam Hyden and Eliza Carter:
1. George Rice S. Hyden, b. 1831
2. John M. Hyden, b. 18 Jan 1835
3. Granville Hyden, b. 30 Jan 1840
4. Mary Jane Hyden, d. in TN
5. Virginia Caroline Hyden, [d. before 1848, when Sam left.]
6. Margaret Texas Hyden, d. Turkey Creek, Lee Co; m. Henry Gibbons
7. Sarah Eveline Hyden; m. _____ Cheek, "over here on the river."

"Sam moved us and set us down here below White Shoals on Powell's River. Sam and Dave Hyden bought a farm together. [Sam] had a new wagon up here. He stayed down there one night, then come up here to get the rest of the stuff ... and he never came back." Sam was a dark complected man, with red hair and red features, gray eyes. He left about 1847-8. Gran served in the Civil War; Eliza (Carter) Hyden died while he was away.

Testimony of John M. Hyden, 69, b. 18 Jan 1835 on Wallin's Creek, Lee Co, VA, s/o Sam Hyden and Eliza Carter, gs/o John and Elizabeth (Brashears) Hyden. He testified that the siblings of Sam Hyden were: Kelly Hyden, d. young in OH; Sam Hyden; John C. Hyden, m. Elizabeth Daugherty; Wilse Hyden, m. Nanny Hargus; Jane Hyden, m. Hamilton.

The judge asked: did you know your grandmother,

Elizabeth Brashears? John answered: "Why, of course I did." She was a middling large woman, blue eyes, fair complected, gray hair. She had a brother named John, and a "boy I forgot," and sisters Dicey Ferguson and Charity Lockheart. The mother of Elizabeth was Nancy, but "we always just called her Grannie."

"Sam left when I was 13 [1848] and he left in April, the Spring. He left one morning ... we had moved 12 miles below here, and the next morning, he harnessed up his team, and we had a wagon we left on Wallin's Creek, and he said he was going up there and load it with a lot of bacon that he had at Henry Daugherty's and would be home the next evening, and also went out and showed me and my older brother [George Rice S. Hyden] where to be at work until he came back, and he didn't come back."

"George R.S. Hyden took another wagon and run off and left his family, was killed over by Van Buren, AR."

John M. Hyden's grandfather was John Hyden Sr. John C. Hyden, brother of his father, Sam, married a McIntosh in KY.

Testimony of Henry T. Ferguson Jr, 71, b. 5 July 1833, Lee Co, VA, s/o Henry T. Ferguson and Dicey Brashears, gs/o Grannie Nancy Brashears. He named Dicey's siblings as above. He was 20 years old when Grannie died in 1853. She was buried on the Ferguson place, with a limestone marker with dates, which he said you could no longer read. Henry thought that his grandmother had never been married, but her husband, [James Brashears, s/o Philip Brashear of Henry Co, VA,] had died well before Dicey and Henry Sr had married; so he just never heard of the husband, and Grannie may have teased him by saying she had never been married.

Henry was 27 when his mother died. Henry thought she might have been born on Wallin's Creek, but the others "came from the east." Henry Sr and Dicey were married in 1821. Elizabeth (Brashears) Hyden was married before Henry Jr knew her; "I reckon all her children are older than I am. They lived on Wallin's Creek, about ½ mile from where I was born."

Henry remembered Sam Hyden as sandy-red haired,

"larger than his sons here, Jackie and Gran." "We was kin folks ... staid all night."

The judgment of the three judges of the Choctaw and Chickasaw Citizenship Court: "not the slightest scintilla of reliable evidence ... that Elizabeth (Brashears) Hyden was daughter of Turner and Nancy (Vaughn) Brashears." The Judges believed that Nancy D. Hyden's testimony was "absolutely untrue." Judge Everidge and his son, Joel, had unwittingly "aided and abetted" Whit W. Hyden's application, which was utterly without evidence. "None of the appellants are entitled to be declared Choctaw citizens, or entitled to any rights or privileges ... and should be struck from the rolls."
"So Ordered."

NAPOLEON BRASHEAR'S CAMPAIGN

On Sept 8 and 9, 1896, in three separate petitions, Napoleon Bonaparte Brashears filed applications with the Dawes Commission for enrollment of his family as citizens by blood of the Choctaw Nation, naming the following persons: Napoleon B. Brashears, La Fayette Brashears, Arthur Brashears, Fred S. Brashears, Sarah E. Salmon, John C. Salmon, Forney (?Fannie) Salmon, Lois Salmon, Ida May Duncan, Dora M. Duncan, and for enrollment of the following as intermarried citizens of the Choctaw Nation: Mary J. Brashears and Ollie Duncan. The petition identifies all but Napoleon as children and grandchildren of Napoleon B. Brashears, who stated that he was entitled to enrollment for the following reason: "My father, Mortimer M. Brashears, was a son of Joseph Brashears, whose father was Zadock Brashears. All these Brashears were Choctaw Indians." Affidavits of James D. Coyle and Lucy J. Jones were attached, affirming "Napoleon B. Brashears is a son of Mortimer M. Brashears, and the said Joseph Brashears was a son of Zadoc Brashears. The above-named Brashears were Choctaw Indians." (See also the attorney's summary of his claim, at the end of the case: "Napoleon B. Brashears, et al." Dawes Commission No. 877. Commission Nos 7-D-195, 7-D-

194, 7-D-187, 7-D-198, 23-929; Government Printing Office, see section called *Five Civilized Tribes in Oklahoma*, pages 315-321.)

Napoleon Bonaparte Brashears, b. Feb 1849, Searcy Co, AR, s/o Mortimer M. Brashear and Sarah Vaughn; m. **Mary Jane Clouch**, b. c1845. (1870 Census, Pope Co, AR: Napoleon B. 21, Mary Jane, 25, #D-1053, p.238). He was "admitted on trial" as a Minister of the Methodist Episcopal Church in Arkansas in 1875, transferred to a Methodist Conference outside Arkansas (unspecified) in 1891 (*Methodism in Arkansas, 1816-1976*). He was an active minister in the Oklahoma Conference all during the time he was trying to get himself and his children enrolled as Choctaws by blood, so that he could get land and annuities payments. According to his applications for himself and his children in 1896 for enrollment as Choctaws, the FHL ancestral file, and testimony before the Dawes Commission in 1906 (p.315, 316), Napoleon's family consisted of the following. See vol 7 for a more complete listing of his family.

d1. **LaFayette Brashears**, (twin) of record 1880, AR (Ancestral file, SLC)

d? **?Lillie B. Brashears**, (twin) of record 1880, AR (Ancestral file, SLC); perhaps died young; not in any of Napoleon's petitions to be recognized as a Choctaw.

d? **Walter W. Brashears**, (twin) of record 1880, AR (ancestral file, SLC); perhaps d. young; not in Choctaw applications. William Walter Brashear, 22 Aug 1904—27 July 1906 (2 yrs old), bur in Pope Co, AR.

d2. **Arthur Brashears**,

d3. **Fred S. Brashears**, of record 1880, MO (Ancestral file, SLC)

d4. **Sara E. Brashears**, of record 1880, AR (Ancestral file, SLC); m.1. _____ Salmon; m.2. _____ Scott

e1. John C. Salmon

e2. Fannie Salmon

e3. Lois Salmon

d5. **Ida May Brashears**, (twin) of record 1880, AR

(Ancestral file, SLC); m. 8 July 1894, **Oliver "Ollie" Duncan**, both of Gowen, I.T. (Book 5, p.28)

  e1. Dora M. Duncan
  e2. Francis E. Duncan
  e3. Myrtle Viola Duncan

d6. **Amanda J. Brashears**, of record 1880, AR (Ancestral file, SLC); m. _____ **Freeze**,

  e1. Damon Freeze
  e2. Raymond Freeze
  e3. Ruby Freeze
  e4. Earl Freeze

d7. **Logan Bonaparte Brashears**, b. 5 Oct 1886, Searcy Co, AR, s/o Napoleon Bonaparte & Mary Jane Brashear.

  e1. **Leo Lester Brashears**, b. between 1896 and 1907
  e2. **Floyd Lafayette Brashears**, b. between 1896 and 1907
  e3. **Alvey Fred Brashears**, b. between 1896 and 1907
  e4. **Helen Marie Brashears**, apparently born after 1907 (listed in Ancestral file, SLC, as living in 1990)
  e5. **Homer Roosevelt Brashears**, b. 1913, OK (Ancestral file, SLC)
  e6. **Jess Winfield Brashears**, b. 1916, OK (Ancestral file, SLC)

On 22 Oct 1896, the Choctaw Nation filed its [?favorable] response to his petition; and the Dawes Commission made decisions on 2, 4, and 8 Dec 1896, <u>denying</u> Napoleon's three petitions. No appeal was filed. He's out, right?

Nevertheless, on 6 Jan 1897, a certificate was issued by the Choctaw Nation, showing the names of the above applicants had been placed on the 1896 Tribal Roll of the Choctaw Nation by the Choctaw Tribal commission, generally known as the "Choctaw Revisory Board." That roll contains the names: Napoleon B. Brashears, William Brashears, LaFayette Brashears, Arthur Brashears, Logan Brashears, Fred Brashears, Ida Duncan, Ollie Duncan, Dora M. Duncan, Amanda Freeze, Damon Freeze, and Raymond Freeze. This certificate was filed in evidence and duly noted by the Dawes

Commission. William Brashears was a legitimate Choctaw, a descendant of Benjamin Brashears, who was a son of R.T. "Turner" Brashears and "a daughter of Taboca."

On 5 June 1899, Napoleon filed a new petition for the enrollment of the above named persons, and added the names: Amanda J. Freeze, Damon Freeze, and Raymond Freeze, "Amanda Freeze being the daughter and Damon and Raymond being the grandchildren of Napoleon B. Brashears." On 6 Oct 1899, Napoleon filed for enrollment of Dora M. Duncan. And on 23 Dec 1902, he applied for enrollment of Ruby Freeze and Earl Freeze.

On 19 Jan and 6 Feb 1905, in two separate decisions, the Dawes Commission refused to enroll these applicants, holding that the "Revisory Board" had no authority to enroll anyone after the actions of the Commission in 1896, no appeals had been filed in response to that ruling, and besides the "Revisory Board" had "no legal existence."

On 17 July 1905, the Department of Indian Affairs, of the Department of Interior, returned the case to the Dawes Commission with directions to permit the applicants to introduce "such testimony as might be necessary for a full presentation of the merits of their case," citing the Assistant Attorney General:

> "There is not sufficient evidence in the record for me to form an opinion upon Brashears's right to be enrolled. Accepting the facts stated in his affidavit, undisputed by the Nation after due-service, I am of the opinion that enough appears to show that Brashears, in due time and in due form under the act of 1896, supra, asserted a right and was entitled to a hearing; that there has been a miscarriage in the proceedings amounting in effect to denial of a hearing, and that a rehearing *de novo* should be ordered."

That is, throw out everything and start over.

On 3 Jan 1906, Napoleon B. Brashears testified at a hearing before the Commissioner of the Five Civilized Tribes.

He was questioned about his enrollment by the "Revisory Board." From the summary, p.316: "He stated that he appeared before the Choctaw Revisory Board at Tuskahoma, [I.T.] on December 20, 1896; that at that time he had received no notice of the action of the Dawes Commission, which had a few days previous thereto rejected his claim; that he had been before the Choctaw census commissioners about two months prior to his appearance before the revisory board and before the action of the Dawes Commission and was told by the commissioners that a certificate would be issued to him later; that it would have to be drawn up and signed by the national secretary; that the national secretary did subsequently issue the certificate, which was offered in evidence. The attorney for the applicants then offered the testimony of a number of witnesses as to the merits of applicants' claim, which the Commissioner of the Five Civilized Tribes *refused to hear.*" (italics added)

On 9 Jan 1906, the Commissioner of the Five Civilized Tribes transmitted the case to the department again, recommending that the denials of 9 Jan 1905 be affirmed.

On 6 April 1906, the department returned the case to the Commissioner, directing that all previous actions be set aside, "to the end that a complete investigation of the merits of the case might be made."

Testimony of Napoleon B. Brashears: Finally, on 9 May 1906, Napoleon B. Brashears testified at a hearing before the Commissioners to the Five Civilized Tribes, as follows (p.317):

"My age is 57. I came to the Choctaw Nation in 1858. I lived in the eastern part of the nation with my father, Mortimer Brashears, who is dead; he died in August, 1863. I remained in the Choctaw Nation until the spring of 1861, except for a short period of time during the year 1859. My father enlisted in the United States Army and was killed. My grandfather was Joseph Brashears, and his father was Zadoc Brashears. Zadoc Brashears was a Choctaw Indian. My grandfather, Joseph Brashears, came to the Choctaw Nation, Ind. T. My mother's maiden name was Sarah Vaughn. I do not know whether she had Choctaw blood. I have been recognized by the officials of the Choctaw Nation as a citizen. I enjoyed the privileges pursuing any and all avocations without being molested. I have lived continuously in the Nation since 1890. During these years I have never been called upon to pay a permit. I held land, improved and cultivated land, and afterward sold the improvement to a Choctaw citizen. My grown sons voted with me in the elections. One of my daughters married a noncitizen in the usual way as prescribed by the Choctaw law. They were married as the Choctaw law prescribed between citizens and noncitizens. I held a greater number of cattle than any but a Choctaw could hold. Myself and family were enrolled by the Choctaw Nation on the tribal roll. I have not drawn money from the tribe, and have not been allotted land. Choctaw citizens were required to pay royalties on hay cut on the public domain. I paid such royalties. A noncitizen was prohibited from cutting such hay. A citizen could do so my making bond. I made bond. A Choctaw county judge approved my bond in open court."

On cross examination: When my father came to the Indian Territory he was a trader and rented a house to live in. I married in Arkansas but did not have a license. I voted in Pope County, Ark. I did not swear that I was a United States citizen. I was not required to do so. I did not tell the election judges that I was a Choctaw. From 1872 to 1886 I lived in Arkansas and conducted myself as a citizen of the United States. In 1886 I took a trip to Colorado, returning to Arkansas same year, where I remained near to Fort Smith until 1890 when I moved to Red Oak, Choctaw Nation, where I lived for four years and rented a place. My mother and father were married in the state of Arkansas. I claim Choctaw blood from both. I do not know how old my father was when he died, but my best judgment is that he was about 40. I do not know positively what degree of Choctaw blood I have. I have heard my mother say she had Choctaw blood, and I have heard my father say he had Choctaw blood. I never saw any of my grandparents. I do not remember who my father's mother was, but I do remember who his father was. My parents told me that my grandfather, Joseph Brashears, was a son of Zadoc Brashears. I can not say that my father told me that Joseph was a son of Zadoc, but he did say he was a descendant of Zadoc. I do not know who the wife of Zadoc Brashears was. I know the Brashears people in the Choctaw Nation. Some of them recognize me as their relative. George and John Brashears both recognize me as a relative. George lives near Ada. John lives in Chickasaw Nation. My father told me that Joseph came to Indian Territory. If there are any brothers and sisters of my father living I do not know it. One sister, Mary J. Coyle, died in the Chickasaw Nation. I had one uncle, William, who lived somewhere in the Choctaw Nation. I never had any uncles living in Arkansas. I saw one uncle on my mother's side in Arkansas. His name was Joseph Vaughn. I do not know where he or his descendants live. I never was called upon to pay a permit when I was renting land.

Redirect: When my father lived in the Choctaw Nation, Vaughn Brashears, who lived on Brushy, in Choctaw Nation, repeatedly visited my father's family. Turner Brashears, who also lived on Brushy, visited my father. Vaughn Brashears urged my father to move into his neighborhood, and said he would give my father an improved farm. When I moved to the Choctaw Nation in 1890, I claimed to be a Choctaw. I bought a lot in town and built a house. Richard Brashears was a slave and belonged to Vaughn Brashears. He is living and is here now. I know of two brothers of Joseph Brashears. Their names were William and Vaughn. If there were any more I do not know of it.

In response to commissioner: My grandfather, Joseph Brashears, was born in Mississippi. It has always been my information that he was the son of Zadoc Brashears; the only thing that I can not be positive about is that my father stated so.

<u>Testimony of Richard Brashears</u>, (p.318): I was born in Alabama in 1821. My home is now in the Chickasaw Nation. I came to the Indian Territory in 1831. I was brought here by Vaughn Brashears. Louis, Benjamin, Jefferson, William, and Tobias Brashears came at the same time. These people were all emigrants as Choctaws to this country. They came from Yazoo River, Miss. I was a slave, and belonged to Vaughn Brashears. I lived with the Brashears family until two years before the Civil War. I know Joseph Brashears. He was a son of Zadoc. I can not say when I last saw Joseph. He came to the country to a place now called Tuskahoma. He went from there to the State of Arkansas. He promised his uncle to come back, but took sick and died there. He went to Arkansas to see about some slaves and never came back. His uncle was Vaughn Brashears. William and Turner Brashears, brothers of Joseph, did not come to the Indian Territory. They lived in Alabama. Zadoc did not come. He was killed in a horse race in Alabama. They lived in Sumter County, on the Tombigbee River, where the Choctaws lived. The Brashears I refer to were mixed with Choctaw and French. The French come from the father's side. Zadoc was French. He married a Vaughn, and she was Choctaw. I do not know what year Joseph came to the Choctaw Nation, [I.,T.]. I saw him at his Uncle's. I was a slave.

On cross-examination: I was born in Alabama and lived there seven or eight years; was then taken to Mississippi, on Yazoo River. I am sure that I lived in Sumter County. It is the southern part of the State. I was told by my old master that I came from Sumter County, Ala.

In response to commissioner: I do not know in what year Zadoc was killed. It was after I left Alabama. His brother Turner told me.

Cross-examination continued: I knew Joseph Brashears. We played boys together. I think he was born in Alabama. He was older than me. When I left Sumter County and went over on the Yazoo he was going to school. He went away to school before they brought me from Alabama. I don't know how long before. I wasn't old enough, and can't recollect. I next saw Joseph Brashears in the Choctaw Nation on the Kiamitia, near Tuskahoma. I did not speak to Joseph, but his uncle told that about him. My master told me he was going to Fayetteville. He also told me that he died there. I know William and Turner were Zadoc's sons, and so was Joseph. We played boys together. William and Turner were younger than Joseph. They were the sons of young Zadoc. Neither Zadoc came to this country. It was young Zadoc that got killed. Turner told me. Zadoc had a son Turner and also a brother Turner. His brother Turner came out here to the Choctaw Nation. The children of old Zadoc Brashears was Jesse, Zadoc, Vaughn, and Turner. Young Zadoc's children were Joseph, William, and Turner.

In response to commissioner: Joseph was older than me. I wouldn't undertake to say how much older. Joseph's two brothers were younger than he. William was next to Joseph, and Turner next. Turner was older than me. I do not know what went with them. We had been here seven or eight years when Joseph came. He had with him some children and women. I can't say how many children. I don't know how big the children were. When I last saw him in Alabama he was not married. He was too young. When I last saw Joseph in Mississippi I was a small boy, and when I again saw him in Choctaw Nation here I was nearly grown. When I left Alabama old man Zadoc Brashears was living. The old man of all. There were two Zadocs, old Zadoc and young Zadoc. Both were living, well as I can recollect. Old Zadoc married a Vaughn. They was mighty near full blood. Spoke a little English. Old Zadoc was a French man. I did not hear of Young Zadoc's death until I got out to this country. Turner, old Zadoc's son, told me he was the cause of his death. Old Zadoc had four brothers. They were all French, and did not have any Choctaw blood as I know of. I do not know whether these applicants are related to those back in Alabama.

<u>Testimony of Nathan Gray</u>, (p.319): I am 56 years old. I live at Atoka. I am a freedman. I was born and raised in the Choctaw Nation, in the eastern part, near the Arkansas line, on the Gray farm. I belonged to the Grays. I knew a Mortimer Brashears. He lived across on the river near Poteau. He stopped at the Grays several times. He was on his way to see Turner Brashears, who lived west of us in the Choctaw Nation. It was a little while before the Civil War that I knew him. During two or three years before the war I saw him frequently. He was there at times when he was not on his way to see his people. He and Mr. Gray hunted and gambled together. Mortimer Brashears was 25 or 30 years old. I used to put up his horse, and he sometimes gave me a dime. I got a licking about his horse.

<u>Testimony of Josephine Jones</u>, June 27, 1906. Before the Commission at Duncan, Ind. T., Josephine Jones testified that she was a granddaughter of Joseph Brashears; that she always understood she was kin to the Indians, but did not know whether by blood or marriage; that she knew nothing of Joseph Brashears's family; that she has always been taught that she had some French blood, and that the Brashears was French; that she never heard of any Scotch blood in the family; that Vaughn Brashears wanted her to come to the Territory and live, and that she refused to do so; that she was of French and Indian blood.

<u>Testimony of Sarah Ann (Moncrief) Harlan</u>: Note by counsel: The following witness was produced by the commissioner for the purpose of contradicting the testimony of the applicant, the affidavit of James D. Coyle and Lucy J. Jones attached to the original application, and especially for the purpose of impeaching the testimony of the freedman, Richard Brashears, and upon whose testimony the decision of the commission was based.

November 7, 1896. Before the commission at Blocker, Ind. T., Sarah Ann (Moncrief) Harlan ([v5]1394) testified as follows (p.319):

I was 77 years old last January [either she or the clerk made a mistake; she was 67]. My father was Sampson Moncrief. My mother was Sophie (Brashears) Moncrief. I am not sure, but I think my mother died in 1854, in Alabama, Sumter County. Her maiden name was Sophia Brashears. Her father was Zadoc Brashears. Her mother's name was Susan. I recollect seeing grandfather Zadoc Brashears only once. I don't know what county he was in when I saw him. I have never heard when he died. He was not living when I left Alabama to come to the Territory. I was a little girl when I saw him, 5 or 6 years old; just a mere recollection. Zadoc Brashears possessed no Indian blood. He was a Scotchman. His wife Susan was a half-breed Indian. She died when my mother was a little girl. I came to Indian Territory in 1850. I do not know the name of my great-grandparents on my grandmother's side. I was a beneficiary under the fourteenth article of the treaty of 1830. I do not know how many children Susan and Zadoc had. I only heard of them through my mother. Jesse Brashears was a brother of my mother. Zadoc Brashears, Jr., was a brother of my mother. Vaughn and Turner Brashears were brothers of my mother. She also had sisters, but don't know that I can name them all— Susan, Elizabeth, Anne, and one more; I don't recollect her name. Jesse died in Mississippi. He never came to the Territory. I do not know what year he died. Anne died in Alabama— I do not know when. Elizabeth died in Alabama when I was very small. Susan died in Jackson, Miss.; I do not know when, but before I came to the Territory. Turner came to this country and died. I don't know when he settled, but he died out here before I came. He never had any descendants. His wife died in Alabama. Vaughn came to this country and died here. I saw him once after I came here; he died somewhere along in 1852 or 1853. He has one descendant that I know of living now, a boy, named Turner. Uncle Zadoc died in Alabama after my birth, but I don't recollect anything about it. I was a mere child. I can't say how long before I came to the Territory he died. Zadoc was married at the time of his death. His wife's name was Anne; I do not know the maiden name. He lived near Moscow, on Bigbee River. I visited his home after his death. His children were Turner, John, and William (who were twins), and Oleana. He had no other children. Turner died near Moscow when young. John died when a boy— just a little boy— in Alabama. William died. Oleana moved with her mother to Texas and I lost track of them. I never heard of Joseph. I never heard of Mortimer Brashears. I never heard of Sarah Vaughn. I have kept up tolerably well with my mother's brothers and sisters. Outside of that I know nothing. When I saw Vaughn Brashears here in the nation he was at Poteau. I have heard it talked of that he brought here a slave by the name of Richard Brashears. If any of the sons of Zadoc lived on Yazoo River, as stated by Richard, I don't know it. I don't know whether Zadoc Brashears was killed in a horse race, as stated by Richard. He was shot at a horse race, is what my mother told me. He wife's name was Anne. The two Zadocs, my grandfather and uncle, are the only ones by that name I ever heard of. I got my information from my mother. I didn't know very much about my relatives. Grandfather Zadoc had no Indian blood. He was Scotch. I testified in the case of Joseph Moncrief that Zadoc Brashears married Susan Vaughn. That was her maiden name. I said she was a half-breed Choctaw. That is correct.

Cross examination by attorney for applicants: I have always heard them say that Dick Brashears was a slave of Vaughn Brashears. In 1853 or 1854, when I went back to visit my mother, she told me all about her sister and brothers, and there was no Joseph in her brothers; and if it had been so she would have told it. I did not ask her about a Joseph. It is correct, as testified by Dick Brashears, that my mother's brother was shot and killed in a horse race. It is correct, as testified by Richard Brashears, that Vaughn Brashears came to the Territory and lived and died here. It is correct, as testified to by Richard Brashears, that Turner Brashears came to the Territory and lived and died here. It is correct, as testified to by Richard Brashears, that Jesse was the oldest child. I never heard of one of the children going away to school, as stated by Richard Brashears. It is correct, as stated by Richard Brashears, that Zadoc Sr, Vaughn, and Jesse Brashears lived in Sumter County, Ala. All the Brashears who lived there were Indians except the old original Brashears. All that came from there were of Indian descent. I only had two come. It is correct that all that died there and all that came here were of Indian descent. There was only two that came. There were no families living there during my time by the name of Brashears who did not have Indian blood. If Napoleon B. Brashears can connect himself with Turner and Vaughn Brashears he would be an Indian, but I have never been able to connect him.

Jan 26, 1907. The commissioner rendered a decision wherein he very briefly summarized the testimony of Sarah Ann (Moncrief) Harlan, and then stated:

I am further of the opinion that the evidence clearly established that the Joseph Brashears through whom the applicants herein claim descent was not a descendant of Zadoc Brashears, Sr., and Susan Brashears (née Vaughn), and that none of the applicants herein are possessed of Choctaw blood.

I am further of the opinion that inasmuch as none of the applicants herein are possessed of Choctaw blood, the enrollment of the applicants whose names appear upon the 1896 Choctaw census roll was without authority of law, and that under the provisions of the act of Congress approved June 28, 1898 (30 Stats., 495), their names should be stricken therefrom.

REV. JOSEPH BRASHEARS

Napoleon was right that a Joseph Brashears was his grandfather, but he had the wrong Joseph. His Joseph was a son of Ignatius "Nacy" Brashear Sr and is so listed in "Nacy's" Bible. Joseph's family, which included Mortimer Brashear, was also listed in the Bible. What I know about Joseph Brashear and his descendants, including Mortimer and his descendants, will be included in Vol 7. *Brashear Families West of the Mississippi*. He is a little preview, with only the data relevant to this case.

[7]11. **Joseph Brashear**, (Back#49, s/o Ignatius Brashear Sr and Frances Permelia Catheral), b. 9 Dec 1778, d. 30 Oct 1845, MO; m. ***Elizabeth Noble***, b. ?, d. 18 Sept 1822, four days after birth of her last child (data from Bible of Ignatius "Nacy" Brashears Sr, and "notations of Cousin Victoria" (inserts in that Bible), in possession (1997) of Mrs. Mary Elizabeth (Gabrielson) Gottlieb, a descendant of Mary Margaret (Brashear) Stevens, sister of Dr. John A. Brashear, the Pittsburg Astronomer. Elizabeth Noble was d/o James Noble.

Thanks to Al Caldwell, P.O. Box 1224, Kelseyville, CA 95451, 707/279-1160, for Xeroxes from the Bible, plus a packet of old newspaper clippings and other notes.

"Rev. Joseph Brashears was an early day preacher of the Methodist faith in Miller County." (Judge Jenkins, *History of Miller Co, MO*, p.141) "In the early thirties, the ... Methodist sent Reverend Brashears to Pleasant Mount" (Jenkins, p.254). Some maps show the place as Mount Pleasant, Miller Co, MO. "The Methodist were early active in the area (Pleasant Mount, Miller Co, MO) with Rev. Brashears preaching to the inhabitants in 1833" (Jenkins, p.261).

Partial Family of Joseph Brashear and Elizabeth Noble:

[8]2. ***Mortimer M. Brashear**, b. 2 April 1809, near Lexington, KY, killed Aug, 1863, Searcy Co, AR; m. 9 Nov 1837, Miller Co, MO, **Sarah Vaughan**, (*MO Marr. to 1850*, "by Stephen A. Blevans, Justice of the Peace")

[8]3. **William W. Brashear**, b. 28 June 1811; m. 24 Jan 1841, Polk Co, MO, **Mary Ann Devenport**, (*MO Marr. to 1850*). Polk Co is three counties southwest of Miller. Napoleon testified: "I had one uncle, William, who lived somewhere in the Choctaw Nation."

[8]5. **Mary Jane C. Brashear**, b. 11 Jan 1815; m. 3 Feb 1834, Gasconade Co, MO, ***John or James Coil***, (*MO Marr. to*

1850). They were in the 1860 census, Gainesville, Cooke Co, TX (#569, p.258). Napoleon's testimony: "One sister [of my father], Mary J. Coyle, died in the Chickasaw Nation" i.e. before 1906. The James D. Coyle who made affidavit in support of Napoleon's claim must have been the son, and Lucy J. Jones (Josephine Jones), the daughter. (Data from Cheryl, Mrs. William Robert Haas, <wrhass2@aol. com>).

[9]1. James D. Coyle, b. c1835

[9]2. Lucy Josephine Coyle, b. c1847, MO (12 in 1860); m. _____ Jones

[9]3. Nancy A. Coyle, b. c1854

[8]6. **Flavilla Melcina Brashear**, b. 18 April 1818; m. 15 Dec 1833, Gasconade Co, MO, ***John Chrisman***. (*MO Marr. to 1850*; Jenkins, p.141). Gasconade is two counties east of Miller County. Both Mortimer and Napoleon named a daughter Sarah Melcena.

Note that Joseph was born 9 Dec 1778. That's about 25 years before Zadock Brashears Jr was born, so it is quite certain that Joseph was not a son of the Choctaw Zadock Brashears, Jr. Zadock Brashears, Jr, b. c1804 could not have had a grandson, Mortimer Brashears, b. c1809.

Rev. Napoleon Bonaparte Brashears was simply lying. And he got a good part of his extended family to lie with him! Greed is a great creator of chicanery.

But the case and others like it also illustrate the multiplying of agencies, the red tape, the contradictions and litigations, the bureaucracy that have hog-tied and hamstrung the Indian in America from the beginning. Who needs guns or roses, when he has the courts and legalese?

Appendix— My Books:

Plan for an 8-vol. "A BRASHEAR(S) FAMILY HISTORY"

by **Charles Brashear**, 26 Tiffany Place, Santa Rosa, CA 95409
e-mail: <brashear@mail.sdsu.edu>

I am and have been for almost 40 years actively engaged in research on the Brashear Family, in all its branches, in all its spellings of the surname. Some years ago, Troy Back and Leon Brashear gave me their blessing and permission to "update" their book, *THE BRASHEAR STORY, A FAMILY HISTORY*, so I started trying to assemble a comprehensive Brashear Family history. But the more data I collected, the more I realized that this family history will never again fit into one volume, especially if you include the amount and kind of detail that I like to include— old photos, maps, deeds and other documents, old family letters. I now have working drafts of eight books on the family history. So this is the plan that has evolved:

Vol 1. *The First 200 Years of Brashear(s) in America* and *Some Descendants in Maryland* (this one was published in Nov 1998 and is still available at $35 for hardcover, $25 for paperback, plus $3 postage and packaging; CA residents add 7.0% sales tax.)

Vol 2. *Robert C. Brashear of North Carolina* and *Some Descendants in TN, KY, MO, TX, etc.* (Published 1 Sep 1999. Available only in hardback. $35, plus $3 p&p and CA tax.) If you order two books at once, sent to the same address, $4 is enough for p&p.

Vol 3. *Robert Samuel Brashear(s)* and *Some Descendants in TN and KY* (Published early in 2001; $40, plus $3 p&p and CA tax if applicable. Vol 1, 2, & 3 at same time: $100, plus $5 p&p.)

Vol 4. *Brashear(s) Families of the Ohio Valley* (Published 20 April 2002. 676 pages (xx + 656) with a 59-page index, about 50 pictures, and 7 maps. $40 + $3 p&p.)

Vol 5. ***Two Brashear(s) Families of the Lower Mississippi Valley*** *and their Choctaw and Other Descendants.* (Here it is!)

Vol 6. ***Basil Brashear(s) and his Brashears, Breshears, Beshears, Boshears and Other Descendants*** (I have a very messy, sprawling first draft of this one; many chapters are finished, but the book needs a great deal of work.)

Vol 7. ***Brashear(s) Families West of the Mississippi River*** (Have been collecting chapters for this one, but it's not very well formed yet.)

Vol 8. ***Brashear(s) Family Strays, Additions, Corrections, and Non-Brashear(s) Families*** (Plenty of stray data, and Plenty of Non-Brashears families; the problem is how to organize it all. And then who would want it?)

If you haven't yet sent me your Brashear family information, please do so now. I'll file it in an appropriate drawer and use it when I'm working on the relevant book.

To order, the printed books (please do NOT order the books not yet printed!) send a note, saying which volume(s) you want and where you want it/them sent, along with a check or money order, to

Charles Brashear, 26 Tiffany Place, Santa Rosa, CA 95409

I'll mail the books as soon as I can put them into the mailing boxes and get to the Post Office.

Please add $3 for postage and packaging for the first book, $1 for each additional book. California residents, please add 7.5% CA sales tax.

If any of you want to order a gift copy for your favorite library, I'll knock $10 off the price (that is, you pay $25 or $30 for the hardback, plus $3 p&p), and I'll send it to the library in your name. Just tell me which library, or let me pick one. (Some 30 libraries already have gift copies of vol 1.)

Vol 1: THE FIRST 200 YEARS OF BRASHEAR(S) IN AMERICA and Some Descendants in Maryland

WARNING! Don't mistake this for something it isn't. (Some

people bought the Brazier/Brasher book and then complained that their Brashear family was not in it.) This is a book about descendants of Robert and Benois Brasseur, French Huguenot immigrants to Virginia, c1635, whose surname was Anglicized as Brashear. Over the years, many branches of the family added an "s" to make it Brashears. Benois Brasseur was naturalized in Calvert Co, MD, in 1662, and became known as Benjamin Brashear; he is the progenitor of virtually all Americans with surnames Brashear, Brashears, Brashares, Breshear(s), Breashear(s), Broshear(s), Beshear(s), Boshear(s), Beshires, often Brasher, Brashers, Brashier, Brashiers, sometimes Brazier, and about 35 other spellings. Also, this book only treats the first 200 years of the family, mainly in Virginia and Maryland, from about 1635 to about 1835, except that the Western Maryland chapter comes up to the last few years. I'm working on other books that will bring many of the Brashear(s) lines down to more recent times.

The book is 7" by 10", 336 pages long (16 pages of front matter, including contents and a review of the deBrassier Family of Carpentras, France; 300 pages of text (see contents below); and 20 pages of 4-column index--about 3500 entries).

Abbreviated CONTENTS of Vol 1:

Vol 2: ROBERT C. BRASHEAR OF NORTH CAROLINA and Some Descendants in TN, KY, MO, TX, etc,

The 1740s were an economically rough time in Maryland (some of our family lost their land and/or spent time in debtors' prison). Newly opened land in the Granville District of North Carolina was an invitation to a new start. Three Brashear brothers--Robert C., Basil, and Otho--migrated to NC in the late 1740s, early 1750s, where Robert and Basil got land grants. Basil went broke again and left about 1766, and Otho simply disappeared, but Robert C. Brashear and his wife, Charity Dowell, stayed on and (we think) prospered. They were patriots during the Revolutionary War, after which newly opening land in western places beckoned again, and the family succumbed to wanderlust or land-hunger; they became part of the American westward movement. This book traces Robert C. Brashear in North Carolina and the families of sons Philip, Asa, and Zaza, and daughter, Ann (Brashear) Ball; Robert Samuel Brashear and Jesse Brashears have to wait for vol. 3 and vol. 5, respectively.

The book is 7" by 10", 316 pages (290 pages of text, about 50 illustrations, and 24 pages of 4-column index--over 4000 entries).

ABBREVIATED CONTENTS of VOL 2

Co-author: Jerri Beshears Kennedy

Vol 3: ROBERT SAMUEL BRASHEARS, "THE ROLLING STONE,"
and Some Descendants in TN and KY.

Very early in the Revolution (or maybe even before), several of
the Guilford Co Brashear(s) again got wanderlust, or they had worn
out the land. At any rate, Robert Samuel Brashears and all of his
children migrated to the frontier, first to Sullivan Co, NC (it would
become Sullivan Co, TN), then to Roane Co, TN. RSB's son, Isaac
Brashears, went on to Perry/Decatur Co, TN, and his son, Capt.
Samuel Brashear (he dropped the "s" on his surname), moved on
to Perry Co, KY. RSB's son, Basil, stayed on in Roane Co. This book
is about these families.

The book is 7" x 10", 496 pages, including 41 pages of index
and about 40 maps, pictures, or other documents. Since it costed
me considerably more to print this one, I have to charge $40 per
copy. Sorry.

Abbreviated Contents of vol 3:

The Rest Are Descendants of Capt. Samuel Brashear

Vol 4. **BRASHEAR(S) FAMILIES OF THE OHIO VALLEY**

Well before the Revolution, a burgeoning population made new land necessary. If you have a family of 12 children, there is no way in the world those 12 families can live on the same land as the parents, especially when the parents' land is already old, nearly worn-out. As early as the 1750s, Americans began crowding Western Maryland, the Monongahela River valley in southwestern Pennsylvania, and by about 1775, the Ohio River Valley. A fair number of Brashear(s) families and their relatives were among these emigrants— the Elder and Younger William Brashears; Otho Brashear and his wife Ruth Brown (along with two of her brothers who had married two of Otho's sisters); Ignatius "Nacy" Brashear; Marsham Brashear (and his father, Benjamin, and brothers, who however moved on to Mississippi); remnants of older Maryland families, like Lt. Rezin Brashears, Nathan Brashears/Brashares Jr, Zachariah Brashears/ Broshars; and strays like Joseph M. Brashears of Steubenville. This book is about these people and their families.

The book is 6" x 9" (different format!), hardbound, 676 pages (xx + 656), with 59 pages of index, about 50 pictures and seven maps. $40, plus $3 postage and packaging.

Abbreviated Contents of Vol 4:

My Historical Fiction

I also write fiction (mainly historical fiction about American Indians) and books about the writing process. If any of you are interested, here are some descriptions:

Killing Cynthia Ann,

a novel, published 1999 by Texas Christian University Press. $21.50. In 1836, blonde, blue-eyed Cynthia Ann Parker was kidnaped by Comanches in East Texas. She refused to be repatriated and lived with the Indians almost 25 years, marrying and raising a family (Quanah Parker, last chief of the Comanches, was her oldest son). In 1860, Texas Rangers captured Cynthia Ann and her toddler daughter, Toh-Tsee-Ah-ne, and took them to East Texas, where her Parker relatives held her prisoner the rest of her life. She wanted nothing but to return to her family on the Comanchería, but her Parker relatives could not imagine why anyone would want to be an Indian. Unwittingly, they psychological tortured her to death. The book is a documentary novel about those last ten years of Cynthia Ann Parker's life. Footnotes in the margins tell the reader where the data comes from.

Comeuppance at Kicking Horse Casino,
and Other Stories,
published in 2000 by American Indian Studies Center, UCLA, $15. This collection of stories is a mix of historical and contemporary

fictions. The historical stories provide a background for the contemporary stories, so that the entire collection becomes a loose chronicle of the Native American experience since the European settlement of North America. A wide range of tribes is represented--Powhatan, Cherokee, Creek, Comanche, Lakota, Navajo, Ute, Keres, Ácoma, Zuni, and an unnamed southern California tribe. Each story highlights some individual's quandry--and often alienation--in negotiating and adapting to a face to face encounter with the whites.

Brain, Brawn, and Will: The Turmoils and Adventures of Jeff Ross

Published in 2001 by 1stbooks Library. 6x9 Paperback: $19.95; electronic book (go to www.1stbooks.com and search for my name): $3.95. Jeff Ross was a quintessential 19th century man. As a child in Tennessee, he lay on the bank of the river and watched the Battle of Shiloh. A few years later, he rode in a vigilante party that gunned down his father's murderer. Thus, he learned early that violence was a socially approved way of achieving social goals. At the same time, he went to college and graduated from Cumberland University Law School in 1872 at the head of his class. He then embarked upon a career in which the mind was the instrument of social progress. Thus, his personality was formed by the twin and contradictory forces that have permeated American culture from the beginning— violence and intellect.

In 1878, at the age of 27, he ran away from his law practice and home. He traveled for a time in New England with a circus, running a "panorama" side show and hawking a "magic solder" for mending pots and pans. He hitch-hiked through Europe for a couple of years, shipped for Rio de Janeiro on a Norwegian freighter, led exploring parties into the interior of Brazil. He then took a job, running a mule team to supply railroad-building enterprises. Soon, he had worked his way to transportation chief, then to construction chief, eventually to a licensed civil engineer, who actually designed and built railroads and bridges.

In 1893, he got involved in the Brazilian revolution— on both sides: he sold to each, what he had discovered from the other. When the police came looking for him, he conned the American Consul in Rio into smuggling him out of the country. In New York, he bought a boat-load of munitions for the Brazilian government, then hired a crew of rebels to transport it.

Back in small town Tennessee, he became a town character, curmudgeon, and philosopher of sorts. He once proposed that "the world" should dam Gibraltar, drain the Mediterranean, and claim a continent of naturally irrigated farm land that would have fed the world for many generations to come. "It would work, too," he told a Memphis reporter in 1924, "if we had the brain, brawn, and will to accomplish it, just as the Panama Canal was accomplished."

The book is a story of his life, told largely through his own letters, essays, fragmentary novels, etc.

Contemporary Insanities:

Short Fictions, by Charles Brashear. Published in 1990 by **THE PRESS OF MACDONALD & REINECKE**, P.O.Box 840, Arroyo Grande, CA 93421-0840. $8.95 (mail orders add $2 postage) ISBN 1-877947-11-3. Ask at your bookstore, or order from the publisher.

Each of these short fictions treats some aspect of everyday life that is common enough, but from some eccentric perspective could be considered an insanity—the cruelty with which we "sane" people treat autism; the little "itches" we torture each other with; the ego-centric, sexual fantasies we trick ourselves with; the artifices we use to present ourselves to the world; the ogres of our nightmares and dreams; the games we play on the young, the aged, the unusual, the famous, and (as a nation) on each other and other nations. The theme that runs through all these fictions makes this a coherent book, not just a collection of miscellaneous stories. Our insanities are greed, pretentions, the exercise of privilege, the failure of our compassion and understanding, disrespect for those who are even a little different from us, the abuse of power.

FIVE BOOKS ON WRITING

Long-time professor of Creative Writing and author Charles Brashear has recently published five books on writing, "The Elements of Writing" Series. For thirty years, Dr. Brashear taught writing and literature at three universities: the University of Stockholm (on a Fulbright grant), the University of Michigan, and San Diego State. He is now retired and devotes full time to writing, research, and travel. This series brings his total to 20 books, including a recent novel, *Killing Cynthia Ann*; a short-story collection, *Comeuppance at Kicking Horse Casino*; and a biography of a remarkable 19th century man, *Brain, Brawn, and Will: the Turmoils and Adventures of Jeff Ross*.

Among his textbooks on writing are: *Creative Writing: Fiction, Drama, Poetry, the Essay* (American Book Co, 1968); *The Structure of Essays* (Prentice-Hall, 1973); and several on creativity in writing.

ELEMENTS OF CREATIVITY:
On Creativity in General and Creative Writing in Particular
(No. 1 in "The Elements of Writing" Series; ISBN: 0-75963-362-2; $19.95)

"Simply the best book on the subject." —pre-pub review

"Brashear has done something amazing in pulling together so many strands in the web of creativity." (pre-pub review)

Elements of Creativity integrates most of what we know about the several creative processes into one handbook. Using research in Psychology, Sociology, Philosophy, Pedagogy, the nature of language, the creative process, and my own experience as a writer and teacher of writing for 30 years, I've illustrated how the human mind works while it is inventing, revising, re-envisioning, and arranging creative ideas.

Chapters 1-6, "Creativity in General," offer a comprehensive understanding of a complex process; chapters 7-16, "Creativity in Writing," offer practical aspects of creating, especially in writing, but also in business and science; chapters 17-19, "Creativity with Others," offer integration and connection with larger social and philosophical issues. I haven't tried to say everything about creativity, but I have tried to touch all the *types* of things there are to say.

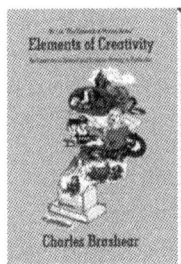

ELEMENTS OF DIALOG, DIALECT,
and CONVERSATIONAL STYLE
(No. 2 in "The Elements of Writing" Series; **ISBN: 0-75963-372-X; $17.95**)

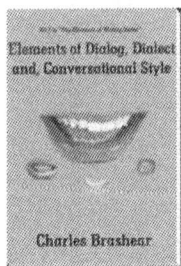

Elements of Dialog, Dialect, and Conversational Style presents the language of talk, its structure, style, grammar, methods of making meaning, aesthetic organization, and much more. Different chapters derive from descriptive linguistics, non-verbal and para-language studies, games theory and transactional analysis, social dialectology, linguistic geography, style studies, even rhetoric. Here are the building blocks of good familiar style. Here are the nuts and bolts, the range of possibilities, the *elements* with which the languages of reports, speeches, informal essays, fiction, poetry, plays, business and personal letters are held together.

"Many current books on writing devote a chapter or a few paragraphs to writing dialog, but there is a lack of books zeroing in on the subject. Here, at last, is a good one. The author's approach is a new one, and he shows great familiarity with linguistics. He covers the subject well, including non-verbal language, explaining how it supplements words as part of dialog. His down-to-earth analyses and examples of dialects and accent can be quite useful. I have never seen the subject covered so thoroughly. His arguments contrasting academic, journalistic, and conversational style were coherent and logical." —U.N. Tejano

"I believe this book will become at least moderately significant among publications for writers. I would, indeed, want it in my personal library." —U.N. Tejano

ELEMENTS OF THE NOVEL: An Update on Forster
(No. 3 in "The Elements of Writing" Series; **ISBN: 0-75963-370-3; $19.95**)

" BREATH OF CLEANSING SEA-BREEZE" —Bill Baeddekker

Elements of the Novel is about the fundamental aspects of the modern novel— story and plot; character and characterization; theme, fantasy, and prophecy; point-of-view and belief; rhythm and pattern; aesthetic structure. It follows and expands the scheme used by E. M. Forster in his classic *Aspects of the Novel*, adding perspectives and insights that have emerged in the last seventy-odd years. It is intended as a handbook and stimulus for people actively involved in writing novels, but would also enrich anyone's novel-reading experience.

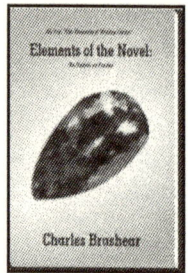

"Whether you think the novel is a vehicle for character study, or a vehicle for story and plot, or for some more "poetic" elements, like aesthetic design and structure, this book is for you. The depth of discussion at every phase is notable and rare in this sort of book. Brashear knows what he's talking about—and does it with clarity and economy." —Joel Black

"Brashear is a modernist, who finds much in Post-Modernism simply nonsense. For those of us who have resisted the waves of absurdities over the last fifty years, he's a breath of cleansing sea-breeze." —Bill Baeddekker

A WRITER'S TOOLKIT: Elements of Writing Personal Essays, Poems, Stories

(No. 4 in "The Elements of Writing" Series; **ISBN: 0-75963-368-1; $23.95**)

"Good book! You'll want it on your shelf." —Jane Wall

A Writer's Toolkit presents the fundamental principles of creative writing and illustrates them with both student and professional writing. Its basic strategy is to offer samples of essays, poems, and stories by way of definition, then ask emerging writers to develop their voices in suggested writing assignments.

The book assumes a writer should develop as many voices and tools as he/she has things to say. It takes a modular approach to fostering writing skills in students. It views basic techniques of writing like intellectual bricks. One has to have the first one in place (let's say control of image) before one can lay the second (let's say the manipulation of image into metaphor). One has to understand scene and character before one can make these ingredients into a plot. However, like a spider, writers have to be constantly attached to the far-flung foundations of their art. Writers are doomed to be always working simultaneously on the strands and anchors of the webs they weave.

"Every beginning writer should know what's in this book. And every experienced writer should be reminded of it once in a while." —Jane Wall

ELEMENTS OF FORM AND STYLE IN EXPOSITORY ESSAYS

(No. 5 in "The Elements of Writing" Series; **ISBN: 0-75963-365-7; $17.95**)

"Highly recommended!" —Howard Koppolo

Elements of Form and Style in Expository Essays is about the techniques of organization and the ingredients of style in the formal, or expository, essay. It deals in detail with the three forms of human understanding and organizing ideas—

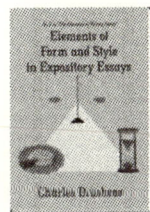

621

chronological sequences, classification/analysis of component parts, and comparison/contrast, as they relate to strategies in short and longer essays. It shows how we make sentences in English, how we make them effective and sensible, and how they mature as we become more skilled at writing. It offers a compendium of organizational techniques and stylistic considerations that we all grapple with as we learn to write well. It is both process-oriented and information-rich.

Strategies and styles of good writing are illustrated with both student and professional samples. The student paragraphs and essays will show an emerging writer how others in his/her situation have dealt with learning to write. The professional writing samples show the sophistication we all ultimately aim toward. The book is both small enough to be usable and full enough to be useful.

"This author makes essay writing seem simple, rather than the arduous task I remember it being. Where was he when I needed him? And his examples, especially those on Washo and Koko, the Ameslan "talking" chimpanzee and ape, are a treat in themselves. Highly recommended!" —Howard Koppolo

INDEX

Note: I have made an effort to index names as they appear in documents, while correcting obvious errors. Where the surname is spelled in more than one way, e.g. both Brashear and Brashears in the same document, you will find that person indexed both ways. Also, check under variant spellings for the object of your search: Breshear(s), Boshears, Beshears, Brasher, Brashers, Brashier(s), etc.

627

628

629

636

637

642

643

644

645

647

648

653

654

655

661

662

663

664

667

668

669

670

671

672

676

ISBN: 0-933362-16-1

www.ingramcontent.com/pod-product-compliance
Lightning Source LLC
Chambersburg PA
CBHW020458100426
42812CB00024B/2705